TO HANOI
AND BACK

TO HANOI AND BACK

THE U.S. AIR FORCE AND NORTH VIETNAM, 1966–1973

WAYNE THOMPSON

SMITHSONIAN INSTITUTION PRESS
Washington and London

By special arrangement with the U.S. Air Force, this publication is being offered for sale by the Smithsonian Institution Press, Washington, D.C. 20560-0950.
ISBN 1-56098-877-0

Library of Congress Cataloging-in-Publication Data
Thompson, Wayne, 1945–
    To Hanoi and back : the United States Air Force and North Vietnam, 1966–1973 / Wayne Thompson
        p.   24 cm.
    Includes bibliographical references and index.
        1. Vietnamese Conflict, 1961–1975—Aerial operations, American. 2. United States. Air Force—History—Vietnamese Conflict, 1961–1975. I. Title.

    DS558.8.T47   2000
    959.704'348—dc21   00-057606

The Author

Wayne Thompson is Chief of Analysis at the Air Force History Support Office in Washington. During the Vietnam War, he served as an Army draftee at an Air Force intelligence station on Taiwan. He did his undergraduate work at Union College in Schenectady, New York, and the University of St. Andrews, Scotland. He earned his doctorate in history at the University of California, San Diego, under Armin Rappaport. In August 1990, Dr. Thompson joined the Checkmate air campaign planning group in the Pentagon. Subsequently he was Senior Historical Advisor for the Gulf War Air Power Survey. In 1995 the Air Force sent him to study bombing operations launched from Italy against Bosnian targets, and in 1999 the crisis in Kosovo turned his attention to air operations over Serbia.

Contents

page

Foreword ix
Preface xi

1 Puzzle 3
2 New Tactics, Old Strategy 37
3 Gradualism on Trial 67
4 Season of Discontent 95
5 Rolling Thunder Subsides 121
6 Protective Reaction 153
7 Prisoners and Other Survivors 175
8 The Lavelle Affair 199
9 Linebacker 219
10 B-52s At Last 255
11 Reverberations 281

Appendices

Maps 293
Statistics 299

Notes 315
Glossary 361
Bibliography 363
Index 399

Foreword

No experience etched itself more deeply into Air Force thinking than the air campaigns over North Vietnam. Two decades later in the deserts of Southwest Asia, American airmen were able to avoid the gradualism that cost so many lives and planes in the jungles of Southeast Asia. Readers should come away from this book with a sympathetic understanding of the men who bombed North Vietnam. Those airmen handled tough problems in ways that ultimately reshaped the Air Force into the effective instrument on display in the Gulf War.

This book is a sequel to Jacob Van Staaveren's *Gradual Failure: The Air War over North Vietnam, 1965–1966*, which we have also declassified and are publishing. Wayne Thompson tells how the Air Force used that failure to build a more capable service—a service which got a better opportunity to demonstrate the potential of air power in 1972.

Dr. Thompson began to learn about his subject when he was an Army draftee assigned to an Air Force intelligence station in Taiwan during the Vietnam War. He took time out from writing *To Hanoi and Back* to serve in the Checkmate group that helped plan the Operation Desert Storm air campaign against Iraq. Later he visited Air Force pilots and commanders in Italy immediately after the Operation Deliberate Force air strikes in Bosnia. During Operation Allied Force over Serbia and its Kosovo province, he returned to Checkmate. Consequently, he is keenly aware of how much the Air Force has changed in some respects—how little in others. Although he pays ample attention to context, his book is about the Air Force. He has written a well-informed account that is both lively and thoughtful.

The bibliography at the end of the volume lists several other Air Force books about the Vietnam War. Our history program is engaged in a constant effort to reevaluate the service's past in light of new research and new perspectives. We welcome criticism of our published work and suggestions for future publications.

RICHARD P. HALLION
Air Force Historian

Preface

When I began to study these events, I thought I would write about one of the saddest portions of the Air Force's history. I may well have done so, but gradually (about as gradually as the Rolling Thunder air campaign of 1965–68 went about its business in North Vietnam) I came to take a more positive view of the Air Force's experience in Southeast Asia. Certainly the pain and death we normally associate with warfare caused many to suffer. Certainly the constraints under which the Air Force had to operate were extraordinarily restrictive and self-defeating. Certainly a reputation for ineffectiveness attached itself to bombing in North Vietnam and made air power seem a much less promising instrument than it was. But after years of seeking a more effective use of limited air power, the Linebacker campaigns over North Vietnam in 1972 joined with aerial mining of the ports there and simultaneous air operations in South Vietnam to make a dramatic difference—albeit a tardy and temporary one.

This rebound of American air power began well before the North Vietnamese invasion of South Vietnam in 1972 and continued long after the end of the war in 1975. The struggle for Southeast Asia helped to transform the Air Force from an almost total focus on potential nuclear warfare against the Soviet Union into a more varied and flexible force wielding increasingly sophisticated conventional weapons. But thinking about air power and about Southeast Asia lagged behind advances in technology. When the ultimate defeat finally came to South Vietnam and its American ally, persuasive victories for the new precision of American air power still lay far in the future.

Although the air campaigns against North Vietnam delivered a smaller tonnage of bombs than parallel efforts in South Vietnam and Laos, the Air Force's intellectual and emotional investment in North Vietnam was greater. There a heavier concentration of air defenses combined with the distance of targets from bases in Thailand and South Vietnam to make air operations more dangerous and more difficult. From its beginnings, the Air Force had defined itself as the service best able to attack targets far from the ground battle or the sea battle. Where troops fought as in South Vietnam, the Air Force provided only a portion of the firepower and a portion of the airlift. But a combination of heavy bombers and air refueling tankers permitted the Air Force to strike hard at great range—a capability not exploited in North Vietnam until the war was nearly over. While the bomber's advantage in long-range striking power had come to be shared not only with Air Force intercontinental nuclear missiles but also with the Navy's submarine-launched nuclear missiles, for long-range conventional attacks Air Force bombers remained the strongest option. When bombers were subtracted from the equation, however, the Air Force contribution lost its uniqueness. Little of North Vietnam was far from the Gulf of Tonkin, where Navy fighters could launch from carriers and reach much of the country without air refueling.

Navy and Marine aircraft joined fully in the bombing of North Vietnam, all the more so because American fears of Chinese intervention restricted the Air Force's heavy B–52 bombers to a very limited role in North Vietnam for much of the war. Partly because the Air Force had concentrated on nuclear warfare preparations, it even found itself using some fighter planes and munitions developed by the Navy.

The B–52s with their radar and large bombload could have dealt a far more severe blow to many North Vietnamese targets from the outset of the war not only in daylight and clear weather but also at night or in the bad weather prevalent over North Vietnam much of the year. The political prohibition against making full use of the B–52's area bombing capability was an ingredient in the stimulation the war gave to the Air Force's search for a precision, all-weather, around-the-clock bombing capability for fighter aircraft. By the end of the war, laser-guided bombs had made true precision a reality, but darkness and foul weather continued to limit the effectiveness of air power.

The closing phase of American participation in the war brought a political situation and a military situation (as well as a technological situation) more favorable to American air power. The Air Force's story in Southeast Asia consequently carried a sense of upward movement even though the service shared responsibility for losing the war.

The defeat of South Vietnam by communist North Vietnam in 1975 was certainly a defeat for American military power (air as well as ground), despite the fact that it was withdrawn from the struggle before the North's successful invasion. Laos and Cambodia also fell under communist control, and over a million Cambodians died as a result. The passage of time and the ultimately favorable conclusion of the Cold War (in which the Vietnam War was embedded) have eased the ache of defeat, as has the growing prosperity of Thailand and other noncommunist countries in Southeast Asia. But a mere mention of the bombing of North Vietnam can still arouse passionate debate among older Americans, many of whom condemn it for being much too harsh or much too weak or simply irrelevant.

For those who debated air power's role in the war at the time and since, the level of passion as well as abstraction was often very high. Readers of these pages should come away with a more concrete sense of air operations and the Americans involved—from the aircrews who risked their lives to the generals who led them and the politicians who sent them. The portrait drawn of the North Vietnamese is necessarily much less sharply defined, and therefore observations on the impact of the bombing are cautious.

Jacob Van Staaveren's *Gradual Failure: The Air War over North Vietnam, 1965–1966* took our story through the belated attempt to destroy North Vietnam's oil storage facilities in the summer of 1966. By then the North Vietnamese had dispersed gasoline and other oil products from tank farms to barrels scattered around the country. It was another lesson in the weakness of a gradual bombing campaign like Rolling Thunder. After eighteen months of bombing, even North Vietnam's airfields were still largely unscathed, not to mention its principal port at Haiphong and its capital city of Hanoi. The Air Force had proposed bombing targets in all those areas at the outset with B–52s, but President Lyndon Johnson kept all air attacks well away from the major cities for months and eventually permitted only fighter aircraft to attack targets near them. No earlier president had so involved himself in the details of target selection and tactics.

Not until 1972, when President Richard Nixon was pulling American forces out of Southeast Asia, did B–52s drop bombs close to Hanoi and Haiphong. While those cities were still largely spared, the Linebacker campaigns contrasted sharply with Rolling Thunder. Not only was there a bigger role for B–52s, but the new technology of laser-guided bombing permitted fighter aircraft to destroy bridges and other targets quickly with a few bombs instead of risking many fighters in repeated raids. This relatively encouraging experience came after years of deadly frustration for the Air Force and years of rebuilding for North Vietnam. Between President Johnson's termination of Rolling Thunder in 1968 and North Vietnam's invasion of South Vietnam in 1972, North Vietnam suffered little bombing. Indeed, Gen. John Lavelle was fired as commander of Seventh Air Force after an airman charged that false reporting hid a few small raids on North Vietnamese preparations for invasion.

General Lavelle is but one of the memorable people readers will encounter here. I never had the opportunity to meet him, but I am acquainted with many of the men who figure in these pages. They have been generous with their time and knowledge; I am especially grateful to the Red River Valley Fighter Pilots Association for including me not only in their stateside reunions but also in their first return to the Thailand bases in 1987. I prize as well the advantage of knowing many of the historians cited in the notes. All of them deserve to be thanked individually, but their names would constitute too long a list and inevitably I would omit people who should be included. Nevertheless, I do want to give some idea of how this book came to be written.

Armin Rappaport at the University of California, San Diego, guided my early study of American involvement in Asia and proved a friend when the Vietnam War interrupted my doctoral work with a tour as an Army draftee at an Air Force intelligence station in Taiwan. After finishing a dissertation on American military control of the Moro Province in the Philippines, I went to work for the Air Force. My first boss in the Air Force history program was Warren Trest—who had been one of the Air Force's most productive historians in Vietnam during the war. When Jacob Van Staaveren retired, I followed Warren to Washington and joined Col. John Schlight's group of Vietnam historians just before they disbanded—leaving Bernard Nalty and me. Bernie and I both had Vietnam books in progress, but for the most part we worked on other projects. Prospects for declassification of my manuscript appeared bleak.

In August 1990 I joined Col. John Warden's Checkmate air campaign planning group in the Pentagon. Subsequently I became Senior Historical Advisor for the Secretary of the Air Force's Gulf War Air Power Survey directed by Eliot Cohen. Several of my colleagues in the survey were Vietnam veterans (including Richard Blanchfield, Paul Bloch, Alexander Cochran, John "Joe" Guilmartin, Richard Gunkel, Thomas Keaney, Col. Emmett "Mike" Kiraly, Col. David Tretler and Barry Watts) and our conversation often shifted to that earlier war. When I returned to my normal office after a three year absence, declassification of my Vietnam manuscript looked feasible. The end of the Cold War had made it possible even to produce an unclassified version of the multi-volume Gulf War survey. Little about the Vietnam War seemed likely to remain classified, and I finished writing the first draft of this book in a year.

To Hanoi and Back does not pretend to be the last word on its subject or even my last word on it. Eventually I hope to cap the Air Force's multi-volume series on the Vietnam War with a one-volume treatment. For this book on operations over North Vietnam, I depended mostly on Air Force records. Although I made considerable use of documents at the Lyndon Baines Johnson Library in Austin, Texas, I had not yet used the papers of Richard Nixon, Melvin Laird, or Henry Kissinger. My view of the Joint Chiefs of Staff, Pacific Command headquarters, and the headquarters of Military Assistance Command Vietnam (MACV) came primarily from older official histories.

While my manuscript was still classified, I was fortunate to get helpful comments on it by historians of the other services: Graham Cosmas (who was writing the Army's MACV history), Mark Jacobsen (a professor at the Marine Corps Command and Staff College who was writing the Navy's volume on Rolling Thunder), and Jack Shulimson (author of three volumes in the Marine series on the war). I also got a careful reading from David Humphrey, who had guided me through the extensive Vietnam materials at the Johnson Library before he joined the State Department to edit Vietnam volumes of the *Foreign Relations of the United States*. After declassification, the manuscript gained several knowledgeable readers, including David Mets, Marshall Michel, John Sherwood, Warren Trest, Barry Watts, Kenneth Werrell and Darrel Whitcomb.

When conducting research for this book, I often called upon individuals in the other services and agencies. In addition to those already mentioned, Edward Marolda and Bernard Cavalcante of the Navy shared their extensive knowledge of the war, as did Dale Andrade, Jeffrey Clarke, Vincent Demma and William Hammond of the Army. W. Hays Parks of the Army Staff's international law division provided many insights over the years. At the Joint Chiefs of Staff,

Walter Poole and Willard Webb were always ready to help. Thomas Johnson, Gary Keeley and Henry Schorreck at the National Security Agency; Deane Allen and Carrie Thompson at the Defense Intelligence Agency; Robert Destatte at the Defense Intelligence Agency and later the Defense POW/MIA Office; and J. Kenneth McDonald at the Central Intelligence Agency provided invaluable assistance. Merle Pribbenow, a retired American expert on Vietnam, generously shared his translation of Hanoi's official history.

Writing history in the Air Force is a cumulative process that begins with field historians gathering documents, conducting interviews, and writing reports. Hundreds of these reports and thousands of attached documents underlay this volume. I am indebted to all the field historians who did their much tougher job and made it possible for me to write this book. I am also a beneficiary of the Air Force Historical Research Agency at Maxwell Air Force Base, Alabama. The agency not only preserves and indexes documents but has conducted hundreds of interviews related to the Vietnam War. Much of the interviewing was done by Hugh Ahman and James Hasdorff; after retiring, Dr. Hasdorff went on to conduct for the Air Force Academy interviews with former prisoners of war, and I am indebted to Duane Reed of the Academy library for providing me with copies of those transcripts as well as many other kindnesses. There is probably not a person at the Historical Research Agency who has not assisted me on some project. For this one, I should thank at least Thomas Dean, Archie Difante, Judy Endicott, Lynn Gamma, Richard Gamma, Robert Johnson, James Kitchens, MSgt. Barry Spink and Warren Trest; also Robert Young, who was at the agency before he moved to become historian of the National Air Intelligence Center at Wright-Patterson Air Force Base in Ohio.

I frequently exploited my colleagues in the Washington office of the Air Force history program—in this case especially Vicky Crone, Sheldon Goldberg, William Heimdahl, Yvonne Kinkaid, Marcelle Knaack, Maj. John Kreis, Eduard Mark, Karen Fleming Michael, Lt. Col. Vance Mitchell, Walton Moody, Bernard Nalty, Jack Neufeld, Diane Putney, Col. John F. Shiner, George Watson, Col. George Williams and Richard Wolf. During two summers I had the assistance of talented interns: Cadet Robert Cummings of the Air Force Academy studied the North Vietnamese rail system, and Janis Gibbs of William and Mary surveyed the American press's treatment of air operations in North Vietnam.

My principal mentor was Herman Wolk. I could not have written the volume without his support and the support of three chiefs of the Air Force history program: Maj. Gen. John Huston, Richard Kohn, and Richard Hallion. The demanding task of declassifying my manuscript was undertaken by a team of Air Force declassifiers under Maj. William Coburn. I was very fortunate to have my manuscript put into the competent hands of David Chenoweth, the Air Force's most experienced editor of books on the Vietnam War.

Finally, I want to honor my most formative influences. Clarence and Elaine Thompson brought me into the world when he was a navigator in a B–24

Liberator bombing Germany. Lillian Hurlburt Thompson married me before I was drafted, joined me in Taiwan, became an international businesswoman, and helped to build a humane context for my study of war.

To Hanoi and Back

The United States Air Force and North Vietnam
1966–1973

Chapter One

Puzzle

At the end of the twentieth century, after communism collapsed in Europe and lost momentum in Asia, Americans still could not agree what course their country should have taken in Vietnam. Without American intervention, communists were poised to wrest control of all of Vietnam, Laos, and Cambodia from the French in the decade following the Second World War. The postponement of communist victory until 1975 came at a high price for those Southeast Asian countries and for the United States. But on the periphery of carnage grew a prosperous, noncommunist Southeast Asia. In the long rivalry between Vietnam and Thailand, the Vietnam War helped Thailand move ahead economically with an infusion of dollars from U.S. Air Force wings based there. Thailand's communist insurgency sputtered, while Vietnamese communism struggled first against American firepower; later against Chinese communist invaders and their Cambodian communist allies (who had exterminated hundreds of thousands of Cambodians); and finally against the inertia of an aging leadership more adept at fighting a war than building an economy.

Whatever the merits of waging the Vietnam War, the Air Force and its sister services could not avoid the puzzle of how best to fight the war within constraints imposed by technical capabilities, by the physical geography of Southeast Asia, and by the changing complexity of the world's political geography—as it was filtered through the perceptions of Presidents Lyndon Johnson and Richard Nixon. Johnson's rejection of the Air Force's original proposal to send the big Boeing B–52 Stratofortress bombers against targets throughout communist North Vietnam left Air Force and Navy fighter aircraft to nibble at targets gradually doled out by the President. During the long Rolling Thunder air campaign over North Vietnam from March 1965 to November 1968, Johnson confined B–52 targets in North Vietnam to supply depots and transportation routes near the border with South Vietnam and Laos. Even these marginal B–52 raids on the North did not begin until April 1966. Meanwhile, B–52s had been pounding the jungles of South Vietnam in hope of hitting communist insurgents and regular North Vietnamese units trying to overthrow a government closely tied to the United States.[1]

After failing to give the French enough support to suppress the communist rebellion led by Ho Chi Minh in the 1940s and 1950s, the U.S. government wanted to contain communism in North Vietnam—the half of the country that lay north of the seventeenth parallel. In the south the United States tried to establish a new country under Ngo Dinh Diem, a nationalist who had buried a brother killed by the communists. Unfortunately, Diem was a Roman Catholic in a predominantly Buddhist country.* Unrest among Buddhists led in 1963 to a military coup that cost Diem his life and left Vietnamese veterans of the former French colonial army in charge. Eventually, Gen. Nguyen Van Thieu pushed ahead of the more flamboyant Air Marshal Nguyen Cao Ky.

The association of Thieu and Ky with French colonialism tarred their administration from the outset. Their claims to national leadership were also undercut by an increasing American presence in South Vietnam and by the public American guarantee that the existence of communist North Vietnam would not be threatened. Thieu and Ky were unable to offer the prospect of a reunified Vietnam—only the communist regime of North Vietnam offered that. While the United States proved all too willing to Americanize the war in South Vietnam with half a million American troops, as well as planes, those troops were forbidden to invade North Vietnam. President Johnson did not want to risk a massive communist Chinese intervention of the kind that had pushed U.S. forces out of North Korea in 1950. But North Vietnam could move beyond supporting insurgency to full-scale invasion of South Vietnam. Although such invasions did not occur until 1972 and 1975, the South Vietnamese government and its American ally acted under the assumption that an invasion might come much sooner. In the meantime, at least fifty thousand North Vietnamese regulars were operating inside South Vietnam by 1967. It was a great strength of the communist position that its opponents could not focus on the insurgency in South Vietnam at the expense of preparing to meet the conventional threat from North Vietnam (and vice versa).

In contrast to communist exploitation of their opponents' weaknesses, the Johnson administration even felt constrained to forbid an American invasion of the Laotian panhandle, down which the North Vietnamese were sending troops and supplies into South Vietnam. The "Ho Chi Minh Trail" became an increasingly elaborate network of dirt roads carrying trucks at night through a gauntlet of American bombing, punctuated in later years by gunfire from AC–130s (converted air transports called "gunships").[2] North of the panhandle, American air power helped Laotian government forces defend themselves from communist attack. The Geneva Agreement of 1962 had supposedly guaranteed Laotian neutrality, and the country's beleaguered government preferred to maintain the fiction that Laos was not being used as a conduit for communist supplies.

---

* For most Vietnamese, religion was a mixture of Buddhist, Confucian, and Taoist elements with folk traditions.

Hence, the Laotian government did not want the unavoidably overt introduction of large American ground forces to cut the Trail—but did agree to air operations for the same purpose. U.S. air forces (like North Vietnamese ground forces) pretended in public that they were not operating in Laos. America's transparent pretense also suited the Soviet Union, which thereby found it easier to avoid confronting the United States over Laos. This situation was one of the Vietnam War's open secrets helping to persuade many Americans that their government was dishonest.

*   *   *

The government of Thailand also tried to keep its own role in the war quiet. U.S. Air Force planes taking off from bases in Thailand were not permitted to bomb in South Vietnam, and the Air Force was required to pretend that missions into North Vietnam and Laos had actually launched from bases in South Vietnam. Not until 1967, long after air operations from Thailand became common knowledge, would the Thai government relinquish this fiction to permit B–52 missions from Thailand against targets in South Vietnam. Until then, Air Force pilots in Thailand got no publicity, except on those rare occasions when they were sent to give a press briefing in Saigon under the pretense that their missions over North Vietnam had been launched from South Vietnam. Some pilots relished this publicity, but others considered it a jinx after the commander of the 67th Tactical Fighter Squadron, Lt. Col. Robinson Risner, followed his appearance on the cover of *Time* magazine with a long stay in North Vietnam's prison system; he was shot down on September 16, 1965.

The Air Force was not entirely unhappy with Thailand's reluctance to have planes based there bomb in South Vietnam, since that policy had the effect of fencing off substantial air power that could be used only against North Vietnam and Laos. Not until 1968 would Thailand permit fighter aircraft based there to strike targets in South Vietnam and then only in the northern area called I Corps. Except for the 366th Tactical Fighter Wing at Da Nang Air Base in I Corps, Air Force fighters based in South Vietnam rarely ventured deep into North Vietnam. Army and Marine demands for air power in South Vietnam surpassed anything ever seen. Of the eight million tons of ordnance that would fall from the sky on Southeast Asia, more than half would fall on South Vietnam; less than a million tons would fall on North Vietnam and little more than two million on Laos. Although these figures were impressive when compared with the less than four million tons dropped by the United States and the United Kingdom in all theaters during World War II, most of the bombs in World War II fell in and around cities—unlike Southeast Asia, where most of the bombs fell in the jungle, along with the bulk of the eight million tons of rounds fired by American artillery.

The American air war over North Vietnam and Laos was waged mostly from Air Force bases in Thailand and Navy carriers in the Gulf of Tonkin. Where Thailand's Korat plateau bulged north of Cambodia to the Mekong River and the Laotian panhandle, as little as seventy miles separated Thailand and Vietnam. The Air Force used three bases in eastern Thailand near the Mekong, and four nearer the capital at Bangkok, about three hundred miles west on the Gulf of Thailand. Five hundred miles lay between the western Thailand bases and the North Vietnamese capital at Hanoi. Depending on the location of bases and targets, bombing missions from Thailand to North Vietnam could last from one to three hours.

At the beginning of the war, there were only three bases in Thailand with runways long enough to handle fully loaded jet fighters comfortably: Don Muang, just north of Bangkok; Takhli, a hundred miles north up the Chao Phraya River from Bangkok; Korat, on the southwestern edge of the Korat Plateau, about a hundred miles northeast of Bangkok. Facilities were best at Don Muang, but since it also served as the Bangkok airport, the Thai government was reluctant to permit obvious Air Force operations there. Except for a few air defense interceptors, transports, and refueling tankers, the Thais reserved Don Muang's military ramp for their own air force of old American F–86 fighters.

At Takhli and Korat, however, the Thais were soon submerged by about ten thousand American airmen with more than a hundred Republic F–105 Thunderchief fighters. This force had to be constantly replenished, because the F–105 was the Air Force's principal fighter-bomber used in the Rolling Thunder campaign, and more than three hundred F–105s were shot down over North Vietnam and Laos.* Attrition would have been even worse had it not been for the protection provided by supporting aircraft. Two dozen EB–66 electronic warfare aircraft, for example, shared the Takhli facilities with the F–105s and attempted to jam enemy radars from a distance; the EB–66s were too slow to survive over the better defended areas in North Vietnam.

During the 1950s, the Air Force had concentrated on building its capability to wage nuclear war. The Strategic Air Command then absorbed most of the service's resources, and Tactical Air Command spent much of the remainder developing its own capacity to drop nuclear bombs. The F–105 was designed for that, but instead of carrying a nuclear bomb in its bomb bay, the F–105 carried conventional bombs on its wings. Those relatively small wings had been intended to help the F–105 penetrate at high speed close to the ground; at higher altitude they limited the F–105's maneuverability. Pilots gave the F–105 unflattering nicknames like "Lead Sled" or more commonly "Thud"—a nickname that in Southeast Asia would become more affectionate than derogatory. The Air

---

* For aircraft loss figures, see the statistics appendix.

Force's awkward attempt in 1964 to use Thuds for its air-show demonstration team, the Thunderbirds, came to a quick and inglorious end. But combat forged a proud bond between pilots and their Thuds. While it could not maneuver agilely in a dogfight, the Thud could carry more bombs further than any other Air Force fighter in 1966 and could outrun enemy fighters at low altitude.

The only Air Force fighter that could better handle North Vietnamese air defenses was the newer, more maneuverable McDonnell F–4 Phantom II (a descendant of the Navy's first carrier jet fighter, the McDonnell FH–1 Phantom of the late 1940s). "Phantom" was a most unsuitable name for this big two-engine fighter known for leaving a highly visible trail of black smoke. Only by using its afterburners could the F–4 avoid the smoke that in daylight continually gave the plane's position away. Nevertheless, "Phantom" was one of the few official names that aircrews actually used. The Phantom did get most of the night bombing missions, for which its two-man crew was better suited than a lone Thud pilot. Someone caught the humor in the name "Phantom" by drawing a cartoon of a funny little man (with the delta shape of the fighter) wearing a cape, broad-brimmed hat, and tennis shoes. In their daytime air-to-air combat with enemy fighters, Phantom aircrews had to resign themselves to the fact that there was nothing stealthy about their plane.

Although nearly as heavy as the single-engine Thud, the Phantom's two engines and bigger wings permitted it to climb faster—a virtue that came at the price of higher fuel consumption and shorter range. In one respect, the Phantom was less well prepared for air-to-air combat than the Thud, for early in the war the Phantom had no gun. The Navy had developed the Phantom to protect the fleet with radar-guided Sparrow missiles that could down attacking aircraft at long range—usually more than a mile—if the radar could be kept "locked on" the target during a missile's entire flight. Over North Vietnam, however, ground clutter could interfere with the radar guidance system; in any case, the presence of so many Navy and Air Force planes obliged aircrews to identify an enemy aircraft visually before attacking—often putting the Phantom too close to use a Sparrow effectively. Despite the ability of the Phantom's heat-seeking Sidewinder missiles to find an enemy plane's tailpipe at fairly close range, Phantom crews sometimes found themselves too close for anything but the gun they did not have. Not until 1967 would Air Force F–4s begin to use a gun mounted in a pod under the fuselage, and only as Rolling Thunder ended in 1968 would new F–4s with a built-in gun deploy to Southeast Asia.[3]

While most Thuds had only one seat, each Phantom had two on the theory that a second crew member was required to operate the plane's radar; he would try to lock his radar on an enemy fighter so that the Phantom's pilot could fire a Sparrow missile. The Navy gave this backseat job to a navigator called a "radar intercept operator." During Rolling Thunder, the Air Force gave the radar job to a second pilot, but no pilot liked to ride in the back seat and the Air Force ultimately followed the Navy's example. The Air Force's backseat navigator would be called officially a "weapon system officer" (WSO, pronounced "wizzo"), because he often handled not only air-to-air missile radar but also the new precision bombing systems that were developed late in the war. Unofficially, he would assume the nicknames of the backseat pilot who preceded him: "guy in back (GIB)" or simply "backseater."

The fact that the Air Force's Phantom backseaters were originally pilots may have made other fighter pilots somewhat less hostile to giving backseaters equal credit with the frontseat pilot for any enemy aircraft shot down. Shooting down at least five enemy aircraft had long been a milestone in a fighter pilot's career, for then he was called an "ace." When the war finally produced its first American aces in 1972, all Phantom backseaters were navigators and three of them (two Air Force, one Navy) became aces.[4]

At the beginning of Rolling Thunder, the Air Force had about six hundred Thuds and six hundred Phantoms. The production line for the single-seat Thud had closed, but the Air Force received more than two hundred new two-seat Phantoms every year. While a portion of the growing Phantom force was used for less risky bombing in South Vietnam, Thuds were reserved for the more dangerous missions in North Vietnam and Laos. Not only were most Thuds older than most Phantoms, but the loss of a single-seat Thud cost at most one crew member rather than two. Air Force Phantoms operating in North Vietnam were expected to protect Thuds from North Vietnamese fighter aircraft; this less expensive mission absorbed much of the Phantom effort there during Rolling Thunder. When Rolling Thunder ended in 1968, more than half the Thuds were gone, and most of the remainder were soon replaced by Phantoms.

When the Air Force Phantoms were first deployed to Southeast Asia in 1965, runways had to be lengthened at two bases in northeast Thailand near the Mekong. At first, the Phantom's reconnaissance version (the RF–4) shared Udorn with RF–101s and F–104s, but these older aircraft were entirely replaced by more RF–4s and F–4s in 1967. Two hundred miles down the Mekong from Udorn, Ubon became the principal Phantom base in Thailand. Another two hundred miles east of Ubon across the Laotian panhandle in South Vietnam, Da Nang's Phantoms could be used in North Vietnam and Laos as well as South Vietnam. Altogether, the three bases had about ninety F–4s and twenty RF–4s in 1966; in subsequent years the Phantom presence in Thailand would grow. Of the more than five hundred Air Force F–4s and RF–4s lost in Southeast Asia, two-thirds were shot down over North Vietnam and Laos.

Many of the Phantom and Thud losses could be attributed to two poor design features they shared. At the beginning of Rolling Thunder, neither type of fighter had self-sealing fuel tanks and both had hydraulic control systems with backup lines close enough together that a single hit could render the aircraft uncontrollable or cause the fuel tank to explode. Self-sealing fuel tanks were heavier, and aircraft designers tried to save weight in these already heavy aircraft by using lighter tanks. While some Thuds eventually got self-sealing fuel tanks and a more survivable arrangement of their control systems, the Phantoms kept the maneuverability afforded by their lighter, more vulnerable fuel tanks. Late-model Phantoms did benefit from the addition of a backup electrical system for pitch control.[5]

Men shot down had a better than even chance of surviving. About a third were rescued in North Vietnam, and almost as many survived years of captivity there. More were rescued in Laos, where lighter air defenses threatened rescue aircraft less, and friendly as well as enemy forces were on the ground. But during the prisoner exchange in 1973, only thirteen Americans captured in Laos would come home. Of the more than five hundred Air Force men shot down there, about a third met a fate unknown; some may have been killed by Laotian communist troops, for whom prisoners were too much trouble, or by North Vietnamese communist troops who were pretending not to be in Laos.

Before rescue helicopters at Udorn would venture into Laos or North Vietnam, downed aircrew would be located and protected by small propeller-driven Douglas A–1 Skyraiders (or "Spads" as pilots dubbed them after the famous French fighters flown by Americans in World War I). In addition to the squadron of A–1s at Udorn, a squadron at Nakhon Phanom lay just across the Mekong from the Ho Chi Minh Trail in the Laotian panhandle. The Air Force opened "NKP" (as Americans called the new base) with a runway made of pierced steel planking that corrosion soon necessitated replacing with aluminum matting. Only propeller aircraft like the Spads could use NKP regularly, but jet aircraft could land there in an emergency and many fighters shot up over North Vietnam were able to make it back to NKP to land or at least permit their crews to bail out where they could be easily rescued.[6]

When F–105s and F–4s made their longer three-hour raids into North Vietnam, they required refueling in the air from Boeing KC–135 tankers soon after takeoff and again after leaving North Vietnam. Routine use of air refueling for combat missions was an innovation. Before the Vietnam War, air refueling had usually facilitated the deployment of aircraft rather than their employment. By the end of 1966, there were about thirty KC–135s in Thailand: ten at Takhli and twenty at U-Tapao, a new base seventy miles south of Bangkok on the Gulf of Thailand. Fuel could be brought in by ship to U-Tapao, an arrangement much preferable to trucking fuel to bases further north.

Each KC–135 could transfer about fifty thousand pounds of fuel per sortie, enough to top off four fighters in less than half an hour and have plenty left; after a morning mission, a KC–135 could land, reload, and come up again for an afternoon mission. Getting the most out of the tanker force drove mission scheduling. Every morning and afternoon the tankers flew over northern Thailand in oblong orbits called "tracks," topping off fighters on their way north and later meeting them over Laos with enough fuel to get them home.[7]

Other KC–135s took off from the Japanese island of Okinawa to refuel B–52s on ten-hour missions from Guam, two thousand miles east of Vietnam and Laos; each of the big bombers soaked up an entire tanker load. Even with aerial refueling, a B–52 could not carry its maximum thirty tons of bombs so long a distance, and bomb loads were cut to twenty tons or less. This was still ten times the load carried by an F–105 or F–4 on missions to North Vietnam. The Air Force worked to persuade the Thais to permit B–52 operations from the new base at U-Tapao, since from there the big bombers could reach targets with full bomb loads without air refueling.

The B–52s and KC–135s belonged to the Strategic Air Command, which tried to keep conventional warfare from crippling the command's ability to perform its nuclear bombing mission. Since B–52s flew sorties above twenty thousand feet over Southeast Asia (above thirty thousand feet over North Vietnam), Strategic Air Command feared that its crews would lose their skill at flying low-level missions of the kind envisioned for a nuclear war with the Soviet Union. Consequently, B–52 crews rotated back to the United States after six-month tours of temporary duty in the Pacific. Although this policy made less sense for KC–135 crews, they too came to the Vietnam War on temporary duty. While fighter squadrons also began the war on temporary duty, their pilots, like the ground personnel at all the bases (including U-Tapao), eventually found themselves "permanently" assigned—but in Southeast Asia, "permanently" turned out to mean twelve months or less.

Through much of 1965, fighter squadrons arrived for four months of temporary duty in Thailand from Japan and the United States. Toward the end of that year, squadrons began to stay for the duration of the war. Each of the fighter bases in Thailand had a single fighter wing with up to four fighter squadrons (more than seventy fighters sharing a crowded field with an assortment of other aircraft). By late 1966 the fighter wings had acquired the numerical designations that they would keep through the end of Rolling Thunder: the 355th Tactical Fighter Wing at Takhli (F–105s), the 388th Tactical Fighter Wing at Korat (F–105s), the 8th Tactical Fighter Wing at Ubon (F–4s), and the 366th Tactical Fighter Wing at Da Nang, South Vietnam (F–4s). The mixture of reconnaissance aircraft (RF–101s and RF–4s) and fighters (F–104s and later F–4s) at Udorn composed the 432d Tactical Reconnaissance Wing.

Most nonflying personnel cycled through on one-year tours. Every year on the anniversary of a squadron's arrival, many of its people would leave to be replaced by new people usually without any experience in Southeast Asia. Aircrew were on a different schedule, since they could go home after completing one hundred missions over North Vietnam—just as F–86 pilots in the Korean War had gone home after a hundred missions over North Korea. Commonly, meeting this standard took seven or eight months, but that depended on how the tour meshed with seasonal and political variations in the intensity of the American effort over North Vietnam. When not flying there, aircrew operated over Laos where they might get shot at, but would not receive mission credit toward the necessary one hundred "counters."

While some aircrew volunteered to come back for a second or even a third tour, most did not want to push their luck flying against North Vietnamese air defenses. Not until much later did the Air Force require many who had completed a "permanent" tour in Southeast Asia to serve there again, but backseat F–4 pilots sometimes returned voluntarily to get into the front seat. The prevalence of one tour in Southeast Asia for most Air Force personel contrasted not only with the repeated stints of temporary duty allotted to aircrews of the Strategic Air Command, but also with repeated cruises in the theater for Navy carrier personnel. Nevertheless, the one-tour policy spread the risks as well as the career advantages of combat service through much of the force. All the good it did for morale, however, came at a considerable cost in the depth of Southeast Asian experience available in the theater. Nor was that the only price to be paid. Early in the war most Air Force fighter pilots went into combat after years of flying fighters elsewhere, but replacement training units in the United States sent an increasing proportion of new pilots and those who were cross-training into fighters from bombers and transports.

For nonflying personnel, the one-year tour seemed less equitable. A year in Southeast Asia could be spent far more pleasantly in Thailand than in South Vietnam. The South Vietnamese bases were subject to frequent rocket, mortar and sapper attacks. The Thai bases were attacked only a few times (all by sappers) and the first attack did not come until 1968. Indeed, Bangkok was a favorite choice for the rest and recuperation week available to those serving in South Vietnam. Yet it was a grievance among ground personnel in Thailand that they could not participate in the rest and recuperation program; nor did they get an income tax break available to all personnel in South Vietnam. Aircrew in Thailand eventually did get these benefits, but of course, Thailand was then a more dangerous assignment for aircrew than South Vietnam.[8]

The practice of assigning Air Force ground personnel for one-year tours in Thailand made less and less sense as the years passed. When the Thai bases were undergoing expansion in 1965 and 1966, living conditions were primitive in comparison with the relative luxury of later years. Some early expedients did not work: inflatable shelters collapsed when the glue in the seams melted in the tropical heat, and the herd of goats acquired to keep the grass short at Takhli became a smelly nuisance until replaced by lawnmowers. In 1967, a visitor from the Pentagon to Takhli and other Thailand bases could report that "wing commanders are focusing their attention and diverting energy to base development and upkeep (green grass etc.) to a much greater extent than one would reasonably expect in a combat zone."[9]

Swimming pools made a successful early appearance at the Thailand bases—all the more popular in the tropical heat because getting air conditioners for sleeping quarters proved difficult even for aircrew. Club bars provided a ready release from the tension of combat or the boredom of desk duty. Just off base, Thai prostitutes did not want for customers, and the dispensary at each base was handling about a thousand venereal disease cases a year. American men and Thai women also developed more enduring relationships. There was something intoxicating about the gracious culture of Thailand. Even for the men who had to fly north where survivors were bound to lose friends, Thailand would provide fond memories.[10]

However much their country might seem like a paradise for young American men, Thailand's leaders managed to exploit their relationship with the United States without being swallowed by it. During the nineteenth century, the kings of Siam (as Thailand was then known) had succeeded in maintaining their country's independence as a buffer between British Burma and French Indochina. A tilt toward the British in those years was more than counterbalanced by collaboration with the Japanese in World War II, when Thailand declared war on the United Kingdom and the United States. Together with land reform, Thailand's independence of the western colonial powers had inoculated the country against the appeal of communism. Even after losing authority to military dictators in the 1930s, the Buddhist king remained a potent symbol of Thai nationalism.

The poorest and most vulnerable part of Thailand was the Korat plateau, where American air bases began to inject some much needed money. On the other hand, communists naturally scented opportunity in the conjunction of American bases with a population not only poor but closely tied to Laos. More Lao (a Thai people) lived in Thailand than in Laos, and the communist movement seemed to have excellent prospects for spreading across the Mekong. But this insurgency never made much progress except among Vietnamese refugees. Sappers caught in the handful of attacks on American bases in Thailand turned out to be Vietnamese.[11]

Since Thailand was a bulwark against communism, the United States was not inclined to be very critical of its dictatorial form of government. Indeed, the military aid supplied by the United States since the 1950s had strengthened the hold of the Thai army on the government. When Field Marshal Sarit Thanarat died in 1963 (leaving a wife and more than fifty mistresses), he was succeeded as prime minister by his less colorful deputy, Gen. Thanom Kittikachorn. Thanom continued Sarit's policy of working with the U.S. Army to prepare ground defenses against Chinese invasion. The small Thai air force lacked influence and did not much figure in Thanom's plans.[12]

The U.S. Air Force presence in Thailand grew up largely outside the established American military apparatus for doing business there. Of the thirty-four thousand American military personnel in Thailand by the end of 1966, twenty-six thousand were Air Force. Yet the commander of the U.S. Military Assistance Command, Thailand, was still an Army officer: Maj. Gen. Richard G. Stilwell (who was not, as many thought, a son or nephew of Gen. Joseph W. Stilwell, commander of American forces in the China-Burma-India theater during World War II). While the U.S. Air Force sought to bring more men and planes into Thailand, Stilwell tried to be the Air Force's sole channel to the American ambassador, Graham A. Martin, who was supposed to conduct all negotiations with General Thanom and his government. But Martin had served in the Army Air Forces during World War II, and the Air Force had ready access to him through the air attaché, Col. Roland K. McCoskrie.[13]

Despite Colonel McCoskrie's best efforts with Ambassador Martin, the Army-managed approval process in Thailand often proved frustrating for the Air Force. In January 1966, the Air Force sought to strengthen its position by sending a major general to Udorn to oversee Air Force assets in Thailand. The new commander, Maj. Gen. Charles R. Bond, Jr., had been one of Maj. Gen. Claire L. Chennault's Flying Tigers in China during World War II, when he shot down nine Japanese aircraft. Bond would take his orders on operations over North Vietnam from the Air Force commander in South Vietnam, Lt. Gen. Joseph H. Moore. Moore's command was called Second Air Division until the spring of 1966, when it became Seventh Air Force. To make this arrangement more palatable to the Thai government (which wanted to disguise Thailand's connection with the war in Vietnam), the Air Force made Bond subordinate to Thirteenth Air Force in the Philippines for all nonoperational matters. Therefore, Bond was said to be deputy commander of Seventh/Thirteenth Air Force.[14]

Since the Seventh Air Force commander and his staff dealt directly with the wings at each base in Thailand, Bond could not be said to command anything. He had one of the oddest jobs in the history of the Air Force. When he tried to mediate between his two Air Force bosses, the ambassadors in Thailand and Laos, and General Stilwell, Bond often encountered more discord than harmony. Stilwell took a very dim view of Bond's role and complained that neither Stilwell himself nor the ambassador nor General Thanom had been consulted about Bond's assignment. In fact, the Chief of Staff of the Air Force, Gen. John P. McConnell, had obtained Ambassador Martin's approval during a visit to Washington. When confronted by Stilwell, Martin could only slap the Air Force's wrist for not providing a formal request through channels.[15]

*   *   *

A few months after sending General Bond to Thailand, the Air Force Chief of Staff sent Lt. Gen. William W. Momyer from Air Training Command to replace General Moore as commander of Seventh Air Force in South Vietnam. General McConnell decided to make this change on the advice of a retired Air Force general, Elwood R. "Pete" Quesada, a famous fighter commander in World War II and the first commander of Tactical Air Command after the war. In retirement, Quesada had continued to be an influential defender of fighter aircraft during an era when the Air Force was dominated by Strategic Air Command's bombers and missiles. Senator Stuart Symington (Democrat, Missouri), who had been the first Secretary of the Air Force, asked Quesada to visit Southeast Asia and determine whether anything could be done to improve the Air Force's performance there. Quesada concluded that Moore was too subservient to the joint commander in South Vietnam, Army Gen. William C. Westmoreland. Moore and Westmoreland grew up together in Spartanburg, South Carolina, and had remained close over the years—too close, as far as Quesada was concerned.[16]

Moore had come to South Vietnam in 1964 with Westmoreland and took command of the Second Air Division (subsequently Seventh Air Force) at Tan Son Nhut Air Base on the edge of the capital, Saigon. Although Westmoreland's U.S. Military Assistance Command Vietnam, (MACV) was headquartered in downtown Saigon at that time, he would eventually move it to a large new building informally dubbed "Pentagon East" at Tan Son Nhut. Westmoreland's joint headquarters consisted mostly of Army officers, and many in the Air Force complained that air matters were not getting sufficient attention. Quesada wanted to replace Moore with a far less agreeable general, one well known for his convictions about the best way to employ fighter aircraft. "Spike" Momyer was already a fighter group commander in North Africa during World War II, when the Army Air Forces developed enduring doctrine under fire. No Army commander was apt to get the best of an argument with Momyer over air power. He had a disciplined and practical intellect befitting the son of a lawyer who had once taught at the University of Chicago.

The death of his father when Momyer was fourteen both liberated the boy from becoming a lawyer and forced an early end to playing sports, as he had to take a job after school. By then he had already seen Charles A. Lindbergh and his *Spirit of St. Louis* land at an Army Air Corps base near the Momyer home in Muskogee, Oklahoma. After his mother moved the family to Seattle, Momyer worked his way through the University of Washington and straight into the Army Air Corps. He never stopped working hard, and five years out of college, he was commanding a fighter group in combat. The weight of early responsibility made him far less fun-loving than most fighter pilots.[17]

The staff at Seventh Air Force headquarters soon found that their new commander was all business and that he made their business his business. His quick mind and appetite for work permitted him to avoid delegating much of his authority, and he acted as virtually his own deputy for operations. Some were intimidated by his intellect and by his unusual austerity, symbolized by a smoking ban during staff meetings. He did not like the laid-back style common in a combat theater. He expected proper uniforms and clean quarters and flower beds—this last idiosyncrasy a subject of humor.[18]

By the time Momyer took command of Seventh Air Force, many airmen suspected that the U.S. was in for a much longer war and possible defeat in

Southeast Asia. He bent his efforts to helping the Air Force come through the experience in the best shape possible, and for him that meant an Air Force with the most versatile technology available. He was, at most, lukewarm about the extensive use of old propeller aircraft in South Vietnam and Laos; no matter how well suited they were to fighting insurgents, propeller aircraft could not survive in Europe against Soviet air defenses. On the other hand, he opposed the development of technology designed to meet too specific a threat. Since the U.S. could never predict exactly what situation its armed forces would encounter, he favored multirole jet aircraft. Of the aircraft already in the inventory, the F–4 was his clear favorite, since it could be used against enemy fighters in the air or targets on the ground.[19]

Momyer was an especially able exponent of the need for unity in the command of air power. But unity of command was not to be found in Southeast Asia anywhere above a wing commander. His efforts to change that were unavailing. He doubted that Thai sensitivities were really behind denying him command of the wings in Thailand and giving him only operational control. His repeated interrogations of Ambassador Martin on this point gave Momyer the impression that the admiral who ran the Pacific theater from Hawaii (Adm. Ulysses S. Grant Sharp, Commander in Chief of Pacific Command) and his Air Force component commander (Gen. Hunter Harris, Commander in Chief of Pacific Air Forces) wanted to deny Momyer command of the Thailand wings because he was Westmoreland's air deputy—by denying Momyer command, they were really denying Westmoreland and keeping air operations against North Vietnam under their control.[20]

From Momyer's point of view, there should have been a separate Southeast Asia theater with Westmoreland in charge and with all air operations (including those of the Navy and Marine Corps) under Momyer. As it was, Momyer's authority did not even extend to the Strategic Air Command B–52s that were dropping more than a third of the bombs in South Vietnam. Since the same aircraft also had a nuclear mission in case of a wider war, Strategic Air Command refused to give them to Momyer. Nor did Westmoreland consult Seventh Air Force about targets for the B–52s, and Momyer was not mollified by the presence of an Air Force colonel in Westmoreland's targeting shop. Westmoreland decided what he wanted the B–52s to hit and passed the list to Strategic Air Command. Momyer was appalled by the enormous tonnage of bombs the B–52s were dropping on the South Vietnamese jungle with little evidence of much physical effect on the enemy, however psychologically upsetting to enemy troops in the vicinity. Strategic Air Command's ownership of tankers was less onerous for Momyer, since Westmoreland did not get involved. Momyer's main gripe about tankers was Strategic Air Command's unwillingness to let them fly far enough north in Laos to save returning fighters especially low on fuel. In practice, however, tanker pilots often broke Strategic Air Command rules to save fighters.

The fact that Seventh Air Force worked for General Westmoreland in Saigon on operations in South Vietnam and for General Harris in Hawaii on operations in North Vietnam contributed to handling those operations separately by establishing "in-country" and "out-country" control centers. This way of dividing the work preceded Momyer and might well have occurred even if Westmoreland had controlled the whole war, since the two regions made different demands. Indeed, Westmoreland did control air operations over a portion of North Vietnam adjacent to South Vietnam (not to mention sharing control of operations in Laos with the U.S. ambassador there), but those operations were handled by the out-country control center. The in-country "tactical air control center" answered ground unit requests for air support in South Vietnam. This tactical air control center included South Vietnamese personnel and (only to maintain political appearances) its director was a South Vietnamese colonel; the real director was an American brigadier general who reported to Momyer's deputy for operations.*

The out-country U.S.-only "command center" (with the radio call sign "Blue Chip") developed daily orders to send a few large formations against major targets in North Vietnam and many smaller formations, including two-plane patrols on armed reconnaissance of transportation routes there and in Laos. These daily orders were called fragmentary orders or "frags," because each wing received only a fragment of the order and because information that did not change on a daily basis (like rules of engagement) was not sent on a daily basis. Fragmentary orders permitted Seventh Air Force to send the necessary information in electronic messages without overwhelming the telecommunications network. The in-country tactical air control center also issued fragmentary orders, but they provided a more routine framework through which the control center could react to changing circumstances on the battlefield in South Vietnam. Fragmentary orders were prepared and executed on a three-day cycle; while part of the staff planned operations for the day after next, another group drafted the next day's orders, and a third group monitored the current day's operations. Teams of operations and intelligence personnel specialized in preparing fragmentary orders for daylight or nighttime operations.[21]

Momyer's headquarters was near Westmoreland's at Tan Son Nhut Air Base just north of Saigon. South of the city lay the fertile rice paddies of the Mekong Delta. North for seven hundred miles, most of the way to China, stretched a narrow coastal plain pressed against the sea by rugged hills, until the Red River provided another delta, smaller and less fertile. There lay the North Vietnamese capital of Hanoi, the principal North Vietnamese port of Haiphong, and many of the targets of greatest interest to Momyer. When he sent planes to

---

* B–52 missions, in-country and out-country, were controlled by the Strategic Air Command and scheduled by the SAC Advanced Echelon (SACADVON) at Seventh Air Force headquarters.

the Red River, they were too far from his command center at Tan Son Nhut to communicate easily. In the summer of 1966, a control center for operations over North Vietnam began functioning (with radio call sign "Motel") on Monkey Mountain, which dominated a peninsula jutting into the South China Sea at Da Nang, about half way between Saigon and Hanoi.

The progress of strike forces over North Vietnam was also monitored by the control center at Udorn Air Base, Thailand. If Monkey Mountain went off the air, Udorn was in control. Both sites had long-range radar, but they could not see the Red River Delta. That far north only a Navy radar ship and Air Force Lockheed EC–121 radar planes could offer some radar coverage while keeping their distance from enemy fighters and missiles. Unlike the Boeing E–3 Airborne Warning and Control System (AWACS) planes produced after the Vietnam War, the EC–121's radar could not "look down" successfully and aircraft would be lost in ground clutter on the EC–121's radar screens. In truth, neither the EC–121s nor the ground stations at Monkey Mountain and Udorn could do much to control air operations over the Red River.

Over the less defended Laotian panhandle, other even more vulnerable converted transports could survive. Lockheed EC–130s each carried an Airborne Battlefield Command and Control Center (ABCCC) without radar, but with the communications equipment and battle staff necessary to control interdiction strikes against trucks in the Laotian and North Vietnamese panhandles. An ABCCC aircraft often coordinated interdiction strikes through forward air controllers (FACs) surveying the panhandles in either light propeller planes or jet fighters (beginning in 1967 over North Vietnam where enemy air defenses made the slower propeller planes too vulnerable). Each FAC patrolled the same stretch of road and jungle every day, so that in daylight he had the best chance of seeing elusive enemy trucks and directing strike aircraft sent his way by an ABCCC.

While ABCCC aircraft and Motel were closer to the bombing, Blue Chip was closer to the boss. On his out-country staff as well as his in-country staff, Momyer found somewhat more harmony among operations planners and intelligence analysts than had once been the case. The creation of teams combining operations and intelligence personnel in the spring of 1966 had broken down some of the bureaucratic walls, but a barrier remained between photographic intelligence and electronic signals intelligence, especially radio communications intercepts. Security procedures meant to protect signals intelligence also made integration with other intelligence sources difficult. In any case, photographic intelligence could not always meet demands for up-to-date imagery of targets. Weather often interfered with photographic reconnaissance, and among the hundreds of targets, many were new or altered. Even when good imagery was acquired, getting it reproduced and filed in the target folders at each wing was another matter. Like air commanders before and after him, Momyer was rarely completely satisfied with the speed or comprehensiveness of bomb damage assessment. Like other air commanders, he wanted to avoid unnecessarily repeating strikes on a target since the enemy usually responded by increasing air defenses.[22]

Seventh Air Force's reliance on photographic and signals intelligence was even heavier because American efforts to maintain South Vietnamese reconnaissance teams in North Vietnam had failed. Although the Military Assistance Command Studies and Observations Group continued to insert teams and supply them, those that still sent radio reports were correctly suspected of having fallen under enemy control. Nothing so vividly illustrated the plight of South Vietnam as its inability to sustain agents in North Vietnam while communist agents held positions in the Saigon government.[23]

*   *   *

As the new commander of Seventh Air Force, General Momyer's ability to shape the Rolling Thunder air campaign against North Vietnam was sharply limited by men in the complex chain of command above him, from Saigon to Hawaii to Washington. At Pacific Command headquarters in Hawaii, Admiral Sharp simplified the problem of allocating targets by dividing North Vietnam into seven geographical areas or "route packages."* The Pacific Fleet conducted most of the bombing in four route packages along the coast (from south to north, Route Packages Two, Three, Four, and Six B) that aircraft launched from carriers in the Gulf of Tonkin could reach without air refueling. Pacific Air Forces was responsible for bombing in northwestern Vietnam (Route Packages Five and Six A), while General Westmoreland gained responsibility for Route Package One just across the "Provisional Military Demarcation Line" from South Vietnam; this boundary ran down the middle of the Ben Hai River flowing into the South China Sea, and a "Demilitarized Zone" about six miles wide buffered the line for its entire length of about forty miles from the coast to the Laotian border. In the summer of 1966, after months of watching the North Vietnamese use the Demilitarized Zone as a sanctuary for their forces, the United States at last began to bomb it. General Momyer took his orders from Westmoreland for Route Package One (and the Demilitarized Zone) and from General Harris at Pacific Air Forces headquarters in Hawaii for Route Packages Five and Six A.

The rigidity and fragmentation built into the route package arrangement grated on both Momyer and Harris, who had tried to talk Sharp out of it. But neither Harris nor the Chief of Staff of the Air Force, General McConnell, could persuade the Navy to integrate air operations over North Vietnam under the Air Force. Sharp did permit the Seventh Air Force commander to chair a coordinat-

---

* See North Vietnam map, page 297.

ing committee with representatives from Seventh Fleet's Task Force 77, whose carriers bombed North Vietnam. But any disagreement had to be referred to Sharp, and for the most part the two services conducted separate operations in their own route packages.[24]

Sharp's position on route packages did not surprise Harris, nor did it embitter him. The two men got on well and shared a belief that air power had been used far too timidly over North Vietnam. Like Momyer, Harris was deeply concerned about what the Vietnam War was doing to the reputation of air power. Limited strikes against North Vietnam had been portrayed in the press as an all-out effort. "It troubles me and many others, of course," Harris wrote McConnell in March 1966, "that for all our military superiority we have been out-maneuvered by a third-class power. I can't help but believe that a defeat . . . will tend to relegate the military instrument to an essentially defensive role aimed primarily at forestalling a direct attack on the U.S. with all that this means for our future military capability vis-a-vis our world interests."[25]

Given Admiral Sharp's decision to allocate targets by route package and Washington's domination of target selection, the principal role of Pacific Command headquarters in Rolling Thunder became one of lobbying for better targets. Sharp did not take "no" for a final answer and repeatedly requested targets that had been denied time and time again. This persistence paved the way for a longer target list, but did not endear him to his civilian bosses.

No President had ever taken the interest in target selection that Lyndon Johnson did. Through the long years of Rolling Thunder, he personally scrutinized lists of proposed targets and weighed their potential for civilian casualties, bad press, or Soviet and Chinese involvement. During his first term in the Senate, China had intervened powerfully in the Korean War when American troops had moved into North Korea. Johnson had supported President Harry Truman's firing of Gen. Douglas MacArthur, who shared the administration's underestimation of the danger of Chinese intervention and then publicly challenged Truman's decision not to bomb China. In Vietnam, President Johnson was taking no chances with his generals. Not only did he forbid an invasion of North Vietnam, he would not even permit the kind of urban bombing there that Truman had permitted in North Korea from the early weeks of the Korean War. Johnson's fears of massive Chinese intervention were clothed in the all too sophisticated "signalling" analysis proffered by advisers. According to this line of thought, threatening destruction was a more influential signal of American determination than destruction itself—it was better to hold important targets "hostage" by bombing trivial targets.[26]

On August 4, 1964, after North Vietnamese torpedo boats attacked an American destroyer in the Gulf of Tonkin on one occasion if not twice,*

---

* There has been much controversy about whether North Vietnamese boats made a second attack on two U.S. destroyers at night in bad weather. For evidence supporting the

President Johnson authorized the first air raid into North Vietnam; on August 5, U.S. Navy planes hit North Vietnamese navy boats, bases and a fuel depot. This "tit for tat" raid seemed appropriate to the Congress, which passed a resolution authorizing Johnson to "take all necessary measures" to prevent further communist aggression in Southeast Asia. Rather than make immediate use of this broad charter, Johnson won a landslide election in November by assuring the American public that American boys would not fight a war for Asian boys. He sought successfully to contrast his views with the hawkish reputation of his Republican opponent, Senator Barry Goldwater (Arizona), who was a major general in the Air Force Reserve. Johnson made no military response when, a few days before the election, communist forces attacked Bien Hoa Air Base near Saigon, killing five Americans and destroying six American B–57s.

Even after the election, Johnson did not retaliate when, on Christmas eve, a car bomb killed two American officers and wounded more than fifty in Saigon's Brinks Hotel. By then, however, he had already told his advisers that if he did decide to bomb North Vietnam, he would not follow the Air Force's recommendation to send intensive air raids including B–52s against ninety-four targets throughout North Vietnam. His gradual Rolling Thunder campaign was finally triggered in early February 1965, when more than thirty American military personnel died in communist attacks on installations at Pleiku and Qui Nhon, South Vietnam.[27]

The weak bombing operations of Rolling Thunder did not dissuade the North Vietnamese regime from continuing intervention in South Vietnam, but they did serve as a prelude to sending American ground combat units to fight there. No longer would the American presence be limited to twenty thousand military "advisors" (including Air Force "advisors" who flew combat missions in South Vietnam). Beginning with two battalions of Marines to protect the American air base at Da Nang, Johnson increased American military strength in

---

reality of a second attack, see Edward Marolda and Oscar P. Fitzgerald, *The United States Navy and the Vietnam Conflict, Vol II: From Military Assistance to Combat, 1959–1965* (Washington, 1986). For a contrary view by a carrier pilot who could not find the enemy that night, see Jim and Sybil Stockdale, *In Love and War* (New York, 1984). Stockdale's view has received support from Edwin E. Moise, *Tonkin Gulf and the Escalation of the Vietnam War* (Chapel Hill, NC, 1996). In 1997, former Secretary of Defense Robert McNamara asked Gen. Nguyen Dinh Uoc in Hanoi whether the second attack had occurred and was told that according to Gen. Vo Nguyen Giap, it had not occurred. But McNamara was also told that even the first attack was executed on the orders of a local commander. See Robert S. McNamara, James G. Blight, and Robert K. Brigham, with Thomas J. Biersteker and Col. Herbert Y. Schandler, *Argument Without End: In Search of Answers to the Vietnam Tragedy* (New York, 1999), pp 202–5. Long before this affair, the U.S. response to the communist insurgency in South Vietnam had included sending South Vietnamese sapper teams into North Vietnam to blow up targets, and at the end of July 1964, gunboats (supplied by the U.S. but with South Vietnamese crews) began to fire on North Vietnamese installations.

South Vietnam to seventy-five thousand by July 1965, when he announced that he would send another fifty thousand and decided on fifty thousand more. In three years he would have half a million troops in Vietnam, where they joined a South Vietnamese army that grew to more than half a million.

A few days before the beginning of Rolling Thunder, the most ardent advocate of a more forceful air campaign retired from the Air Force. Although Gen. Curtis E. LeMay had served as a four-star general for a record thirteen years and worn stars for more than twenty, he was still a vigorous fifty-eight. Already a major figure in the Second World War, when he led B–17 bombers over Germany and commanded the B–29 fire-bombing of Japanese cities, LeMay became best known for building the Strategic Air Command after the war. He was far less successful as Air Force Chief of Staff in Washington, where his views seemed simple-minded to the youthful professors surrounding President John F. Kennedy.[28]

Ten years younger than LeMay, Secretary of Defense Robert S. McNamara brought to the Pentagon a team of still younger "whiz kids"—a term once applied to McNamara when, after World War II, he and a few other statisticians got out of the Army Air Forces and sold their services to the Ford Motor Company. During his wartime tour in the China-Burma-India theater and in the Pacific, McNamara, a lieutenant colonel, had admired General LeMay's tactical brilliance. But as Secretary of Defense, McNamara treated LeMay with the same disdain most generals received from the new secretary and his whiz kids. McNamara's condescending opinions seemed bloodless abstractions rather than perceptive responses to the realities of warfare. After Kennedy's assassination in November 1963, LeMay's hope for better treatment from the Johnson administration evaporated when President Johnson chose to keep McNamara and other Kennedy advisers.[29]

LeMay's prestige with influential legislators like Senator Symington made both Presidents Kennedy and Johnson fearful of replacing this forceful Chief of Staff. But when LeMay's first two-year term expired in June 1963, Kennedy extended him only for a single year. Johnson chose to extend him again rather than deal with the wrath of LeMay's friends during an election year. Instead of granting him a full fourth year, Johnson prescribed that LeMay would retire February 1, 1965, upon completing thirty-five years of service. He did not go quietly. When a reporter asked him what he thought of Washington, LeMay growled that it made him sick.[30] He went on to elaborate in a memoir that included a memorable passage about North Vietnam: "My solution to the problem would be to tell them frankly that they've got to draw in their horns and stop their aggression, or we're going to bomb them back into the Stone Age."[31] His critics would never let him forget a phrase that he would come to regret: "That sort of gave me the reputation of being somebody whose solution to every problem was bombing hell out of them. That's not my idea of the solution to every problem."[32]

LeMay was a man of few words. The stories of his intimidating taciturnity were legion, but when he did remove his cigar to speak, he often nailed down the essence of a situation from his point of view. He admonished Washington to quit just "swatting flies" in South Vietnam and go after the "manure pile" in North Vietnam.[33] The general who had fire-bombed Tokyo did not yet propose to level the North Vietnamese capital at Hanoi. He was ready to try using B–52s against ninety-four targets that had garnered the approval of the Joint Chiefs, but not yet ready to make full use of area bombing in populated areas. If bombing the initial targets proved inadequate, more should be added. LeMay opposed publicly ruling out the use of nuclear weapons against North Vietnam. It was a principle with him that the nuclear threat was too valuable to discard, even if the United States had no intention of actually using nuclear weapons. As early as 1954, when American support was proving insufficient to keep the French from losing their empire in Indochina to communist take-over, LeMay had suggested to a group of American officers: "In those 'poker games' such as Korea and Indo-China, we have never raised the ante—we have always just called the bet. We ought to try raising the ante sometime."[34] But he also told the same group that he opposed going to war in Indochina.[35]

In the 1950s, LeMay's anticommunism was focused on the Soviet Union. He was not much concerned about Chinese communism, let alone Vietnamese communism. During the Second World War, when he was commanding B–29s in China, LeMay had persuaded Mao Tse-tung and his Chinese communists to supply weather data and help with rescuing downed American pilots. Further south the American fighter commander in China, General Chennault, got the same kind of cooperation from the Vietnamese communist leader, Ho Chi Minh. Only in the 1960s would LeMay come to favor a bigger American role in Vietnam (and then only in the air and only if the United States was willing to do what was necessary to end the war quickly).

LeMay argued that a vigorous prosecution of the war could save friendly and enemy lives by ending the war sooner. Gradualism might lose the war while costing more lives. But President Johnson feared that LeMay's way of going to war might mean a wider war with China or perhaps even the Soviet Union, not to mention a very bad press for Lyndon Johnson. The President hoped to keep the war in Southeast Asia as much out of the press as possible. His years as Senate majority leader had equipped him to pass the biggest domestic spending program since the "New Deal" of Franklin Roosevelt, and Johnson was determined to keep the Vietnam War from derailing his "Great Society." On the other hand, he did not want to be charged with losing Vietnam to communism as President Truman had been blamed for losing China. In this frame of mind, Johnson replaced LeMay with a general much more to his liking.[36]

Seven years before selecting "J. P." McConnell to be Air Force Chief of Staff, Johnson had invited the general to stay at the senator's LBJ Ranch in the Texas hill country west of Austin. McConnell was then LeMay's director of plans at Strategic Air Command and had testified before Johnson several times. The majority leader spent the weekend showing McConnell his ranch, introducing him to neighboring ranchers, even personally serving him breakfast in bed—all the while learning about Strategic Air Command. It was a quintessential Johnson performance, which would give McConnell the impression that they had a personal relationship, even though they would not have another private meeting until 1964 when McConnell was commanding the U.S. Air Forces in Europe and the President wanted him to replace LeMay. That summer McConnell became Vice Chief of Staff with the understanding that he would become Chief of Staff in six months.[37]

Born the same year as the President (1908) in a small town in Arkansas, McConnell had no trouble getting along with Johnson. Both men combined southern earthiness with quick, practical minds. Graduating magna cum laude from a little college in Arkadelphia, Arkansas, when he was only nineteen, McConnell then attended the U.S. Military Academy at West Point and joined the Army Air Corps. After serving on the staff of South East Asia Command under Adm. Lord Louis Mountbatten (Royal Navy) during the Second World War, McConnell went to China where he was Chiang Kai-shek's American air adviser after the war. Throughout his career he was an agreeable staff officer with a persuasive smile.

Although not LeMay's choice for Chief of Staff, McConnell did advocate LeMay's plan to use B–52s based on Guam against North Vietnam. But McConnell did not put up much of a fuss when he was overruled, and in any case he was hardly consulted. President Johnson received his military advice mostly from Secretary of Defense McNamara, who relied more on his assistant for international security affairs, John T. McNaughton (formerly a law professor at Harvard), than on the Joint Chiefs of Staff. Even the Chairman of the Joint Chiefs, Army Gen. Earle G. Wheeler, was often excluded from important meetings. Wheeler did form a committee in the Joint Staff to recommend bombing targets, and two months after the beginning of the Rolling Thunder campaign, McConnell was finally able to have Col. Henry H. Edelen from his target intelligence staff serve on the committee.[38]

Early in Rolling Thunder, Johnson liked to have a weekly Tuesday luncheon meeting with McNamara and Secretary of State Dean Rusk. On these occasions and at other times when the three got together, McNamara often presented a list of proposed targets that had already been coordinated with the State Department. He gave the President estimates of possible civilian casualties and any other risks associated with the prospective targets. Johnson would approve perhaps a dozen targets, usually fewer, and these would have to be hit within the week or Johnson's approval would have to be sought again. Since only fighter aircraft were used and they lacked much capability to bomb in bad weather, the clouds prevalent in March 1965 over North Vietnam assured that some or all of the few targets authorized might not be attacked in the assigned week. Not until

September 1965 were any targets approved indefinitely. In 1966, weekly bombing programs were replaced by five multiweek programs (Rolling Thunder Forty-eight, Forty-nine, Fifty, Fifty-one, and Fifty-two) each lasting from one to four months. By the end of 1966, the President had personally approved more than two hundred targets, but he had also steadfastly disapproved many on the original list of ninety-four.[39]

*   *   *

The Joint Chiefs of Staff target list for North Vietnam included, at the outset, a dozen route segments. For example, the railroad and highway running south about 150 miles from Hanoi to Vinh were each divided into two segments by the major bridge at Thanh Hoa. Although the Thanh Hoa bridge was a separate target, smaller bridges were part of a route segment that could be approved as a whole for "armed reconnaissance"—fighter aircraft patrolling the route could attack targets of opportunity like trucks or trains as well as fixed targets like bridges whose destruction would interfere with the movement of supplies. As President Johnson approved targets gradually from the southern panhandle northward, route segments were abandoned in favor of a bomb line south of which armed reconnaissance was permitted unless a particular target was specifically exempted or unless the President's rules of engagement prohibited a strike (e.g., in a heavily populated area).[40]

The armed reconnaissance line crept north through the spring and summer of 1965. After reaching 20 degrees north at the beginning of April, the armed reconnaissance line did not reach 20 degrees 30 minutes until September. This east-west bomb line was joined by a north-south line at 105 degrees 20 minutes east that permitted armed reconnaissance in northwestern North Vietnam (so long as the bombs stayed at least thirty nautical miles south of the Chinese border). The two lines fenced off Route Package Six (the "northeast quadrant" containing the major cities of Hanoi and Haiphong) from armed reconnaissance until the spring of 1966, when rail and road segments were targeted there. Finally in July 1966, all of North Vietnam was opened to armed reconnaissance except three restricted areas: (1) along the Chinese border, a buffer zone thirty nautical miles deep west of 106 degrees and twenty-five nautical miles deep east of there; (2) around the port of Haiphong, a circle with a radius of ten nautical miles; (3) around the capital at Hanoi, a circle with a radius of thirty nautical miles. Armed reconnaissance was permitted on some route segments within the Hanoi circle, including one segment only twelve miles from the city center.*[41]

---

* Areas restricted in the rules of engagement were measured in nautical miles—each about 15 percent longer than a statute mile.

In fact, air defenses around Hanoi were so formidable that armed recon-naissance patrols were deemed too risky. Consequently, armed reconnaissance in Route Package Six was really just a matter of hitting fixed targets and any associated targets of opportunity that might appear. Although a lot of air patrol-ling was done along transportation routes in the panhandle of North Vietnam, even there armed reconnaissance sorties went after a rapidly growing lists of fixed targets.

Through separate target lists, the Joint Chiefs of Staff, the Pacific comman-der in chief, and the Seventh Air Force commander each tried to gain control over what was being bombed and what was not being bombed. At the beginning of the war, the Defense Intelligence Agency had a list of about five thousand possible targets in North Vietnam. Very little was known about most of these facilities, and the Joint Chiefs of Staff selected only eighty-two of them togeth-er with a dozen route segments for their original North Vietnam target list. As the joint list grew to more than double its original length, it was as much a "no-fire" list as a target list. These were the targets the Johnson administration was most reluctant to approve for fear of Chinese and Soviet reaction or a bad press at home.[42]

Meanwhile, Pacific Command and Seventh Air Force developed their own lists of targets with their own numbering systems. The Joint Chiefs of Staff also departed from Defense Intelligence Agency target identification numbers, which were deemed too long and cumbersome for wartime use. The problem with this proliferation of simplified numbering systems was the confusion caused by each target having as many as four identification numbers—more when area targets were divided into smaller precision targets (each of which might have four different numbers). Eventually, Seventh Air Force's list of tar-gets would include over six thousand in North Vietnam and Laos.[43]

The Seventh Air Force commander, General Momyer, believed that the most important of those targets were in the Red River Delta, homeland of the Vietnamese for perhaps four thousand years. Here the Vietnamese had built a network of dikes and canals to produce the rice that sustained their economy. Here they persistently sought to free themselves from Chinese domination. From here, some moved south, settling along the banks of the next river and the next, until their descendants took control of the Mekong's much bigger delta from the Cambodians. The southern Vietnamese grew powerful enough to break away from the north for the two hundred years before 1802, when a southern emperor reunited the country with its capital at Hue on the central coast. The stature of the old northern capital at Hanoi was revived by the French, who made it the capital of French Indochina (including Laos and Cambodia as well as Vietnam).[44]

When Ho Chi Minh's communist forces took control of North Vietnam after the Second World War, they inherited an economic infrastructure built under French auspices. In addition to administrative buildings, residences and churches, the French had directed the construction of harbor facilities at Haiphong and a railroad that not only linked the port with Hanoi, but also ran south to Saigon and its French rubber plantations as well as north to China. While the southern line ran along the coast and competed with ships, the French hoped that the route from Haiphong west through Hanoi and splitting there into northeast and northwest lines to China might make Haiphong the principal port for all of southern China—might even make France the dominant power in southern China.[45]

The result of disappointed French ambitions was the curious fact that North Vietnam's railroad became an essential link between China's interior Yunnan Province and coastal Kwangsi Province. Copper, tin, and lead from Yunnan rode North Vietnamese rails to coastal China, while equipment, food, and consumer goods made the return trip. Early in Rolling Thunder, more than a hundred thousand Chinese laborers and air defense artillery troops came south to maintain and defend North Vietnam's railroads. In preparation for war with the United States, Mao Tse-tung embarked upon an expensive program to move vulnerable industries from along the Chinese coast to the remote interior, while laying an east-west rail link in southern China. Completion of this railroad in the summer of 1966 freed North Vietnamese rails of Chinese domestic traffic, making way for more supplies to move into North Vietnam. The longer northwest railroad link between Yunnan and Hanoi became much less important than the seventy-five mile northeastern rail link between Hanoi and Kwangsi.[46]

About a third of North Vietnam's imports came down the northeast railroad from China, and most of the rest came by sea through Haiphong. Since North Vietnam imported almost all its military supplies, including gasoline, General Momyer deemed it essential to close the port of Haiphong and the rail connection with China. But Soviet ships at Haiphong caused President Johnson to worry that an international incident might lead to a wider war. The President refused to approve Navy bombing or mining of Haiphong harbor, and the Air Force was left to bomb the northeast railroad without much hope of making a critical difference. In any case, bridges along the route were hard to hit with unguided bombs in the teeth of heavy enemy air defenses. Johnson had not even approved striking the biggest bridges across the Red River at Hanoi and across the parallel Canal des Rapides for fear of civilian casualties. Nor were railyards promising targets without the heavy bomb loads only forbidden B–52s could carry. Trains could make a quick run from the Chinese border to Hanoi at night, skipping the intervening yards, and the downtown yard was, of course, off limits.[47]

Not only did the North Vietnamese struggle to keep their railroad open under Rolling Thunder, they even built new track. The Chinese helped them complete a line from the northwest railroad through Thai Nguyen and its ironworks to the Gulf of Tonkin at Hon Gai, a smaller port north of Haiphong near the country's major coal deposits. The new line crossed the northeast line at

Kep, and when the Kep-Thai Nguyen section opened in the fall of 1966, the North Vietnamese could bypass the southern portion of the northeast line. Meanwhile, far to the south in the panhandle, the North Vietnamese had pushed the railhead past Vinh toward Dong Hoi and South Vietnam. They had destroyed much of this line during their war with the French and had not completed rebuilding the portion south of Vinh when Rolling Thunder began. North of Vinh at Thanh Hoa, they had rebuilt over the Song Ma a bridge that they had destroyed by arranging a collision between two locomotives filled with explosives. The North Vietnamese took seven years to rebuild it so that it would be very hard to destroy again. They called it Ham Rong or "The Dragon's Jaw," and wedged powerfully between two hills, it withstood repeated air attacks by the Air Force and the Navy throughout Rolling Thunder.[48]

Navy air did manage to keep the lighter bridges on the route south of Thanh Hoa in sufficiently bad shape that the North Vietnamese rarely used normal trains, but resorted to trucks with rail wheels pulling small two-axle cars. Below Vinh it was necessary to shuttle freight with trucks between interdicted sections of track until the railroad gave out fifty miles north of South Vietnam. Supplies might be moved along the coast by boat, or trucked through the mountain passes to Laos, or carried on backs and bicycles directly across the Demilitarized Zone, or stored for a future invasion force in caves, tunnels, and bunkers just north of the zone. Late in the summer of 1966, B–52s began to bomb the Demilitarized Zone and a narrow strip along it reaching about ten miles into Route Package One. This area just north of the Ben Hai River would become the primary focus of the more than two thousand B–52 sorties that struck North Vietnam during Rolling Thunder; while less than 1 percent as many as the fighter sorties that bombed North Vietnam in the same years, each B–52 carried at least ten times the bombs carried by a fighter, and they were all directed at a relatively tiny portion of the country. In some places B–52 bombing would produce hundreds of craters clustered so close together that pilots would compare them to a moonscape. Yet in those tunnels that did not collapse from the pounding, North Vietnamese men, women, and children continued to live and maintain a flow of supplies to communist forces there and in South Vietnam.[49]

While fighter aircraft could hit trucks and trains moving south in daylight, the night gave good protection. Truck drivers each learned a short segment of the route so that they could drive without headlights. Fighter pilots tried to dispel the darkness with flares and managed to destroy trucks that way, but too many other trucks ran the gauntlet successfully. A bridge might be out or a road badly cratered, but there was usually a ferry or a pontoon bridge or another route that could be used until repair teams could complete their work. American radar sites in South Vietnam and Thailand did permit ground controllers to give fairly precise bomb release instructions to B–52s and fighter aircraft for fixed targets in the panhandle of North Vietnam—such targets could be hit at any hour in any weather. Moving targets, however, proved too difficult a problem at night and in bad weather. Across the mountains in Laos, the roads were patrolled with propeller-driven attack aircraft or even lumbering cargo planes fitted with guns and night sensors. But only B–52s and jet fighter aircraft proved survivable strike vehicles in North Vietnam, and they were not well suited to finding trucks or destroying them.

The Annamite Mountains separated not only countries but also weather systems. While the clouds of the northeast monsoon masked much of North Vietnam from November to April, the sky was often clear over the Laotian panhandle. As dirt roads dried, thousands of imported trucks rolled down the Ho Chi Minh Trail road network in Laos toward South Vietnam. During the peak of the northeast monsoon, more than half the monthly total of about twenty thousand fighter sorties attacking North Vietnam and Laos would strike the Laotian panhandle. The share hitting targets in the Red River Delta would drop to much less than a twentieth. This share would not exceed a fifth even during the southwest monsoon from May to October. The delta got most of its heavy rainfall during the southwest monsoon, but at least the storms were interspersed with periods of clear weather. During the dry northeast monsoon, in contrast, the pervasive cloud cover over the delta rarely broke. Consequently, sorties were often diverted to the North Vietnamese and Laotian panhandles, which were much more heavily bombed than the Red River Delta.[50]

Superimposed on the natural division between delta and panhandle were Admiral Sharp's route packages. The Air Force sent many more sorties against Route Package One than scheduled, because the service usually had nowhere else in the panhandle to send them when bad weather forced diversions from the Red River Delta; the other panhandle route packages were under Navy control. During the southwest monsoon, the Air Force diverted as many as a thousand sorties a month to Route Package One. Even after Sharp's decision in August 1966 to permit Air Force sorties in the western portion of the Navy's panhandle route packages, General Momyer in South Vietnam and the Air Staff in Washington continued to push for more. Except for the roads leading to Laos, most of targets in the North Vietnamese panhandle were near the coast, and Momyer wanted his forces to be authorized to attack them.[51]

The squabble over panhandle route packages came to a head in early November 1966. The Air Staff in Washington prepared a script that General Moore, vice commander of Pacific Air Forces and former commander of Seventh Air Force, used to brief Sharp. The Air Staff's rationale for Air Force bombing in the coastal area of Navy route packages was built upon the old concept of interdiction belts. Employed in the Italian campaign of 1944, this concept emphasized the importance of blocking parallel lines of communication at choke points so that a blocked route could not be bypassed easily. The concept had already been resurrected by Moore a few months earlier under the name "Gate Guard" for use in Route Package One and Laos, but so far as Sharp could see, North Vietnamese repair efforts had been able to stay ahead of the bombing. Sharp had developed such an aversion to the words "Gate Guard" that Moore deleted them from the briefing. He did argue for establishing interdiction belts in Navy route packages with Air Force planes.[52]

As Moore informed the Air Staff afterward, his session with Admiral Sharp grew "rather tense."[53] Adm. Roy L. Johnson, commander of the Pacific Fleet, accused the Air Force of trying to take control of Navy route packages. Sharp rebuked both sides, declared that he was fed up with excuses, and emphasized his expectation that the route package system would be made to work. The Air Force would not be permitted to control Navy route packages, but Sharp expected his Air Force and Navy subordinates to negotiate arrangements for sending sorties into all parts of each other's areas.[54]

The resulting arrangements did not permit Air Force interdiction belts in the Navy portion of the North Vietnamese panhandle, and the Air Force ceased to push that idea. General Momyer in Saigon was more interested in bombing the Red River Delta, as was Admiral Sharp. Momyer tended to express his preference for bombing the delta in terms of the greater concentration of enemy supplies there. Nor did Sharp argue in terms of cutting off the flow of supplies to South Vietnam (he did not believe this was possible), but in terms of hurting the North Vietnamese economy as a whole. Both men thought that bombing in the delta was apt to have more impact on the enemy leadership located there than bombing in the panhandle.[55]

In any case, interdiction belts in the panhandle became tainted by their similarity to Secretary of Defense McNamara's barrier concept, which sought to replace the bombing of North Vietnam with a physical barrier to infiltration along the northern edge of South Vietnam and across the Ho Chi Minh Trail in Laos. The South Vietnamese portion of this "McNamara Line" was to consist of fortifications manned by American troops, but President Johnson's refusal to send regular ground forces into Laos meant that there the McNamara Line would have to depend upon air power, albeit air power aided by electronic sensors and a few ground reconnaissance teams.[56]

Secretary McNamara's disillusionment with the bombing of North Vietnam moved in a direction opposite from that of most of his military subordinates. They had strongly disapproved of Rolling Thunder's gradualism from the outset, but continued to argue for gradually increasing the campaign's intensity as the best approach they could get from the President. McNamara had argued for gradualism until late 1966 when he wanted to end Rolling Thunder, but he was not yet ready to propose its elimination to a President who was likely to feel betrayed by this about-face.[57]

The Secretary of Defense was confirmed in his pessimism by the failure of Rolling Thunder's operations against North Vietnamese oil storage facilities in the summer of 1966. The Air Force and the Navy had sought permission to go after oil from the beginning of the war. Without gasoline, North Vietnamese trucks would be useless. But the big tank farms were in the cities of Haiphong and Hanoi, where President Johnson hesitated to do any bombing. By the time he gave the go-ahead, the enemy had dispersed gasoline around the country in drums and small underground tanks. When bombing caused the tank farms to go up in billowing flames and smoke, their significance had already been reduced to a minimum. Planes spent the rest of the summer chasing gasoline drums, while the trucks kept moving.

The chief civilian proponent of bombing oil was a man of sufficiently optimistic temperament that these less than encouraging results did not dissuade him from recommending more bombing. Walt Whitman Rostow had been a close student of bombing since the Second World War, when as a young major in the Office of Strategic Services he belonged to a targeting team in London. He was an economic historian, and economics seemed fundamental to targeting. In the 1960s, as in the 1940s, he was partial to bombing oil and bridges; he had argued in 1944 against the insistence of the British analyst Solly Zuckerman that allied bombing focus on railyards rather than oil and bridges in the months before the invasion of France. Since then, Rostow's academic career at the Massachusetts Institute of Technology had been cut short when President Kennedy brought him to Washington. In the spring of 1966, he replaced McGeorge Bundy as President Johnson's National Security Adviser. In the fall, Rostow's older brother Eugene became Under Secretary of State for Political Affairs; Bundy's older brother William was already Assistant Secretary of State for Far Eastern Affairs. All four had attended Yale in the 1930s and all four had a hand in the bombing of North Vietnam, but the Rostow brothers maintained their enthusiasm for it longer.[58]

Walt Rostow provided a warmer welcome for men in uniform than had his predecessor. Although much military analysis seemed a little crude to Rostow, he had found an officer with whom he could work closely. Col. Robert N. Ginsburgh's doctorate from Harvard, his lack of flying experience, and his Second World War service in Army artillery set him apart from most Air Force generals, but thanks in great measure to Rostow he would join their ranks. Ginsburgh's career also benefited from associations gained through his father, a brigadier general who left the Army to join the new Air Force in 1948 as deputy director of public relations; after developing a warm relationship with Secretary of the Air Force Symington, the elder Ginsburgh went on to serve four secretaries of defense before his retirement in 1953 and death in 1958. The younger Ginsburgh first worked with Rostow on the State Department's policy planning staff, and Rostow arranged for him to come to the White House as the Joint Chiefs of Staff liaison in Rostow's office. Since General Wheeler was not in the inner circle of the President's advisers, the Chairman often had to rely on Ginsburgh for information about decision making in the White House. For more than a year, Ginsburgh made little progress in getting invitations for Wheeler to Tuesday lunches and other meetings when President Johnson,

Secretary of Defense McNamara, Secretary of State Rusk, and Rostow discussed target selection.[59]

Ginsburgh's compatibility with Rostow did not mean that the two men saw eye to eye on the bombing of North Vietnam. Like most Air Force officers, Ginsburgh believed in at least ratcheting up the bombing dramatically, if not bombing massively from the outset. Rostow, on the other hand, wanted a very gradual increase in pressure under which he hoped the enemy would break at some point. As a student of economic development, Rostow did favor bombing North Vietnam's powerplants and its few examples of modern industry in the Red River Delta, but he did not favor focusing the air effort on the delta. Rather, the National Security Adviser wanted just enough bombing in the delta to keep North Vietnamese air defenses and repair capabilities concentrated there as a way of assisting interdiction bombing further south.[60]

Ginsburgh was more interested in the Red River Delta. It seemed to him that the best way to hurt North Vietnam's rice economy was to bomb the dike system. He was influenced by Robert F. Futrell's history of the Air Force in the Korean War; Futrell indicated that the bombing of irrigation dams near the end of the war had helped to bring a cease-fire. Neither Rostow nor President Johnson would countenance so controversial a move, and even General McConnell, the Air Force Chief of Staff, doubted the feasibility of breaching the big earthen dikes.[61]

*   *   *

In Rolling Thunder the Johnson administration devised an air campaign that did a lot of bombing in a way calculated *not* to threaten the enemy regime's survival. President Johnson repeatedly assured the communist rulers of North Vietnam that his forces would not hurt them, and he clearly meant it. Government buildings in downtown Hanoi were never targeted. Even the government's ability to communicate was left almost untouched. The location of the principal telephone switches next to the Soviet Embassy and the Hanoi offices of the International Control Commission guaranteed the switches' immunity to bombing. Created by the Geneva Accords of 1954 ending the Vietnamese communist war of independence from the French, the International Control Commission was composed of representatives from India, Canada, and Poland; their peace-monitoring mission had long been superfluous.

The North Vietnamese leaders were too formidable a group not to make the most of the advantages Johnson gave them. Ho Chi Minh was looking more frail than ever in his seventies, but he was still at least the symbolic "Uncle Ho" around whom the Vietnamese communist party coalesced. His assumed name meant "Bringer Of Light" and was the last of a series of aliases used for propaganda or disguise. His real name was Nguyen, the most common family name in Vietnam. Like most of his younger colleagues, he had been raised on the central coast of Vietnam. His father was an educated man with just enough money to send his son to the National Academy at Hue, where Ngo Dinh Diem and many other Vietnamese nationalists also got their start. After working as a cook on ship and in London, he helped to found the French communist party. Ho spent most of the 1920s and 1930s in Russia, China, and Thailand as an agent of the Communist International.[62]

In 1966, Americans could not be sure which of the men in Ho's inner circle wielded the most power. When Ho died three years later, Le Duan, already very influential, would emerge as the dominant leader. Since much of his career as a communist organizer had been spent in the Mekong Delta, he could be expected to insist on pursuing victory there. Truong Chinh was thought to be less dedicated to the struggle in South Vietnam, and he had taken the blame for the severity of North Vietnamese land reform—a bloody process that may have killed fifty thousand of the former owners. He was also thought to be much too enthralled with the Chinese; even his name was an alias meaning "Long March" in honor of Mao. Pham Van Dong, the prime minister who appeared to mediate between Le Duan and Truong Chinh, had enjoyed a comfortable childhood and suffered a long imprisonment under the French.

Since Pham Van Dong was one of the Vietnamese communists who had attended Chiang Kai-Shek's Whampoa Military Academy, he might have been Ho's general. But Ho chose a history teacher, Vo Nguyen Giap, to lead the troops. It was an inspired choice. General Giap's victory in 1954 at Dien Bien Phu, a heavily defended French outpost near the Laotian border two hundred miles west of Hanoi, made him more famous than any of the American generals opposing him a dozen years later. Still in his fifties, he was the youngest of the men in Ho's inner circle. Apparently more cautious and less influential than Le Duan, Giap's prestige inside his army and beyond assured him at least an important role in the implementation of strategy (if not always in its formulation).[63]

During Rolling Thunder, Giap commanded a large army. In a North Vietnam of eighteen million, he had half a million under arms, including a quarter of a million regulars. Fifty thousand of those regulars were in South Vietnam, where they supported four times that many armed insurgents in a population of about sixteen million. Outnumbered in South Vietnam, Giap relied upon the jungle and the villages to give him the initiative; his forces could hide until they were ready to fight. In the north, however, American air power presented him with some new problems. His old enemies the French had controlled the cities, and Giap's forces had been able to hide in the jungle. But now Giap had his own cities, his own railroads, and his own harbors to protect.

When this new war's bombs first fell on North Vietnam in August 1964, Giap was not well prepared. Since 1956 his little air force had been slowly taking shape at airfields in China and the Soviet Union, while his own airfields were under construction. The Soviets provided Mikoyan-Guryevich MiG–17s—faster offspring of the Soviet MiG–15s the Chinese had used against Americans in the Korean War. The Vietnamese learned to fly and maintain the MiGs in China until Giap's principal airfield at Phuc Yen near the village of Noi Bai, fifteen miles north of Hanoi, was finally ready for jet fighters in the summer of 1964. The day after the first American air strikes on North Vietnam, Giap's three dozen MiGs flew from China to Phuc Yen. But American bombing did not resume for another six months.[64]

Communism, for a time, overcame some of the ancient hostility between China and Vietnam. For several years the Chinese had been more helpful than the Soviets, but that changed with the ouster of Nikita Khrushchev as Soviet leader in the fall of 1964. The new Soviet leaders, Leonid Brezhnev and Alexei Kosygin, competed with the Chinese for influence in Vietnam. While the Chinese provided manpower, the Soviets could offer more in the way of technology. Hanoi was eager to embrace Soviet technology in preference to too many Chinese troops. When bombs again fell on the panhandle of North Vietnam in February 1965, Kosygin was in Hanoi with the Soviet minister of aviation and the commander of the Soviet air force.

Using aid to reap prestige in Hanoi and elsewhere in the communist world, the Soviets also expected concrete returns. North Vietnam was a laboratory for Soviet equipment and doctrine pitted against American equipment and doctrine. The Soviets secured samples of downed American aircraft and other American hardware that they could use to develop defenses or imitations. But the North Vietnamese were not always as cooperative as the Soviets thought appropriate, and the Soviets complained that the Chinese received preferential treatment. One irritant was the slow unloading of Soviet ships at Haiphong where their mere presence protected nearby antiaircraft artillery against American air attack. Also irritating were incessant requests for more equipment while earlier shipments sat in the open unused and corroding. None of these frustrations stopped the Soviets from competing ardently with the Chinese for North Vietnam's allegiance.[65]

The North Vietnamese proved adept at exploiting Sino-Soviet rivalry, though it made delivery of Soviet equipment somewhat challenging. While the Chinese agreed to let the Soviets transport goods across China by train, each cargo plane overflight had to be approved. Rail transport became risky during Mao's "Cultural Revolution" of 1966–68, when student mobs attacked Mao's critics (including Soviets). Americans, on the other hand, eased Giap's problem by leaving North Vietnam's principal port of Haiphong wide open to Soviet and other ships. The fact that the Chinese were keeping larger forces on the Soviet border than on the Vietnamese border did little to ease President Johnson's concern that China might wage full-scale war in Southeast Asia. Nor was the Johnson administration willing to risk making much use of North Vietnam's fear of dependence on massive Chinese intervention; had the United States forced the North Vietnamese to rely more heavily on China by threatening the survival of their regime, it was at least conceivable that the North Vietnamese might have looked for ways to avoid bringing in an overwhelming Chinese presence—even if avoidance meant postponing their take-over of South Vietnam.[66]

By the fall of 1966, Giap had more than forty MiGs at Phuc Yen, plus ten at Hanoi's Gia Lam airport and five at Kep airfield thirty miles northeast of Hanoi. He also had two useable airfields at Haiphong, and he was building new airfields at Yen Bai (fifty miles northwest of Hanoi) and Hoa Lac (only ten miles west of Hanoi). Meanwhile, the Chinese had been building their own new airfields close to North Vietnam. Thus far the Americans had ignored their own doctrine (that called for striking airfields at the beginning of a campaign) and left all the major airfields in the Red River Delta untouched; the Johnson administration feared not only that Soviet and Chinese advisers might be killed in airfield attacks, but also that the North Vietnamese air force would move to China and generate pressure from the U.S. Air Force and its friends to bomb the Chinese bases. Further south, the old airfields at Vinh and Dong Hoi as well as the one under construction at Bai Thuong near Thanh Hoa were bombed out of commission so that North Vietnamese aircraft could not attack South Vietnam or interfere with American planes bombing the North Vietnamese and Laotian panhandles.

Giap's air force included fourteen MiG–21s that were newer and faster than MiG–17s; the latter usually relied on their guns against opposing fighters, while MiG–21s depended mostly on their heat-seeking air-to-air missiles.* Giap also had six old Soviet light jet bombers, Ilyushin Il–28s. Getting the planes was easier than training the pilots. Most flight training had to be done in China and the Soviet Union. By the spring of 1965, MiG–17s were engaging American aircraft, and less than a year later MiG–21s joined the fray.

Although inferior to the F–4 in speed and range, the smaller single-seat MiGs did not leave a smoke trail and were harder to see at a distance—an advantage multiplied by the American reluctance to risk hitting their own aircraft by using radar-guided missiles beyond visual range. A MiG–17's tighter turns could also make it a formidable opponent in a dogfight. A MiG–21, on the other hand, had difficulty turning inside an F–4, and poor cockpit visibility to the rear was a handicap against an F–4's second pair of eyes. The greatest American advantage at the outset was superior training. But since the air-to-air battle took place over North Vietnam, that country's pilots had a better chance of returning to action after being shot down. As the months and years went by,

---

* American pilots observed MiG–21s firing only five radar-guided missiles during the entire Vietnam War. See the June 1974 report of the USAF Tactical Fighter Weapons Center, Project Red Baron III, Vol III, Part 1, p 25.

North Vietnamese pilots became more experienced while the American rotation policy emphasized inexperience. In any case, MiGs did not need to shoot down American aircraft to help defend North Vietnam—every time an American fighter jettisoned its bombs to confront an attacking MiG, the MiG had already won a victory.[67]

In the Soviet tradition, MiG activity was kept on a tight rein by Senior Col. Dang Tinh, who used a radar network to command both the air force and the hundreds of antiaircraft guns that ringed Hanoi. He also had a newer weapon at his disposal, if not under his command. In the spring of 1965, the Soviets began to construct SA–2 surface-to-air missile (SAM) sites, and on July 24 a Soviet missile crew shot down an Air Force F–4.[68]

The U.S. response to SAMs was almost as inadequate as its failure to attack North Vietnamese airfields. In April 1965 when American reconnaissance began to observe the construction of SAM launch sites within twenty miles of Hanoi, Secretary of Defense McNamara took Assistant Secretary McNaughton's advice and forbade attacks on the sites. In May when President Johnson raised the possibility of taking them out, McNamara argued that the SAM sites could not be attacked until B–52s had bombed the airfields—a suggestion which promptly diminished Johnson's interest in attacking the SAM sites.[69] Thanks to the gradualism of American bombing, Hanoi was not under attack, and consequently a ring of launch sites there seemed to pose little immediate threat to American aircraft. For a while it was even possible for some to speculate that the sites were intended only as a signal not to bomb Hanoi. But the F–4 shot down forty miles west of Hanoi in July alerted the Johnson administration that the North Vietnamese had built at least two launch sites further from the city than the original five. Sites six and seven were thirty miles west of Hanoi.

The first SAM shoot-down caught the Johnson administration in the middle of deliberations over whether to Americanize the ground war in South Vietnam. General McConnell and the other chiefs had already been called to the White House, where the President had polled them on this major change of policy for South Vietnam. McConnell supplied the expected affirmative, but he would promise only that American forces in the south plus more bombing in the north would permit the United States to "do better than we're doing."[70] Harold Brown, the young physicist recently chosen by McNamara to be the next Secretary of the Air Force, was no more enthusiastic: "It seems that all of our alternatives are dark."[71] Neither man had much real say in Johnson's ground force decision. Nor were they called back to advise Johnson on what to do about the SAMs.

The Chairman of the Joint Chiefs, General Wheeler, at least participated in the White House SAM discussions on July 26. He presented the recommendation of the chiefs that all SAM sites be attacked at once—failing that, at least sites six and seven. None of the civilians present favored going after the sites closer to Hanoi, but even Under Secretary of State George Ball (a World War II Strategic Bombing Survey veteran who opposed his country's deepening involvement in Vietnam) agreed that if sites six and seven were the beginning of an outer SAM perimeter they would have to be eliminated. Secretary of State Rusk noted that while killing Soviets at the sites would be risky, it would also be a useful warning. Secretary of Defense McNamara told the President that bombing targets within range of the SAM sites would no longer be wise unless the sites were attacked first. McNamara recommended bombing sites six and seven using fighters at low level where they would not be vulnerable to SAMs.[72]

President Johnson decided to take out SAM sites six and seven, but this proved easier said than done. On July 27, 1965, the Air Force sent fifty-four F–105s against the two sites and nearby barracks where SAM personnel were thought to be living. Per Washington's instructions the F–105s went in below five hundred feet—only to encounter a flak trap with a dummy missile and enough guns to shoot down four F–105s. Two more were lost in a collision on the way home when one attempted to inspect the other's flak damage. It was by far the most costly air strike of the war so far.[73]

Subsequently the Air Force and the Navy tried to avoid turning SAM sites into flak traps and limited the force attacking a site to four planes or less. The number of sites rapidly increased, much more rapidly than the number of SAM launch battalions—each of which could move up to six launchers from one site to another in a few hours. Instead of waiting for the SAMs to kill and move before sending a retaliatory strike, the Air Force sent "Iron Hand" hunter-killer flights ahead of the big strike packages to threaten the SAM launch teams. For several months, each F–105 Iron Hand flight was led by a two-seat F–100F "Wild Weasel" hunter that had detection equipment to find a site's radar; the F–100F could then use its rockets to mark the site for the F–105s to bomb. By the summer of 1966, two improvements had been made to Iron Hand. The slower F–100Fs were replaced by two-seat F–105F Wild Weasels (like the two-seat F–100Fs, originally trainer aircraft with the space necessary for detection equipment plus an electronic warfare officer* to use it), and the target-marking rockets were replaced by the Navy's radar-seeking Shrike missiles. The Shrike warhead's thousands of small steel cubes did not appear to have much success destroying revetted radar equipment but did threaten launch personnel sufficiently for them to shut down radar operations temporarily. After the addition of white phosphorus to the Shrike warhead, detonation could at least reveal a SAM site's location so that it could be bombed.[74]

Although Wild Weasel crews could rarely be certain a Shrike had hit enemy radar, they could detect the radar going off the air—often in response to the mere presence of Wild Weasels. As much as possible, the SAM crews

---

* Unlike the F–4 backseater, the F–105F electronic warfare officer was a navigator (rather than a pilot) from the outset. He was often called a "bear."

(increasingly North Vietnamese rather than Soviet) began to use off-site surveillance radar for tracking and turned on the site tracking radar only at the last minute. Meanwhile, aircraft had considerable success outmaneuvering the lumbering SAMs, often likened to flying telephone poles, but were driven down within reach of the guns. Although the Wild Weasels also attacked radar controlling the biggest antiaircraft guns and tried to stay above the effective range of the smaller guns most of the time, North Vietnamese air defenses continued to make Iron Hand an especially dangerous mission. Of the eleven F–105F Wild Weasels that deployed to Thailand in the spring of 1966, only four were left by mid-August. Replacements soon arrived, but it was not always possible to send a pair in each Iron Hand flight of four; sometimes the older practice of one Wild Weasel per mission was all that could be managed.

Since SAMs proved too mobile and antiaircraft artillery too numerous and most of the MiG fields were off limits, all three arms of North Vietnam's air defense remained deadly. They worked increasingly well together through practice and through a growing radar-communications network. By putting SAMs and guns on or near dikes, hospitals and schools, the North Vietnamese found they could put American pilots in a no-win situation—either permit these units to fire unhampered or give the North Vietnamese the kind of publicity that could win friends in the United States and threaten a pilot's career. There was plenty of time to move some of the machinery in Hanoi to underground locations outside Hanoi in case the Americans eventually did decide to bomb the city. The citizenry could be engaged in digging bomb shelters, including tens of thousands of relatively small holes (each big enough to hold one person) as well as larger shelters. In areas already subject to bombing, some of the more trustworthy citizens were issued rifles; instead of diving into shelters, they fired at American aircraft with an enthusiasm that seemed at least psychologically beneficial.[75]

In such ways did North Vietnam's rulers seek to persuade their own people, as well as Americans, that American high technology could be beaten. The U.S. government cooperated to a remarkable degree by giving Rolling Thunder a gradual, even tentative character of self-imposed sanctuaries and bombing pauses. Since the North Vietnamese took the position that they would not negotiate while they were being bombed, the Johnson administration found itself under pressure to stop bombing to prove its interest in a negotiated peace. As early as April 1965, Senator Robert F. Kennedy of New York visited Johnson to argue for a bombing pause. The slain President's brother was Johnson's principal rival in the Democratic Party, and Johnson sought to keep his own grip on President Kennedy's political legacy.[76]

Johnson's first bombing pause in May 1965 lasted six days. He had intended a five-day pause, but before it was over, Secretary of Defense McNamara argued that the *New York Times* expected a full week of seven days and Johnson split the difference.[77] Any hope Johnson had that the pause would quiet his critics was disappointed. They protested that the pause was too brief for North Vietnam and its communist allies to make a positive response. McNamara became the principal voice within the administration for a longer pause. In July 1965 he began to talk about a pause lasting six to eight weeks (beginning in December). Secretary of State Rusk could see little point in stopping the bombing when there was no indication that the North Vietnamese were ready to talk, but Johnson agreed to a five-week pause from December 24, 1965 to January 31, 1966. The North Vietnamese could only have been encouraged by the spectacle of dozens of their enemy's emissaries scrambling around the world in a "peace offensive."[78]

Secretary McNamara and Assistant Secretary McNaughton prepared for the long pause's failure by presenting it as only a step toward another long pause proposed for the end of 1966. But President Johnson lost patience with long pauses, and although he would agree to short pauses and revived sanctuaries from time to time, not until after the communist Tet offensive of 1968 would he agree to another major cutback. Meanwhile, he tried to fine tune the bombing so that it complemented more than forty "peace initiatives" or "peace feelers" as these diplomatic exercises were called. Not privy to the "peace feelers," the Air Force became all the more puzzled by the President's bombing policy.[79]

Chapter Two

New Tactics, Old Strategy

The northeast monsoon arrived a little early in 1966. By the middle of October, it hid Hanoi and Haiphong under dense clouds often reaching below a thousand feet. Although violent storms were common from May to September, the October overcast rarely broke into a downpour. For six months the low ceiling would cover the Red River Delta. This fact of nature exerted a greater influence on American bombing operations in late 1966 than it had a year earlier. At that time, the gradually escalating campaign had rarely touched the heart of North Vietnam. Not until June 1966, sixteen months after the campaign had begun, did Rolling Thunder's bombs begin to explode frequently near Hanoi and Haiphong. Pressure on the Red River Delta could not be sustained through the northeast monsoon, however, without using B–52s or without a better all-weather fighter bombing capability than the United States possessed. The clouds of October guaranteed respite for the delta unless the United States conducted area bombing and multiplied civilian casualties. This the United States would not do.

Even during the northeast monsoon, some raids struck the delta. Cracks in the weather permitted strikes on a railyard just north of Hanoi, on a truck depot just south of the city, and on an ironworks thirty-five miles away. None of these targets had been hit before, and the strikes foreshadowed heavier bombing. The Air Force emerged from the northeast monsoon more able to cope with North Vietnam's air defenses. By April 1967, Air Force fighter-bombers carried electronic countermeasures pods to jam radars guiding surface-to-air missiles and antiaircraft guns. The pods permitted fighter-bombers to fly over the delta at a higher altitude where SAMs had formerly held sway; no longer were F–105s and F–4s exposed to low-altitude flak before diving toward a target; no longer did they have to pop up before diving. By April, fighter-bombers pulled out of their dives above the worst flak, and most formations over the delta included a flak suppression flight whose cluster bombs could kill or intimidate gun crews. When better bombing weather at last arrived, Seventh Air Force finally began to bomb MiG bases and then exact a toll in the air on increasingly aggressive MiGs. Thenceforth, F–4s escorted most F–105s bound for the delta so that

F–105 pilots could focus on bombing and not have to jettison bombs or switch the plane's attack control system to its air-to-air mode.

Despite important changes, bombing tactics remained routine and predictable. On a day when the weather looked at all promising, as many as two hundred combat aircraft flew to the delta from Thailand and the Gulf of Tonkin. The Air Force scheduled up to four formations a day—two in the morning and two in the afternoon, each with from eight to twenty-four strike aircraft surrounded by escorts and sometimes outnumbered by them. The need to refuel fighter-bombers en route to the delta from Thailand tied them to the tanker schedule. There were not enough tankers to refuel large formations both morning and afternoon without giving the tankers several hours at midday to land for more fuel. Since carriers were closer than Thailand bases to North Vietnam, Navy aircraft were less dependent on refueling.* The Navy's somewhat greater flexibility in the timing of strikes also stemmed from Task Force 77's preference for smaller formations. In any case, North Vietnamese radar picked up attackers more than a hundred miles out, leaving very little possibility of surprise. The most that electronic countermeasures could do was to hide the exact location of individual aircraft; they made the strike force's presence as a whole even more obvious.[1]

Gradual escalation had given the North Vietnamese time to protect the Red River Delta with air defenses very difficult to destroy. An estimated twenty-five SAM battalions (with six missile launchers each) rotated among approximately 150 sites. The practice of sending strike teams to kill SAMs was falling into disuse, because SAM sites recently active often turned out to be nothing more than flak traps. The North Vietnamese were at least as quick to move their anti-aircraft guns as to move their SAMs; not requiring elaborate site preparation or good roads, the guns could be moved more easily. Their movement and the display of dummies created an exaggerated impression of the scope of North Vietnamese air defenses. As American intelligence agencies saw through this illusion, they reduced their estimate of the number of North Vietnamese antiaircraft guns with a caliber of at least thirty-seven millimeters (ranging up to a hundred millimeters) from more than seven thousand in early 1967 to less than a thousand in 1972. However many guns there were, they were most numerous in the Red River Delta, where they were coordinated with about 150 SAM launchers and over a hundred MiGs. The most important components of the air

---

* Although the carriers had their own KA–3 tankers aboard, Navy aircraft did sometimes require refueling from the Air Force's bigger and more numerous KC–135s. On May 31, 1967, a KC–135 refueled a Navy KA–3 while it was refueling a Navy F–8—said to be the first tri-level air refueling. Two Navy KA–3s and four Air Force fighters were refueled before that KC–135 landed. Its crew (Maj. John J. Casteel, Capt. Dean L. Hoar, Capt. Richard L. Trail, and MSgt. Nathan C. Campbell) received the National Aeronautic Association's Mackay Trophy for the most meritorious Air Force flight of 1967. See Charles K. Hopkins, *SAC Tanker Operations in the Southeast Asia War* (Offutt AFB, 1979), pp 68–69.

defense system were the more than two hundred radar facilities that provided warning and guidance for MiGs, SAMs, and guns.[2]

Since the attacks could not achieve surprise, sustained pressure was all the more desirable. But limited capability to make accurate strikes at night and in bad weather robbed Rolling Thunder of sustained pressure and frustrated attempts to take advantage of poor visibility by flying under enemy radar coverage. In the densely populated, strongly defended Red River Delta, American aircraft had great difficulty striking at night or in bad weather while avoiding civilian casualties. The Johnson administration's caution did not deter North Vietnamese propagandists from making the most of relatively light casualties during the northeast monsoon of 1966–1967. Notwithstanding attempts to achieve accuracy necessary for extending the delta campaign into darkness and bad weather, American bombing there usually occurred in daylight and fair weather.

*   *   *

On November 10, 1966, President Johnson approved a bombing program that featured several new targets in the Red River Delta. They included the Thai Nguyen ironworks; the cement plant and two powerplants in Haiphong; the Yen Vien railyard and the Van Dien truck depot, both near Hanoi; and fuel dumps at Ha Gia and Can Thon. Though he had taken three months to approve this target list, Johnson soon deferred four of its major targets: the ironworks, the cement plant, and the two powerplants. Three more months would pass before the President would begin to release these targets. Meanwhile, he waited for another peace initiative to run its course.[3]

The target list approved and partly deferred in November was the product of several proposals made in August. At that time the campaign to destroy North Vietnam's oil supplies had passed from dramatic destruction of tank farms to the frustrating search for gasoline drums buried underground, hidden in the jungle, or stored along village streets outside bounds set for the campaign by the Johnson administration. Pacific Air Forces had recommended progressing to more substantial targets like the Thai Nguyen ironworks, the Yen Vien railyard, and the Van Dien truck depot. Although Sharp advocated these targets by November, in early August he had still favored pursuing the oil campaign. At the top of his list had been the Ha Gia and Can Thon tank farms, which had not been authorized earlier because of their nearness to airfields at Phuc Yen and Kep. The Johnson administration feared that attacking MiG bases might provoke a Soviet or Chinese reaction. When the two target lists from Hawaii reached Washington, the joint staff combined them and added Haiphong's powerplants and cement plant.[4]

The Haiphong cement plant was North Vietnam's only one. Its importance had been affirmed by the Central Intelligence Agency in March 1966, when the agency counted itself among those calling for an oil campaign coupled with closing the port of Haiphong and bombing the northeast railroad to China; even if the railroad could not be severed for an extended period, the agency had hoped to overload it with fuel and cement as well as other goods that had been entering by sea. The CIA recommendation had been implemented only partially. In addition to oil strikes, the northeast railroad had been bombed regularly enough to became a leading flak trap, but the trains continued to roll. Haiphong's cement plant, like its port, remained unstruck and busy.[5]

The target recommendations of all military organizations from the Joint Chiefs of Staff (JCS) down sometimes hinged as much on their judgment of what the President might approve as on what was most needed. Though closure of the port of Haiphong was widely considered to be a key objective, General Wheeler avoided tiresome repetition of that recommendation. Sharp and others down the line were less restrained, but even they did not push for Haiphong every time. Despite Wheeler's restraint, the Johnson administration frequently balked at JCS recommendations. The President was slow to approve the August 1966 target list, which in November at last became the fifty-second bombing program ordered since the beginning of Rolling Thunder. Early in the campaign, bombing programs had lasted a week, but the fifty-first had lasted four months. Now that gradualism had brought bombing to the outskirts of Hanoi and Haiphong, the administration hesitated to go farther.[6]

When, on November 11, President Johnson deferred four targets he had just approved, his military advisers believed that the deferment would be short lived. Wheeler explained to Sharp that the targets would be deferred only until after the Moscow visit of George Brown, British foreign secretary. Brown was scheduled to leave Moscow on November 25, and Wheeler had been assured that the deferred targets could then be struck. As it turned out, the deferment held through Tet in February 1967. While Sharp and Momyer could only stew about this delay in ignorance of its cause, the Johnson administration was once again exploring the doubtful possibility that leaders might be willing to talk seriously about a settlement acceptable to the United States. This round of diplomacy began with Brown's visit to Moscow in November and ended with a visit to London in February by a Soviet leader, Alexei Kosygin. The centerpiece was an aborted Polish attempt to arrange a meeting between North Vietnamese and American officials in Warsaw.[7]

The State Department, which named each peace feeler after a flower, called Poland's initiative "Marigold." Since the summer of 1966, the Polish representative on the International Control Commission in Vietnam had tried to find common ground in the American and North Vietnamese positions. On November 30, he gave Ambassador Lodge in Saigon a list of ten points that the North Vietnamese government was said to have approved as a basis for conversation with American officials in Warsaw. Despite State Department reservations, the American ambassador in Warsaw was told early in December to inquire whether conversations with the North Vietnamese could be arranged through the Polish foreign minister. At this point, Marigold died. According to the Polish foreign minister, American bombing near Hanoi killed North Vietnamese interest in making contact.[8]

So it was that the care taken in November to defer targets which might endanger negotiations did not save the Johnson administration from incurring accusations of doing just that. Two of the targets not deferred were close to Hanoi: the Yen Vien railyard (five miles northeast of Hanoi's center) and the Van Dien truck depot (four miles southeast of Hanoi's center). Not since the Air Force strike against the Hanoi tank farm on June 29 had bombs fallen that close to downtown Hanoi. For three weeks after Johnson's approval of these targets, weather prevented an attack. On December 2 the clouds cleared enough for the Navy to strike the truck depot. Two days later the Air Force hit the railyard. When told that the timing of the raids was the result of weather and not of Marigold, the Polish foreign minister objected that policy was more important than weather. The State Department, nevertheless, informed its ambassador in Warsaw that no change would be made in the current bombing program. On the other hand, the President gave an equally negative response to General Wheeler's request that the deferred targets be attacked. Wheeler let Sharp know that the delay was due to "certain political problems."[9]

When weather over the delta improved again on December 13 and 14, Air Force and Navy aircraft returned to the same targets they had hit two weeks earlier. After these strikes, the Polish foreign minister told the American ambassador that the North Vietnamese were no longer interested in talking to the American government. President Johnson attempted to salvage the Warsaw connection by offering to prohibit strikes within ten nautical miles of the center of Hanoi, if the North Vietnamese and Viet Cong would refrain from attacking within ten miles of the center of Saigon. In the absence of any North Vietnamese response, Johnson unilaterally established a prohibited zone with a radius of ten nautical miles for Hanoi; strike aircraft were not even to fly over the prohibited zone, let alone expend ordnance there. Over the course of the next year, however, the President would permit a number of attacks on targets within the prohibited zone.[10]

The Hanoi prohibited zone added one more limitation to those already confining American pilots and encouraging North Vietnamese air defenses to concentrate near authorized targets. Around the prohibited zone, the thirty-mile restricted zone remained in place. There pilots had gradually gained some freedom of operation: SAM sites and fuel storage could be struck as well as any previously authorized target that had not been specifically withdrawn; in addition, armed reconnaissance was permitted along railroads. Haiphong was also protected by a restricted zone (ten nautical miles from the center) and would later be given a prohibited zone (four nautical miles from the center). The buffer zone along the Chinese border remained off limits as did all targets on the JCS list that had not been authorized.[11]

*   *   *

President Johnson's prohibition on bombing near Hanoi came at the beginning of the most important North Vietnamese propaganda initiative before the Tet Offensive of 1968. TASS, the Soviet news agency, issued reports that the December 1966 bombing attacks had killed civilians in downtown Hanoi, capturing headlines in the United States and Europe. That was only the beginning. For the first time under Rolling Thunder, North Vietnam permitted a visit by an American reporter. From the many who had requested a visa, North Vietnam chose Harrison Salisbury, an assistant managing editor of the *New York Times*.[12]

After Salisbury's articles began to appear, the British government called for immediate talks on a cessation of hostilities. The Chairman of the Senate Foreign Relations Committee, J. William Fulbright (Democrat, Arkansas), held hearings. Senator Vance Hartke (Democrat, Indiana) called for an end to bombing and an independent evaluation of the entire war effort by former Under Secretary of State George Ball and former Ambassador to India John Kenneth Galbraith. On the other side of the question, the Chairman of the House Armed Services Committee, L. Mendel Rivers (Democrat, South Carolina), suggested that the United States "annihilate" Hanoi if necessary: "Give them two weeks to get out and then level the city."[13] While Defense Department public affairs specialists tried to calm public controversy, their boss contributed to it. Arthur Sylvester, Assistant Secretary of Defense for Public Affairs, openly attacked "Harrison Appallsbury" of the "New Hanoi Times."[14] Years later, author Tom Wolfe would skewer Salisbury as the "ocarina" that the North Vietnamese had used "as if they were blowing smoke up the pipe and the finger work was just right and the song was coming forth better than they could have played it themselves."[15]

The North Vietnamese had done a good job of choosing a reporter. Salisbury represented America's most prestigious newspaper, and he opposed bombing North Vietnam. For months he had been trying to get North Vietnam's permission to enter that country. In June he had talked to the North Vietnamese consul in Phnom Penh, Cambodia, and had filed his visa application there. A letter to Hanoi was written in his behalf by Anne Morrison, a Quaker whose husband was said to have become a hero in North Vietnam after burning himself to death in front of the Pentagon. On December 15 the North Vietnamese government cabled Salisbury that his visa was waiting in Paris. He arrived in

Hanoi on December 23 and remained for two weeks. His front-page articles began appearing on Christmas day.[16]

Salisbury stayed in Hanoi's old Metropole Hotel, which had been renamed the Thongnhat (Reunification), illustrating North Vietnam's plans for South Vietnam. While he was there, the hotel hosted the deputy director of TASS; four American women on a visit arranged by David Dellinger, a prominent pacifist; and a seven-member delegation seeking evidence for British philosopher Bertrand Russell, who was preparing a mock trial of President Johnson and other American "war criminals." Each of the groups and Salisbury were taken on separate, but similar, tours of North Vietnamese bomb damage.[17]

Salisbury first saw sites in Hanoi, where about three hundred homes were said to have been destroyed and ten people killed. This downtown destruction was about five miles from either the Yen Vien railyard or the Van Dien truck depot. He described the truck depot (North Vietnam's largest truck repair facility with 180 buildings) as a "large, open area with light buildings and compounds that may or may not have been a truck park."[18] Salisbury was more interested in the destruction of the Vietnam-Polish Friendship high school "probably three-quarters of a mile from the presumed United States target."[19] He made no mention of casualties in this case. As to the Yen Vien railyard, he was told that buildings destroyed and damaged near the tracks were apartments. Air Force bomb damage reports described extensive damage to a warehouse complex associated with the country's largest railyard. Salisbury's account made no mention of warehouses.[20]

On Christmas day Salisbury was driven sixty miles southeast to Nam Dinh. Here was the principal exhibit in North Vietnam's case against American bombing. According to Salisbury's guides, the city had been struck fifty-two times in a year, eighty-nine people had been killed, and 13 percent of the city's housing had been destroyed. Salisbury concluded that U.S. aircraft were "dropping an enormous weight of explosives on purely civilian targets."[21]

Johnson administration attempts to refute Salisbury's articles seemed awkward, mostly because it was Salisbury's interpretation that was objectionable rather than his data. True, his statistics were supplied by the North Vietnamese government, but for the most part they did not conflict with American estimates. Indeed, Secretary McNamara was upset to learn from the CIA that bombing deaths in North Vietnam might already total as many as twenty-nine thousand, including more than two thousand civilians who were not war workers. It did not follow, however, that civilians were being targeted. Had they been, the number of casualties would have been radically higher.[22]

The Johnson administration had taken extraordinary measures to minimize the number of civilian casualties, yet had difficulty countering Salisbury's charge that it had done the opposite. The problem was that the administration had not educated the public about the limitations of bombing. Even if a pilot correctly identified a target, most of his bombs were apt to miss. When bombing through heavy flak, only about half the bombs dropped by F–105s (which usually carried six 750-pound bombs apiece) were likely to hit within five hundred feet of the aiming point. Americans who did not know that bombing precision was unlikely in the face of a determined defense could hardly be blamed for accepting Salisbury's conclusions.[23]

Salisbury saw little of North Vietnam's formidable air defenses. Nam Dinh was well known to Navy pilots for a concentration of antiaircraft artillery and SAMs that greeted them when they entered the Red River Delta by the most direct route from the south. According to the Defense Intelligence Agency, Nam Dinh's normal complement was about a hundred guns with a caliber of at least eighty-five millimeters and about fifty smaller caliber guns of at least thirty-seven millimeters, not to mention a battalion of six SAM launchers. Yet Salisbury did not report seeing any antiaircraft weapons in Nam Dinh. Since he visited during the Christmas cease-fire, no attacks occurred to provoke shooting. Nam Dinh ran three alerts anyway, presumably in response to reconnaissance aircraft.[24]

Salisbury misled his countrymen by telling them that the only targets in Nam Dinh other than people were dikes and a cotton textile mill. Though the largest in North Vietnam, the textile mill had not been targeted. An adjacent powerplant had been bombed several times, and stray bombs had damaged the mill; its twenty thousand workers had dispersed to smaller factories. Throughout the war, the North Vietnamese claimed that the United States was bombing the dike system essential to rice cultivation. If bombed after heavy rain, during the southwest monsoon, breached dikes might cause extensive flooding. While antiaircraft guns firing from dikes were sometimes attacked, pilots were never authorized to attack the dikes. Because Nam Dinh was only twenty miles from the coast, most strikes there were flown by the Navy, and the Navy had bombed a river transshipment facility with dikes nearby. Be that as it may, no extensive flooding was caused by bombing anywhere in North Vietnam. Major targets in Nam Dinh were the tank farm, the powerplant, the railyard, the transshipment facility, and the air defense sites. None of these were described in Salisbury's articles.[25]

Though Salisbury reported much greater damage for Nam Dinh than for Hanoi, the latter was harder to explain, since the nearest authorized targets were about five miles away. Part of the mystery was solved when a reconnaissance photo indicated that some Air Force pilots had mistaken the Gia Lam railyard for the Yen Vien railyard. Gia Lam was half way between Yen Vien and downtown Hanoi. The two yards were easy to confuse through scattered clouds because Yen Vien was east of the Canal des Rapides Bridge and Gia Lam was east of the Paul Doumer Bridge over the Red River. South of the latter bridge lay the heart of Hanoi. The exact nature of the mistake was not made public, however. The administration would only say that some kind of accident may have occurred.[26]

Nor did the Johnson administration comment publicly on speculation about damage caused by aircraft jettisoning bombs, air-to-ground missiles, or fuel tanks when jumped by MiGs. The danger of explosion was sufficient to discourage pilots from landing with bombs on board. For this reason and to conserve fuel, unexpended bombs were dropped at sea or in mountainous areas on the way home. Though bombs could be jettisoned without arming them, a 750-pound bomb jettisoned from several thousand feet could cause considerable damage even without exploding. The failure of the administration to talk freely about the obvious question of jettisoning reduced the credibility of explanations that were made. The administration stressed that one consequence of heavy antiaircraft fire was damage caused when disintegrating projectiles fell back to earth. This was a plausible explanation for light damage of the kind Salisbury reported for the Chinese and Rumanian embassies. American pilots had seen SAMs go haywire and detonate on the ground; this could explain more extensive destruction.[27]

North Vietnam sent a fairly complex message to the American people through Harrison Salisbury. The message was not simply one of American transgression, but also one of North Vietnamese resistance. North Vietnamese officials were careful not to exaggerate bomb damage in a way that might suggest any potential for bombing to reduce their effort in South Vietnam. They told Salisbury that they expected Hanoi to be destroyed and that they had prepared blueprints for a complete new capital city. He was told that much of the urban population and their work had already been moved to the countryside. In Nam Dinh, only twenty thousand were said to remain of the ninety thousand who had made that city the third largest in North Vietnam. With this information, low casualty figures could be reconciled with extensive damage, and perhaps Americans could be persuaded that any attempt to bomb industry or population would be futile. Salisbury could see for himself that many who stayed in the cities could hide in shelters. Though he did not witness an attack, numerous air raid alerts featured civilians with rifles ready to fire at American aircraft. North Vietnamese officials bragged that South Vietnam would not dare arm its civilians. But the grim determination evident in Hanoi was not the whole story. Since bombing attacks were confined largely to daylight, shops and streets bustled during the evening.[28]

Salisbury saw thousands of fifty-five gallon fuel drums lining village streets and scattered through rice paddies. Bombing had destroyed the large tank farms, but it could not combat dispersion. Similarly, repair materials were piled along railroads and highways. Damage could be quickly repaired by road crews, and a steady stream of traffic flowed through the night. In a book published three months after his return, Salisbury expanded on this theme. Why, he asked, were so many trivial targets bombed while obviously important targets like the Doumer Bridge and the Hanoi powerplant were left unscathed? It was the very question Admiral Sharp and General Momyer had been asking. Within four months of the book's publication, both targets would be bombed.[29]

Escalation of the air war followed a February 1967 opinion survey conducted by Lou Harris, who found that 67 percent of Americans favored bombing North Vietnam. An equally interesting finding was that 85 percent of Americans agreed that the bombing was killing innocent civilians. Henceforth, the debate over bombing veered from humanitarian considerations and centered on its cost and effectiveness.[30]

*   *   *

The cost of Rolling Thunder received a great deal of official attention in late 1966 and early 1967. The onset of frequent raids into the Red River Delta had sharply raised the price Americans were paying. From the beginning of July 1966 to the end of September, fifty-one American aircraft fell in Route Package Six, which encompassed most of the delta; forty-four of them belonged to the Air Force, which suffered a loss rate there exceeding twenty-five attack aircraft per thousand attack sorties. Before the delta raids, American losses had rarely exceeded three per thousand anywhere in Southeast Asia and averaged less than one per thousand. An especially painful aspect of losses in the delta was the near impossibility of rescuing downed airmen in a region so densely populated and well defended.[31]

The Air Force's heavy losses in Route Package Six contrasted vividly with the comparatively light losses of the Navy—seven Navy aircraft lost from July through September (compared with the Air Force's forty-four) for a loss rate of less than three attack aircraft per thousand attack sorties. During this period, the Navy had sent more attack sorties into Route Package Six than had the Air Force (1,695 compared with the Air Force's 1,557). Before the delta raids of mid-1966, the loss rates over North Vietnam of the two services had been about the same, with the Navy's only a little lighter. The extreme variation experienced during the mid-1966 campaign did not persist into the next year, though the Navy's loss record remained slightly better throughout. One explanation sometimes offered for the overall superiority of the Navy's loss record was the nearness of Navy targets to the coast, which meant shorter routes over defended territory; Route Package Six remained divided into a Navy B section along the coast and an Air Force A section inland. But since most losses occurred near targets, the location of Navy targets could not alone explain the pronounced variation in losses that occurred in 1966. The Navy's major technical advantage was that most of its attack aircraft carried electronic countermeasures devices which transmitted false positions when triggered by North Vietnamese radar.[32]

During 1967, Air Force losses in Route Package Six declined to less than ten attack aircraft per thousand attack sorties. This improvement owed primarily to three changes: increasing altitude of bomb release, growing use of cluster bombs to suppress flak, and introduction of electronic jamming pods.[33]

The higher a dive bomber released its bombs and pulled off the target, the higher was the probability of its surviving and the lower the probability of its bombs hitting the target. As the Air Force undertook heavier bombing of the Red River Delta in 1966 and 1967, the concentration of antiaircraft guns there forced the wings to raise recommended bomb release altitude from less than six thousand feet to as much as nine thousand feet, which raised pullout altitude from less than four thousand feet to as much as seven thousand feet. Unfortunately, the increase in bomb release altitude also increased probable circular error (the radius within which half the bombs were apt to fall) from less than three hundred feet to more than five hundred feet.[34]

Although both Air Force and Navy bomb release altitudes were rising over the Red River Delta in 1966 and 1967, Navy pilots reported release and pullout altitudes about a thousand feet lower than those reported by Air Force pilots. This surprising fact did not seem to fit with the Navy's comparatively low loss rate—not only for Route Package Six in general, but for dive and pullout in particular. Some pilots may have reported releasing bombs at recommended altitude when in fact they had released them at a higher or lower altitude. But it can not be shown that inaccurate reporting was more common in one service than the other. Part of the explanation may have been the Navy practice of tailoring recommended release altitude for each target rather than making a blanket recommendation for Route Package Six. In dealing with more heavily defended targets, Navy pilots were told to release their bombs at higher altitude.[35]

Higher bomb release altitude seemed to be responsible for a significant reduction in aircraft losses over Route Package Six. During August 1966, six F–105s had been lost to ground fire while diving toward or pulling off targets in Route Package Six. During May 1967 (when the Air Force flew about a thousand sorties there, or more than twice as many as in August 1966) only three F–105s were lost in that way. Four of the F–105s lost in August 1966 were reportedly hit below four thousand feet. Only one of the F–105s lost in May 1967 was reported to have been hit that low. Although antiaircraft gunners raised their sights, they were foiled not only by altitude, but also by cluster bombs bursting around them.[36]

The cluster bomb, a modern version of shrapnel, was a canister designed to release hundreds of spinning bomblets whose detonation sent thousands of steel pellets flying in all directions. Though a cluster bomb had little effect on guns, it could force gun crews to take cover or suffer severe wounds. Early models of cluster bombs could not be used in the strongly defended Red River Delta, because they required delivery at about three hundred feet. In 1966 the Air Force introduced a cluster bomb that could be dropped in a dive above three thousand feet. With increasing availability of the new model, a flight of four aircraft could use cluster bombs to suppress flak while the rest of a formation struck a target. To discourage gun crews from promptly resuming their posts, later models were modified so that bomblets would detonate randomly for two hours; eventually the period of detonation was reduced to twenty minutes—few attacks lasted longer. A big shortcoming of dive cluster bombs when first introduced was their scarcity. Not until early 1967 was the production rate adequate to make a significant difference. Even then, the monthly rate of about five hundred was only an eighth of Seventh Air Force's stated requirement, and the Navy also wanted them.[37]

The cluster bomb reduced losses during dive bombing runs, but it did less for a strike force en route. Before fighter-bombers rolled in toward their target, they had most to fear from SAMs, which had a range of about twenty miles. The dispersal of launch sites meant that pilots had to begin watching for missiles at least sixty miles from Hanoi. Until December 2, 1966, the American response to SAMs had seemed adequate. Only thirty-four aircraft had been lost to the approximately eleven hundred missiles thought to have been launched. On December 2, however, a record eight American aircraft went down, including five hit by SAMs. None of these was part of the Navy's strike that day against the Van Dien truck depot on the outskirts of Hanoi. All but one went down attempting to attack oil tank farms, with the Air Force losing four (including three to SAMs) during a strike on the Ha Gia tank farm near Phuc Yen airfield (twenty-five miles northwest of Hanoi). However, SAMs would have few days as successful as that—over the next year, American estimates of the North Vietnamese SAM success rate would continue to decline from an already dismal one kill for thirty launches to less than one kill for fifty launches.[38]

The major new factor in combating SAMs after December 2, 1966 was the growing number of jamming pods. None of the aircraft shot down by SAMs on December 2 was carrying a jamming pod. A few weeks later, enough pods had arrived so that most F–105s on missions in the delta were carrying one. By mid-1967, F–105s and F–4s would be carrying two pods apiece.[39]

Pod jamming supplemented jamming already provided by EB–66 electronic warfare aircraft, converted bombers with room in their bomb bays to carry large transmitters. These slow jammers were vulnerable to missiles: two EB–66s had been shot down by SAMs in 1966, and a third would fall in February 1967. When out of SAM range, EB–66 jamming was not powerful enough to hide F–105s and F–4s as they neared Hanoi. With jamming pods, F–105s and F–4s supplied their own electronic fog. The location of an aircraft with one or two pods, however, was not disguised adequately unless that aircraft flew in formation with other pod-equipped aircraft. This weakness was the result of the relatively small transmitters that could be carried in pods on the wings of a fighter, but a bonus accruing from the fighters' adjustment to space limitations was an ability to move pods easily from aircraft to aircraft.[40]

In late 1966 and early 1967, the F–105 wings in Thailand experimented with various formations to see which offered better electronic protection.

Eventually they chose formations which put each flight of four aircraft within a box about a mile wide and a thousand feet deep, so that their jamming created as large an area of uncertainty as possible for North Vietnamese radar; if a flight spread much farther, each aircraft appeared separately on enemy radar scopes. Flight boxes drew together in a larger box so that the whole formation gave the illusion of a single undifferentiated mass on radar screens—a more difficult set of targets for SAMs but, unfortunately, a more predictable target set for MiGs. Before pods, there had been wide separations within a long string of loosely formed flights giving aircraft room for jinking thought necessary to evade SAMs. The Navy was able to avoid the rigidity of Air Force pod formations, because electronic countermeasures devices on board Navy aircraft gave false locations rather than attempting to cloud radar screens with jamming; the drawback was that amid the false targets thus produced, Navy aircraft also appeared on enemy radar screens. The Navy adjusted its formations to make the best use of the deception device and kept them loose enough to facilitate evasive maneuvers.[41]

Air Force ingress tactics were not uniform, and F–105 wings in Thailand differed markedly in their employment of jamming pods. The 388th at Korat was quicker to develop a new approach, while The 355th at Takhli was far more distrustful of the pods and held longer to old tactics. The 355th continued to enter the delta at about five thousand feet and pop up above twelve thousand before diving on a target.

The 355th's old ingress procedure offered some terrain protection from radar, especially northwest of Hanoi. Here a small range of mountains rising about four thousand feet reached to within thirty miles of the city. F–105 pilots transferred the ironic nickname of their aircraft to "Thud Ridge" in rueful acknowledgement that as much as the ridge helped them, it was also a grave stone for many friends. The ridge was not the only reality that kept the 355th at five thousand feet. At that altitude an aircraft was apt to be under the clouds where its pilot could see SAMs launch and dodge them before they gained full speed. Since pod jamming interfered with the F–105's SAM radar warning device, 355th pilots often turned off their pods.[42]

Despite such justifications for conservatism, the 388th embraced pods and the freedom offered by them to use higher altitude. Instead of approaching a target at five thousand feet and popping up above twelve thousand, the 388th came in above twelve thousand and avoided the necessity to pop up. This technique gave pilots more time to look for targets and lessened the effectiveness of anti-aircraft fire during ingress before diving. Replacing a loose string of flights with a tighter box formation brought the entire formation over the target much more quickly, so that gunners had to choose among them. But there was then the problem of bunching if each flight did not roll in fast enough. Rolling toward the target from a pod formation proved less than satisfactory with respect to accuracy also, because only the lead aircraft in each flight could easily attain the preferred forty-five degree dive; the other three were likely to have a more shallow dive (both less accurate and more dangerous) since they started farther from the target.[43]

For reasons just discussed, the 355th persisted in dissolving pod formation before a dive. But at the end of March 1967, the 355th began ingressing above twelve thousand feet in good weather and climbing out of pod formation to fifteen thousand before diving. The 355th retained a preference for ingressing under a low ceiling so as not to be surprised by SAMs breaking through clouds.[44]

Differences in wing attitudes toward ECM pods grew out of differences in combat experience. Since Korat was close enough to the North Vietnamese panhandle for unrefueled missions, the 388th had drawn more sorties in the "easy packs" than had the 355th at Takhli a hundred miles farther west. Economical use of tankers meant that Takhli F–105s, which required refueling anyway, had been sent more often to the Red River Delta. Takhli's losses had been much greater, but its leadership believed that the wing had learned to take care of itself the hard way. Though the 355th had been the first wing to receive jamming pods, it was the least impressed with them. Most impressed was the 8th Tactical Fighter Wing, the F–4 wing at Ubon. Pod protection from SAMs permitted F–4s to fly at higher altitudes from which MiGs could be spotted more easily. Higher altitude also increased the F–105's need for F–4 protection. At low altitude, F–105s could outrun MiGs, but at higher altitude an F–105's small wing made it less maneuverable than a MiG or an F–4.*[45]

*   *   *

When F–105 use of jamming pods increased in December 1966, North Vietnamese MiGs became more aggressive as if they were attempting to substitute for SAMs and take advantage of the more rigid pod formations. There may

---

 * The 355th Tactical Fighter Wing did not fully convert to the ECM pod formation employed by the 388th Tactical Fighter Wing until August 1967, when Col. John C. Giraudo took command. Before assuming command at Takhli, Giraudo stopped at Korat to visit a former boss, Brig. Gen. William S. Chairsell, who was about to leave after a year commanding the 388th. Giraudo was all the more interested in tactics that might lower losses, because he had already been shot down and taken prisoner during both World War II and the Korean War. Unlike Chairsell, however, Giraudo himself flew many missions into North Vietnam. See Lt. Col. Charles M. Heltsley's interview with Maj. Gen. John C. Giraudo, Treasure Island, Florida, 8–12 January 1985, AFHRA 1105191. For a view of the 388th under Chairsell, see the USAF film *There Is a Way* (i.e., a way to survive a hundred missions over North Vietnam). For a view from the 355th before Giraudo, see the well known books by the wing vice commander in 1966–67, Col. Jack Broughton (*Thud Ridge* and *Going Downtown*).

not have been a direct relationship between pods and MiGs, since the MiGs may simply have been reacting to attacks unusually close to Hanoi, Haiphong, and Phuc Yen. Another possible explanation was the training cycle of MiG pilots, whose confidence had appeared to be growing for several months. Whatever its cause, MiG activity worried officers in Southeast Asia and Washington. In December, MiGs shot down two F–105s at a cost of one MiG. On the three days of heaviest activity, MiGs persuaded nineteen out of seventy-four strike aircraft to jettison bombs and, in several cases, jamming pods.[46]

The MiG problem came under discussion at a Pacific Air Forces commanders conference held in the Philippines. General Momyer and Col. Robin Olds, new commander of the F–4 wing at Ubon, exchanged views over cocktails. Both men had been fighter aces in World War II, and Olds' father had risen to the rank of major general in the Army Air Forces before succumbing to a heart attack. Aside from their shared experience, Momyer and Olds were very different—the short general's cerebral asceticism contrasting with the tall colonel's fun-loving boisterousness. Like many of his men, Olds sported a regulation-breaking mustache, and his marriage to a film actress added a certain luster to his reputation.

Olds' conversation with Momyer led to an imaginative operation code-named Bolo (a Philippine knife), which cost the North Vietnamese perhaps 7 of their 115 MiGs. Because the Air Force and Navy were not permitted to attack MiG bases, the MiGs could be destroyed only by drawing them into air-to-air combat. Colonel Olds succeeded in doing so by attempting to persuade the North Vietnamese that F–4s trimmed for air-to-air engagement were F–105s loaded with bombs, and that these "F–105s" intended to bomb the country's major MiG base at Phuc Yen.[47]

Jamming pods played an important part in the ruse, because thus far they had been used only by F–105s. The pods would help to disguise F–4s as F–105s, and if the North Vietnamese chose to send up SAMs rather than MiGs, F–4s would benefit from pod protection. The number of available pods determined the size of the MiG sweep: at one pod per aircraft, fifty-seven pods permitted twelve flights of four F–4s with plenty of backup. Olds planned to use seven flights from his 8th Tactical Fighter Wing and five from the 366th at Da Nang. These would be supplemented by an EC–121 radar plane, an EB–66 electronic intelligence and jamming plane, eight F–104s to guard the EB–66 and assist the F–4s if necessary, twenty-four F–105F Wild Weasels to threaten SAMs, and twenty-five KC–135 tankers to refuel aircraft on the way to North Vietnam and again on the way home. The force was designed to look like an unusually big strike, with formations heading for the MiG bases from west and east simultaneously. The Navy and Air Force sometimes achieved this pincer effect through parallel operations. In this case, the Navy agreed to stand down while the Air Force sent Ubon F–4s in from the west and Da Nang F–4s in from the east.[48]

The New Year's cease-fire allowed enough time to transfer pods from F–105s to F–4s without causing a suspicious change in F–105 bombing routine. C–130s carried the pods from Takhli and Korat to Ubon and Da Nang—much to the displeasure of F–105 pilots, who could not be told what was afoot. Throughout New Year's night, maintenance crews worked to attach pods to F–4 wing pylons. Adapter kits had been rushed from the United States, but the kits had to be supplemented with parts welded in Thailand.[49]

Most of the men who took off in the early afternoon of January 2 had never even seen an enemy aircraft, let alone fired at one. Olds had shot down thirteen German aircraft during the Second World War, and his operations deputy, Col. Daniel "Chappie" James, Jr. (later the Air Force's first black four-star general), had seen action during the Korean War, but even they had yet to encounter North Vietnamese MiGs. Though F–4s often patrolled a target area looking for MiGs, they had been jumping F–105s and avoiding F–4s.*[50]

Bolo's execution varied considerably from its plan. The Da Nang force judged the weather inadequate and did not penetrate the delta. Olds decided to risk taking his force over solid cloud cover. He had planned to make a traditional run down Thud Ridge at five thousand feet, partly so that he could see any SAMs. But with cloud tops at seventy-five hundred, he guessed that he might not get under the ceiling, and so proceeded at twelve thousand. A high ingress would soon be standard, but his reliance on pods was then considered daring. Four SAMs came up and missed the attackers by a wide margin. Olds had expected MiGs to challenge him as soon as he started his run down Thud Ridge. When his lead flight made its first pass over Phuc Yen at about three in the afternoon, the MiGs had still not taken off. Then perhaps a dozen MiG–21s came up; according to American intelligence, there were only thirteen MiG–21s in North Vietnam. Some of North Vietnam's nearly one hundred MiG–17s and MiG–15s took off from airfields east of Hanoi. These older, slower, more maneuverable fighters did not enter the battle northwest of Hanoi, but they probably would have been encountered by the Da Nang force had it penetrated the delta airspace.[51]

The battle above Phuc Yen lasted less than fifteen minutes, only time enough for Olds' first wave of three flights to enter at five minute intervals. Without a loss, the F–4s claimed to down at least seven MiGs.[†] When Olds' second wave arrived ten minutes later, the surviving MiGs had already ducked below the clouds and landed. If all had gone according to plan, the spacing between F–4 flights would have made it difficult for MiGs to land, forcing them

---

* During World War II, Olds served in the 479th Fighter Group under Lt. Col. Hubert "Hub" Zemke, who had become famous as commander of the 56th Fighter Group, "Zemke's Wolfpack." In Southeast Asia, the 8th Tactical Fighter Wing would come to be known as "Olds' Wolfpack."

† Istvan Toperczer found that the North Vietnamese lost only five MiG–21s that day. See his *Air War Over North Vietnam: The Vietnamese People's Air Force* (Carrollton, Texas, 1998), p 17.

to engage or run out of fuel. A MiG could fight over its own field for about an hour; F–4s, even with refueling during ingress and egress, could stay over Phuc Yen for at most twenty minutes and only five minutes using afterburner—hence the five-minute intervals between flights. But the clouds, which had helped to disguise the F–4s as F–105s until the last minute, also permitted surviving MiGs to escape.[52]

On this occasion, North Vietnam's radar proved a mixed blessing at best. It encouraged an inflexible dependence on ground control, and the controllers failed to distinguish between F–4s and F–105s. Then too, American missiles had a far better day than the enemy's guns and rockets. If the MiGs were carrying any missiles, they were not fired. On the other hand, F–4s had no guns at this time. The Americans had taken extra care to make sure their missiles were properly adjusted. Four kills were attributed to Sparrow radar-guided missiles and three to heat-seeking Sidewinders. Olds and his backseat radar officer, 1st Lt. Charles C. Clifton, downed one MiG with a Sidewinder. Three more victories in May would make Olds the leading MiG killer of the war until 1972, when the Air Force and Navy would finally produce five aces (with at least five kills each).[53]

Less than a week after Bolo, two F–4s pretended to be a single reconnaissance aircraft by flying so close together that they gave a single radar return. This ruse also worked, and two more MiG–21s went down without loss of an F–4. But the MiGs did not cooperate with an attempt to repeat Bolo on January 23. Olds argued against repeating Bolo, and he did not lead the mission. The MiGs stayed on the ground and SAMs came up; one F–4 did not make it back.[54]

MiG pilots would not again be so badly fooled. As their self-confidence returned, MiGs would once more become a dangerous nuisance. For a time F–4s would accompany F–105 formations. When a formation was jumped by MiGs, the F–4s would jettison bombs and go after the MiGs. Later, F–4s would be stripped of bombs and left to the more free-wheeling combat patrol duty they had performed since the first year of the war. The most effective response to MiGs would come when the Johnson administration at last permitted the bombing of MiG bases.[55]

*   *   *

Early in 1967, the Johnson administration had yet even to release targets deferred in November, let alone authorize bombing MiG bases. On February 22, the President approved one of the deferred targets, the Thai Nguyen ironworks. General Wheeler thought he saw a major change in Johnson's attitude that promised release of more targets in the Red River Delta when the weather improved.[56]

Wheeler told Admiral Sharp that this "new sense of urgency" was due in part to the heavy flow of supplies from the Red River Delta southward during the recent Tet cease-fire (February 8–13).[57] Intelligence estimates exceeded twenty thousand tons. Since the cease-fire did not apply to Laos, little of the supply surge moved down the Ho Chi Minh Trail. Most came by boat along the coast toward the Demilitarized Zone, north of which the North Vietnamese had two divisions, with a third on the way. According to the Defense Intelligence Agency, twenty thousand tons of supplies could support at least one North Vietnamese division for six months. Seventh Air Force estimated that twenty thousand tons could support eight North Vietnamese divisions or thirty Viet Cong divisions for a year, if each division experienced only one day of combat per month. In any case, the Tet supply surge was a substantial contribution to the North Vietnamese troop buildup along the Demilitarized Zone.[58]

Despite intelligence reports about the North Vietnamese supply effort, the Tet pause in bombing North Vietnam had been extended from four days to six days while Harold Wilson, British Prime Minister, discussed peace prospects with Alexei Kosygin, Chairman of the Soviet Council of Ministers. Midway through the talks, Wilson learned about a hardened American negotiating position prompted by fears that the North Vietnamese would send three divisions across the Demilitarized Zone if bombing stopped. President Johnson now demanded that North Vietnam's infiltration into South Vietnam end before a bombing halt; the American position had been that bombing would stop if the North Vietnamese gave private assurance that infiltration would then cease (perhaps days or weeks later). Johnson sweetened his proposal with an offer to quit augmenting American forces in South Vietnam in addition to halting the bombing of North Vietnam after infiltration stopped. He sent his proposal by letter to Ho Chi Minh as well as through Wilson and Kosygin.[59]

During the night before Kosygin's departure from London, Johnson agreed to extend the bombing pause if North Vietnam would give assurance that it would immediately cease sending soldiers and supplies into South Vietnam. Otherwise bombing would resume soon after Kosygin left London. Though time for getting North Vietnamese agreement was extremely short, Kosygin supported the proposal. According to an intelligence translation of his telephone conversation with Communist Party leader Leonid Brezhnev, Kosygin said that there was "a great possibility of achieving the aim, if the Vietnamese will understand the present situation. All they need to do is give a confidential declaration."[60]

Before bombing began again that day, February 13, Hanoi radio broadcast a letter to Pope Paul VI from Ho Chi Minh, who demanded an unconditional halt to bombing. Two days later, Ho sent a rejection to Johnson. The fruitless Wilson-Kosygin talks in London closed an especially intense period of diplomatic maneuvering that had begun with British Foreign Secretary Brown's visit to Moscow in November.*[61]

At long last, the Air Force could proceed with bombing the Thai Nguyen ironworks. This showpiece of North Vietnamese industrialization was located thirty-five miles due north of Hanoi and about three miles south of the small city of Thai Nguyen. The Chinese began construction of the plant in 1958 to take advantage of iron ore deposits on the northern edge of the delta. Pig iron production began in 1963, and by 1967 the plant made barges and fuel drums out of imported steel. The plant's own steel mill was nearly ready to begin operation. There were only two other ironworks in the country, both of them much smaller. While they produced perhaps fifteen thousand metric tons a year, the Thai Nguyen works were designed to produce three hundred thousand of pig iron and two hundred thousand of steel. The complex, including its powerplant, occupied two square miles along the railroad that connected it with Hanoi. About ten thousand people worked at this, the largest industrial facility in North Vietnam.[62]

By March when the Air Force began to strike the ironworks, Thai Nguyen bristled with exceptionally strong antiaircraft defenses. On eight days in January and February, the Air Force had struck the city's railyard and supply depot with about a hundred attack sorties. While only one aircraft was lost on these early missions, the defenders took a heavy toll when the Air Force returned to attack the ironworks.[63]

More than two weeks after President Johnson approved that target, the weather cleared enough for a strike on March 10. Korat F–105s led the way over the target without loss, but the Takhli formation behind them ran into trouble. A flight of four Iron Hand F–105s (including two Wild Weasel F–105Fs) preceded the rest of the Takhli formation. Antiaircraft artillery knocked down the lead aircraft and damaged the second as they dove toward a SAM site. While the Takhli strike force dropped its bombs on the ironworks, the other two Iron Hand aircraft attacked the SAM site. Capt. Merlyn H. Dethlefsen, pilot of the third aircraft (an F–105F), was later awarded the Medal of Honor for making five runs on the site. Despite opposition from MiG–21s and flak damage to his aircraft, he ran the gauntlet repeatedly—first expending his Shrikes and

---

* While the North Vietnamese refused to stop sending soldiers and supplies into South Vietnam, they did begin to advertise that peace talks might follow a cessation of the bombing. On January 28, 1967, Foreign Minister Nguyen Duy Trinh said as much to the Australian communist journalist Wilfred Burchett, and soon thereafter, Senator Robert Kennedy learned in Paris that the North Vietnamese considered Trinh's remark an important policy statement. For recent American and Vietnamese views on the significance of this initiative, see Robert S. McNamara, James G. Blight, and Robert K. Brigham, with Thomas J. Biersteker and Col. Herbert Y. Schandler, *Argument Without End: In Search of Answers to the Vietnam Tragedy* (New York, 1999), pp 278–83.

cluster bombs, then strafing. His backseat electronic warfare officer, Capt. Kevin A. Gilroy, won the Air Force Cross. [*][64]

A flight of bomb-laden F–4s from Ubon followed the Takhli F–105s. Twenty-five miles from the target, one of the F–4s was hit by antiaircraft fire and began to leak fuel. While diving on the target, a second F–4 was hit. Unable to get all the way back to the tankers, both crews bailed out over Laos and were rescued.[†][65]

When fighter-bombers returned to Thai Nguyen on the following day, March 11, the wings switched places so that the 355th from Takhli hit the target first. Korat's 388th once again bombed without loss, while three F–105s from Takhli went down—two hit by flak and one by a SAM. The Takhli wing persisted with its low-level ingress, but all its losses occurred over the target, while either diving or pulling up. Six American aircraft having been lost attempting to destroy it, the ironworks still operated. It remained the Air Force's primary target for the next month and a half. But thanks to effective flak suppression, the Air Force lost no more aircraft there during that time. In addition to continuing use of cluster bombs, an effort was made to destroy guns with general purpose bombs. Aircraft losses on the first day caused the second day's strike force to make gun sites principal targets. At least one gun (eighty-five millimeters) was thought to be destroyed. A discouraging development was the appearance for the first time of hardened sites whose crews could function while protected from cluster bombs by concrete revetments.[66]

The necessity of returning again and again for a total of nearly three hundred attack sorties (or about 750 tons of bombs) was the result of both target size and bombing inaccuracy. To obtain greater accuracy, three F–105s from Korat made a bold, low-level run against the complex's powerplant. The success of this mission on March 16 led to a similar mission on March 30, when three F–4s from Ubon attempted to hit the blast furnaces; subsequent intelligence estimates were skeptical of claims that the strike had done significant damage. Nevertheless, by the end of April the ironworks no longer functioned, and occasional raids would keep it shut down.[67]

*   *   *

The new commander of Pacific Air Forces, Gen. John D. Ryan, was unhappy about taking more than two months to close the Thai Nguyen ironworks.

---

* A month later another Takhli Wild Weasel team earned the same pair of medals. Like Dethlefsen and Gilroy, Maj. Leo K. Thorsness and Capt. Harold E. Johnson returned safely from their award-winning performance, but Thorsness was shot down eleven days afterward and spent the rest of the war in North Vietnamese prisons.

† For the remarkable story of how the two damaged aircraft made it to Laos, see chapter 11, page 290.

Bad weather caused his wings to cancel or divert more than sixty strikes against that facility. "The largest problem we faced there in the air war was weather," Ryan would say later, "and we didn't have an all-weather capability."[68]

When he took command from General Harris in Hawaii at the beginning of February 1967, Ryan had just stepped down from the top position in Strategic Air Command. The unusual measure of sending the SAC commander to PACAF sparked gossip about an Air Force plot to take Pacific Command away from the Navy. But his move to Washington in 1968 as Vice Chief of Staff of the Air Force would indicate that he was being groomed for Chief of Staff. Throughout his stay in Hawaii, Ryan was a strong voice for developing a capability to bomb in bad weather and at night.[69]

Ryan had been in Hawaii less than a month when he asked the Air Staff in Washington for comparative data on the radar bombing capability of available aircraft. After the Air Force conducted an extensive series of tests on the F–105, the F–4, and the new General Dynamics F–111, the Air Staff concluded that the F–111 was the best hope for sufficient accuracy in times of low visibility. The accuracy of the F–105 and F–4 was inadequate for effective use against point targets. But no F–111s could be sent to Southeast Asia before 1968.[70]

Meanwhile, Ryan tried to use the F–105 for night and all-weather bombing. The original impetus for putting the F–105 in this role had come from the 388th Tactical Fighter Wing at Korat. As early as September 1966, the 388th had depended on aircraft radar to bomb the Mu Gia Pass at the top of the Ho Chi Minh Trail; the steep slopes offered a good return for aircraft radar, and accuracy could be checked using ground radar in Thailand. Encouraged by results in the pass, the 388th asked Seventh Air Force for permission to try radar bombing in the Red River Delta. When Ryan took command of Pacific Air Forces, the Korat proposal was waiting for him.[71]

Ryan wanted a radar bombing aircraft as successful as the Navy's Grumman A–6 Intruder. The A–6, however, boasted far greater accuracy than the F–105 could possibly achieve at night or in bad weather. Ryan was sensitive about Navy help with night raids against Thai Nguyen and other Air Force targets. "The Navy could have made us look very immature and not very capable at that time if they had taken advantage of it," he would recall, "because they had the A–6 and the A–6 is a damned fine all-weather bomber."[72] Like Ryan, Admiral Sharp thought that Task Force 77 ought to send more A–6s against the delta and fewer against the panhandle. Sharp was able to alleviate this situation somewhat by persuading General Westmoreland to permit the twenty-four Marine A–6s based in South Vietnam to fly raids into the panhandle, freeing the eighteen carrier A–6s to make more raids in the delta. But the aircraft's complex electronic systems were plagued by maintenance problems, and there was little likelihood of increasing the number of A–6s in Southeast Asia before late 1967.[73]

For his night and all-weather bomber, Ryan chose the F–105F Wild Weasel. Like the A–6, the F–105F carried a crew of two and had a terrain avoidance radar (though one not nearly as good as the A–6's). During March and April, twelve crews trained for the new mission in Japan, where their aircraft were undergoing modification. In addition to making improvements in the radar presentation, maintenance technicians at Yokota Air Base put a bomb release switch in the rear cockpit. Though the Korat wing had been planning penetration and bombing runs at about twelve thousand feet, Ryan insisted on gaining surprise with as low an altitude as possible, preferably below a thousand feet. This was the technique used by the A–6, and the F–105 had itself been designed for low–level bombing. But the inadequacy of the F–105F radar's terrain avoidance mode meant that a crew flying below a thousand feet was risking collision with the ground, to say nothing of ground fire.[74]

Ryan's emphasis on low-level bombing was an expression of established doctrine in the tactical air commands as well as the Strategic Air Command. During the Korean War, the Air Force had developed a toss-bombing computer enabling a fighter-bomber to make a low-level nuclear bombing run.* Before release, the aircraft would begin to climb rapidly. After tossing the bomb, the aircraft would reverse direction with an Immelman flip. Since the bomb had been tossed upward, the aircraft had time to move away before detonation. Designed for delivering a nuclear bomb, the F–105 had a toss-bombing computer. There was no need to toss 750-pound conventional bombs, but the computer could be used to improve the accuracy of a night drop. Once the target appeared on the radar screen, the aircraft held a steady course and the computer released the bombs automatically. Achieving significant damage with conventional bombs, however, required much greater accuracy than with a nuclear bomb. Even if an aircraft radar operator could correctly identify a target, the computer was unlikely to provide the accuracy necessary.[75]

Four crews of Ryan's Raiders, as they called themselves, reached Korat in late April 1967. All eight men were pilots. However, after the first twelve crews, navigators already serving as electronic warfare officers would be trained to use the radar, and the same crews could fly F–105Fs either as Wild Weasels or as Ryan's Raiders. As far as the original all-pilot crews could tell, they had been picked at random. The usual unhappiness of pilots told to sit in the back seat was exacerbated by suspicion that their dangerous mission was more a matter of competing with the Navy's superior A–6 than doing significant damage to North Vietnam. At any rate, Ryan had made much of Navy success when he talked to his raiders in Japan before they flew to Thailand. The crews caught the grim humor of their situation by adopting a patch that featured an F–105F with a gold screw through the back seat.[76]

Ryan's Raiders flew their first missions on the night of April 24. One aircraft was sent against the ferry at Ron in the panhandle and another against the

---

* The inventor of the Low Altitude Bombing System was Maj. John A. Ryan, Jr., no relation to General John D. Ryan.

railyard at Yen Bai on the Red River about seventy-five miles northwest of Hanoi. The tracks provided a good radar return, but darkness inhibited bomb damage assessment, as did craters left by earlier bombing. Impressive results were not produced by these raids or those that followed against Thai Nguyen and other targets in the delta. Then on the night of May 12, an F–105 was lost on a raid against the Ron ferry. The cause of the loss was unknown, and it was feared that the aircraft had flown into a hill. Three days later, another F–105F was downed by gunfire on a night raid against the Kep railyard northeast of Hanoi. The North Vietnamese hit the raiders with searchlights and barrage fire, forcing the F–105Fs to quit flying missions in the delta.[77]

While F–105F night activity was restricted to Route Package Five and the panhandle, some F–4D night missions were flown in the delta. The F–4D, whose bombing computer made better use of radar returns, began replacing F–4Cs in Southeast Asia before the end of May. Unlike F–105Fs, F–4Ds bombing at night in the delta penetrated and dropped their bombs at about twelve thousand feet. Using jamming pods, the F–4Ds flew in flights of four. As with F–105s, however, radar bombing was not very accurate. Bombs dropped at night with radar by either F–4Ds or F–105Fs landed an average of three thousand feet from the aiming point, or twice the distance normal for the A–6. The Air Force hoped that the F–111 would be able to drop most of its bombs within two hundred feet of the aiming point. Meanwhile, F–4Ds and F–105Fs harassed the enemy as best they could. General Ryan readily admitted the limitations of his raiders. "But that," he asserted, "was a hell of a lot better than just sitting on our duffs waiting for the weather to clear."[78]

*　　　　*　　　　*

In mid-April 1967, a week before Ryan's Raiders flew their first mission, the weather over the Red River Delta began to clear. The monsoonal shift in wind pattern from northeast to southwest broke up the cloud cover. Clearing skies gave the Navy an opportunity to bomb the Haiphong powerplants, targets that had been deferred in November and authorized again by President Johnson toward the end of March. Weather had combined with a second deferment (while Johnson visited Latin America) to protect the powerplants for another month. On April 20, the Navy sent fifty-three attack sorties against the powerplants. Another forty-two would finish the job before the end of May.[79]

One of the powerplants was little more than a mile from the center of Haiphong. (The oil tank farm hit the previous summer was two miles from the center.) At a Pentagon press conference, the new Assistant Secretary of Defense for Public Affairs, Phil Goulding, dodged a question as to whether bombing the powerplants was escalatory: "We do not characterize it in any fashion whatsoever."[80] Others were less cautious. Senator Richard Russell (Democrat, Georgia), Chairman of the Armed Services Committee, said he hoped the strikes were the first step toward closing the port of Haiphong.[81] Even that step would not be escalatory, Secretary of State Rusk told a group of Illinois Republicans, since the communists had already mined Saigon harbor.[82]

On April 22, in the wake of the powerplant strikes, President Johnson approved a new target list. The Haiphong cement plant, the only target yet to be struck of those deferred the previous November, could now be bombed. Since it was the primary customer of one of the bombed powerplants, the cement plant was already in trouble. Navy aircraft promptly put it out of operation, and North Vietnam had to begin importing cement. The prohibition imposed in December on striking within ten nautical miles of the center of Hanoi was lifted enough to permit attacks on three targets: an electrical switching station, a railyard, and a bridge.[83]

The central link in North Vietnam's major electrical power system was the switching station and transformer at Dong Anh, seven miles northwest of downtown Hanoi. This switch could transfer power from an area with an operational powerplant to one with a plant closed down by bombing. The switch connected Hanoi's 32,500-kilowatt coal-burning powerplant to smaller coal-burning plants at Viet Tri (on the Red River thirty miles northwest of Hanoi), Thai Nguyen, Bac Giang (twenty-five miles northeast of Hanoi), Haiphong, Uong Bi (ten miles north of Haiphong), and Hon Gai (on the coast twenty miles east of Uong Bi). The network also reached south through the Hanoi plant to Nam Dinh.[84]

By April 22, all powerplants in the delta network had been bombed except the largest one at Hanoi. Outside the network, there were several other fixed plants and a growing number of mobile generators. The largest of the latter were three 1,500-kilowatt coal-burning plants from Czechoslovakia; these could be joined into an installation as large as the smaller fixed plants. The Soviet Union furnished hundreds of 200-kilowatt diesel generators. The North Vietnamese also were thought to have about seventy-five small hydroelectric generators, most of them less than 50-kilowatts. As the North Vietnamese decentralized electrical power in deference to American bombing, construction was stopped on the 112,500-kilowatt Lang Chi hydroelectric project sixty miles up the Red River from Hanoi. Thanks to the gradualism of the campaign against electrical power, the North Vietnamese had been able to adjust through decentralization just as they had in the case of motor fuel. Though the Dong Anh switch should logically have been struck early, it was not authorized until after most of the fixed powerplants had been hit. The Dong Anh switch proved a difficult target, and not until November 1967 would Seventh Air Force succeed in knocking it out.[85]

Seventh Air Force had better luck with other Hanoi targets. F–105s could now bomb legitimately the Gia Lam railyard, which had been bombed accidentally in December. The yard was less than two miles northeast of the center of Hanoi. Seventh Air Force was also told to bomb the rail and highway bridge that crossed the Canal des Rapides a mile northeast of Gia Lam. On April 29, sixteen F–105s each attempted to hit the bridge with a 3,000-pound bomb and three 750-pound bombs; two of the six spans collapsed, cutting Hanoi's link with both railroads to China. The railroad to Haiphong, however, lay south of the canal; it could best be separated from Hanoi and routes south at the Doumer Bridge over the Red River west of Gia Lam. Because destroying the Doumer Bridge would also cut the railroads to China, from a military point of view the attack on the canal bridge might better have been directed at the Doumer Bridge. But the Johnson administration was not quite ready to make a strike so close to the center of the city. Meanwhile, the North Vietnamese began to repair the canal bridge and build a bypass bridge.[86]

President Johnson's target selections of April 22 not only sent the fighter-bombers back to Hanoi, but for the first time permitted them to strike MiGs on the ground. The key jet airfields at Phuc Yen and Gia Lam remained out of bounds, together with two others near Haiphong, but Johnson authorized limited attacks on Kep (thirty-seven miles northeast of Hanoi) and Hoa Lac (nineteen miles west of Hanoi). The runways at both fields had recently been lengthened, and Hoa Lac was able to take jets for the first time. Admiral Sharp had recommended light strikes on two of the five MiG bases in the hope of overcoming administration fears that airfield strikes would cause the North Vietnamese to move all their MiGs to China. Perhaps a fourth of about 120 North Vietnamese MiGs could already be found near Mengtzu, fifty miles north of the border. Forcing the North Vietnamese MiGs to operate out of China put them at a disadvantage, since fuel limitations would permit them much less time over the delta. But the Johnson administration was nervous about increasing China's involvement in the war.[87]

Ever since May 1966, when an F–105 had shot down a MiG inside China, the administration had gone to great lengths to keep combat aircraft from invading Chinese airspace. Fighters coming close to the Chinese border were warned by Air Force EC–121s, comparable Navy radar aircraft, or radar ships. With limited ability to pick out aircraft from ground clutter, an EC–121 tracked friendly aircraft primarily by sending a signal that triggered their identification transponders. When escaping or chasing MiGs near the border, pilots had been known to turn off their transponders. The Air Force consequently found it difficult to refute China's repeated claims that American fighters had violated its airspace.[88]

Nevertheless, the Johnson administration finally opened some of the North Vietnamese airfields to attack. Seventh Air Force directed the 8th Tactical Fighter Wing commander, Colonel Olds, to hit MiGs on the ground at Hoa Lac. On April 24, he led eight F–4s against the new target. Their cluster bombs caught about a dozen MiGs on the ground. The attackers lost an aircraft, but

Maj. Thomas M. Hirsch, pilot of the first F–4 to bomb the MiGs, claimed destruction of five; his comrades claimed at least two more. These were the first of fifty aircraft reportedly destroyed on the ground before the end of May. None of these claims could be verified, and MiGs which suffered even numerous hits from cluster bomb pellets could be repaired. Nevertheless, Air Force raids on Hoa Lac and Navy raids on Kep may well have helped to spur unusually aggressive MiG behavior that permitted destruction of many in air battles.[89]

Air Force F–4s and F–105s shot down twenty-one MiGs in May at a cost of two F–4s, while Navy fighters got three MiGs without a loss. A third of the Air Force's victories were attributed to gunfire, including the first three won by F–4 guns. While F–4s did not yet have built-in guns, a twenty-millimeter gun could be carried in a pod mounted under the fuselage. But the gun's rate of fire had been thought too slow for success in air-to-air engagements. The new operations officer at Da Nang's 366th Tactical Fighter Wing, Col. Frederick C. "Boots" Blesse, persuaded General Momyer to permit the wing to experiment with gun pods. Persuasion was required, because Momyer had long opposed putting a gun on the F–4. Blesse was a Korean War fighter ace well known in the Air Force as the author of "No Guts—No Glory," a vivid guide to air-to-air tactics first published in the *Fighter Weapons Newsletter* of January 1954. He took a dim view of the F–4's lack of a built-in gun. MiGs could get too close for an F–4 to fire its missiles successfully, and ground clutter could interfere with missile guidance systems at low altitude. Blesse's analysis was reinforced by the success F–105 pilots had with their guns under those circumstances.[90]

The gun pods helped the 366th to get one more victory than Ubon's 8th Tactical Fighter Wing in May 1967 (the month with the most air-to-air engagements during Rolling Thunder). This was especially noteworthy because the 366th had not participated in the air-to-air mission for several months and could never give it as much attention as the 8th. Despite the 366th's success, however, the 8th got more publicity. Colonel Blesse blamed the disparity not only on the glamour surrounding the 8th's commander, Colonel Olds, but also on the 8th's nickname: "The Wolfpack." The press naturally preferred to write about "the Wolfpack" rather than "the 366th Tactical Fighter Wing." Blesse's men soon came up with their own sobriquet—"The Gunfighters"—and painted what they claimed was the biggest wing insignia in the world on the roof of a hangar. From miles away pilots could see the huge comic phantom carrying his gun and proclaiming not only new unit pride but also an old confidence that no enemy aircraft could ever get near Da Nang. Indeed, after the spring airfield raids and air-to-air victories in North Vietnam, the North Vietnamese air force would make few appearances anywhere for the next two months.

American political reaction to the airfield raids followed familiar patterns. Congressman Rivers said that they were "one of the most gratifying developments of the war."[91] Former Vice President Richard Nixon assured the press that there was no danger of a war with China, which would "not dare have a confrontation with the United States."[92] Senator Fulbright thought it "very likely" that the war would expand to "include the Chinese and probably the Russians."[93] Senator George McGovern (Democrat, South Dakota) agreed with Fulbright about the risk the administration was taking: "They are really going for broke."[94] Senator Robert Kennedy (Democrat, New York) praised the courage of McGovern's speech calling for a total bombing halt throughout Vietnam.[95]

The Joint Chiefs of Staff cautioned Admiral Sharp that the airfield attacks had been too vigorous. A few days later, however, President Johnson demonstrated his readiness to increase pressure on North Vietnam by adding another MiG base (Kien An, near Haiphong) to the approved target list, as well as several targets near Hanoi. Returning to the list were the Yen Vien railyard and the Van Dien truck depot—targets that had aroused so much controversy in December.[96]

At last on May 16, after months of discussion within his administration, Johnson authorized bombing Hanoi's powerplant. He had been very reluctant to approve a target in downtown Hanoi. The powerplant was less than a mile from the Ministry of National Defense and not much farther from the President's Palace. But Johnson was persuaded that the Navy's new Walleye television-guided bomb was so accurate that there would be little chance of civilian casualties except for workers at the plant.[97]

The Walleye was the first of a family of guided bombs that would provide the accuracy needed to strike urban targets with minimal civilian casualties. Most of that family would not be ready before the United States stopped bombing the Red River Delta in 1968. An Air Force project to develop laser-guided bombs was over a year away from production when Navy Walleyes reached the Gulf of Tonkin in early 1967. By May the Navy had dropped several Walleyes with great accuracy. Aircraft survivability also improved, because a pilot could drop a Walleye more than three miles from a target and leave immediately—before the bomb had hit its target. Once the bomb's television guidance system had locked onto a picture with sharp contrast (part of the outline of a building, for instance) the bomb was supposed to proceed straight to the origin of the image. In time, pilots would learn that the bomb could be fooled. For instance, the television camera's focus might jump from one bridge support to the next (their outlines were so similar) until the bomb hit a river bank. The major disappointment so far had been the inability of direct hits by the 1,100-pound bomb to bring down the steel bridge at Thanh Hoa (seventy miles south of Hanoi), but that bridge had long since proved itself the most durable target in North Vietnam. The Hanoi powerplant was much more vulnerable.[98]

After scrutinizing detailed maps and photographs, the President approved a strike on the plant by two aircraft each carrying one Walleye. If possible, the raid was to be accomplished before May 22, Buddha's birthday and the beginning of a visit by British Foreign Secretary Brown to Moscow. Since the television guidance system required clear weather, a long wait would probably have been necessary during the northeast monsoon. But the southwest monsoon had brought reasonably good bombing weather, permitting the Navy to strike the powerplant on May 19—Ho Chi Minh's seventy-seventh birthday. Though two escort fighters were shot down, a Walleye hit the target. The Navy struck again two days later, losing an escort fighter but hitting the target. The Hanoi plant appeared to be out of commission, leaving only one small plant fifty miles south of Hanoi to supply power for the network.[99]

The powerplant raids made headlines as the first against downtown Hanoi. Since Walleye's existence was classified, the special accuracy of this new weapon could not be disclosed and the Johnson administration could not take public credit for its careful restraint. In a more visible exercise of restraint, the President called a halt to bombing near Hanoi. On May 22, only a month into the southwest monsoon with its relatively favorable bombing weather, Johnson put his foot on the brake. Bombing within ten nautical miles of Hanoi's center again required his approval for each strike. Johnson withheld approval for several weeks while his divided administration reconsidered the future of Rolling Thunder.[100]

Chapter Three

Gradualism on Trial

The gradual intensification of the American air war against North Vietnam paralleled a gradual buildup of American ground forces in South Vietnam. Although these two forms of gradualism were related, they were shaped by different constraints. The buildup of ground forces in South Vietnam pressed against the weakness of the local economy, the capacity of America's logistical apparatus, and the unwillingness of the Johnson administration to risk alienating American voters by calling up reserves. President Johnson sought to wage a war in Southeast Asia within fiscal and political parameters that would not interfere with his domestic programs. From the outset, however, B–52 bombers could have struck targets throughout North Vietnam in any weather at any hour. Instead Johnson doled out targets one at a time to fighter-bombers poorly equipped for striking in bad weather or at night. Fears of a wider war restrained the air campaign, while hopes for a war on the cheap restrained the ground buildup. Despite Johnson's gradualism, or because of it, critical voices grew louder and more numerous inside as well as outside the administration.

Little by little, the number of authorized targets in North Vietnam increased, as did the number of American soldiers in South Vietnam—until a decision for a major addition could require fairly dramatic action, such as a reserve callup or mining North Vietnam's ports. In this context a little more bombing with fighter aircraft could seem the safest form of escalation, the last chance for gradualism. When, in March 1967, General Westmoreland asked that his troop ceiling of 470,000 be increased by at least 80,000 and as much as 200,000, he began a long debate that would first cool the air war in May and then heat it up in August.[1]

General McConnell, the Air Force Chief of Staff, injected the bombing issue. He doubted that sending more troops would be enough to achieve victory, but he agreed to 100,000 if the Joint Chiefs of Staff would also recommend expanding the air and naval campaign against North Vietnam. The other chiefs agreed and once more linked troops in South Vietnam and bombs in North Vietnam. In a memorandum to Secretary of Defense McNamara, they supported sending 100,000 more troops to South Vietnam, calling up the reserves, and expanding the air and naval campaign to include mining North Vietnam's ports.[2]

In late April 1967, President Johnson had Westmoreland come home to make a speech in New York and another to Congress. Westmoreland also joined the Chairman of the Joint Chiefs, General Wheeler, in meetings at the White House, where they argued that the recommended buildup would permit shallow invasions into Laos, Cambodia, and North Vietnam. Only the President's National Security Adviser, Walt Rostow, showed any interest in sending ground forces across South Vietnam's borders. Dramatic ground action of that kind could make the air war look tame by comparison, and Wheeler raised the possibility of mining North Vietnam's ports. While this proposal made no more headway than did the invasion plans, his remark that the bombing campaign was running out of targets provided grist for those who were seeking to cut back the bombing.[3]

Secretary of Defense McNamara and his assistant for international security affairs, John McNaughton, used Wheeler's remark in a draft presidential memorandum arguing for a bombing cutback. They quoted Wheeler as saying that "the bombing campaign is reaching the point when we will have struck all worthwhile fixed targets except the ports."[4] The memorandum concluded that all bombing should be concentrated south of the twentieth parallel—i.e., south of the Red River Delta. McNamara had first raised this possibility in the fall of 1966, when it became obvious that North Vietnam had dispersed oil storage to cope with American bombing. He seemed to prefer an unconditional bombing halt as more likely to lead to negotiations, but he knew that even a cutback to the twentieth parallel would face strong opposition from men in uniform and their allies in Congress.[5]

During the winter of 1967, McNamara had been quietly winning adherents to his view within the administration. His effort was facilitated by a small discussion group that met every Thursday afternoon in the office of Under Secretary of State Nicholas Katzenbach. These meetings had gained President Johnson's approval in November 1966 to consider quietly the administration's major problems in Vietnam. In January 1967, when the President asked Rostow to look into setting up a committee to examine the bombing of North Vietnam, Rostow steered the job to Katzenbach's committee. Rostow did consult with Clark Clifford, an influential Washington lawyer who had served in the Truman administration and had known Johnson for many years. Clifford urged a small, secret group whose existence the President could deny by saying there was "no committee" or that the President talks to "a great many people on a great many subjects."[6]

Rostow recommended that while the President might later want to call upon Clifford and other outsiders to undertake a study of the bombing, the time was not yet ripe. So Rostow, Under Secretary of Defense Cyrus Vance, McNaughton, and William Bundy (Assistant Secretary of State for Far Eastern

Affairs) focused on that problem during their weekly cocktail meetings in Katzenbach's office. McNamara often came, as did Richard Helms, Director of Central Intelligence; Rusk sometimes joined them. They called themselves the "No Committee" or the "Non Group." Although not even told about their meetings at the outset, General Wheeler was eventually informed and may have participated occasionally.[7]

By May the No Committee was leaning toward a bombing cutback. Walt Rostow told the President that the group unanimously rejected both mining Haiphong and systematically bombing the rail lines to China. Rusk's worries about possible Chinese and Soviet reactions bolstered McNamara's arguments against the cost-effectiveness of bombing the Red River Delta. Even Rostow doubted air power's ability to close the "top of the funnel" by mining Haiphong and striking the railroads. Since his days as a target planner in England during World War II, Rostow had believed oil and electricity to be vital targets, but he had always been skeptical about bombing railroads. He was especially impressed by an estimate that North Vietnam's import capacity of seventeen thousand tons per day exceeded actual imports by more than eleven thousand tons. Rostow and the No Committee were ready to cut back bombing north of the twentieth parallel as soon as the Hanoi powerplant had been destroyed.[8]

McNamara hoped that hitting the Hanoi powerplant would also make the Joint Chiefs amenable to a bombing cutback. But that hope only illustrated how far he and the No Committee had moved from the military point of view. Walt Rostow grew fearful of a public breach. "The question," he told President Johnson, "is what kind of scenario can hold our family together in ways that look after the nation's interests and make military sense."[9] Rostow suggested withdrawing approval to bomb targets in Hanoi and Haiphong until after McNamara and Wheeler could visit South Vietnam. Then the manpower and bombing recommendations could be considered together. Johnson took Rostow's advice, and when the Navy had made its second strike against the Hanoi powerplant on May 21, 1967, the President reinstated the prohibition against attacks within ten nautical miles of the center of the city.

For the next month, much of the administration's energies were absorbed by the Six Day War between Israel and its Arab neighbors. In the wake of the Arab defeat, Alexei Kosygin, Chairman of the Soviet Council of Ministers, met with President Johnson at Glassboro, New Jersey. Kosygin brought a message from Hanoi that the North Vietnamese were ready to begin talks a day or two after the bombing stopped. Johnson agreed to stop bombing North Vietnam if he was assured that talks would begin immediately and that the five army divisions in North Vietnam near the Demilitarized Zone would not attack South Vietnam. There was no response from Hanoi.[10]

Meanwhile, opposition had begun to build against ending the bombing of North Vietnam's Red River Delta. Director Helms of Central Intelligence supported further concentration of strikes in the southern route packages, but warned Johnson that a total cessation of bombing in the Hanoi-Haiphong region would be seen as a victory in Hanoi. Air Force Secretary Brown argued for the status quo; he considered mining Haiphong too risky, but did not want to reduce bombing in the Red River Delta without getting something in return.[11]

Since becoming Secretary of the Air Force in 1965, Brown had been confronted with an increasing divergence between Chief of Staff McConnell and Secretary of Defense McNamara. By the end of 1966, the crux of Brown's problem was McNamara's plan to build an infiltration barrier near the demilitarized zone: ground forces, minefields, and fences would reach across the northern edge of South Vietnam, while air forces would attempt to interdict the Ho Chi Minh Trail area of Laos with the help of electronic sensors. McNamara brought together a group of academic scientists in the summer of 1966 to study the feasibility of a barrier, and as soon as they had recommended it, he ordered a joint task force under Army Lt. Gen. Alfred D. Starbird to have the barrier ready by September 15, 1967.[12]

It was obvious to the Joint Chiefs that the barrier could profoundly change the character of the war in ways that they believed would reduce the chance for a satisfactory outcome. General Westmoreland would have to transfer ground forces from search and destroy missions to defending McNamara's wall; McNamara talked in terms of 20,000, but the Chiefs feared that the number of soldiers required would be many times higher. Westmoreland's own preferred method of interdicting the Ho Chi Minh Trail was to send his ground forces into Laos. Instead, the Air Force and Navy would be expected to focus their efforts there, while McNamara might succeed in persuading the President to end the bombing of North Vietnam.[13]

Secretary Brown labored to convince Chief of Staff McConnell and the Air Force that the barrier was a good idea which would supplement rather than replace bombing North Vietnam. Indeed, the Air Force ultimately invested more heavily in the barrier than did the other services. Most of the ground portion was never built, but the effort to use electronic sensors for air interdiction in Laos would become a major preoccupation of the Air Force for the next four years. In the short run, Brown also helped to keep the bombing campaign alive over North Vietnam. More influential advocacy of bombing, however, would come from senators on the Armed Services Committee and airmen in Southeast Asia.[14]

*   *   *

South of the twentieth parallel in North Vietnam's panhandle, where Secretary of Defense McNamara proposed to concentrate bombing, Air Force and Navy aircrew were already flying eight thousand attack sorties a month—

more than two-thirds the total sent against North Vietnam. The railroad south of Vinh had long since ceased to function and few trucks moved on the roads in daylight. Even at night the Air Force was sending more than fifteen hundred sorties a month, usually F–4s armed with flares as well as bombs. Whatever gains in effectiveness were to be had by increasing the already abundant air power directed at the panhandle seemed slight in comparison with opportunities thereby lost in the Red River Delta.[15]

Much of North Vietnam's military and economic strength was concentrated in the delta. Here were gathered the essential supplies provided by the Soviet Union and China. Through the port of Haiphong came perhaps forty-three hundred tons of imports a day, and possibly another fifteen hundred tons came down the northeast railroad from China. Most weapons arrived by rail, while trucks and oil came through Haiphong. According to one American estimate, communist forces in South Vietnam required only fifteen tons of supplies a day from North Vietnam—less than six thousand tons a year. To undertake an offensive, however, the communists required far more; during the northeast monsoon of 1967–1968 they would (by Hanoi's own count) employ about five thousand trucks attempting to move sixty thousand tons of supplies through Laos. Even that large an effort proved difficult to bomb when hidden by night and jungle. Trucks destroyed in the North Vietnamese panhandle or on the Ho Chi Minh Trail in Laos could have a more immediate effect on the communist supply situation in South Vietnam than could the destruction of railyards and warehouses in the Red River Delta, but strikes on those more vulnerable delta targets could have far greater impact on North Vietnam's military and economic strength as a whole.[16]

While the Air Force and the Navy continued to seek wider authority to mine the ports and bomb the railroads in the Red River Delta, McNamara's proposal to quit bombing there put a premium on showing some progress within the authority already granted. Since mining Haiphong was prohibited, the Navy went to work on the ground transportation routes radiating from the port—especially Haiphong's only rail line, which, as it passed west through Hanoi, intersected with the only line running south. Armed reconnaissance was prohibited within either Haiphong or Hanoi, so the Navy paid special attention to Hai Duong, where the railroad crossed a bridge about midway on the sixty-mile journey to Hanoi. At the end of June, Walt Rostow informed the President that the Navy had found a bottleneck. A week later, Rostow could report that the raid of July 2, 1967, on Hai Duong caused a serious disruption in the rail traffic headed for Hanoi.[17]

Meanwhile, the Air Force had strengthened its effort to interdict the northeast railroad from Hanoi to China. More than a third of the ninety-mile route lay within zones that President Johnson had forbidden American aircraft to attack. A buffer zone twenty-five nautical miles deep along the Chinese border was intended to ensure that American aircraft would not cross into China. Here

Soviet and Chinese arms arriving on standard-gauge railroad cars could be stored or loaded onto meter-gauge cars for the night run to the Hanoi sanctuary.

Chinese laborers were adding a third rail to the northeast line, so that by the end of 1967 it would no longer be necessary to transfer supplies from China's standard-gauge cars to North Vietnam's meter-gauge cars. Chinese rail construction in China, as well as in Vietnam, had already made the North Vietnamese rail system more valuable to North Vietnam and less vulnerable to American bombing. Before the summer of 1966, the Chinese had depended on North Vietnam's northeast and northwest railways as coastal China's only rail connection with the mineral-rich interior of southwest China. The completion of a direct Chinese rail line to Kunming freed North Vietnam's rails to carry more supplies required by its war effort. At the same time, Chinese workers in North Vietnam completed a dual-gauge line from Hanoi running north to the ironworks at Thai Nguyen and then east to join the old northeast line at Kep on the edge of the delta. American aircrews became very familiar with the rail triangle thus formed; they called it the Iron Triangle.[18]

The targets that could contribute most to backing up traffic on the northeast line (together with its Thai Nguyen branch) lay within the ten-mile prohibited zone which President Johnson had reinstated around Hanoi on May 21, 1967. Before that, he had permitted some attacks on the rail system within the zone. Unfortunately, the timing and sequence of these attacks limited their impact. North Vietnam's largest railyard, the one at Yen Vien five miles northeast of downtown Hanoi, was struck in December 1966. Thanks to the subsequent outcry in the American press, this yard had not been struck again. Three miles closer to downtown Hanoi, the Gia Lam yard, with North Vietnam's principal railroad car repair shops, had also been struck in December—by accident.[19] Johnson authorized another strike on it in April and, at the same time, authorized a strike on the railroad and highway bridge over the Canal des Rapides (Song Duong). Since the canal bridge was north of Gia Lam and south of Yen Vien, closure of the bridge stalled rail traffic from China in Yen Vien (which also remained off limits to bombing) rather than in Gia Lam.[20]

While the North Vietnamese repaired the canal bridge and built alternates, enough rail traffic backed up on the northeast railroad and its Thai Nguyen branch to give the F–105s and F–4s more rolling stock to bomb than usual. Seventh Air Force tried to prolong this state of affairs by repeatedly striking the bridges and railyards that lay between the Hanoi prohibited zone and the China buffer zone. Though many of these bridges and yards had been struck during the past year, the pounding reached a crescendo in the summer of 1967.

The principal bridges on the main line crossed the Song Cau at Dap Cau near Bac Ninh, about fifteen miles from Hanoi, and the Song Thuong at Bac Giang, another ten miles north. Even when the main line could be broken, there was the alternate that ran from Yen Vien through Thai Nguyen and rejoined the main line at Kep a little less than halfway to China. None of the bridges on the alternate line were nearly as long as those at Dap Cau or Bac Giang. Even with the longer bridges, the North Vietnamese and their Chinese allies had become adept at making repairs and providing parallel bridges or ferries. A bridge that appeared down might require only a prefabricated span that lay in wait near-by.[21]

Since nearly all bombing of the northeast railroad occurred in daylight and most trains ran between sanctuaries at night, it was remarkable that any rolling stock was ever caught by the fighter-bombers. Yet aircrews reported seeing more than twenty-five hundred cars on the northeast railroad and its Thai Nguyen branch from the middle of May to the end of June. Of these, they claimed to have destroyed or damaged about one thousand. The number destroyed was probably far smaller, and the Chinese apparently replaced many of the losses. At any rate, U.S. intelligence estimates would place the North Vietnamese rolling stock inventory at about two thousand at the end of the sum-mer—only six hundred less than at the beginning of the year.[22]

In the short run, however, it was possible to be more optimistic about the progress being made. This was especially true in Washington. At the end of June, the Air Force's Vice Chief of Staff, Gen. B. K. Holloway, wrote the Pacific Air Forces commander, General Ryan, that it was time to focus on North Vietnamese locomotives. Holloway believed that North Vietnamese rolling stock had been reduced from twenty-six hundred to six hundred, while the loco-motive count had come down only 15 from 120 to 105. However exaggerated Holloway's picture of the rolling stock situation, it was certainly true that the North Vietnamese rarely left their locomotives in the open during daylight. A locomotive campaign would have to be a night campaign, and General Ryan's attempts to increase night sorties in the Hanoi region had met with little success so far.[23]

Ryan's Raiders* at Korat, with their two-seat F–105Fs, ceased to fly night missions into the delta in mid-May less than a month after they began them. Their last mission in the delta was, as before, only a single sortie that penetrat-ed at low level, perhaps a thousand feet. It was shot down over the target, the Kep railyard. The F–4Cs of the 497th Tactical Fighter Squadron at Ubon then tried their hand at low-level missions in the delta. The aircrews of the 497th were known as the Night Owls, thanks to their nightly visits to Laos and the panhandle of North Vietnam. In less well defended areas they could use flares, but they did not much care to do this even in the panhandle. Certainly in the delta they would not use flares, and their luck proved little better than that of Ryan's Raiders.[24]

On the evening of 22 May, 1967, the Night Owls sent four F–4Cs to attack railyards near Kep. They penetrated at an altitude of five hundred feet or less, and two of the aircraft were hit by antiaircraft fire near the railroad. One

---

* See above, chapter two.

crashed immediately, killing both crew members. The other aircraft almost made it to the coast north of Haiphong before the crew had to bail out. Maj. Richard D. Vogel, the pilot, injured his back during ejection and was captured. The backseater, 1st Lt. David L. Baldwin, was rescued by a Navy helicopter. So ended the last in a series of Night Owl attempts to penetrate the delta at low level. A few days later F–4D aircraft arrived at Ubon from Florida, and the Night Owls used their improved radar for occasional night raids at more than ten thousand feet above the delta. But the accuracy of the night missions had always been questionable, and the increase in altitude did nothing to enhance it. In any case, such meager night raids could be no more than harassment at best.[25]

If most of the air assault on the northeast railroad was limited to daylight, at least the weather in June 1967 cooperated with a string of unusually clear days. Of the six thousand attack sorties Seventh Air Force sent into North Vietnam that month, about fifteen hundred went into Route Package Six with more than three thousand tons of bombs; as usual the bulk of Air Force sorties struck Route Package One in the panhandle just north of the Demilitarized Zone. Nevertheless, the effort against the delta was among the strongest of the war and was concentrated on the railroad. Only two aircraft fell to enemy air defenses. On June 2, an F–105 was hit by ground fire at sixteen thousand feet just before diving on a railyard near Kep. The North Vietnamese or Chinese gunners scored another victory on June 14 when they downed an F–4 that was attempting to penetrate the delta below eight thousand feet. Usually ingressing aircraft tried to stay well above that altitude even if it meant a cloud layer might block their view of surface-to-air missiles. Using jamming pods to deceive the missiles, pilots were able to stay above accurate flak.[26]

As for MiGs, they were rarely seen in June. On only a couple of occasions did fighter-bomber pilots jettison bombs to deal with attacking MiGs; in September 1966 this had occurred more than sixty times. The spring 1967 strikes on airfields and consequent air-to-air battles had nearly eliminated the MiG problem for the time being. On June 11, however, two F–4s collided while guarding an F–105 strike force against the possibility of MiG attack. Aside from this accident, escort fighters had an easy month.[27]

The success with which fighter-bombers were now penetrating the Red River Delta, as well as the destruction of more box cars than usual, encouraged airmen to believe that they might be able not only to head off Secretary of Defense McNamara's proposed cutback in bombing north of the twentieth parallel, but even to increase the bombing there. They hoped to eliminate (or at least reduce) the sanctuaries established by President Johnson along the Chinese border and around Hanoi and Haiphong. Johnson did permit the Navy to return to Hanoi in June to hit the powerplant again and to hit the Van Dien supply depot with its support facility for surface-to-air missiles. But all other targets within the sanctuaries remained off limits, and authority to attack in the

Haiphong area was reduced further after two Soviet ships were strafed in North Vietnamese harbors.[28]

The first incident involving a Soviet ship took place on June 2, 1967, in the port of Cam Pha, forty miles up the coast from Haiphong. A flight of four F–105s were leaving North Vietnam, when the pilot of the third aircraft decided to pay a visit to a well known antiaircraft site on the coast; his wingman followed. As the element leader dove on the site, he thought he saw a ship in the roadstead firing at him, and he strafed it. When the pair returned to Takhli Air Base that evening, the element leader tried to retrieve his gun camera film, but the young airman unloading the camera would not break the rules. Before long the problem was put into the hands of the acting wing commander, Col. Jacksel M. Broughton, who destroyed the evidence by exposing the film.[29]

Unfortunately for Colonel Broughton, this incident was not to be closed so easily. The Soviet Union immediately complained that its ship *Turkestan* had been fired upon by an American aircraft, killing one of the crew. The Commander in Chief, Pacific, Admiral Sharp, assured Washington that there was little to the Soviet claim; possibly the ship had been hit by debris from antiaircraft fire. Walt Rostow told President Johnson that Secretary McNamara and General Wheeler were convinced that the United States bore no responsibility. The State Department informed the Soviets that aircraft attacking targets in the area had been investigated and that none had attacked a ship.[30]

Two weeks later Soviet Ambassador Dobrynin told Secretary of State Rusk that the *Turkestan* had docked at Vladivostok with an unexploded round from an F–105; Foreign Secretary Gromyko was considering bringing it to the United Nations when he and Kosygin visited in a few days. That was more than enough to reopen the investigation, and within a week the United States had to apologize. From Colonel Broughton's perspective, his court martial for destroying evidence was just the final frustration of many that he subsequently described in his books *Thud Ridge* and *Going Downtown*.* From the perspective of more cautious men in Washington, the *Turkestan* incident was proof that enemy sanctuaries needed more emphasis from the President.[31]

Washington was still very sensitive about the incident when on June 29, the Soviet ship *Mikhail Frunze* was apparently strafed in Haiphong harbor by two Navy fighters. This led immediately to the declaration of a prohibited zone with a radius of four nautical miles from the center of Haiphong. Like the ten-mile Hanoi prohibited zone that had been declared in December 1966, no strike was to be made within the new zone without special authorization from the President. In the prohibited zones, U.S. aircraft were not even to react to antiaircraft fire. Such reaction was permitted in the restricted zones, which ran out

---

* Colonel Broughton's court martial conviction was set aside by the Office of the Secretary of the Air Force. Instead, Broughton was fined six hundred dollars and retired.

to thirty nautical miles from the center of Hanoi and ten nautical miles from the center of Haiphong.[32]

The establishment of the Haiphong prohibited zone seemed less foreboding to airmen than it might have, because only a day earlier the Preparedness Investigating Subcommittee of the Senate Armed Services Committee had announced that it was going to hold hearings on the conduct of the air war over North Vietnam. Since most subcommittee members were known to be sympathetic to a more decisive use of air power, air leaders in the Pacific had reason to feel more confident about Secretary of Defense McNamara's forthcoming visit to Vietnam and chances for defeating his proposal to eliminate bombing north of the twentieth parallel.[33]

McNamara came to Saigon in early July with the troop issue largely resolved. He announced that there would be no reserve call-up, so that the biggest troop increase Westmoreland could get would be 42,000, or a total force of 525,000. But the Secretary was clearly in no position to announce a bombing cutback, and he was subjected to a series of briefings carefully prepared to talk him out of pursuing one. A couple of weeks before McNamara's arrival, Admiral Sharp had sent the text of his own briefing to General Westmoreland, General Momyer, and Vice Adm. John J. Hyland, the Seventh Fleet commander; then Sharp had watched Momyer and Hyland rehearse their briefings. But it turned out to be Sharp's briefing that rubbed the Secretary of Defense the wrong way. After hearing Sharp's call for mining Haiphong and lifting most restrictions on bombing, McNamara showed his irritation by thanking Westmoreland for the briefings while ignoring the theater commander.[34]

Momyer's presentation, however, was more persuasive. He emphasized Seventh Air Force's recent success attacking the northeast railroad with relatively few aircraft losses. Though suggesting that it was time to "broaden and increase our effort," he left specific recommendations to Sharp.[35] Momyer's cerebral style and his impressive marshalling of data found favor with his audience. After McNamara's return to Washington, there was speculation in the press that he had been converted to bombing in the delta. But, in fact, McNamara told Johnson that the air leaders were much too optimistic about bombing results.[36] General Wheeler was able to dilute McNamara's influence by giving Momyer's briefing transcript to the President, who was so impressed with it that he read passages to the cabinet.[37] Johnson also sent it to former President Eisenhower, who liked Momyer's argument that the reduction in antiaircraft fire, including surface-to-air missiles, might be a result of railroad interdiction.[38]

While Momyer's briefing may have contributed to Johnson's willingness to continue bombing in the Red River Delta, the President was not yet ready to authorize a major expansion of the bombing. When, on July 20, 1967, Johnson approved a list of fifteen new targets, none of these lay within the ten-mile Hanoi prohibited zone, the four-mile Haiphong prohibited zone, or the China buffer zone. Indeed, Johnson specifically disapproved any attack on Hanoi's Doumer Bridge across the Red River. He also vetoed three Hanoi targets that had been struck at least once during the preceding year: the powerplant, the Yen Vien railyard, and the Van Dien truck depot. Nor would the President approve hitting the major MiG base at Phuc Yen, about fifteen miles northwest of Hanoi.[39]

The most significant increase in bombing authority granted by President Johnson on July 20 opened to armed reconnaissance all major transportation routes (road, rail, and water) radiating from the Hanoi prohibited zone. Between the circumference of the prohibited zone (with a radius of ten nautical miles) and the circumference of the restricted zone (with a radius of thirty nautical miles) lay a region whose shape inspired airmen to call it the Hanoi "donut." Hanoi's entire restricted zone had often been called a donut before creation of the prohibited zone. Henceforth, the term "donut" sometimes included the prohibited zone and sometimes excluded it as merely the donut hole. The new expansion of bombing authority concerned lines of communication in the donut ring. When fighter aircraft began to bomb north of the twentieth parallel in the summer of 1965, Johnson had established the restricted zone to keep them away from Hanoi. Subsequently, he had permitted some armed reconnaissance on certain routes within the zone. In the case of the northeast railroad, for example, the thirty-mile circle crossed just north of Bac Giang, but armed reconnaissance was permitted from there to Bac Ninh, less than twenty nautical miles from the center of Hanoi. The new rule permitted armed reconnaissance all the way to the ten-mile circle, not only on the northeast railroad, but for other routes coming into Hanoi.[40]

Since June 30, the Haiphong donut also had a hole. On that day, President Johnson had declared a prohibited zone (with a radius of four nautical miles) inside Haiphong's previously established restricted zone (with a radius of ten nautical miles). The Haiphong donut ring differed from its Hanoi counterpart in that no armed reconnaissance was authorized. Hence, the Navy might be permitted to bomb a bridge in the donut ring, but traffic that backed up between the bridge and the port could not be struck. Although Haiphong was principally a Navy responsibility, the Air Force was very concerned about it. Interdicting the northeast railroad could not have a major impact so long as imports could flow freely through Haiphong. General McConnell proposed that the Haiphong donut ring become the focus of an intensive interdiction campaign, with armed reconnaissance permitted on all the major routes carrying traffic inland from the port. In addition, McConnell wanted to shrink the donut hole, the prohibited zone, from a radius of four nautical miles to a radius of one and a half nautical miles.[41]

In the fall of 1966, when the Air Force had proposed to establish interdiction belts across Navy route packages in the panhandle of North Vietnam, Admiral Sharp had rejected the proposal on the ground that it was an Air

Force attempt to control part of Navy territory. This time the Air Force did not make the mistake of trying to launch a campaign of its own against the Haiphong donut. By lobbying for the Navy, the Air Force irritated Sharp only slightly. He pointed out that Navy airmen had been attempting to isolate Haiphong for some time, but he welcomed any increase in their authority to do that job.[42]

McConnell's Haiphong donut plan also met a favorable reception from Walt Rostow, who saw that it offered a way around President Johnson's usual objections. Johnson was firmly opposed to mining the port or bombing the docks. Nor did he like General Wheeler's proposal in the spring of 1967 to "shoulder out" shipping from the harbor by bombing targets that were progressively closer to the docks. McConnell's plan promised to reduce the flow of imports through Haiphong without risking further incidents involving Soviet ships. On the last day of July, Rostow sent the plan into Johnson with the advice that this was a "quite serious and interesting proposal."[43]

A little more than a week later, President Johnson authorized armed reconnaissance in the Haiphong donut ring. At the same time, he approved several railroad targets within the Hanoi prohibited zone and within the China buffer zone. To a degree, this expansion in bombing authority reflected the growing optimism of some of Johnson's advisers. Rostow told him that the No Committee now believed they were on the "winning track" and favored more bombing of transportation and electric power targets in the Hanoi-Haiphong region. Support inside the administration probably had far less to do with Johnson's decision, however, than political pressure from outside. The morning after Johnson expanded Air Force and Navy bombing authority, the Preparedness Investigating Subcommittee of the Senate Armed Services Committee opened its investigation into the bombing of North Vietnam.[44]

*   *   *

During his years in the Senate, Lyndon Johnson had chaired the Preparedness Investigating Subcommittee of the Armed Services Committee. The current Chairman, John Stennis (Democrat, Mississippi), had often acted in that capacity even when Johnson was in the Senate, since Johnson was absorbed by his more important duties as majority leader. Though Johnson's increasingly liberal stance on civil rights had disturbed Stennis, he had supported Johnson for the presidency in 1960. Even after Johnson entered the White House and pushed for civil rights legislation, Stennis had continued his support on most other matters, including the war in Vietnam. But he was becoming very uncomfortable with Johnson's preference for increasing pressure on North Vietnam only gradually.[45]

Fearful that Americans might continue to die in South Vietnam for years to come, some of the military's strongest supporters in the Senate began to think that a pullout would be preferable to gradualism. On August 1, 1967, Senator Ernest F. Hollings (Democrat, South Carolina) warned Walt Rostow that the President's policies were troubling some of his key backers, like Stennis and Senator Richard Russell (Democrat, Georgia), the Chairman of the Armed Services Committee. During his Senate years, Johnson had been considered a Russell protege. Now, according to Hollings, Russell was so fed up with gradualism that he wanted to declare war or get out of Vietnam. Stennis too felt that the U.S. was overcommitted and that it had surrendered the initiative to the enemy.[46]

On matters relating to air power, the most influential and outspoken member of the Stennis subcommittee was Senator Stuart Symington (Democrat, Missouri). Since serving as the first Secretary of the Air Force in the late 1940s, he had been a persistent advocate for the service during more than a dozen years in the Senate. He had been appointed to the Armed Services Committee by Lyndon Johnson, then majority leader. Their friendship had cooled in the period before the 1960 presidential campaign, when they both sought the nomination of their party. Since then, they had continued to be political allies, but Symington had grown increasingly disenchanted with the war in Vietnam.[47]

Symington visited Southeast Asia several times in an attempt to understand the war. As he talked to pilots and generals about the restrictions under which they were operating, he grew especially hostile toward the President's ban against striking North Vietnam's airfields. Even after some of these were at last added to the authorized target list in the spring of 1967, he continued to push for attacking the others, including the principal MiG base at Phuc Yen. When he learned that Secretary of Defense McNamara was attempting to cut back bombing, Symington called for an investigation.[48]

Symington's colleagues on the Stennis subcommittee shared his dissatisfaction with the way the war was going. In addition to Stennis, the other Democrats were Henry M. Jackson of Washington, Howard W. Cannon of Nevada, and Robert C. Byrd of West Virginia; the Republicans were Margaret Chase Smith of Maine, Strom Thurmond of South Carolina, and Jack Miller of Iowa. In closed session August 9–29, 1967, the subcommittee questioned seven generals, three admirals, and the Secretary of Defense. From the subcommittee's point of view, the score was ten to one, with McNamara alone on the losing side.[49]

The first to testify was the Pacific commander, Admiral Sharp, who was accompanied by his two principal subordinates in Hawaii, the commanders of the Pacific Fleet (Adm. Roy Johnson) and Pacific Air Forces (General Ryan). They and their questioners could congratulate themselves that their hearings had already produced an expanded target list even before their proceedings had begun. On the morning of the opening session, President Johnson had approved railroad targets within ten nautical miles of Hanoi (including the Red River bridge) and within twenty-five nautical miles of the Chinese border, not to mention permitting armed reconnaissance within ten miles of Haiphong. Sharp stressed at the outset, however, that he would be asking for more targets: "It is important that we continue to take these good targets and get in there and strike where it hurts."[50]

President Johnson's attempt to take the wind out of the senators' sails served chiefly to redirect their energies away from investigating moves toward a bombing cutback. Only Senator Smith showed much interest in the origins of McNamara's barrier concept and any connection it might have with cutback proposals. Sharp assured her that the barrier could never be "a substitute for the bombing."[51] Since the possibility of a cutback appeared to have faded, the subcommittee focused on the need to mine Haiphong harbor and bomb Phuc Yen airfield.

Senator Symington explained that he had called for the hearings because he feared that "the way our air power over North Vietnam has been handled, it was being denigrated before the people to a point where one of the great arms of both our services, Navy and Air Force, would eventually be eliminated."[52] The tactical air forces had been made to look weak. Pilots in Southeast Asia had pleaded with him to be allowed to hit Phuc Yen airfield. Why had Sharp been refused authorization to hit Phuc Yen? "I have not been given a reason," the admiral replied.[53]

Walt Rostow thought at first that Symington wanted to bomb Fukien Province in China. The National Security Adviser solemnly warned the President that such an attack would mean war with China. But one point Symington was trying to make was that Phuc Yen airfield should not have been an especially sensitive target. It was a military installation more than ten miles from Hanoi. If the Pacific commander had not even been told why Phuc Yen should not be bombed, a reasonable inference was that the military leadership was not fully involved in the target selection process.[54]

On the question of military consultation, the President could be put in a bad light since he rarely included admirals or generals in meetings with his principal advisers. Even the Chairman of the Joint Chiefs of Staff, General Wheeler, had not been present during most of the critical discussions in 1965, and he had participated only occasionally since then. With Wheeler's testimony scheduled to follow Sharp's, Rostow suggested to Johnson a "roundup session" for Wheeler which would enable him to say that he had been consulted on all targets.[55] But when Wheeler testified, he took a somewhat more open approach. He claimed only to have been "frequently" present, particularly for "major" bombing programs. Senator Thurmond wanted to know if targets had ever been turned down in Wheeler's absence. Wheeler answered in the affirmative, while noting that targets were also turned down when he was present.[56]

Though Wheeler tried to mute his criticism of the administration as much as possible, he could not duck direct questions about his views on Haiphong. He favored mining Haiphong; the other chiefs favored it; the President and the

Secretary of Defense opposed it. Symington asked Wheeler whether he thought it was fair to criticize generals for the alleged failure of a gradual bombing policy which they had not recommended. Wheeler agreed that such criticism was unfair. On the matter of Phuc Yen airfield, however, he confined himself to saying that the Joint Chiefs had for two years recommended bombing it, but that they had not been permitted to because of its nearness to Hanoi, the probable cost in terms of American pilots and aircraft, and the weakness of the MiG threat.[57]

Symington's advocacy of bombing Phuc Yen was then quietly undermined by the Seventh Air force commander, General Momyer. As in his briefing for McNamara in Saigon, Momyer argued persuasively for the increasing effectiveness of American aircraft against North Vietnam's air defenses, especially MiGs. The airfield attacks and air-to-air battles of the spring had broken MiG resistance. "We have driven the MiGs out of the sky for all practical purposes."[58] MiG pilots would soon give Momyer reason to regret that sentence, but for the moment it took the steam out of Symington's criticism.

When President Johnson met with his principal advisers, Secretary of Defense McNamara was full of praise for Wheeler and Momyer. Wheeler was present on this occasion and noted that while Symington had been the roughest questioner, he was "on Phuc Yen like a broken record."[59] McNamara predicted that the subcommittee would fail in its attempt to find a chasm between himself and Wheeler or between them and the President: "sure there are small differences but these are worked out."[60]

Wheeler's testimony had tried to paint a picture of growing harmony between the civilian and military leadership. After all, many targets once forbidden had since been approved, and he was confident that more approvals lay just ahead. Indeed, during the hearings, President Johnson approved thirteen targets (in addition to the sixteen he approved just before the opening session). When Senator Smith asked the Air Force Chief of Staff about this, General McConnell offered the opinion that McNamara's recent trip to Vietnam may have caused him to appreciate for the first time the value of the air war in the north. But, McConnell added, "I haven't talked to him about it at all."[61]

Whatever success the Joint Chiefs had in portraying McNamara's conversion to their point of view evaporated when McNamara testified. The Secretary of Defense dismissed enthusiasm about the release of so many new targets. The new targets were of no great importance, and he had not changed his mind about the air war. In McNamara's view, there never had been a significant disagreement between himself and the Joint Chiefs over bombing—just a difference of opinion about the allocation of only 5 percent of the sorties sent against North Vietnam. Symington interjected that attacking an octopus in the head seemed "pretty fundamental" even though the head was only 5 percent of the octopus. "But if you were attacking 95 percent of the octopus simultaneously," McNamara replied, "the analogy doesn't hold . . . ."[62]

The subcommittee did not accept McNamara's contention that attacking new targets would make little difference. They sided with the witnesses in uniform, who had stressed the critical importance of closing North Vietnam's ports, especially Haiphong. McNamara attempted to disparage the value of Haiphong by arguing that communist operations in South Vietnam needed only a small quantity of supplies: if less than 1 percent of North Vietnam's imports were required by communist forces in South Vietnam, surely enough supplies could be brought ashore in lighters at countless points along hundreds of miles of North Vietnamese coastline or carried overland from China. During the year since American bombers had destroyed oil off-loading facilities, North Vietnamese lighters had been delivering fuel in barrels.[63]

The subcommittee's frustration with McNamara's testimony was evident. Senator Howard W. Cannon (Democrat, Nevada), a major general in the Air Force Reserve, noted that imports coming through Haiphong supported the communist war effort whether or not those supplies crossed the border into South Vietnam. As to McNamara's argument that the North Vietnamese would simply find other ways to import necessary supplies, Cannon protested that if Americans were going to throw their hands in the air over such difficulties, they might just as well say, "Let us get out then because we cannot handle this problem." Symington seconded this view.[64]

At the end of August 1967, the Stennis subcommittee published its report. "What is needed now," the subcommittee stated, "is the hard decision to do whatever is necessary, take the risks that have to be taken, and apply the force that is required to see the job through."[65] But the substance of the subcommittee's recommendation was somewhat less bold than this rhetorical flourish. According to the subcommittee, it was necessary to close the port of Haiphong, but it was not necessary to subject North Vietnam's cities to area bombing or even to use B–52s against targets near those cities.

None of the witnesses had called for using B–52s against the densely populated Red River Delta. Admiral Sharp expressed concern about the possibility that a surface-to-air missile might bring down a B–52.[66] General McConnell noted that North Vietnam's air defenses were much stronger in 1967 than in 1965, when he had supported using the B–52s against targets in the delta.[67] General Wheeler declared that "no responsible military commander that I know of has ever yet advocated the attack of population as a target."[68] Wheeler left little doubt that his category of responsible military commanders did not include General LeMay, whose famous proposal to bomb the North Vietnamese back to the Stone Age was interpreted by Wheeler to mean attacking the population. While Wheeler was anxious to demonstrate that the bombing he favored would spare most civilians, McNamara used this claim as an argument against new targets. "There is no basis to believe," McNamara asserted, "that any bombing campaign, short of one which had population as its target, would by itself force Ho Chi Minh's regime into submission."[69] But no one at the hearings suggested that bombing in North Vietnam should be anything more than a partner of the ground war in South Vietnam.

After more than two years of gradualism, there seemed little room for dramatic action. Generals and senators might regret the failure to use B–52s against the Red River Delta in 1965, but the North Vietnamese had been permitted to grow accustomed to bombing gradually and build their defenses against it. In any case, no one at the 1967 hearings quarreled with the Johnson administration's decision not to threaten the existence of the communist government of North Vietnam. As much as the senators on the subcommittee disliked gradualism, following most of their recommendations could yield little more than another gradual escalation in the bombing campaign. Only their call for closing the port of Haiphong promised action of a relatively dramatic character.

The Stennis subcommittee report revealed the chasm between Secretary of Defense McNamara and the Joint Chiefs. At a press conference on the following day, President Johnson insisted that while there might be differences of opinion, there was "no deep division."[70] In any case, the Joint Chiefs could come directly to him anytime they chose. Differences of opinion were natural in the American system of government, and Johnson recalled that in the late 1940s, Secretary of the Air Force Symington had asked a congressional committee for an opportunity to testify on behalf of a bigger Air Force than the Truman administration thought feasible. As to McNamara, Johnson insisted that there was no truth to the rumor that the Secretary of Defense had threatened to resign if the bombing program expanded: "He doesn't go around threatening anything or anyone."[71]

Only three months later, Johnson would announce McNamara's departure from the Defense Department to become president of the World Bank. McNamara's defense of administration policy at the Stennis hearings had not endeared him to the President. Although Johnson continued to oppose mining Haiphong, he was ready to conciliate proponents of bombing by authorizing less risky targets. McNamara's bleak assessment of the bombing's effectiveness at the hearings and his backstage search for a way out of Vietnam both served to weaken his influence. His testimony was frequently praised by critics of the bombing, including the North Vietnamese representative in Paris.[72]

In late November, when he raised the possibility of McNamara's departure at a National Security Council meeting, President Johnson felt obliged to emphasize that no member of the Joint Chiefs of Staff had talked to him about resignation. General Wheeler immediately affirmed that no member of the Joint Chiefs had threatened to resign: "As far as I am concerned any report like that is a lie."[73] Nevertheless, gossip about resignation threats continued to circulate. According to one version, some or all of the Chiefs had threatened to resign in May. According to another version, Wheeler had called a meeting of the Chiefs on the evening after McNamara's testimony to the Stennis committee in late

August; all had agreed to resign, but by the next morning Wheeler had changed his mind and they all kept quiet. When the latter version was published in 1989, the only surviving Chiefs from 1967, Adm. Thomas Moorer (Chief of Naval Operations) and Gen. Wallace M. Greene, Jr. (Commandant of the Marine Corps), both flatly denied that the Joint Chiefs had ever agreed to resign.[74]

While withdrawing support from McNamara, President Johnson developed a warm relationship with Wheeler. The President's top general was a consummate staff man without combat experience. Less than a week after the Stennis hearings, a heart ailment sent Wheeler to the hospital. Having had a heart attack of his own, Johnson was inclined to be sympathetic. When Wheeler offered to resign as Chairman of the Joint Chiefs, Johnson put his arm around him and told him that the President could not afford to lose him. Wheeler would remember proudly that on this occasion Johnson also praised him for never giving a bad piece of advice. Henceforth, Wheeler would be a more regular participant at Johnson's meetings on bombing North Vietnam.[75]

*   *   *

As a result of the Stennis hearings, the list of targets authorized by President Johnson grew somewhat longer. A few hours before the hearings began on August 9, 1967, the President approved new targets on the northeast railroad. For the first time, American aircraft would be permitted to strike railyards and bridges in the buffer zone along the Chinese border—i.e., within twenty-five nautical miles of China. At the other end of the northeast railroad in Hanoi, the Doumer Bridge over the Red River at last became a target.

In communist Hanoi, the Red River bridge was called the Longbien Bridge. Its French name, the Paul Doumer Bridge, was still used by American airmen, though few knew who Doumer was. More than four decades had passed since the assassination of President Doumer of France, and the bridge was a product of his service in Vietnam at the turn of the century. As governor general of French Indochina, Doumer had tried to centralize the administration of French colonies in the region and make them profitable for France. He pushed for the construction of railroads that would link northern Vietnam with southern Vietnam and with China. Though the railroads were built, they did not spur the rapid economic development Doumer had expected. But when the communists began to develop North Vietnam in the 1950s, Doumer's railroad system played an important role in their plans.[76]

The linchpin of Doumer's railroad system was his Red River bridge at Hanoi. Rail traffic carrying goods from China or from the port of Haiphong had to pass over the Doumer Bridge to reach Hanoi and points south all the way to Saigon. This bridge was one of the most obvious targets in North Vietnam, and it had been spared so long only because its southern end projected into downtown Hanoi. Though well defended by antiaircraft artillery and surface-to-air missiles, the bridge's great length made it vulnerable. This, the longest bridge in Vietnam, stretched for more than a mile, ten times the length of the hard-to-hit bridge at Thanh Hoa.[77]

The long, frustrating, and still unsuccessful campaign to destroy the Thanh Hoa bridge weighed heavily on planning for the Doumer strike. While the precision television guidance system of the new Walleye bombs would have been very desirable for hitting the Doumer Bridge and avoiding the population, the 1,100-pound Walleye with its 825-pound warhead had proved too weak for the Thanh Hoa despite direct hits. Therefore, the Air Force decided to use 3,000-pound unguided bombs. On August 9, President Johnson directed that the Hanoi powerplant be struck again with Walleyes and that only after a week had passed could the Doumer Bridge be attacked. The next day, however, the President agreed to reverse the order of attack in deference to a temporary problem with the Walleyes.[78]

On the morning of August 11, 1967, Seventh Air Force told the F–105 wings at Takhli and Korat, together with the F–4 wing at Ubon, to bomb the Doumer Bridge that very afternoon. Aircraft already loaded with 750-pound bombs had to be reconfigured with a pair of 3,000-pound bombs. The strike force of thirty-six fighters penetrated North Vietnam at ten thousand feet and flew down Thud Ridge before popping up to thirteen thousand and diving on the target. Though the unguided bombs were released more than a mile above the bridge, it was hit several times—destroying one of the nineteen rail spans and portions of the highway that ran along both sides of the track. As Walt Rostow commented to President Johnson, "dropping a span of that bridge the first time around was a quite extraordinary feat."[79] Not everyone was so impressed, however. Two weeks after the raid, Secretary of Defense McNamara told the Stennis subcommittee that the target had been just another bridge: "We have struck tens if not hundreds of bridges of a similar kind."[80]

Since the North Vietnamese could no longer send trains across the Doumer Bridge, they had to transfer cargo to trucks and ferry them across the river, delaying cargo moving west from Haiphong as well as south from China. Southbound traffic soon experienced additional delay after the Air Force bombed two bridges over the Canal des Rapides about four miles northeast of the Doumer Bridge. In response to the first strike on the original Canal bridge in May, the North Vietnamese had built a bypass bridge and repaired the old one; in August both ceased to function. The efficiency of the northeast railroad was further reduced by attacks on railyards and bridges in the buffer zone along the Chinese border.[81]

So much interference with traffic on the northeast railroad had the desired consequence of increasing the number of box cars stalled in railyards. The largest yard in North Vietnam at Yen Vien just north of the Canal des Rapides had been struck in December 1966, but since then it had been off limits along with most other targets within ten nautical miles of Hanoi. On August 21, 1967, about 150 box cars sat open to attack in the Yen Vien yard. Twenty F–105s and eight F–4s damaged more than half the box cars and trapped the remainder in the yard, where they were struck again two days later. These strikes, however, cost the Air Force men and planes. On the 21st, two F–105s were lost to anti-aircraft artillery, as was an F–4 on the 23d. But more surprising and dismaying was the loss of a pair of F–4s to MiG–21s on the 23d.[82]

After suffering heavy losses in the air-to-air battles of May 1967, the MiGs had stood down. When they attacked on August 23, they employed new hit-and-run tactics. Having passed low under a strike force on its way down Thud Ridge, two MiG–21s climbed quickly and fell upon the force from the rear—a single pass and two heat-seeking Atoll missiles destroyed two F–4s. The most remarkable aspect of this incident was that nothing like it had occurred before over North Vietnam. American airmen on their way to strike a target had grown used to looking for a MiG ahead, though they had all been taught to "check six"—i.e., watch their "six o'clock" (or rear). The old admonition at once seemed more relevant. North Vietnam's ground radar control system had demonstrated that it could guide MiGs into the deadly six o'clock position.[83]

F–4 and F–105 strike aircraft on the Yen Vien raid that day were escorted by a flight of F–4s armed only for air-to-air combat and led by the commander of the 8th Tactical Fighter Wing, Col. Robin Olds. A World War II ace, Olds' four victories in North Vietnam made him the top MiG-killer of the war so far. His flight was just behind the F–105s and just ahead of the strike F–4s. "I heard them scream," he would recall, "I turned, and all I saw were two burning objects . . . ."[84] His compassion turned to anger when he learned that Seventh Air Force intelligence officers had known for several days that the MiGs were practicing this new tactic. He declared that had he been told, he would have split his escort flight of four into two elements and sent both elements ahead of the strike force—one element low and the other high, with the latter swooping back over the strike force as they came down Thud Ridge. Olds thought that this maneuver would have caused the North Vietnamese ground controller to call off the attack.[85]

Unfortunately, the MiG–21s on August 23 took their toll and were only part of the Air Force's problems that day. Another F–4 was shot down by anti-aircraft artillery at the Yen Vien railyard; a fourth ran out of fuel and flamed out over Thailand. Adding an F–105 hit by ground fire in Route Package Six and an F–4 in Route Package One, losses totalled six Air Force jets and one Navy jet over North Vietnam for the 23d and caused pilots to call it "Black Wednesday." It was the worst day in the air over North Vietnam since "Black Friday," December 2, 1966, when five Air Force jets and three Navy jets were lost.[86]

Black Wednesday made relatively little impression in Washington, where American aircraft losses usually received less attention than enemy civilian casualties. A major exception to this general rule, however, had occurred only two days earlier, when two Navy A–6s strayed into China and were shot down by Chinese MiG–19s. That got Washington's attention, but in the end disappointed those who expected this incident to bolster their argument against bombing targets near the Chinese border. The A–6s had bombed a railyard near Hanoi far from the border and were trying to return to the carrier Constellation when a thunderstorm caused them to fly north of their intended route. The carrier and its radar aircraft attempted to warn the A–6s of their impending border violation, but the warnings were apparently not received. The Chinese limited their response to shooting down the A–6s and blaming the border violation on a conspiracy between President Johnson and Soviet Premier Kosygin. Far from discouraging strikes near the border, this relatively restrained Chinese reaction raised administration confidence that the Chinese would not increase their involvement in the war.[87]

While continuing to permit bombing near the Chinese border, President Johnson renewed his prohibition on bombing within ten nautical miles of the center of Hanoi—beginning August 24, only two weeks after he had authorized targets there. No one in the Pacific was told the reason for this about-face, which had to do with the activities of Henry A. Kissinger, then director of the defense studies program at Harvard. Kissinger was acquainted with a microbiologist in Paris, Herbert Marcovich, whose friend Raymond Aubrac had been close to Ho Chi Minh. During Ho's negotiations with the French at Versailles in 1946, he had stayed in Aubrac's villa. Now Aubrac was working for the United Nations in Rome and offered his services as an intermediary. With the encouragement of the State Department (conveyed informally through Kissinger), Aubrac and Marcovich visited Hanoi in July 1967. They proposed a variation on the two-phase formula that had become the American negotiating position.[88]

Since late 1966, the Johnson administration had expressed a willingness to stop bombing (phase A) before North Vietnam reciprocated by ceasing to infiltrate troops and supplies into South Vietnam (phase B). Since the two phases would not be connected overtly, North Vietnam would be able to claim that the United States had stopped bombing unconditionally. After consulting with Kissinger, Aubrac and Marcovich altered phase B, so that the North Vietnamese would only commit themselves not to increase their infiltration; the question of reducing that infiltration would be considered during negotiations that would promptly follow a bombing halt. Hence, the United States would trade a bombing halt merely for negotiations. After the North Vietnamese expressed interest, President Johnson approved the new two-phase formula on August 18; the next day he agreed to suspend bombing near Hanoi from August 24 to September 4 so that Aubrac and Marcovich would have plenty of time for a bomb-free second visit there.[89]

North Vietnam used the mid-August air strikes in the Hanoi area to justify denying Aubrac and Marcovich permission for a second visit. They had to conduct their business through the North Vietnamese representative in Paris, Mai Van Bo. For two months, the North Vietnamese let the new two-phase proposal dangle, while President Johnson extended the prohibition on bombing within ten nautical miles of the center of Hanoi. Johnson made the American offer public in a speech at San Antonio, Texas, on September 29, 1967, and henceforth this proposal was called the San Antonio formula. But on October 20th, Mai Van Bo refused to see Aubrac and Marcovich; on the same day Wilfred Burchett, an Australian communist journalist, reported from Hanoi that the North Vietnamese were "in no mood for concessions or bargaining."[90]

The coincidence of the Kissinger initiative and the Stennis hearings was very awkward for President Johnson. As usual, he tried to balance the conflicting demands of those who sought negotiations and those who wanted to increase the pressure on North Vietnam. After giving airmen two weeks to destroy the bridges over the Red River and the Canal des Rapides, he gave the North Vietnamese two months to rebuild them. As a sop to the Stennis committee, he authorized new targets further from Hanoi, including one opposed during the hearings by Secretary McNamara—the coal exporting port of Cam Pha, but only when no ships were present. Since there were always ships at Haiphong and usually Soviet ones, Johnson rejected the Stennis committee demand that North Vietnam's major port be closed by mining or bombing.[91]

As the Kissinger initiative dragged on, the President grew impatient. At a Tuesday lunch meeting with his advisers on September 12, he wanted to know whether Kissinger was a dove. Secretary of State Rusk assured him that Kissinger was basically on the administration's side, though Rusk doubted productive talks would really follow a bombing halt; in Rusk's view, a bombing halt would thus prove to be only temporary. Walt Rostow worried that Kissinger might go soft in a crunch. But Rostow was himself becoming more amenable to a bombing halt, because he believed that the communists were losing the war in South Vietnam and therefore that bombing North Vietnam was no longer essential. So Rostow's optimism, Rusk's skepticism, and McNamara's pessimism all pointed toward a bombing cutback. In the fall of 1967, however, President Johnson paid more heed to calls for harsher bombing from the Joint Chiefs of Staff and their allies in the Senate.[92]

*   *   *

While waiting for the Kissinger initiative to die and thus release targets near Hanoi, the Joint Chiefs sought Johnson's approval for striking North Vietnam's major MiG base at Phuc Yen—more than ten miles from the center of Hanoi. During the Stennis hearings, Senator Symington's repeated demands that Phuc Yen be hit were undercut by General Momyer's claim that the MiGs had been driven from the sky in May. Even before the hearings were over, however, the MiGs began to display new aggressiveness and effectiveness. In September, bad bombing weather and the prohibition against bombing near Hanoi cooled the air-to-air battle and the MiGs got only one kill, but forty-eight American aircraft jettisoned bombs while fending off the MiGs.[93]

In mid-September, Richard Helms at the Central Intelligence Agency called Walt Rostow to report that Senator Symington was in a very black mood as he prepared to leave Washington for another trip to Southeast Asia. Symington was worried about the economic burden imposed by America's gradual escalation of the war. Rostow cabled Ambassador Ellsworth Bunker in Saigon that he would need to do a lot of missionary work on Symington. But no amount of missionary work could dissuade the senator from his growing conviction that the United States must either hit North Vietnam hard or quit.[94]

Upon returning to Washington, Symington proposed that the United States cease all military action in both North Vietnam and South Vietnam—but that if productive negotiations did not follow, American airmen should be free to conduct a much harsher bombing campaign. This proposal immediately ran into opposition at both the Defense Department and the State Department. Under Secretary of State Katzenbach protested that the "only purpose of formulating cessation of military actions in this way would be to justify major escalation."[95] General Wheeler, on the other hand, deemed it "improbable that any feasible post-pause increase in the scope and intensity of our combat operations could offset rapidly the advantages which the enemy would acquire during the proposed cessation of hostilities."[96]

Before Symington circulated his new cease-fire proposal, President Johnson had already moved to satisfy the senator's longstanding demand that the Air Force be permitted to bomb the MiG base at Phuc Yen. But Johnson had no more than approved the target on September 26, 1967, when he was persuaded to withdraw it the very next day. The White House belatedly discovered that the Rumanian Prime Minister, Ion Gheorghe Maurer, was due to land at Phuc Yen within hours of the planned strike. The State Department was grooming Maurer as the vehicle for its latest peace initiative and had promised him a bomb-free visit to Hanoi. The Central Intelligence Agency took this opportunity further to delay a strike on Phuc Yen by pointing out that there were perhaps two hundred Soviet advisers there.[97]

The Central Intelligence Agency got support from a surprising ally when Col. Robin Olds visited the White House on October 2. Olds had given up command of the F-4 wing at Ubon to become commandant of cadets at the Air Force Academy. He confirmed that the change in MiG tactics was causing problems, but he was opposed to striking Phuc Yen: "I'd rather knock them out of the skies . . . . I would rather have them coming from Phuc Yen, because I know where they are."[98]

The Air Force Chief of Staff, General McConnell, would have been appalled to hear Olds' advice to the President on Phuc Yen. After the postponement of the Phuc Yen strike, North Vietnamese MiGs knocked down three more American aircraft. When McConnell stood in for Wheeler at a meeting with Johnson and his principal advisers on October 11, McConnell pushed for an attack on Phuc Yen. He hoped to destroy at least eight of the sixteen MiGs there even if it cost as many as three American aircraft. Secretary of Defense McNamara dismissed Phuc Yen as militarily marginal, and Secretary of State Rusk agreed. But Rusk also said that he was not too concerned that any unfortunate consequences would result from bombing Phuc Yen—he only wanted the strike postponed for a few more days. With the collapse of the Kissinger peace initiative a week later, President Johnson approved a strike on Phuc Yen together with restrikes against the Hanoi bridges and powerplant.[99]

Phuc Yen airfield was located in Route Package Six's western half, where the Air Force usually did any bombing that was permitted. But other services wanted a share in attacking the principal MiG base. Both of the Navy's carriers then serving in the Gulf of Tonkin participated in the Phuc Yen strikes of October 24 and 25, as did a Marine A–6 from South Vietnam. The Air Force, of course, was also well represented. In addition to providing F–4 escorts for the F–105s from Takhli and Korat, Ubon sent F–4s loaded with bombs.

Although the target was ringed with especially heavy defenses, this was a mission that many aircrew were eager to fly. When three out of four aircraft in one Ubon flight were not loaded in time for the first strike on the 24th, the flight leader borrowed an F–4 from another squadron for his wingman and they took off as an element of two—deprived of the mutual protection (especially in terms of electronic jamming) provided by a flight of four. Yet no losses were suffered either by this foolhardy flight or by any of the other Air Force flights attacking Phuc Yen on October 24. The Navy was not so fortunate, losing two F–4s on the 24th and an A–4 on the 25th—when the Air Force also lost a plane, an F–105 diving to bomb the guns that hit it.[100]

These initial attacks cratered Phuc Yen's runway and damaged its tower, thanks to a direct hit on the latter by a Navy Walleye guided bomb. Most of the eighteen MiGs then based at Phuc Yen were caught on the ground; reconnaissance photography indicated that perhaps a dozen of them suffered severe damage. On October 24, two MiG–21s had taken off against the first wave of attackers—Air Force F–105s and F–4s from Thailand. As the MiGs were attempting to get behind the attacking force, an F–4 escort used a twenty-millimeter cannon to shoot down one.[101]

With its gun still carried in a pod rather than built into the aircraft, the F–4 relied on its missiles during most air-to-air engagements. Indeed, that would continue to be the case even after the built-in gun arrived in 1967. The most effective air-to-air weapon during the first two and a half years of the war was the heat-seeking Sidewinder missile. When chasing an enemy aircraft, the

Sidewinder could be fired several hundred feet closer than the F–4's other missile in those years, the radar-guided Sparrow. Beginning in the fall of 1967, nevertheless, the Sparrow supplanted the Sidewinder as the Air Force's preeminent air-to-air weapon in Southeast Asia. This turnabout was a consequence of the introduction of a new aircraft model, the F–4D, which did not carry the Sidewinder. Instead the F–4D's Sparrows were paired with a heat-seeking version of the Falcon, which had been developed as a radar-guided missile. Unfortunately, the heat-seeking Falcon proved less effective than the Sidewinder in Southeast Asia.

The dismal record of the Falcon was especially disappointing to the Air Force, because this missile had been developed under Air Force auspices. The Sidewinder and Sparrow, on the other hand, were (like the F–4) products of Navy development. Unfortunately, the Air Force pursued its own cheaper Falcon rather than adopt the improved Sidewinder that the Navy introduced in 1966. All three missiles shared the drawback of having been designed for defense against relatively slow-moving bombers. On paper at least, the supersonic Falcon appeared to have an advantage over subsonic Sidewinders and Sparrows. With a capability for hitting a target being chased at a range of less than two thousand feet, the Falcon might have been expected to be more useful in a dogfight than either the Sidewinder or the Sparrow. But the Falcon was fatally handicapped by a very small warhead that lacked a proximity fuse. Unlike the Sidewinder and the Sparrow, the Falcon had to make a direct hit to destroy an aircraft. The Falcon was also more cumbersome to fire, because the Falcon's infrared seeker required cooling (unlike the Sidewinder's), and the cooling mechanism (which had to be turned on before firing) would literally run out of gas in two minutes.[102]

Col. Robin Olds was finishing his tour as commander of the 8th Tactical Fighter Wing at Ubon in the summer of 1967, when F–4Ds began to replace his wing's F–4Cs. He liked the radar bombing capability of the F–4Ds and their toss-bombing computer, which permitted better accuracy with a higher pull-out (above seven thousand feet rather than below five thousand feet); even the F–4D's Walleye television-guided glide bombs showed promise, despite the fact that half malfunctioned. But Olds reviled the F–4D's substitution of the Falcon for the Sidewinder. Indeed, he blamed the Falcon for robbing him of a fifth kill in Vietnam.*[103]

---

* Colonel Olds often resisted changes imposed from Washington. In the case of the Falcons, he had F–4Ds rewired to carry Sidewinders. This makeshift arrangement did not produce any MiG kills, but eventually the Air Force did again equip all its F–4s with Sidewinders. Early in his stay at Ubon, Olds had objected strongly to "Rapid Roger," a test designed to answer a question from the Secretary of the Air Force. Secretary Brown asked whether sortie rates could be increased; instead of going to the expense of deploying more aircraft, he wanted to increase the number of sorties flown by aircraft already deployed. The sortie rate for bases in Thailand was about .8 or less than one sortie per day per aircraft

An F–4D did not down a MiG with a Falcon missile until October 26, 1967, after the departure of Olds and all F–4Cs from Ubon. In the wake of the initial strikes on the MiG base at Phuc Yen, a flight of four F–4Ds returned as escorts for a reconnaissance mission. During ingress they were warned by an EC–121 radar surveillance aircraft that MiGs were heading in their direction. As the F–4s headed southeast down Thud Ridge at eighteen thousand feet, they spotted six MiG–17s at ten thousand feet. Instead of waiting for the F–4s to come down where the slower, more maneuverable MiG–17s could fight to best advantage, the MiG pilots made the fatal mistake of climbing to sixteen thousand feet. Here they went into a wagon wheel formation, which could be effective in a dogfight since the MiGs were well positioned to cover each other's tail. But the F–4s sped through the wheel repeatedly with their own version of hit and run. While one element of two F–4s was breaking through the MiGs, the other element was gaining distance to fire its missiles. Two of six Sparrows launched found their mark, as did one of three Falcons, while the F–4s all emerged unscathed. More than four years would pass before the Air Force could boast another day with three air-to-air victories. During the remaining months of Rolling Thunder, MiG pilots would be more careful to engage only when the odds were heavily in their favor.[104]

North Vietnamese MiGs continued to harass American aircraft despite repeated attacks on most airfields in North Vietnam—most, but not all. Hanoi's Gia Lam airport remained out of bounds, and MiGs could always be assured of sanctuary there, as well as across the border in China. The Bac Mai airfield on the southern edge of Hanoi did not have a runway long enough to handle MiGs, but a bunker there housed an air defense command post. President Johnson would not countenance an attack on Gia Lam, which was used regularly by diplomats (including those working for the International Control Commission established by the Geneva Accords of 1954). In the case of Bac Mai, however, he proved amenable, despite the presence of American prisoners at a camp near the airfield.[105]

Bac Mai was believed to play an important role in controlling not only MiGs, but also surface-to-air missiles and antiaircraft artillery. As they had throughout the war, artillery and missiles continued to down more American aircraft than did the MiGs. On October 27, there occurred an especially severe reminder of this fact during a strike on the bridges over the Canal des Rapides.

---

possessed. In South Vietnam and on the Navy's carriers, sortie rates could exceed 1.2 because the distance to targets was much shorter. The only way Ubon could hope to achieve that high a sortie rate over an extended period was to use the same aircraft for day and night missions. Maintenance crews were not able to keep up with the demands of this situation, and some aircrews took off without wingmen. When Rapid Roger finally came to an end, Olds' men buried a black casket in its name and urinated on the grave. See Ralph F. Wetterhahn, "Change of Command," *Air and Space*, Aug/Sep 1997, pp 62–69; hist, USAF Tactical Air Warfare Center, Jan–Jun 1967; hist, 8 TFW, Jul–Dec 1966.

Two F–105s crashed after being hit by surface-to-air missiles, while artillery took a third. Later in the day, another F–105 was downed by artillery fire while attacking a missile site. Missiles, artillery, and MiGs worked together in a close coordination that the Air Force hoped to disrupt by striking Bac Mai. The raid of November 17, however, failed to make a noticeable difference in North Vietnam's air defense network, even though one bomb exploded on a mound believed to cover the command bunker.[106]

The impact of an air raid like that on Bac Mai can be measured in many ways, some of them very personal. For Capt. Gene I. Basel, Bac Mai was the raid that took his close friend and element leader, Maj. Charles E. "Cappy" Cappelli, whose F–105 encountered a surface-to-air missile. Basel would remember that before the raid "Cappy" had breached an unwritten rule by promising to do some paperwork when he got back: "It's not done. You don't talk about coming back."[107] The death that caught the eye of the press, however, was that of an Indian staff sergeant at the International Control Commission office in downtown Hanoi, more than two miles from Bac Mai. Whether he died from stray munitions of the attackers or the defenders, his death underlined once more the political cost of bombing near cities.[108]

*   *   *

In November 1967, the northeast monsoon ended Rolling Thunder's last stretch of good bombing weather over the Red River Delta. At that time the drizzle appeared to represent no more than a repetition of the five-month hiatus experienced during each of the previous two years. Few expected that before another five months had passed, President Johnson would call off bombing in the delta. The Stennis hearings had shaken down targets long withheld: the Doumer Bridge in Hanoi, the rail targets close to China, the principal MiG base at Phuc Yen, and the air defense control center at Bac Mai. But President Johnson had few major targets left to grant without authorizing those he considered so sensitive that they might break the bounds of gradualism and threaten a wider war. He continued to draw the line on escalation at Haiphong harbor, and not even the Joint Chiefs were recommending strikes against the Red River flood control dikes, the population of North Vietnam, or Chinese airfields.

The concept of gradualism had lost most of its adherents. Secretary of Defense McNamara and other early advocates now wanted a bombing cutback. Those like Generals LeMay and McConnell who had favored a more vigorous bombing campaign in 1965 found that much of their original target list had been gradually bombed or mined—with the major exception of Haiphong harbor. Having once lost the opportunity for a surprisingly sharp blow, there seemed little chance of retrieving it. Even had President Johnson authorized mining Haiphong harbor, that action could no longer have quite the impact it might have had at the outset as part of a rapid campaign against most major targets. All that the proponents of a sharp blow had been able to achieve was an occasional quickening in the pace of gradualism.

Despite its faults, gradualism finally reached after two years an intensity that seemed to cause the North Vietnamese real difficulty. In September 1967, when John Colvin left his post as British consul general in Hanoi, he judged North Vietnam "no longer capable of maintaining itself as an economic unit nor of mounting aggressive war against its neighbor."[109] He attributed the subsequent communist offensive to forces and supplies already gathered before the summer bombing, which he believed capable of causing a collapse of the North Vietnamese government—if the bombing had continued and if the North Vietnamese ports had been closed. Moreover, in Colvin's view, such a state of affairs could have been achieved in 1965 with a more serious air campaign.

Whatever might have been, American intelligence was far less sanguine about the progress of Rolling Thunder. While finding that North Vietnam's rail system was in the worst shape ever, the Central Intelligence Agency and the Defense Intelligence Agency reported that essential military and economic traffic continued to move on highways and waterways; communist allies supplied necessities no longer available from North Vietnam's devastated industries. As to the impact of Rolling Thunder on the ground war in South Vietnam, the intelligence agencies repeated their old view that the North Vietnamese retained their ability to support operations in South Vietnam and Laos "at present or increased combat levels." The intelligence agencies did concede that the air strikes had "degraded" North Vietnam's capability to sustain large-scale conventional operations.[110]

American airmen in Southeast Asia paid a high price for gradualism. It gave North Vietnam ample opportunity to build formidable defenses against them. As with all attrition campaigns, the question seemed to be which side would wear down first. But that question was not to be answered in the air over North Vietnam, for the communists were to end bombing there by attacking cities in South Vietnam. In the two months remaining before the Tet offensive, Rolling Thunder once again failed to maintain its power through the persistent clouds of the northeast monsoon.

Chapter Four

Season of Discontent

The fourth and last northeast monsoon of Rolling Thunder brought all the usual frustrations in greater measure. From November 1967 to March 1968, American airmen had to deal with the worst bombing weather over North Vietnam that they had encountered. Their attempts to bomb accurately through clouds achieved few demonstrable successes; nor did seeding transportation routes with mines that were too easy to sweep in water and too easy to see on land. The previous northeast monsoon had at least offered the compensation of major progress in coping with North Vietnam's air defenses. This time the MiGs were fewer, but they were flown with greater skill. Despite radar jammers now carried in a pair of wing pods on each American fighter, North Vietnamese guns and surface-to-air missiles could still be deadly—especially when an aircraft left a formation and the protection of jamming pods carried by other aircraft, or when the North Vietnamese fired a barrage at a large formation, or when they used optical tracking instead of radar tracking.

After a year of considerable progress in the air war, a nearly total loss of momentum weighed heavily on airmen. General Momyer, the Seventh Air Force commander in Saigon, and General Ryan, the Pacific Air Forces commander in Hawaii, began to get on each other's nerves. They had different views of what Seventh Air Force should be doing during the bad weather months. Ryan's years in the Strategic Air Command predisposed him to place special emphasis on the all-weather bombing problem. During his first winter in Hawaii, he had sponsored an attempt to use two-seat F–105Fs for low-level raids in bad weather. Despite the inability of Ryan's Raiders to overcome inadequate radar (inadequate both for flying at low level and for dropping bombs accurately), he continued to support their ineffective high-level strikes. Momyer, on the other hand, saw little merit in Ryan's preference for using F–105Fs as bombers rather than as Wild Weasels combatting enemy SAMs.[1]

Momyer had spent his career in the tactical air forces. Gen. Gabriel P. Disosway, then in charge of the Tactical Air Command (TAC), would later say that "Spike knew more about TAC, I guess, than anybody" except perhaps Gen. Otto P. Weyland, who had commanded Far East Air Forces during the Korean

War. According to Disosway, Momyer was a hard man to deal with because he was "so much smarter than most people" that he was very impatient—he already knew the answer before other people had even started to think about the question.[2] In the case of all-weather bombing, Momyer was convinced that, given the available equipment and the prohibitions on area bombing of urban targets, little could be done.[3]

During bad weather, Momyer preferred to concentrate on enemy air defenses—especially MiGs. Although airfield attacks and air-to-air battles had reduced the number of MiGs based in North Vietnam from more than a hundred at the beginning of 1967 to about twenty at the end of the year, the pilots of the remaining MiGs demonstrated increasing ability and aggressiveness. In December they forced more than 10 percent of the sorties bombing Route Package Six to jettison bombs before reaching the target. Having reduced the jettison rate to less than 1 percent earlier, Momyer did what he could to regain control of the situation. He increased the ratio of escort and patrol sorties to strike sorties from less than one-to-five to more than two-to-one. That brought the jettison rate down to about 3 percent but did not increase the rate of MiG shoot-downs, which continued to limp along at four or five a month.[4]

While MiGs destroyed in North Vietnam could always be replaced by those stationed in China, air-to-air victories might take a toll on North Vietnam's best pilots. Momyer had reason to be proud of his role in planning Operation Bolo, which had destroyed perhaps seven MiGs in the air on January 2, 1967. But when he tried a similar sweep on January 6, 1968, fewer MiGs came up and none were destroyed. Instead of F–4s pretending to be F–105s as in Bolo, Momyer's new sweep featured thirty-four F–105s stripped of their bombs and ready to dogfight. Most of them crossed Thud Ridge at fourteen thousand feet and turned east as if intending to strike Kep airfield or the railroad bridge at Mo Trang, fifteen miles west of Kep on the line to Thai Nguyen. Not surprisingly, their ruse was soon discovered, when two pairs of MiG–21s attacked from the rear. Typical of North Vietnamese tactics since August, it was a hit-and-run attack out of the late afternoon sun. The MiGs and the strike force traded heat-seeking missiles without doing any damage, and the MiG pilots escaped to tell their controllers that the F–105s were not carrying bombs. The best opportunity for destroying an enemy aircraft that afternoon came a few minutes later, when an F–105 pilot noticed an Il–14 Crate transport several thousand feet below, headed for Hanoi. While the F–105 pilot was getting his force commander's permission to attack this gray cargo plane with a red star, it dove into the nearest cloud; the F–105 got off one burst of gunfire and missed.[5]

"In my opinion," Ryan informed Momyer, "this type of operation is not very productive . . . . The firing on the Crate . . . appears to be in violation of rules of engagement."[6] Momyer had to agree that there was a rule prohibiting attacks on enemy transports, but he protested that it was a "strange rule" in view of repeated enemy gunfire against American civilian airliners in South Vietnam (not to mention military transports). As to the fighter sweep as a whole, Momyer insisted that while he had no illusions about another Bolo, there was nothing better to do with his aircraft during the northeast monsoon.[7]

Ryan combined his short sermon on MiG sweeps with a proposal to make more use of Walleye television-guided bombs, but Momyer was less than enthusiastic. Since their introduction in Southeast Asia during 1967, the Walleyes had been in short supply. But their accumulation in storage at Ubon Air Base, Thailand, did not convince Momyer that they should be used while the weather was so unfavorable. Rarely could he count upon the clear sky necessary for F–4s to release Walleyes on a target. Furthermore, the Air Force Walleye was not yet as good as the Navy original. Momyer complained that the Air Force version had been "pushed into combat" despite limitations which constrained him to use it only under optimal conditions at high noon. "Nevertheless," he told Ryan, "we will use the Walleye wherever it appears worthwhile."[8]

Momyer also indicated that he had resorted to a fighter sweep only after trying other means for defeating the MiGs. He had sent F–4 escorts ahead of the strike force by as much as a quarter of an hour; he had added a flight of them at forty thousand feet, far above the strike force; he had sent two flights below enemy radar to pop up and surprise the MiGs; he had combined a close escort with a roving flight. But the fundamental problem remained that Seventh Air Force was "operating with less than real time information, while the enemy has this information available to him."[9]

One of Momyer's major objectives had been to improve Seventh Air Force's warning and control system while impairing North Vietnam's. MiG effectiveness depended upon ground control, which could be reduced by jamming early warning and intercept radars. The relatively small transmitters carried in pods by American fighters were used to jam SAM and artillery control radars, leaving early warning and MiG intercept radars to more powerful, but more distant, jammers carried by Douglas EB–66s. In 1965, EB–66s had accompanied strike forces to within a few miles of targets in the Red River Delta, but MiGs and SAMs had forced the EB–66s farther and farther away. By the summer of 1967, two or three EB–66s were orbiting near the intersection of the twentieth parallel and the Laotian border, seventy-five miles southwest of Hanoi, while a like number orbited over the Gulf of Tonkin.[10]

On November 15, 1967, Seventh Air Force sent two EB–66s north of Thud Ridge for the first time since 1966. This boldness was encouraged partly by the movement of SAM launchers away from the ridge southeast into Hanoi and the panhandle. EB–66s had also been vulnerable to MiG attack, especially because their jamming transmitters interfered with communications from fighter escorts and the EC–121 radar warning aircraft. A new radio remedied that problem, and permitted the experiment of November 15. Two EB–66s flew long-abandoned orbits without difficulty on that day.[11]

Five days later, however, an EB–66 orbiting north of Thud Ridge was attacked from the rear by a pair of MiG–21s, one diving and one climbing. Two F–4 escorts weaving behind the EB–66 saw the MiGs and warned the EB–66 to break into a downward spiral—just in time to evade a heat-seeking Atoll air-to-air missile fired by the climbing MiG. Although the EB–66 and its escorts escaped unharmed, the F–4 aircrews from Ubon Air Base, Thailand, were unhappy with their performance. Weaving behind an EB–66 seemed an unsatisfactory way to accommodate its slower speed, and they were confident that they could work out better tactics through discussion with the EB–66 aircrews at Takhli Air Base, Thailand. No such planning had yet taken place, nor would it. Seventh Air Force decided that one close call was enough and required EB–66s to stay far south of Hanoi.[12]

During the next month, Seventh Air Force tried to improve jamming by increasing the number of EB–66s operating during a strike to as many as fourteen. This augmented force began to drop chaff timed to interfere with North Vietnamese radar detection of an ingressing strike force and of the EB–66s themselves. On January 14, 1968, however, only five EB–66s were orbiting in support of late afternoon strikes on targets in Route Package Five. A pair of MiG–21s took off from Phuc Yen and flew south toward Thanh Hoa. Before reaching the twentieth parallel, they turned west and attacked an unescorted EB–66 orbiting near the Laotian border. An Atoll air-to-air missile struck the EB–66 in the right wing. All seven crew members managed to get out of the crippled plane. The pilot, instructor navigator, and an electronic warfare officer were rescued two days later, together with five members of a helicopter crew who had crashed while trying to pick up the EB–66 crew in bad weather. The EB–66's remaining three electronic warfare officers and the navigator spent the rest of the war in captivity. Theirs was the last EB–66 permitted to fly over North Vietnam. Henceforth, EB–66 orbits were limited to Laos, the Gulf of Tonkin, and South Vietnam; a barrier patrol of fighters began to protect the EB–66s in Laos, just as Navy fighters had long provided protection for Air Force EB–66s operating over the gulf.[13]

The EB–66's failure to provide effective jamming of MiG ground control radars was partially offset by an improvement in Seventh Air Force's ability to guide its own fighters. Since much of the airspace over North Vietnam could not be surveyed by American ship radar, let alone more distant ground radar, Seventh Air Force used airborne radar carried by propeller-driven Lockheed EC–121s from the Air Defense Command. The "Connie" was a variant of the Super Constellation commercial transport. Its radar had been designed to detect bombers approaching North America over water. Looking down over land the Connie's radar screens were filled with clutter, but a Connie skimming fifty feet above the Gulf of Tonkin could look up to survey the sky over Hanoi above ten thousand feet.[14]

Far more valuable than its radar was the Connie's ability to interrogate radio identification transponders carried by American and North Vietnamese aircraft. If a transponder was turned on, it could be triggered by a radio signal to transmit its identity and location. At first, the Connies could only interrogate friendly aircraft, and they irritated fighter pilots by policing those who flew too near the Chinese border in pursuit of MiGs; American fighter pilots turned their transponders off to avoid being interrogated by the Connies. The adversary relationship between EC–121 crews and fighter pilots had come to a head in February 1967, when Ubon's F–4 wing was forced to share its facilities with the Connies. They moved out of the Seventh Air Force headquarters base at Tan Son Nhut to make room for other functions. Ubon's 8th Tactical Fighter Wing commander, Colonel Olds, was at first unhappy about his new neighbors, but worked to change their emphasis from border monitoring to MiG warning. In early 1967, the best the Connies could do was use their radar to announce that there was a MiG within a sector thirty miles by thirty miles. Olds found this information to be less than helpful: "Forty-five thousand cubic miles of sky, and you tell me there's a bloody MiG in there."[15]

After a January 1967 test of the equipment necessary to interrogate enemy aircraft, the Connies began routine interrogation of MiGs that summer. For a while, the Connies labored under a National Security Agency restriction intended to prevent the North Vietnamese from discovering the new capability, but by the fall of 1967, transponder interrogation had replaced radar as the principal and much more exact way of tracking enemy aircraft.[16]

Fuller use of the Connie's capabilities was stimulated by the arrival in Thailand of "Rivet Top," an experimental Connie sponsored by the Tactical Air Command. Rivet Top could not stop pilots from turning off their transponders, but it did persuade General Momyer that Connies could contribute to shooting down MiGs.[17] The impact of Rivet Top could be attributed partly to its improved capabilities and partly to its sponsorship. General Disosway at Tactical Air Command was in a better position to influence Momyer (an obvious choice to succeed Disosway) than was Lt. Gen. Arthur C. Agan, Jr., at Air Defense Command. The Seventh Air Force commander and his fighter pilots warmed to Rivet Top in a way they never had to Air Defense Command Connies, which had been moved from crowded base to crowded base and berated for the slovenly appearance of aircraft and crews. Rivet Top was embraced as a help against MiGs rather than as a border policeman restraining F–4s and F–105s. Although this fighter-pilot discrimination aroused resentment among Air Defense Command controllers, Rivet Top broke down barriers that had been preventing the other Connies from playing a more significant role.[18]

Even when Air Defense Command Connies were at last permitted unfettered interrogation of enemy aircraft, however, they were not quite as well equipped as Rivet Top to track MiGs. While Air Defense Command Connies could interrogate most of North Vietnam's Soviet-made transponders, Rivet Top could interrogate a few more. Rivet Top could also compare SAM radar emissions with a computer data base on launch sites; unfortunately, this missile detection system could only deal with three sites at a time and was often overloaded. A more useful innovation was the inclusion of Air Force Security Service equipment and personnel, so that Rivet Top could bring together radar and communications intelligence on MiG activity.[19]

Faced with competition from Rivet Top, Air Defense Command moved to upgrade its version of the plane. By the summer of 1968, Air Defense Command Connies were also carrying Air Force Security Service personnel. This reinforced General Momyer's decision of October 1967 to permit direct communication between Connies and fighters. Other intelligence gatherers continued to break rules against talking directly to aircrews. Anonymous warnings were often repeated by pilots again and again, contributing to a nervous babble.[20]

Since 1966, Seventh Air Force had been trying to insert its Monkey Mountain control center (near Da Nang, South Vietnam) between intelligence sources and users. Monkey Mountain was intended to be a "fusion center" where the intelligence picture was put together and made available to aircrews flying over North Vietnam. Using equipment developed to help Air Defense Command protect North America, Seventh Air Force was building a command post at Monkey Mountain to provide direction for fighter pilots engaged with MiGs. Control centers at Udorn Air Base, Thailand, and Tan Son Nhut Air Base near Saigon were to be similarly equipped, but in late 1967, only Monkey Mountain was beginning to use an automated processing and display system. Seventh Air Force was far behind Seventh Fleet in automating air control. Monkey Mountain computers at last permitted Seventh Air Force to tie into the Navy and Marine tactical data systems in March 1968.[21]

Meanwhile, MiGs continued to surprise American strike forces. Although Connie warnings were often more precise and communicated directly to the appropriate aircrews, sometimes communications were inadequate or MiGs simply were not detected in time. Even a force designed specifically to destroy MiGs in the air, like Momyer's big sweep of January 6, 1968, could be hit by MiG–21s without warning from a Connie or from Monkey Mountain, let alone guidance necessary to intercept MiGs. "We are still behind the enemy," Momyer explained ruefully to Ryan.[22]

*　　　　　*　　　　　*

While General Momyer was especially disheartened by failure to make much progress in overcoming North Vietnam's air defenses, General Ryan's principal frustration was a lack of success in bombing during the cloudy weather extending from November to April. The Navy's Grumman A–6 Intruder, a subsonic jet with terrain-following radar, was the most effective bad-weather bomber available in Southeast Asia. Ryan succeeded in getting some Marine A–6 sorties allocated to Air Force targets in the Red River Delta, but there were not enough Marine and Navy A–6s to do much more than harass the North Vietnamese. He was eager to deploy the Air Force's new tactical bomber, the General Dynamics F–111, which promised to be still more accurate than the A–6.[23]

Soon after six F–111s reached Takhli in March 1968, however, three of them crashed. The wreckage of one of these, together with that of another crash in Nevada, indicated a weak weld in a tail control rod. This was but one in a series of problems that had plagued the F–111 development program ever since Secretary of Defense McNamara had attempted to marry Air Force plans for a tactical bomber with Navy plans for an air superiority fighter. The novel ability to change configuration in flight using variable sweep wings did not bridge the gap between these two functions, and while Air Force F–111s were crashing in Southeast Asia, the Navy was pulling out of the program altogether.[24]

Few of the Takhli F–111 missions went according to plan—a lone aircraft weaving through mountains at night and skimming across the coastal plain of the North Vietnamese panhandle to drop bombs on truck parks and storage depots. Returning F–111 pilots and weapon systems officers reported little hostile fire, but they had difficulty identifying their target in time to make a satisfactory bomb run. Of seventy-one sorties sent against North Vietnam, only eighteen had good runs with measurable results. Half their bombs fell within five hundred feet of the target—equal to daylight dive bombing in clear weather and superior to the A–6 in bad weather, but disappointing in a program that hoped to put half its bombs within two hundred feet of the target.[25]

The Air Force received considerable criticism for sending a new weapon system into battle before it was ready. Chief of Staff McConnell shrugged off this criticism with the observation that there was much to be gained from testing equipment in combat and that F–111s were also lost in the United States during testing.[26] Secretary Brown doubted that the Soviets would learn a great deal from F–111 debris in North Vietnam.[27] But General Ryan regretted having lobbied hard for the F–111's early deployment.[28] It was not ready yet and, in any case, did not reach Southeast Asia in time to make a real difference. Only a few days after the F–111's arrival in Thailand, the United States ceased to bomb targets in the Red River Delta. Not until 1972 would the F–111 have an opportunity to display its capabilities against the most heavily defended targets in North Vietnam. During the northeast monsoon of 1967–68, the Air Force had to make do with older aircraft.

A year earlier, General Ryan had sent two-seat F–105Fs on low-level raids in bad weather. But the plane's terrain-following radar and bombing computer had proved inadequate. So Ryan's Raiders had climbed to altitudes above ten thousand feet, where their bombing was even less accurate. There they were joined by F–4Ds whose newer equipment proved no more effective—strikes with average bombing errors of three thousand feet were common for both types of aircraft. Part of the problem was a shortage of targets with good radar signatures. Usually it was necessary to relate the target to a landmark in the area and offset the bomb drop accordingly. As aircrews gained experience and the radar film library grew, bombing accuracy improved.[29]

Meanwhile, in South Vietnam, the Air Force had less difficulty bombing through clouds. There ground controllers used "Skyspot" bomb-scoring equipment to track B–52s and other aircraft; when the bomber reached the correct position, the controller signaled the bomber to drop bombs. Control stations near the demilitarized zone and at Nakhon Phanom, Thailand, enabled the Air Force to employ this system in the panhandle of North Vietnam. But the Red River Delta remained out of range until a control station could be established about 125 miles west of Hanoi in Laos.[30]

As with all other Air Force activity in Laos, the Site 85 control station at Phou Pha Thi had to be approved by the American Ambassador, William H. Sullivan. He at first opposed it, because he suspected that the Prime Minister, Prince Souvanna Phouma, would not want Laos involved in directing offensive operations against North Vietnam—even though North Vietnamese troops were engaged in offensive operations in Laos. Indeed, a problem with the proposed location at Phou Pha Thi was its vulnerability to North Vietnamese attack. Nevertheless, Souvanna Phouma did permit establishment of the new control station, provided that it was not manned by American military personnel. The Air Force worked around this prohibition by having its controllers wear civilian clothes and sign paperwork temporarily releasing them from the service; fresh teams of controllers arrived by helicopter from Thailand. In a further effort to disguise Phou Pha Thi's role, the controllers there communicated with attacking fighter-bombers via an EC–135 radio relay aircraft.[31]

The mountain of Phou Pha Thi guarded a major route from Hanoi to central Laos. The Meo forces of Gen. Vang Pao defended it for its own sake, and the Central Intelligence Agency had established an airstrip at the foot of the mountain to resupply them. Before putting controllers on top the mountain, the Air Force had already set up a radio navigation beacon for fighter-bombers on their way to North Vietnam. The controllers had been at Phou Pha Thi just two months, when on January 12, 1968, the North Vietnamese made it the target of their first air attack on ground forces. At least two old Soviet-made Antonov An–2 biplanes fired rockets and dropped crude bombs (converted from mortar rounds) before ground fire and an Air America helicopter brought them down.[32]

Despite a substantial investment in Phou Pha Thi, the Air Force doubted that Vang Pao could hold it; explosives were attached to all the equipment on the mountain in preparation for a quick getaway. But when the communists overran Phou Pha Thi in March 1968, General Momyer and Ambassador

Sullivan had waited too long to order evacuation. Twelve of eighteen Americans at the site were dead or missing, and their equipment was not destroyed.* The Air Force had to bomb the control station, while Momyer and Sullivan entered into a heated debate about responsibility for the failure either to defend the site or evacuate in time.[33]

From November 1967 to March 1968, controllers at Phou Pha Thi directed nearly a hundred "Commando Club" missions (about five hundred sorties) against the Red River Delta. But ground controlled bombing proved disappointing in this part of Vietnam. The control site was too far from its targets for anything more accurate than area bombing. Hence, to do much damage, the Air Force needed to send a big force against a big target. When such a raid was attempted against Phuc Yen airfield, its heavy defenses destroyed four F–105s and caused the rest of the strike force to jettison bombs. The 388th Tactical Fighter Wing at Korat Air Base, Thailand, lost its commander, Col. Edward B. Burdett, only three weeks after its vice commander, Col. John P. Flynn, was shot down over Hanoi. Unlike Colonel Flynn, Colonel Burdett and three men downed with him would not come home at the end of the war.[34]

The unfortunate ground-controlled raid against Phuc Yen occurred on the morning of November 18. A dozen F–105s carrying bombs were protected from MiGs by four F–4s and from SAMs by eight more F–105s. Half the latter constituted the normal Iron Hand flight with Shrike radar-seeking missiles, whose presence encouraged the North Vietnamese to keep their SAM guidance radar turned off as much as possible; the remaining flight of four F–105s carried radar jamming pods to supplement those carried by strike aircraft. Five EB–66s nearly a hundred miles south of the target added their jamming power, while three EC–121 radar surveillance aircraft watched for MiGs.[35]

The strike force's troubles began forty miles west of Phuc Yen when the Iron Hand flight was attacked by two MiG–21s making a single pass from the rear. Heat-seeking Atoll missiles destroyed a two-seat F–105F and crippled a single-seat F–105D; the rest of the flight escorted the crippled aircraft back to Laos, where the pilot ejected and was rescued. They had been warned by an EC–121 three times about MiGs, but those warnings were garbled by competing communications between the strike force and the ground controller at Phou Pha Thi.[36]

Deprived of its weapon for attacking SAM sites, the strike force now had to depend entirely on electronic jamming. A single aircraft's pair of jamming pods could not give it much protection, so each flight flew a formation tight enough

---

* One of the twelve was killed on board a helicopter after extraction. In 1990 an Air Force officer reported that, according to his interview with a Laotian general, Americans captured at Phou Pha Thi were sent to Hanoi. A year later when MSgt. William Gadoury of the U.S. Joint Casualty Resolution Center asked Gen. Singkapo Sikhotchounamaly about this claim, he said that he had been misunderstood. See Timothy N. Castle, *At War in the Shadow of Vietnam: U.S. Military Aid to the Royal Lao Government, 1955–1975* (New York, 1993), pp 96–97, and *One Day Too Long: Top Secret Site 85 and the Bombing of North Vietnam* (New York, 1999), pp 196–200.

for the pods of all four aircraft to work together—but loose enough to create for enemy radar operators as large an area of uncertainty as possible. This pod formation could not be used over the target. Ground-controlled bombing required that aircraft move closer together for a tighter bombing pattern, since they would all drop their bombs simultaneously with the lead aircraft. Ninety seconds before reaching the bomb release point, the aircraft in each flight reduced horizontal spacing from fifteen hundred to five hundred feet.[37]

Straight and level flying in tight formation at eighteen thousand feet provided a tempting target for SAMs. The North Vietnamese fired a barrage of about twelve, and destroyed two more F–105s (including Colonel Burdett's). This unusually high kill ratio led to speculation that enemy radar operators had been able to distinguish each flight, because flights had not closed as tightly together as had aircraft within flights. Hence, missiles could be aimed at the relatively small jamming pattern produced by the pods of each compressed flight. Despite the possibility that altering the shape of a large formation might produce better results, Seventh Air Force ceased experimenting with ground controlled bombing over the Red River Delta by formations larger than one flight. Although SAMs did not destroy any aircraft on these smaller Commando Club raids (as the Air Force had labeled all ground-controlled missions over the Red River Delta), aircrews remembered the big raid on Phuc Yen and called the smaller raids Commando Kaze.[38]

Experimentation with ground control of big formations might have continued if losses on the big Phuc Yen raid had not been perceived as part of a larger crisis. In just four days, North Vietnamese SAMs brought down ten American aircraft. Nothing like this had occurred since December 2, 1966, when SAMs took five Air Force fighter-bombers. But those "Black Friday" missiles had destroyed aircraft not yet equipped with electronic jamming pods. Such pods had reduced the SAM average kill ratio from about three aircraft destroyed for every one hundred missiles launched to less than two. Since most of the aircraft hit by SAMs in November 1967 were not engaged in ground-controlled bombing, Seventh Air Force might have concluded that once other problems were solved, large ground-controlled strikes could resume. A sense of crisis, however, was encouraged by the arrival of a team of analysts from the Air Staff and the Air Force Systems Command. They made several recommendations and Seventh Air Force tried to implement all of them, including ones calling for the elimination of large ground-controlled strikes in the Hanoi area.[39]

While ground-controlled bombing formations may have been part of the SAM problem, the Air Staff team could see that the problem had other dimensions. Losses to SAMs over Phuc Yen on November 18, 1967, may have been the result of a departure from jamming pod formation, as F–105s closed to get a tighter bombing pattern. Similarly, in clear weather a flight usually drew closer together just before rolling into a dive—a departure from jamming pod formation that may have contributed to two more SAM kills that week. But at least one aircraft lost on November 19 was thought to be part of a full flight of four in correct jamming pod formation. Since the North Vietnamese were now firing barrages of six to thirty missiles, they may simply have been lucky.[40]

There were other possible explanations, however, and all of them troubled the Air Staff team. North Vietnam may have been using radar at frequencies lower than those being jammed. While jammers could be adjusted accordingly, there was the more dangerous possibility that the North Vietnamese were interrogating radio transponders carried by American aircraft—just as American EC–121 radar surveillance aircraft were already interrogating North Vietnamese MiG transponders. Certainly the North Vietnamese had shot down enough American aircraft to obtain American transponders.[41]

In addition to possible improvements in North Vietnam's ability to track American aircraft electronically, SAM controllers seemed to be using an optical tracking system on clear days. Turning off a fighter-bomber's identification transponder or jamming North Vietnamese radar could not deceive optical tracking. But a missile's communications with its ground controller were always vulnerable to jamming. In December 1967, Air Force fighter-bombers began to jam the frequency used by the radio beacon in each missile. North Vietnamese controllers might be able to track an American aircraft, but henceforth they encountered greater difficulty in tracking their own missiles. Of all the measures taken to reduce the SAM threat in late 1967, this was probably the most effective.[42]

Efforts to thwart SAMs electronically grew out of an inability to destroy them. About 150 launchers were clustered in groups of up to 6 at about 30 of more than 200 prepared sites. The North Vietnamese and their Soviet advisers moved the launchers frequently, so that an American attack on a site recently occupied might encounter only heavy flak. The Air Force's F–105F Wild Weasels rarely tried to do more than suppress SAM activity for the duration of a bombing raid by firing or threatening to fire radar-seeking Shrike missiles at SAM radars. The North Vietnamese usually turned off their radar transmitters when threatened. Since the North Vietnamese quickly turned on their radar again as soon as the Wild Weasels were gone, most major strike forces had both a vanguard and a rear guard of Wild Weasels; each of these guard positions was held normally by an Iron Hand flight consisting of two Wild Weasel F–105Fs leading two F–105Ds.[43]

During 1967, Seventh Air Force expended 1,322 Shrikes, and by the end of the year the F–105 wing at Takhli was complaining about a shortage. In early 1968, a new radar-seeking missile (AGM–78) arrived. It flew faster and farther than the Shrike at ten times the cost—two hundred thousand dollars each. It did not have time to prove itself in the delta, however, and the Air Force made little use of it in the panhandle for fear that its long range might permit a misguided missile to hit one of the Navy's ships or an Army radar site just south of the Demilitarized Zone.[44]

The radar at a SAM site could stay off the air until just before launch if the site was connected to radars at other locations. In addition to more than 100 missile and antiaircraft artillery radars, the North Vietnamese had more than 150 early warning and MiG-control radars. American airmen faced a radar network that could easily compensate for a few losses scattered through the system. Admiral Sharp, the Pacific commander in Hawaii, once again began to think about the possibility of attacking North Vietnam's entire air defense system within a few days. Proposals to do this had always run aground on the failure of reconnaissance to produce photographs of active missile sites in time to bomb them before their launchers moved. The addition of a new photo reconnaissance capability in the spring of 1967, however, caused Admiral Sharp to wonder whether this old hurdle could now be surmounted.[45]

Admiral Sharp was excited about photographs of North Vietnam sent to him by the National Photographic Interpretation Center in Washington. These had been taken by a Lockheed A–12, an older brother of the SR–71 Blackbird. Area surveillance photography of North Vietnam was also provided by satellites, but these rarely passed over North Vietnam more than a couple of times a month. For example, a Corona satellite with KH–4A cameras made two passes over North Vietnam during a mission (June 17–22, 1967) which orbited over the Soviet Union and China as well. Cloud cover made nearly half the Corona imagery worthless. The A–12 could be sent much more often and could take advantage of breaks in the weather.[46]

The A–12's predecessor, the Lockheed U–2, was now considered too vulnerable to risk over the Red River Delta; the MiGs and the SAMs would have too good a shot at it. The A–12 could fly a little higher (over eighty thousand feet) and much faster (more than Mach 3). In clear weather it could photograph all of the Red River Delta on a single mission. When President Johnson authorized the use of A–12s over North Vietnam, he hoped that the new planes would be able to give the earliest possible warning of the presence of surface-to-surface missiles that would threaten ships in the Gulf of Tonkin. The same photographs would also track changes in SAM deployment.[47]

The great defect of the A–12's first mission over North Vietnam was that the film was sent all the way to Washington for processing. This was soon improved by sending film to the Strategic Air Command's U–2 processing center at Saigon's Tan Son Nhut Air Base, headquarters for both the Military Assistance Command, Vietnam and for Seventh Air Force. Tan Son Nhut was a convenient location for U–2 photo-processing, not only because the principal consumers were there, but especially because U–2s flew from nearby Bien Hoa Air Base. But the A–12s flew from Kadena Air Base, Okinawa. Consequently, in September 1967, responsibility for processing A–12 photographs was transferred to Fifth Air Force's 67th Reconnaissance Technical Squadron at Yokota Air Base, Japan. This unit could supply Seventh Air Force with the location of SAM sites one day after an A–12 mission; photographs would follow in another day.[48]

General Momyer underlined for Admiral Sharp the fact that A–12 photographs indicated eight active SAM sites within ten nautical miles of the center of Hanoi—that is, within the prohibited circle which President Johnson had drawn around Hanoi. There American airmen could attack launch sites only when fired upon in the course of bombing authorized targets. Unless this rule was changed, a campaign against missiles was out of the question.[49] A change in the rules, however, could take advantage of a greater concentration of missiles close to Hanoi than in the past; their sites were revetted and launchers rarely moved. Elsewhere in the Red River Delta, the number of launchers had decreased, some moving to the Hanoi sites and others south where they could threaten B–52s striking North Vietnamese supplies and forces just north of the Demilitarized Zone. The southward migration of launchers had reduced the number of active sites in Route Package Six from thirty to twenty-one.[50]

Admiral Sharp wanted a plan to destroy North Vietnam's SAMs, MiG–control radar, early warning radar, and air defense control centers. He told General Ryan to develop such a plan with Admiral Johnson, Commander in Chief of the Pacific Fleet. Admiral Johnson complained that A–12 photographs did not provide aircrews the perspective they would need to attack missile and radar sites successfully, let alone control centers whose locations could not be ascertained using any aerial photograph. The vertical perspective of high-altitude photography made a different impression than the oblique perspective of the camera or pilot at lower altitude. Admiral Johnson asked for plenty of up-to-date low-altitude photography.[51]

While low-altitude drones could photograph some missile sites in cloudy weather, too much good weather and time would usually be required to meet Admiral Johnson's requirements. Nevertheless, General Ryan's plan incorporated Admiral Johnson's specifications and added that even more good weather was necessary, since there was no point in going after air defenses unless there would be ample opportunity to exploit air supremacy by bombing targets whose defenses had been eliminated. Ryan's plan assured that there would be no major campaign against the SAMs at least until better weather returned the following summer—and probably not then.[52]

*　　　　*　　　　*

Although he could sometimes limit the number of aircraft that Momyer used to combat enemy air defenses, Ryan was less successful in finding enough productive missions during the northeast monsoon for Air Force aircraft based in Thailand. As in past years, many sorties were shifted from North Vietnam to Laos, where good weather prevailed over panhandle roads heavily used at night by North Vietnamese trucks heading south. Meanwhile, in North Vietnam itself most roads could be used in daylight as well, for they were commonly protected from air strikes by overcast. Radar bombing strikes and those under the direction of ground controllers did not have sufficient accuracy to destroy bridges, let alone hit trucks and boxcars.

For the first time the Johnson administration permitted river mining north of the twentieth parallel, and between rare breaks in the weather when bridges could be bombed, Air Force F–4Ds and Navy A–6s tried to discourage ferrying and bridge repair by dropping Mk–36 Destructor mines. The weather inhibited accurate placement and intelligence about the effectiveness of mining, but results appeared to be at best modest. Three boxcars were believed to have been destroyed while being ferried across the Red River at Hanoi and a tug and two barges sank in the Cam River at Haiphong.[53]

The technological weaknesses of the newly developed Mk–36 limited its usefulness. It was a five hundred-pound Mk–82 bomb with a magnetic trigger that would respond to an iron hull or the metal in an engine. Unfortunately, the trigger was too sensitive, so that the mine often exploded while the target was too far away, and a wire fishing net or empty oil barrels could be used to detonate the mines. Later versions of the Mk–36 would provide a less sensitive trigger that shut off periodically so that a sweeper could never be sure he had completed his job. Whatever the deficiencies of the original Mk–36 mines, however, they could lay in wait for North Vietnamese traffic during long spells of cloudy weather when bombing was difficult. The mines were also dropped on land with even less probability of success, for they were easier to find there.[54]

While mines frequently landed far from their intended destination, on two occasions seeding errors were unusually obvious. A few hours before the end of 1967, the 8th Tactical Fighter Wing at Ubon Air Base, Thailand, reported that a flight of F–4s had dropped forty-eight Mk–36s into international waters about five miles off the North Vietnamese coast and about forty miles north of the Demilitarized Zone. Less than a week later, on January 4, an A–6 from the *Kitty Hawk* dropped mines directly on a Soviet transport ship, the *Pereslavl-Zalesskiy*, anchored in Haiphong's Cam River. The aircrews flying this A–6 and two others had been trying to place Mk–36s near a bridge upriver, but an error in a map's margin scale had led to plotting errors. In addition to mines hitting the ship and detonating, others lay armed in the water nearby. This situation caused concern in Washington, where Secretary of State Rusk gave Soviet Ambassador Dobrynin a map showing the approximate location of the mines as well as their planned target area.[55]

As he had so often in the past, President Johnson responded to the latest incident by establishing a zone where bombing and mining were prohibited. When Navy fighters had been accused of strafing the *Mikhail Frunze* in June 1967, Johnson had announced a prohibited zone with a radius of four nautical miles from the center of Haiphong. This time he extended the radius to five nautical miles. Only a few days earlier, on January 3, he had established a prohibited zone reaching five nautical miles from the center of Hanoi. While Hanoi's new prohibited zone was much smaller than the old ten-mile zone proclaimed a year earlier, that one had made way during the summer for strikes on several targets including the Doumer Bridge over the Red River.[56]

President Johnson's rationale for the new prohibited zone around Haiphong seemed obvious enough, but why prohibit further strikes on Hanoi's Doumer Bridge—not to mention an end to mining the river there? Airmen had become accustomed to not being told why these decisions were made. Once again Hanoi had secured a restriction on bombing by dangling the prospect of negotiations.

In late November 1967, several weeks after Rumanian Prime Minister Ion Gheorghe Maurer returned from a visit to Hanoi, President Johnson sent his roving ambassador W. Averell Harriman to Bucharest. Since Maurer had been in Hanoi when Johnson delivered his September 29 speech at San Antonio, Harriman wanted to know why the North Vietnamese leadership had turned down Johnson's offer to stop bombing North Vietnam in exchange for talks— so long as the North Vietnamese did not take advantage of the halt to increase the southward flow of soldiers and supplies. Maurer said that he did not know, because the text of Johnson's speech had not reached Pham Van Dong before the conclusion of their discussions. But Harriman knew that the same offer had been sent privately to Hanoi as early as August.[57]

Nevertheless, one of Maurer's recollections did give some slight cause for hope. Pham Van Dong indicated that if the bombing ceased, Hanoi "would" enter into discussions with the United States. "I questioned his use of 'would,'" Harriman cabled Secretary of State Rusk. Hanoi usually used "could," but Maurer was uncertain which word had been used; he said that it did not matter, because Pham Van Dong's French was too poor for such nuances.[58] So barren had been the record of Hanoi's interest in negotiations that Washington was ready to grasp at straws. The State Department's executive secretary, Benjamin Read, thought that the Rumanian channel might prove to be a "winner" and dubbed it "Packers" after the championship Green Bay Packers football team.[59]

In mid-December 1967, Rumania's First Deputy Foreign Minister, Gheorghe Macovescu, visited Hanoi. There the North Vietnamese Foreign Minister, Nguyen Duy Trinh, read to Macovescu a new statement of his government's position: after "unconditional cessation" of the bombing, North Vietnam "will enter into serious discussions" with the United States.[60] Not only did Trinh use "will," but he dropped the word "final" from the usual "final and unconditional cessation." Macovescu later told Harriman that when asked about this omission, Trinh said firmly that the shortened phrase was his government's position. On December 29, a week after Macovescu's departure, Trinh made the same statement public at a Mongolian reception. The addition of the word "will" and the deletion of the word "final" were enough to stop all bombing and mining within five nautical miles of the center of Hanoi.[61]

The Chairman of the Joint Chiefs of Staff, General Wheeler, was sufficiently impressed by Washington's reaction to the Trinh statement that he alerted Admiral Sharp and General Westmoreland to prepare for a bombing halt.
Wheeler professed to see some merit in this development, since he thought it
might mean that the North Vietnamese would reduce their activity near the
Demilitarized Zone and enable Westmoreland to divert forces from there to the
rest of South Vietnam.[62] Westmoreland and Ambassador Bunker had already
cautioned Secretary of State Rusk to be wary of North Vietnamese peace initiatives in light of a buildup in North Vietnamese forces just north of the
Demilitarized Zone.[63] Sharp immediately fired off a reply to Wheeler: "In summary, I perceive no advantage and see greatest disadvantage from cessation of
bombing . . . ."[64]

From the airman's point of view, North Vietnamese concessions could only
be gained by military pressure. Even had airmen been privy to all the diplomatic niceties, it is doubtful that they would have been in sympathy with President
Johnson's logic. The Trinh-Macovescu meetings had occurred during a break in
the weather lasting five days, the longest period of good bombing conditions
during the northeast monsoon stretching from November 1967 through March
1968. Whether or not Trinh's word changes were really significant, they came
together with bombs falling on the Doumer Bridge less than a mile away.

*   *   *

The raids of December 14 and 18, 1967, once again crippled Hanoi's
Doumer Bridge over the Red River. About fifty F–105 sorties attacked the
bridge with two three thousand-pound bombs apiece. These unguided bombs
proved even more accurate and destructive than their predecessors in August
and October. Seven of nineteen spans fell into the water. The October raid had
kept the bridge closed for only a month, but after the December raids it would
not begin to carry traffic again for six months. Indeed, the North Vietnamese
made no attempt to repair the bridge until bombing ceased in the Hanoi area at
the end of March; nor did they install a bypass pontoon bridge until then.
Meanwhile, they used ferries to link Hanoi with Haiphong and China.[65]

No aircraft were lost attacking the Doumer Bridge during December's one
week of good weather, but two F–105s and two F–4s went down during raids on
other targets in the Hanoi area. In one respect, the six Air Force officers on
board these aircraft would turn out to be an unusually fortunate group, for all
would come home at the end of the war.[66] All but one were victims of the most
active MiG defense since the spring of 1967. As many as twenty MiGs came up
on December 17 and perhaps fourteen two days later. In addition to MiG–21s
with their usual hit-and-run attacks, MiG–17s tried to draw the Americans into

low-altitude dogfights. The resulting melees continued over the target area, where SAM inactivity made room for MiG activity. While MiG–21s came away from the American good-weather campaign of December 14–19 with another two victories and no losses, the MiG–17s did not fare so well. Their lone victory was won at the price of four losses.[67]

Although the commander of Pacific Air Forces, General Ryan, objected to independent fighter sweeps, he had no objection to air-to-air combat arising out of escort duty. Indeed, he had reason to be especially proud of an F–4 victory over a MiG–17 on December 17, because his eldest son (1st Lt. John D. Ryan, Jr.) was in the back seat of the F–4. This victory was also exceptional in two other respects: the pilot, Capt. Doyle D. Baker, was a Marine on exchange duty, and the weapon was a heat-seeking Falcon missile. The Falcon's lack of a proximity fuse would keep its total of kills to a mere five, but on this occasion it went up the MiG's tailpipe.[68]

Under the rules then in effect, Lieutenant Ryan received half a credit for his part in downing a MiG, and Captain Doyle got the other half. Four years later (two years after young Ryan's death in an aircraft accident) when General Ryan was Chief of Staff and the Air Force was once again bombing North Vietnam, he would get the rule changed so that a pilot and his backseater each got full credit for a victory; the revised rule was retroactive to 1965. Until General Ryan changed the rules governing victory credits, Colonel Olds' four victories in F–4s gave him only two credits and tied him for top honors with the pilot of a single-seat F–105, Capt. Max C. Brestel, who had shot down two MiG–17s on March 10, 1967. Their nearest competitors were Lt. Col. Robert F. Titus and his backseater, 1st Lt. Milan Zimer, who shared the credit for three victories.[69]

Moving into fifth position on December 19 was 1st Lt. George H. McKinney, Jr., an F–4 backseater from Bessemer, Alabama. Like Lieutenant Ryan and Lieutenant Zimer, Lieutenant McKinney had been trained as a pilot, and may well have been less than enthusiastic about having to serve in the back seat as a radar operator. Later this job would be turned over to men with navigator training. So long as men with pilot wings sat in the back seat, they were officially designated "pilots" and the actual pilots in the front seat were "aircraft commanders." No matter what titles were used, a backseater sometimes found his situation a little demoralizing—especially when he was a veteran of many sorties over North Vietnam and a newly assigned pilot sat in the front seat. Prospects for backseaters improved in November 1967, when they were at last permitted to move into the front seat without first completing their tour and returning to the United States for training.[70]

The equal sharing of victory credits was another attempt to raise the morale of backseaters. Moreover, their role was often essential in air-to-air combat; when they did not pick up a MiG on radar, they might be the first to see it attacking from the rear. Their most important job was to "lock" the radar onto a MiG within parameters that would permit a missile kill. Whatever the backseater's contribution to a particular victory, however, he was awarded as much credit as the pilot. Lieutenant McKinney had won a full credit on November 6, when Capt. Darrell D. Simmonds in the front seat shot down two MiG–17s with the twenty-millimeter gun carried in a pod on their F–4.[71]

While only two airmen had been granted a pair of victory credits in Southeast Asia, several had one credit. McKinney got ahead of the latter group by winning a quarter of a credit on December 19. This time the man in the front seat was Maj. Joseph D. Moore, son of Lt. Gen. Joseph H. Moore (Westmoreland's boyhood friend, Momyer's predecessor as commander of Seventh Air Force, and Ryan's second in command at Pacific Air Forces before becoming Inspector General of the Air Force in August 1967). Once again the pod gun was used, but it was not working well and its slow rate of fire was not enough to bring the MiG–17 down. After a two-seat F–105F Wild Weasel finished the job, the victory credit was split four ways.[72]

Despite losing two MiGs without downing an American aircraft, the MiG effort could be counted a success on this last afternoon of a rare week of good weather. Of forty strike aircraft, twenty-four jettisoned their bombs. "I tried to find where the MiG–17 had impacted," Major Moore recalled, "but I couldn't tell an airplane crash from all the bomb detonations."[73] Whatever they blew up, it was not part of the railyards targeted. So ended a brief renewal of the previous summer's campaign against rail lines between Hanoi and the Chinese border.[74]

Five days was simply too short a time to attack a large proportion of the rail targets. The Doumer Bridge was by far the longest in North Vietnam, but many others also carried the rails reaching down from China. The old Canal des Rapides Bridge (three miles northeast of the Doumer Bridge) was struck on December 15, but it was necessary to strike the canal's two bypass bridges as well. All three were short and easily repaired, so the effect was at best temporary. In any case, the weather closed in again before much could be done to attack rolling stock backed up in railyards and on rail spurs. The big railyard at Yen Vien was hit, as was the rail car repair shop at Gia Lam, but the North Vietnamese put over a hundred cars on spurs that had not been authorized for attack. On the last day of clear weather, Seventh Air Force's request to hit these rail spurs was making its way too late through channels to Washington; approval did not reach Saigon until early the next morning.[75]

Although no one knew it then, the Doumer Bridge strike of December 18, 1967, was to be the last major bombing success in Hanoi for more than four years. Most of the damage was done by F–105s from the 388th Tactical Fighter Wing, Korat Air Base, Thailand. Three days later the wing commander, Col. Neil J. Graham, learned that President Johnson was about to visit Korat. In the month since Graham had taken command after Colonel Burdett was shot down over Phuc Yen, Graham had been visited by the Chief of Staff of the Air Force (General McConnell), the Commander in Chief of Pacific Air Forces (General Ryan), and Congressman Joseph Y. Resnick (Democrat of New York), among others; entertainer Bob Hope's visit was to follow the President's. The combination of bad bombing weather and celebrity visitors provided a brief respite in the grim toll Rolling Thunder was taking on the Korat wing and its leaders. Having recently lost a wing commander and vice commander, the wing deputy for operations, Col. James E. Bean, would be shot down and captured early in January and Colonel Graham would die from a heart attack later in the month.[76]

It was not, of course, the wing's final triumph over the Doumer that drew President Johnson across the Pacific. On December 21, he attended the funeral of Prime Minister Harold Holt of Australia—one of the few countries that had sent any troops to Vietnam. Johnson turned this trip into an around-the-world Christmas ritual, with visits to American soldiers in Southeast Asia and the Pope in Rome. Johnson had first visited Vietnam as Vice President, and he had slipped away from the Manila conference in 1966 to shake hands with Army soldiers at Cam Ranh Bay. Before returning to Cam Ranh Bay on December 23, 1967, he spent a night at Korat Air Base. There a new and as yet unoccupied dormitory helped to house the presidential entourage of about three hundred, including some seventy-five reporters. George Christian, the President's press secretary, told reporters that for security reasons they could not file stories until after the President left early in the morning. But the Thai press broke the story, and reporters spent all night using telephones and typewriters at wing headquarters.[77]

The press was barred from Johnson's evening session at the officers club with General Momyer and pilots representing wings throughout Thailand. They described the Doumer Bridge strikes and the air war generally. One of the briefers was Lieutenant McKinney, who talked about air-to-air combat. No backseater had ever been given so much limelight. Before dawn the next morning at a flightline ceremony attended by about five thousand, the President presented Distinguished Flying Crosses to McKinney and five frontseat pilots. McKinney's medal-winning performance had occurred on September 19 with Maj. Lloyd W. Boothby in the front seat; Boothby was also on hand to receive a Distinguished Flying Cross. Their F–4 had been hit by ground fire while attempting to bomb a rail siding north of Hanoi; despite a damaged control system, they had managed to get back to Thailand before bailing out.[78]

President Johnson had heard a great deal from Senator Symington and others about pilot frustration with trivial targets and overly restrictive rules of engagement. In recent months Johnson had given these pilots better targets, including the Doumer Bridge that they had just struck again. Now he gave them a pep talk. "Guerrilla combat provides no easy targets," he explained. But a few airmen were "pinning down" more than half a million North Vietnamese trying to keep transportation routes open. He praised the discipline, restraint, and steadfastness of Americans in uniform. At times he seemed to be giving himself a pep talk too. "The spirit of America is not to be read on the placards or posters," he declared. "No man can come here for even a short period and shake your hand or look you in the eye and have the slightest bit of a doubt for a moment that America is going to hold firm and that America is going to stay faithful throughout the course until an honorable peace is secured." [79]

Although the base collected a bigger crowd for comedian Bob Hope a few days later, President Johnson seemed very pleased with his visit to Korat. Back at the White House, Walt Rostow told his Joint Chiefs liaison officer that "Momyer made a hell of a good impression at Korat."[80] This praise was passed on to the Air Force Chief of Staff, General McConnell, who was also told that the Air Force should get "maximum mileage" out of the President's speech there.[81] McConnell liked the speech so much that more than a year later (after Johnson and he had both retired), he would raise it with an interviewer as a "very well thought-out" statement of Johnson's appreciation for airmen who fought under restrictions deemed necessary by the President.[82]

Indeed, the Korat speech marked the apex of good feeling between President Johnson and the military. Since the Stennis hearings in August, he had approved some long-sought targets and shown Secretary of Defense McNamara the door. Long before McNamara sought to reduce the bombing of North Vietnam, many senior officers had been uncomfortable with his cerebral style and his focus on quantitative measures of progress. Few generals or admirals were displeased by Johnson's announcement in late November that McNamara would leave the Defense Department before long to head the World Bank.[83]

Johnson's efforts to mollify those who wanted to prosecute the war more vigorously could only infuriate those protesting American involvement in the war. Whatever the reservations of the military about his policies, Johnson was always assured a friendly reception when he visited the young Americans who were risking their lives to carry out those policies. But elsewhere, less friendly young Americans booed his speeches and paraded outside the White House daily. On October 23, more than twenty thousand protesters marched from the Mall to the Pentagon for an all-night vigil.[84]

Protesters were a nuisance, but they may have worked to the administration's advantage; obscene slogans, communist flags, and long-haired young men grated on the sensibilities of most Americans. Their dislike of demonstrations, however, could not ensure their continued support for a long and distant war. With presidential elections only a year away, Johnson learned in the fall of 1967 that, according to a Gallup poll, only 38 percent of his countrymen approved of the way he handled his job.[85]

Gallup trial heats for the presidency showed Johnson trailing several political rivals: in his own party, Senator Robert Kennedy of New York; in the Republican Party, Governor Nelson Rockefeller of New York, former Vice President Richard Nixon, and Governor George Romney of Michigan.[86] Rockefeller's silence on Vietnam may have helped make him the most popular. After a spring 1967 visit to Vietnam, Nixon had urged a harsher bombing campaign against North Vietnam that would include the mining of Haiphong harbor. Subsequently, Romney had tried to move away from his earlier support of the war by complaining that the generals and diplomats had "brainwashed" him—now he wanted a reduction in the bombing.[87]

Before the summer of 1967, nearly all prominent Republicans had been supportive of the war effort; their criticism was limited to calls for more decisive prosecution of the war. The Senate minority leader, Everett Dirksen of Illinois, was one of Johnson's closest friends and one of his warmest supporters in debates on the war. But Romney's was not the only Republican defection. In addition to Senator George Aiken of Vermont (an early critic of the war), Senator Mark Hatfield of Oregon and Charles Percy, the junior senator from Illinois, began to attack the extent of American involvement—as did Congressmen Paul Findley, also of Illinois, and F. Bradford Morse of Massachusetts. They used arguments already made familiar by the war's more numerous Democratic opponents (including Senator Kennedy), who took their lead from the outspoken Chairman of the Senate Foreign Relations Committee, William Fulbright of Arkansas. The most influential of the war's newly hatched Republican "doves" was Senator Thruston Morton of Kentucky, a former national chairman of the party.[88]

Like most other vocal opponents of the American role in Vietnam, Senator Morton wanted to begin reducing that role by stopping the bombing of North Vietnam. Although Johnson would eventually attempt to appease his critics by granting their first wish, he had ample reason in the fall of 1967 to think that the bombing was one of his most popular programs. The same polls that registered growing dissatisfaction with his presidency and with the war also registered continued support for bombing North Vietnam. While Americans were getting tired of the war, they were impatient for at least a semblance of victory. In October, a Gallup poll found that 65 percent opposed stopping the bombing of North Vietnam without a promise of something in return; 55 percent favored continuing to bomb at the current level; and 42 percent were even willing to use atomic bombs. This poll, however, also found that 60 percent favored abiding by a United Nations decision on South Vietnam's future, and 71 percent wanted to turn the fighting over gradually to South Vietnamese soldiers.[89]

President Johnson had become seriously concerned about popular support for the war in August 1967, when his Gallup approval rating dropped steeply from 47 percent of American voters to 40 percent. The Stennis hearings of that month aired some of Secretary of Defense McNamara's differences with the Joint Chiefs of Staff over the bombing of North Vietnam. More damaging to the President's popularity, however, was the proposal he sent to Congress on August 3 for a 10 percent income tax surcharge. The cost of the war, added to the cost of Johnson's social programs, had enlarged the federal debt and more than doubled the inflation rate (which in the early 1960s had held steady at about 1 percent a year). To prevent inflation from worsening, Johnson believed that he had to ask for higher taxes. This was bound to be unpopular and to increase pressure on him for measurable progress, so that he could justify the war's cost in dollars as well as in lives.[90]

Ever since he had first sent fighter-bombers against North Vietnam, President Johnson had tried to avoid arousing the passions of the American people. He was afraid that they might push him toward a wider war. But as opposition to his policies swelled in the summer of 1967, he began to talk about changing the character of his war effort on the home front. At a meeting with his closest advisers on August 18, he complained that the United States could not win without parades, songs, and bond drives. He proposed that a colorful general like Douglas MacArthur be sent to talk to the press in Saigon.[91] Apparently no one more colorful than General Westmoreland could be found. In October, when the President asked for the Air Force general best able to defend the bombing of North Vietnam, he received a list headed by Lt. Gen. George Brown, assistant to the Chairman of the Joint Chiefs. While Brown's reputation for competence and cordiality was taking him to the top of his profession, the adjective colorful was rarely, if ever, attached to his name.[92]

It appeared to many officers that President Johnson had fired the most colorful general of the 1960s, General LeMay. In the case of President Truman and General MacArthur, there had been no doubt. Colorful generals were inclined to disagree with their President—an inclination that had contributed to their scarcity. Johnson himself was a vivid personality in private, but this rarely came across in his public speeches. When he thought that the American people needed a pep talk, he turned for help to the blander men he had retained or placed in charge of his military and civilian agencies.[93]

On October 5, Johnson lectured the Cabinet about their responsibility to speak on the war. He recalled the vigor with which Franklin Roosevelt had been defended by Secretary of the Interior Harold L. Ickes and Secretary of the Treasury Henry Morgenthau, Jr. "You have got to come out of your caves and stop being so modest," Johnson urged. "Dirksen is the only one standing up for us now." After Vice President Humphrey noted that a "massive effort" would be needed to turn the "tide of discouragement," the President suggested that perhaps "we should close up our Public Affairs offices and get all new people."[94]

President Johnson's efforts to build a more favorable public image seemed to work for awhile. His Gallup poll approval rating crept upward from a low of 38 percent at the beginning of November to 48 percent by late January. Bad weather over the Red River Delta of North Vietnam assisted his public relations efforts by keeping fighter-bomber raids off the front pages of American newspapers. Johnson had some of the advantages of a bombing pause without having to incur the wrath of the "hawks." Meanwhile, he assured the American public that the war in South Vietnam was being won. To convince them, he brought General Westmoreland and Ambassador Bunker back to the United States for a week of upbeat speechmaking. But whatever the short-term benefit of this exercise, it made Hanoi's subsequent Tet offensive all the more shocking.

Leaders

TOP: Lt. Gen. William W. Momyer (right), Seventh Air Force commander, welcomes Gen. John D. Ryan (right), Pacific Air Forces commander, to Saigon.

ABOVE: South Vietnam's vice president, Nguyen Cao Ky (left), talks with Lt. Gen. Momyer (center) and Gen. John P. McConnell (right), Air Force Chief of Staff.

Weapons

RIGHT: Sparrow and Sidewinder air-to-air missiles on trailers before loading on F-4 fighter aircraft at Da Nang Air Base, November 1966

BELOW: Air Force ground crew technicians prepare F-105 fighter aircraft at Korat Air Base for a bombing mission over North Vietnam.

Targets

ABOVE: The North Vietnamese responded to bridge bombing by building bypass bridges, here three at one site.

RIGHT: First raid on Phuc Yen airfield, October 1967

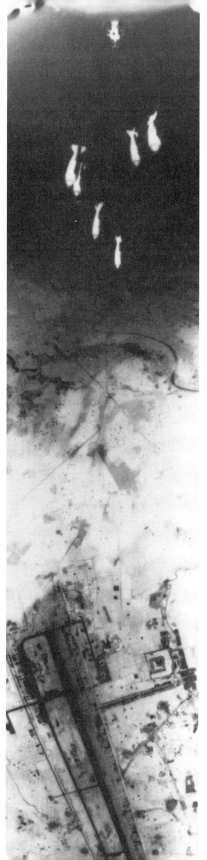

Air Defenses

TOP: A North Vietnamese SA-2 surface-to-air missile

ABOVE: A North Vietnamese MiG-21

Chapter Five

Rolling Thunder Subsides

In 1968 the lunar new year began on January 30. As usual, the South Vietnamese prepared to celebrate for several days before and after Tet (new year's day), but the government bowed to American pressure and announced a cease-fire lasting only thirty-six hours. Although the communist National Liberation Front had advertised a cease-fire extending an entire week, General Westmoreland was persuaded that this time they might break their word with even greater abandon than in the past. For months, intelligence reports had warned of an impending offensive. Westmoreland was particularly concerned about the I Corps area, the northern quarter of South Vietnam, where two North Vietnamese divisions were besieging a Marine outpost in the hills at Khe Sanh; he canceled the cease-fire for American forces in I Corps.[1]

Before the sun rose on the morning of Tet, communist forces attacked government facilities in seven cities, only two of them in I Corps. These premature beginnings of a much larger offensive gave the Americans and the South Vietnamese time to cancel the cease-fire throughout the country and recall soldiers before the onslaught of the following night. Then the communists used perhaps eighty thousand men to attack their enemies in Saigon and more than a hundred other cities and towns. Despite the surprising number and intensity of the assaults, which brought large-scale fighting into the cities for the first time, American and South Vietnamese forces required less than a week to blunt the offensive. Only in the Citadel at Hue in I Corps did communist attackers manage to hold an important objective until late February. For the first time the communists had shown themselves in large numbers under conditions that did not permit them to slip away into the jungle. General Westmoreland thought that his men were winning the greatest victory of the war.[2]

Few American reporters saw an American victory in the Tet offensive. Many of them had long since grown cynical about Westmoreland's claims of progress. Now the war had come to Saigon in a way that both shocked them and confirmed their cynicism. Since most of the reporters assigned to Vietnam were in Saigon, much of their initial coverage concentrated on that city and the story of nineteen communists penetrating the wall of the American embassy compound and remaining on the grounds for several hours before being killed or captured. The suicidal nature of such attacks won for the communists much admiration and sympathy, especially when Americans saw on television and on the front page the image of the Saigon police director, Brig. Gen. Nguyen Ngoc Loan, shooting a captive. Little noted was the fact that communists had just killed one of Loan's men as well as the man's wife and children.[3]

In the weeks that followed the offensive, military public affairs officers took Saigon reporters on field trips to other cities where attacks had been repelled. A casual reading or watching of the resulting stories could give the mistaken impression that the offensive continued to rage throughout South Vietnam. Even when American and South Vietnamese forces were given credit for quickly defeating communist attacks, the heavy use of firepower came in for severe censure. After one of the early field trips to Ben Tre in the Mekong Delta, Peter Arnett of the Associated Press quoted an unidentified American major explaining that it had been "necessary to destroy the town to save it."[4] Perhaps even more damaging to the Johnson administration was the verdict of CBS's influential news anchorman, Walter Cronkite, who after a brief visit to South Vietnam told his television audience that the Vietnam War was a "stalemate" with no end in sight.[5]

The news from Vietnam inverted a recent upturn in President Johnson's Gallup approval rating, which now dropped from 48 percent to 36 percent of Americans polled (slightly lower than it had been in early November before Westmoreland's pep talks in Washington).[6] Since 1968 was a presidential election year, Johnson had ample incentive to change his Vietnam policies. But it was not at all obvious what changes would improve Johnson's domestic political situation, let alone improve matters in South Vietnam. As so often in the past, the administration's debate over Vietnam policy focused on bombing and troop deployments. In many respects this debate was a rehash of the one that occurred in May 1967, except that the outcome changed with respect to bombing. This time, Secretary of Defense McNamara's old proposal to cut back the bombing of North Vietnam to south of the twentieth parallel was reborn as Secretary of State Rusk's proposal. It finally got the President's approval—shortly after Johnson had replaced McNamara with Clark Clifford, a Washington lawyer and presidential adviser since the Truman administration.[7]

McNamara might well have gotten his proposal approved by Johnson in the spring of 1967 had it not been for the Senate Armed Services Committee. When Senator Symington called for hearings under the auspices of Senator Stennis's investigating subcommittee, the President dropped consideration of a bombing cutback and approved new targets, including Hanoi's Doumer Bridge. But the committee did not repeat that performance after the Tet offensive.[8]

The first member of the Senate Armed Services Committee to react publicly to Tet was a Republican, Strom Thurmond of South Carolina, who was speaking on the floor against a civil rights bill when he was given the news. He put aside his prepared remarks and began to talk darkly of the connection between events in South Vietnam and the seizure only a week before of the Navy's radio intelligence ship Pueblo by North Korean patrol boats. In his view, the origin of America's problems in Vietnam was the acceptance of stalemate in the Korean War; it was high time the United States started using its power. "Use your power to close the port of Haiphong," he urged. "Use your power to bomb them so they cannot take it—the kind of bombing we did in World War II, if necessary."[9]

Subsequently, Thurmond and his fellow committee members had little more to say in public about expanding the bombing campaign. Nor did they come forth to dispute the lead editorial in the Sunday *New York Times*, which declared that if the "spectacularly successful" Tet offensive proved anything, it proved that the bombing of North Vietnam had failed to reduce either the enemy's will or his capacity to fight.[10] Of course, the committee's own long-standing criticism of the bombing's inadequacy was well known, but none of those senators had ever said that the current level of bombing was making no contribution at all.

Three days into the Tet offensive, the Senate Armed Services Committee began previously scheduled closed hearings on the defense authorization bill for the next fiscal year. The opening witnesses were Secretary of Defense McNamara, who still had a month to serve in the Pentagon, and General Wheeler, the Chairman of the Joint Chiefs. Since Senator Russell was ill, Senator Stennis was in the chair. He was even more gracious than usual, going so far as to say that McNamara was the "most effective Secretary of Defense I have ever seen or known."[11] The same senators who had grilled McNamara on the air war in August, now barely raised the subject. They did ascertain from General Wheeler that the Joint Chiefs still favored mining Haiphong.[12]

Three weeks later, after the initial shock of the Tet offensive had worn off, the Secretary of the Air Force and the Chief of Staff appeared before the committee. During the morning session Senator Stennis warned General McConnell that after lunch he would be expected to discuss the restrictions under which the bombing had been conducted. Later when reciting the rules of engagement, McConnell said that he did not want to express disagreement with "policies or restrictions which are imposed by the President."[13] That statement bothered several members of the committee. While lecturing McConnell and Secretary Brown on the importance of speaking out, the senators suggested that the public silence of the Air Force leadership had contributed to a dire situation with implications for the credibility of air power that spread far beyond Southeast Asia.[14]

This criticism disturbed McConnell so much that he dropped his usual cordiality to confront it. He protested that he had made his position clear to his superiors and that he had answered the committee's questions honestly. "When I have done that," he concluded, "then I have done everything I should do, and I should not go out and try to convince the American people what my attitude is."[15] But what would the general do in North Vietnam if he had a free hand? McConnell's answer demonstrated the degree to which he had tailored his speaking and perhaps his thinking to political realities in Washington: "If I were given a free hand to do everything I wanted to do in North Vietnam, I don't have the slightest idea of what I would do, Senator, because that would be a responsibility which I have never considered having thrust upon me."[16]

For all their frustration with the Air Force Chief of Staff's willingness to go along with administration bombing policy, the senators on the Armed Services Committee did not themselves try to arouse the public on behalf of more bombing. While the Senate Armed Services Committee met in closed session, the Senate Foreign Relations Committee met before the television cameras to interrogate Secretary of State Rusk for two days. Not since 1966 had Rusk agreed to appear before that committee in open session, and in turn the Foreign Relations Committee had refused to meet with Rusk in closed session. Now the Chairman of Foreign Relations, Senator Fulbright, made the most of his opportunity to attack the administration before a national audience. Although Fulbright's tie bore an image of doves and olive branches, they did not symbolize his attitude toward the Secretary of State.[17]

The Foreign Relations Committee and the Armed Services Committee had only one member in common, and he was the one most closely associated with the Air Force because he had been the service's first secretary in 1947. Increasingly disenchanted with the war, Senator Symington had returned from each of his trips to Southeast Asia less inclined to support the administration. By the summer of 1967 he had favored hitting North Vietnam hard or getting out of the war. After the Tet offensive, he emphasized the latter half of his proposal. He took his turn during the televised hearings to explain the change in his thinking. The war had become too expensive for the American economy, he thought, and the American policy of gradualism was a failure partly because Americans had underestimated the "durability and patriotism of the Vietcong and the North Vietnamese."[18] Nevertheless, he continued to believe that the United States could have destroyed "the enemy's capacity for aggression" if air and sea power had been used in "normal fashion" during 1965. But he indicated that this was no longer as attractive an approach, because "it is probably true that the defenses of North Vietnam have been built up to a point where it is now the most sophisticated defense in world history."[19]

*   *   *

A problem for many bombing advocates was that they no longer wanted to risk over North Vietnam the one type of aircraft capable of delivering a lot of bombs in bad weather—the B–52. Even General McConnell had indicated his own reluctance during the Stennis hearings in August, and the Stennis subcommittee's report had not recommended using the B–52s.[20] Without using B–52s, there was little that could be done over North Vietnam to respond to the Tet offensive, since the weather would minimize fighter operations at least until the middle of April.

Within the administration, B–52s had long been out of the question as one of those rash moves that might lead to a wider war. The President's National Security Adviser, Walt Rostow, did suggest mining Haiphong harbor as something that could be done in bad weather.[21] Rostow's principal source of information on mining was an Air Force officer, Brig. Gen. Robert N. Ginsburgh, the Joint Chiefs liaison to the White House. Ginsburgh told Rostow that mining North Vietnam's harbors might prove to be a good bargaining tactic, since they might be able to get the North Vietnamese to negotiate merely by offering not to renew the minefields. Mining was also a lot less risky than other options like invading North Vietnam, bombing the flood control dikes, or destroying North Vietnamese cities from the air after warning the inhabitants to evacuate.[22] But, of course, mining Haiphong was a step that the President had often rejected before, and its impact on the North Vietnamese would be much reduced if the railroads from China to Hanoi could not be interdicted at the same time. They could not be, at least until the northeast monsoon abated and permitted the fighter-bombers to operate more effectively.

Any interest President Johnson might have had in taking more extreme action was dampened by speculation in the press that he was contemplating using nuclear weapons at Khe Sanh. Johnson was upset to learn that his subordinates had, in fact, been looking into this possibility. Recalling that the use of nuclear weapons had been discussed as a way to break the Vietnamese communist siege of the French position at Dien Bien Phu in 1954, Walt Rostow had raised the matter with General Ginsburgh, who raised it in turn with General Wheeler, who sent a message to Admiral Sharp and General Westmoreland. The commanders in Hawaii and Vietnam were already having the option studied, but they replied that they did not think it would be necessary to use nuclear weapons. Meanwhile, General Eisenhower, who had been urging Johnson to step up the bombing of North Vietnam ever since the seizure of the Pueblo, now indicated to the press that nuclear weapons should not be ruled out at Khe Sanh (even though as President he had not used them at Dien Bien Phu). President Johnson had to assure a press conference that he had received no recommendations to use nuclear weapons, and Secretary McNamara had to call several concerned citizens to convince them that there would be no such recommendation.[23]

Talk of employing nuclear weapons in Southeast Asia reinforced President Johnson's determination not to make any dramatic increase in his use of air power. Although the Joint Chiefs hoped that the Tet offensive would lead to an enlargement of their bombing authority, they assumed that Johnson would veto mining Haiphong harbor and did not ask to do it. They could not guarantee that mining Haiphong would not lead to a confrontation with the Soviet Union, but the Chiefs did hope to persuade Johnson there was now less cause to be as careful of civilian casualties when bombing North Vietnam. After all, many South Vietnamese civilians were dying at the hands of the communists. The Chiefs asked Johnson not only to remove the prohibition on bombing fixed targets in Hanoi and Haiphong, but also to permit armed reconnaissance of water, rail, and truck traffic nearer to the centers of those cities.[24]

Since the summer of 1967, the President had permitted armed reconnaissance on the principal routes radiating through his Hanoi and Haiphong "donut rings," the portion of each restricted bombing zone lying outside each prohibited bombing zone. The Hanoi restricted zone (within which fixed targets required Presidential approval) had a radius of thirty nautical miles, while the Hanoi prohibited zone had a radius of ten nautical miles. In January, the President had established a new prohibited zone with a radius of five nautical miles, but armed reconnaissance was kept outside the ten nautical mile limit. With respect to Haiphong, however, January's new prohibited zone radius of five nautical miles extended further than the old one of four nautical miles, pushing the inner edge of the donut ring outward (while the outer edge remained at ten nautical miles, the radius of Haiphong's restricted zone). Discussions of this matter tended to be somewhat confused, and the Joint Chiefs hoped to simplify it in a way that would give them a freer hand. They wanted to replace all the old zones with one new one for each city, Hanoi's having a radius of three nautical miles and Haiphong's a radius of one and a half nautical miles.[25]

General Wheeler proposed the smaller restricted zones to the President at the first Tuesday Lunch following the onset of the Tet offensive. Secretary of State Rusk objected that this might lead to large civilian casualties. Secretary of Defense McNamara added that aircraft losses would go up and the military effect would be slight. Wheeler protested that the North Vietnamese had a fine warning system which sent the civilian population into shelters. Any increase in North Vietnamese casualties would not compare with the "butchery" of South Vietnamese. Clark Clifford, the Secretary of Defense in waiting, weighed in on the side of Wheeler with the argument that the Tet offensive was a clear rejection of President Johnson's offers to negotiate. Rusk then proposed as a compromise that the President remove his recent prohibition on bombing fixed targets within five nautical miles of the center of each city, and authorize again those fixed targets which he had authorized in the past. Johnson took this advice, giving the Air Force its old targets in Hanoi (including the Canal Bridge and the Doumer Bridge) and the Navy its Haiphong targets.[26]

Since little good bombing weather could be expected until late April, the Joint Chiefs could only hope that any new target authorizations precipitating out of the Tet offensive would remain in effect for at least three months. Meanwhile, the airfields were the only targets in North Vietnam about which they felt much urgency. Il–28 light jet bombers had returned to Phuc Yen Air

Base, where they had not been seen since the spring of 1967. Unlike the newer and smaller MiG–21 fighters at Phuc Yen, the Il–28s had sufficient range to reach Da Nang without staging out of a base in the North Vietnamese panhandle. When General Wheeler raised this problem with the President on February 7, Johnson expressed immediate interest in attacking Phuc Yen and Wheeler assured him that it would be attacked as soon as weather permitted.[27]

Seventh Air Force did not wait for good weather. General Momyer had already given the order to destroy the Il–28s, and on the very next day the 8th Tactical Fighter Wing at Ubon Air Base, Thailand, launched a daring low-level raid. A single flight of four F–4s entered North Vietnam as if on a reconnaissance mission. While half the flight announced their presence at high altitude by turning on their radio identification transponders (which the North Vietnamese were thought to be capable of interrogating), the volunteer crews on board the other two F–4s skimmed across Phuc Yen at 250 feet. The attackers thought that their cluster bombs must have damaged at least one Il–28. The North Vietnamese were not sufficiently surprised, their flak crippling one engine of the lead F–4, which still managed to get to Laos where Capt. Tracy K. Dorsett and Capt. John A. Corder bailed out, evaded enemy search parties, and scrambled aboard a rescue helicopter. Back at Ubon they were reunited with fellow volunteers Maj. Larry D. Armstrong and 1st Lt. James H. Hall. All four received the Air Force Cross.[28]

Two days later, the 8th Tactical Fighter Wing made a second novel attempt to eliminate the Il–28 presence at Phuc Yen. A large formation of sixteen F–4s with cluster bombs (escorted by eight other F–4s and eight F–105s) managed to strike Phuc Yen in bad weather without suffering any losses. This feat was accomplished by having the strike F–4s pull up five miles from the target and loft their bombs.[29]

On February 14, 1968, Ubon launched yet another raid against Phuc Yen. This time a single flight of F–4s was to use their onboard radar to drop their bombs, but the clearest weather in a month permitted dive bombing. Neither then nor subsequently were the Il–28s or MiG–21s caught on the ground. Nor were they ever sent to attack targets in South Vietnam. Henceforth, the North Vietnamese kept only two Il–28s at Phuc Yen, and these would fly north and orbit at the approach of American aircraft. Five other Il–28s were at bases north of the Chinese border with the bulk of North Vietnam's MiG force. Since the airfield raids of the previous year, North Vietnam had based more than a hundred MiGs in China, while fewer than twenty remained at Phuc Yen, Gia Lam, and Kep airfields (with others thought to be hidden in the nearby countryside and hauled to the bases by helicopter when needed).[30]

Although the Valentine's Day raid on Phuc Yen caught no MiGs on the ground, several were encountered in the air. As usual a couple of MiG–21s attempted to hit-and-run from above thirty thousand feet (without success this time since they were spotted early) while at least five MiG–17s waited below fifteen thousand feet. The MiG–17s did manage to draw each of the F–4 escort flights into separate skirmishes, but the MiGs won no victories and suffered two losses (one to gunfire and the other to a Sparrow radar-guided missile). Maj. Rex D. Howerton and Col. David O. Williams, Jr., shared the credit for these last Air Force confirmed air-to-air victories of Rolling Thunder with their back-seaters, 1st Lt. Ted L. Voight II and 1st Lt. James P. Feighny, Jr.[31]

In addition to the planned raid on Phuc Yen, Seventh Air Force used the rare day of clear weather to attack Hanoi's Canal Bridge, one of the targets President Johnson had again released only a week earlier. Since the bridge raids of December, the Canal Bridge had returned to operation, while the Doumer Bridge over the Red River was still down. Late in the afternoon, strike forces from Takhli and Korat converged on the bridge from opposite directions. Sixteen bomb-laden F–105s from the 355th Tactical Fighter Wing at Takhli came down Thud Ridge from the west, with eight F–105 escorts to threaten the SAM sites and eight F–4s to guard against the MiGs. A similar force escorted a like number of F–105s from the 388th Tactical Fighter Wing at Korat as they penetrated North Vietnam from the Gulf of Tonkin. Although the two wings dropped forty-eight 2,000-pound and 3,000-pound bombs, only one hit the bridge, and three days later trains were using it. An escort F–105 from Korat was lost to a SAM and the pilot, Capt. Robert M. Elliot, was never seen by Americans again.[32]

In yet another attempt to make use of clear weather on the 14th, a flight of four F–4s from Ubon dropped Walleye television-guided bombs on the thermal powerplant associated with the Thai Nguyen ironworks, some thirty miles north of Hanoi. At least one of the Walleyes made a direct hit. Two were obscured by dust and smoke that may also have interfered with their guidance systems. Although the Walleye could be very accurate, its relatively small warhead sometimes failed to do enough damage even when right on target. At any rate, the powerplant was soon operating and remained on the target list.[33]

During the weeks of bad weather which followed, there was little more that Seventh Air Force or the Seventh Fleet could do in the Hanoi-Haiphong region. Meanwhile, Thailand finally permitted fighter aircraft based there to be used in South Vietnam, nearly a year after Thailand-based B–52s. Thus, the principal response of the Thailand-based fighters to the Tet offensive came in the hills around Khe Sanh, where they joined B–52s and other fighters in delivering an unprecedented tonnage of bombs on so small an area—a hundred thousand tons in a few weeks, about as much as the Hanoi-Haiphong region had suffered in three years.[34]

Since B–52s were not used near Hanoi and Haiphong, most major targets in North Vietnam were adequately protected from American air power by the northeast monsoon. The solo missions of Navy and Marine A–6s and the less accurate flights of four F–4s or four F–105s (guided by the radar at Phou Pha Thi in Laos) could do no more than harass the enemy. Some of the Red River port facilities on the south side of Hanoi were attacked for the first time without much damage. Unfortunately the most prominent target given the bad weather attackers was one demanding greater accuracy than they could muster. They were supposed to turn off the voice of Hanoi Hannah by bombing Radio Hanoi. Not surprisingly they failed, while the White House paid close attention. After an A–6 attempt, Walt Rostow was informed that Radio Hanoi had kept to its usual schedule "which would indicate that our plane missed."[35]

*   *   *

Since the beginning of Rolling Thunder in 1965, the Johnson administration had linked American bombing in North Vietnam to American ground forces in South Vietnam. Marines had been sent with the immediate purpose of protecting Da Nang Air Base, where some raids against North Vietnam were launched (while others launched from Thailand had to pretend that they came from Da Nang). When Marine and Army ground forces began to take the offensive, the administration's rationale turned around so that the bombing of North Vietnam was then justified as a way of reducing American casualties in South Vietnam.[36]

Even critics of President Johnson's handling of the war often reinforced the linkage between bombs and troops. As early as April 1965, CIA Director John McCone had warned that sending American ground forces to South Vietnam would never win the war unless North Vietnam was subjected to much harsher bombing. Although the CIA stopped calling for more bombing after McCone's replacement by Helms, CIA analysts continued to report that the gradual escalation of American bombing was having little effect. Nor were they sanguine about the value of sending more troops to South Vietnam.[37]

Parallel increases in troop deployments and bombing came to an end in the summer of 1967, when the administration said no to Westmoreland's request for two hundred thousand more troops and promised him only forty-two thousand. Despite McNamara's proposal to end bombing of the Red River Delta, President Johnson went along with some of the demands of the Senate Armed Services Committee for more targets there. But through diplomatic channels and in his speech at San Antonio, Johnson offered to quit bombing North Vietnam if only the North Vietnamese would agree to negotiate seriously while not increasing their rate of infiltrating troops and supplies into South Vietnam.

The Chairman of the Joint Chiefs, General Wheeler, looked with greater equanimity on the possibility of a bombing halt than did his colleagues in the Air Force and Navy. After the San Antonio speech he formed a study group in the Joint Staff to examine the question of a bombing halt with particular attention to the question of what North Vietnamese actions should trigger a resumption of bombing. Of eleven officers, seven were Army and only one was Air

Force. They predicted that North Vietnamese infiltration would increase during a bombing halt, but that the increase would be hard to measure and therefore possibly inadequate to justify resumption.[38]

While these were predictions with which most military men could agree, many in the Air Force and Navy were alarmed that the Chairman and his study group were even considering the possibility of a bombing halt. General Ginsburgh, the Air Force officer who served as Wheeler's liaison on the National Security Council staff, told the Chairman that the study group's report should stress the need to mine the ports and bomb the flood control dikes. The Joint Chiefs finally joined in a memorandum that called for resumption of bombing after thirty days if the North Vietnamese had not by then consented to withdraw all their forces from South Vietnam.[39]

The Tet Offensive revealed the flimsiness of support within the White House, the Congress, and even the Joint Chiefs for mining Haiphong or for using B–52s against the Red River Delta—the only two dramatic air actions that could have been taken in the cloudy weather of February and March 1968. A major troop increase was another matter, however. General Wheeler thought that the Tet crisis might produce the same willingness to expand the military that the Chinese offensive had generated during the Korean War.

The President's initial response to Tet encouraged Wheeler, and on February 3, the Chairman cabled Westmoreland that the President had asked whether his field commander needed reinforcement. At this point Wheeler's principal obstacle seemed to be Westmoreland, who was slow to take the hint. Westmoreland thought that his men were giving the communists a drubbing, and while additional forces were always nice to have, he felt no particular need for them at the moment.[40]

Meanwhile, the President was eager to send reinforcements immediately, but still reluctant to call up reserves. Only a few days earlier, he had called up ten thousand air and naval reservists in response to the Pueblo crisis. Already complaints were coming from relatives and employers that these men were not doing useful work. Over the objections of the Joint Chiefs of Staff, Johnson insisted on sending to Westmoreland an Army airborne brigade and a Marine regimental landing team totalling eleven thousand men—without calling up reserves. In Wheeler's view the Army was already drawn much too thin, with only one deployable division, the 82d Airborne at Fort Bragg, North Carolina. The President's new deployment took a third of that division.[41]

In late February, Wheeler traveled to Saigon, where he and Westmoreland discussed a troop request that President Johnson could not meet without a major reserve call-up. Wheeler wanted to use the Tet crisis to rebuild the American military, but he was also much more nervous about the situation in Vietnam than was Westmoreland. Tired and gloomy at the outset of his visit, Wheeler became more uneasy when an enemy rocket exploded near his quarters and he asked to move into the Combat Operations Center with

Westmoreland. In any case, Westmoreland was happy to comply with Wheeler's desire for a big troop request. Having been turned down when he requested such an increase in 1967, Westmoreland had then followed the Johnson administrations's drift toward gradually turning the war over to the South Vietnamese. But the enormous communist losses of the last month together with the prospect of a major infusion of American troops now had him once again thinking of winning the war.[42]

Echoing his 1967 request, Westmoreland joined Wheeler in asking for about 200,000 men—this time precisely 206,000. Half these were to go to Vietnam in the next few months. The rest might go by the end of the year if necessary, but Westmoreland did not think they would be necessary and thus could be kept in the United States. Even if all 206,000 were deployed (including fifteen fighter squadrons) raising the number of American servicemen in Vietnam above 700,000, stateside forces would have to grow to provide the necessary logistical tail. In fact satisfying the 206,000 request would have expanded the armed forces by about 500,000 (or nearly 15 percent), partly by lengthening terms of service, partly by increasing draft calls, and partly by calling up more than 250,000 reservists.[43]

When Wheeler's proposal reached Washington on February 27, the President was at his ranch in Texas. He was due back the following day for the first of Secretary of Defense McNamara's two retirement ceremonies. In Johnson's absence McNamara and his replacement, Clark Clifford, met to discuss the troop request with a small group of the President's closest advisers, including Secretary of State Rusk. Wheeler's report dramatized the Tet offensive as "a very near thing," a declaration which preyed upon their fears that the communists might soon launch an even more powerful offensive.[44] After all, most of the North Vietnamese forces in South Vietnam had been withheld so far—not to mention all the enemy's forces in Laos and North Vietnam itself.

As McNamara saw it, the President had to make a choice between a big reserve call-up and higher taxes on the one hand and an end to Westmoreland's search and destroy strategy on the other. Westmoreland could be told to withdraw his forces from the hills and use them only to defend the heavily populated coastal areas. In that case a big reserve call-up would not be necessary. If they went with the reserve call-up, they might combine it with a new peace offensive. Rusk suggested that they might offer to cut back the bombing of North Vietnam or end it altogether in exchange for a North Vietnamese withdrawal from Quang Tri Province, the northernmost in South Vietnam. Clifford said that they should consider sending Westmoreland much more than 206,000 men, perhaps as many as a million, though he also said that he was not pushing the idea; given the widespread impression that the United States was losing the war, how could they avoid creating the impression that they were "pounding troops down a rathole?"[45] Clifford thought that they needed to evaluate their entire posture in South Vietnam before making a decision.

Walt Rostow conveyed these sentiments to Johnson and suggested he give Clifford the job of chairing a task force to evaluate the situation and recommend a course of action. Johnson had long placed great stock in Clifford's advice and was enormously pleased to have him take over from McNamara. Although Clifford had joined George Ball in the summer of 1965 to oppose a major troop commitment in South Vietnam, he had subsequently supported the Johnson war policy. Clifford's counsels of caution were usually as welcome as his encouragements to stay the course. As recently as December, he had joined McNamara and Rusk in arguing against a Joint Chiefs' proposal to send B–52s against targets in Cambodia; rather than underline Rusk's fears of a Chinese reaction (always persuasive with Johnson), Clifford had simply questioned the utility of B–52 bombing in the jungle.[46]

Johnson had known Clifford since the 1940s, when Clifford had risen from being President Truman's assistant naval aide to being one of Truman's most influential civilian advisers. Like Clifford's closest friend, Stuart Symington, Clifford was part of Truman's Missouri political family; and like Senator Symington, Clifford would soon come to believe that the United States was on the wrong course in Southeast Asia.

After a very difficult month, the President gladly put the Wheeler proposal in Clifford's hands and left town again, this time for a weekend at Ramey Air Force Base, Puerto Rico. Johnson took along a son-in-law, Patrick J. Nugent, an Air National Guard enlisted man whose unit had been called up as part of Johnson's response to the Pueblo crisis. In the family pattern set by Johnson's other son-in-law, Marine Captain Charles S. Robb, Nugent expected to go to Vietnam in the next few weeks. Johnson was proud that his family was contributing in this personal way to the war effort, while most sons of the country's government and business leadership had managed to avoid military service.

The other major participant in the President's weekend trip was the Chief of Staff of the Air Force, General McConnell. They went through the motions of inspecting Ramey, but their days were filled with golf. While they played for money according to the President's rules (as McConnell would remember with amusement), much of the Washington bureaucracy was hard at work preparing a position paper for the President.[47]

Since Clifford was in charge of this "A to Z reassessment," others in the bureaucracy (JCS, CIA, State, Treasury) sent their inputs to the Office of the Secretary of Defense, where a team of action officers under the Assistant Secretary for International Security Affairs, Paul Warnke, drafted a paper for the President. Some members of this team, including its leader, Leslie Gelb, were already engaged in a project launched by McNamara to compile a classified documentary history of America's involvement in Vietnam—a history that one of the authors (Daniel Ellsberg) would three years later leak to the *New York Times* for publication as *The Pentagon Papers*. Long before the Tet offensive, Warnke, Gelb, and many other civilians working for the Secretary of

Defense had turned against the war. McNamara had given them a sympathetic hearing and tried to cut back the bombing of North Vietnam. They were uneasy about his replacement by Clifford, long a defender of the President's Vietnam policies. The "A to Z reassessment" seemed an opportunity to change Clifford's thinking and perhaps even the President's.[48]

"A to Z" meant that once again the bombing of North Vietnam was considered in conjunction with the troop question. The bombing, however, was not uppermost in the minds of the drafters. They contented themselves with merely objecting to any increase, especially mining Haiphong harbor or reducing the restricted and prohibited zones around Haiphong and Hanoi. General Wheeler managed to get the discussion of bombing moved to an appendix, where the Joint Chiefs' diametrically opposed view was also included.[49]

With General McConnell out of town, Gen. Bruce K. Holloway, the Vice Chief, was left to direct the Air Staff's response to Clifford's request for alternative strategies. The Air Staff's preferred alternative was a much harsher bombing campaign, and they even went so far as to suggest using B–52s over the Red River Delta, as well as targeting the flood control dikes and mining Haiphong harbor. Secretary of the Air Force Brown opposed such measures. He wanted to reduce bombing in the Hanoi-Haiphong region (already very slight owing to the weather, but due to grow in the spring) and increase bombing in the North Vietnamese panhandle (which throughout Rolling Thunder had suffered the bulk of the bombing anyway).[50]

The Under Secretary of the Air Force, Townsend Hoopes, insisted that the Air Staff also study the possibility of substituting tactical air power for Westmoreland's search and destroy operations in South Vietnam. Until October 1967, Hoopes had worked for Warnke in the Office of the Secretary of Defense and was thoroughly in tune with McNamara's desire to cut back the ground war in the south and the air war in the north. Hoopes had already written Clifford a personal letter advocating an end to the bombing of North Vietnam. The Air Force under secretary advised Clifford to heed a study of the bombing completed in 1967 for the JASON division of the Institute for Defense Analyses by a group of university scientists—for the most part the same group of "Jasons" who had in the summer of 1966 developed the rationale for McNamara's proposal to build an electronically monitored barrier against infiltration into South Vietnam (and thereby render the bombing of North Vietnam unnecessary). Once again the Jasons stated in the strongest possible terms that the bombing was a complete failure because the rate of infiltration had increased.[51]

While Clifford may have been interested to learn that the Air Force civilian and military leadership was divided on bombing policy, his immediate concern was Wheeler's troop request. The drafting team reflected that concern. The primary purpose of the Gelb draft was to implement McNamara's suggestion that Westmoreland's search and destroy strategy should be discarded in favor of protecting the heavily populated coastal areas of the country. Wheeler fought this change by warning that it would ensure continued fighting in the populated regions. He got the words about a change in ground strategy stricken from the draft. Though he could not get Clifford to endorse a major troop increase for Westmoreland, the new Secretary of Defense did agree that 262,000 reserves should be called up to rebuild the military in readiness for deployment whenever and wherever necessary.[52]

When the President returned to Washington, he called his principal advisers to the White House for Clifford's report. Clifford explained that his group had not yet been able to agree on bombing policy or otherwise complete a thorough reassessment of the administration's Vietnam posture, but that it should be done before sending Westmoreland major reinforcements. In the meantime Clifford recommended sending only 22,000, while calling up 262,000 reserves to rebuild the active military. Johnson made no immediate decision other than to approve the continuation of Clifford's reassessment. At this point Rusk raised again the possibility of a partial bombing halt during the ongoing northeast monsoon, and the President latched onto Rusk's suggestion as the bright spot in the meeting: "Really get your horses on that."[53]

It took a month for the partial bombing halt to become a reality. That month of March proved even more difficult for President Johnson than February had been, despite the fact that on the ground in South Vietnam the outlook for government and American forces continued to improve. Hue was recaptured at the beginning of March. Although North Vietnamese troops still surrounded the Marines at Khe Sanh, the Marines were adequately resupplied by air while their besiegers suffered the heaviest conventional bombardment of all time. In another month Westmoreland would send a relief column that would arrive after enemy survivors had once again slipped away into the jungle. But meanwhile, March brought a series of new blows to Johnson's presidency, all of them aftershocks of the Tet offensive.

On March 10, the *New York Times* published a front page story on Westmoreland's request for 206,000 men and on the ensuing debate in Washington. This story seemed to confirm all the speculation since Tet that American forces in South Vietnam were in deep trouble. President Johnson was furious, but he was unable to discover the source of the leak, though he suspected that it came from a Pentagon civilian. Only years afterward did a reporter reveal that the original tip came from Townsend Hoopes, the Under Secretary of the Air Force.[54]

On March 12, Democratic voters in the New Hampshire primary failed to give President Johnson the overwhelming support expected. Senator Eugene McCarthy of Minnesota, who was running against the war in Vietnam and Johnson's handling of it, got almost as many votes as the President. True, McCarthy's name was on the ballot and Johnson's was not, but a landslide of write-in ballots for the President was expected. At the time, McCarthy's votes in New Hampshire were thought to indicate support for withdrawing from

Vietnam. Later analysis indicated, however, that most of McCarthy's supporters in New Hampshire were disgusted with Johnson for not prosecuting the war more vigorously.[55]

On March 16, Senator Robert Kennedy announced his candidacy for the presidency. As recently as January 28, he had said that he did not intend to run. But shortly after McCarthy's strong showing in New Hampshire, Kennedy presented an ultimatum to Clifford—either Johnson appoint a commission of prominent Americans, including Kennedy, to reassess the administration's Vietnam policy, or Kennedy would enter the race. The President refused.[56]

"Lady Bird" Johnson had noticed in early March a serenity emerge in her troubled husband. This new equilibrium was upset by the political tremors of that month. On the morning of Kennedy's announcement, the President told a meeting of the National Alliance of Businessmen that the United States was going to win in Vietnam: "To meet the needs of these fighting men, we shall do whatever is required."[57] Two days later he asked the National Farmers Union to join "a total national effort to win the war."[58] He warned them that this would require a more austere economy, which should mean at least enactment of the 10 percent income tax surcharge he had proposed a year ago.

The President's sudden bellicosity passed quickly away. Political realities in Washington no longer permitted a truly national war effort. Clifford's discussions with Senators Russell, Stennis, and Symington (among others) indicated that the administration would have a hard time selling a reserve call-up of even 100,000, let alone the 262,000 Clifford had originally contemplated. By the end of March, the President decided to call up only 62,000 reservists and send to Vietnam nothing beyond those forces already scheduled for deployment; the troop ceiling in Vietnam would not go above 549,000. Johnson also announced that he would bring Westmoreland home that summer to be Chief of Staff of the Army. Westmoreland's replacement in Saigon would be his deputy commander, Gen. Creighton W. Abrams, Jr., who had been giving much of his attention to building the South Vietnamese army.[59]

Ever since the Tet offensive, President Johnson had been thinking about making a televised speech on Vietnam. When he met with his advisers on March 19 to plan the speech, he showed less interest in a new peace initiative than he had earlier in the month. Supreme Court Justice Abe Fortas, a close friend of Johnson's, attended the meeting and encouraged his inclination not to confuse matters by mixing a peace initiative into a speech on troops and war. Within three days, however, Johnson again changed his mind. He told his advisers on March 22 that he wanted to take advantage of the few remaining weeks of bad weather over North Vietnam by giving a speech that featured a bombing cutback—perhaps only a renewed prohibition of bombing near Hanoi and Haiphong.[60]

For a month, Secretary of State Rusk had argued in favor of a bombing cutback to the panhandle of North Vietnam, leaving not only Hanoi and Haiphong but most of the country free from bombing. When he had first raised this proposal in late February, he had talked about trading a bombing cutback for a North Vietnamese withdrawal from South Vietnam's northern province of Quang Tri. But he soon abandoned the idea of a trade and insisted like McNamara a year earlier that since the North Vietnamese had always called for an unconditional halt to the bombing, the administration would be wise to cut back while not expressing conditions and see what the North Vietnamese would do. Whenever Rusk would make this argument, however, Secretary of Defense Clifford would object to cutting back the bombing without a promise of anything in return. Clifford suggested trading a cutback for an end to North Vietnamese artillery shelling from the Demilitarized Zone and over it.[61]

Meanwhile, some of Clifford's civilian subordinates got the impression that their new boss was waging a one-man battle to persuade the President and all his other top advisers to cut back the bombing of North Vietnam. During Clifford's confirmation hearings in January, his testimony on a possible bombing halt had first given Pentagon doves hope that he was not an irredeemable hawk. Clifford had been asked about President Johnson's San Antonio speech, which had expressed a willingness to stop bombing North Vietnam when a halt would lead promptly to productive discussions and if the North Vietnamese would not "take advantage" of the halt. Clifford explained that the North Vietnamese could continue their normal rate of infiltration of men and materials into South Vietnam but not exceed it. The doves believed that making this interpretation explicit would inhibit Johnson from taking a harder line.[62]

The surprising sympathy with which Clifford heard the views of Pentagon doves, together with their longstanding suspicion of Secretary of State Rusk, led them to make some unwarranted assumptions about the discussions Clifford was having with Johnson and his principal advisers. Soon after the end of the administration, Townsend Hoopes would publish a memoir, *The Limits of Intervention*, propounding the view that Clifford had turned the President around. Clifford's own account in *Foreign Affairs* would fail to mention either his objections to Rusk's bombing cutback proposal or even the fact that Rusk had made the proposal which was adopted by Johnson.[63]

Both the President and his new Secretary of Defense were adjusting their thinking during that difficult month of March, but they were headed in different directions. Clifford was becoming convinced that it was time to begin extricating the United States from Vietnam. Johnson, on the other hand, was looking for a way to salvage the war effort amid a more difficult political environment. He needed to avoid the additional controversy sure to be caused by a big reserve call-up and thus encouraged Clifford to propose a smaller one. Meanwhile, Secretary of State Rusk moved to provide a new peace initiative that might relieve some of the political pressure already weighing on the President.

In the legend about Clifford's conversion of the President, an important turning point was a March 26 meeting between Johnson and several former government officials. From the early days of his administration, Johnson had sought the advice or at least the support of men who had spent their careers rotating between important posts in the government and lucrative posts in the private sector, especially in prestigious law firms and financial institutions. He was not very comfortable with this "Eastern Establishment," but he tried to draw from it as much political support as he could. To begin with, his principal connection with such men was his first National Security Adviser, McGeorge Bundy, who would invite the "Wise Men" (as Bundy dubbed them) to meet Johnson usually one at a time. After Bundy's departure from the administration, Johnson relied upon Clifford (the Wise Man with whom Johnson was most comfortable) to tell him which of the others could still be trusted.[64]

Prior to the March 26 meeting, Johnson had last met with the Wise Men as a group on November 2. In preparation for that earlier meeting Clifford had indicated that former Secretary of State Dean Acheson seemed hostile toward Johnson and, in any case, could not be trusted to keep secrets. That got Acheson demoted temporarily to a list of alternates, but not everyone on the November invitation list accepted. As so often in the past, Robert A. Lovett (Assistant Secretary of War for Air in World War II and Secretary of Defense during the Korean War) pleaded ill health. In other respects, the President got exactly what he wanted at the November meeting. Acheson and nine of his colleagues supported the President's Vietnam policy; these supporters included two former Chairmen of the Joint Chiefs, Generals Omar Bradley and Maxwell Taylor. Only former Under Secretary of State George Ball dissented, as he had from the beginning of the war.[65]

Even at their November meeting, the Wise Men expressed some discontent with bombing in the Hanoi-Haiphong region. The President himself indicated that he might begin to reduce bombing there, and his San Antonio speech had made clear his willingness to trade the bombing for productive talks. Dean Acheson suggested trading a bombing halt for an end to communist attacks across the Demilitarized Zone. General Taylor thought it would be much better to trade the bombing for a lower level of enemy activity throughout South Vietnam. McGeorge Bundy warned that weather made it difficult to relate bombing pauses to "specific military actions" by the enemy.[66]

Bundy sought a more routine bombardment that would avoid cities and civilian casualties. In a memo to Johnson after the meeting, Bundy recalled the advice of Henry L. Stimson, Secretary of War during World War II, who had said that airmen would never pay as much attention to the question of civilian casualties as they should; he had pointed particularly at Henry H. "Hap" Arnold, Commander of the Army Air Forces in World War II. "I first learned this lesson from Colonel Stimson," Bundy wrote Johnson, "when he was telling me how he was hornswoggled by Hap Arnold on just this point."[67]

Before the Wise Men met in March, the kernel of discontent about the bombing of North Vietnam had grown into agreement with George Ball that the

United States should begin disengaging from South Vietnam. Only General Bradley, General Taylor, and former Ambassador Robert Murphy strongly disagreed. Clifford knew that most of the Wise Men had changed their minds, and he suggested that Johnson hold the March meeting. The President was also in a position to know that the Wise Men would express themselves much differently than they had in November. Not only was he familiar with the change in Clifford's thinking, but Johnson had been talking to McGeorge Bundy and Dean Acheson.[68]

Although Johnson may not have been surprised by the general tenor of the advice he received on March 26, he was irritated about briefings that the Wise Men received on the preceding evening from Philip C. Habib of the State Department, Maj. Gen. William E. DePuy (Army) of the Joint Staff, and George Carver of the Central Intelligence Agency. Johnson thought that those briefings had drawn too bleak a picture of communist gains in the South Vietnamese countryside after government forces had been withdrawn to fight in the cities. As a counterweight, Johnson began his meeting with the Wise Men by introducing General Wheeler and General Abrams (who was paying his first visit to the President after selection as Westmoreland's replacement). Both Wheeler and Abrams had just come from a meeting with Westmoreland at Clark Air Base in the Philippines. Wheeler insisted that everything had turned around for the better since his February visit. Abrams stressed that South Vietnamese government forces had performed very well and that in time they would be able to assume a larger proportion of the fighting.[69]

While the President had a more positive view of developments in Vietnam than did most of the Wise Men, he was as depressed as they were about political developments in the United States. He had already expressed interest in a partial bombing halt as a way to mollify his critics, and he ensured that the question of a bombing halt would receive plenty of attention by inviting Arthur Goldberg, Ambassador to the United Nations, to meet with the Wise Men. Goldberg had been urging a total bombing halt over all of North Vietnam. George Ball, of course, agreed with him, as did a second new addition to the roster of Wise Men, Cyrus Vance, former Deputy Secretary of Defense. Ball, however, thought that the President should not raise the matter of a bombing halt publicly until it had been suggested by the Pope or the Secretary General of the United Nations. General Bradley agreed that a bombing halt was a good idea if the Pope would suggest it. The rest of the group was more wary of stopping the bombing when Westmoreland's forces near the Demilitarized Zone were threatened by communist forces on both sides of the border.[70]

A partial bombing halt would permit Johnson to bomb communist forces and supply routes north of the border—and still avoid the outcry that accompanied bombing near Hanoi and Haiphong. During the three days immediately preceding his meeting with the Wise Men, Johnson had been talking to speech writer Harry C. McPherson, Jr., and Secretary of State Rusk about stopping the bombing north of the twentieth parallel (which would free all of North Vietnam except the panhandle from American attack). The meeting of the Wise Men at least did not divert Johnson from this important ingredient of his televised speech on March 31. Johnson told House and Senate leaders afterward that his meeting with the Wise Men led directly to the speech. In his memoirs, however, he would be at pains to show that the major points of his speech had taken shape before his meeting with the Wise Men (and thus, Secretary Clifford's role in the speech was less than advertised). Johnson's memoirs seem nearer the truth than his effort at the time to associate the Wise Men with his decision. He frequently called upon influential "advisers" to share the responsibility for a decision he had in fact already made.[71]

The President's announcement of a bombing cutback gained enormously in its impact (at least on the American public) from its coupling in the March 31 speech with his statement that he would not run for reelection. He had raised this possibility with his principal advisers as early as October 1967, but he caught even them by surprise. In less than three days, his surprising speech was followed by North Vietnam's surprising agreement to meet with representatives of the U.S. government. During the summer of 1967, Johnson had offered them a complete bombing halt over North Vietnam for formal peace negotiations. Now they accepted a partial halt for informal talks. Only two months after the Tet offensive had seemed to shut the door on peace initiatives, the North Vietnamese were at last ready to talk to American government officials.[72]

The first strong evidence that the North Vietnamese might be changing their position had come in late February through the Indian ambassador in Washington. The Central Intelligence Agency also reported on March 1 that the North Vietnamese were ready to talk while fighting—in the belief that a bombing halt would not only help them rebuild their economy and their forces in South Vietnam, but also help to discourage and thus destabilize the South Vietnamese government.*[73]

Hopes for peace talks had often been dashed before. Had Johnson been rebuffed again, the bombing probably would have been resumed when the good weather arrived in May—and it was at least conceivable that political opposition to Johnson's policies might then have swollen so dramatically as to force a rapid withdrawal from Vietnam. But the North Vietnamese chose a talk and fight strategy which would permit Johnson's successor a disengagement so gradual that it could still seem possible for South Vietnam to survive free from communist control.

---

* In the summer of 1967, North Vietnamese planning for the next winter-spring offensive had apparently embraced the possibility that a successful offensive would lead to negotiations while fighting continued. See Ronnie E. Ford, *Tet 1968: Understanding the Surprise* (London, 1995), especially pp 67-86.

Had the North Vietnamese failed to respond to Johnson's bombing cutback, his opponents on Capitol Hill were ready to lay the blame at the President's door. During the brief interval between the March 31 speech and North Vietnam's positive answer, Senator Fulbright castigated Johnson for misleading the country by promising to stop the bombing of North Vietnam "except in the area north of the Demilitarized Zone." How could the President's promise be reconciled with the next day's naval air attack on a truck park near Thanh Hoa, more than two hundred miles north of the Demilitarized Zone and less than one hundred miles south of Hanoi?[74]

Senators Mike Mansfield, Richard Russell, and John Stennis rose to the President's defense on this point. They had been consulted by Johnson about his speech before he made it, and he had told them that there would be no bombing north of the twentieth parallel. Thanh Hoa lay just south of the twentieth parallel. Senator Mansfield of Montana, the Majority Leader, pointed out that the President was correct in his statement that 90 percent of the North Vietnamese people lived in the region no longer being bombed. While Thanh Hoa was more than two hundred miles from South Vietnam, the intervening panhandle was so narrow that it constituted less than a third of North Vietnam.[75]

Senator Russell, Chairman of the Senate Armed Services Committee, made it very clear that he did not approve of the cutback and that he had advised the President against it "unless there was some indication of reciprocity on the part of the North Vietnamese." But the President "as has often been the case in the past" did not take the advice of his old friend Senator Russell, who had been opposed to getting into the war and opposed to the way it had been fought. For two years he had urged a naval blockade of the coast of North Vietnam. "We have been about two years behind what we should have been doing in fighting the war ever since it started." Russell had "no solution of my own to bring the war to a successful conclusion without considerable escalation."[76] He predicted that the President's speech would not lead to a "fruitful conference" with the North Vietnamese—a prediction Senator Thurmond modified by warning that another kind of peace talks might well be in the offing. During the Korean War negotiations, Thurmond recalled, the United States lost almost as many men in combat as had been lost before negotiations began.[77]

The character of President Johnson's support in the Senate did not embolden him to stand his ground at the twentieth parallel. He may have regretted taking Under Secretary of State Katzenbach's advice to delete any mention of the twentieth parallel in the March 31 speech, but once challenged by Fulbright, the President immediately retreated to the nineteenth parallel. Thanh Hoa and the top third of the panhandle joined the sanctuary that then protected all North Vietnam except a narrow strip less than 50 miles wide stretching from Vinh south 150 miles to the Demilitarized Zone.

A virtue of retreating to the nineteenth parallel was that it eliminated a possible source of friction between the Air Force and the Navy over bombing responsibilities. The eighteenth parallel evenly divided the new target area and was also near the boundary between long-established route packages. The Air Force's Route Package One lay between the eighteenth parallel and the Demilitarized Zone (at the seventeenth parallel), while to the north, the Navy's Route Package Two and part of Route Package Three were between the eighteenth and nineteenth parallels.

Into this relatively small area, the Air Force and Navy poured all the firepower they had formerly spread throughout North Vietnam. Some proponents of the bombing cutback liked to present this compression as a very dramatic improvement in the effectiveness of interdiction.* Secretary of Defense Clifford had become a firm supporter of the cutback, especially once the North Vietnamese had agreed to talk. His subordinates in the military were presented with a familiar dilemma: having argued against the cutback, should they now go along with their boss in looking for its bright side. As usual much of the military leadership decided that the new bombing policy had a lot of merit, especially in comparison with no bombing at all.

The Chairman of the Joint Chiefs, General Wheeler, told President Johnson on April 9 that the United States had lost nothing by ceasing to bomb in the Hanoi-Haiphong region, but that there was a need to bomb Thanh Hoa—that is, return to the twentieth parallel. Given the cloudy weather that had not yet broken over the Red River Delta, relatively little bombing could be done there for a few weeks, though conditions over Thanh Hoa were not much better. It was certainly true that Thanh Hoa was increasing daily in importance as a supply storage and transportation center. After all, it was the southernmost city in North Vietnam no longer subject to bombing, and the North Vietnamese were quick to take advantage of that fact. Wheeler may well have guessed (probably correctly) that the President would be more likely to return to the twentieth parallel than to bomb the Red River Delta. In the old game of gradualism, the objective was always the next little bit.[78]

Secretary of Defense Clifford attempted to stave off efforts to return to the twentieth at first by downplaying enemy truck traffic through the North

---

* This argument was also apparently made by Premier Zhou Enlai of China to censure North Vietnam's acceptance of peace talks in exchange for a bombing cutback. On 29 June 1968 in Beijing, Zhou reportedly said to Pham Hung: "In reality, recently, bombing has become fiercer, concentrated on a smaller area, thus causing you more obstacles for your assistance to the South. That you accepted their partial bombing, and agreed to talk with them has bettered their present position compared with the one they were in in 1966 or 1967. Though you still maintain your principles in negotiation, you have reduced the amount of their difficulties in this election year. It is the fault of the Soviets." See Odd Arne Westad, Chen Jian, Stein Tonnesson, Nguyen Vu Tung, and James G. Hershberg, ed., "77 Conversations Between Chinese and Foreign Leaders on the Wars in Indochina, 1964-1977," Woodrow Wilson International Center for Scholars, Cold War International History Project, Working Paper No. 22, May 1998, p 138.

Vietnamese and Laotian panhandles. When the *New York Times* quoted him as saying that he was "not aware of any increase in infiltration," Clifford felt obliged to draft a letter explaining to the President that this "reprehensible" reporting was a willful misunderstanding of the way the Secretary of Defense and the Secretary of State had decided to handle this question. Clifford and Rusk were merely saying that there had been an increase starting before Johnson's March 31 speech and that the increased flow had continued. "We are not taking the position that there has been any specific increase since March 31 because that increases the burden on the President for restricting the bombing as of that date."[79]

Wheeler's argument in favor of bombing Thanh Hoa was strengthened in May when the communists launched a second offensive in South Vietnam. Although this offensive was much smaller than the Tet offensive and focused mostly on Saigon, the Johnson administration worried that something bigger was coming from the North Vietnamese forces in and near the I Corps region of northern South Vietnam. At the outset of the second offensive on May 4, Secretary of State Rusk said that he was willing to bomb Thanh Hoa. Clifford argued that they should save Thanh Hoa for a major offensive that might come much later in the negotiating process. The President was not ready to return to the twentieth parallel, but Clifford's influence with him was crumbling. When Clifford asserted that the May offensive was merely a reaction to the administration victory in getting the North Vietnamese to accept Paris as the negotiating site rather than Warsaw, the President curtly remarked that the North Vietnamese really preferred Paris.[80]

Attacks on Saigon prompted Ambassador Bunker to recommend that one of the conditions for a bombing halt over North Vietnam should be an end to communist assaults on South Vietnamese cities. In Bunker's view such restraint fell within the meaning of President Johnson's San Antonio formula—that the communists not "take advantage" of a bombing halt. When passing along Bunker's views to Johnson, Rusk suggested that the time had come to move beyond the narrow Clifford interpretation of the San Antonio formula, which permitted the North Vietnamese to do anything but increase their rate of infiltration (a rate that had tripled since the President's San Antonio speech in September).[81]

Toward the end of May the President seemed ready to bomb north of the nineteenth parallel. He was much affected by Wheeler's argument that the MiG base at Bai Thuong (about twenty miles west of Thanh Hoa) posed a danger not only to Navy pilots operating near Vinh, but also to American forces in South Vietnam. The Chairman stressed that the North Vietnamese were using their sanctuary, that MiGs and Il–28s were busy training—possibly for an attack on the American air base at Da Nang. Wheeler's proposal to bomb Thanh Hoa and Bai Thuong gained in attractiveness when contrasted with his other proposal of late May to send B–52s against communist forces and supplies in Cambodia. Upon hearing Wheeler's Cambodian initiative, the President declared that he was ready to send the fighter-bombers back to the twentieth parallel and instructed Rusk and Clifford to figure out how to do it quietly. This quiet bombing escalation apparently eluded the Secretaries of State and Defense, if indeed they bothered to look for it. Never again would President Johnson order fighter-bombers north of the nineteenth parallel.[82]

*   *   *

Left with a smaller field of action, Seventh Air Force tried to make the best of it. Chasing trucks in Route Package One was at least less dangerous than bombing targets in the Red River Delta, and the North Vietnamese did less than expected to change that situation in the summer of 1968. They did nearly double their antiaircraft guns in the panhandle to perhaps twenty-six hundred, but most of their surface-to-air missile batteries remained near Hanoi and Haiphong—with only four or five active sites near the nineteenth parallel. There was no effort in 1968 (as there had been in 1967) to install missiles near the Demilitarized Zone. Hence the Navy bore the brunt of the remaining SAM threat as well as the MiG threat.[83]

The Air Force had only to worry about antiaircraft artillery, which was less deadly when divorced from SAMs and MiGs. Nevertheless, Route Package One boasted more guns than Route Packages Two and Three, and the Air Force lost fifty-two aircraft there in the remaining six months of Rolling Thunder; fifty-six of the men were not rescued, of whom only eleven came home at the end of the war. These losses were slightly more severe than Navy losses in Route Packages Two and Three, but much less severe than the two services had experienced in Route Package Six (the Hanoi-Haiphong region). In some months, Route Package Six losses had exceeded twenty per thousand sorties, while the rate stayed below two per thousand in Route Package One.[84]

The North Vietnamese panhandle was, nevertheless, a much more deadly place for pilots than the Laotian panhandle. In Laos the Air Force was beginning to have some success finding and strafing trucks with guns mounted on a relatively slow, propeller-driven transport aircraft (a Lockheed C–130 Hercules), but such a fixed-wing gunship could not survive in the North Vietnamese panhandle. Nor could forward air controllers (FACs) use their customary light propeller-driven aircraft to look for targets and call in fighter-bombers. Instead the FACs flew in two-seat F–100F jets. They were fortunate indeed to see a truck in daylight from forty-five hundred feet at four hundred knots, and most North Vietnamese trucks did not take to the road until after dark.[85]

A FAC could see better from the back seat of an F–100F than he could from the back seat of an F–4, and the F–100F could loiter over the panhandle longer. But the old F–100Fs were in short supply as they neared retirement. In the summer of 1968, the Air Force began to supplement the F–100Fs with Da

Nang F–4s for FACs working in Route Package One. The Da Nang F–4s did well enough that subsequently Thailand F–4s would join them in taking the jet FAC concept to Laos, where communist air defenses were improving.

Meanwhile, many F–4 crews were introduced to night interdiction. Only the F–4s of the 497th Tactical Fighter Squadron at Ubon Air Base, Thailand, had specialized in night work over the North Vietnamese panhandle. In the spring of 1968, the Night Owls began to teach night flying to the other squadrons in the 8th Tactical Fighter Wing. Truck traffic on the roads in Route Package One was plentiful enough so that aircrews claimed to see about three thousand trucks a month in May, June, and July; of those sighted, they claimed to have destroyed or damaged about 20 percent. Of course, the same trucks were no doubt sighted repeatedly. No American knew how many were using the roads, let alone how many had actually been destroyed.[86]

Many of the trucks moving south through Route Package One in the summer of 1968 were carrying ammunition and supplies for North Vietnamese units located in and just north of the Demilitarized Zone dividing North from South Vietnam. The North Vietnamese had never had much problem infiltrating forces through the Demilitarized Zone, and perhaps thirty thousand of their soldiers operated in the I Corps region of South Vietnam. Supplying these forces through the zone was much more difficult than infiltrating them. Most trucks with supplies for communist forces in South Vietnam went around the Demilitarized Zone by driving west through the mountain passes into Laos.

Because the arrival of heavy rain in May made truck travel on dirt and gravel roads in Laos difficult, the North Vietnamese emphasized resupply of units in South Vietnam during the dry northeast monsoon of November through April. The southwest monsoon brought rain to the North Vietnamese panhandle as well, but the amount was somewhat less on the lee side of the mountains and the roads were somewhat better. From the North Vietnamese point of view, the major problem with the seasonal character of their resupply system was that the seasons favored American air attack in Laos. When the roads were dry in Laos, there were relatively few clouds overhead to protect the trucks from the planes. The fighter-bombers, however, rarely got such good weather in North Vietnam, because the relatively dry northeast monsoon produced heavy cloud cover along the coast and over the Red River Delta. The best opportunities to bomb Hanoi and Haiphong had occurred during the breaks between the heavy rains of the southwest monsoon when the skies did clear. Hence the American bombing had focused on the Laotian panhandle during the northeast monsoon, but during previous southwest monsoons the American effort had necessarily been divided between North Vietnam's panhandle and the Red River Delta.

Even in the summer of 1967, at the height of bombing in the Red River Delta, more than half of the Air Force's fighter-bombers attacking North Vietnam had bombed the North Vietnamese panhandle. Whenever clouds over the delta did not permit attack, Air Force fighter-bombers had been diverted to Route Package One. Seventh Air Force had frequently argued that this practice produced in Route Package One an overabundance of air power which might better have been used in the Navy route packages farther north. After the bombing cutback in 1968, Seventh Air Force had the resources to double the number of strike sorties sent into Route Package One to more than six thousand a month. While absorbing Air Force sorties that had formerly struck the northern route packages, Route Package One could be bombed without using a high percentage of attacking aircraft for suppression of enemy defenses. Occasionally Seventh Air Force would send a big formation of strike aircraft with escorts into Route Package One, but only to practice the technique in case the President once again permitted them to bomb targets near Hanoi.[87]

Although Seventh Air Force thought of Route Package One primarily in terms of interdiction, the Marines holding outposts just south of the Demilitarized Zone wanted close air support as well. North Vietnamese artillery in and just north of the zone exchanged heavy fire with Marine and South Vietnamese artillery units on hills south of the zone. As in many similar situations over the years, the Air Force thought it could best limit North Vietnamese firepower by interdicting the enemy's supply of ammunition rather than by attacking the guns themselves, which were well protected in their earthworks. A steady pounding from B–52s had not silenced the North Vietnamese guns, and the Air Force would have moved the target areas for the big bombers farther north had not the Johnson administration feared to threaten the Paris talks with any change that might be perceived as escalation of the war. Certainly Seventh Air Force did not want to expend much of its fighter-bomber force on the border guns.[88]

Throughout northern I Corps there was a tug of war in progress between the Air Force and the Marines over control of air power. Seventh Air Force had long controlled aircraft from the Marine air wing in Route Package One, where they contributed about a fifth of the interdiction sorties. Early in 1968 during the massive use of air power to break the siege at Khe Sanh in I Corps, the Seventh Air Force commander, General Momyer, became "single manager" for fixed-wing air operations within South Vietnam, thereby gaining some control over Marine in-country air operations. For the most part, Air Force and Marine officers managed to cooperate reasonably well within complex control structures and under the pressures of interservice rivalry. Seventh Air Force tried to coordinate air operations in I Corps, while interfering as little as possible in the smooth close air support relationships that years of practice had developed between Marine air and ground forces.[89]

During the first week in July 1968, Seventh Air Force joined a major effort to destroy North Vietnamese artillery in and near the Demilitarized Zone, dedicating nearly half its effort in Route Package One to bombing the Cap Mui Lay Sector on the eastern end of the zone. Encompassing the six-mile wide Demilitarized Zone and an adjacent strip about the same width in North

Vietnam, this sector ran from the coast for twenty miles inland. Beneath what had been agricultural villages in the vicinity of Vinh Linh, underground tunnels hid important military supply depots, while (above ground) mobile artillery fired into South Vietnam from more than four hundred prepared positions; these guns were defended from air attack by their own mobility, by antiaircraft guns that moved among an even larger number of positions, and by surface-to-air missiles. For a week the firepower of all four U.S. services made a coordinated attack on the Vinh Linh area. The Marines and Navy carriers each matched Seventh Air Force's tactical air effort, and Strategic Air Command's B–52s dropped a greater tonnage than the tactical aircraft of all three services combined. To eight thousand tons of bombs, Marine and Army artillery and Navy ship guns added more than forty thousand rounds (about two thousand tons). While a smaller total than expended by a similar operation covering a broader region along the Demilitarized Zone for six weeks in the fall of 1967, the effort in 1968 was much more intense.[90]

The bombardment went on around the clock all week at the rate of a ton of explosive a minute. Artillery spotters and forward air controllers were even able to fly their light planes into the sector (without much concern for enemy fire, but with great concern for friendly fire). While the joint headquarters for the operation claimed destruction of nearly two hundred field artillery positions and nearly eight hundred antiaircraft artillery positions, the Air Force estimate of destruction was much more modest: about a hundred field artillery positions and three hundred antiaircraft positions. Seventh Air Force doubted that most of these positions were occupied when they were struck. Photography could confirm the destruction of only two occupied field artillery positions and eleven occupied antiaircraft positions. The best that could be said with any certainty was that for several weeks after the operation, North Vietnamese artillery fire from that sector was much less frequent.[91]

Although B–52s continued to bomb enemy positions in and near the Demilitarized Zone, Air Force fighter-bombers returned their focus to interdicting truck traffic. The new Army commander in Vietnam, General Abrams, favored interdiction because he feared that the communists were preparing a third offensive that would be bigger than their May offensive and perhaps surpass their Tet offensive. Since their earlier two offensives had depleted their supplies in South Vietnam, the North Vietnamese would have to depart from their normal seasonal supply cycle if they were going to launch a third offensive within South Vietnam in 1968.[92]

As usual during the southwest monsoon, the North Vietnamese had concentrated on sending supplies to units stationed just north of the Demilitarized Zone. But even if they chose to invade across the Demilitarized Zone and abandon their pretense that there were no North Vietnamese soldiers in South Vietnam, the communists would still need to prepare their forces within South Vietnam for the struggle. That meant sending more trucks through Laos in the rainy season, and by early July traffic was growing on roads leading to the Mu Gia and Ban Karai mountain passes along the Laotian border.[93]

Seventh Air Force attempted to block use of mountain passes by closing the roads leading to them. The passes themselves, as well as the roads in Laos, had been heavily bombed by fighter-bombers and B–52s, but were rarely closed for more than a few hours. Early in the war, bombing sometimes blocked a road with a rock slide, but repeated bombing of the same points had turned the rock to gravel, which North Vietnamese road repair crews used to their advantage. Despite this experience in Laos, Seventh Air Force thought that there were places on the North Vietnamese side of the passes where bombing might close roads at least for a few weeks.[94]

The most ardent supporters of road closing (as opposed to truck destruction) were air intelligence officers. Their capability of analyzing aerial photography had not been very helpful in the truck destruction campaign, since trucks moved faster than film could be processed. Photo interpreters did sometimes turn up evidence that a particular area in the jungle was being used as a truck park, but pilots doubted that they were really bombing a target of value to the enemy unless bomb detonations were accompanied by secondary explosions. In the case of an interdiction choke point, the target at least stayed put and (once chosen by intelligence analysts) was fairly easy for pilots to find—especially after they had returned to it daily with more and more bombs.[95]

As trucks moved south from Vinh, they could take either Route 1 through the coastal lowlands or Route 15 into the mountains toward the Mu Gia Pass and Laos, a journey of about seventy-five miles. Trucks bound for the Ban Karai Pass left Route 15 twenty miles north of the Mu Gia Pass and followed Route 101 forty miles south to Route 137, which crossed the mountains into Laos forty miles from the Demilitarized Zone. Under the direction of Brig. Gen. George J. Keegan, Jr., Seventh Air Force's Deputy Chief of Staff for Intelligence, analysts chose one choke point on each of the three North Vietnamese roads connecting Vinh with the mountain passes.[96]

Just north of its intersection with Route 101, Route 15 was a single lane road winding sharply through steep cliffs. From the middle of July this Xom Ve choke point was bombed repeatedly as was a less promising point on Route 101. Neither of these efforts was very successful, though the Xom Ve choke point was thought to be closed almost a third of the time. More satisfactory was a choke point on Route 137 recommended by Col. Frederick I. Brown, Jr., Chief of Intelligence for the 432d Tactical Reconnaissance Wing at Udorn Air Base, Thailand. Route 137 bent around a cliff where a river passed underneath the road and into a limestone cave. Brown had visions of damming the river and flooding the road permanently. That did not happen, but whenever it rained the road was covered with a pool dubbed "Brown's Lake" by aircrews. There was enough rain in late July to keep Route 137 closed two-thirds of the time.[97]

In August, Seventh Air Force added three more choke points to the target list. The six targets were bombed so frequently that they soon looked like former choke points in Laos that had been worn out by bombing. But interdiction bombing in Laos was performed during the dry northeast monsoon. The rainy southwest monsoon proved more conducive to the choke point method, since rain turned worn out choke points into mud. Tropical Storm Rose of mid-August was followed by Tropical Storm Bess and Typhoon Wendy in early September. General Keegan was delighted with what he took to be the result: "A 90 percent reduction of the enemy's net logistic tonnage through-put into Laos was accomplished."[98] Years later Hanoi's official history of the People's Army of Vietnam would acknowledge Seventh Air Force's success helping the rain to cut roads in the panhandle of North Vietnam during the summer of 1968.[99]

General Keegan's confidence that he could measure the amount of truck traffic from North Vietnam to the Laotian panhandle had been increased by the introduction of electronic sensors to detect movement and sound. The sensors were a legacy from former Secretary of Defense McNamara's project to build a barrier against infiltration into South Vietnam. Although "McNamara's Wall" had not been built, parts of the project continued to grow. South of the Demilitarized Zone, Marines strengthened their major positions except for Khe Sanh, from which they had withdrawn after breaking the communist siege. As they had for the first time at Khe Sanh, Marines in northern I Corps used electronic sensors to warn of enemy movement. Neither the Americans nor the South Vietnamese, however, came anywhere near constructing an impenetrable line of fortified positions from the coast to the mountains.[100]

The western, mountainous portion of McNamara's Wall had never been intended to be more than strings of sensors monitored by the Air Force, which would send aircraft to attack when enemy trucks and soldiers were detected. In South Vietnam and Laos, sensors could be planted by ground teams or dropped from the air. By the summer of 1968, Seventh Air Force was also dropping sensors into Route Package One. EC–121 radar surveillance aircraft from Korat Air Base, Thailand, picked up sensor signals and transmitted them to a control center at Nakhon Phanom Air Base on the eastern boundary of Thailand, just across the Mekong River from Laos.[101]

Electronic sensors confirmed aircrew observation that there was much less traffic on the mountain roads between North Vietnam and Laos. This result led General Keegan to write that Seventh Air Force's effort against those roads during the southwest monsoon of 1968 was "one of the most successful interdiction campaigns in modern history."[102] Not everyone agreed. Those who favored truck destruction were embarrassed to find that the Navy claimed to have destroyed or damaged nearly four thousand trucks from July through October 1968, while the Air Force could claim fewer than twelve hundred. This result, however, did not flow simply from Seventh Air Force's dedication of a fifth of its sorties to bombing choke points. Fewer trucks were seen on the roads even in the Navy route packages, and still fewer reached Route Package One.[103]

General Abrams seemed less impressed with either closing mountain roads or truck destruction than with the sharp decline in truck traffic throughout the panhandle. But he may have given airmen more credit for that change than they deserved. As early as August 23, Abrams informed Walt Rostow that air interdiction had been "the primary agent" in reducing trucks detected in the North Vietnamese panhandle from more than 1,000 a day to between 150 and 200 a day.[104] This was misleading. In mid-July truck detections had briefly surged to an unprecedented level, but the daily average for the heavy traffic months of May, June, and July was only about 200 a day. Thereafter, detections fell below 150 a day for most of the next three months, a somewhat steeper decline than had been experienced during the typhoon season a year earlier.[105]

President Johnson was glad to get evidence of an 80-percent decline in the number of trucks detected in North Vietnam (the misleadingly large drop from one thousand to two hundred). He released General Abrams' data to newsmen and also used it in a letter to McGeorge Bundy, Walt Rostow's predecessor as National Security Adviser and subsequently the youngest Wise Man. Bundy, like so many others, was now calling for an unconditional bombing halt (that is, stopping without getting anything in return from the North Vietnamese). Johnson faced a party platform fight on this very issue at the Democratic National Convention, which got underway in Chicago the following Monday, August 26. Although student protesters fought police outside the hall, a badly divided convention did manage to select Vice President Humphrey as their nominee for President, with a platform supporting administration policies.[106]

In August the administration's reluctance to halt the bombing was based at least in part on an expectation that the communists would launch a third offensive. Meanwhile, a lull in the fighting throughout South Vietnam had spurred the *New York Times*, among others, to ask why the President did not reciprocate by halting the bombing. On August 19, the new Commander in Chief, Pacific, Adm. John S. McCain, Jr., warned Washington that while the North Vietnamese were ready to launch a third offensive, they might hold back in hope of encouraging Americans who were advocating a bombing halt. As the level of violence increased for a couple of weeks in late August, including renewed rocket attacks on Saigon, the administration was uncertain whether the third offensive had at last arrived. If it had, it did not amount to much.[107]

*   *   *

Rolling Thunder was a one-term bombing campaign. It had not begun until after President Johnson's reelection in 1964. A few days before the 1968 election, Rolling Thunder came to an end, and its timely demise was almost enough to return the Democrats to the White House.* But prospects for peace and for Hubert Humphrey dimmed considerably on the very first day of the bombing halt, November 1, when President Thieu of South Vietnam told his National Assembly that he was not yet ready to participate in the Paris talks.

Thieu had gained the impression that the Republican candidate, Richard Nixon, was less likely than Humphrey to let South Vietnam come under communist control. During the campaign Humphrey had put enough distance between himself and Johnson to declare that a Humphrey administration would end the bombing of North Vietnam. Nixon's position was more difficult to decipher. He had permitted his party to insert a peace plank in their platform, and he claimed to have a secret plan to end the war. But the President of South Vietnam did not have to rely solely on vague public statements when assessing Nixon's plans.[108]

For months President Thieu had been hearing about Nixon's views from the chairwoman of Republican Women for Nixon, Anna Chennault, China-born widow of Maj. Gen. Claire L. Chennault. Her husband had served in China during World War II as commander first of the American Volunteer Group (the "Flying Tigers") and subsequently of the Fourteenth Air Force. The Chennaults had moved to Taiwan with the government of Chiang Kai-shek in 1949, when China fell under communist control. After General Chennault's death in 1958, Anna Chennault continued to build her connections with anticommunist political leaders not only in Taipei and Washington, but also in Saigon.[109]

Whatever Anna Chennault told Thieu or his ambassador in Washington, Bui Diem, Nixon soon disappointed them all. Less than a week after his election, Nixon's messengers, including Senate minority leader Everett Dirksen, started to call upon Bui Diem with the message that Nixon wanted the Thieu government to participate in the Paris peace talks. Anna Chennault refused to

---

* The election was complicated by the strong third-party candidacy of Governor George Wallace of Alabama and his running mate, General Curtis LeMay (USAF, retired). They pulled nearly ten million votes (out of about seventy million) from the major party candidates in a close election. Theodore H. White's *The Making of the President 1968* (New York, 1969) argued that Wallace would have done better had he not chosen LeMay as a running mate, because Wallace supporters tended to be former enlisted men who disliked generals like LeMay. To bolster this argument, White recalled meeting LeMay in China during World War II: "Meeting Curtis LeMay, as I had in Asia, one could not but instantly respect him then, and later, in retrospect, recognize how great a debt the Republic-in-arms owed to him. But one could not love him; and the men of his command loathed the harsh, unsparing, iron discipline by which he made the United States Air Force the supreme instrument of annihilation it became in the skies over Japan." There were, of course, many enlisted men who recalled their service under LeMay with pride, and there were many voters who liked LeMay's gruff talk about the need at least to threaten harsher bombing of North Vietnam. LeMay's friends thought it was a mistake for a man of his stature to run with a politician known for exploiting racial bigotry. LeMay's thinking about the election seemed uncharacteristically muddled. He distrusted Richard Nixon, but preferred him to Hubert Humphrey. See Thomas M. Coffey, *Iron Eagle* (New York, 1986), p 445.

carry that message. Thieu held out until the end of November before giving into the pressure he was getting from both American political parties. Years of talking in Paris then followed the years of bombing in North Vietnam, while fighting continued in South Vietnam with fewer and fewer American soldiers.[110]

President Johnson and his closest advisers may not have admitted even to themselves that the Paris talks might be permitted to drag on for months, let alone years, without a resumption of the bombing of North Vietnam. They thought that their negotiating posture was based on the President's speech in San Antonio a year earlier, when he had offered a bombing halt in exchange for productive talks. Somehow they accepted, in the end, merely North Vietnam's concession that the South Vietnamese government would be permitted to participate in the talks—no matter how unproductive they might be.

When word of North Vietnam's concession reached Washington in mid-October, Johnson and his advisers were surprised, delighted, and suspicious. They knew that Hanoi was trying to encourage Humphrey's election, and they doubted that the talks would be productive. Secretary of State Rusk suggested that they stop bombing and go along with enlarged, formal talks in Paris until December 1, 1968. If a suitable peace agreement had not begun to emerge by then, they should resume bombing. But Johnson did not commit himself to any time limit. After all, the weather was already turning sour over North Vietnam and would not improve for six months.[111]

The President tried to use both the promise of resuming the bombing and the onset of the northeast monsoon to persuade his military leaders to support a bombing halt. He invited the entire Joint Chiefs of Staff (not just the Chairman as usual) to come to the White House on the afternoon of October 14. When he asked for their views about a bombing halt, the Air Force Chief of Staff, General McConnell, immediately raised the question of a possible resumption of the bombing. Johnson assured him that if more bombing proved necessary they would not merely resume—they would move on to unlimited bombing.[112]

The President and Walt Rostow explained to the Joint Chiefs that unproductive talks were not the only possible reason for resuming the bombing of North Vietnam. The Paris negotiating team of Averell Harriman and Cyrus Vance had told the North Vietnamese repeatedly that any bombing halt rested on two "facts of life": no attacks or infiltration across the Demilitarized Zone and no attacks on South Vietnamese cities. The Joint Chiefs expressed considerable skepticism that the administration would resume bombing under any circumstances, particularly if the North Vietnamese merely stalled in Paris. This sentiment was echoed by Senator Russell, Chairman of the Senate Armed Services Committee, who participated in Johnson's October 14 meeting with the Joint Chiefs. Nevertheless, Russell said that a majority of his committee would probably go along with a bombing halt.[113]

When Harriman and Vance returned to Paris, they insisted that the North Vietnamese agree to meet with South Vietnamese government representatives the day after a bombing halt announcement. The North Vietnamese objected because they wished to avoid public acknowledgement that the bombing halt was anything other than unconditional; late in October, they at last reduced from several weeks to a single week their proposed gap between a bombing halt announcement and a meeting with the South Vietnamese. The whole exchange was pointless since the South Vietnamese were not ready to meet with the North Vietnamese anyway. Meanwhile, President Johnson had two weeks to stew about the criticism he would get from Republicans and other Americans for halting the bombing of North Vietnam on the eve of an election.[114]

Before announcing his bombing halt decision, President Johnson consulted two more generals. General Abrams was summoned all the way from Saigon to tell Johnson that a bombing halt was the right thing to do. Since General Momyer had left Seventh Air Force that summer to take charge of the Tactical Air Command (with headquarters at Langley Air Force Base, Virginia), he did not have to travel so far to see the President. Like McConnell, Momyer wanted to make certain that reconnaissance aircraft would keep flying over North Vietnam. Johnson promised to continue reconnaissance flights and said that the North Vietnamese understood this would be the case. His instructions to Harriman and Vance were to commit the United States to cease only "acts of force" against North Vietnam rather than "acts of war." In the State Department's view, reconnaissance was an act of war, but not an act of force.[115]

The President kept his word to Momyer about reconnaissance, but Johnson also confirmed the foresight of those who doubted that he would resume the bombing of North Vietnam. Even after the South Vietnamese government agreed in late November to join the talks, nearly two months were spent arguing about the shape of the negotiating table. The communists wanted a four-sided table to proclaim that North Vietnam and the National Liberation Front of South Vietnam were separate negotiating parties. The South Vietnamese government preferred a two-sided table, with the communists together on one side. Four days before the inauguration of Richard Nixon, the negotiators agreed on a round table. Whether to resume the bombing of North Vietnam was a question that then passed quietly to the man who said he had a secret plan for peace in Vietnam.

Chapter Six

Protective Reaction

The American bombing halt in North Vietnam encouraged people in both countries to believe that the long war was nearly over. Only gradually did they realize that the war had merely entered a new phase. Having suffered heavy losses in the Tet offensive of 1968, communist forces in South Vietnam were much less aggressive for the next three years. They could bide their time and rebuild their strength while the United States slowly withdrew its forces. In exchange for disengaging, the United States asked nothing at the negotiating table in Paris and received nothing.

Meanwhile, the United States tried to build a South Vietnamese army that, with the assistance of American air power, would be capable of stopping a communist offensive. Although South Vietnam's air force was increasingly able to provide close air support for its army, a resumption of full-scale bombing in North Vietnam could be undertaken only by the United States. Whether bombs would again fall on North Vietnam was a question to be pondered not only in Washington, but also, of course, in Hanoi.

When the bombing ceased north of the nineteenth parallel in April 1968, the North Vietnamese quickly began to restore their battered transportation system. In three months, the Paul Doumer Bridge over the Red River at Hanoi was carrying rail traffic once again. Hundreds of smaller bridges were rebuilt, and locomotives pulled trains in daylight as far south as Thanh Hoa. After bombing ended throughout North Vietnam in November, the railroad was reopened between Thanh Hoa and Vinh. Thousands of boats operated free of harassment along the coast and on the rivers, and thousands of trucks moved rapidly on sunlit roads free of bomb craters. The road network grew especially in the southern panhandle, so that trucks could delay crossing into Laos (where bombs continued to fall) until they were just north of the Demilitarized Zone. An oil pipeline, which had begun to appear in July 1968 while the bombs were still falling, extended steadily southwest from Vinh through the Mu Gia Pass into Laos. A second pipeline was then built from Quang Khe (a port about ninety miles south of Vinh) passing into Laos just north of the Demilitarized Zone. If bombing resumed, these oil pipelines would be even harder to hit in daylight than trucks had been at night, and trucks would be free to carry other supplies.[1]

The rapidity with which the transportation system was rejuvenated contrasted with the leisurely pace of reconstruction elsewhere. Neither the North Vietnamese nor their allies were eager to provide new targets for American bombers. In the case of the Chinese, this reluctance was reinforced by a new coolness in their relations with North Vietnam. China had opposed the Paris negotiations, and the Central Intelligence Agency received reports that a Chinese offer of combat troops had been spurned by North Vietnam. Indeed, many of the more than one hundred thousand Chinese in North Vietnam had gone home. In the absence of American bombing, they were no longer needed to work on North Vietnam's railroads or man its antiaircraft artillery. The Chinese also left behind the ruins of their major industrial project in North Vietnam, the ironworks at Thai Nguyen. North Vietnam postponed plans to open a steel mill there indefinitely and did not even attempt to resume production of pig iron.[2]

That the failure to rebuild Thai Nguyen was not merely the result of worsening relations with China could be seen by looking at other industrial projects sponsored by the Soviet Union and its East European allies. Before Rolling Thunder, Hanoi and Haiphong had been served by several coal-burning electric powerplants tied together in a grid. American bombs destroyed the grid's control switch and left the plants operating at less than a third of their former capacity. The North Vietnamese had turned to hundreds of small diesel generators imported during the bombing, and (even in the absence of bombing) the bigger plants only slowly and partially recovered. The North Vietnamese tried to hide restoration of productive capacity by replacing bombed smoke stacks with underground flue systems. Meanwhile, the control switch at Dong Anh was not repaired, and construction progressed slowly on the Soviet hydroelectric project on the Red River at Lang Chi, sixty-five miles northwest of Hanoi. Completing this project would provide more electricity than all the old coal powerplants combined. American intelligence estimated that the Soviets and North Vietnamese could rush Lang Chi into production within nine months, but they took three years.[3]

The citizens of North Vietnam were considerably less cautious than their leaders. The government's preference for dispersed population and industry could not long keep former residents of Hanoi away from their homes when bombs no longer fell on the Red River Delta. In any case, throughout the war very few bombs had fallen on Hanoi itself, one of the safest places in Vietnam. Although more than half a million people had left the city during the bombing, within three years Hanoi exceeded its prewar population of about a million. So quickly did they return, that their number often outran the government's ability to feed them, and a black market grew to fill the need. In Hanoi as elsewhere, the passage of time dissipated euphoric expectations that the bombing halt would soon be followed by the end of the war.[4]

Hanoi's problems were exacerbated in August and September 1968 by typhoons that drowned the new rice crop and severely damaged the city. Unlike American bombers, the typhoons made no effort to avoid Hanoi. On September 9, falling trees brought down power lines and cut off electricity for several days. The city authorities responded to this emergency with remarkable sluggishness. Many cranes, tractors, and trucks sat idle while too few rescue workers made slow progress. One British observer noticed a victim pinned under a tree for six hours and wondered how well the city would have handled an air raid.[5]

In Washington, the Johnson administration was pleased to end its management of the war by having nature do work that the political climate no longer permitted bombers to do. Although not focused on particular targets, typhoon damage was widespread in North Vietnam. With his usual enthusiasm, Walt Rostow informed the President that the recent typhoons had probably done more damage than six months of bombing.[6]

*   *   *

For a year and a half after the bombing halt of November 1968, the United States limited its air attacks on North Vietnam to retaliation against air defense sites that fired upon American aircraft. At the peak of Rolling Thunder in 1967, the United States had sent more than a hundred thousand attack sorties to strike North Vietnam (not counting nearly as many escort, reconnaissance, and refueling sorties). In 1969, there were about five thousand reconnaissance sorties there, supported by more than fifteen thousand fighter sorties. While contributing about 60 percent of the reconnaissance sorties, the Air Force provided fewer fighter escorts than did the Navy.[7]

The first reconnaissance planes to venture over North Vietnam after the bombing halt flew without escorts. Fourteen sorties in four days penetrated the panhandle before the North Vietnamese reacted. On the night of November 7, 1968, a Navy RA–3B was fired upon in Route Package Three. Although President Johnson thereafter permitted fighter escorts, the North Vietnamese continued to shoot. On the afternoon of November 23, an Air Force RF–4C was hit by gunfire at about three thousand feet while attempting to photograph a surface-to-air missile site northwest of Dong Hoi. The crew of the escort fighter could not see parachutes, but Capt. Mark J. Ruhling, the navigator of the downed plane, soon contacted them on his radio and told them that he was surrounded by enemy forces. Ruhling spent the rest of the war as a prisoner, and his pilot, Capt. Bradley G. Cuthbert, was presumed dead.[8]

Only two days later, another pair of Air Force planes ran into antiaircraft fire near Dong Hoi while photographing a road from a thousand feet. This time the escort fighter went down. Once again radio contact was made with the crew,

Maj. Joseph C. Morrison and First Lt. San D. Francisco, but neither would come home at the end of the war. Although Navy reconnaissance aircraft were each escorted by two fighters (rather than the single escort at first used by the Air Force), the Navy lost an RF–4C near Vinh, also on November 25. That added up to three losses in only two days. In retaliation, American fighter planes bombed the responsible antiaircraft sites. When Secretary of Defense Clifford reported these developments at a National Security Council meeting, he complained that it would be tragic if the reconnaissance problem was allowed to derail negotiations with the North Vietnamese in Paris. But the Chairman of the Joint Chiefs, General Wheeler, urged that reconnaissance of North Vietnam was essential to the security of American forces just south of the Demilitarized Zone in South Vietnam.[9]

President Johnson kept the reconnaissance program he had established. American planes could retaliate when fired upon, but he did not choose to make North Vietnamese attacks on American reconnaissance a reason for resuming the bombing of North Vietnam. His emissaries did complain to the Soviet ambassador in Washington and to the North Vietnamese in Paris. Although the United States lost another plane in December (an Air Force RF–4 whose crew was rescued), that would be the last loss for more than a year. The North Vietnamese apparently decided not to press their luck, and thenceforth their gunners rarely fired at American reconnaissance planes or their escorts.[10]

Contributing to Hanoi's caution may have been concern about the new Republican administration that took charge in Washington at the end of January 1969. President Richard Nixon was reputed to be one of America's most ardent foes of communism. He had first achieved national prominence in 1948 when, as a young congressman from California, he played a leading role in the investigation of Alger Hiss, president of the Carnegie Endowment for International Peace and former State Department official. Nixon's persistent effort to prove that Hiss was a communist spy was the beginning of an enduring estrangement from liberals, including many reporters. Their hatred of Nixon grew during his harsh, successful run for the Senate against Helen Gahagan Douglas.[11]

Despite his anticommunist rhetoric, Nixon had avoided being too closely identified with the right wing of the Republican party. In the presidential race of 1952, when the party had to choose between Senator Robert A. Taft (the very conservative son of former President William Howard Taft) and General Dwight D. Eisenhower, Nixon cast his lot with the more moderate and more popular Eisenhower. It was a shrewd decision. Nixon had just turned forty when he became Vice President.

During his eight years under Eisenhower, Nixon traveled the world. Once again his anticommunist speeches were better publicized than his increasingly sophisticated view of the world's complexities. In the fall of 1953, he spent two months touring an Asia where the United States and communist China had only recently agreed to a cease-fire in Korea and were shifting their attention to

Indochina. When Nixon's plane touched down at Hanoi, Ho Chi Minh's communist forces controlled the hills around the Red River Delta. After spending the night with the French Commissioner General, Nixon flew on a French transport to a village on the edge of the delta. There he watched an artillery barrage and dined on *boeuf bourguignon* served with wine. He was offended by the haughty attitude of the French toward their Vietnamese soldiers, and he insisted on visiting the Vietnamese mess and giving them the same pep talk he had given the French.[12]

A few months later when the French were losing the decisive battle at Dien Bien Phu, Nixon told the American Society of Newspaper Editors meeting in Washington that he would favor sending American troops to Indochina if that was the only way to save it from a communist takeover.[13] His failure to succeed Eisenhower in 1961, however, left it to Democrats to send American divisions to Vietnam. When Nixon became President in 1969, the country clearly expected him to bring the troops home.

Yet Nixon had managed to avoid saying how he would end the war. His secret plan echoed Eisenhower's equally vague promise of 1952 to end the Korean War. In recent years Eisenhower had made no secret of the fact that he had threatened China with nuclear destruction. He told the press in early 1968 that nuclear weapons should not be ruled out in Vietnam, and he urged President Johnson to prosecute the conventional air war against North Vietnam more vigorously. When Nixon took office in January 1969, Eisenhower was in failing health and died two months later—before he could witness the unfolding of Nixon's stratagems for ending the war in Vietnam.[14]

Far from threatening China with nuclear weapons, Nixon envisioned a normalization of relations with that country. In a 1967 article in *Foreign Affairs*, he had proposed that in the long run the United States should try to pull China "back into the world community."[15] He warned that it would be a mistake to enter into an alliance with the Soviet Union against China, for that would divide the world by race. During the first year of his presidency, he had a chance to take his own advice when the Soviet Union secretly proposed that Soviet and American nuclear forces join in attacking Chinese nuclear plants. Instead of taking sides, Nixon began to play one side against the other and managed to improve American relations with both. Ultimately, this change in the international climate would enable the United States to bomb North Vietnam without any risk of a reaction from China or the Soviet Union.[16]

Meanwhile, Nixon wanted to find some way to threaten North Vietnam without stirring up discontent in the United States. After his election, even university students were relatively quiet about the war while they waited to see what Nixon would do. Liberal journalists were reassured by Nixon's selection of Henry Kissinger to be his National Security Adviser. David Kraslow and Stuart H. Loory of the *Los Angeles Times* had recently published *The Secret Search for Peace in Vietnam*, which included a description of the Harvard professor's role in negotiating with North Vietnam through French intermediaries during the summer of 1967.[17]

Nixon met Kissinger in December 1967 at Claire Boothe Luce's Christmas party. Although Kissinger was then serving as foreign policy adviser for New York Governor Nelson Rockefeller, a liberal rival for the Republican nomination, Nixon made a point of recalling that he had sent a letter praising Kissinger's first book ten years earlier. Indeed, *Nuclear Weapons and Foreign Policy* had apparently persuaded Nixon that he and Kissinger thought alike. It had also turned an obscure young instructor (denied tenure by the government department at Harvard) into a celebrated strategist whose wisdom was prized in Washington as well as Cambridge.[18]

The book responded to worries about the strategy of massive retaliation, which sought to deter communist expansion by threatening all-out nuclear attack on the Soviet Union. Kissinger agreed with those who claimed that such threats were not credible, but he offered an alternative to the great expense of matching Soviet strength in conventional forces. Kissinger advocated reliance on tactical nuclear weapons that he thought would deter or, if necessary, win wars without escalation to strategic nuclear weapons. In Kissinger's view, a limited war might also be a war fought with tactical nuclear weapons.[19]

Nuclear Weapons and Foreign Policy won Kissinger more friends among politicians and civilian defense thinkers than among military officers. They mistrusted the work of civilian strategists in general, and Kissinger tied his strategic thinking to a proposal for reorganizing the Department of Defense. He wanted to replace the services with a strategic force (commanded by an air officer) and a tactical force (commanded by a ground officer). "It may well be," Kissinger wrote, "that the separation of the Army and the Air Force in 1948 [*sic*] occurred two decades too late and at the precise moment when the distinction between ground and air strategy was becoming obsolescent."[20] It would have been better, he thought, to "mix the two organizations more thoroughly."[21]

A Jewish refugee from Hitler's Germany, Kissinger knew a lot about European politics and history, but much less about Asia. In 1965 he was invited to visit South Vietnam by the American ambassador, Henry Cabot Lodge. During this and subsequent visits, Kissinger grew skeptical about prospects for an American military triumph. On the other hand, he believed that the United States had committed too much of its resources and prestige to abandon South Vietnam. He hoped that a way out might be found through negotiations.[22]

Kissinger's role in secret negotiations with the North Vietnamese during the summer of 1967 strengthened his connections with the Johnson administration. When open negotiations began in Paris the next year, Kissinger maintained his contacts there and at the State Department. The Johnson administration's negotiating team would have been disturbed to learn that Kissinger was passing information acquired in this way to the Republican presidential candidate. While not giving Nixon details of the negotiations, Kissinger did warn him during the campaign that a bombing halt might be near.[23]

Shortly after President Johnson stopped the bombing of North Vietnam, Kissinger submitted an article entitled "The Viet Nam Negotiations" to *Foreign Affairs*, which published it in the wake of Nixon's announcement that Kissinger would be his National Security Adviser. It was, consequently, an article thoroughly and widely scrutinized for clues to the new administration's policy. While making no criticism of President Johnson for halting the bombing, Kissinger stated that Hanoi should have "little doubt that the bombing halt would not survive if it disregarded the points publically [*sic*] stated by Secretary Rusk and President Johnson," that is, if North Vietnam violated the Demilitarized Zone or attacked South Vietnamese cities.[24]

Kissinger did criticize the Johnson administration for insisting on Saigon's participation in the Paris talks. While he thought that the shape of South Vietnam's government should ultimately be a matter for the Vietnamese to work out on their own, the "mutual withdrawal" of American and North Vietnamese forces could best be discussed by those two countries independently. The growing hostility in relations between the Soviet Union and China should somehow impel North Vietnam to seek a settlement with the United States. However, if the North Vietnamese refused to withdraw, then "we should seek to achieve as many of our objectives as possible unilaterally" by avoiding American casualties, strengthening the South Vietnamese army, and withdrawing at least part of our forces.[25] This would prove to be the fatal weakness of the Nixon administration's policy: the North Vietnamese had no incentive to withdraw so long as they thought that the Americans were going to withdraw unilaterally.

While scattering reassuring words in several directions, the Kissinger article fell far short of delivering a plan for peace in Vietnam, and Nixon's "secret plan" remained secret. Indeed, a major attribute of administration plans and decisions on Vietnam would be extreme secrecy that would permit participation to spread as little beyond Nixon and Kissinger as possible. Nixon distrusted the bureaucracy's ability to keep secrets and its loyalty to him. Even the Secretary of State, the Secretary of Defense, and the Director of Central Intelligence would often be left in the dark. Director Helms was a holdover from the Johnson administration retained largely at Kissinger's insistence. William P. Rogers, the new Secretary of State, had been Attorney General in the Eisenhower administration and knew little about foreign affairs. His appointment proclaimed Nixon's intention to be his own Secretary of State. For Secretary of Defense, Nixon had wanted Senator Henry M. Jackson (Democrat, Washington), who could be counted on to help win votes in a Democratic Congress. When Jackson turned the President down, Nixon turned to Congressman Melvin R. Laird (Republican, Wisconsin), longtime member of the House Appropriations Committee.[26]

Laird proved to be the most formidable member of the new cabinet. Nixon and Kissinger could not entirely exclude Laird from their deliberations, because he had many allies in the Congress and in the Republican Party at large. He was a very forceful Secretary of Defense, but better liked by the service chiefs of staff than his immediate predecessors because he paid more heed to military advice. The principal purveyor of that advice to Nixon as well as to Laird might have been the Chairman of the Joint Chiefs, General Wheeler, had it not been for his declining health and Laird's determination that the Secretary of Defense should be the conduit of such advice to the President. Among the service chiefs an increasingly influential role was assumed by Adm. Thomas H. Moorer, the Chief of Naval Operations, who replaced Wheeler as Chairman in 1970.[27]

When General McConnell, the Air Force Chief of Staff, retired in the summer of 1969, he was replaced by his Vice Chief, General Ryan, who had come from Pacific Air Forces the previous summer. Although McConnell had groomed Ryan to take the top job, the two men were very different. While subordinates often encountered a crusty McConnell, he had enjoyed warm relations with many Washington politicians, including President Johnson. Neither Nixon nor Ryan were suited to such cordiality, and Ryan's aloofness may well have lost his service some support on Capitol Hill. But the new Air Force Secretary, Robert C. Seamans, Jr. (an aeronautical engineer from the Massachusetts Institute of Technology), definitely liked the change. After a few months of dealing with a "salty" and inflexible McConnell, Seamans found Ryan to be a refreshing change of pace: "I guess I've never worked with anybody that I respected so much, who was so direct and so open and so pragmatic."[28]

Seamans also liked the man who was already expected to succeed Ryan, Gen. George S. Brown. Formerly General Wheeler's assistant, Brown had moved to Saigon as commander of Seventh Air Force in the summer of 1968. Even before taking over as Chief of Staff, Ryan told Brown that he was next in line.[29] They were both West Point graduates whose careers had got an early boost from World War II. Brown had led a bomber group on the famous raid against the oil refineries at Ploesti, Rumania, in August 1943, and after a little more than a year he became a full colonel when he was only twenty-six. He was still a colonel thirteen years later when he became executive officer for the Chief of Staff, Gen. Thomas H. White. Brown's calm, good-humored diplomacy kept him in the Pentagon as military assistant for two Secretaries of Defense, first Thomas S. Gates and then McNamara. That Brown was able to remain on good terms with both McNamara and White's successor as Chief of Staff, General LeMay, seemed miraculous and eventually led to Brown's selection as Wheeler's assistant and subsequently command of Seventh Air Force.

The transition from General Momyer to General Brown as commander of Seventh Air Force was an even more dramatic change than the Air Staff experienced in going from McConnell to Ryan. Momyer was an authority on tactical air warfare, and he continually involved himself in the details of operations. His intelligence chief, Maj. Gen. George Keegan, would later recall that "Momyer ran every aspect of that war and hardly used his staff."[30] Brown, on the other hand, delegated authority. He had been too tall to become a fighter pilot, and he claimed no special expertise in fighter operations. Handsome and athletic, Brown took time for a daily game of tennis. He told subordinates not to bother him with their problems unless they wanted him to make a decision they could not make. A wing commander who called Brown in the middle of the night to report an enemy rocket attack was quietly told to call back if there was something that Brown could do about the situation.[31]

When Momyer was in Saigon he had found himself in repeated disagreement with the commander of Pacific Air Forces, General Ryan. Brown was more fortunate in this regard, not so much because his diplomatic skills were exceptional or because Ryan had been replaced by Gen. Joseph J. Nazzaro, but mostly because Rolling Thunder came to an end. Without Rolling Thunder, the Commander in Chief, Pacific, and his immediate subordinates in Hawaii (the Commander in Chief, Pacific Air Forces, and the Commander in Chief, Pacific Fleet) lost much of their influence on the prosecution of the war. During Rolling Thunder, the Pacific commander, Admiral Sharp, had reluctantly given General Westmoreland control of air operations in Route Package One of North Vietnam as well as in Laos—to the extent that the American ambassador in Laos permitted military control there. From Brown's point of view, Sharp had thus written his successor (Adm. John S. McCain, Jr.) out of the war. Since the manned tactical reconnaissance mission in North Vietnam continued to be conducted along the old service lines (Air Force in Route Package One and Navy in Route Packages Two and Three), only in the Navy route packages did McCain have much of a role. Unlike Momyer, Brown had to worry about only one military boss, Westmoreland's successor in Saigon, General Abrams.[32]

Brown thought his principal achievement as Seventh Air Force commander was persuading Abrams that at least half the air effort should be expended in Laos. When Brown arrived in the summer of 1968, about 60 percent of the Air Force's attack sorties were going to South Vietnam. Brown thought that many of these could be better used in North Vietnam or Laos. After bombing stopped in North Vietnam, Brown made certain that Laos picked up the extra sorties and not South Vietnam. As Abrams reduced the exposure of American ground forces to combat, he was willing to divert more and more sorties to the interdiction campaign in Laos.[33]

Laos became the sole preoccupation of Air Force crews in Thailand, and their lives became much safer. Aircraft losses dropped from nearly two hundred a year to less than fifty (out of about six hundred U.S. Air Force planes based in Thailand). Thailand crews still ran greater risks, however, than their counterparts in South Vietnam, and there was considerable resentment among the former when it appeared that the Internal Revenue Service might deprive them of their income tax exemption for combat service. In South Vietnam, the income of all American enlisted personnel was exempt from taxation as was the first five thousand dollars of every officer's pay. In Thailand, only aircrews flying over North Vietnam were eligible for this benefit. Since the United States continued to pretend that it had no forces fighting in Laos, the end of bombing in North Vietnam threatened the tax exemption for aircrews in Thailand.[34]

General Brown raised the tax exemption question when he visited President Nixon at the White House in early February 1969. Nixon was concerned that aircrew morale might have been hurt by the bombing halt. Brown assured him that while there was a morale problem, it could be remedied by maintaining the tax exemption. Nixon replied that depriving the Thailand aircrews of their tax break was "ridiculous" and told Kissinger to fix it.[35]

Brown came away from his conversation with Nixon impressed that unlike every other civilian Brown talked to in Washington, the new President said nothing about withdrawing forces from Southeast Asia. In fact, it was Brown who counseled restraint and Nixon who seemed ready to do more. Since the weather would have permitted little bombing of North Vietnam during the past three months even without a bombing halt, Brown was able to say truthfully that the halt had not yet really hurt the American war effort. When the President wondered whether more could be done in South Vietnam, Brown cautioned him against the political repercussions of permitting American casualty rates to rise. Nixon seemed especially eager to curb enemy use of his sanctuary in Cambodia and even told Brown that if Abrams employed "dirty tricks" in Cambodia, the President would stand behind him.[36]

Nixon was perhaps surprised by Brown's caution, since the new President had already heard the Chairman of the Joint Chiefs voice his support for bombing North Vietnam. In his first meeting with the new President on January 30, Wheeler had argued for bombing and Secretary Laird had argued against. The rest of the Joint Chiefs soon made plain their agreement with Wheeler that resuming the bombing of North Vietnam and mining Haiphong harbor could bring the war to a favorable conclusion. But their opinion reached the President together with the dissenting views of the Office of the Secretary of Defense and the Central Intelligence Agency—both of which thought that North Vietnam would not be intimidated and would be able to import whatever it needed across the Chinese border under any bombing campaign. The replay of this old argument together with many others was staged by Henry Kissinger, who persuaded Nixon to send the bureaucracy a long list of questions about the war. Many of these questions were prepared by Daniel Ellsberg of the RAND Corporation, who had been working on a history of the war for the Office of the Secretary of Defense.[37]

The list of twenty-eight major and fifty subsidiary questions was ready when Nixon was inaugurated, and on his first full day in office he sent them out over his signature as National Security Study Memorandum 1. Kissinger, in this way, made clear at the outset that his potential rivals throughout the government not only still disagreed about the war, but disagreed according to a pattern established during the Johnson administration. The most positive view of the ability of American military force to gain a favorable outcome in the war came from the military and Ambassador Bunker. By contrast, the Office of the Secretary of Defense, the Central Intelligence Agency, and the State Department took a much more skeptical stance.[38]

The familiarity of the bureaucracy's responses could be partly attributed to the fact that the new administration had yet to fill many appointed positions with its own people. But those responses did indicate a continuity in thinking about the war within segments of the two administrations. This continuity was most striking in the Office of the Secretary of Defense. While the Joint Chiefs of Staff found the new secretary to be a more congenial boss than McNamara or Clifford, Laird was determined to get American forces out of Vietnam. He hoped to do this by turning the fighting over to South Vietnamese forces.[39]

Before Laird could convince President Nixon to begin a unilateral withdrawal, the communists launched a light offensive in South Vietnam. On February 23, 1969, just as Nixon was beginning a tour of the Europe, they began to fire rockets into Saigon and other cities. But those cities were spared ground attacks, while communist ground forces assaulted targets only in remote areas. Although sporadic rocket attacks continued through March, this offensive was barely worthy of the name. It did demonstrate, however, that President Nixon was not going to enforce the understandings upon which President Johnson's bombing halt was supposed to have depended.

President Johnson had publicly implied that the United States would resume bombing North Vietnam if communist forces violated the Demilitarized Zone or attacked South Vietnam's cities. The Johnson and Nixon administrations had chosen not to react in that way against North Vietnam's continued infiltration of troops and supplies through the Demilitarized Zone. Rocket attacks on Saigon could not be ignored, however, since they were given ample coverage in the press. When Nixon was asked by a reporter on March 4 whether the communists in Vietnam were testing the new administration, Nixon admitted that the rocket attacks might be "technically" a violation of the October 1968 understandings. But he was still considering whether the violation was "so significant" that it would require a response.[40]

Another reporter then asked if a resumption of bombing might be an appropriate response? Nixon replied that there were "several contingency plans" but that he would not threaten North Vietnam with mere words. He did not, of course, reveal any of those plans, which included mining Haiphong and bombing targets in the vicinity. He told the press that he preferred to let his deeds speak for themselves: "I will only indicate that we will not tolerate a continuation of this kind of attack without some response that will be appropriate."[41]

The President's only public response was sending Defense Secretary Laird and General Wheeler to visit South Vietnam. Although General Abrams urged a return to bombing up to the nineteenth parallel, Secretary Laird found that the communist rocket attacks were not sufficiently significant to warrant bombing North Vietnam. General Wheeler agreed the enemy's offensive was weak, but thought an American failure to respond would confirm North Vietnam's claim that the bombing halt had been unconditional. The Chairman's position on this issue had little or no chance of overcoming administration reluctance to endure the political uproar sure to follow renewed bombing.[42]

The Seventh Air Force commander offered a related reason not to bomb. In General Brown's view, the North Vietnamese might be trying to spur the United States to bomb and thereby revive the antiwar movement. Brown sent General Abrams a memorandum suggesting alternative courses of action said to be less politically incendiary: "neutralize" enemy base areas near South Vietnam's borders in Cambodia and Laos; mine Haiphong harbor; blockade the Cambodian port of Sihanoukville. Brown's options seemed likely to produce much more domestic furor than he indicated, but (as Brown knew) Abrams and President Nixon were already strongly interested in eliminating the border sanctuaries.[43]

Shortly after Brown had met with Nixon in early February, Abrams had asked permission to send B–52s against the Cambodian sanctuaries. Of all the ideas that came to the new President about Vietnam during the early weeks of his administration, Nixon liked this one the best. Since the beginning of the year, he had been talking with Kissinger about the enemy buildup in Cambodia. The B–52 proposal offered a way to retaliate against North Vietnam without arousing the war's critics in the United States—if the B–52 strikes could be kept secret from them. Secrecy seemed possible, because North Vietnam denied that it had forces in Cambodia and thus would not be apt to complain about their being bombed; in this respect the situation in Cambodia was very much like the one that had long been characteristic of Laos. With Nixon's approval, the Strategic Air Command's big B–52 bombers commenced a year of covert bombing just over the Cambodian border.[44]

So began a cancer that would destroy the Nixon presidency and eat away at the integrity of the Air Force. The Cambodian bombing was so secret that the military's normal classified reports were not trusted to protect it. Instead, those reports were filled with false information about B–52 bombing in South Vietnam. Air Force officers began to lie for the President, and the lies did not stop when, a few weeks into the bombing, the *New York Times* exposed it.[45] Indeed, that very exposure caused Nixon and Kissinger to authorize wiretaps on their subordinates in hope of identifying those who were leaking to the press.[46]

Although the Secretary of Defense had favored bombing in Cambodia, he was distrusted in the White House—as was his military assistant, Air Force Colonel Robert E. Pursley, who had served in the same capacity under Secretaries McNamara and Clifford. Consequently, the Federal Bureau of Investigation tapped Pursley's telephones, but the wiretaps turned up nothing damaging to Pursley or to his boss, who continued to provide Nixon and Kissinger with sometimes unwelcome advice for the next three years.[47]

Nixon's suspicion of Laird did not inhibit the President from embracing the Secretary's efforts to put a better face on the administration's actions. Some of Laird's descriptive phrases were adopted by the administration and the press. Nixon saw merit in using Laird's "Vietnamization" in preference to "De-Americanization" as way of describing and rationalizing withdrawal of American forces from Vietnam. Another of Laird's useful phrases, "protective reaction," was coined during his first visit to Vietnam. The *New York Times* reported that a hundred U.S. marines had occupied a few hills in Laos for a week. When asked whether this was an escalation of the American war effort, Laird refused to confirm the story, but said that American commanders had long had authority to take actions necessary to protect their troops. In the months and years to come, his phrase "protective reaction" would provide an all-purpose label for a wide range of military activities, including American air strikes retaliating against air defense sites in North Vietnam.[48]

*   *   *

Except for the secret bombing of Cambodia, President Nixon had trouble finding a way to intimidate North Vietnam without arousing American critics of the war. During his first year in office, his threats remained empty, and most of his actions revealed the weakness of his position. After his initial decision not to resume the bombing of North Vietnam, Nixon's next opportunity to display greater toughness came in April 1969 when a Navy EC–121 radio intercept plane was shot down off the coast of North Korea and all thirty-one crew members were lost. Arguing that this incident would be seen as a test of the administration's resolve not merely in Pyongyang, but also in Moscow, Beijing, and Hanoi, Kissinger supported a retaliatory strike against a North Korean airfield. Secretary of Defense Laird urged restraint and, on his own, canceled all American reconnaissance flights, not only near North Korea, but also near China, the Soviet Union, the Mediterranean, and Cuba. Although Nixon was furious with Laird, the President decided not to risk a war with North Korea. Nixon would later say that he told Kissinger: "They got away with it this time, but they'll never get away with it again."[49]

Knowing that withdrawal of American forces would undercut any influence he might yet have on North Vietnam, Nixon did not announce removal of the first twenty-five thousand troops until June 1969. The long-awaited beginning of Vietnamization helped to quiet protests in the United States against American search and destroy tactics, which had led in May to the bloody battle of Hamburger Hill. At Ap Bia near the Laotian border, the North Vietnamese had not melted away into the jungle as usual but had chosen to stand and fight. In repeated assaults on the hill, more than fifty Americans were killed. After taking the hill, American troops then abandoned it, for their objective there and elsewhere had not been gaining positions, but killing the enemy. Although enemy losses were thought to be much greater than American and South Vietnamese losses, American public opinion had turned against expending American lives in this way.[50]

Less than a month before his first troop cutback announcement, Nixon had gone on television to propose a cease-fire followed by withdrawal of most American and North Vietnamese troops. Since the United States was beginning to withdraw unilaterally, there was little incentive for North Vietnam to make such an agreement and withdraw its forces. To give Hanoi the necessary incentive, Nixon decided in early July that he would secretly send an ultimatum.

President Nixon's first messenger was Jean Sainteny, a Paris businessman who had served as France's Delegate-General in Hanoi. Nixon's letter to Ho Chi Minh urged peace, but Nixon instructed Sainteny to tell the North Vietnamese that unless there was a negotiating breakthrough by November 1 (the first anniversary of the bombing halt) Nixon would resort to "measures of great consequence and force."[51] Nixon's ultimatum may not actually have accompanied his letter to Ho. North Vietnam denied Sainteny a visa, and he had to give Nixon's letter to Mai Van Bo in Paris. Kissinger, who served as translator for Nixon's conversation with Sainteny, would claim in his memoirs to have known nothing about Nixon's ultimatum for another two weeks. With or without the ultimatum, a few days later the North Vietnamese proposed a secret meeting in Paris between Kissinger and Xuan Thuy, their senior representative at the peace negotiations.[52]

Kissinger began his covert negotiations in Paris under the guise of reporting to the French government on Nixon's late July tour of Asia. The image of weakness conveyed by Nixon's tour may well have carried more weight in Hanoi than his secret ultimatum whenever it arrived, but the President intended his journey to advertise American strength. On July 23, he flew to the carrier *Hornet* in the South Pacific, where he greeted astronauts returning from the first visit to the moon. In an ebullient mood, Nixon told them that "this is the greatest week in the history of the world since the Creation," a remark he later had to explain to the evangelist Billy Graham.[53]

From Hanoi's point of view, Nixon's confession of weakness came during his press conference on Guam. The President proclaimed his determination to avoid being "dragged" into other conflicts like Vietnam. In the future, allies were going to have to fight their own battles short of nuclear war—perhaps with American arms, but not with American soldiers.[54] This "Nixon Doctrine" was warmly received in the United States, but neither that reception nor the doctrine itself could have done anything other than undercut Nixon's threat of harsh action against North Vietnam.

During his visits in Asian capitals, Nixon told his hosts about his determination to take action if negotiations with North Vietnam did not begin to make progress by November 1. Kissinger then presented Nixon's ultimatum directly to the North Vietnamese in Paris during the first week in August.[55] At the end of the month, a letter arrived from Ho Chi Minh rejecting Nixon's proposals and ignoring his ultimatum.[56]

Three days later Ho died at the age of 79. Since his heart had been troubling him for several years, he had already delegated much of his authority to associates who had worked together for decades. Nevertheless, in Washington and Saigon, some thought that a struggle might develop among Ho's possible successors. Few were as optimistic as President Thieu, who told the press that if party secretary Le Duan emerged on top, his moderate, pro-Soviet views might permit a quick negotiated end of the war.[57] This was a rather curious assessment, since Le Duan had led communist forces in the south against the French and was usually said to be a leading proponent of total victory there. Although Le Duan did appear gradually to gain the most influential position in the government, there was no obvious squabbling in Hanoi, nor any change in policy.

President Nixon wanted to find a way to make the North Vietnamese believe in his ultimatum and respond to it. Kissinger's National Security Council staff and the Joint Chiefs of Staff had been quietly exploring ways to implement the ultimatum, including mining North Vietnam's harbors and invasion as well as a resumption of bombing.[58] Some attention may also have been given to the possibility of using nuclear weapons for contaminating transportation routes with radiation.[59] Unlike President Eisenhower's handling of the Korean War, however, Nixon did not try to end the Vietnam War by explicitly threatening to use nuclear weapons. He did decide to let North Vietnam know that he was considering invasion and mining Haiphong. Nixon leaked these options to the press by briefing several senators.[60]

Nixon also tried to pressure the Soviet Union into using its leverage with North Vietnam to end the war. When Soviet ambassador Anatoly Dobrynin asked to see Kissinger in late September, the President and his National Security Adviser staged a little performance. As they had planned, a call from Nixon interrupted the meeting, and after putting down the telephone Kissinger somberly told Dobrynin that in the President's words the "train had left the station and was heading down the track."[61] Dobrynin replied that he hoped it was a plane rather than a train, because a plane could still change course.[62]

In October, Nixon attempted to underline the seriousness of his ultimatum to Moscow and Hanoi without contributing to the revival of antiwar protest in the United States. On October 10, the Chairman of the Joint Chiefs, General Wheeler, ordered the Strategic Air Command and the unified commands to begin a readiness test that would generate actions "discernible to the Soviets, but not threatening in themselves."[63] General Bruce K. Holloway, the SAC commander, nearly doubled the number of B-52s on ground alert to 144.

Almost two-thirds of the rest of his bombers were loaded with nuclear weapons on October 25, and two days later B–52s carried nuclear weapons on airborne alert for the first time since January 1968 (when a B–52 crashed near Thule, Greenland). But on October 28, the administration ended the readiness test.[64]

Nixon's campaign to convince Moscow and Hanoi that he was serious about his ultimatum had opened persuasively on October 13, the first day of the readiness test, when his press secretary announced that the President would make a televised address to the nation on November 3. The timing of the speech was meant to suggest the possibility that Nixon might use the occasion to announce the dire measures he had been threatening.[65] But the communists called his bluff, and the first week in November passed without escalation of the war.

Nixon blamed the failure of his ultimatum on the antiwar movement, which rose to new heights after a year's quiescence. Since the bombing halt, student unrest had mostly involved racial problems. After black students at Cornell University got their way in the spring of 1969 by carrying rifles, Nixon was not alone in fearing what a revival of the antiwar movement might bring. But the threat of violence at Cornell, following the skirmishing between police and demonstrators at the Democratic convention in Chicago the preceding August, caused the development of new tactics within the antiwar movement. During the summer of 1969, organizers planned a nationwide "moratorium" for October 15, when people were asked to take time out from their normal routine to protest the war. The idea was to involve as much of the American middle class as possible—to shed the disreputable "hippie" image of earlier demonstrations in favor of cleancut respectability. Those in sympathy with the moratorium were asked to wear black armbands. In addition to marches, there would be a range of other activities, including lectures and candlelight vigils.

Growing support for the moratorium on the east and west coasts seemed to indicate that many Americans wanted out of the war immediately, without regard to the consequences for South Vietnam. A Gallup poll found that more than half the Americans surveyed favored withdrawing completely by the end of 1970.[66] President Nixon tried to derail the antiwar movement by announcing a second installment of thirty-five thousand troops to be withdrawn from South Vietnam. He also removed Lt. Gen. Lewis B. Hershey (U.S. Army) as Director of the Selective Service System. Ever since the United States had begun to draft young men into the military during World War II, Hershey had managed the proceedings, and during the Vietnam War he had become a favorite target of the antiwar movement. Within a year, continuing withdrawals from Vietnam combined with a new draft lottery (that quickly exempted most young men from the draft) would deprive the antiwar movement of much of its impetus, but Nixon's gestures in the fall of 1969 did less to curb it than to rob his ultimatum of any weight in Hanoi.

North Vietnam's leaders took undisguised pleasure in the American antiwar movement's activities. The day before the moratorium, North Vietnam's delegation in Paris gave the press an open letter from Premier Pham Van Dong to "American friends" wishing them a "great success" in their "autumn struggle."[67] President Nixon would later recall that when he heard about Pham Van Dong's letter, "I knew for sure that my ultimatum had failed."[68]

Not only was the moratorium of October 15 the first time the antiwar movement had succeeded in coordinating major events in several cities simultaneously, but the same groups were already organizing much larger gatherings for Washington and San Francisco in mid-November. Only two days after the moratorium, Kissinger advised the President that perhaps it might be best to postpone plans to act more forcefully against North Vietnam.[69] On the same day, Nixon got similar advice from a British authority on counterinsurgency, Sir Robert Thompson, who suggested that the United States needed to convince Hanoi and Saigon of its ability to stay, not escalate.[70]

The Soviet Union hammered home the final nail in the coffin of Nixon's ultimatum. On October 20, Ambassador Dobrynin presented Nixon with his government's agreement to enter into strategic arms limitation talks. At the same time, Dobrynin voiced Soviet unhappiness with Nixon's overtures to the Chinese. Left unspoken was the bad time Nixon was bound to have with the American press if he risked a Soviet arms agreement to escalate the Vietnam War. Nixon took the opportunity to lecture Dobrynin at length on the Soviet Union's failure to help end the war. "If the Soviet Union will not help us get peace," Nixon threatened once again, "then we will have to pursue our own methods for bringing the war to an end."[71] He added that the Soviets should not expect much progress on other matters until the war was over.[72]

Having decided not to announce any dramatic new actions in the war, Nixon was left with the problem of what to say to the American people on November 3. Fortunately they did not know about his ultimatum, and he used the occasion to shore up his dwindling support on the war. He reminded his television audience that when the communists took Hue during the Tet offensive of 1968, they had executed about three thousand civilians.[73] He repeated his offer to withdraw American forces from South Vietnam if the North Vietnamese would do the same, and he read Ho Chi Minh's letter rejecting that proposal. But Nixon said that his plan for ending America's role in the war did not depend on negotiations with Hanoi. Through Vietnamization, he would gradually replace American forces with South Vietnamese forces. If North Vietnam ever tried to take advantage of this situation by introducing greater force against the remaining American troops, Nixon promised that he would "not hesitate to take strong and effective measures to deal with that situation."[74]

While Hanoi now had plenty of reasons to doubt Nixon's willingness to make good on his threats, he appeared forceful and reasonable to much of his audience that evening. He reached to them past the demonstrators who were beginning to harry him as they had harried President Johnson. Nixon acknowledged that Vietnamization would take more time than protestors marching in the streets seemed inclined to give him, and he called upon "the great silent majority" of Americans to support him.[75]

A Gallup telephone poll taken after Nixon's speech found that more than three-fourths of those who heard the President did support him.[76] For the first time more than two-thirds of the American people seemed to approve of Nixon's performance in the White House.[77] His leading critic in the Congress, Senator Fulbright, decided to postpone new public hearings on the war. Representative James Wright (Democrat, Texas) and about three hundred other House members signed his resolution supporting the President's "efforts to negotiate a just peace in Vietnam."[78] Nixon thanked his congressional supporters on November 13 by making speeches to the House and the Senate, his first there as President.

As Nixon spoke on Capitol Hill, protestors were gathering in Washington for the biggest demonstration ever held there, surpassing even the great civil rights March on Washington of 1963. At least a quarter of a million people participated in 1969 and perhaps two or three times that many. Meanwhile, more than a hundred thousand demonstrated in San Francisco, and there were dozens of smaller demonstrations in the United States and Europe. In Washington the three-day event began with a "March Against Death" from Arlington Cemetery to Capitol Hill, where forty-six thousand marchers each deposited a placard bearing the name of an American killed or a Vietnamese village destroyed into one of forty black coffins. The bulk of the youthful crowd maintained the discipline sought by organizers, but a rough fringe element broke windows, damaged police cars, and flew a Vietcong flag over the Justice Department before being scattered by tear gas.[79]

Although President Nixon had proved the existence of a relatively silent majority, a large and influential minority was obviously becoming increasingly vocal. The North Vietnamese government could take comfort in this, as well as in Nixon's failure to enforce his ultimatum. In any case, Nixon seemed committed to withdrawal—only the pace of withdrawal remained in question. A few days before the big demonstration in Washington, there was a "solidarity rally" in Hanoi addressed by visiting American antiwar activists Richard J. Barnet (co-director of the Institute for Policy Studies in Washington) and William Meyers (director of the Lawyers Committee on American Policy Toward Vietnam in New York). Urging immediate withdrawal of all U.S. forces, Barnet said that he and the North Vietnamese were fighting the same aggressors.[80]

*   *   *

November 1969 would have been a poor time to start an air campaign against North Vietnam unless the big B–52 bombers were used against area targets. As occurred every November, the northeast monsoon began to cover the Red River Delta with clouds and drizzle. Meanwhile, the sky cleared over the Laotian panhandle and as the roads dried there, North Vietnamese trucks were detected in increasing numbers headed south. By the end of the year, more than six hundred B–52 sorties a month (40 percent of those available for all of Southeast Asia) were dropping more than ten thousand tons of bombs on the Ho Chi Minh Trail in Laos.[81]

Apart from political repercussions, another argument against using B–52s over the Red River Delta was their vulnerability to surface-to-air missiles. Earlier in the war, North Vietnamese SAMs had not bothered B–52s over Laos, but on December 19, 1969, a site on the North Vietnamese side of the Ban Karai Pass launched two missiles against a cell of three B–52s in Laos. One of the missiles narrowly missed the third B–52. The Seventh Air Force commander, General Brown, requested permission to bomb the offending SAM site and any other SAM sites in North Vietnam threatening his forces in Laos. The Chairman of the Joint Chiefs, General Wheeler, decided not to present this request to Secretary Laird. But Wheeler did pass along another Brown request to permit F–105G Wild Weasel aircraft to operate in North Vietnam.[82]

Since the bombing halt over North Vietnam, the two-seat Wild Weasels had been limited to flying along the Laotian side of the North Vietnamese border, a restriction that inhibited maximum use of radar detection equipment, radar-seeking air-to-ground missiles, and other munitions against missile sites in North Vietnam. President Nixon did not approve use of Wild Weasels in North Vietnam until late January 1970. On January 28, a pair of F–105G Wild Weasels escorted an RF–4C reconnaissance aircraft into North Vietnam. After evading two SAMs launched from a site near the Mu Gia Pass, the Wild Weasels dropped a dozen 500-pound bombs on the site. One of the Wild Weasels then strafed a second site a few miles north of the first and was hit by ground fire while pulling off the target. The pilot, Capt. Richard J. Mallon, and the electronic warfare officer, Capt. Robert J. Panek, both ejected.[83]

An unsuccessful rescue effort came to a sad end less than three hours later when a rescue helicopter orbiting nearby in Laos was shot down by a MiG–21's heat-seeking missile. The helicopter exploded in the air and all six crew members were presumed to have died instantly: Maj. Holly G. Bell, Capt. Leonard C. Leeser, SMSgt. William D. Pruett, MSgt. William C. Sutton, SSgt. William C. Shinn, and Sgt. Gregory L. Anderson. Nor would Captains Mallon and Panek come home at the end of the war.[84]

Dismayed by these losses and disappointed that he had not been granted permission to mount a campaign against missile sites near the Laotian border in North Vietnam, General Brown resolved to make maximum use of the authority he did have. Since the fall of 1968, there had been little change in the basic rules of engagement for operations in North Vietnam. Brown could send reconnaissance aircraft with escorts as far north as the nineteenth parallel. If fired upon by MiGs, SAMs, or antiaircraft artillery, the escorts could return fire—unless the offending SAM or artillery site lay north of the nineteenth parallel. Beginning in the summer of 1969, Brown sometimes authorized a flight of four fighters to orbit in readiness to join a reconnaissance mission when attacked, so that Seventh Air Force could react with more force than afforded by the pair of escorts which then normally accompanied a reconnaissance aircraft. Now, early in 1970, Brown took the advice of his second in command, Maj. Gen. Robert J. Dixon, and expanded the reaction force to at least a dozen aircraft. An aide would recall that this was one of the few times he saw Brown display much emotion: Brown banged the table and declared he wanted "every damned plane we can get airborne."[85]

On February 2, 1970, Seventh Air Force had two RF–4C reconnaissance aircraft (each with two F–4 escorts) fly over North Vietnamese SAM sites near the Laotian border. Orbiting in Laos were fifteen other F–4s. Although one of the reconnaissance flights was fired upon by antiaircraft artillery near the Mu Gia pass, neither encountered a SAM. After the escorts alone bombed the offending artillery, Seventh Air Force sent the orbiting force against another artillery site near the Ban Karai Pass (midway between the Mu Gia Pass and the Demilitarized Zone). That artillery site had fired on American aircraft in Laos the day before, and reaction was permitted within twenty-four hours. General Brown hoped that a SAM site north of Ban Karai would respond to so large a force and it did. After launching a SAM, the site was bombed by eight F–4s led by Col. Donald N. Stanfield, commander of the 8th Tactical Fighter Wing (Ubon, Thailand). This was an unusually effective strike: at least two missiles were thought to be destroyed on the ground, while launch facilities and associated artillery sites were heavily damaged.[86]

Just a week after the Ban Karai strike, President Nixon not only extended the time for reaction against fire in North Vietnam to three days, but permitted preemptive strikes on SAM and antiaircraft artillery sites near the Laotian border. When bad weather prohibited any attacks on those sites during the first week after his authorization, Nixon expressed his impatience—only to withdraw the authorization a day later. Early in March, he reinstated the three-day period for permissible reaction and subsequently permitted reaction as far north as the twentieth parallel, but he did not again give a blanket authorization for preemptive strikes. Instead, he began to consider authorizing an air campaign much broader in scope.[87]

The occasion for Nixon's renewed interest in bombing North Vietnam was the overthrow of Prince Sihanouk's government in Cambodia by Gen. Lon Nol, who wanted American forces to drive North Vietnamese forces out of his country. Having tossed aside Sihanouk's delicate compromise between American and North Vietnamese interests, Lon Nol was immediately at war with the large North Vietnamese forces on the Cambodian side of the South Vietnamese border. For a year, B–52s had been secretly bombing those forces, and General

Abrams had long wanted to send his soldiers against this enemy sanctuary with its Cambodian port at Sihanoukville. Lon Nol renamed the port Kompong Som and closed it to communist supplies. If Abrams could destroy supplies stored along the border before Vietnamization stripped him of most of his own forces, South Vietnam's chances for survival would improve—as would those of Lon Nol and American forces remaining in South Vietnam.[88]

When President Nixon decided to attack North Vietnamese forces in Cambodia, he knew that he would face an uproar on Capitol Hill, in the press, and on college campuses. He suggested to Kissinger that they might as well go the whole way and resume the bombing of North Vietnam to include mining the ports. Kissinger did not believe the President was serious, and brushed aside the suggestion by commenting that they had a full plate already. But after the war, Kissinger would doubt that he had given good advice on this occasion: "The bane of our military actions in Vietnam was their hesitancy; we were always trying to calculate with fine precision the absolute minimum of force or of time, leaving no margin for error or confusion, encouraging our adversary to hold on until our doubts overrode our efforts."[89]

Although Nixon did not resume a full-scale bombing campaign against North Vietnam, he did decide to bomb North Vietnamese supply dumps just north of the Demilitarized Zone and near the mountain passes on the Laotian border. During the first four days in May, when American troops joined South Vietnamese troops fighting in Cambodia, Air Force and Navy fighter planes flew more than seven hundred sorties against North Vietnam. Nothing like this had occurred since the bombing halt of November 1968. The size of the operation overwhelmed North Vietnam's defenses, and the Air Force and the Navy each lost only one aircraft. Fortunately, both crew members of the downed Air Force F–4D were rescued.[90]

Pacific Command intelligence officers believed that the May strikes had been very damaging, but the evidence did not permit their estimates of destroyed supplies to be more precise than somewhere between ten thousand and fifty thousand tons.[91] At any rate, as President Nixon had guessed, the public relations cost of the raids seem considerably lessened by their occurring in the midst of the clamor over Cambodia. When National Guard troops killed four students on the campus of Kent State University in Ohio, students at hundreds of universities went on strike, and about one hundred thousand came to Washington for the last major demonstration of the war.

In this context, the air raids on North Vietnam received relatively little attention. When the press was informed about the just concluded raids on May 4, 1970, the Defense Department briefer did not know that the Navy had struck the Mu Gia Pass area and therefore denied that this attack had occurred—an error that was rectified the next day. But the press was given far more information about the raids than military officers in Hawaii put in their own classified reports. In the insidious fashion set by Strategic Air Command's falsified reporting about B–52 raids on Cambodia, Pacific Command and Pacific Air Forces deleted the raids from their Top Secret reports. Pacific Air Forces' long, detailed monthly summary of operations in Southeast Asia, for example, stated that there had been only three strike sorties sent against North Vietnam during the entire month of May.[92]

Although the Nixon administration was more honest than that with the press, there was plenty of deception for reporters as well. The administration latched onto Secretary of Defense Laird's "protective reaction" phrase to defend the raids. There was a certain irony in this, since Laird was again out of favor in the White House, this time for opposing the invasion of Cambodia. Nevertheless, he was defending the administration in public and insisting that if the North Vietnamese retaliated after the Cambodian operation by attacking across the Demilitarized Zone, he would favor resuming the bombing of North Vietnam.[93]

Several months earlier, Laird had applied the phrase "protective reaction" to retaliation against North Vietnamese air defenses.[94] By then, his phrase (originally applied to small Army operations from South Vietnam across the Laotian border) was already closely associated with the end of search and destroy missions by American troops in South Vietnam—where "protective reaction" implied that American troops would no longer go looking for trouble, but would merely react when attacked.

During the first year of the Nixon administration, Vice President Spiro T. Agnew had often served as the administration's lightning rod in its battles with the press. Once again he stepped forward to defend the President's actions on a television interview program. When asked about the raids on North Vietnam, he said that American attacks there had "traditionally been ones that we call protective reaction. As far as I know, these attacks that you are referring to fit into that category."[95] Secretary of State Rogers also emphasized that American air attacks were directed at North Vietnamese air defenses, and Defense Department spokesmen confirmed this view while indicating that the size of the raids was new by calling them "reinforced protective reaction strikes."[96] No one in the administration publicly admitted that, although air defense targets were of course included, the principal targets of the raids were enemy supply dumps.

Despite the drubbing President Nixon took on campus and in the press during the Cambodian operation, he continued to hold the support of a majority of Americans. A Gallup poll found that more than 80 percent of adults over the age of twenty-one objected to students going on strike to protest "the way things are run in this country."[97] President Nixon had finally taken a dramatic public action which may well have surprised North Vietnam's leaders. On the other hand, the vigor of American dissent may also have reassured them that he would be unlikely to take such action again. If the North Vietnamese came to that conclusion, Nixon would prove them wrong.

Chapter Seven

Prisoners and Other Survivors

On May 1, 1970, while American troops pushed into Cambodia and F–4s bombed the panhandle of North Vietnam, more than a thousand American military wives and parents gathered in Washington to deal with the war's special impact on their families. Although some of their husbands and sons had been imprisoned or missing in Southeast Asia since as long ago as 1964, no such meeting had occurred before. The Johnson administration had discouraged these families from organizing; they were told that quiet diplomacy was the best way to secure the safe return of their men, whose survival might be threatened by publicity. But the families grew suspicious of quiet diplomacy, especially after an avalanche of publicity about the USS *Pueblo* (the Navy intelligence ship whose crew was captured by North Korea in January 1968 and released at the end of that year).[1]

The Nixon administration decided to join in publicly condemning North Vietnam's cruelty toward its American prisoners and failure even to reveal which men it had captured. Secretary of Defense Laird unveiled the administration's decision to publicize the plight of captured Americans in May 1969. Three prisoners subsequently released by North Vietnam in August 1969 were encouraged to tell the press about the grim realities of imprisonment in North Vietnam—a subject that had been discussed only in classified debriefings by six prisoners released in 1968. The American member of the United Nations Commission on Human Rights complained about conditions in North Vietnam's prisons to a committee of the General Assembly in November 1969. Meanwhile, wives of Americans missing in Southeast Asia visited the North Vietnamese delegation at the peace talks in Paris to inquire whether they were wives of prisoners or widows. They got no answer, and when Philip Habib replaced Henry Cabot Lodge as America's chief negotiator at the talks in December, he devoted his entire opening statement to the prisoner of war issue.[2]

In March 1970, Senator Robert Dole (Republican, Kansas) proposed that the new National League of Families of American Prisoners and Missing in Southeast Asia come together for a meeting at Constitution Hall in Washington on International Law Day, May 1. Many family members were flown to Washington by the Air National Guard. Although Secretary Laird and Vice President Agnew spoke to the group, much of the expected publicity was submerged in the controversy over Cambodia. But this was to be the first of many national gatherings, and the League established an office in Washington to promote its interests.[3]

Senator Dole's concern reflected Kansas's military ties in addition to his own experience as a severely wounded veteran of World War II. Fort Riley had sent its First Infantry Division to Vietnam, and many of the Army's field grade officers had attended Command and General Staff College at Fort Leavenworth. But it was McConnell Air Force Base near Wichita that had trained F–105 pilots who attacked targets in North Vietnam.[4]

While few Americans missing in South Vietnam or Laos were thought to be still alive, imprisonment seemed much more likely for the aircrews of more than nine hundred aircraft shot down over North Vietnam. Although fewer than a hundred of those men had been rescued, evidence of captivity had emerged for about four hundred, and there was hope that some of the other missing flyers were also in captivity. As the replacement training center for F–105 pilots, McConnell had not only contributed many of the prisoners and missing, but its staff included officers who had fought in the skies over North Vietnam.[5]

A year after President Johnson's March 1968 bombing halt in the Hanoi-Haiphong region, veterans of Rolling Thunder had flown to McConnell for their first stateside "practice reunion." They called it a "practice reunion" because they declared that a "real reunion" could not occur until their friends imprisoned in North Vietnam could join them. About a hundred pilots parked their military aircraft on the ramp, while several hundred others came to Wichita by commercial air or automobile. They partied for three days, adopted a charter, and elected another Johnson, Col. Howard C. "Scrappy" Johnson, as their president.[6]

Colonel Johnson had launched the first practice reunion in Thailand. When he became the operations officer at Korat Air Base in 1966, his chief claim to fame was that he had set an altitude record in the F–104. But he had also flown F–51 missions during the Korean War, and he thought that men fought better in the air if they knew each other on the ground. With the force attacking North Vietnam scattered among several bases and aircraft carriers, coordination of the air war was often too impersonal to permit a full sharing of ideas and experience. So Johnson persuaded his wing commander, Brig. Gen. William S. Chairsell, to invite the other wings to a tactics conference at Korat.[7]

The Korat conference on May 22, 1967, was the occasion for an exuberant release from the tensions of war. Visiting dignitaries were hoisted atop elephants and paraded through the base to the music of a marching band. Similar gatherings were held at Ubon, Takhli, and Udorn before the bombing halt. Thus was born the Red River Valley Fighter Pilots Association. They called themselves the River Rats, and they took as members all who had flown into Route Package Six, plus all who were imprisoned in North Vietnam. Air Force, Navy and Marine fighter pilots flew to the gatherings, and other participants in the air war also came—helicopter rescue crews were especially welcome.

To differentiate the many squadrons represented, River Rats took to wearing "party suits," flight suits in the squadron's color with the most imaginative insignia the wearer could create. The tailoring of these flight suits became a major enterprise outside the gates of the Thailand bases. At Udorn, Maharajah Clothiers grew into an establishment employing more than eighty seamstresses who made party suits for officers from throughout Seventh Air Force. The "Maharajah," Amarjit Singh Vasir, formerly a civil servant in India, frequently attended squadron parties wearing the appropriate party suit (bought by the squadron). His clients (who included several generals) made him an honorary six-star general, and the shoulders of his party suits bore the stars to prove it.[8]

Two favorite activities at River Rat parties were "dead bug" and "MiG sweep." At the command "dead bug," the last man to assume the proper position (on his back with legs and arms in the air) bought drinks for the rest. Those participating in a "MiG sweep" linked arms and attempted to knock down everyone else in the room. When Navy pilots were present, "carrier landings" were added—a wet table assuming the role of an aircraft carrier and a pilot assuming the role of an aircraft.

High jinks and party suits were much in evidence at Wichita in 1969 when Colonel Johnson became CINCRAT. But as before in Thailand, a more serious purpose underlay the festivities. After the bombing halt and their own return to the United States, the River Rats took as their new mission the welfare of the families of friends killed, missing, or held prisoner in Southeast Asia. Members were enjoined to check on those families and make sure they were getting as much financial and moral support as possible. The River Rats raised money to provide scholarships for the children of their unfortunate comrades; it was a commitment the Rats would sustain for more than two decades until all those children were educated.

By the time the River Rats met for their second annual stateside practice reunion at San Antonio in May 1970, they had acquired in Thailand a "liberty bell" that would not be rung until the prisoners were released. Like many other Americans, River Rat families began to wear bracelets bearing the names of the prisoners and the missing—with promises to wear them until the prisoners came home.

In this way, the prisoners began to be seen as the most celebrated group of heroes in a war that some Americans thought lacking in heroism. During earlier wars, fighter pilots had looked to aces as their principal celebrities, but in 1970 no pilot had yet shot down the requisite five aircraft. Although there had often been a stigma attached to being shot down by another fighter, most of the pilots lost in North Vietnam were shot down by ground fire. Those who took greater risks by diving lower to get better accuracy made themselves more vulnerable. For every prisoner whose lack of skill or experience may have contributed to his fate, there were others whose abilities were widely respected. In any case, the length and hardship of the prisoners' ordeal commanded the sympathy and respect of fellow fighter pilots as well as of Americans generally.[9]

Demands for return of the prisoners reverberated through American society. In June 1970 an exhibit of their living conditions opened in the U.S. Capitol building. A life-size mockup of a North Vietnamese cell showed a prisoner whose only companions were a rat and some cockroaches. Nearby, a mockup of a Viet Cong bamboo cage showed a prisoner whose feet were shackled. Although this exhibit made no attempt to portray torture, visitors were dismayed at the grimness of what they saw.[10]

The Capitol exhibit was provided by a young and wealthy Dallas businessman, H. Ross Perot, who, after graduating from the Naval Academy in 1953, had made a quick fortune in the new computer industry. His interest in the prisoners and the missing had been engaged in 1969 when some of their wives asked him for funds to visit the North Vietnamese delegation in Paris. Not only did he provide those funds, but he immediately began to put hundreds of thousands of dollars into a campaign to advertise the plight of the prisoners. For Christmas 1969 he gathered tons of Christmas packages (with food, clothing, and medicine) for the prisoners, but the North Vietnamese authorities did not permit his cargo planes to land. The North Vietnamese also refused to meet with him when he flew to Laos or Paris, and they turned down his offer of one hundred million dollars in exchange for the prisoners.[11]

One result of Perot's offer, together with the publicity generated by him and others, was that the North Vietnamese knew without question that their few hundred American prisoners were an asset whose value was increasing. By contrast, the North Vietnamese showed nothing but disdain for the thirty-six thousand communist prisoners in South Vietnamese hands and indicated no interest in getting any of them back. North Vietnam would not even admit that about seven thousand of those prisoners were North Vietnamese, for North Vietnam continued to insist that there were no North Vietnamese forces in South Vietnam. If the Americans wanted the return of American prisoners, the Americans would have to trade something far more important than the communist prisoners in South Vietnam.[12]

When the Nixon administration offered to cut back B–52 bombing in South Vietnam in exchange for the prisoners, the North Vietnamese said they would take nothing less than the full evacuation of American forces from South Vietnam—and even that they could expect to get anyway as the end result of Vietnamization.[13] After all, the Nixon administration was already cutting back B–52 sorties and withdrawing troops without any concession by the North Vietnamese. It was not difficult to discern that, unless there was a sea change in American politics, the Nixon administration would want to have most of its forces out of South Vietnam by the next presidential election in 1972. But the North Vietnamese were willing to trade the prisoners to have their desires met sooner, for it was the essence of the Nixon administration's policy to prolong Vietnamization as long as possible (up to the 1972 election) so that the South Vietnamese government would have some chance of standing on its own.

The Nixon administration could not use the prisoner issue either to maintain American support for the war or to improve the situation of the prisoners without increasing the negotiating value of the prisoners to the North Vietnamese. But the administration's negotiating position was already so weak, it hardly mattered. So long as Vietnamization promised that American forces would be withdrawn eventually in any case, the North Vietnamese had little incentive to agree to the withdrawal of their own forces from South Vietnam. And once American forces had all gone home, what was to stop the North Vietnamese from simply keeping their American prisoners indefinitely?

In August 1970 President Nixon sought to heighten awareness of North Vietnam's mistreatment of American prisoners by sending Col. Frank Borman, a former astronaut recently retired from the Air Force, as his special emissary to fourteen countries (including the Soviet Union). Borman had come to Nixon's attention on Christmas Eve 1968 when the astronaut read to the world from the Book of Genesis while orbiting the moon. Later he had made a good impression speaking to a joint session of Congress and visiting several foreign capitals. Now Nixon wanted him to perform in a similar way on behalf of the prisoners.[14]

The Borman tour came on the heels of revelations about harsh conditions in the South Vietnamese prison on Con Son Island, fifty miles off the coast. This facility had been built by the French (who called the island Poulo Condore) nearly forty years before to house the colonial government's most recalcitrant prisoners (including Pham Van Dong and Le Duc Tho). Don Luce of the World Council of Churches had persuaded two congressmen to tour the prison. Augustus F. Hawkins (Democrat, California) was an early opponent of the Vietnam War, which he condemned for soaking up funds needed by his black constituents in the riot-torn Watts area of Los Angeles. William R. Anderson (Democrat, Tennessee) was a retired Navy captain who had commanded the Navy's first nuclear-powered submarine, the *Nautilus*. They were both shocked by what they saw. In one building they looked down through floor bars into concrete cells they dubbed "tiger cages." Each cell held as many as five prisoners (men or women) confined to a space measuring about six feet by ten feet. One man claimed that his fingers had been cut off as punishment. Others complained about being shackled so long that they had been paralyzed.[15]

By the end of July 1970, photographs of the "tiger cages" on Con Son Island were featured in *Life*, and Gloria Emerson of the *New York Times* was doing her best to spread Don Luce's version of the story. Luce, who had gone to

South Vietnam in the 1950s from Cornell University as an expert on sweet pota-toes, now became a hero of the antiwar movement. He found an antidote to the evil reputation the North Vietnamese were earning for their mistreatment of American prisoners of war.[16]

When Frank Borman reached Saigon at the end of August, he too asked to see the prison on Con Son Island. By then the "tiger cages" were no longer in use and some had been torn down. He came away convinced that the only pris-oners of war still on Con Son Island were a few convicted of crimes in the ordi-nary prison camps like the one he visited at Phu Quoc—camps frequently inspected by the International Red Cross. In his speech to a joint session of Congress on September 22, 1970, Borman urged once again that "we continue to press for the use of the International Red Cross in inspection of the prison camps in North Vietnam."[17]

*   *   *

The International Committee of the Red Cross had sponsored a conference in 1949 at its headquarters in Geneva, Switzerland, to draft new conventions for the protection of war victims. One of these conventions governed the treatment of prisoners of war. By 1958, the Geneva Conventions were accepted by both North and South Vietnam, as well as the United States. But North Vietnam fol-lowed the lead of the Soviet Union in agreeing to the convention on prisoners of war only with a most important reservation: North Vietnam did not accept arti-cle eighty-five, which stated that "prisoners of war prosecuted under the laws of the Detaining Power for acts committed prior to capture shall retain, even if convicted, the benefits of the present Convention."[18]

Throughout its struggle with the United States, North Vietnam insisted that the American airmen who fell into its hands were criminals, not prisoners of war. Since the North Vietnamese called the bombing of their country a crime rather than an act of war, they refused to comply with the pertinent Geneva con-vention—inspectors from the International Committee of the Red Cross would not be welcome in North Vietnam. American complaints that the North Vietnamese were failing to live up to provisions of the convention on prisoners could be dismissed simply by noting that North Vietnam rejected the applica-bility of those provisions.

Even within the terms of its own reservation, North Vietnam's treatment of American prisoners was indefensible.[19] Although North Vietnam threatened them with prosecution, war crimes trials never took place in Hanoi. The British philosopher Bertrand Russell did sponsor mock war-crimes trials in Sweden and Denmark, but of course, his purpose was to foment international opinion against the Johnson administration rather than to weigh the criminal liability of individual pilots.[20] The best justifications North Vietnam could produce for denying American rights under the prisoner of war convention were the confessions extorted by torturing prisoners in violation of that convention.

Without the protection afforded by the Geneva Conventions, Americans captured in North Vietnam had reason to doubt that they would survive captivity. Bernard Fall's widely read *Street Without Joy* described the deaths of hundreds of French prisoners in communist camps there during the early 1950s; few of them were killed—most of the dead were victims of infection, disease, and malnutrition. During their war against the French, the communist forces often operated as guerrillas, and guerrillas rarely took prisoners or treated well those taken. Before their war with the United States, the North Vietnamese had inherited the French prisons and could more easily provide humane treatment if they so desired.[21]

Instead the North Vietnamese not only ignored the Geneva Conventions, but looked to Chinese and North Korean practices in the Korean War for a model of how to treat American prisoners. The American public had been dismayed in that war when American airmen in Chinese prison camps confessed to germ warfare. Although those germ warfare allegations had been discredited, the North Vietnamese were eager to get at least confessions of intentionally bombing hospitals, schools, homes, and other civilian targets. The North Vietnamese became adept at using torture to extort such "confessions"—for the most part without killing and often without permanently disfiguring their valuable American prisoners.[22]

North Vietnamese torturers commonly used ropes to pull a prisoner's arms behind him, squeezing his elbows together and increasing the pressure and the pain—sometimes until his shoulder joints dislocated. Prisoners were also forced to torture themselves: great pain could be inflicted simply by kneeling on a concrete floor for enough hours. Prisoners who were injured when they ejected from their aircraft were tortured and denied medical treatment until they "confessed." Yet the prisoners who survived knew of only twelve men who died in North Vietnam after capture. This at least was a welcome contrast to the Korean War, when more than a third of seven thousand Americans captured were known to have died—many because they did not receive adequate protection from sub-zero weather.[23]

A new prisoner might face the terrible initial weeks or months of his captivity shackled in isolation from other prisoners. When he yielded to torture, he did not know that most of his fellow prisoners had also relented but had learned to gather their strength to resist again. Sometimes even before his captors relieved his isolation by giving him a cellmate, veteran prisoners made contact with the new prisoner and taught him to communicate by tapping on walls or writing messages on toilet paper with ink made from cigarette ash. For a few prisoners who spent years in solitary confinement, secret communications were especially cherished.

The tap code was introduced to Hanoi's Hoa Lo Prison by Capt. Carlyle S. "Smitty" Harris whose F–105 was shot down in April 1965 while bombing the Thanh Hoa Bridge. At this early stage the North Vietnamese had not yet begun to torture their American prisoners, whose rapid increase in number soon led to Harris being put into a cell with three other Americans. He taught them the tap code he had learned in survival school at Stead Air Force Base, Nevada.

The code had not been a formal part of Harris's training, but one sergeant teaching the course had told a story about prisoners communicating by tapping on a pipe. Thinking they had used Morse Code, Harris asked the sergeant how they had differentiated between dots and dashes. The sergeant explained that each tap indicated a letter's position in a square matrix of five rows and five columns. The letter "A" was signaled by one tap for the row and one tap for the column; the letter "Z" by five taps for the row and five taps for the column; the letter "K" was dropped from the matrix in favor of "C," leaving only the twenty-five letters necessary to fill the matrix.[24]

The increasing number of American prisoners soon led to the separation and relocation of Harris and his first three cell mates—spreading the tap code to others. Over time variations of this code would develop. If transmitting hand and receiving eye were close enough together, sign language could be used. Capt. Kyle D. Berg, whose F–105 went down along with four others on July 27, 1965, had a deaf stepsister and taught his cellmates how to sign.[25]

Until September 1965, almost all American prisoners in North Vietnam were kept in Hoa Lo Prison, which had been built by the French near the center of Hanoi some seventy years before. Although the "Hanoi Hilton" (as American prisoners called Hoa Lo) was big enough to hold at least four hundred prisoners, the North Vietnamese decided not to concentrate Americans there. Instead a large part of Hoa Lo continued to house Vietnamese criminals, while other facilities in and around Hanoi were converted to prisons for Americans.

The largest of the improvised prisons was a former film studio at Cu Loc on the southern edge of Hanoi; about two hundred prisoners could be kept there in what they called the "Zoo." A somewhat smaller prison was established in some sheds on the grounds of a mansion that had been the French mayor's home. Here at the "Plantation" (or "Country Club"), foreign journalists and American antiwar activists came to meet prisoners in the "Big House" (or "French House"). A few cells were fixed up to show visitors. Prisoners being considered for early release were sent to the "Plantation," while some of the least cooperative prisoners were sent to "Alcatraz," a small jail behind the Ministry of National Defense.[26]

Since it was possible that the United States might eventually bomb Hanoi, dispersion of the prisoners may have been intended to ensure that some of them would survive. On the other hand, one group of prisoners was deliberately put in harm's way during the summer of 1967, when they were moved onto the grounds of the Hanoi thermal powerplant. The plant was one of the few targets ever bombed within the city. The North Vietnamese may have hoped that casualties among the prisoners might make the United States more reluctant to bomb Hanoi.[27]

In any case, scattering the prisoners inhibited their attempts to organize. Within each facility prisoners still sought to communicate and determine the identity of their senior ranking officer. This dangerous responsibility soon fell upon Lt. Col. Robinson Risner, a Korean War ace shot down in September 1965. After a couple of weeks at the Hilton, he was among the first prisoners sent to the Zoo. Although he continued to be kept in solitary confinement, he had already learned the tap code and was even able to have whispered conversations with a prisoner in a neighboring cell. Risner's stay at the Zoo was a short one of only a few weeks. His efforts to organize the prisoners and present their demands for decent living conditions brought his early return to the Hilton, where he spent the next month in stocks and was one of the first prisoners to be tortured.[28]

The prison authorities were on the lookout for signs of leadership emerging among the prisoners and would torture and isolate anyone caught assuming a leadership role. Navy Cmdrs. James B. Stockdale and Jeremiah A. Denton, Jr., frequently found themselves in risky leadership positions at the Hilton or the Zoo or Alcatraz, as did Majors Lawrence N. Guarino and James H. Kasler (a Korean War ace like Risner) at the Zoo. Such men took turns leading and suffering the consequences. Their fragile communication networks were sometimes disrupted, but rarely did American prisoners lack American leadership for long. On the other hand, for more than two years the North Vietnamese were successful in completely isolating from other American prisoners within the Hilton four colonels captured in 1967 and 1968.[29]

The leaders among the prisoners were in their forties, while most of the men were captains about thirty years old. A few of the older men were veterans of World War II. Major Guarino had even strafed Japanese rolling stock on the railroads around Hanoi, and Capt. Richard P. "Pop" Keirn had been captured by the Germans; Keirn had been shot down on his tenth B–17 mission in Europe and on his fifth F–4 mission in Southeast Asia— his fifteen missions led to more than eight years in prison.[30] Although the younger men had not joined a military service until after the Korean War, they too looked to America's recent wars for examples of how a prisoner of war should behave. Filtered through movies, novels, and training manuals, those examples contributed to confusion among the prisoners who needed them.

For several days after arriving at the Hilton, Colonel Risner thought that it was just a processing center and that he would soon be "moved to a compound to start the life of a regular prisoner of war."[31] The Zoo was hardly what he had in mind. Where were the open barracks in which prisoners played cards and planned escapes? Clearly the relatively mild experience of American prisoners in Germany during World War II was not going to be relevant in Hanoi's prisons. Even the deadly brutality of Japanese prison camps lacked the ideological and propagandistic thrust of imprisonment in North Vietnam. The most appropriate reservoir of experience for American prisoners in Hanoi was the same one the prison authorities there were using—the Chinese and North Korean prison camps in the Korean War.[32]

Concern about the behavior of American prisoners in the Korean War led President Eisenhower in 1955 to approve a Code of Conduct for members of the armed forces.[33] From its birth the Code was a compromise among the services. They did not agree on its meaning in 1955, and they continued to teach their contradictory interpretations of the Code throughout the Vietnam War. Consequently, Americans shot down in North Vietnam carried these disagreements into prison.

Article V of the Code stated that a prisoner of war was "bound to give only name, rank, service number, and date of birth"—that he would "evade answering further questions to the utmost of my ability." Ever since the Hague Convention of 1899, international law had required that prisoners of war give their captors name and rank; in 1929 the first Geneva Convention Relative to the Treatment of Prisoners of War included service number, and the Geneva Convention of 1949 added date of birth. These "big four" items of information enabled countries at war to notify each other of the identity of those captured so that the family of each prisoner might learn that he was alive.

International law did not require, of course, that prisoners refuse to answer other questions. Every country interrogated its prisoners of war, and usually elicited useful intelligence. In the Air Force's view, Article Five of the Code of Conduct was merely a restatement of international law with an added injunction to "evade" giving information detrimental to the United States. While "evade" seemed to imply that a prisoner was free to do more than simply refuse to talk, Article Five's blanket reference to "further questions" might mean that the prisoner should confine his answers to the "big four" or that he should not give truthful answers to even the most trivial questions beyond the "big four."[34]

The Defense Advisory Committee on Prisoners of War, which had drafted the Code of Conduct, also drafted a training guide to go with it. In this document the other services permitted the Air Force to have its way. Recommended training included "the use of ruses and stratagems to evade and avoid the disclosure of important information."[35] Individuals engaged in special operations were also to be taught "the use of cover stories."[36] But only the Air Force implemented these training recommendations. The other services maintained that most of their personnel needed the simplicity of "the big four and no more"—if they started talking they would not know where to stop.

While the other services were reacting to collaboration by young enlisted prisoners during the Korean War, the Air Force was trying to deal with germ warfare "confessions" by officers. During that war, the Strategic Air Command had given its aircrews training in answering the questions of enemy interrogators without divulging important information. None of the men who received this training and subsequently endured imprisonment were among those who confessed to germ warfare, but it was not clear how evasiveness had stopped the Chinese from extorting lies.[37]

Most American prisoners in the Korean War had received an assortment of conflicting guidance. At the beginning of the war the Joint Chiefs of Staff authorized prisoners to divulge any information that the enemy already knew. Even when accurately communicated to those who might need it, this directive was hard to apply in practice and was soon replaced by an injunction to be vague when talking to an enemy interrogator. In the wake of the germ warfare "confessions," Far East Air Forces ordered its men not to give the enemy any information beyond name, rank, serial number and date of birth.[38]

After the Korean War, the Air Force discarded Far East Air Forces' "big four" reaction in favor of the Strategic Air Command's training program in ruses and stratagems. The Strategic Air Command's survival school at Stead Air Force Base, Nevada, was expanded into an Air Force survival school under Air Training Command. Navy officers who attended the school complained about its departure from complete reliance on name, rank, serial number, and date of birth. The Air Force insisted that few men could hold that line against torture and continued to teach fallback techniques which involved talking without divulging important information.[39]

But the problem for prisoners in North Vietnam (and earlier in North Korea) was not so much safeguarding classified information as it was avoiding exploitation for enemy propaganda. The North Vietnamese had ample opportunity to observe American air tactics and they had acquired American hardware ranging from undetonated bombs to aircraft. The routine character of American air operations over North Vietnam meant that as the war went on there was less and less an American pilot could tell the North Vietnamese that they did not already know. North Vietnamese interrogators lost interest in gathering intelligence, but they were increasingly interested in getting confessions of war crimes.

However much or however little a prisoner talked, he might be required to write a "confession" or tape one or recite one to visiting journalists. Most prisoners could be tortured into confessing, but many learned to sabotage these confessions. While Navy officers may have been less prepared than Air Force graduates of Stead for failure to hold the line at name, rank, serial number and date of birth, some of the Navy prisoners proved especially successful in undermining North Vietnamese propaganda. When Commander Stockdale was selected for a filmed interview, he pounded his face black and blue with a mahogany stool. When Commander Denton was giving a filmed interview, he blinked the word "torture" in Morse Code. When Cmdr. Richard A. Stratton appeared before a group of visiting journalists, his face assumed a vacant expression and he complied with the North Vietnamese requirement that prisoners bow by bowing repeatedly and stiffly like an automaton; thanks to a *Life* magazine photographer, the North Vietnamese were soon getting complaints from around the world that they must be "brainwashing" their American prisoners. When Navy Lts. Charles N. Tanner and Ross R. Terry talked to a Japanese television interviewer, they told him that Lt. Cmdr. Ben Casey and Lt. Clark Kent had been court-martialed for refusing to fly missions. Upon learning that "Ben Casey" was the fictional surgeon on a popular American television show and "Clark Kent" was better known as Superman, the North Vietnamese were considerably less amused than the American public.[40]

North Vietnam's effort to use its American prisoners for propaganda purposes often seemed to backfire. Sometimes this was because the real target of the propaganda was not in the United States or Europe but in North Vietnam itself. The prisoners were trophies whose display could arouse the martial ardor of the North Vietnamese people. When prisoners were first captured, they usually had to run the gauntlet in several villages whose inhabitants naturally enjoyed beating a man who had dropped bombs in their vicinity. After bombing began near Hanoi in the summer of 1966, fifty-two American prisoners were paraded through a mob in downtown Hanoi and endured countless rocks, bottles, and fists. Film of this event spurred even the antiwar leaders in the Senate (including Fulbright, McGovern, McCarthy, Morse, and the Kennedys) to warn Hanoi not to put its American prisoners on trial for war crimes.[41]

Thereafter, the government of North Vietnam showed more restraint in displaying American prisoners. Often the government was content merely to put their uniforms in a museum. At the end of 1969, for example, Hanoi opened a large exhibit in honor of the air defense forces. Model aircraft on wires fought above a relief map of Hanoi, from which little missiles arose as tape-recorded antiaircraft fire boomed; a dozen aircraft models bearing American insignia fell while a narrator described the capture of American "air pirates." Col. Norman C. Gaddis's uniform was displayed together with the uniforms of two of North Vietnam's leading aces, Capt. Nguyen Van Coc and Capt. Nguyen Van Bai.* Colonel Gaddis, the assistant deputy commander for operations of the 12th

---

* By most accounts, at the end of the war Nguyen Van Coc was still North Vietnam's leading ace with nine victories. Nguyen Van Bai's seven victories were matched or exceeded by Nguyen Hong Nhi (eight), Mai Van Cuong (eight), Pham Thanh Ngan (eight), and Dang Ngoc Ngu (seven). There were ten other North Vietnamese aces, for a total of sixteen—all pilots. Only two American pilots and three weapon systems officers would achieve ace status during the Vietnam War, all in 1972; see Chapter 9. While both an F–4 pilot and his backseater each received full credit for their kills, it was also common for several North Vietnamese MiG pilots to receive credit for the same kill. Indeed, when an American aircraft went down, credit sometimes may have flowed simultaneously to MiGs and ground fire. Then too, MiG pilots received credit for shooting down reconnaissance drones. See especially Istvan Toperczer, *Air War Over North Vietnam: The Vietnamese People's Air Force* (Carrollton, Texas, 1998).

Tactical Fighter Wing at Cam Ranh Bay, was shot down near Hanoi in his F–4 by a MiG–17 on May 12, 1967; the 12th did not operate in Route Package Six, but Gaddis was visiting Da Nang and asked to go along.[42]

Although their propaganda about American prisoners could be clumsy, the North Vietnamese sometimes used the sophisticated services of Wilfred Burchett, an Australian communist writer who had disseminated China's germ warfare propaganda during the Korean War. After that war, Burchett had come to live in Hanoi for a couple of years before taking up residence in Moscow. During the Vietnam War, he returned to live in Phnom Penh and write books and articles attacking the United States and glorifying North Vietnam. In March 1966 he conducted a filmed interview in Hanoi with Major Guarino, who stoutly defended American policy and conduct in Southeast Asia. When the interview was broadcast on American television, most viewers (including Guarino's own family) could not fully appreciate the great courage of the prisoner's performance. Rather they could only marvel that the North Vietnamese permitted such freedom of expression.[43]

By the spring of 1967 the North Vietnamese were preparing to take a bolder step to advertise their "lenient" treatment of American prisoners in a way that could persuade the American public and divide the prisoners. One day the usual dose of propaganda broadcast to the prisoners over loudspeakers included the announcement that repentant prisoners might be permitted to go home early— before the end of the war. Commander Stockdale dubbed this the "fink release program" and the senior officers opposed it with the policy that all would go home together.[44]

Lacking volunteers, the program's first candidates for early release may have been a dozen prisoners at the Zoo who were placed under a Cuban officer they called "Fidel." The Cuban's approach was to torture these men until they were so compliant that they would do anything—even express gratitude for an early release and (most unlikely) not divulge their torture afterward. The North Vietnamese never agreed that this was the sort of prisoner they would be wise to send home anytime soon. Fidel's experiment finally ended when he encountered two especially resistant prisoners. Major Kasler (still suffering from infection in a severe leg wound received when he ejected from his aircraft two years before) and Capt. Earl G. Cobeil endured days of floggings. Cobeil went out of his mind, stopped eating, and died.[45]

While Hanoi's prison authorities sorted through their American prisoners for suitable candidates to release, the Viet Cong freed three American soldiers held in South Vietnam. They were sent to Phnom Penh, where they were turned over to an American antiwar activist, Thomas E. Hayden. A founder of the major left-wing student organization in the United States, the Students for a Democratic Society, Hayden had just paid his second visit to Hanoi. On his first visit in 1965 he had come as a junior partner of two historians, Herbert Aptheker (a communist) and Staughton Lynd (a Quaker professor at Yale). In the fall of 1967, Hayden led a group of young activists, including Rennard C. Davis (who would join Hayden the following year to organize demonstrations at the Democratic National Convention in Chicago). Having hosted many such visitors, the North Vietnamese took Hayden's group to see the usual attractions—bomb damage, bombs that had not detonated, and American prisoners. The activists quarreled among themselves about whether to believe a prisoner who said not only that he was treated well but that he opposed the war. They had been urging the communists to release some prisoners as a step toward negotiations, and Hayden agreed to escort from Phnom Penh to New York three American soldiers captured in South Vietnam.[46]

Three months later during the communist Tet 1968 offensive, Hanoi freed three American pilots shot down over North Vietnam. This time the American peace movement sent Father Daniel Berrigan and Professor Howard Zinn of Boston University to escort the three. Berrigan and his brother Philip had persuaded many young men to burn their draft cards; these two priests would themselves go to prison for destroying government records kept by a draft board. At a press conference in Hanoi, Berrigan condemned American bombing of North Vietnamese women, children, schools, hospitals and churches. While all three pilots made obligatory statements thanking the North Vietnamese for humane treatment and release, the most junior (Ens. David P. Matheny) was alone designated by the North Vietnamese to talk to the press.[47]

The only way Americans could enter and depart Hanoi peacefully was by means of the weekly International Control Commission plane from Vientiane, Laos. Berrigan took his charges to Vientiane, where he planned to transfer them to a commercial flight. But Ambassador William H. Sullivan met the Commission plane when it landed and explained to Air Force Lt. Col. Norris M. Overly (the senior prisoner released) that the White House preferred they return by military air, which they agreed to do despite heated objections from Berrigan and Zinn.

The willingness of Overly, Matheny, and Air Force Capt. Jon D. Black to accept early release disgusted fellow prisoners, but Washington was eager to get the intelligence they brought with them. Although the North Vietnamese had been careful to select pilots recently captured and held under relatively mild conditions at the Plantation, the three were able to convey useful information. Thanks to the excellence of prison communications, they could name many prisoners they had not met and recount examples of torture they had not experienced. Matheny had memorized more than seventy names and said that he himself had been subjected to the rope torture.

Overly spent most of his five months in prison caring for two badly injured cellmates, Lt. Cmdr. John S. McCain III and Maj. George E. ("Bud") Day. McCain was the son of an admiral who would soon become Commander in Chief, Pacific, and the North Vietnamese may have wanted Overly to convey the message that McCain (who had broken three limbs and a shoulder ejecting from his A–4) was receiving good medical care. Overly did report that McCain believed his surgeons were respected by other Vietnamese. On the other hand, McCain had been beaten and denied medical attention until he agreed to talk and his captors discovered the identity of his father.[48]

When McCain was put in Overly's cell, Overly was already attending to the needs of his other cellmate, Major Day, who despite a broken arm and wrenched knee had managed to escape from his captors near the Demilitarized Zone. While he struggled through the jungle for two weeks, Day was wounded by an American bomb or rocket and by Viet Cong bullets. He made it to South Vietnam before being recaptured and severely tortured to the point of breaking his wrist. After the war and more than five years in prison, Day would come home to receive the Medal of Honor.[49]

For fear of retarding negotiations and in the hope that more prisoners might be released, the Johnson administration chose to keep quiet about mounting evidence of torture. That evidence was not limited to the testimony of released prisoners. Other intelligence illuminated the grim recesses of the prisoners' predicament. Instead of making public revelations, however, the Johnson administration sought to protect intelligence sources.[50]

It did turn out to be the case that Hanoi's periodic releases of American airmen stopped for three years after the Nixon administration permitted returning prisoners to talk publicly about torture. By then nine prisoners (three groups of three) had come home from Hanoi. The second and third groups took commercial flights from Laos to New York for fear of hurting chances for further releases by offending Hanoi and the antiwar activists. The second group included Maj. James F. Low, one of the three Korean War aces imprisoned in Hanoi. The other two aces, Colonel Risner and Major Kasler, led fellow prisoners in resisting their captors. Although Low was tortured at first, he was careful to refer to the experience as "punishment" and to hide the fact that he was an ace. The North Vietnamese had read about Risner and Kasler in the American press, but they did not learn about Low's aerial victories until after he was released in August 1968.[51]

The third group of three prisoners was not released by Hanoi until August 1969. Since air operations (and therefore aircraft losses) over North Vietnam had been curtailed in 1968, this third group had been held in captivity much longer than its predecessors. They knew a lot about prison life in Hanoi, and one of them, Seaman Apprentice Douglas B. Hegdahl, came home with the approval of the prisoner leadership. Hegdahl was a special case in many respects. He was not aircrew—he had fallen off his ship in the spring of 1967. With this beginning, the North Vietnamese were inclined to view him as a stupid boy rather than a war criminal like the airmen. Hegdahl was bright enough to play the role of dunce to the hilt.[52]

Hegdahl and the two officers in the third group had memorized more than three hundred names of fellow prisoners. In addition to information of that kind, the three also brought a request for official guidance on the propriety of accepting early release. Through a prearranged signal, the U.S. government was to tell prisoners which of four policies they were to follow: no early release; or early release of sick and wounded only; or early release of sick, wounded and longtime prisoners only; or anyone is free to accept early release. The bureaucracy wrestled with this question for months. Although against trying to give the prisoners guidance, the Air Force agreed with the Navy that the fourth alternative was preferable to the others. The Army's preference for the third alternative was largely overridden in the ultimate compromise: "The U.S. approves any honorable release and prefers sick and wounded and longtime prisoners first."[53]

When directed to introduce the new policy into training programs, Lt. Gen. Sam Maddux, Jr. (Air Training Command) objected that it ran counter to Article III of the Code of Conduct: "I will accept neither parole nor special favors from the enemy."[54] This was precisely the view of the prisoner leadership in Hanoi. After the revelations of torture emerging from the 1969 release, Hanoi did not give its American prisoners a chance to act on the new U.S. policy until 1972. In any case, most of them continued to believe that early release was a violation of the Code of Conduct.

The prisoners' stance on early release might have inhibited a gradual exchange of prisoners had the North Vietnamese been so inclined. Following North Vietnam's first release in early 1968 of three American airmen, three captured North Vietnamese sailors had been returned to Hanoi on the International Control Commission plane. Accompanying them were two American editors, Harry S. Ashmore of the *Encyclopaedia Britannica* and William C. Baggs of the *Miami News*, who had been asked by the State Department to seek a broader prisoner exchange. The North Vietnamese seemed uninterested, and in any case this initiative was submerged in the excitement over President Johnson's bombing cutback and announcement that he would not seek another term.[55]

American visitors to North Vietnam tended to have more sympathy for the North Vietnamese than for their American captives, especially because such visitors disapproved of the bombing campaign that the prisoners had waged. Prospective visitors likely to think otherwise were not given visas. During the Ashmore-Baggs visit, the most famous Americans staying at Hanoi's Thong Nhat (Reunification) Hotel were CBS television correspondent Charles Collingwood and novelist Mary McCarthy. In McCarthy's case, lack of sympathy for American prisoners hardened into disdain. After talking to Colonel Risner and another prisoner, she pronounced them "pathetic cases of mental malnutrition" who must make their charming captors wonder about the quality of an American college education—"naive, rote-thinking, childish."[56] She did guess that the prisoners did not entirely trust her, but the suspicion that they might have been tortured apparently never crossed her mind.[57]

Although Hanoi consistently rebuffed any proposal that would have involved the release of a large number of American prisoners before a cease-fire, the U.S. government continued to seek such an exchange especially after the Nixon administration took office. Secretary of Defense Laird was sensitive about having promised the prisoners' families that the prisoners would not be left stranded by Vietnamization. When American forces had left South Vietnam, how much leverage would the United States have to get a prisoner exchange? Laird sought an exchange as soon as possible, but of course, the North Vietnamese had little incentive to cooperate other than the return of their own men—an outcome they seemed in no hurry to achieve.[58]

In early 1970, Laird enlisted the State Department in his campaign to persuade the South Vietnamese government to release as many as possible of its seven thousand North Vietnamese prisoners. President Thieu refused to release any able-bodied prisoners without assurance that the North Vietnamese would respond in a similar fashion, but he did send sixty-two disabled prisoners of war and twenty-four fishermen back to North Vietnam in July 1970.[59]

Although North Vietnam made no gesture in return, Thieu agreed in May 1971 to send more than five hundred sick and wounded prisoners. After the International Red Cross determined that only thirteen of these men wanted to return to North Vietnam, however, the North Vietnamese refused to accept any. It was an episode reminiscent of the Korean War, when the reluctance of Chinese prisoners to go home was for two years an impediment to a cease-fire. In both cases, the United States opposed forced repatriation and the communist governments sought to avoid the bad publicity surrounding the refusal of their men to return. There was also a superficial resemblance between the attitudes toward release of North Vietnamese and American prisoners, but the Americans desperately wanted to go home—all together—and their countrymen were increasingly desperate to get them back.[60]

*　　　　*　　　　*

The same article of the Code of Conduct that enjoined American prisoners of war to refuse "parole," also urged them to "make every effort to escape and aid others to escape."[61] In contrast to the very strict interpretation most prisoners made of the "parole" clause (extending it to almost every kind of early release), they were inclined to water down the "escape" clause. Colonel Risner discouraged escape planning in 1966 by insisting that escape would not be feasible without outside help.[62] While Americans might be able to break out of jail, they could not blend into the local population.

The best opportunities for escape occurred soon after capture, especially near the Demilitarized Zone. In addition to Major Day's almost successful attempt, Capt. Lance P. Sijan had evaded capture for six weeks and after capture managed to escape briefly. But starvation, injury, and torture took their toll, and Sijan did not survive to receive the Medal of Honor in person; he was the first Air Force Academy graduate to win that medal, and the Academy named a dormitory for him.[63]

Once a prisoner reached Hanoi, his chances for escape diminished. Only two escape attempts were mounted there during all the years of American captivity. The first and most promising grew out of the North Vietnamese decision to open a new prison in old buildings near the city's powerplant while it was under air attack in the summer of 1967. The prisoners called the main facility "Dirty Bird," because the powerplant's coal dust covered everything. When Navy Lt. (j.g.) George T. Coker and Air Force Capt. George G. McKnight were put into the nearby "Dirty Bird Annex," they saw opportunity in lax security procedures and proximity to the Red River. On the night of October 12, they removed the locks from their makeshift cell doors and stole away to the river. The current helped them swim perhaps fifteen miles before dawn forced them to seek cover on the bare, muddy bank. There they were discovered by peasants and recaptured.[64]

An encouraging aspect of the Coker-McKnight escape attempt was the lack of severe punishment afterward either for the recaptured men or their fellow prisoners. But the next attempt would lead to the worst weeks of torture experienced by prisoners at the large Zoo prison on the south side of Hanoi. There the abundance of airmen shot down in 1967 had led to the construction of an annex filled with more than seventy junior officers. Many of them and their fellow prisoners in the Zoo would suffer from the aborted escape of Air Force Captains John A. Dramesi and Edwin L. Atterberry.

Although Maj. Conrad W. Trautman, the senior officer in the annex, had grave doubts about an escape and refused to approve it, he could not bring himself to veto it. On a rainy Saturday night, May 10, 1969, Dramesi and Atterberry emerged from the roof of their cell, crossed the prison yard, and climbed the wall. Thanks to Atterberry's experience as a telephone lineman, he knew how to short out the exposed electric wires running along the top of the wall. While the guards tried to get the lights back on by fiddling with the switch box, Dramesi and Atterberry slipped over the wall and used provisions laboriously gathered for months to disguise themselves as peasants carrying baskets on a shoulder pole. They passed through the streets undetected, but fearing daylight they hid in some bushes hours before dawn. There a few miles from the Zoo they were found by the soldiers sent to look for them.[65]

Atterberry died at the hands of North Vietnamese torturers. Dramesi again proved himself exceptionally tough. This was his second escape attempt—he had embarked on his first with a bullet wound in the right leg and a sprained left knee shortly after being shot down near Dong Hoi. Both times he survived his punishment ready to plan another escape. But Dramesi's intolerance of those less able to withstand torture and his persistent advocacy of escape had already made him unpopular. Many who endured torture on his account grew fervent in their opposition to escape attempts.[66]

The relationship between Dramesi's second escape attempt and torture was all the more memorable because this suffering was followed by a dramatic improvement in prison life. For most prisoners there was little or no torture after the death of Ho Chi Minh at age seventy-nine on September 3, 1969. Whether replacement of the prison system's commander and other positive changes flowed more from Ho's death or publicity about North Vietnamese torture, few prisoners wanted to risk a return to torture for the sake of escape attempts with little prospect of success.

If outside help would be necessary for a successful escape, as Colonel Risner argued, then inmates of Hanoi's prisons could not have much hope of going home (on terms acceptable to most of them) before the end of the war. Short of invasion, American forces would have a hard time extracting prisoners from so well defended a city. Prospects for a rescue improved for prisoners held outside Hanoi. In the spring of 1970, Air Force intelligence analysts used photography to prove that American prisoners were being held in a compound about twenty-four miles west of Hanoi near the village of Son Tay. Construction to expand the facility had drawn attention, and the prisoners signalled their presence by arranging laundry and piles of dirt.[67]

This was not the first time that a prison camp had been established at Son Tay. During World War II the Japanese had imprisoned Vietnamese soldiers there, and at that time Nguyen Cao Ky (the future vice president of South Vietnam) was a boy in the village. Twenty-five years later in the summer of 1970, an American joint task group rehearsed a Son Tay rescue at Eglin Air Force Base, Florida, where Air Force special operations training had been conducted throughout the Vietnam War.[68]

Brig. Gen. Leroy J. Manor commanded both the Air Force's Special Operations Force and the joint task group for the Son Tay raid. His combat experience dated back to World War II, when he had flown P–47s in Europe. While commanding the 37th Tactical Fighter Wing at Phu Cat Air Base, South Vietnam, in 1968, Manor had flown missions into Route Package One. His second in command of the Son Tay task group was Col. Arthur D. "Bull" Simons from the Army's Special Warfare Center at Fort Bragg, North Carolina. Simons (a colorful veteran of World War II special operations in the Philippines) would lead the raiders to Son Tay, while Manor oversaw the operation from the communications center on Monkey Mountain, near Da Nang. Night after night the raiders practiced at Eglin with a Son Tay mock-up that was dismantled during the day to prevent observation by a Soviet reconnaissance satellite.[69]

Manor's task group was ready in October, but President Nixon decided to postpone the operation until November—after the midterm election and after Nixon had been able to make an overture to China for better relations. A November date would also be further removed from Nixon's October 7 speech offering a cease-fire (with all forces left in place) and an exchange of all thirty thousand communist prisoners in South Vietnamese prisons for the much smaller number of prisoners of war held by the communists. Since Manor wanted a quarter moon to provide enough but not too much light, the only suitable nights were November 21–25.[70]

Manor's task group arrived at Takhli Air Base, Thailand, on November 18, 1970. After five years of combat operations there, the F–105s of the 355th Tactical Fighter Wing had just left Southeast Asia as part of Nixon's drawdown. Unfortunately Takhli no longer had secure telecommunications with Seventh Air Force headquarters or the command center on Monkey Mountain. While a makeshift system was put in place, two T–39s shuttled weather reports from Saigon to Takhli, where Manor remained until a few hours before the raid. By the 20th of November, Manor was convinced that Typhoon Patsy would make the mission doubtful for any of the designated nights (November 21–25), and he decided to launch it one night early.[71]

Colonel Simons loaded the fifty-five soldiers in his raiding party aboard a transport plane, which took them to Udorn Air Base where they were transferred to three of the six Air Force helicopters headed for Son Tay. After aerial refueling over Laos, the six helicopters and five A–1 propeller-driven attack aircraft were led into North Vietnam by two C–130E four-engine transports equipped for special operations. When they reached the prison camp, the C–130s climbed to fifteen hundred feet and dropped flares over both the prison and a nearby army training center.[72]

Fire-fight simulators were also dropped near the training center to decoy enemy troops there. This measure proved unnecessary, because Simons' helicopter landed at the training center (possibly staffed by Chinese soldiers) instead of at the prison as planned—a fortunate error that killed and wounded scores of enemy soldiers without loss to Simons' force. The prison itself was less well defended, for the prisoners had been moved out three months earlier, even before Manor's task group had been formed.* The raiders penetrated

---

* The Son Tay prison camp was south of the Red River near the Song Con, a river which flooded in the summer of 1970. The fact that the high water almost reached the camp was probably why the North Vietnamese decided to move the prisoners. Benjamin F. Schemmer's *The Raid* (New York, 1976) discussed a possible link between the flooding and American rainmaking operations in Laos. While information about these operations had been tightly held during the war, Senator Claiborne Pell (Democrat, Rhode Island) succeeded in getting Defense Department personnel to give his Foreign Relations Subcommittee a top secret briefing on the subject in March 1974; this hearing was declassified and made public in May 1974 under the title *Weather Modification*. Operation Popeye (the most well known of its designations) had begun in Laos in late 1966, and over the next two years RF–4s also seeded clouds in adjacent portions of the North Vietnamese panhandle. After the end of Rolling Thunder, WC–130s and RF–4s continued to seed clouds in Laos until July 1972; rainmaking operations in North Vietnam never resumed after 1968. All told about twenty-six hundred sorties dropped nearly fifty thousand seeding cartridges (only about eleven hundred of which fell in North Vietnam). It is very doubtful

almost to the heart of North Vietnam and came home with one slight bullet wound, a broken ankle, and no liberated prisoners.[73]

Henry Kissinger would blame raiding this empty prison on an "egregious failure of intelligence," but a few days before the raid the Defense Intelligence Agency had concluded that the prisoners had probably been moved.[74] Secretary of Defense Laird and Admiral Moorer, the Chairman of the Joint Chiefs, went ahead with the raid anyway, probably after talking to Nixon (if not Kissinger) about the latest intelligence estimate.[75] When Laird testified before the Senate Foreign Relations Committee, he omitted any mention of that estimate and repeatedly declared that reconnaissance cameras could not see through roofs.[76]

Senator Fulbright and many of his colleagues on the committee were upset, not only about the raid, but also about air strikes that had been conducted the next day against the panhandle of North Vietnam. Indeed, there was considerable confusion between these two operations. The administration initially announced only the strikes conducted in the panhandle on November 21. But Hanoi complained to the press about bombing near Hanoi and even claimed that American prisoners had been wounded when their prison was attacked. In the wake of these charges, Secretary Laird began to tell the nation about the Son Tay raid.[77]

Laird introduced Manor and Simons at a press conference and told how Navy airmen had drawn enemy attention away from the raiders by dropping flares near Haiphong (they were not permitted to drop bombs). Unfortunately, even then Laird held important parts of the story back. Gradually the press learned that both Navy and Air Force fighters had distracted enemy air defenses by firing Shrike missiles at enemy surface-to-air missile radars near Hanoi and Haiphong, that one of these fighters (an Air Force F–105 Wild Weasel) had been hit by a SAM and could only return as far as Laos before the crew had to eject (they were both rescued), that Air Force A–1s had strafed a bridge near the prison to cut off enemy troops, and that the Son Tay raiders had attacked another enemy installation near the prison. Poor handling of the Son Tay story left many Americans with the impression that their government had resumed bombing in the Red River Valley and then lied about it.[78]

The Nixon administration had displayed a certain wisdom in running two politically risky operations back to back. As with the Cambodian incursion and

---

that rainmaking in Southeast Asia made any significant difference. It did not (and was not intended to) raise overall rainfall in the region. Success in meeting its objective of inducing greater rainfall on the Ho Chi Minh Trail could never be measured, because in any specific location rainfall varied from year to year in any case. Rainfall throughout Southeast Asia was always heavy. As to the Red River delta of North Vietnam, the most important factors in abnormal flooding were typhoons spawned at sea. On Operation Popeye, see also Van Staaveren, *Interdiction in Southern Laos*, pp 226–28; John F. Fuller, *Thor's Legions: Weather Support to the U.S. Air Force and Army, 1937–1987* (Boston, 1990), pp 291–94; Charles C. Bates and John F. Fuller, *America's Weather Warriors* (College Station, Tex., 1986), pp 224–32; and Craig Stevaux, "The Weather War," *Vietnam*, Dec. 1997, pp 31–36.

bombing of the North Vietnamese panhandle in the spring, the level of criticism spurred by two operations did not appear greater than would have accompanied only one. Indeed, even in failure the Son Tay raid caught the imagination of many sufficiently to blunt barbs aimed at bombing in the panhandle.

On the other hand, it was difficult to prove that six hours of bombing in the panhandle had accomplished much. As with the bigger operation in the spring, the Nixon administration called the strikes of November 21 "protective reaction," but now anonymous Defense Department officials readily leaked the fact that fighter-bombers were attacking not only SAM and gun sites but also supplies stored in preparation for the dry season surge down the Ho Chi Minh Trail. Soon the network of roads in Laos would dry sufficiently to support the heavier truck traffic necessary to carry those supplies to South Vietnam.[79]

As for SAMs and antiaircraft artillery in the North Vietnamese panhandle, they threatened not only reconnaissance planes in North Vietnam itself, but also B–52s and fighter-bombers attacking the transportation system in Laos. It was nonetheless true that the Nixon administration hoped to persuade the North Vietnamese to quit firing at reconnaissance planes over North Vietnam. After the May 1970 strikes, reconnaissance planes had encountered little resistance until an Air Force RF–4C was shot down on Friday, November 13, with the loss of both crew members.[80]

The Freedom Bait protective reaction strikes of November 21 lasted only six hours because Typhoon Patsy was bearing down on the Vietnamese coast. Seventh Air Force and Seventh Fleet managed to send more than two hundred strike sorties (mostly Air Force F–4s and Navy A–7s) before weather closed the operation. Needless to say bomb damage assessment amounted to anybody's guess. The crews claimed to have hit perhaps ninety trucks and started fires at three fuel dumps, but were less certain about SAM sites. As the Commander in Chief, Pacific, Admiral McCain, informed Admiral Moorer, four SAM sites may have been hit, but "only two indications of possible SAM associated equipment were noted."[81]

Afterward the wings involved made known their unhappiness with the way Freedom Bait had been run. On the evening of November 20, Seventh Air Force had informed the wings at Udorn, Ubon, and Korat, Thailand, as well as Da Nang and Phu Cat, South Vietnam, that they would soon launch the sorties for which they had already been sent sealed target materials. Not until after midnight were they permitted to look at those materials and then only for targets assigned to the particular wing. That restriction was especially irritating to the 388th at Korat, which was expected to provide Wild Weasel support for the other wings.[82]

Scarcity of time to prepare for Freedom Bait was the result of the special demands for secrecy thought necessary if the Son Tay rescue mission was not to be endangered. Freedom Bait orders were sent in the most secure and slowest "back channel" messages. Seventh Air Force started sending the fragmentary order specifying the contributions of Udorn's 432d before 7 p.m. on November 20, but the wing did not receive the order until after midnight.[83]

Meanwhile, the wings were flying routine night missions as well as supporting the Son Tay rescue and preparing to fly the routine day missions that they had already been assigned. The latter were not cancelled until 7 a.m., little more than three hours before the wings launched their biggest operation in six months. As they scrambled to prepare for Freedom Bait, the wings had trouble believing that they would actually fly these missions in the face of the oncoming typhoon. But at 4 a.m. on the 21st, as soon as the Son Tay raiders had returned, the wings were told to execute Freedom Bait.[84]

Per instruction the wings hit their Freedom Bait targets with waves of a dozen strike aircraft very much in the fashion of the old Rolling Thunder strikes in Route Package Six. The aircrews would have preferred breaking the waves down into flights of four or elements of two in the armed reconnaissance mode customarily used in Route Package One and on the Trail. Panhandle air defenses and targets did not appear to justify the more cumbersome formation that permitted many trucks spotted by forward air controllers to escape unscathed.[85]

As so often in the air war over North Vietnam, Freedom Bait and the Son Tay raid had less to do with hurting the enemy than with signalling to him. This time the signal did some good, while costing no American lives and only one aircraft—the F–105 Wild Weasel lost defending the raiders. The principal beneficiaries of the raid were the American prisoners in North Vietnam. Fearing another rescue attempt, the North Vietnamese emptied the outlying prison camps and concentrated their American prisoners in downtown Hanoi at Hoa Lo, the "Hanoi Hilton." Even the "Zoo" on the edge of the city was vacated for a time. At the Hilton, more than three hundred American prisoners had to be housed in open bay cells, with twenty to fifty men in a cell.[86]

The sudden privilege of associating openly with many of their fellow prisoners was a great morale boost, and the men dubbed their open bay cells "Camp Unity." The senior prisoner, Col. John P. Flynn, took command of the 4th Allied Prisoner of War Wing—so called because Americans were engaging in their fourth allied war effort of the twentieth century and a few of their South Vietnamese and Thai allies were imprisoned with them. The North Vietnamese were soon sending prisoners deemed troublemakers away from Camp Unity, some of them to camps outside Hanoi. But for most of North Vietnam's American prisoners, prison life had finally come to resemble the German prison camps in World War II.[87]

The Nixon administration portrayed the Son Tay raid as an attempt not only to shorten imprisonment but, more than that, to save American lives. The North Vietnamese had recently given Cora Weiss, an antiwar activist from New York City, the names of seventeen Americans who had died in North Vietnam—including eleven for whom the United States had evidence of capture. In the case of Air Force Capt. Wilmer N. Grubb, the North Vietnamese had released photographs of him in apparent good health after his capture in January 1966. In November 1970 they revealed not only that Grubb had died but also that his death had occurred only nine days after capture—before communist newspapers published his photograph.[88]

Although release of the dead men's names was a positive step in the somewhat more humane policy that North Vietnam had begun to implement a year earlier, those names conveyed the impression of a situation more desperate than the prisoners' ameliorating plight had become. With regard to Son Tay, this impression was made all the more vivid by reasonable but unfounded speculation that the North Vietnamese might send away from Hanoi the prisoners in worst shape so that they would not be seen by visitors.

The sense of urgency stirred by the Weiss list helped to blunt qualms of the prisoners' families about the risks that the Son Tay raid necessarily took with the prisoners' lives. Although the raid's positive impact on the prisoners could not then be known by their wives and parents, the League of Families applauded the raid as proof that the Nixon administration really wanted to do something for the men who had been imprisoned for so long. A few of the families broke with their leadership, and one wife criticized the rescue attempt as a cynical ploy that "wiped the bombing raids right out of the headlines."[89] Most of the families who spoke to the press, however, were enthusiastic.

The wife of Air Force Capt. Howard J. Hill, for example, did not know that her husband was about to be moved to a better environment at the "Hilton" from a camp west of Hanoi. But she told the press that she was "screaming with sheer joy" and that the raid would not lead to worse conditions for her husband: "If anything, I think Hanoi will afford them better treatment. If the helicopters had brought out men in terrible condition, some maybe on the verge of death, how would that have looked for North Vietnam?"[90]

Chapter Eight

The Lavelle Affair

Curiosity about the attempt to rescue prisoners at Son Tay was especially strong among those who knew men imprisoned in North Vietnam. Many within the Air Force had worked with those men, and occasionally personal relationships ran back further than service together. Lt. Gen. John D. Lavelle had first met Colonel Flynn, the highest ranking prisoner, when they were boys attending the Catholic schools of Cleveland, Ohio. Lavelle was six years older and had dated Flynn's sister. But Lavelle had a still more direct connection with the raid, and the fragile character of that connection confirmed the depth to which his own career seemed to have fallen.[1]

Although Lavelle was Vice Commander in Chief of Pacific Air Forces, he was told nothing about the raid in advance or even afterward—until he watched Secretary Laird brief the nation on television. Lavelle's boss, Gen. Joseph Nazzaro, had been briefed together with key members of his staff, a group from which Lavelle was obviously excluded. During the raid, Nazzaro was away from headquarters on one of his frequent trips to see his farflung units; as usual he was accompanied by the key members of his staff. When intelligence reported a very high volume of North Vietnamese radio traffic, Lavelle tried to inform Admiral McCain, Commander in Chief, Pacific, and was finally told by one of McCain's subordinates to ignore the whole matter.[2]

After years of pressure-filled jobs of considerable importance, Lavelle found himself merely minding the store. An early attempt to make a decision while his boss was away was quickly quashed when Nazzaro returned. Yet despite a lack of authority, Lavelle was expected to remain on Hickam Air Force Base, Hawaii, whenever Nazzaro was off base even for a few hours. This meant that every time Lavelle wanted to leave the base, he had to ask Nazzaro for permission.[3]

Lavelle blamed his predicament on the Air Force Chief of Staff, General Ryan, with whom Lavelle had some disagreements during his previous assignment. They were very different personalities. Ryan was careful, quiet, almost taciturn. Lavelle was gregarious and impulsive.

Before his encounters with Ryan, Lavelle's impulsiveness had already caused him difficulties. As Seventeenth Air Force commander in 1967, Lavelle nearly sent his alert force at Wheelus Air Base, Libya, to intercept unidentified Algerian MiGs on their way to land at a nearby airport; any confrontation might have been explosive, because Libyans were already rioting against American support of Israel in the Six Day War. Lavelle got in trouble even for having his men start their engines, but he held them on the ground. Although his next assignment came sooner than expected, it was an important one.[4]

For nearly three years, Lavelle directed the Defense Communications Planning Group, the joint organization that had been set up in Washington to implement Secretary of Defense McNamara's plans to build a physical and electronic barrier against North Vietnamese infiltration into South Vietnam. Lavelle took over the group just before McNamara's departure and helped refocus the project on its Air Force component, a sensor field on the Ho Chi Minh Trail monitored by Task Force Alpha at Nakhon Phanom Air Base, Thailand.[5]

In pushing the Air Force component of the barrier project, Lavelle got little opposition from the other services. The Marines had been expected to build a well-defended fence along the Demilitarized Zone from the coast thirty miles inland, and they were glad to avoid their participation in what seemed to them a bad idea. But General Ryan was skeptical about the effectiveness of the sensors and he did not want to contribute the specially equipped F–4s necessary to drop them accurately—using Long Range Navigation (loran) electronic ground beacons. At one point Lavelle even offered to resign both from his joint job and the Air Force. Nevertheless, Ryan did perceive advantages in Lavelle's project (including funding for new munitions, plus loran's utility for all-weather bombing even without sensors), and the Ryan-Lavelle relationship did not run aground on the barrier.[6]

Sensing that his career prospects might improve if he returned to the Air Force, Lavelle made it known that he wanted an Air Force assignment. When Ryan raised the possibility of Lavelle tackling cost overruns at the Lockheed plant that manufactured the controversial C–5 giant transport, Lavelle took his arguments against Air Force management of the plant to Undersecretary John L. McLucas and Secretary Robert Seamans. Ryan seemed so angry that Lavelle believed his career was finished, an interpretation which in his view was reinforced regularly by his new boss, General Nazzaro.[7]

Less than a year after assigning Lavelle to Hawaii, however, General Ryan gave him a fourth star and sent him to Saigon as Seventh Air Force commander. When Lavelle took command at the end of July 1971, he looked like a natural choice, because his predecessor at Seventh Air Force, Gen. Lucius D. Clay, Jr., had also preceded him as Vice Commander in Chief of Pacific Air Forces; now Clay was returning to replace Nazzaro, who was retiring. But Lavelle was not inclined to give Ryan much credit for the promotion that Lavelle concluded was the result of a recommendation by his new Army boss, General Abrams.

Lavelle had become well acquainted with Abrams while working on the barrier, and Lavelle had learned that Clay's predecessor as Seventh Air Force commander, General Brown, had lobbied for either Lavelle or Gen. J. C. Meyer (Ryan's Vice Chief of Staff) to become Seventh Air Force commander when Ryan gave Clay the job.[8]

While Ryan this time went along with Lavelle's promotion, there was evidence that the Chief of Staff saw the job of Seventh Air Force commander as one of diminishing importance. After all, most American armed forces were apt to be out of South Vietnam well before the 1972 presidential election, and Thailand was less and less enthusiastic about playing host to large American forces. Before going to take command in Vietnam, Lavelle spent a week in Washington trying to see Ryan, but had to settle for a meeting with the Vice Chief of Staff. Meyer gave no instructions other than to improve relations with the Army.[9]

Lavelle found that the trouble which had been brewing between Military Assistance Command, Vietnam, and Seventh Air Force in Saigon revolved around the two intelligence chiefs. Since Lavelle's intelligence chief was about to rotate anyway, this problem was soon resolved. But Lavelle's major problems were only just beginning.

As the southwest monsoon spent itself, the North Vietnamese began to prepare for their annual supply surge through the Laotian panhandle from November to March. It became increasingly apparent that this year's surge was going to be much better protected than ever before. In addition to the antiaircraft artillery that had been the mainstay of air defense in the adjacent Laotian and North Vietnamese panhandles, the North Vietnamese increased the number of active surface-to-air missile sites in the North Vietnamese panhandle from two or three to a dozen, and for the first time sites were suspected in Laos itself. Meanwhile, the North Vietnamese had built a new all-weather pierced-steel-plank runway at Quan Lang on the Ca River, about fifty miles northwest of Vinh, and they were repairing the fair-weather airfield at Dong Hoi only thirty-five miles north of the Demilitarized Zone.[10]

The air defense environment in the panhandles of North Vietnam and Laos was beginning to bear a resemblance to the more formidable one near Hanoi and Haiphong. Fears for the survival of B–52s in such an environment increased on October 4, when, for the first time, a MiG tried to intercept B–52s in Laos, and on November 20, when a MiG fired a missile at a B–52 near the Mu Gia Pass. Although no B–52s were lost to MiGs or SAMs during the 1971–72 supply surge, a SAM did bring down a C–130 gunship in Laos at the end of March. By then, General Lavelle's efforts to combat North Vietnam's buildup and its air defenses had got him into a lot of trouble.[11]

On March 23, 1972, General Lavelle was recalled to Washington, where General Ryan secured his relief as commander of Seventh Air Force for employing a system of false reporting to cover up unauthorized raids into North

Vietnam. General Lavelle insisted that he had been encouraged by his bosses to conduct such raids and that false reporting was the result of misunderstanding and overzealousness on the part of subordinates.[12]

*   *   *

One of the odd aspects of the Lavelle affair was the relatively inconsequential bombing that he was charged with conducting illegitimately—fewer than 30 missions, about 150 sorties—when on specific occasions he was authorized to make much larger raids on North Vietnam. But unlike his illegitimate raids, the timing of those bigger, authorized raids was determined by political factors over which Lavelle had no control.

Before Lavelle took command, the Nixon administration had preferred to attack North Vietnamese targets when it was taking heat for some other unpopular action anyway. The first big protective reaction strikes had been associated with the invasion of Cambodia in the spring of 1970 and the second batch with the Son Tay raid in the fall. When South Vietnamese ground forces attacked North Vietnamese supply centers in the Laotian panhandle during February and March of 1971, American air forces were authorized to hit SAM sites, trucks, and supply depots in the North Vietnamese panhandle with about three hundred sorties; a few of these were sent on February 20, 21, and 28, but most went on March 21 and 22, while South Vietnamese troops were retreating from Laos.[13]

In September 1971, less than two months after Lavelle took command, he was given his first legitimate opportunity to send a major strike into North Vietnam. This time there was no parallel initiative to share the load of criticism that inevitably accompanied bombing in North Vietnam. Lavelle was not enthusiastic about orders restricting him to targets within twenty miles of the Demilitarized Zone, and he was even less happy about going in bad weather. But Washington would agree to no more than a day's postponement, and on September 21, Lavelle sent nearly two hundred sorties against three gasoline tank farms. The weather was so bad that the Navy sent only four sorties, and Seventh Air Force relied entirely on specially equipped F–4 pathfinders guided by the loran ground beacons Lavelle had done so much to install as part of McNamara's barrier. Without losing an aircraft, he claimed destruction of about thirty buried gasoline tanks with a total capacity of more than 150,000 gallons. In Lavelle's, view this amount of destruction was not worth the effort, but he was proud of having directed the first big loran fighter strike.[14]

Lavelle was never told why he was authorized to send that first loran strike, but he would not have been surprised to learn that it was part of the negotiating process. Henry Kissinger's secret talks with the North Vietnamese in Paris had come to nothing. Despite President Nixon's offer in May 1971 of a cease-fire which would not require North Vietnamese troops to withdraw from South Vietnam, the North Vietnamese government was demanding that the Thieu government in South Vietnam be eliminated before a cease-fire. The loran strike served as Nixon's response to the collapse of the secret talks.[15]

Although talks with the North Vietnamese were not going well, Nixon and Kissinger were emboldened by their progress in getting better relations with China and the Soviet Union. Nixon was scheduled to make unprecedented presidential visits to Beijing and Moscow in 1972. Indeed, the surprise announcement in July 1971 that the Chinese would play host to Nixon in February 1972 had chilled relations between North Vietnam and China. By the same token, Nixon had gained enough popular support in the United States to risk some of it on limited bombing of North Vietnam. Convinced that the North Vietnamese were preparing an offensive for 1972, Nixon authorized in December 1971 by far the biggest bombing raids on North Vietnam since the end of Rolling Thunder.[16]

Seventh Air Force and the Seventh Fleet sent about a thousand strike sorties against North Vietnam from December 26 through December 30, a period bounded by the Christmas and New Year's holidays. For the first time since Rolling Thunder, strikes were permitted as far north as the twentieth parallel— more than two hundred miles north of the Demilitarized Zone, only seventy-five miles south of Hanoi. Although Christmas day had been clear, the weather closed down on the morning of December 26 just as two flights of Air Force F–4s were approaching the Thanh Hoa barracks and truck repair shop. The attackers got under a fifteen-hundred-foot ceiling and lost an F–4, apparently to ground fire. The rest of the five-day operation had to be conducted through clouds. Seventh Air Force F–4s guided by loran pathfinders made two thirds of the strike sorties, while Navy A–6s used their onboard radar to guide carrier-based F–4s and A–7s to their targets.[17]

Aside from indicating that the Nixon administration might be willing to resume full-scale bombing of North Vietnam, the December 1971 raids did not achieve very impressive results. Effective loran bombing required photography annotated to show the target's exact relationship with the navigation beacons; this painstaking work had not yet been done for most of North Vietnam. In any case, the greater the distance from the beacons, the lower the accuracy. Only about a fourth of the bombs hit close enough to their targets to show up on bomb damage assessment photography.[18]

The strike on Quan Lang airfield was among the most accurate, with more than 160 craters appearing in photographs after about two hundred bombs had been dropped. But even here the pierced-steel-plank runway was broken in only fourteen places and was quickly repaired. East German television did indicate that two MiG–21s were blown on their backs. As to the thirteen buried gasoline tank farms attacked that week, estimates of destruction ranged from a total of

194,000 gallons up to 870,000 gallons out of a capacity of about 3,500,000 gallons.[19]

*   *   *

General Lavelle was not content with rare opportunities to bomb North Vietnam in bad weather. He wanted routine authority to hit North Vietnam's air defenses and its gathering invasion force at times of his own choosing. But the Nixon administration would not grant Lavelle this much authority, at least officially. Privately, Nixon groused about what seemed to him the Air Force's poor performance and the lack of imagination found among military leaders as a whole. While he admired the courage of airmen, soldiers, and sailors, Nixon had a low opinion of generals and admirals. The President liked to quote H.G. Wells' comment that military minds were mediocre because bright people would not subject themselves to a military career.[20]

From the beginning of Nixon's term, he had been expecting to end the war even while withdrawing ground forces from South Vietnam and not resuming a sustained bombing campaign in North Vietnam. Since the Air Force had proved unable to work this miracle for him, he blamed air leadership and promised his aides that he would bomb North Vietnam thoroughly before pulling out entirely. So far, however, Nixon had been careful to keep overt bombing of North Vietnam within time limits that minimized protest. By sending the biggest raids while most American college students were home for Christmas, Nixon had further dampened student opposition already cooled by the draft lottery, reduced draft calls, and reduced American participation in ground combat. The situation in Vietnam would have to get worse before the President was ready to authorize sustained bombing operations over North Vietnam.[21]

Meanwhile, Lavelle was repeatedly told to make maximum use of the authority he had. There was nothing new in this dialogue. General Clay and General Abrams had been requesting expanded authority for months, and Secretary Laird had repeatedly refused. On July 24, 1971, just before Lavelle took command, the Chairman of the Joint Chiefs, Admiral Moorer, conveyed Laird's latest refusal to the Commander in Chief, Pacific, Admiral McCain, with the admonition to "take full advantage" of the current rules.[22] Admiral McCain in turn urged "maximum use," and General Abrams in one of his first formal messages to General Lavelle spelled out an interpretation of the current rules:

> Interlocking and mutually supporting NVN air defenses constitute unacceptable hazard to air crews attempting to identify a particular SAM/AAA firing site. Accordingly, on occurrence of any SAM or AAA firing or activation against our air-

craft, it is considered appropriate for escort forces to direct immediate protective reaction strikes against any identifiable element of the firing/activated air defense complex.[23]

The words "interlocking" and "firing or activation" would provide key ingredients of General Lavelle's rationale for his way of making maximum use of the rules. Before his taking command, F–105 Wild Weasel crews had already been authorized to fire their radar-seeking missiles at any SAM site whose radar was tracking an F–105 or the aircraft it was escorting. An F–105 did not have to wait for a SAM site to fire; activation of its radar was sufficient—as indicated by radar warning gear carried by the F–105 and the F–4. In General Lavelle's view, it was foolish to wait for a signal from the radar warning gear, especially because that gear would only sound the alarm for SAM radars. In an interlocking system, North Vietnam's early warning and MiG-control radars could feed their data to the missile launch sites, which consequently would not have to come on the air until the last minute. Lavelle argued that Seventh Air Force should assume the enemy air defense system was activated every time American aircraft entered North Vietnam. Hence, any aircraft that attacked an air defense target in North Vietnam necessarily did so after activation of the North Vietnamese air defense system and therefore was operating within the rules of engagement as interpreted by Lavelle.[24]

Lavelle's interpretation permitted Seventh Air Force to plan attacks on North Vietnamese air defenses and execute the plans without waiting for the North Vietnamese to shoot first. While his superiors were encouraging a liberal interpretation of the rules of engagement, this was probably not what they had in mind. The customary way of stretching the rules, and one employed to especially good effect by the Navy, was "trolling." Reconnaissance aircraft were used as bait; as soon as the North Vietnamese reacted, previously selected targets were hit by a force waiting nearby. The Navy's superiority in trolling was their use of a bigger strike force. While Lavelle approved of that, he did not like using his men as bait. Trolling seemed to him a silly and unnecessarily dangerous game.

Lavelle claimed that much of his thinking about bending the rules was confirmed by a visit of the Chairman of the Joint Chiefs to South Vietnam in early November 1971. At that point Lavelle was concerned about the presence at Quan Lang airfield of two MiG–21s which were threatening B–52 operations in Laos. As Lavelle would recall their conversation, Moorer indicated that an Air Force protective reaction strike could hit the airfield even though it was in an area normally patrolled by the Navy. Moorer's recollection, on the other hand, would be that he and Lavelle discussed only photoreconnaissance, not a protective reaction strike.[25]

On November 8, an Air Force RF–4 with two F–4 escorts flew over Quan Lang. They reported being fired upon and attacking the airfield. The MiGs were nowhere to be seen, but the F–4s did leave some craters near the runway.

Lavelle showed Moorer photographs of the empty airfield just before the Chairman left Vietnam. Soon Lavelle learned from General Clay that General Ryan was complaining about how little damage this Quan Lang raid had done. Lavelle concluded that his error had been in sending so small a force armed mostly with cluster bombs for flak suppression.[26]

This was not the first time that Washington had seemed to encourage using routine protective reaction strikes against targets other than air defenses firing on reconnaissance planes. In the wake of the Son Tay raid, President Nixon had told a press conference that if American planes were fired upon, he would "order that the missile site be destroyed and that the military complex around the site which supports it also be destroyed."[27] By then, of course, Nixon had already sent special strikes against supply dumps in North Vietnam under the rubric of protective reaction.

In the spring of 1971, Secretary Laird had even suggested using routine protective reaction strikes to hit field artillery.[28] When Laird came to Saigon in early December, he talked to Lavelle at Ambassador Bunker's home. As Lavelle would recall their conversation, Laird indicated that Lavelle should not ask the Secretary of Defense to make a more liberal interpretation of the rules, but that if Lavelle made a more liberal interpretation, Laird would stand behind him or at least not question him.[29]

Lavelle thought that a similar message was conveyed by Lt. Gen. John W. Vogt, an Air Force officer who was Director of the Joint Staff. Vogt represented Admiral Moorer at a conference held in Hawaii to discuss ways of better protecting B–52s over Laos. Gen. Bruce K. Holloway, the SAC Commander in Chief, had become so concerned about the MiG threat that he had grounded the B–52s in Southeast Asia for a couple of days. Lavelle's vice commander, Maj. Gen. Winton W. Marshall, returned from Hawaii with a report that Moorer wanted a liberal interpretation of the rules and that the conference had decided to increase both the number of reconnaissance missions and the number of fighters escorting reconnaissance aircraft as well as B–52s.[30]

In mid-December, Lavelle attended an Air Force commanders conference at Andrews Air Force Base near Washington. While he was there, five Air Force F–4s were lost over Laos—three of them to MiGs in northern Laos where the North Vietnamese were engaged in an offensive. It was the worst three days the Air Force had experienced since the end of Rolling Thunder. Lavelle would later recall that General Meyer, the Vice Chief of Staff, invited him to the Pentagon to hear a briefing on how to destroy the Moc Chau radar, which controlled MiGs over northern Laos. But Moc Chau was in North Vietnam far north of the twentieth parallel and off limits to reconnaissance planes not to mention their escorts. As Lavelle remembered the meeting, he was not quite being told to bomb Moc Chau—just how to bomb it.[31]

Subsequently, a pair of F–105 Wild Weasels struck Moc Chau with Standard antiradar missiles. The radar stayed on long enough to be hit, because the F–105s disguised themselves as F–4s (not armed with Standards or older Shrikes) by flashing the appropriate electronic identification code. Tactical deception was rare in the air war over Southeast Asia, and this instance of it was designed by Seventh Air Force in preference to the Air Staff plan. When Seventh Air Force reported this new expansion of protective reaction, Admiral Moorer informed General Abrams that attacking a MiG control radar was not authorized—nor were operations of any kind north of the twentieth parallel except hot pursuit of a MiG. Before the end of January 1972, however, Moorer got Laird's approval to authorize protective reaction strikes against MiG-control radars outside Route Package Six whenever MiGs in the air threatened American aircraft.[32]

Although the Moc Chau strike was one of Lavelle's first attempts to stretch the rules of engagement, it was the last time he reported the details to his bosses. When he sent five F–4s against Dong Hoi airfield on January 23, the aircrews reported that there had been no enemy reaction before they bombed the airfield. Lavelle was in the Seventh Air Force command post when this early report arrived, and he complained to his deputy for operations, Maj. Gen. Alton D. Slay, that the crews could not report "no enemy reaction."[33]

The Dong Hoi attack and most of the subsequent illegitimate attacks were performed by the 432d Tactical Reconnaissance Wing at Udorn Air Base, Thailand, under the command of Col. Charles A. Gabriel. Unlike the other wings in Thailand, the 432d had reconnaissance aircraft as well as fighter aircraft, and thus it was the natural arm of protective reaction, real or pretended. Lavelle's new reporting requirement gave Gabriel problems that Lavelle may well have known nothing about. There was no honest way of translating into the prescribed after-action message format General Lavelle's theory that the North Vietnamese air defense system was always activated against American aircraft. The after action message had to state exactly the nature of the enemy reaction—what gun fired or what SAM radar locked on.[34]

General Slay and Colonel Gabriel worked out a reporting system that put false data into the formal after-action messages for Washington and accurate data into back channel messages that went from Gabriel to Slay only. This procedure resembled one authorized by President Nixon three years earlier to disguise B–52 raids in Cambodia. Since Lavelle apparently never saw the formal messages (which could be read easily only by those familiar with a fill-in-the-blank format designed to build a computer data base), he could assume that they merely made a vague reference to activation of the enemy air defense system. In fact they often specified enemy gunfire that had not occurred.[35]

Slay and Gabriel called their commander's special strikes "heavies" since they involved four to twelve "escorts," rather than the usual two. Crews were told to drop their bombs whether or not the enemy fired. The targets were usually not enemy guns, SAM sites, or even airfields, but increasingly SAM transporters and trucks. Once the trucks crossed into Laos, they were legitimate targets, but while still in North Vietnam the best rationale available was that they were supplying the air defense sites. In the case of tanks, which were gathering in the North Vietnamese panhandle to invade South Vietnam, Lavelle could not find a rationale to attack them even with his interpretation of the rules governing protective reaction; he left the tanks unscathed. Meanwhile, Slay and Gabriel decided that the formal after-action messages should not claim truck kills, but merely use the often true formula "results not observed."[36]

Lavelle's illegitimate strikes might well have gone unremarked in Washington had it not been for a young intelligence debriefer at Udorn, Sgt. Lonnie D. Franks, who wrote about them to one of his Iowa senators, Harold E. Hughes, a Democrat and prominent critic of the war effort. General Ryan sent the Air Force Inspector General, Lt. Gen. Louis L. Wilson, to investigate. Little investigation was required, because Lavelle, Slay, and Gabriel readily told what they had been doing. Lavelle explained that he had not kept Ryan and Clay fully informed because that might put them in an awkward position. General Abrams was supportive of Lavelle but claimed not to have realized that breaches of the rules of engagement had occurred.[37]

*   *   *

In the formal chain of command, the Chief of Staff of the Air Force had no authority over the Seventh Air Force commander, who worked for joint commanders wearing Army or Navy uniforms in Saigon and Hawaii. But each service was expected to clean up its own scandals as quietly as possible. While General Lavelle and his many friends thought that General Ryan should have defended Lavelle instead of retiring him, Ryan tried to minimize political damage to the Air Force. False reporting (rather than stretching the rules of engagement) seemed to Ryan the major problem.

It was not the first time Ryan had removed an officer who had tried to disguise rule breaking. In the summer of 1967, while commanding Pacific Air Forces, Ryan had discovered that Col. Jacksel M. Broughton, the wing vice commander at Takhli, had destroyed evidence that his men had strafed the Soviet ship *Turkestan*. Although Broughton was court-martialed, Ryan and Secretary of the Air Force Seamans agreed that court-martial proceedings for Lavelle would invite unwelcome publicity. They advised Secretary of Defense Laird to remove Lavelle from command and have them brief the chairmen of the Senate and House Committees on Armed Services and Appropriations.[38]

Laird, however, was even more cautious and kept the Air Force leaders from talking to congressional leaders on this issue. He told Seamans and Ryan that publicity about Lavelle's bombing could provide the North Vietnamese an excuse for the invasion they were about to launch. Laird himself talked to

Senator Symington and a few others, but apparently did not give them the full story.[39]

Laird's quiet removal of Lavelle soon came under a spotlight. Senator Hughes persisted in his effort not only to increase the severity of General Lavelle's punishment, but to punish others as well. The senator did not like the fact that because Lavelle's retirement came before his formal relief from command of Seventh Air Force, he would receive the retired pay of a four-star general even though the Senate refused to approve Ryan's recommendation of Lavelle's advancement from permanent major general to lieutenant general (let alone full general as customary) on the retired list. Four-star pay for Lavelle was made possible by a rule that applied only to a medical disability retirement—which also sheltered much of his income from taxation. It was not uncommon for officers to serve a full career and then get a disability retirement, but in Lavelle's case this practice aroused suspicion; among his disabilities was a heart problem that would lead to his death seven years later.[40]

Senator Hughes was on the Armed Services Committee, which held hearings on Lavelle in connection not only with his advancement on the retired list but also with the nomination of General Abrams as Army Chief of Staff. These hearings were the committee's most dramatic investigation of the bombing of North Vietnam since 1967, when the committee had supported the Joint Chiefs in their effort to remove restraints imposed by Secretary of Defense McNamara and President Johnson. Once again, Senator Stennis was in the chair, but this time the committee seemed in favor of restraints or at least opposed to any breach of civilian control over the military.[41]

General Abrams, Admiral Moorer, and General Ryan all denied they had told Lavelle to break the rules of engagement. Lavelle claimed only that he believed his liberal interpretation of the rules was supported by their injunctions to make full use of the rules. If he had received more explicit instructions, he said almost nothing about them to the Senate committee—either because he wanted to protect his superiors or because he believed with some justification that his interpretation of the rules was winning support in Congress. Earlier hearings by the House Armed Services Committee had been more friendly, and that group applauded Lavelle for showing the initiative to do something about the enemy buildup.[42]

In the case of Quan Lang airfield, however, Lavelle did tell a story with potential for getting his superiors in trouble. Admiral Moorer and General Ryan had some difficulty refuting Lavelle's contention that they expected his crews to strike MiGs on the ground. Moorer claimed that he was only interested in photographs to determine whether the MiGs were there, but Ryan had complained about the quality of the bombing and his testimony did not entirely dispel the impression that the targets missed were more than antiaircraft guns. The rules of engagement sought to confine attacks on MiGs to those in the air; those on the ground and their runways were off limits. The only legitimate targets on the ground for routine protective reaction were the guns and SAMs that had fired on or were at least tracking American aircraft. There was apparently not much interest among senators on the Armed Services Committee in pursuing this issue.[43]

Senator Hughes turned his attention from Lavelle and his superiors to Lavelle's subordinates. For two years Hughes monitored promotion lists to stop the promotion of any officer who had been involved in illegitimate missions or false reporting. But in 1973 revelations about the false reporting system authorized by President Nixon for the bombing of Cambodia undercut Hughes' campaign against Lavelle's subordinates. In any case, most of Hughes' colleagues saw merit in General Ryan's position that General Lavelle's subordinates had no way of knowing how high was the source of the orders they were getting from Lavelle. Three of those subordinates achieved four stars (Slay, Gabriel, and Gabriel's vice commander, Jerome F. O'Malley), and one of them became Air Force Chief of Staff (Gabriel).[44]

Not only the men directly affected, but all officers had reason to ponder the actions of General Lavelle. Like him, they might be subject to pressure from above to bend the rules. Like him, they might want to bend the rules to help subordinates deal with problems. General Lavelle's greatest strength as a commander was his concern for the welfare of his men. But in Vietnam his concern got him into trouble, got them into trouble, got the Air Force into trouble—all for the sake of bombing too slight to make much difference. A less generous man might have risked the lives of his men trolling to bend the rules in a more acceptable way. A wiser man would have avoided the risks to his and their integrity for so little benefit to the war effort. Even before he could be retired, a North Vietnamese invasion of South Vietnam made both the military justification and the military insignificance of his illegitimate bombing obvious.

Leaders

ABOVE: Gen. John W. Vogt (right), Seventh Air Force Commander, and an F-111 pilot (left) who has just arrived at Takhli Air Base, September 1972

RIGHT: Gen. John D. Lavelle took command of Seventh Air Force in the summer of 1971 but was forced to resign in April 1972.

Contest for Air Superiority

ABOVE: An F-4 returns to Udorn Air Base, home of the 432d Tactical Reconnaissance Wing, which led the battle against the MiGs in 1972.

LEFT: Col. Scott G. Smith (center), 432d commander, with two aces, F-4 pilot Capt. Richard S. (Steve) Ritchie (left), and weapon system officer Capt. Charles B. DeBellevue (right)

Reconnaissance and Warning

TOP: Technicians remove the film from the camera bay of an RF-4 while the crew is leaving the cockpit.

ABOVE:An EC-121 radar surveillance aircraft that warned friendly aircraft of potential border violations and approaching MiGs

Air Refueling

Because of the distances involved, KC-135 aerial tankers refueled many aircraft before a mission over North Vietnam and sometimes after. Refueling a flight of F-4s (above), and a B-52 seen from over the shoulder of a boom operator (right).

Guided Bombing

TOP: In April 1968 Air Force munitions men load a 2,000-pound bomb with a laser seeker on an F-4 that will drop it on the test range at Eglin Air Force Base, Florida.

ABOVE: The Thanh Hoa Bridge had withstood repeated attacks by unguided bombs during Rolling Thunder but did not fall until laser-guided bombs were used in May 1972.

B-52s

ABOVE LEFT: Ground crew members struggle to move bombs for loading into a B-52.

BELOW LEFT: A D model B-52 with drag chute deployed lands at U-Tapao Air Base, Thailand.

Linebacker II

ABOVE RIGHT: The principal targets of B-52 Linebacker II bombing were railyards. One was Gia Lam, just across the Red River from Hanoi.

BELOW RIGHT: A misplaced load of B-52 bombs hits Kham Thien Street near the Hanoi railyard.

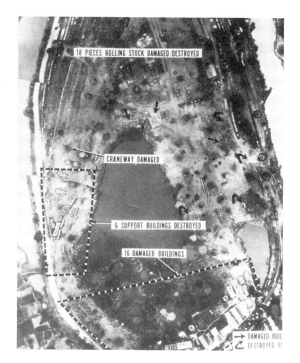

18 PIECES ROLLING STOCK DAMAGED/DESTROYED

CRANEWAY DAMAGED

6 SUPPORT BUILDINGS DESTROYED

16 DAMAGED BUILDINGS

DAMAGED BUIL
DESTROYED B

DAMAGED BUILDINGS

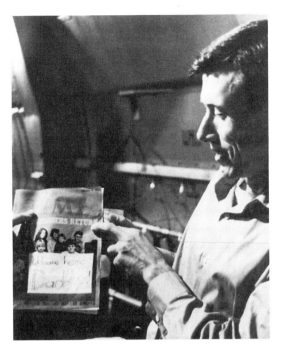

Homecoming

For married POWs their release was particularly poignant. Maj. Joseph S. Abbott Jr. enjoys a Time magazine with his family on the cover (above), and Maj. (later General) Charles G. Boyd and his wife Millicent renew their wedding vows (right).

Chapter Nine

Linebacker

North Vietnam's invasion of South Vietnam in the spring of 1972 came too soon to topple the Thieu government. While nearly all American ground forces had been evacuated, substantial American air power remained in the theater and more was quickly added. President Nixon proved willing to use that air power in a less restrained fashion than his predecessor, and North Vietnamese ground forces exposed themselves to air power when their tanks moved on the roads and their artillery fired steadily in support of conventional operations.

Air power's achievement in stopping the North Vietnamese invaders would be overshadowed by the collapse of South Vietnam under a similar offensive only three years later, when the U.S. Congress withheld American air power from the struggle. But in 1972, President Nixon used air power to better advantage than President Johnson, and the Air Force demonstrated that it had a potent new weapon in the laser-guided bomb.

Since bringing them to Southeast Asia in 1968, the Air Force had found few good targets for laser-guided bombs and used thousands of them to cut roads in Laos before the North Vietnamese offensive of 1972 yielded better targets. To repel that offensive, the Air Force would expend about four thousand in North Vietnam alone, and by the end of the war, the total dropped in Southeast Asia exceeded twenty-eight thousand—triple the number used in the short Gulf War two decades later, but introduced in Southeast Asia against a narrower range of targets and with much less publicity than subsequent guided bombing in Southwest Asia.[1] The accuracy provided by laser guidance often meant dispensing with the old practice of dropping scores of bombs to get one or two on target. A single F–4 with two laser-guided bombs could now drop a bridge span, perhaps two. But these "smart" bombs required good weather, and against the heavy air defenses of North Vietnam they were dropped only in daylight (because jet fighters did not yet carry night target identification equipment reliable above ten thousand feet). Fortunately, the North Vietnamese launched their offensive only a few weeks before the best bombing weather.

By waiting until March 30 to begin their invasion, the North Vietnamese had made the fullest use of the cloudy but dry northeast monsoon for moving supplies into stockpiles near jump-off positions. Two divisions attacked across the Demilitarized Zone between North and South Vietnam and a third moved east from Laos toward Quang Tri. Within a week, more North Vietnamese divisions were in action further south—two of them in the Central Highlands, where they threatened to cut South Vietnam in half by joining forces with Viet Cong units already operating along the coast. Saigon lay in the path of another North Vietnamese division and two Viet Cong divisions descending from Cambodia on An Loc. Altogether, this Easter offensive employed more than one hundred thousand soldiers and hundreds of tanks in widely separated thrusts.[2]

*   *   *

Before the rains of the southwest monsoon periodically washed the clouds and fog away and permitted American jet fighters to attack, North Vietnamese soldiers had two weeks relatively free from accurate air strikes. As frustrating as this was for American airmen, it was even more frustrating for their President. When he met with the Chairman of the Joint Chiefs on April 4, Nixon told Admiral Moorer to convey to the American commander in Saigon, General Abrams, the need for "maximum aggressiveness" in the use of air power.[3] Nixon was upset that only 136 tactical air sorties had flown against the invaders near the Demilitarized Zone in the last twenty-four hours. Moorer explained the weather problem and noted that the B–52s were bombing through the clouds. Although this appealed to the President's personal preference for B–52s, he was not appeased. Nor was his National Security Adviser, Henry Kissinger. Moorer had been authorized on April 2 to send fighter strikes up to twenty-five nautical miles north of the Demilitarized Zone. "It seemed to me that our entire Air Force consisted of delicate machines capable of flying only in a war in the desert in July," Kissinger would later recall. "I suggested that if they could not fly maybe they could taxi north for twenty-five miles."[4]

The next day Nixon complained to Attorney General John Mitchell that the weather was not really the problem: "It isn't bad. The Air Force isn't worth a— I mean, they won't fly."[5] Despite his impatience, Nixon indicated that he was ready to play the hand he had been dealt. "The bastards have never been bombed like they're going to be bombed this time," he declared, "but you have to have weather."[6]

In this frame of mind, he met with the new commander of Seventh Air Force, Gen. John W. Vogt, who had been Director of the Joint Staff. Nixon told Vogt he had to do the job no matter what the weather was—make maximum use of the B–52s. If Vogt did not succeed in Vietnam, the President noted, the Air Force could not expect White House support on major procurements; moreover, this might well be the last major battle fought by the Air Force and it would be tragic for the service to end its combat career in disgrace. Recalling the complicated chain of command and restrictions that had hampered earlier commanders of Seventh Air Force, Vogt asked for sufficient authority to do the job—he wanted to be General Abrams' deputy commander and not merely deputy for air; Nixon told Kissinger to make it happen, and it did two months later. In any case, Nixon advised Vogt to go around Abrams and communicate directly with Washington. Nixon assured Vogt he had all the authority he needed, but Vogt would later regret that the President did not put this assurance in writing.[7]

Although Nixon no doubt wanted to give his air commander a free hand, there were built-in constraints with which Vogt was as familiar as anyone. His own selection as Seventh Air Force commander underlined the continued intimate involvement of the Pentagon and the White House in the direction of the air war. He was the consummate staff officer, close to his most recent boss, Admiral Moorer, and on good terms with Henry Kissinger. Indeed, Kissinger had recommended Vogt to Nixon as Lavelle's replacement.[8] Vogt's Ivy League education (Yale, Columbia, and Harvard, where he first met Kissinger), long series of key staff assignments, and lack of command experience set him apart from most Air Force generals. Not since the 1940s, when he was a fighter ace and squadron commander in Europe, had Vogt commanded a unit in the field. But he had been heavily involved in developing plans and policy for Southeast Asia since 1954, when he was sent to Paris after the fall of Dien Bien Phu. At the beginning of Rolling Thunder, he was in the Office of the Secretary of Defense, helping McNamara and Paul Nitze massage target lists. For most of Rolling Thunder, Vogt was the plans and operations deputy at Pacific Air Forces in Hawaii where he worked for General Ryan (before Ryan became Air Force Chief of Staff).

In Saigon, Vogt found himself answering frequent telephone calls from Admiral Moorer. While sometimes burdensome, these calls indicated the increased stature of the Seventh Air Force commander. Since most American ground forces had already gone home, air was what counted. In any case, Vogt's Army boss in Saigon, General Abrams, was out of favor with the Nixon administration. Nixon and Kissinger blamed Abrams for the sad fate of the South Vietnamese incursion into Laos early in 1971. Abrams seemed to them a tired and frustrated commander who after three years of routine drawdown was unable to adjust to the new combat demands.[9]

Nixon made a lame effort to cure what Kissinger called the "institutionalized schizophrenia" of the route package system dividing responsibility for the air war over North Vietnam.[10] But when Secretary of Defense Laird and Admiral Moorer opposed attempting organizational changes in the midst of crisis, Nixon backed down. Thanks to a solid base of support in the Congress, Laird continued to exercise authority essentially independent of the President. The two men responded very differently to the North Vietnamese invasion. Laird saw the invasion as a good test of Vietnamization. Consequently, he thought it best to do nothing special for the South Vietnamese, and he strongly opposed the resumption of bombing in North Vietnam; in this opposition he had the quiet support of Secretary of the Air Force Seamans. As in earlier crises, Nixon sought to work around Laird by working directly with Admiral Moorer in Washington and Ambassador Bunker in Saigon; Bunker conveyed "backchannel" guidance from Kissinger to Generals Abrams and Vogt. Meanwhile, Laird could put his own pressure on Moorer, and the upshot was that Laird was sometimes able to put restrictions on renewed bombing in North Vietnam.[11]

Moorer's situation was especially awkward because his relationship with Kissinger had recently been buffeted by charges that Moorer's liaison officers on Kissinger's staff, RAdm. Rembrandt C. Robinson and his successor, RAdm. Robert O. Welander, had used Yeoman Charles Radford to steal sensitive papers (about China and Pakistan) from Kissinger on behalf of Moorer. The yeoman, who had also passed some of these secrets to newspaper columnist and fellow Morman, Jack Anderson, was quickly reassigned, as was Welander, and Kissinger closed the liaison office. Perhaps because Nixon was himself becoming suspicious of Kissinger's appetite for diplomatic triumphs well-publicized in the press, Moorer's relationship with the President did not suffer.[12]

Both Nixon and Kissinger continued to need Moorer as a way of getting around Secretary of Defense Laird's opposition to their use of military power. Many of the confrontations between the White House and Laird took the form of heated telephone conversations between Kissinger's military assistant, Maj. Gen. Alexander M. Haig, Jr. (Army), and Laird's military assistant, Maj. Gen. Robert E. Pursley (Air Force). Haig had graduated from the U.S. Military Academy at West Point in 1947 two years ahead of Pursley. They had both won promotion to brigadier and major general thanks to their civilian bosses. After earning a master's degree in business administration from Harvard, Pursley had served as military assistant to three secretaries of defense, beginning with Robert McNamara in 1966. It was Laird, however, who twice promoted him. Meanwhile, Haig had served as military assistant to Army secretary Cyrus Vance before becoming a battalion commander in Vietnam.[13]

An especially destructive incident in the relationship between Pursley and Haig (and their civilian bosses) had been North Korea's shoot-down of an EC–121 reconnaissance aircraft on April 15, 1969. Nixon ordered a naval task force into Korean waters, and he became impatient when no movement took place. Haig's repeated calls to Pursley left Haig with the impression that Pursley was being evasive. Finally concluding that Laird had not transmitted the President's orders, the White House sent the orders directly to the Navy.[14] In the three years since that bad beginning, the White House had wiretapped Pursley's telephone. He was still ignorant of that fact in the spring of 1972, when he visited Haig to improve relations. Haig's revelation that the White House had been keeping a record on Pursley spurred the Air Force general to announce his retirement, but Laird talked him into accepting an assignment in Japan.[15] As for Haig, he was becoming increasingly influential with the

President. Since Haig did not share Kissinger's inclination to fine tune the bombing of North Vietnam in the service of diplomacy, Haig could consistently bolster Nixon's inclination to make stronger use of air power.

Nixon and Moorer moved quickly to get more air power into Southeast Asia. While Vietnamization had left considerable American air power in the theater, the remainder was much smaller than the force that had confronted the Tet offensive in 1968. Then the Air Force alone had more than 1,700 aircraft on South Vietnamese and Thai bases, not to mention other aircraft within reach, like the B–52s on Guam and Okinawa. Now there were fewer than 800 Air Force aircraft in Southeast Asia, and the half of these in South Vietnam were slated either to move to Thailand or return to the United States. Nixon permitted most of the scheduled moves to take place, but he altered the result by squeezing 350 F–4s and 50 B–52s into Thailand, with another 150 B–52s on Guam.[16]

Fighters deploying to Thailand included the new F–4Es that each had a 20-millimeter gun built into the nose. Seventy-two F–4Es from North Carolina and Florida crowded onto Udorn and Ubon Air Bases with the more than one hundred F–4s already there. But older F–4Ds also came to Thailand. Indeed, the entire 49th Tactical Fighter Wing of seventy-two F–4Ds flew from New Mexico to reintroduce an American presence at Takhli Air Base. Since the 355th Tactical Fighter Wing's departure in 1970, the American side of the base had been stripped of electricity, water, bedding, and furniture. Such deficiencies were ameliorated just in time to handle the 366th Tactical Fighter Wing, which moved from Da Nang to Takhli in June. The 388th Tactical Fighter Wing at Korat (home of F–105 Wild Weasels and EB–66 jammers) also absorbed more F–4s, and these, like the Takhli F–4s, dedicated much of their effort to hitting North Vietnamese ground forces in South Vietnam. That left the principal responsibility for fighter operations in North Vietnam to the 8th Tactical Fighter Wing at Ubon and the 432d Tactical Reconnaissance Wing at Udorn.[17]

While there were 150 fewer Air Force jet fighters than had been available during the Tet offensive, Navy carriers operating in the Gulf of Tonkin increased from two to five before dropping back to four, one more than commonly operated on the line in 1968. The Marines sent two squadrons of F–4s and a squadron of A–6s to a nearly bare base at Nam Phong, fifty miles south of Udorn; the Marines moved into tents, planted a single rose bush, and dubbed their new home the "Rose Garden." With twice as many B–52s as had ever been used in Southeast Asia and an abundance of the new laser-guided bombs for the Air Force F–4s, Nixon gathered a more formidable (if less numerous) air armada than the North Vietnamese had yet encountered.[18]

Nixon repeatedly underlined his demand for more B–52s. As early as February, he had responded to Abrams' call for renewed bombing of North Vietnam by sending 29 B–52s to Guam. U-Tapao Air Base, Thailand, already carried its maximum of 51 B–52s and nearly as many tankers. Thanks to their proximity to Vietnam, the U-Tapao B–52s were far more valuable than those that had to be based twenty-four hundred miles away on Guam. But Guam was as close as newly deployed B–52s could get. Kadena Air Base on Okinawa could no longer be used as a B–52 base, because Nixon had already agreed that Okinawa would revert to Japanese control in May. The Japanese would permit tankers, but not bombers, to operate from Kadena. Guam would have to absorb some 150 B–52s, far more than Andersen Air Force Base could handle comfortably.[19]

Nixon's immediate response to the Easter Offensive was to deploy 54 B–52s to Guam and 36 F–4s to Ubon Air Base, Thailand. That gave him a total of 134 B–52s to use in the theater, but he soon found that his plans to use them in North Vietnam were constantly meeting objections from Abrams and Laird to use every available B–52 in South Vietnam on the invading forces. In exasperation, Nixon called in May for another 100 B–52s. No one in the Pentagon or the Pacific could figure out how to cram an additional 100 B–52s on Guam. After failing to talk Nixon out of this new deployment, Moorer told his staff a story about a farmer who managed to carry four tons of turkeys in a truck with a capacity of two tons by keeping half the turkeys in the air.[20]

Eighth Air Force on Guam finally did manage to absorb another 58 B–52s by closing one of Andersen's two runways and using it to park them. The old B–29 hardstands from World War II simply could not handle the bigger B–52s. The commander of Eighth Air Force, Lt. Gen. Gerald W. Johnson, later recalled that a B–29 stub "would barely take the main gear and everything else would be hanging over the sides . . . and after they rolled on the stubs a couple of times, we'd go out to get the airplanes and find they'd sunk into the pavement about a foot."[21] For two months while Navy Seabees constructed new hardstands and enlarged old ones, Johnson had only one runway for takeoffs. He had the weeds cleared from an old World War II runway for emergency landings, and the Naval Air Station was also used for this purpose.[22]

Housing the people who came with the newly deployed B–52s caused more problems. Andersen Air Force Base, which only a few weeks earlier had fewer than three thousand people, now had to support more than nine thousand. For a couple of thousand people, that meant living in tents; for a couple of hundred, it meant living off base in luxury hotels normally populated by Japanese tourists. Both these new housing options were widely preferred to crowding into the hot Quonset huts of "tin city." Most people were working too hard and long to care much about housing. After years of routine "milk runs," Andersen and its sister B–52 base at U-Tapao, Thailand, began to fly missions both more dangerous and more obviously critical to the survival of South Vietnam.

The new dangers facing the B–52s were posed not only by surface-to-air missiles near the Demilitarized Zone and even in South Vietnam, but also by President Nixon's decision to send the B–52s deep into North Vietnam. At least since the covert B–52 raids into Cambodia in 1969, Nixon had taken a special interest in B–52s. During Rolling Thunder, B–52 raids into North Vietnam had been confined to the southern end of the panhandle and the mountain passes into Laos. But Nixon did not share Johnson's fear of triggering a reaction in Moscow and Beijing, which had both responded favorably to Nixon's overtures. Nor was he deterred by the possibility that the heavier air defenses surrounding Hanoi and Haiphong might take a toll on the B–52s.

Yet Nixon did not order the immediate bombing of Hanoi and Haiphong. It took more than a week for him to approve a series of shifts in the northern bombing limit even to nineteen degrees, where it had been during the last six months of Rolling Thunder. He seemed to want Moorer to propose dramatic actions for the President's approval. But Moorer did not yet have in place much of the abundant air power that would soon descend on Southeast Asia, and Laird was opposing any bombing in North Vietnam. Nevertheless, on April 8 when Nixon complained again that there had been only "routine" operations so far, Moorer did promise that at least six B–52s would strike a target deep in North Vietnam before sunset on April 10.[23]

Twelve B–52s from U-Tapao hit the Vinh oil tank farm and the Vinh railyard before dawn on April 10. To get these twelve bombers into North Vietnam, an armada of fifty-three other aircraft played supporting roles. Navy A–6s and A–7s began the attack by striking surface-to-air missile sites. Air Force F–105 Wild Weasels then threatened those sites, while twenty F–4s laid a chaff trail for the B–52s. This was the first major use of chaff since World War II. The F–4s could not reach the altitude of the B–52s (above thirty-five thousand feet), and the B–52s wanted to stay as far above most flak as possible. As a result, the B–52s rode along above their chaff trail, which both hid their exact location from North Vietnamese radar and alerted that radar to their general flight path.[24]

The North Vietnamese began firing surface-to-air missiles at the attackers even before they had passed over the border from Laos to North Vietnam. More than thirty of the missiles arced through the bomber formation, hitting nothing but still disrupting plans to fly straight and level. The B–52 pilots did follow their orders to "press on" despite SAM or MiG interference, and the MiGs did not come up to challenge this nighttime raid—so far, they were a daytime phenomenon. The twelve B–52s dropped a total of nearly eight hundred bombs, mostly 750-pound and 500-pound high-explosive bombs, but including some cluster bombs. The raid, however, was not very effective, probably because the crews tried to use the skyspot system for ground radar direction of bombing. Vinh was too far from the radar sites in Thailand and South Vietnam, even if the B–52s had managed to maintain a straight and level bomb run.[25]

Moorer ordered another raid for April 13, this one to penetrate farther north with six additional B–52s (a total of eighteen), all dropping high-explosive bombs only and all using onboard bombing radar rather than skyspot. Mindful of the inaccuracy of the Vinh raid, the new target was chosen for its relative isolation from the civilian population as well as for its importance to the war effort.

Just south of the twentieth parallel lay Thanh Hoa's Bai Thuong Airfield, part of North Vietnam's expanded airfield complex to support a growing air force of more than two hundred MiGs (almost double the size it had been during Rolling Thunder). Once again the B–52s struck just before dawn. They destroyed a MiG–17 on the ground and none came up to oppose them; they left seventeen craters in the runway. The North Vietnamese fired their surface-to-air missiles in as great a profusion as before and with as little result.[26]

The Joint Chiefs had already triggered planning in Hawaii for a third raid to strike three days after the second. This time the targets would be Haiphong and Hanoi. A proposal to increase the size of the raid to forty B–52s, however, gave way to sending eighteen B–52s against an oil tank farm at Haiphong before dawn followed by more than a hundred Navy and Air Force fighters attacking Haiphong and Hanoi targets in daylight. Even the reduced force of B–52s, however, was too much for Abrams, who objected to diverting any of them from South Vietnam while An Loc was under so much pressure. When he got Abrams message, Nixon was upset because he suspected that if the land battle went sour he would be blamed for the diversion. Kissinger, who had supported the raid, now had second thoughts. But Moorer pointed out that the B–52s had already launched and would have to ditch their bombs in the Gulf of Tonkin. Nixon decided to let the mission run its course.[27]

One of the B–52s aborted with mechanical problems, but the remaining seventeen dropped their bombs before dawn on Sunday, April 16, and destroyed or damaged more than thirty oil tanks at Haiphong. Despite the failure of the chaff to disperse sufficiently to form a trail, more than a hundred surface-to-air missiles missed the B–52s and most of their escorts. But a missile did shoot down an F–105 Wild Weasel that had been protecting F–4s dropping chaff. After daybreak the Navy lost an A–7 attacking warehouses in Haiphong.[28]

The Air Force F–4 raid on a tank farm near Hanoi came off without a loss, and supporting F–4s flying combat air patrol even managed to shoot down three MiG–21s. Yet General Vogt was not entirely pleased with the day's work. Some of his discomfiture may have come from his own peripheral role in the planning, which had been done mostly in Hawaii by a joint team dominated by an admiral and a colonel from Strategic Air Command. Since the Hanoi tank farm was considerably smaller than the Haiphong tank farm and since seventeen B–52s could drop almost ten times as many bombs as thirty-two F–4s, Vogt's F–4 raid was necessarily not as spectacular—even though the F–4s were credited with a higher percentage of destruction. At the time, Vogt bragged that this F–4 raid was "one of the best ever executed" in the Hanoi area.[29] But he was bothered by bombs that missed the target area entirely; they had a potential for exacting civilian casualties and spurring Washington to put important targets off-limits. Vogt became more and more determined to make maximum use of guided bombs.[30]

Whatever Vogt's reservations, for the first time since the beginning of the Easter offensive the President was not disappointed. "Well," Nixon told his chief of staff, "we really left our calling card this weekend."[31] In the glow of this assessment, B–52 raids in North Vietnam were bound to continue for a while longer. About a week later, a pair of strikes on April 21 and 23 used nearly forty B–52 sorties to hit warehouses near Thanh Hoa. Most of the fighter sorties scheduled to hit other Thanh Hoa targets, like the famous bridge that had withstood so many attacks during Rolling Thunder, were canceled due to bad weather. The B–52s did get their usual escort of F–4s and F–105 Wild Weasels, but for the first time over North Vietnam a B–52 was damaged by a surface-to-air missile. The damaged B–52 completed its bomb run and landed at Da Nang with three of its eight engines shut down. This was only the second B–52 to sustain combat damage, the first having been hit by a surface-to-air missile three weeks earlier near Quang Tri city, South Vietnam.[32]

The Thanh Hoa raids were intended to strengthen Henry Kissinger's hand during his visit to Moscow of April 20–24. While advocating strikes south of the twentieth parallel, Kissinger urged the President not to bomb again near Hanoi and Haiphong at least until Kissinger had talked to the Soviets in Moscow and the North Vietnamese in Paris, where he was scheduled to meet Le Duc Tho on May 2. Kissinger hoped to bring to fruition Nixon's long-planned "summit meeting" in Moscow, where in late May the President would sign an agreement limiting strategic arms. But Nixon thought that threatening to call off the summit might persuade the Soviets to put pressure on the North Vietnamese. During Kissinger's April visit in Moscow, he simply ignored Nixon's instructions.[33]

By the time Kissinger met with Le Duc Tho, the North Vietnamese had overrun the city of Quang Tri and were in no mood to bargain. The National Security Adviser returned to Washington without a strong diplomatic argument against the President's desire to use B–52s against Hanoi. Kissinger turned to a military alternative he had first considered in 1969—mining the North Vietnamese ports and interdicting their ground transportation routes by attacking them with fighter aircraft. Rolling Thunder's attempts to interdict the roads running from North Vietnam into Laos and South Vietnam had left Haiphong and North Vietnam's other harbors free to import goods from the Soviet Union, China, and elsewhere. The Cambodian port of Sihanoukville had also been a conduit for supplies to the communist forces in South Vietnam until the new Lon Nol government had closed it to the communists in 1970. Since North Vietnam's conventional invasion of South Vietnam was consuming large quantities of ammunition and other supplies, Kissinger saw great potential in simultaneous land and sea interdiction.[34]

Nixon's "detente" had proceeded far enough with the Soviets and the Chinese for him not to share President Johnson's old fear of sharply increased military intervention on their part. Nixon had already had his summit meeting in Beijing in February 1972. The Soviets might pull out of the May summit, but they were not apt to do more militarily than try to resupply the North

Vietnamese—a task that could be made far more difficult by mining the ports. The Soviets would then be forced to transport those supplies through a less than friendly China, if the Chinese would permit it. Nixon very much liked the boldness of the proposal, and for a time it did distract him from sending the B–52s north again. On May 4, he terminated military planning for B–52 and fighter raids on Hanoi and Haiphong scheduled for May 6 and 7.[35]

Nixon wanted to make sure that his own actions in Vietnam contrasted sharply with those of his predecessor. Former President Johnson contributed directly to White House resolve on this occasion by sending word that his mistakes had been a consequence of following advice against his own instincts. Nixon told his close aides that he had experienced the same problem. When the North Koreans shot down the EC–121 in 1969, he should have followed his instinct to bomb North Korea. When he sent American forces into Cambodia in 1970, he should have followed his instinct to mount a full-scale bombing campaign against North Vietnam instead of the few sorties sent then. "If we'd done that then, the damned war would be over now."[36]

Having embraced mining and interdiction as the bold action required, Nixon made his preparations in the greatest secrecy. By the time Nixon permitted his National Security Council to discuss the proposal on May 8, he had already decided to go ahead. Nevertheless, he went through the motions of listening to his critics. As expected, Secretary of Defense Laird opposed the plan, and he was supported in his opposition by the Central Intelligence Agency. They argued that the North Vietnamese already had sufficient supplies stockpiled for the offensive and in any case that air power would fail to interdict the roads from China to North Vietnam. Kissinger would later claim in his memoirs his own agreement at the time that the effects of the campaign would come too late to affect the North Vietnamese offensive: "I agreed, but I was concerned with Hanoi's actions after the offensive."[37]

Four days before the National Security Council meeting, Nixon had called Admiral Moorer into his private office in the Old Executive Office Building to get the Chairman's views and get him planning in the quietest way. Moorer assured the President that Moorer himself had already planned such an operation eight years earlier when he commanded the Seventh Fleet and that the necessary preparations could be made without the press hearing anything about it. Moorer was as good as his word. When Nixon made his television announcement on the evening of May 8 that the new campaign was already underway, he caught Americans and North Vietnamese by surprise.[38]

General Abrams, the U.S. commander in Saigon, was among the Americans surprised by the mining of Haiphong. Suddenly the Navy withdrew gunfire support from scheduled ground operations in South Vietnam. Relations between Abrams and the Commander in Chief, Pacific, in Honolulu, Adm. John McCain, were already tense. This time Abrams complained bitterly to a visiting assistant secretary of defense about the Navy's lack of cooperation only to learn that the Navy ships had been pulled off to support the mining of Haiphong. That this came as news to him was the clearest sign yet that Abrams had lost the administration's confidence. At least he would no longer have to argue daily against siphoning B–52s from targets in South Vietnam to strike North Vietnam. For a while that job would be left to fighter and attack aircraft.[39]

*   *   *

When President Nixon went on national television to tell his fellow citizens about mining North Vietnam's ports, it was nine o'clock on the evening of May 8, 1972. The time in Haiphong was nine o'clock on the morning of May 9. While Nixon spoke, A–6 aircraft from the carrier *Coral Sea* dropped sea mines into the narrow channel connecting North Vietnam's principal port with the Gulf of Tonkin. As Nixon explained, the mines would not activate for three days, during which the twenty-eight foreign ships in Haiphong harbor would be free to leave. That they did not leave appeared to result from North Vietnamese refusal to provide tugboats until the ships had unloaded their cargo. Their stay would be a long one lasting into the following year. The failure of the North Vietnamese to send a minesweeper into the channel confirmed Admiral Moorer's good judgment in restricting the minefield to simple magnetic mines; his own Navy would sweep them in the end.[40]

On the day following the mining of Haiphong, an interdiction campaign began against land routes from China through North Vietnam. During April, Air Force and Navy tactical aircraft had flown nearly two thousand attack sorties into North Vietnam, the bulk of them hitting the panhandle in a campaign called "Freedom Train"; tactical aircraft had also joined B–52s in attacking a few targets north of the nineteenth parallel. Now the B–52s were withdrawn from North Vietnam, and when they returned in June, it would be only to the panhandle. The number of fighter attack sorties in North Vietnam, on the other hand, tripled to six thousand a month—including about a thousand in Route Package Six.[41]

Although the first strikes of May 10, 1972, flew under the old rubric of "Rolling Thunder," this new campaign would be called "Linebacker." Campaign designations often were drawn randomly from approved lists and had no other significance, but "Rolling Thunder" and "Linebacker" seemed more than chance selections. Just as the label "Rolling Thunder" had conveyed the gradualism of that campaign, "Linebacker" was football terminology suggesting the defensive nature of the new campaign. Perhaps it was no mere coincidence that many air planners were avid football fans as was their president; Nixon had even been known to compare international politics to his favorite sport. Instead of tackling football runners or blocking passes, this bombing campaign would attempt to interdict North Vietnamese supply lines.[42]

Yet Rolling Thunder had also been in large measure an interdiction campaign. Why would Linebacker be any more successful? Linebacker's proponents were encouraged by the fact that large North Vietnamese conventional forces were for the first time rapidly expending munitions and other supplies in South Vietnam, while Nixon had moved boldly to close North Vietnam's ports. The other hopeful factor in the new equation was the laser-guided bomb.

"Laser" is an acronym for "light amplified by stimulated emission of radiation." This intense beam of light was produced for the first time at Hughes Aircraft in 1960. Army researchers at Huntsville, Alabama, began to explore the laser's utility for missile guidance. By relying on a pulsed laser beam rather than a steady one, they reduced the weight of a laser generator enough for aircraft to carry it. The pulsed laser beam could designate (or "illuminate") a target sufficiently for a missile with a laser sensor to hit it.[43]

When Army money for laser research dried up in 1965, the Huntsville team took their idea to the Air Force Systems Command. Col. Joseph Davis at Eglin Air Force Base steered the effort away from missiles to free-fall bombs. An F–4 could easily carry a laser designator mounted near the weapon system operator in the back seat, while laser-seeker kits combining sensors and control fins (or "canards") could be attached to bombs already in the inventory. Davis encouraged competing proposals for a laser-seeker kit from several companies; Texas Instruments and North American Aviation entered the competition. Prototype tests in 1966 favored the cheaper Texas Instruments design.[44]

Although early work on laser guidance had used 750-pound bombs, testing in Southeast Asia during the summer of 1968 reinforced a growing conviction that the 2,000-pound bomb was more suitable. Laser-guided bombs were obviously more expensive than unguided bombs of any weight, and the Air Force wanted enough punch to take out a bridge span with one bomb. After brief use in the North Vietnamese panhandle, the end of Rolling Thunder meant that for three years, laser-guided bombing was done mostly in Laos, where there were few good targets. Destroying small bridges and penetrating cave entrances were among the most appropriate tasks there, but breaching dirt roads was more common.[45]

Even had the White House authorized raids into the Hanoi-Haiphong area during the "protective reaction" years, laser-guided bombs probably would not have been used. The problem was not merely that laser guidance required relatively clear weather to function, but also that the Air Force had not yet developed a way to designate the target without exposing the designating aircraft to the high risk of being shot down wherever enemy defenses were heavy. Since the target had to be illuminated throughout the bomb's glide, the designating aircraft had to orbit over the target until all the bombs dropped by other F–4s had struck.

Although only the F–4 was certified to drop laser-guided bombs, communist air defenses in Laos and South Vietnam were sufficiently light to permit AC–130s, C–130s, and OV–10s as well as F–4s to orbit with laser designators. F–4s could use the same orbiting tactic for laser designation in the panhandle of North Vietnam, but dropping laser-guided bombs in the heavily defended areas closer to Hanoi and Haiphong demanded a new designation technology. Fortunately, by the spring of 1972, Seventh Air Force had a wing pod that hung the laser designator on a gimbal—permitting it to track the target by swiveling independently of the F–4's maneuvers; the designating F–4 no longer had to orbit and could drop bombs itself. Unfortunately, Seventh Air Force had only six of these "Pave Knife" pods and had no prospect of getting new ones that summer.[46]

General Vogt therefore designed the Air Force's portion of Linebacker to make maximum use of his six Pave Knife pods while preserving them. That meant escorting them with big formations much like those he had developed for the B–52s in April. At first, eight F–105 Wild Weasels led the way, but later these were joined by F–4s in hunter-killer teams, since the F–105's antiradiation missiles only attacked radars and not the surface-to-air missile launchers themselves; the F–4s carried CBU–52 cluster bombs, which could do more damage to equipment than the CBU–24 antipersonnel cluster bombs of Rolling Thunder. Normally the chaff force was considerably smaller than the twenty F–4s used with the B–52s—usually eight F–4s dropping chaff, but sometimes as many as sixteen. At first these were unescorted, but as the MiGs became more active and skillful, up to eight other F–4s were added to escort the chaff F–4s. The strike force itself rarely exceeded eight F–4s, because the dust and smoke kicked up by their bombs soon interfered with the laser guidance of additional attackers. The strike force had a close escort of eight F–4s, not to mention yet another dozen or more F–4s flying combat air patrol in the vicinity. At the outset of Linebacker, supporting combat aircraft outnumbered strike aircraft by more than three to one; by early summer, the ratio exceeded five to one, and that did not count supporting aircraft operating at a distance, like the EB–66 jammers, the EC–121 warning aircraft, and the KC–135 tankers.[47]

Vogt's big strike packages did preserve four Pave Knife pods through the campaign. Only two pods were lost, both in July—the first when the designating F–4 was shot down by a surface-to-air missile and the second when an F–4 caught fire after blowing a tire on take-off.[48] Vogt resisted pressure from Washington and Hawaii to increase the number of aircraft dropping bombs at the expense of his escorts. Only when the weather began to sour in August and September, did he permit greater use of unguided bombs in Route Package Six with smaller escort packages. Even then the total of Air Force, Navy, and Marine sorties dropping bombs on North Vietnam usually did not much exceed the two hundred daily with which Linebacker had begun; this was about a third of the available U.S. attack sorties available for all of Southeast Asia. By the end of the summer, the fighters had been rejoined over the panhandle of North Vietnam by about twenty B–52 sorties daily (a fifth of those available).[49]

From the beginning of Linebacker, two hundred attack sorties a day for North Vietnam seemed much too little to President Nixon. "I am concerned by the military's plan of allocating 200 sorties for North Vietnam for the dreary 'milk runs' which characterized the Johnson administration's bombing . . . ." he wrote Kissinger in May. Nixon emphasized that the U.S. had sufficient power to destroy North Vietnam's "war-making capacity," and that the only question was whether the administration had the will to use that power. "What distinguishes me from Johnson," he declared, "is that I have the *will* in spades."[50]

But Nixon did not simply order the military to increase the weight of effort over North Vietnam. Rather he instructed Kissinger to have the military and the National Security Council staff come up with "some ideas on their own."[51] The only consequence of this instruction was planning during the summer to send the B–52s to Hanoi. Meanwhile, the steadily improving situation in South Vietnam diminished Nixon's insistence on doing something more drastic in North Vietnam.

Nevertheless, General Vogt did continue to hear from Admiral McCain in Hawaii on the subject of increased sorties over North Vietnam, especially Route Package Six. As a result of Vogt's emphasis on laser-guided bombing, the Air Force's war over North Vietnam in 1972 looked much different than the Navy's. The Navy was sending about twice as many attack sorties against North Vietnam as the Air Force, and the Navy's sorties were scattered against many more targets. Not only would the Navy plan to attack more fixed targets each day (often four or five while the Air Force targeted one or two), but Navy armed reconnaissance sorties often hit a dozen or more fixed targets in addition as far north as Route Package Six.[52]

Vogt confined Air Force armed reconnaissance in North Vietnam almost entirely to Route Package One, where few of the targets were fixed and where laser-guided bombs also played an important role against artillery and tanks (the same target sets pursued by laser-guided bombs in South Vietnam, where Seventh Air Force did about half its laser-guided bombing). In Route Package One and South Vietnam, Vogt could use his older laser-guidance systems with the designating aircraft orbiting over the target. This emphasis on guided bombs was not shared by the Navy, which dropped fewer than five hundred laser-guided and TV-guided bombs on North Vietnam while Seventh Air Force was dropping about four thousand.[53]

Vogt persisted with laser-guided bombing because it was yielding remarkable results far superior in accuracy to any previous bombing. He could count on every mission destroying its target unless cloudy weather got in the way. Seventh Air Force, however, ceased to use television-guided bombs in Route Package Six, even though both the Navy and the Air Force had developed a heavier 2,000-pound version (and thus corrected a major deficiency of the

Navy's Walleye during Rolling Thunder). While F–4 aircrews were effective dropping laser-guided bombs from medium altitude above ten thousand feet, getting adequate contrast for a good lock-on with the much more expensive television-guided bomb required them to fly lower into enemy air defenses.[54]

Laser guidance was not without its own drawbacks. In high-threat areas it could not be used at night since the F–4 lacked adequate night sensors and had to rely on aircrew seeing the target with the naked eye. Not only could clouds prevent initial designation of the target, but a passing cloud could interfere with the laser at any time during the bomb's glide. Dust and smoke could also cause the bomb not to guide. The North Vietnamese of course tried to exacerbate this problem with smoke pots, but more often than not a breeze would clear the target long enough for it to be hit. After a couple of hits, however, the resulting dust and smoke could cause later bombs to miss.

The scarcity of laser-guidance systems led Seventh Air Force to concentrate most of them in the 8th Tactical Fighter Wing at Ubon Air Base, Thailand. This one wing did all Air Force laser-guided bombing in Route Packages Five and Six and most guided bombing in Route Package One and South Vietnam as well. During Rolling Thunder, the 8th had called themselves the "MiG Killers" and specialized in air-to-air operations, while the F–105s at Takhli and Korat dropped most of the bombs. During the "protective reaction" period, the famous 555th "Triple Nickel" squadron and much of the air-to-air job had passed to the 432d Tactical Reconnaissance Wing (assisted by the 366th and 388th wings). Under Col. Carl Miller, the 8th Tactical Fighter Wing in Linebacker would earn the new nickname of "Bridge Busters." Miller had flown F–84s during the Korean War and F–100s in South Vietnam as recently as 1967. He would personally lead many of the pioneering laser-guided bombing missions into North Vietnam.

Miller could not focus on guided bombing alone. In April his four F–4 squadrons had made room for two F–4 squadrons from Seymour Johnson Air Force Base, North Carolina. These two temporary-duty squadrons joined AC–130s supporting South Vietnamese ground forces, as well as flying missions in Laos and Cambodia. Miller's four permanent F–4 squadrons also had other duties besides guided bombing. They dropped chaff for the B–52s and for their own bomb droppers, and they provided forward air controllers in Route Package One, both day and night. To perform these many functions, Miller had a base crowded with about a hundred F–4s and a dozen AC–130s.[55]

As their nickname "Bridge Busters" testified, it was guided bombing for which the 8th Tactical Fighter Wing aircrews would be best known in 1972, and their principal targets were bridges. The development of guided bombs had been closely associated with bridge bombing ever since World War II. While bridges like those across the Seine River in France were severed by unguided bombs, fighter pilots had to take severe risks flying low-level runs to hit those bridges. By the end of the war, however, the U.S. Army Air Forces had developed a radio guidance kit that could be attached to 1,000-pound and 2,000-pound bombs. These early precision bombs could be guided in azimuth only, not range. Although a B–24 bomber dropping them could stay above eight thousand feet, it had to remain over the target while the bombardier tried to guide a bomb all the way. These precision bombs were used only in Burma, where air defenses were relatively light and where fewer than five hundred radio-guided bombs succeeded in destroying more than twenty bridges.[56]

During the Korean War, the Air Force used improved radio-guided bombs. The addition of range control, however, did little to improve the accuracy of radio-guided bombs and nothing to reduce the vulnerability of bombers dropping them. While B–29 bombardiers where able to judge the correct azimuth, they had great difficulty judging range. In Korea, 1,000-pound guided bombs encountered bridges for which they were inadequate, stimulating the Air Force to try a 12,000-pound version. When it hit a bridge, the big bomb destroyed it, but aircrews discovered to their dismay that the bomb could not be jettisoned without detonating when it hit the ground; a wounded bomber creeping home at low altitude could be blown up if it tried to get rid of its big guided bomb.[57]

Again in North Vietnam, the Navy and the Air Force at first used guided munitions too light for some bridges. The Navy's Bullpup missiles (also used by the Air Force) were descended from the Korean War radio-guided bombs with the addition of a rocket engine, but this did not permit much standoff safety because the aircraft had to remain close enough for the crew to see the target—and the rocket engine smoke helped enemy gunners judge the aircraft's position. The 250-pound Bullpup did little damage. In any case, the Bullpup could not be used against the heavy air defenses prevailing throughout most of North Vietnam. The Navy's Walleye television-guided bomb was used against better defended bridges, because it permitted the aircraft to leave the area after initial lock-on. But the version of Walleye available during Rolling Thunder was too light (1,100 pounds with an 825-pound warhead) to down spans in the stronger bridges.[58]

The toughest bridge in North Vietnam crossed the Song Ma at Thanh Hoa. Only two spans meeting on a central concrete abutment, this bridge took seven years to build and was not completed until 1964. The communists may have taken special care in its solid construction not only because it carried the only railroad running south of Hanoi together with the principal highway, but also because they had themselves blown up its predecessor during their rebellion against the French. Their technique of arranging a head-on collision between two locomotives loaded with explosives could not be imitated by Americans. During three years of Rolling Thunder, hundreds of sorties had suffered eleven losses while fruitlessly attacking the Thanh Hoa Bridge with Walleyes, Bullpups, mines and unguided bombs. Transport aircraft even dropped 5,000-pound mines upriver at night so that they would float into the bridge abutment, but this attempt also failed—costing a C–130 and its crew. The Thanh Hoa

Bridge still stood, no span had ever fallen, and none of the damage done had made this bridge unusable for very long.[59]

On April 27, 1972, two weeks before the mining of Haiphong, eight Air Force fighters returned to the Thanh Hoa Bridge with a new generation of guided bombs. One flight carried 2,000-pound laser-guided bombs and the other 2,000-pound television-guided bombs. Although laser-guided bombs would prove to be normally a little less sensitive to weather, on this occasion it was the television-guided bombs that got a good enough lock-on for five of them to be dropped; the cloud cover was sufficient to make it unlikely that a laser beam could be kept on the target long enough for bombs to complete their glide, and so no laser-guided bombs were dropped. The television-guided bombs closed the bridge to traffic but did not down a span.[60]

When the 8th Tactical Fighter Wing came back to the Thanh Hoa Bridge on May 13, 1972, the fourth day of Linebacker, five of the fourteen strike F–4s carried their heaviest weapons, 3,000-pound laser-guided bombs, while the others had 2,000-pound laser-guided bombs or 500-pound unguided bombs. The weather cooperated, and for the first time a span of the Thanh Hoa Bridge went down. Nevertheless that was not to be the last raid on this bridge. While rail traffic would not cross the bridge for the rest of the year, trucks were soon using it again. The Air Force revisited the bridge twice more, and the Navy came no less than eleven times. Nor did the North Vietnamese fail to use pontoon bridges across the Song Ma. While guided bombs facilitated interdiction, they did not make it easy.[61]

Altogether, the Air Force destroyed more than a hundred bridges in Linebacker, some of them several times. The first to go down, even before the Thanh Hoa Bridge, was the much longer Doumer Bridge over the Red River at Hanoi. Because of its location, it had been a forbidden target during Rolling Thunder until August 1967, when it was attacked by F–105s and F–4s with unguided bombs. On that 1967 raid, F–105s with 3,000-pound bombs collapsed one of the nineteen spans. Although they were dropping bombs from seven thousand feet and pulling out as low as four thousand feet, none of the attacking aircraft was shot down; an F–105 and an F–4 were damaged, both managing to land in Thailand. The backseater in the damaged F–4, Lt. Thomas "Mike" Messett, returned to Southeast Asia as a captain in 1972 and sat in the front seat of another F–4 during the first two Linebacker raids on the Doumer Bridge. Most of his fellow pilots were making their initial visits to Hanoi.[62]

On the morning of May 10, 1972, sixteen F–4s attacked the Doumer Bridge from twelve thousand feet with guided bombs. Colonel Miller led the first flight of four over the target and dropped television-guided bombs, none of which hit the target. The experience soured both Miller and his boss in Saigon, General Vogt, on television guidance. The other three flights dropped 2,000-pound laser-guided bombs that severely damaged the bridge but failed to down a span. Vogt sent a single flight of four F–4s back the next day with a pair of 3,000-pound laser-guided bombs as well as six more 2,000-pounders. This time three spans broke away. Not only did the bigger bombs prove as effective as unguided bombs had in 1967, but keeping the laser designator on target was easier in the face of the lighter air defenses that confronted the smaller force.[63]

*   *   *

While all the strike aircraft attacking the Doumer Bridge on May 10 and 11 completed their missions unharmed, two escorting F–4s were shot down by Chinese-made MiG–19s. These MiG–19s (or J–6s as the Chinese versions were called) were less maneuverable than the older MiG–17s and slower than the newer MiG–21s. Like the MiG–17s and unlike the MiG–21s, the MiG–19s in North Vietnam relied primarily on their guns to combat other aircraft. Altogether the Chinese provided more than thirty MiG–19s after the end of Rolling Thunder—or about a seventh of North Vietnam's fighter force in 1972. While these MiG–19s did not give North Vietnam a major new capability, they were the first Chinese-made aircraft in the North Vietnamese inventory. As early as September 1965, a Chinese MiG–19 had downed an Air Force F–104 that had strayed into China, and a pair of Navy A–6s had been lost in the same way two years later. Now Air Force and Navy aircraft would have to deal with MiG–19s in North Vietnam, and these first losses were especially costly for the Air Force.[64]

The Air Force's leading contenders in the 1972 race to win five air-to-air victories and become aces, Maj. Robert A. Lodge and his backseater, Capt. Roger C. Locher, of the 432 Tactical Reconnaissance Wing at Udorn, were shot down by a MiG–19 on May 10 just after winning their third victory. Major Lodge was killed together with Capt. Jeffrey L. Harris and Capt. Dennis E. Wilkinson, whose F–4 went down in the same skirmish. Preoccupied with MiG–21s, the F–4s were surprised from the rear by MiG–19s. Captain Locher not only parachuted to survival, but evaded capture for three weeks and was rescued only sixty miles northwest of Hanoi in one of the deepest helicopter penetrations of the war.[65]

These losses were just part of the most intense day of air-to-air fighting in the Vietnam War. In exchange for the two Air Force F–4s, eleven MiGs fell; Air Force F–4s shot down three MiG–21s with Sparrow radar-guided missiles; Navy F–4s shot down seven MiG–17s and one MiG–21, all with Sidewinder heat-seeking missiles. The Navy managed this feat without an air-to-air loss, but did lose an F–4 to ground fire and another to a surface-to-air missile. The latter plane was the very one whose crew had just succeeded in shooting down three MiGs in a single afternoon. Having suddenly won their fifth victory and become the first aces of the Vietnam War, Lt. Randy Cunningham and Lt.(j.g.) William Driscoll were dumped into the Gulf of Tonkin. Fortunately they were rescued. Driscoll (the backseat radar intercept officer) was the first crew member other than a pilot to get official credit for five victories since World War I; the Army Air Forces had not recognized the claims of bomber gunners in World War II because the large number of gunners involved in most engagements had made conflicting claims difficult to sort out.[66]

Not until late in the summer would Capt. Richard "Steve" Ritchie and his weapon system officer, Capt. Charles B. DeBellevue, become the Air Force's first aces of the war. They won their initial victory on May 10 in the melee that killed Lodge, Harris, and Wilkinson. The rarity of such heavy air-to-air engagements meant that the Vietnam War would produce only one more American ace, Capt. Jeffrey S. "Fang" Feinstein, an Air Force weapon system officer. Only DeBellevue would get as many as six victories. The Korean War, in contrast, had produced eight times as many American aces, and the leading ace won sixteen victories in about a hundred sorties (the usual number flown in a full tour over North Vietnam).[67]

While another day like May 10, 1972, would not occur in the Vietnam War, there would be too many occasions when a North Vietnamese MiG picked off F–4s. This misfortune occurred far more often to Air Force planes than to Navy planes. During 1972, the Air Force lost twenty-three F–4s and one F–105 Wild Weasel to MiGs; the Navy lost just two F–4s and one RA–5 reconnaissance plane in this way. The disparity was partly caused by the distribution of enemy air assets. The MiG–21s at Phuc Yen dealt mostly with Air Force raids in the Hanoi area, while the MiG–17s at Kep concentrated on Navy sorties nearer the coast. The MiG–21s specialized in a single pass from the rear, while the slower MiG–17s depended on their maneuverability in dogfights. The MiG–21s attacked more often, exacting a higher cost and suffering greater losses. Air Force chaff flights had to fly above twenty thousand feet, at an altitude more favorable to MiG–21s and higher than Navy aircraft in Linebacker or both service's aircraft in Rolling Thunder. Air Force F–4s in Linebacker faced an upgraded version of the MiG–21 with longer range and four missiles rather than the two usually carried in Rolling Thunder. Altogether, Air Force F–4s shot down forty-seven MiGs in 1972 (including thirty-nine MiG–21s), while Navy F–4s shot down twenty-four MiGs (fourteen of which were MiG–17s).[68]

Many of the Air Force air-to-air victories came late in the summer, however. In May and June, Air Force F–4s shot down only twelve MiGs, while MiGs were shooting down thirteen F–4s. It was the first time the Air Force had been on the losing end of an air-to-air ratio, and the sting was all the sharper because Navy F–4s won nineteen victories with no losses during the same two months. The Seventh Air Force commander was not left to solve this problem entirely on his own. The Air Force Chief of Staff took a very active interest. General Ryan paid a visit to Saigon in July, and decided to replace General Vogt's chief of operations, Maj. Gen. Alton D. Slay, with Ryan's own director of operations, Maj. Gen. Carlos M. Talbott.[69]

General Slay had also served as General Lavelle's chief of operations and became a focus of some of the controversy surrounding Lavelle's relief. In the summer of 1972, much of the Air Force was divided between supporters of Lavelle and supporters of the man who fired him, Ryan. Lavelle insisted that he did not know about the false reporting that brought him down, and many of his friends blamed Slay for the false reporting scheme.* That summer, however, Slay found himself in trouble not only with Lavelle's friends, but also with Ryan. The Chief of Staff did not like the way operations were being run at Seventh Air Force.[70]

Slay's replacement, General Talbott, had already served in Saigon in 1966 as deputy director of the tactical air control center. His reassignment to Saigon broke the unwritten rule that the Air Force did not send its generals to Southeast Asia for a second tour. He found a very different headquarters from the one he had left six years earlier. In a combat environment more demanding than the one that had prevailed then, the number of headquarters personnel shrank day by day. The operations center for the out-country war had been combined with the tactical air control center for the in-country war, and this new combined center moved across Tan Son Nhut Air Base to become the Military Assistance Command's operations center. Like nearly everyone else at Seventh Air Force headquarters, Talbott "wore a second hat"—that is, he held the same job in the joint headquarters that he did in Seventh Air Force. The consolidation had many advantages, not least the elevation of General Vogt to be deputy commander under the Army's new MACV commander, Gen. Fred C. Weyand.

Slay refused to talk to his replacement and left a few hours after Talbott arrived. Talbott's impression was that Slay had been cut out of much of the day-to-day management of operations. The intelligence chief dealt directly with Vogt on targets, and there were no daily staff meetings to review yesterday's results and plan tomorrow's operations. Talbott attributed this way of doing business to Slay's lack of operational experience. In any case, those like Talbott who believed Slay's career was over proved mistaken. He would gain two more stars and eventually take charge of Air Force Systems Command.[71]

By the time Talbott reached Saigon in August, Vogt had already taken a number of actions to improve his command's performance. In response to pressure from Ryan, he called his commanders to Saigon in July and told them to hold frequent Linebacker after-action meetings at Udorn. From mid-August through December, flying and control units sent representatives to a daily meeting at Udorn to assess the previous day's missions. There was no precedent for this much coordination, and it meant pulling aircrews and controllers away from their jobs for trips to Udorn. During Rolling Thunder, there had been only

---

* See Chapter 8.

the occasional "practice reunions" that emphasized camaraderie as much as exchanging information.[72]

A major objective of the daily Linebacker conferences in late 1972 was to improve the process by which controllers warned strike forces of impending MiG attacks. Indeed, General Vogt believed that Seventh Air Force's principal problem with the MiGs was a lack of warning. In December 1971, a few F–4Ds had started to exploit their own new capability to interrogate MiG identification transponders and not rely on an EC–121 to make such interrogations. Six months later, only three F–4Ds with the necessary "Combat Tree" equipment survived at Udorn until twenty more arrived in July. In some situations, this identification capability permitted F–4s to launch Sparrows from beyond visual range, but the North Vietnamese caught on to the change and turned their transponders off much of the time. The Navy radar control ship in the Gulf of Tonkin received information from several sources about MiG activity in the coastal portion of North Vietnam where Navy planes were operating. Vogt wanted something comparable for the Air Force to bring together information from all available reconnaissance sources (including North Vietnamese radio communications). During Rolling Thunder, Seventh Air Force had attempted to perform this "fusion" function at Monkey Mountain near Da Nang.* But in 1972, Seventh Air Force was moving out of South Vietnam, and Vogt established his new fusion center at Nakhon Phanom Air Base, Thailand, with the call sign "Teaball." Vogt expected Teaball to provide the earliest possible MiG warning for his strike packages.[73]

Vogt's belief that Teaball turned the air-to-air situation around seemed to be supported by the obvious correlation between Teaball's commencement of operations in early August and Seventh Air Force's dramatically improved performance against MiGs. During the next three months, the score was twenty MiGs down at a cost of only four Air Force F–4s. During and after the war, however, many of the fighter pilots involved questioned the importance of Teaball. In Vogt's view, the pilots' low esteem for Teaball derived from their lack of sufficient security clearances to know about Teaball's sources.[74]

The Air Force's Tactical Fighter Weapons Center at Nellis Air Force Base, Nevada, systematically gathered documents on air engagements and interviewed crew members. The Fighter Weapons Center concluded that Teaball's contribution was relatively minor and that the Navy radar control ship continued to provide more useful warnings even to Air Force planes. Teaball's defenders objected that the Fighter Weapons Center was concerned only with the utility of warnings that led to shooting down MiGs—Teaball's real purpose was preventing the shoot-down of F–4s. But since F–4 escorts and patrols had borne the brunt of losses to MiGs as well as winning nearly all victories against them, escorts and patrols were the aircraft that most needed the warnings for

---

* See Chapter 4.

defensive as well as offensive purposes. It was true that other aircraft maneuvered in response to MiG warnings. But of the seven Air Force chaff, strike, and Wild Weasel aircraft lost to MiGs in 1972, three were lost after the introduction of Teaball.[75]

A major part of Teaball's problem was communications, especially communications from Nakhon Phanom to the strike forces. Because of its great distance from Hanoi, Teaball had to use a radio relay aircraft. For some reason this relay often failed to work well. One theory was that interference from EB–66 jamming aircraft caused the trouble, but this idea surfaced only at the end of the year—too late for any remedy to be applied.[76]

How then to account for the dramatic improvement in Seventh Air Force's performance against MiGs? The Fighter Weapons Center not surprisingly emphasized the importance of aircrew experience. Navy pilots did better at the outset of Linebacker because the Navy had established its Top Gun air-to-air training program after Rolling Thunder. The Air Force had no such program, and its pilots required a few months of combat to become skilled enough to defeat the MiGs. This argument was sufficiently persuasive for the Air Force to establish its Red Flag exercise program at Nellis, where air-to-air and bombing skills could be honed together in the face of air defenses—including an "aggressor squadron" of T–38s and F–5s mimicking MiG–21s. One outcome of more realistic training would be an Air Force decision to abandon its "fluid four" fighter formation in favor of the Navy's "loose deuce." While the "fluid four" had always been intended to break into two pairs of fighter aircraft, an Air Force pair had at least theoretically been much tighter and less flexible than a Navy pair. The loose deuce formation would encourage every wingman to fly at a greater distance from the lead aircraft and take the lead role in an engagement with enemy aircraft when feasible.[77]

During Linebacker, the Air Force did what it could to support its pilots with better tools. The sad performance of air-to-air missiles received a lot of attention. Despite all attempts to improve them, the probability of a missile destroying its target remained less than 20 percent. The Sparrow's fundamental problem was that it was designed for a different kind of war—a war in which American pilots would be permitted to fire Sparrows far beyond visual range. In Southeast Asia, pilots were usually required to identify the enemy aircraft visually before they could launch a Sparrow. On at least one occasion, an F–4 was shot down while speeding ahead of its flight to make sure that a targeted aircraft was in fact a MiG. Allegations that this F–4 was hit by a Sparrow launched by another F–4 in the flight were discounted by the Air Force, which concluded that a second MiG–21 had done the job. In any case, the requirement to visually identify MiGs collided dangerously with the requirement for sufficient range to use the Sparrow.[78]

In 1972, Seventh Air Force was using a so-called "dogfight Sparrow," but it still could not be launched from as close to a MiG as the Sidewinder heat-seeking missile could. Aircrews often had difficulty launching either missile within required parameters of range and direction. Even when those parameters were satisfied, the fragile Sparrow frequently malfunctioned. An F–4 maintenance officer at Korat discovered that some of the Sparrow's problems could be attributed to the shaking the missiles received when a munitions tractor pulled them across foreign-object-damage (FOD) bumps at the edge of the flight line; these metal FOD strips were intended to shake out rocks, screws, and other objects that might be sucked in by jet engines.[79]

At sea, conditions for the Sparrows were even worse, and the Navy chose to rely almost entirely on Sidewinders. Their version of the Sidewinder was reputed to be better in some respects than the Air Force's. Sidewinders were, in any case, the most appropriate missiles for close-range, maneuvering dogfights with MiG–17s. The Sparrows, on the other hand, were more suitable for dealing with the faster MiG–21s and their one-pass tactic. Because of this tactic, in 1972 Air Force crews found less use for their Sidewinders. As Air Force pilots gained combat experience using the Sparrow, it became more effective in their hands and continued to be used more than the Sidewinder even after an improved version of the latter reached Udorn Air Base in August. The Air Force's improved Sidewinder did down two MiG–19s on September 9, the fifth and sixth victories for Captain DeBellevue—and the first two of three for his pilot on this mission, Capt. John A. Madden, Jr.[80]

MiG–21 hit-and-run tactics also made the F–4 gun less relevant. Aircrew complaints about the F–4C's lack of a gun had led to deployment of F–4Ds with gun pods in 1967. After Rolling Thunder, F–4Es with a gun built into the nose reached Southeast Asia. The North Vietnamese invasion spurred the deployment of F–4E squadrons, but F–4Ds still outnumbered F–4Es by two-to-one at the two bases (Udorn and Ubon) that sent the most sorties into the high-risk portions of North Vietnam. Thanks to upgrades of the F–4D, it was in most respects comparable to the F–4E and some F–4Ds could determine the location of MiGs beyond visual range by triggering their identification transponders. Indeed, the F–4Ds experienced less than half as many losses as the F–4Es to MiGs in 1972 while downing more MiGs; all three Air Force aces scored victories in both versions of the F–4. F–4E guns did bring down a MiG–19 and four MiG–21s; an F–4E gun combined with a Sidewinder to destroy another MiG–21, and an F–4D gunpod eliminated a sixth MiG–21.[81]

At least as important as improvements derived from Air Force combat experience was the degradation in MiG capability during Linebacker. The North Vietnamese had launched their spring offensive in 1972 with a considerably stronger air force than they had during Rolling Thunder. When American air power had finally begun to attack North Vietnamese airfields in the spring of 1967, the North Vietnamese had about 150 MiG fighters. Those that were not destroyed could not remain on their bases near Hanoi and had to use bases in southern China. But the North Vietnamese air force in late 1967 could take comfort from the fact that their 20 MiG–21s were beginning to shoot down U.S. planes with the new tactic of making a single pass from the rear. After the end of Rolling Thunder in 1968, the North Vietnamese built a stronger air force. The number of MiGs increased to nearly 250, including more than 80 MiG–21s. With the exception of about 30 MiG–17s, North Vietnam's entire air force was pulled out of China and returned to North Vietnamese bases. Many of the aircraft were housed in caves or bomb shelters. North Vietnam built new bases in the panhandle within reach of South Vietnam.[82]

Soon after the beginning of the spring 1972 offensive, American planes resumed bombing North Vietnamese airfields. Most of these raids targeted the panhandle airfields, and the North Vietnamese were not able to move their planes south during Linebacker. On the other hand, operations never ceased for more than a few hours at North Vietnam's four principal airfields: Phuc Yen (mainly MiG–21s), Yen Bai (mainly MiG–19s), Kep (mainly MiG–17s), and Hanoi's airport at Gia Lam. The Air Force did not attempt to bomb aircraft in shelters or caves. Several raids did attack the air defense command bunker at Bac Mai airfield on the southern outskirts of Hanoi. General Vogt was convinced that his crews finally penetrated the bunker, but the intelligence agencies were skeptical that much damage had been done; the bunker was hard to see from above ten thousand feet.[83]

North Vietnamese air defenses continued to function throughout Linebacker. The MiGs did not flee to China as they had in 1967. Nevertheless, their effectiveness diminished. While the skill of American aircrews increased, the MiG force shrank from nearly 250 to fewer than 200. About half the MiG–21s were destroyed. These losses probably included some of North Vietnam's most aggressive pilots and required difficult adjustments in so small an air force.[84]

Although the MiG pilots for a time outshined their Air Force opponents, they managed to destroy in 1972 only one more American aircraft (twenty-eight) than they had in 1967. Indeed, the overall experience of American planes over North Vietnam in 1972 was much healthier than in 1967. While flying about 25 percent fewer sorties into North Vietnam, losses there dropped by 50 percent to about a hundred aircraft. The big difference in 1972 was the much diminished effectiveness of North Vietnamese antiaircraft artillery. In 1967, artillery had accounted for about two-thirds of Air Force aircraft losses in North Vietnam; in 1972, artillery accounted for less than a third.[85]

American estimates of the number of North Vietnamese antiaircraft artillery pieces with a bore of at least thirty-seven millimeters declined from nearly eight thousand in 1967 to fewer than a thousand in 1972. Much of this remarkable decline could not be accounted for by pieces destroyed or moved to Laos and South Vietnam. American intelligence analysts became more adept at distinguishing real artillery pieces from dummies. North Vietnam's antiaircraft artillery inventory may have been nearly as large as it had ever been, especially if guns of somewhat smaller caliber were counted. The North Vietnamese had perhaps three thousand pieces with a twenty-three millimeter bore.[86]

It was not so much North Vietnamese antiaircraft artillery that changed, but rather the Air Force tactics used against it. General Vogt and laser-guided bombs had moved Air Force strike packages higher in altitude beyond the reach of most artillery. But Navy planes continued to dive lower, and artillery exacted about half the Navy's losses.[87]

At the medium altitudes favored by Seventh Air Force, the principal foes were MiGs and surface-to-air missiles. These also bothered Navy planes en route to their targets and returning to their carriers. Indeed, the Navy was suffering more losses to SAMs than was the Air Force, perhaps because the Air Force made heavy use of chaff. The ability of F–4s to lay a chaff corridor improved in July with the introduction of a dispenser that released the chaff steadily rather than in the widely separated bunches characteristic of the chaff bombs used earlier in the year.[88]

The F–4s did not rely solely on chaff. The introduction of jamming pods during Rolling Thunder had been a great success, and F–4s in 1972 each carried two jamming pods (rather than the one customary in 1967).* For six weeks F–4s with laser-guided bombs dropped them from a formation designed to get maximum protection from the jamming pods. Later the 8th Tactical Fighter Wing discovered that it could still get good results using just one laser designation pod in each flight, if the flight abandoned jamming-pod formation for about a minute to climb and dive so that all four F–4s could drop their bombs into the laser "basket" formed by the lead F–4's laser designator.[89]

While Seventh Air Force continued to depend on jamming pods, it was noted that no F–4 had been shot down in a chaff corridor. The price the Air Force paid for protecting its laser-guided bombers with chaff was a series of MiG attacks on its big formations. General Vogt could take satisfaction, however, in the fact that MiGs rarely got through his F–4 escorts and patrols to hit either his chaff-dropping F–4s or his strike F–4s. The F–4 escorts and patrols took losses, but succeeded in their mission of protecting the strike packages.[90]

Neither chaff nor jamming pods eliminated the game of cat and mouse played with SAM sites by F–105 Wild Weasels. The Standard antiradiation missile introduced toward the end of Rolling Thunder now saw heavy use, but it was in short enough supply and suffered frequent enough malfunctions to keep the older, slower, shorter-ranged Shrike in business as well. All the Southeast Asia Wild Weasels were based at Korat, and the F–4Es there joined them in hunter-killer teams that used new antimateriel CBU–52 cluster bombs in an attempt to destroy SAM sites and not just suppress them. The CBU–52

---

* Improvements in the jamming pods permitted a less rigid formation than during Rolling Thunder, and in 1972 (while not yet adopting the Navy's "loose deuce" tactics) the Air Force F–4 wings developed looser, weaving formations that helped aircrews watch for MiGs.

was certainly more potent than the CBU–24 of Rolling Thunder, but claims of success against SAMs were usually hard to prove—whether or not SAM equipment was damaged, it could be moved.[91]

Although SAMs turned out to be a manageable problem for Seventh Air Force, they did give officers in Southeast Asia and Washington some worries. The inventory was thought to have increased since Rolling Thunder from perhaps 180 SA–2 launchers to perhaps 240. As it happened, Americans estimated that the North Vietnamese launched roughly the same number of SA–2s in 1972 as in 1967—about 4,000. Even if only half that many were actually launched, fewer than 4 percent brought down an aircraft.* But for several months, aircrews and intelligence analysts feared that SA–4s with mobile launch vehicles had been introduced into North Vietnam. Aircrews often reported seeing a new SAM that they called the "Black SAM." New jamming pods for F–4s were rushed to Thailand before analysts finally concluded that this "Black SAM" was a Chinese version of the SA–2 and definitely not an improvement. Not until early 1973 would the presence of SA–3s (more effective against aircraft flying at lower altitudes) be confirmed in North Vietnam. The only really new SAM to plague Seventh Air Force in 1972 was the small, shoulder-launched SA–7 that threatened slow aircraft flying low in South Vietnam.[92]

*   *   *

The most effective North Vietnamese air defense had always been weather. From May through mid-July, American planes enjoyed the least cloudy weather of the year in the Red River Delta (which meant that about half the planned sorties could strike their original targets and not have to be canceled or diverted to the panhandle). With better luck, these relatively clear conditions might have

---

* According to American estimates, North Vietnamese SA–2 effectiveness declined from about thirty missiles required to destroy an aircraft in 1966 to about sixty in 1972. In 1998, however, a retired Russian general published SA–2 expenditure data from 1972 that cast doubt on the American estimates. See Mark Vorobyov, "Dvina: Guarding Vietnam's Skies," *Military Parade*, Jul–Aug 1998, pp 101–3. Vorobyov argued that the ratio of SA–2s expended to aircraft destroyed in 1972 was less than five to one. His ratio, however, depended on a greatly inflated estimate of US aircraft losses. When Vorobyov's SA–2 expenditure data are compared with US loss data, the ratio is about thirty SA–2s launched for each aircraft destroyed in 1972. Unfortunately, Vorobyov did not provide annual SA–2 expenditure data for earlier years, although he did state that total wartime expenditure of SA–2s plus those "found faulty" was about sixty-eight hundred. He also indicated that SA–2 effectiveness in 1966 of about four missiles launched for destruction of one aircraft declined sharply in 1967 to about ten to one and recovered in 1972. It may be that the ratio of SA–2s launched to aircraft destroyed did reach more than fifty to one in late 1967 before reversing direction in 1972. I am indebted to Barry Watts for his analysis of Vorobyov's article.

continued well into September. In 1972, however, six weeks of unusually cloudy weather intervened before a few more weeks of good weather in September. After that, the beginning of the northeast monsoon brought with it the increasing cloudiness and mists that would rule out most laser-guided bombing for the next six months.[93]

The Air Force Chief of Staff, General Ryan, had a long familiarity with the problems posed by the northeast monsoon. As commander of Pacific Air Forces in 1967, he had sought to provide at least a limited bad-weather bombing capability by converting the two-seat F–105F Wild Weasel aircraft into a radar bomber. But while it would have been adequate for nuclear bombing, the F–105's radar could not provide enough accuracy for conventional bombing. "Ryan's Raiders" were not up to the job; nor were the F–4s. Ryan had to wait until six of the new General Dynamics swing-wing F–111s could be deployed in March 1968. Since their arrival came shortly before the Rolling Thunder cutback to the panhandle of North Vietnam, the F–111s did not have many targets with a good radar return. But their big problem in 1968 seemed to be the terrain-avoidance radar that was essential to survival on their low-level missions. Three quick F–111 losses ended their first combat deployment after only one month. While a maintenance problem was known to have caused one of the losses, inability to explain the other two fed speculation that they had flown into a mountain.[94]

The F–111's first visit to Southeast Asia in 1968 further tarnished that aircraft's already controversial reputation as the product of Secretary of Defense McNamara's aborted attempt to develop a multirole fighter for both the Air Force and the Navy. The Navy managed to get out of the deal, and the Air Force got a fighter that might be able to bomb but could not fight MiGs. Ryan did not give up on the F–111, for he saw it as the Air Force's best hope for an all-weather bomber. Its accuracy was much better than Ryan's Raiders. Bridge bombing was not a good choice, because the F–111 did not yet have a laser target designator. But railyards, airfields, and supply dumps were suitable targets for the F–111's unguided bombs in bad weather and at night.[95]

When Ryan visited Saigon in July 1972, he urged Vogt to embrace the return of F–111s to Southeast Asia. Vogt had been Ryan's operations deputy in Hawaii during Rolling Thunder, and both men were keenly aware of the Air Force's need for an accurate all-weather bomber. Vogt could see merit in using F–111s rather than B–52s, not only because the F–111s were more accurate, but also because the F–111s could penetrate North Vietnam on their own without the big escort packages required by the B–52s. On the other hand, Vogt was not enthusiastic about Ryan's proposal to send forty-eight F–111s to Takhli in place of the ninety-five F–4s already there. Those F–4s, together with more than fifty at Korat, had been the backbone of Seventh Air Force's effort in South Vietnam.[96]

After hearing Vogt's objections, Ryan proceeded with plans to replace the Takhli F–4s with F–111s that began arriving near the end of September. A few days later, Vought A–7s began replacing the F–4s at Korat. Although the Navy, which had developed both the F–4 and the A–7, had been using its carrier version of the A–7 in Southeast Asia since the end of 1967, this was the first time the Air Force version was deployed to the theater. The Korat A–7s, which had bad-weather capability superior to the F–4s, would attempt to do the work that the Takhli and Korat F–4s together had been doing in South Vietnam. But with communist ground forces retreating in South Vietnam, Ryan wanted Vogt to use most of his resources in North Vietnam. Unfortunately, neither A–7s nor F–111s could replace Korat and Takhli F–4s in protecting strike packages from MiGs, and the air-to-air mission now fell entirely on the Udorn F–4s. On the other hand, since A–7s and F–111s could reach their targets without aerial refueling, Ryan was able to withdraw from Thailand and Taiwan more than a quarter of the 172 tankers that had been operating in Southeast Asia. Indeed, Thailand's insistence that tanker operations from the Bangkok airport cease by mid-October bolstered Ryan's argument for replacing F–4s with F–111s and A–7s.[97]

While the F–111 and the A–7 would both prove valuable additions to Vogt's arsenal, he had to put up with a lot of redeployment in the midst of war. Even at Thailand bases which got to keep the F–4, Ryan made matters difficult by insisting that they all participate fully in the disruptive service-wide transition from squadron maintenance organizations to consolidated base maintenance organizations. The early F–111 sorties would do little to put a brighter face on the changes imposed by Washington.

A few hours after the first F–111s arrived at Takhli, five of them took off on separate missions into Route Package Five. Before it could be spotted by North Vietnamese radar, each F–111 was to drop to a thousand feet and go as low as five hundred feet for the bomb run. One of these F–111s did not return and was presumed to have flown into the ground. Although F–111 combat operations were called off for a week while the two-man crews practiced in Thailand, three more F–111s disappeared in the next six weeks. But Takhli's 474th Tactical Fighter Wing was sending out at least twenty F–111 sorties a night, and the loss rate was not bad enough to ground the fighters with the most accurate bad-weather bombing capability. A squadron bulletin board warned: "Flak effectiveness is 5%—missile effectiveness is 8%—ground effectiveness is 100%—AVOID GROUND."[98]

Meanwhile, General Vogt was pursuing another approach to bad-weather bombing that proved fairly successful in the panhandle, but did not help much in the Red River Delta. When dropping sensors on the Ho Chi Minh Trail in Laos, Seventh Air Force had required a precise navigation system. As the operations director at Pacific Air Forces during Rolling Thunder, Vogt encouraged using a Coast Guard Long Range Navigation (loran) system for this purpose as well as for bad-weather bombing. An aircraft could determine its location by measuring the time difference in the reception of signals sent by two loran ground stations. Despite its name, loran's range was insufficiently long to reach dependably to Hanoi from the ground stations in Thailand.[99]

Nevertheless, Vogt did what he could to make loran function as well as possible. Even when the ground station signals could be received, loran could not produce accurate bombing unless the exact location of the target was known. During good weather in September, Vogt sent the RF–4s of the 432d Tactical Reconnaissance Wing at Udorn on repeated missions to secure the necessary grid-annotated photography. The RF–4s also served as loran pathfinders for F–4s to drop test bombs in good weather as well as bad. By dropping a type of 1,000-pound bomb not used before, distinctive craters could tell photo-analysts where loran bombs were hitting and permit refinements in the loran signal time delays associated with each target. These loran sorties were accompanied by other F–4s engaged in unguided bombing without benefit of loran. Together they partly answered demands from Washington and Hawaii for more Air Force attack sorties in the northern route packages. With fewer laser-guided bombing missions, more F–4s could bomb instead of performing escort or patrol duties. Loran missions did not get the big escort packages allotted the laser-guided missions, and F–111s did not get any at all.[100]

*　　　　*　　　　*

As the northeast monsoon moved into North Vietnam in October and brought a natural end to the bridge-busting campaign, American intelligence agencies remained largely unconvinced that Linebacker had much reduced North Vietnamese imports or stopped the resupply of North Vietnamese forces in South Vietnam. When South Vietnamese forces regained Quang Tri city in September, they captured some North Vietnamese troops who had not eaten in a few days and were short of ammunition. But such shortages could be attributed to a local distribution problem. In the absence of conclusive evidence, the campaign's critics and advocates retreated into shrill assertion. When Secretary of the Air Force Seamans optimistically told the press that perhaps only a quarter of the supplies the North Vietnamese were sending south reached their destination, he found himself in trouble with the White House for being so pessimistic publicly.[101]

Laser-guided bombs had limited the railroads to shuttling between downed bridges, but sometimes aircrews did exaggerate their prowess. On May 22, the 8th Tactical Fighter Wing attacked eight bridges with fifteen laser-guided bombs and claimed six bridges destroyed; subsequent photo-analysis found three of the claimed bridges still operational. Quite apart from the difficulty of assessing bomb damage when inflicted, bridge repair often quickly permitted at least trucks to cross. For example, on July 30, thirteen bridges were down on the northwest railroad from China to Hanoi; a week later only four remained closed to all traffic. In the case of longer bridges like some of those on the more important northeast railroad also connecting China and Hanoi, bridge repair might require a month or more. Few, if any, of the downed bridges could not be bypassed at least by ferry or pontoon bridge. A moveable bridge could be hidden along shore in daytime and put across a river at night.[102]

Nevertheless, the Air Force relied almost entirely on the laser-guided bombing of bridges for interdiction in Route Packages Five and Six. This was a departure from Rolling Thunder, when a considerable effort had been made to destroy locomotives and rolling stock. While the Navy in 1972 had some success against such targets in the panhandle, neither service made much of an attempt along the routes from China to Hanoi. There were a few raids on the railyards there, but little rolling stock was hit and the North Vietnamese continued to use more than two thousand railcars. As in Rolling Thunder, the yards close to the Chinese border remained off limits, as did the one in downtown Hanoi. The much greater success against bridges permitted by laser-guided bombs encouraged the abandonment of riskier raids against rolling stock. Indeed, laser-guided bombs seemed to point the way to a new kind of warfare much less bloody for attackers and attacked.[103]

The bridge campaign in 1972 was sufficiently successful to force the North Vietnamese for the first time to rely heavily on trucks to get supplies from China to Hanoi. South of Hanoi, the North Vietnamese had relied on trucks during Rolling Thunder as well, but with Chinese help had been able to keep the rail routes open from China to Hanoi. When laser-guided bombs disrupted rail transport north of Hanoi in 1972, the North Vietnamese turned to trucks. For this form of transport they were also heavily indebted to the Chinese.

Since China's largest truck factory at Chang Chun in Manchuria produced some sixty-five thousand trucks a year, replacing North Vietnam's truck losses of at most four thousand in 1972 was not unmanageable. Throughout the year, American intelligence estimates put North Vietnam's truck inventory at more than twenty thousand or about double its inventory during Rolling Thunder. In the panhandle of North Vietnam, the 8th Tactical Fighter Wing's "night owl" squadron pursued the trucks with flares to pull away the cover of darkness. Most of North Vietnam's truck losses in the summer of 1972 occurred in the panhandle. Such armed reconnaissance was deemed too dangerous in Route Packages Five and Six, where trucks were free to roam night and day.[104]

Until about June 7, 1972, traffic on the ninety miles of highway paralleling the northeast railroad from China to Hanoi was ten trucks per mile. Then suddenly the thousands of trucks filling big truck parks along the Chinese border emptied, and traffic density rose to perhaps forty trucks per mile all the way to Hanoi. The month's delay after the commencement of Linebacker before the big surge in truck traffic has sometimes been attributed to deliberate

Chinese stalling in retribution for North Vietnam's warm relations with the Soviet Union. But the closure of Haiphong may have required a month to reroute supplies inland. In any case, traffic on the northeast railroad continued to move until June 7. Only when bombing closed the railroad did truck traffic surge.[105]

While attacking trucks when they could be found in the panhandle, Seventh Air Force tried to reduce truck traffic in Route Packages Five and Six by destroying bridges, maintenance facilities, and supply depots. "We all know we cannot stop truck traffic," General Vogt told his commanders in July.[106] North Vietnam had ensured a reliable fuel supply for its trucks by opening a new oil pipeline from China to join with the one that already connected Haiphong and South Vietnam. During Rolling Thunder, trucks had to carry barrels of gasoline south to refuel themselves. Now they were relieved of that load, and the pipelines gave them a dependable source of fuel. The pipelines were hard to hit even with laser-guided bombs; if hit, the pipelines were very easy to repair. Given this durable link with imported oil, attacks on oil tank farms in North Vietnam could have only fleeting impact.[107]

The trucks continued to roll, but no one in the American intelligence community could be certain whether they carried enough supplies to replace the flow that used to come through Haiphong. It was certain that the North Vietnamese were having to import food. Long-term agricultural problems had been aggravated by a severe typhoon in the summer of 1971. A year later the North Vietnamese had yet to complete repair of the earthen dike system that controlled the Red River and made possible good rice crops. It was typhoon season again. What if more dikes were breached by bombing?[108]

Repeated North Vietnamese allegations that the U.S. was targeting the dikes may well have stemmed from concern that North Vietnam's food supply was in real danger. During Rolling Thunder, the Defense Department had studied the possibility of bombing the dikes, but most analysts judged that several bombs hitting close together would be required for each breach in one of the big dikes (levees) along the Red River; these were eighty feet across at the high-water line. The smaller dikes were judged too numerous and too easy to repair. Nevertheless, some analysts could foresee promising results from bombing the Red River dikes when the water was high during the summer typhoon season—yielding flood damage not only to the rice crop, but also to many facilities near the river in Hanoi.[109]

The belief that flooding would damage targets that were clearly military bolstered the legal case for bombing the dikes. Toward the end of the Korean War, the Air Force had justified the bombing of irrigation dams as a way to flood a railroad—but even then it was the obvious threat to North Korea's food supply that seemed to contribute significantly to a cease-fire. Probably the most influential Air Force officer to take an interest in dike bombing during Rolling Thunder was General Ginsburgh, Joint Chiefs liaison on the National Security Council staff. The Air Force Chief of Staff at the time, General McConnell, thought that agriculture was a legitimate target but eventually concluded that bombing the dikes would be "a pretty fruitless operation."[110]

The questionable legality of attacking targets so closely linked to agriculture, together with the likelihood of a very bad press, discouraged experimentation with bombing dikes in Rolling Thunder and continued to do so even in 1972—after laser-guided bombs had improved its feasibility. The few bombs that did hit dikes either strayed from a nearby target or sought to destroy air defense artillery or missiles mounted on the dikes. In late July, when many American reporters were disseminating Hanoi's claims about deliberate American bombing of dikes, President Nixon declared publicly that if the United States wanted to breach the dikes, it could do so in a few days. Many found this argument persuasive, and some suggested that the North Vietnamese government was simply trying to blame American planes for its own failure to get typhoon-damaged dikes repaired. In any case, North Vietnam escaped a bad typhoon and severe flooding in 1972.[111]

The dikes were not the only potential targets that the U.S. continued to deny itself during Linebacker operations very much as it had in Rolling Thunder. Although the rules of engagement were less restrictive in 1972, they still put three key regions of North Vietnam mostly off limits: Hanoi, Haiphong, and the northern frontier along the Chinese border. The old restricted circle around Hanoi was reduced from a radius of thirty nautical miles to ten nautical miles—within which every target required the approval of Secretary of Defense Laird. The comparable radius at Haiphong had always been ten nautical miles and remained so.[112]

Similarly, the buffer zone along the Chinese border kept its former depth: twenty-five nautical miles from the Gulf of Tonkin across the northeast railroad to the 106th parallel; thirty nautical miles from there across the northwest railroad to Laos. As in Rolling Thunder, raids on rail targets were permitted to penetrate the border buffer zone; the depth of penetration was increased from ten nautical miles to fifteen nautical miles on the northeast railroad (and from fifteen nautical miles to twenty nautical miles on the northwest railroad). This enabled key bridges in the border buffer zone to be bombed, but left nearby truck parks unscathed.

Since many potential targets lay within the restricted areas, Secretary Laird's veto power could make a considerable difference. During Rolling Thunder, President Johnson, Secretary of Defense McNamara, and Secretary of State Rusk had winnowed targets over lunch—reinforcing each other's caution by cutting targets not already cut by McNamara. In Linebacker, President Nixon's advocacy of bolder moves was diluted by his leaving to Laird the authority to veto targets.

In May and June, Laird approved more than a hundred targets, about two-thirds of them in the restricted areas; the rest required his approval because they also carried a risk of civilian casualties. Laird began to say "no" more often.

When the Joint Chiefs of Staff asked him to approve forty-four targets on June 6, Laird authorized only twenty-eight. For the most part he stood by his vetoes, which included Hanoi's Gia Lam airport (heavily used by MiGs). In a few cases, like a communications site in Hanoi, he eventually relented. But when Admiral Moorer asked for twenty-nine targets on August 30, Laird denied them all.[113]

One target repeatedly vetoed by Laird was the Hanoi thermal powerplant, which the Navy had successfully struck with Walleye television-guided bombs in 1967. After that strike, the North Vietnamese had kept American prisoners at the site for a several months. This did not eliminate the target from consideration, but Laird opposed hitting any target so close to downtown Hanoi—with the major exception of the Doumer Bridge. Although Laird did approve bombing most other powerplants, Moorer had to go to Nixon for approval to bomb the big new Lang Chi hydroelectric plant about seventy miles northwest of Hanoi.[114]

Since Lang Chi's three generators could meet about half of North Vietnam's demand for electricity, their destruction was deemed essential. Unfortunately, the generators sat on top a concrete spillway in the middle of an earthen dam, a forbidden target like dikes. Seventh Air Force was expected to destroy the generators without breaching the dam. Even with laser-guided bombs, this was a tall order. General Vogt personally visited Ubon to make certain that Colonel Miller and his crews understood the importance of not breaching the dam. Vogt joked that if they hit the dam they should just fly on to India, where he would join them in exile.[115] When they managed to destroy all three generators on June 10 and still leave a solid dam, Vogt was so relieved that he told a reporter the raid was "the greatest feat in modern bombing history."[116]

Except for attacks on electrical production and distribution, Linebacker remained focused on targets with a more direct connection to interdiction. During Rolling Thunder, the interdiction rationale had been stretched to cover targets like the cement plant at Haiphong (road and runway repair) and the ironworks at Thai Nguyen (barge construction), but these targets received less attention in 1972. The Defense Intelligence Agency even advised the joint targeting committee in the Pentagon to cut the ironworks from the target list. This was not done and the ironworks were bombed in late June. Other more typical targets at Thai Nguyen were also hit—including a railroad repair shop, an army supply dump, and a powerplant.[117]

Although attacks on transportation and electricity added to the difficulty of life in North Vietnam, Linebacker otherwise made only feeble attempts to reduce the ability of the North Vietnamese authorities to govern their people. The Air Force did drop more than half a billion leaflets on North Vietnam. C–130s and B–52s dropped the bulk of the leaflets; many were released over the Gulf of Tonkin in an often vain hope that they would drift against the prevailing wind and reach the Red River Delta. In December 1967, a C–130 had been lost in Route Package Five after dropping leaflets near Hanoi. F–4s and drones were the only leaflet-carriers flying over Hanoi in 1972, and they could not carry anywhere near as many leaflets.[118]

Besides warning people to stay away from targets, leaflets talked about the need for the North Vietnamese government to sign a cease-fire bringing an end to bombing in the north and troop casualties in the south. Some "inflation" leaflets counterfeited North Vietnamese currency; captured prisoners reported that they had been able to spend this fake currency for awhile in the evening, but its washed-out color did not pass muster in daylight. In another attempt to provide a propaganda tool more attractive and influential than the usual leaflet, the Air Force dropped small radios to enable more people to hear broadcasts from South Vietnam. None of these psychological operations bore much obvious fruit.[119]

Ever since the beginning of Rolling Thunder, direct attack on North Vietnam's leadership in Hanoi had been ruled out. The Johnson administration had committed the U.S. not to threaten the overthrow of the communist government in Hanoi—while the communists were making every effort to overthrow the noncommunist government in Saigon. Although Nixon sometimes seemed ready to do more, through the summer of 1972 he kept within the bounds of the old policy. The Air Force asked to bomb the Ministry of National Defense facility in downtown Hanoi, but the Defense Intelligence Agency raised the possibility that American prisoners might be held there and questioned whether it was still an important headquarters. The only leadership facility Secretary Laird permitted the Air Force to attack was the air defense control bunker at Bac Mai airfield.[120]

Even within the constraints of a bombing policy that put enemy leadership off limits, a much stronger effort might have been made to sever the leadership's telecommunications links with its forces and its people. Unfortunately, the two principal telephone switching centers in North Vietnam were located next to facilities in Hanoi that inhibited bombing; one was adjacent to the International Control Commission and the other to the Soviet embassy. But the location of a dozen other communications nodes (including Radio Hanoi) was known, and yet they too were not attacked.[121]

Linebacker subordinated all else to interdicting supplies coming into North Vietnam and heading south. Given the volume of truck traffic that continued to move, the campaign's effectiveness could be questioned. Air operations in South Vietnam had a more obvious role in stopping the enemy offensive there. Certainly the Air Force put the preponderance of its war effort in South Vietnam. Most of the heavy tonnage of unguided bombs (dropped by B–52s and fighters) fell in South Vietnam, and much of the remainder in Route Package One. About half the laser-guided bombs expended in 1972 were used against targets in South Vietnam and Laos, especially artillery and tanks.[122]

North Vietnam had gradually built up its stockpiles of invasion supplies before launching its spring offensive. Rapid expenditure of those supplies in the spring and summer of 1972 meant that the stockpiles could be maintained only by a much more intense supply operation. Linebacker, together with min-ing, made it difficult for North Vietnam to continue sending supplies south at the same rate, let alone a much increased rate. To the extent that the Hanoi regime did try to resupply the invasion forces, it had to reduce the supplies available to its people in North Vietnam who were having to cope with daily bombing raids.

By the fall, both the North Vietnamese offensive and the South Vietnamese counteroffensive had lost momentum. North Vietnamese invaders had been dri-ven away from the cities of South Vietnam but not out of the country. The prin-cipal remaining leverage the U.S. had on North Vietnam was the demonstrated capability to bomb targets there—and that leverage was weakened by the north-east monsoon.

*   *   *

On October 23, 1972, President Nixon stopped bombing north of the twen-tieth parallel. Military leaders like General Vogt thought this was a poor move to make in advance of a cease-fire agreement. Henry Kissinger argued that he and Le Duc Tho had agreed on all important points in Paris; Le Duc Tho had finally conceded that the Thieu government would not have to resign before a cease-fire. But President Thieu did not welcome this news. Although he had for more than a year seemed ready to accept a cease-fire in place (with North Vietnamese forces remaining in South Vietnam), he had not expected or wanted such an agreement. In any case, the spring invasion greatly increased the size of North Vietnamese forces that would be left in South Vietnam.[123]

As a reward to the North Vietnamese and a signal to Saigon that it was time to settle, Kissinger wanted to stop the bombing of North Vietnam entirely. This Nixon would not do. "I was not going to be taken in by the mere prospect of an agreement as Johnson had been in 1968," Nixon later wrote.[124] By cutting back to the panhandle at the beginning of the northeast monsoon, Nixon gave up mostly what the weather would no longer permit him to do. F–111, A–6, and F–4 loran bombing could have continued in the Red River Delta, but the weath-er would make bridge-busting with laser-guided bombs usually impossible. Only B–52s could make a major difference in the delta during bad weather, and for months they had been restricted to the panhandle. Since Nixon's problem was at the moment more with Saigon than Hanoi, he was not yet ready to send the B–52s to bomb the Red River Delta.[125]

Nixon's disagreement with Kissinger about continuing to bomb North Vietnam was part of their larger disagreement about how to negotiate a cease-fire. For months Nixon had been uncomfortable with Kissinger's use of restric-tions on bombing to facilitate negotiations. Secretary of Defense Laird, on the other hand, was happy to indulge Kissinger in this practice. Consequently, the Chairman of the Joint Chiefs found himself making changes he did not like. "Kissinger endeavored to orchestrate the bombing," Moorer later recalled. "I personally don't think the North Vietnamese had any idea whether we sent a hundred bombers or eighty bombers or whether we sent them up above the twenty-first parallel or the twentieth parallel."[126]

Before going to Moscow in May, Nixon had insisted that there be no reduction in bombing during the summit meeting. But, in fact, bombing was forbidden within ten nautical miles of the center of Hanoi or five nautical miles from the center of Haiphong during that meeting. Later for a week in mid-June, strikes were forbidden not only in those normally restricted areas, but also anywhere in Route Packages Five and Six—to avoid an incident while Soviet President Nikolai Podgorny visited Hanoi (even though Kissinger had only promised the Soviets not to bomb Hanoi and Haiphong). After Podgorny left Hanoi, bombing resumed throughout North Vietnam except in the restricted areas (Hanoi, Haiphong, and the buffer zone along the Chinese border); there no strikes were permitted until Kissinger completed his own visit to Beijing in late June. Since Nixon also wanted to use improving relations with the Soviets and the Chinese to pressure the North Vietnamese, he went along with Kissinger's limitations on bombing.[127]

The most fundamental disagreement between Nixon and Kissinger on cease-fire negotiations concerned timing. Kissinger believed that the U.S. could get a better deal by reaching an agreement before the November presidential elections. But Nixon came to expect a landslide over his Democratic opponent, Senator George McGovern of South Dakota, without a cease-fire. Although McGovern had himself bombed Germany During World War II as a B–24 pilot, he now promised to pull out of Southeast Asia even before making arrangements for the return of the communists' American prisoners. Public opinion polls indicated that Nixon's Vietnam policies, including the bombing of North Vietnam, were popular. A cease-fire before the election could only raise questions about his political motives, just as he had questioned President Johnson's four years earlier.[128]

Johnson's failures and fortitude continued to affect Nixon, even inspire him. When the Democratic candidate for vice president, Sargent Shriver, called Nixon "the number-one bomber of all time," Nixon joked with Johnson's former press secretary that Johnson should be pleased. "I don't believe so," George Christian replied. "LBJ never likes to be number two in anything."[129] But Nixon was already contemplating how he could use B–52s after the election in a more dramatic way than they had ever been used.

Chapter Ten

B–52s at Last

During eleven of the twelve nights from December 18 to December 29, 1972, B–52s pounded railyards and other area targets from the outskirts of Hanoi and Haiphong almost to the Chinese border. The big bombers' airborne radar permitted them to work regardless of weather. F–111s used their terrain-following radar to make low-level attacks on airfields just before the B–52s arrived over North Vietnam. In daylight, other fighters bombed through the clouds by using weak signals from distant loran transmitters in Thailand. When the weather cleared briefly on three occasions, F–4s attacked targets in or near downtown Hanoi with laser-guided bombs. Only on Christmas day did the bombing pause. Nevertheless, the press called this campaign the "Christmas Bombing." The Joint Chiefs of Staff called it "Linebacker II."

Linebacker II was by far the heaviest two weeks of bombing in the Hanoi-Haiphong region. All of the massive air power gathered in and near Southeast Asia was focused on this one region. The two hundred B–52s based in Thailand and Guam dropped about fifteen thousand tons of bombs in Route Package Six, and fighters added more than two thousand tons.[1] This was enough tonnage to have leveled Hanoi and Haiphong, but the Nixon administration wanted B–52s to bomb only on the periphery of the cities—close enough to scare city dwellers while not killing many of them. Although a few strings of bombs went astray and enemy dead numbered perhaps two thousand, that contrasts with the tens of thousands killed in a single night by bombing raids during World War II.[2]

While B–52 losses were less than the Air Force's prediction of 3 percent for the whole campaign, they were double that on the third night and surface-to-air missiles ultimately destroyed fifteen B–52s (less than 3 percent of more than seven hundred sorties).[3] This came as a shock to B–52 crews accustomed to years of sorties further south without a loss until one in November 1972 during a raid on Vinh. Now in two wrenching weeks they saw more than thirty of their comrades killed and more than thirty captured. After six B–52s fell on the third night, tactical changes reduced B–52 losses to no more than two per night. Throughout Linebacker II, the B–52s remained above effective artillery fire and the MiGs seemed able to do little more at night than gauge B–52 altitude for surface-to-air missiles. MiG–21 pilots did claim to have shot down two

B–52s, but the U.S. attributed all B–52 losses to SAMs. Meanwhile, B–52 gunners claimed to have shot down at least two MiGs; two escorting F–4s were also fired upon by B–52 gunners—fortunately with less accuracy.[4]

Air Force and Navy F–4 crews destroyed four MiGs at a cost of two F–4s and a Navy RA–5 reconnaissance aircraft. Meanwhile, North Vietnam's initial lavish expenditure of missiles led to American attacks on storage and launch sites, followed by a decline in the number of launches. Although attacks on launch sites did not do much damage, the attacks on warehouses where the North Vietnamese were believed to assemble imported SAMs may have contributed to a shortage of usable missiles—or expenditure may simply have outrun supply.[5]

President Nixon chose not to exploit Hanoi's apparent shortage of missiles by further bombing, however, when North Vietnam agreed to return to the negotiating table in Paris. Nixon's many critics emphasized that the cease-fire agreement signed in January 1973 was little better than the one North Vietnam had agreed to in October. There was some new language about respecting the Demilitarized Zone, but (as Nixon wrote to President Thieu of South Vietnam) none of the provisions of the agreement meant as much as the ability to enforce them in the absence of American ground forces. Linebacker II concluded Nixon's demonstration of what American air power could do in that regard, and the campaign may have helped persuade the South Vietnamese government to acquiesce in a cease-fire agreement. In any case, Nixon left the South Vietnamese with little choice, and by the time they needed his air power again, he had been forced out of the White House.[6]

*   *   *

Air Force plans to bomb Hanoi with B–52s had been pushed aside ever since 1964. After North Vietnam acquired surface-to-air missiles in the summer of 1965, General McConnell became more wary of using B–52s. But his successor as Chief of Staff, General Ryan, thought that B–52 losses over Hanoi would be acceptably low.[7] In President Nixon the Air Force gained a leader far more willing than President Johnson to send the B–52s north. Nevertheless, after five raids above the twentieth parallel in April 1972, the B–52s were pulled south before striking Hanoi. General Abrams' desire to use all the B–52s nearer the battlefields of South Vietnam was reinforced by Henry Kissinger's preference for avoiding political and diplomatic complications by using only fighter-bombers against the urban north.

Throughout the summer of 1972, the new Commander in Chief of Strategic Air Command, Gen. John C. (usually called "J. C.") Meyer, urged Admiral McCain in Hawaii to send the B–52s north. While McCain could not authorize so dramatic an escalation on his own, he did tell Meyer and the commander of Pacific Air Forces, Gen. Lucius D, Clay, to plan some B–52 raids on North Vietnamese airfields. Since Meyer and Clay were more interested in using the B–52s against railyards and supply dumps, McCain agreed to recommend Meyer's first choice—the Kinh No railyard north of Hanoi. But the Joint Chiefs turned it down. When McCain retired late that summer, he was replaced by Adm. Noel Gayler. The focus of B–52 planning for North Vietnam then shifted back to airfields, and in the fall, newly arrived F–111s were added to B–52s in the airfield strike plans.[8]

An unusual feature of Admiral Gayler's approach to B–52 planning was his decision to put coordination of the operation under the commander of the Pacific Fleet, who delegated the responsibility to the commander of Seventh Fleet, who further delegated the job to the commander of Task Force 77, Adm. Damon W. Cooper. Meyer had to send his plans to Cooper for integration with fighter attack and support sorties.[9] When Linebacker II was executed in December, however, the dominant role in coordinating fighter support reverted to General Vogt at Seventh Air Force. In any case, Linebacker II was mostly Meyer's show, and the fighter commanders were often left to throw together their support packages at the last minute.

The return of the B–52s to the northern route packages came in gradual increments. Through the summer, they had been restricted to Route Package One and points south. With the onset of the northeast monsoon in the fall, however, laser-guided bombing was rarely possible—strengthening the argument for using B–52s in the northern route packages. In October, General Ryan took advantage of serving as acting Chairman of the Joint Chiefs to propose sending B–52s as far north as the nineteenth parallel. Although the Joint Chiefs approved Ryan's proposal, they subsequently pulled the B–52s back to Route Package One when intelligence indicated that the North Vietnamese were getting advance warning of targets and strike times. Secretary of Defense Laird was so concerned that he launched an investigation into the vulnerability of American air operations to enemy intelligence. But there had never been much surprise involved in bombing North Vietnam—due to the smallness of the country, the limited choice of targets, the dependence on air refueling with all its regularities, and the ease with which enemy eyes could observe aircraft taking off from bases throughout Southeast Asia. The Soviet trawler lying off Guam could give especially early warning of B–52s launching there. Even without communications intercepts and headquarters spies (both of which may have been abundant), American air operations tended to be big and obvious.[10]

Whatever the risk to the B–52s and their crews, President Nixon wanted to use them to show the North Vietnamese that American eagerness to settle had not yet deprived him of his all-weather air weapon. That eagerness had grown in October together with public knowledge of the South Vietnamese government's unwillingness to go along with the tentative cease-fire agreement. Only two days after Nixon had cut back the bombing of North Vietnam to the twentieth parallel, Radio Hanoi broadcast the terms of the tentative cease-fire agreement and accused the United States of reneging on it. When Henry Kissinger went on national television to explain the need for revising the agreement, he raised expectations unduly by declaring that "peace is at hand."[11]

Under the circumstances, Nixon knew that any overt escalation of the air war was bound to be unpopular. But he quietly enlarged the scope of the B–52 attacks in early November with an upper limit first set at eighteen degrees forty-five minutes and then nineteen degrees fifteen minutes. After his reelection on November 7, Nixon approved B–52 bombing as far north as the twentieth parallel. There the limit stayed while Kissinger returned to Paris with South Vietnam's proposed changes in the cease-fire agreement.[12]

Nixon had been less disappointed than Kissinger when negotiations with the North Vietnamese stumbled on the eve of the election. Given an overwhelming lead in the polls over the Democratic challenger, Senator McGovern, Nixon did not need a cease-fire to win the election. Indeed, moves toward a pre-election settlement had opened the President to accusations of playing politics with the issue. Moreover, after the election, Nixon could use the B–52s in controversial ways without worrying about their impact on reelection. Despite his crushing victory on November 7, however, Nixon found himself with little room to maneuver on Vietnam. His election strategy of remaining in the White House above the political battle had cost him support in Congress.[13]

Even before the election, a majority in the Senate had voted to pull out of Southeast Asia without even getting a cease-fire; the Senate's only condition was the return of the communists' American prisoners of war. Although supporting the President's actions against the North Vietnamese invasion, the American electorate voted for a new Congress still more anxious than its predecessor to end American involvement in the war. Nixon understood that he had less than two months before the new Congress would arrive to cut off funding for further air action. He had to act quickly or not at all.[14]

When Kissinger brought the South Vietnamese demands to Paris, the North Vietnamese were in no mood for further negotiation; the American congressional election results promised to reward uncompromising communists. There was no chance that North Vietnam would agree to Thieu's call for withdrawing their soldiers from South Vietnam. The Nixon administration had long since given up really trying to gain that concession. Kissinger did try to get language affirming respect for the Demilitarized Zone between North and South Vietnam. In conjunction with North Vietnam's promise to stay out of Laos and Cambodia, a truly Demilitarized Zone would in theory seal off South Vietnam from North Vietnamese infiltration. To give such provisions some meaning, Kissinger sought to create an international inspection team large enough to observe violations of the agreement. North Vietnam's chief negotiator, Le Duc Tho, stalled progress by refusing to consider protocols for implementing the basic agreement while it was still in question. From time to time he made a new demand of his own, or he withdrew his approval of a provision previously agreed upon. Kissinger came to the conclusion that the North Vietnamese had decided not to settle before the arrival of the new American Congress. In Kissinger's view, Le Duc Tho continued to negotiate principally to avoid giving Nixon an excuse to escalate the air war. Finally on December 12, Le Duc Tho announced his decision to return to Hanoi for consultations. He and Kissinger had a final fruitless meeting on December 13. With Christmas so near, Le Duc Tho may have thought that there was little risk of Nixon taking dramatic military action.[15]

In fact, Kissinger had been about to break off the negotiations himself, and he had recommended to Nixon an intensification of the bombing of North Vietnam. Unfortunately, the President had already taken Kissinger's advice in late November to cut the number of sorties hitting North Vietnam by a fourth.[16] While Nixon had long favored using B–52s against Hanoi before signing a cease-fire, he now realized that the big bombers could ignite "peace is at hand" sentiment. He blamed Kissinger's press conference for some of that sentiment, but more to blame was the disclosure of North Vietnamese terms acceptable to most Americans. The root problem was Thieu's refusal to go along. Nixon reluctantly concluded that he would have to threaten Hanoi as well as Saigon if he wanted to get out of Vietnam with a respectable cease-fire agreement before the new Congress made matters still more difficult.

On November 30, Nixon alerted a few of his subordinates to the possibility that he would order B–52s against Hanoi if the North Vietnamese refused to complete a cease-fire agreement—or having signed one, broke it. He said as much in a meeting that day with Secretary of Defense Laird and the Joint Chiefs of Staff; Kissinger was also in Washington during an intermission in the Paris talks and attended the meeting with his assistant General Haig. Over the next two weeks, the administration wrestled with the question of whether to escalate and how much. Laird opposed any escalation in the bombing. As usual, Moorer found himself caught between Laird and Nixon. Until Nixon made his decision, Moorer remained sufficiently cool toward using B–52s against Hanoi that Laird could tell Nixon that Moorer also opposed it. When Haig called to check on this, Moorer insisted that Laird misunderstood him. Moorer may well have been of two minds. He had learned from the Air Staff to expect both B–52 losses and Soviet gains in knowledge about the aircraft with its advanced radar jamming capabilities. These costs may have seemed too much when the Defense Department was writing off Vietnam and looking to the future.[17]

Kissinger also remained reluctant to use B–52s against Hanoi. He preferred to restrict that job to fighters as in the past and keep the B–52s further south. But the northeast monsoon would prohibit much fighter bombing before spring, and even if the Congress still permitted bombing then, fighters could only provide more of what the North Vietnamese had already experienced. Kissinger could not offer a persuasive alternative to B–52 strikes in the Hanoi-Haiphong region, a course fervently advocated by General Haig. On December 14, Nixon gave the orders to launch a three-day campaign (subsequently extended) in Route Package Six with B–52s and tactical air. According to Nixon's original orders, the bombing was to be preceded by reseeding mines in the harbors. These orders were altered so that the mining followed the commencement of the bombing and did not rob it of surprise. The services gained an extra day to prepare when Nixon decided to begin bombing on Monday, December 18, rather than Sunday; he did not like the symbolism of beginning on Sunday, and Kissinger wanted to wait until after Le Duc Tho left Beijing.[18]

To weather the bad publicity bearing down on him, Nixon chose to remain silent. He sent Kissinger to explain to the press why the talks had broken down, and during Linebacker II the President refused to comment. Administration spokesmen did object to charges that Hanoi had been leveled by B–52 "carpet bombing," but they did not release intelligence photos to prove that point until months later.[19] Although friends of the administration despaired at the President's silence, it did have advantages. Since he had issued no ultimatum, Hanoi could return to the bargaining table with less loss of face. Since he did not seem personally concerned about allegations of leveling Hanoi, he might appear more likely to do just that—the publicity could get no worse. In fact, Nixon was bluffing, and the B–52s were given targets only on the outskirts of Hanoi.

*　　　　　*　　　　　*

During his service in South Vietnam, General Haig had seen B–52s hit enemy forces within a few yards of his American troops. This extraordinary accuracy made a great impression on him, and he assumed that the B–52s over Hanoi could bomb with the same accuracy. Haig did not understand that the ground-controlled skyspot bombing system could not reach into the Red River Delta. There B–52s had to rely on their own radar. There enemy missiles and MiGs made accurate bombing far more difficult than in the more friendly skies of South Vietnam. Under the circumstances, Linebacker II was remarkably accurate. But stray bombs did provide grist for North Vietnamese propaganda by hitting homes and a hospital.[20]

The North Vietnamese had taken care to have American visitors who preferred a communist victory to a continuance of the war. On Saturday, December 16, four Americans arrived in Hanoi with Christmas mail for American prisoners. Through displays of this kind, the North Vietnamese government and the American antiwar movement continued to exploit the plight of the prisoners. Visitors usually provided rave reviews of North Vietnam's treatment of American prisoners—after meeting only those few deemed reliable. In recent months, Hanoi's American visitors had included former Attorney General

Ramsey Clark and film actress Jane Fonda, both of whom performed their propaganda roles with relish. Fonda even posed for a photograph as a crew member on an antiaircraft gun ready to shoot down fellow Americans; she returned home to marry the onetime student radical Tom Hayden, who had visited Hanoi twice during Rolling Thunder.[21]

In this Christmas 1972 group, the regime took the unusual risk of including Telford Taylor, a Columbia law professor who, as an Army brigadier general just after World War II, prosecuted German war crimes cases at Nuremberg. Like other visitors to Hanoi, Taylor had made no secret of his opposition to American involvement in the Vietnam War. But Taylor's familiarity with Nazi Germany and bombing there gave him a standard of comparison sorely lacking among American pilgrims in Hanoi. By the same token, anything favorable he said about the North Vietnamese or critical of American air operations would carry more weight than the less well-informed reactions of his traveling companions: Michael Allen, assistant dean of Yale Divinity School; Barry Romo, "Maoist" and representative of Vietnam Veterans Against the War; Joan Baez, singer and pacifist whose former husband had gone to jail for resisting the draft.[22]

Two days before Linebacker II, the Taylor group entered an Hanoi full of adults and children. As so often in the past, the regime's evacuation orders were widely ignored. The citizens had long since learned that Hanoi was the safest place in Vietnam, north or south. Monday evening, December 18, when the bombs began to fall in unprecedented numbers on the airfields and railyards north and west of the city, a real evacuation began. By the end of the campaign, more than half the residents may have left, at least for a short time. Those who did not go far enough soon found that they had left the relative safety of Hanoi for the suburban target area.[23]

As for the Taylor group, they learned that they could not leave Hanoi either to explore Haiphong and other places in the targeted region or to return home. Their planned one-week visit extended to two weeks, because their flight was canceled after the terminal at Gia Lam airport suffered damage from bombs probably intended for a nearby railyard. An occasional Chinese plane was the only way out of North Vietnam, and Taylor had to beseech the Chinese ambassador for seats. The group left on December 29, a few hours before the last bombs fell in the Red River Delta.[24]

Their stay in Hanoi necessarily conformed to the rhythm of the bombing. At first the B–52s came in three long waves spread through the night. Later a compressed single wave permitted a better night's sleep especially if it came before midnight. Once the B–52 bombing was over for the night, Hanoi could look forward to several quiet hours until the fighters came in the early afternoon searching for a break in the clouds that would permit laser-guided bombing of targets downtown. The quiet morning hours were ideal for showing the American visitors bomb damage, newly captured B–52 crews, and model prisoners. Much of the rest of the day and night was spent in the Hoa Binh Hotel bomb shelter, where Baez sang her songs, tape recording them with the rumble of distant bomb explosions for a new album.[25]

Taylor's first dispatch to the *New York Times* appeared on Christmas day while he was still in Hanoi. He wrote it just after visiting Bac Mai Hospital, which had been hit by bombs intended for warehouses on the opposite side of Bac Mai airfield. Taylor could see the airfield and oil storage tanks; he assumed that they were the targets and not the hospital. In his major exaggeration of damage, Taylor reported that the hospital was "destroyed." Later, some readers would learn that only part of the complex had been destroyed, that patients had been evacuated before the bombing, and that North Vietnamese authorities reported the death of twenty-nine people (none of them patients). While Taylor was moved by the "terrible scene," he knew that (after four days of bombing) "Hanoi looks nothing like the Berlin or Hamburg of World War II," that the bombing had been "relatively concentrated in certain areas," and that "one can drive through the city for many blocks and see no damage whatever."[26]

Amid shrill vituperation of the bombing in the press, including the *New York Times*, Taylor provided some reasonably accurate information. In this respect, his articles were a welcome contrast to Harrison Salisbury's Christmas series five years earlier.[27] Unlike Salisbury, Taylor saw bombing operations as well as bomb damage. Even though he did not approve of those operations, Taylor had definite views about how downed aircrews should be treated. He disliked seeing the North Vietnamese publicly display their new captives. After his first such session at the International Club, he complained to the authorities, and his group was not invited again—even Baez, who deemed the aircrews guilty of genocide and thought that the North Vietnamese officials were handling the prisoners with "great restraint."[28]

Taylor was even more unhappy to discover that American prisoners were not provided with bomb shelters. His group had been taken to the southern outskirts of the city to visit the prison camp called the "Zoo" by its inmates; toward the end of the war, a few cooperative prisoners were segregated there and it became known as a "good guy camp" to the majority of prisoners incarcerated downtown or along the Chinese border. The North Vietnamese apparently wanted to show off some minor roof damage in the compound. After Taylor criticized the lack of bomb shelters, prisoners were given shovels and told to start digging. Fortunately for the North Vietnamese, Taylor did not realize that the conditions about which he was objecting were among the mildest the prisoners had endured.[29]

Taylor's perspective was much different than that of prisoners at Hoa Lo (or the "Hanoi Hilton" as they called it), to whom he was not introduced even though their cells were much closer than the "Zoo" to his hotel. He thought the citizens of Hanoi were bearing up extremely well under the bombs and showing a lot of the "London pride" he recalled from World War II. The prisoners at the Hilton, on the other hand, could compare the behavior of their guards during these raids with what it had been before. For the first time, many of the guards seemed afraid and even deferential. Few made much of an effort to stop the prisoners from cheering the B–52s.[30]

Except for a daytime laser-guided strike on a railyard only a couple of blocks west, the Hilton prisoners were at least a mile away from the bombing until the night after Christmas. Then a load of B–52 bombs fell on shops and homes along Kham Thien Street not far south of the same railyard. More than two hundred people were reported to have died in the most deadly bombing error of the campaign. The natural supposition that the downtown railyard had been the target was wrong. Only laser-guided bombing was permitted against targets near so densely populated a neighborhood. The B–52 targets that night were a couple of miles away.[31]

The Bac Mai error a few nights earlier (a much smaller miss) had probably been the result of a B–52 being hit by a surface-to-air missile just before bomb release. A similar occurrence may well have contributed to the bombing error which demolished the flimsy buildings on Kham Thien Street, but so large an error suggested that a crew may have confused the downtown railyard with one of the four suburban railyards targeted that night: Gia Lam, Kinh No, Duc Noi, and Giap Nhi. The Gia Lam railyard was often called "Hanoi railyard" in the planning documents and distinguished from the downtown Hanoi railyard only by their assigned target numbers, so there may have been a misunderstanding about which yard was to be attacked. More likely, the radar image of the downtown railyard was mistaken for another yard. Like the downtown yard, Giap Nhi was southwest of the Red River. In the case of Kinh No, an exceptionally large supply dump lay next to the yard and bombs were aimed at the supplies outside the yard as well as the rails inside.

On the night of the Kham Thien bombing, two B–52s were hit by surface-to-air missiles near the time they released their bombs. One (whose target was Giap Nhi railyard) crashed southeast of Hanoi—killing two crew members and putting the surviving four in prison. The other crippled B–52 (whose target was the Kinh No railyard and supply dump) limped back to Thailand with a wounded gunner. Rather than bail out over northern Thailand, the pilot was told to bring his wounded gunner all the way back to U-Tapao. But the pilot, the navigator, the radar-navigator, and the electronic warfare officer perished in the crash landing. The wounded gunner pulled himself from the wreckage. The copilot also survived thanks to the courage of Capt. Brent O. Diefenbach, a B–52 pilot who had just landed. He saw the crash, flagged down a Thai truck, and told the driver to take him to the site, where he got the injured copilot out of the cockpit just before the plane exploded.[32]

Each of the two B–52s lost on this the eighth night of Linebacker II was especially vulnerable because another B–52 in its three-ship cell had dropped out with mechanical difficulties. Two-ship cells proved much less effective than three-ship cells in jamming missile radar and guidance signals. Yet Strategic

Air Command continued to insist that two-ship cells "press on," and the next night two more B–52s were shot down in the same way.

To the end of Linebacker II, Strategic Air Command maintained the requirement that each B–52 crew press on unless their bomber developed truly crippling mechanical difficulties; if some of its jammers were not working or if another ship in its cell had to abort, a B–52 was still expected to press on despite its increased vulnerability to enemy air defenses. In other respects, however, Strategic Air Command made major tactical changes after the third night, when six losses spurred criticism from the White House as well as from crews flying the missions. Despite Kissinger's assurances that the B–52 loss rate was bound to decline as the B–52s attacked targets further from Hanoi, President Nixon was upset. "I raised holy hell," Nixon would recall, "about the fact that they kept going over the same targets at the same time."[33] Although Nixon's diagnosis missed key tactical problems with Linebacker II, he was right to think that Strategic Air Command could do better.

Strategic Air Command's major problem was insufficient compression. On the first night, 129 B–52s flew over the Red River Delta one cell of 3 B–52s at a time. They came in three waves at four-hour intervals, each wave requiring a half hour to drop its bombs. The three-wave procedure was repeated on the second and third nights with 90 B–52s each night using basically the same routes. The interval between waves gave the surface-to-air missile launchers enough time to reload. Normally about 70 missile launchers were within reach of the B–52s; at no time were they able to knock down more than 3 B–52s in a single wave even when the wave took a half hour to pass over. Finally, on December 26, Strategic Air Command sent more than 113 B–52s over the delta in only fifteen minutes; the missile launchers could fire only once in less time with more targets—they got 2 B–52s rather than the 6 they had hit on the night of December 20–21, when three widely separated waves had permitted reloading. The compression of December 26 was achieved by sending the B–52s in from seven different directions simultaneously.

Since compression proved to be so significant, why did Strategic Air Command wait so long to adopt it? In fact, Strategic Air Command had thought its opening wave on December 18 was already extraordinarily compressed. Never before had more than forty B–52s hit the same target area in half an hour, and they were part of a strike package of about a hundred aircraft (not counting the tankers that refueled the B–52s from Guam or the tankers that refueled the fighter aircraft from Thailand). Just getting so many B–52s in the air at once was a challenge, not to mention merging B–52s from Guam and Thailand in a single wave. Fears of a mid-air collision were fed by memories of four B–52s lost in two air refueling accidents that killed crew members and a major general.[34]

Strategic Air Command sought to preserve as much as possible of the routine quality of the missions the crews were accustomed to flying in South Vietnam. Each cell of three B–52s would fly nearly the same route over the target area, one cell at a time. If that was not bad enough, SAC planners made the job of enemy missile crews even easier by requiring the B–52s to make a sharp post-target turn as soon as they had dropped their bombs. In theory, this turn would get B–52s out of the target area as soon as possible. In fact, it was a turn into the strong wind with which the B–52s had flown over Hanoi from the northwest.

"They had us turning into a hell of a head wind, about 100 knots from west to east," one crew member recalled. "As a result out [ground speed] was about 200 knots less than it was going in, which didn't help any."[35] Not only would the B–52s have cleared the target area more quickly by continuing to the southeast, but their post-target turn interfered with their ability to jam surface-to-air missile radar; most of the B–52s lost on the first three nights of Linebacker II were hit by missiles in the post-target turn. Especially vulnerable were B–52Gs that had yet to receive new jamming equipment already installed in the older B–52Ds and in some B–52Gs. After the disastrous third night, Strategic Air Command kept the B–52Gs away from targets near Hanoi for the rest of the campaign. The command was slower to abandon the post-target turn that had been adopted years earlier for dropping nuclear bombs. Rather than give it up, Strategic Air Command first tried having the B–52s release chaff during the turn, a technique scorned by the command's own analysts.

To support three waves a night, Seventh Air Force could provide two flights of chaff-dropping F–4s per wave. Since each of these chaff flights could create one corridor, Strategic Air Command was limited to two bomber streams per wave. This restriction proved worse than fruitless, because the high winds above thirty thousand feet played havoc with the chaff corridors, and most of the B–52s flew their missions largely without benefit of chaff until Strategic Air Command and Seventh Air Force agreed to abandon corridors in favor of a chaff blanket. The only way Seventh Air Force could provide enough chaff to blanket Hanoi was to compress the three waves of the early nights into one wave a night—a compression that had the even more important advantages already discussed. While thinking through these changes, Strategic Air Command for four nights simply cut its effort to a single wave of thirty B–52s per night and mostly hit targets many miles from Hanoi. Then, on the night after Christmas, all the principal elements in Strategic Air Command's new approach to bombing near Hanoi came together with a full complement of more than a hundred B–52s, one-wave compression, a chaff blanket, and replacement of the sharp post-target turn by at most a gentle dogleg.[36]

With all these improvements, Strategic Air Command still lost two B–52s on the night of December 26. As already mentioned, both of the B–52s lost that night had been deprived of normal jamming support when one of the three ships in its cell had aborted with mechanical difficulties. But Strategic Air Command did not take the natural next step of requiring an entire cell to abort if one of its three B–52s could not complete the mission. The SAC commander, General

Meyer, insisted that his B–52s "press on" in keeping with Washington's demand for a "maximum effort." This phrase from World War II had been introduced into Linebacker II planning by Lt. Col. Richard Secord, an Air Force special operations officer then serving in the Office of the Secretary of Defense. Secord's insistence on "maximum effort" stimulated Joint Staff questions about its meaning, if any, but it resonated with Meyer—one of the leading fighter aces of World War II.[37]

Meyer called not only for his B–52s to press on, but also for the other two World War II fighter pilots commanding Linebacker II forces to attack surface-to-air missile sites more effectively. Like Meyer, both General Johnson at Eighth Air Force on Guam and General Vogt at Seventh Air Force near Saigon were aces. Like Meyer, both won their victories in Europe. Although Johnson shot down seventeen German aircraft, he himself was shot down, imprisoned, and for a time overshadowed by a Pacific ace with the same name (except a middle initial of "R" instead of "W") and five more victories.[38] Meyer's twenty-four victories ranked him twelfth among American pilots in World War II and he added two more victories as a jet pilot in Korea. While Vogt's eight victories in World War II ran well ahead of what anyone achieved in the Vietnam War, they had not been enough to make him a leading ace in a war with hundreds of aces. He found himself in Linebacker II relegated to third place in a pecking order established three decades earlier in the skies over Germany.

Meyer was clearly in charge, and Vogt usually learned Meyer's plans with barely enough time to throw together support packages. Throughout the Vietnam War, Strategic Air Command had refused to subordinate its contribution to the operational control of the Seventh Air Force commander. This had always irritated the latter, whoever he was. Now Strategic Air Command was not merely going its own way, but instructing Seventh Air Force to follow along smartly. After the severe B–52 losses of the third night, Meyer communicated his frustration to Vogt: "If unable to provide SAM suppression as requested would appreciate your letting me know in some detail."[39] While Vogt promised a "max effort," he noted that Meyer's plan simultaneously to go after targets as widely separated as Hanoi and Quang Te airfield (thirty miles south) would require him to split his missile suppression forces, which were, in any case, inadequate for night work.[40]

During the summer, Vogt had considerable success with hunter-killer teams pairing F–105 Wild Weasels and F–4Es using cluster bombs, but those missions had been in daylight and relatively good weather. Some of his F–105 Weasels were replaced by F–4Cs that he had refrained from sending to the Red River Delta because, in the Weasel configuration, they carried only one jamming pod rather than two. But in Linebacker II, Vogt risked sending the F–4C Weasels north to maximize his missile suppression force. They did have the virtue of flying more easily in formation with F–4Es than had the F–105 Weasels— which were left to operate independently of the hunter-killer teams. If Strategic

Air Command restricted itself to one wave going against targets close together, Vogt could provide five hunter-killer teams (a total of ten F–4s), plus five F–105 Weasels and eight Navy A–7Es.[41]

F–4C Weasels and F–105 Weasels encountered a new problem during Linebacker II. A single radar site appeared to be involved in shooting down about half the eleven B–52s lost on the first four nights. Instead of the Fan Song radar associated with surface-to-air missiles since Rolling Thunder, this deadly new site had a Team Work radar using frequencies that the Weasels could not track. Team Work radars had been active through the summer, but only in support of antiaircraft artillery. Given the Air Force's emphasis on dropping laser-guided bombs from medium altitude, artillery had usually not been able to reach high enough with accuracy. Shifting Team Work radars to missile support suddenly left the Air Force without an effective response. None of the B–52 jammers was very effective against Team Work, and the jamming itself could be tracked adequately to permit barrage firing of surface-to-air missiles.[42]

Vogt attributed the failure of his hunter-killer teams' suppression of surface-to-air missile expenditure during Linebacker II mostly to the difficulty those teams had operating at night. About all they could do then was fire anti-radar missiles at suspected sites just before the B–52s arrived. That might keep the sites from turning on their radar. The Weasels soon ran out of Standard anti-radar missiles and had to rely on their older Shrikes. In any case, they could intimidate only Fan Song radars and not the new Team Work radar. While Meyer was more interested in Vogt's results than Vogt's problems, Vogt did receive vocal support from the commander of Pacific Air Forces, General Clay, who was even more thoroughly cut out of Linebacker II planning than was Vogt. Clay proposed daylight B–52 raids so that the hunter-killer teams could do a better job of suppressing surface-to-air missiles.[43]

Given the prevalence of bad weather, however, F–4Es were unlikely to have much more opportunity to attack missile sites in daylight. Any slight improvement in missile suppression would be purchased at the price of a greater threat from MiGs that would perform better in daylight. Meyer responded that he might try a daylight B–52 raid in the less well-defended parts of North Vietnam, but even there he continued to operate only at night.[44]

Meyer was more taken with the idea of attacking missile sites with B–52s, F–111s, and A–6s. Because Strategic Air Command had originally been told to attack all its targets in three nights, no thought was given then to attempt "rolling back" North Vietnamese air defenses. Now the indefinite extension of Linebacker II and the heavy early losses of B–52s combined to encourage directly attacking those defenses and not just reacting to them with Wild Weasels and hunter-killer teams. When, on the fifth night, all thirty B–52s were scheduled to bomb targets near Haiphong, Strategic Air Command asked the Navy to attack the missile sites in that area with A–6s before the B–52s arrived. The Navy complied, and no B–52s were lost that night. The next night, the

B–52s themselves attacked missile sites, and F–111s also turned their attention to the missile sites after Christmas.[45]

Pacific Air Forces analysts later questioned the wisdom of the planned strikes on missile sites, because those strikes all used high-explosive "iron bombs" rather than cluster bombs. Except for an operating radar's vulnerability to radar-seeking warheads, the scattered equipment at a missile site was hard to hit. Consequently, the hunter-killer teams used the shotgun effect of cluster bombs. But A–6s and F–111s came in over their targets at a few hundred feet and were not permitted to risk shooting themselves down with cluster bombs. B–52s, on the other hand, were capable of dropping cluster bombs safely, but did not. Pacific Air Forces estimated that four B–52s dropping cluster bombs could have been more effective in suppressing a missile site than more than two hundred B–52s dropping iron bombs—which was another way of saying that the twenty-one B–52 sorties actually employed against missile sites had a very low probability of success. Two of thirteen sites attacked by B–52s and F–111s, however, were judged to have suffered 50-percent destruction, and the B–52s got the credit for one of these sites. Another two sites were empty when attacked; since it only took about four hours to move missile launchers away from a site, the attackers were fortunate that this was not more of a problem.[46]

The last B–52 lost in Linebacker II was hit by a missile on December 27 just after bombs away against a missile site. The crew made it back to Thailand before bailing out; for returning his crew safely, Capt. John D. Mize won the first Air Force Cross awarded to a Strategic Air Command pilot in Southeast Asia. His crew had already run into more than their share of trouble when their B–52 was damaged on two earlier nights. This time they thought that their bombs struck the very missile site that got them; they were hit ten seconds after bomb release and their bombs required fifty seconds to reach the target. But Strategic Air Command concluded not only that their bombs had missed the targeted missile site, but that the missile in question had been launched by another very successful site which had already been bombed by B–52s and F–111s—and was about to be struck again by B–52s on the 27th without apparent success.[47]

While missile sites may have been a poor target for F–111s and B–52s, shifting them from attacking airfields was probably a good idea. The MiGs had given the B–52s little trouble at night, and there was slight evidence that airfield attacks had much to do with this outcome. The major factor seemed to be a lack of night-flying experience on the part of the MiG pilots. Although runways were frequently cratered, they were operational most of the time. The F–111s' most successful moment came when a single sortie managed to cause a brief hiatus in operations at Yen Bai airfield after a big raid with forty-four A–7s and F–4s failed to make an impression. But one or two F–111 sorties per airfield could not drop enough ordnance to produce much more than harassment.[48]

Nevertheless, Linebacker II was a breakthrough for the F–111s that until then bore a reputation for flying into the ground. When forty-eight F–111s had arrived at Takhli Air Base, Thailand, less than three months before, they were still under the cloud of the losses suffered during the 1968 deployment. Four losses in the fall of 1972 did not improve their image. There was a strong suspicion that heavy rain had caused the F–111's terrain-following radar to go blank—a fatal shock to crews accustomed to flying low over the deserts of the American West. By mid-December, however, the storms of the southwest monsoon had given way to the incessant clouds and light rain of the northeast monsoon. In Linebacker II, F–111s did not fly into the ground. Indeed, the airfield and missile-site raids were conducted without a loss. Two F–111s were lost on raids closer to downtown Hanoi; one after attacking a radio transmitter and the second after attacking port facilities on the Red River. The latter's crew was the first to gain enough altitude to eject safely and be captured; upon their eventual return to the United States they would report that small arms fire had ruptured their F–111's hydraulic control system. Flying low usually freed the F–111 from missiles and artillery, but brought new risks from less formidable weapons.[49]

Possibly more effective than strikes on airfields or missile sites were strikes on suspected missile storage and assembly facilities. Just before Christmas, Strategic Air Command recommended striking the Quinh Loi storage facility in southeastern Hanoi. Reconnaissance photography indicating missile equipment in the compound led to the inference that at least some of about twenty warehouses might contain missiles. When the Joint Chiefs vetoed using B–52s against this urban target because civilian casualties were likely, General Meyer in Omaha called General Vogt in Saigon. Vogt then asked the Chairman of the Joint Chiefs to permit a daylight bad weather raid by fighter aircraft using the loran transmitters in Thailand. Loran often did not function well at the fringe of its range in the Hanoi area, where heavy antiaircraft fire discouraged F–4 pilots from making a sufficiently straight and level bomb run. Admiral Moorer's authorization of the Quinh Loi raid indicated the seriousness with which Washington viewed the missile threat.[50]

Vogt made the most of this authorization, and sent thirty-two A–7s led by eight loran-equipped F–4s on December 28. A fortunate break in the weather permitted half the force to drop its bombs visually, and five of the warehouses suffered extensive damage. On the next two nights, a total of forty-three B–52s struck the missile support facility at Phuc Yen near the major MiG base; as expected, these much heavier raids (twenty miles northwest of Hanoi) did much more damage than the Quinh Loi raid. Meanwhile, another package of F–4s and A–7s made a daylight raid on the missile support facility at Trai Ca, thirty miles north of Hanoi. This target was also in a rural area and fifteen B–52s struck it that night. But here there were no secondary explosions as at Phuc Yen; the hundreds of bomb craters were scattered through a much less compact facility than the one at Quinh Loi.[51]

Since the number of missile launches detected by American intelligence dropped from seventy-three on December 27 to forty-eight on December 28 to twenty-five on December 29, the Phuc Yen, Quinh Loi and Trai Ca strikes may have been very successful. General Vogt was especially enthusiastic about Quinh Loi, and after the war he liked to tell how "SAC bombers were literally saved by tactical application of all-weather bombing."[52] Apart from the fact that the Phuc Yen raids did more obvious damage, there is the larger question of the effectiveness of all these attacks on missile support facilities during the last two days of the campaign. Admiral Moorer would later recall that American intelligence's assessment of a missile shortage was based not only on missile launches, but also on North Vietnamese complaints about a shortage.[53]

Nevertheless, it should be noted that earlier in Linebacker II, missile launches had declined even more sharply, only to recover. After peaking at more than two hundred on the third night, missile launches dropped to forty on the fourth night and fell to a mere four on the sixth night (December 23). During this period, Strategic Air Command cut B–52 sorties from about a hundred in three waves per night to thirty in one wave per night. Then too, targets were attacked further from Hanoi. On the nearly missile-free sixth night, B–52s began by hitting missile sites for the first time; three sites fifty miles northeast of Hanoi were hit before other B–52s dropped their bombs on the Lang Dang railyard—even farther from Hanoi and protected principally by the three missile sites just struck. To supplement a paltry four surface-to-air missiles launched, the MiGs made an unusually determined effort, but their air-to-air missiles missed. Although a B–52 gunner's claim of two kills could not be verified, it was clearly a very bad night for North Vietnamese air defenses. From this nadir, missile launches rose on the two nights after Christmas to about seventy per wave (a rate equal to that of the first three nights).[54]

Judged solely on missile launches then, there was no guarantee that an extension of Linebacker II would not have been met by a resurgence of missile launches. On the other hand, the North Vietnamese may have been suffering from a real and fairly persistent missile shortage. America's own lavish expenditure had quickly run dry the supply of the newer Standard antiradar missiles, leaving only the older Shrikes. But when American chaff supplies in theater ran short, they were replenished from outside the theater. Similarly, for the North Vietnamese, much may have depended on whether new Soviet missiles were being trucked across the border by the Chinese. At any rate, Linebacker II had no way of stopping truck traffic.

*   *   *

Although Strategic Air Command did make several worthwhile changes in tactics during Linebacker II, B–52 crew members grumbled that those changes should have been adopted much earlier, even before the beginning of the campaign. In November, a crew had bailed out over Thailand after their B–52 had been hit by a surface-to-air missile near Vinh, North Vietnam.* It was the first B–52 ever lost to enemy fire, and bomber crews in Thailand and Guam did not think Strategic Air Command headquarters in Omaha, Nebraska, seemed sufficiently concerned about the loss. The SAC commander's insistence that every B–52 "press on" contrasted with earlier guidance urging avoidance of enemy air defenses. General Meyer expected to take some losses as a consequence, but although he had a computer model for estimating attrition of B–52s on nuclear missions against the Soviet Union, Meyer had nothing comparable for a conventional war. His intelligence chief suspected that Meyer may have applied some "political English"; Meyer's estimate of losing 3 percent of the sorties both alerted the administration that American lives would be lost and indicated that Strategic Air Command could do this job at a cost modest by the standards of World War II.[55]

From the point of view of the B–52 crews, General Meyer was simply too far away in Omaha to confront the reality of their situation adequately. Meyer's own staff had difficulty getting decisions from him early enough in the planning cycle. "After about two days of clock fighting, including handing bags to crews as they were taxiing out," his intelligence chief recalled, "a critical path chart was developed to help 'stimulate' General Meyer to a decision. This chart was approximately 20 feet long, and turned out to be a remarkably useful tool."[56] It made clear to Meyer the many necessary steps that had to be taken in the limited time between his decisions and bombs on target. At any moment during the campaign, the staff was planning strikes two days ahead while making changes in the orders for the next day and getting feedback on the current day. With an eleven-hour time difference, nighttime strikes in Hanoi occurred during the daytime shift at Strategic Air Command headquarters. The staff work went on around the clock there as well as in other headquarters acting in response to orders from Omaha: Eighth Air Force on Guam, Seventh Air Force at Saigon, and Task Force 77 in the Gulf of Tonkin. When final guidance reached the wings and squadrons, there was usually little time to spare.

To begin with, Meyer had been given three days warning to launch a three-day campaign; a fourth day of preparation added for political and diplomatic reasons helped by permitting the timely deployment of more tankers. Compressing the hundred daily sorties into three waves a night (rather than the usual routine of sending B–52s out around-the-clock in cells of three) strained

---

* A few weeks before the first B–52 combat loss, North Vietnamese air defense forces held a conference on the best techniques for using SAMs to bring down a B–52; a manual under development since 1969 was issued after the conference. During Linebacker II, however, departures from following the manual's advice sometimes met with apparent success. See Linh Cuu My's translation of Gen. Hoang Van Khanh's "Taking Aim at the B–52s" in *Vietnam* magazine, Apr 1996, especially pp 30–31. A fuller account of the conference and the initial shoot-down is in Merle Pribbenow's translation of the *History of the People's Army of Vietnam, Vol II* (Hanoi, 1994), Chapter 12, Section 4.

maintenance and control as well as air refueling. Fortunately, Guam had gained some relevant experience a few weeks earlier when a typhoon had required the rapid evacuation of B–52s. Nevertheless, there was a collective sigh of relief when the first night's operations went off reasonably well. The loss of two B–52s that night was within Meyer's prediction of 3 percent, and a loss-free second night seemed to confirm that Meyer knew his business.

The six losses on the third night upset Meyer's subordinates and his superiors. After the first wave lost two B–52Gs (with inferior jamming equipment) and a B–52D attacking the Yen Vien railyard northeast of Hanoi, General Johnson called from Guam and Meyer decided to press on with most of the second and third waves while cancelling a second-wave strike by six B–52Gs on the Gia Lam railyard and repair shops just across the Red River from downtown. The third-wave strike by B–52Ds on Gia Lam was permitted to proceed at the cost of one B–52D. When two B–52Gs in the third wave were lost attacking the Kinh No railyard and storage area northwest of Hanoi, Meyer banished the B–52Gs from the Hanoi area for the remainder of a campaign that President Nixon had extended indefinitely on the second day.[57]

Authorization of new targets sometimes caused Meyer to modify his orders rather late in the planning cycle. For example, on December 23 after giving Eighth Air Force targets for the following night (December 24) in the Thanh Hoa area well south of Hanoi, Meyer received permission to hit the Kep and Thai Nguyen railyards north of Hanoi; he changed the targets for December 24 accordingly, rather than wait until after Christmas to hit the new targets.[58]

Although Meyer kept Linebacker II's reins in his hands throughout the campaign, eventually he did give Johnson on Guam more mission planning responsibility. For the biggest raid right after Christmas, Johnson's orders were to send seven streams of bombers simultaneously from different directions into the Red River Delta—four streams of B–52Ds were to converge on the Hanoi area while three streams of B–52Gs hit Haiphong and Thai Nguyen. Johnson and his Eighth Air Force staff chose the axis of attack and egress for each bomber stream; it was a demanding challenge to synchronize so many converging aircraft without a midair collision.[59]

Secretary of Defense Laird asserted his authority in Linebacker II just as he had in Linebacker. Until December 27, Admiral Moorer had to gain Laird's approval for every target; on that day, Laird agreed to give Moorer the authority to approve targets for tactical aircraft outside the Hanoi and Haiphong control zones and the buffer zone along the Chinese border, provided those targets had been authorized during Linebacker. While approving most targets nominated by Moorer, the Secretary denied a request to hit Gia Lam airfield—where the terminal had already been hit by stray bombs probably intended for the neighboring railyard. On the other hand, he approved a guided-bomb strike on the Hanoi powerplant that had been off-limits throughout Linebacker.[60]

Meyer usually sought Washington's approval to hit a target, but in the case of Lang Dang railyard Moorer repeatedly called for strikes. This yard became the most heavily bombed target in the campaign. More than eighty B–52 sorties dropped about forty-five hundred bombs on Lang Dang in four raids. The principal justification for this target was the large number of freight cars counted in reconnaissance photography. Lang Dang was in the buffer zone along the Chinese border, and the North Vietnamese were using the northeast railroad to bring supplies from China at least as far as Lang Dang. Another attraction of Lang Dang for Moorer may have been the ability of the B–52s to strike it without a loss. The first attack there on December 23 made that point. It was a good place to send the B–52Gs, whose jammers had proved inadequate against Hanoi's air defense radar network.[61]

Despite all the changes in targets and tactics that were making Linebacker II more survivable for B–52 crews, some of the crew members carried a lingering bitterness toward General Meyer. This was especially true on Guam. When he came to Andersen Air Force Base after the campaign to present medals, tension would lead to stories about a near riot—albeit one that occurred mostly within the minds of those hostile to Meyer.[62]

Although U-Tapao Air Base had the only B–52 crew member who refused to fly a Linebacker II mission, less discontent boiled up there than on Guam.[63] On the first three nights, U-Tapao suffered only two losses compared to Guam's seven. All of Eighth Air Force's vulnerable B–52Gs were based on Guam, and at first the more important targets near Hanoi were assigned mostly to the Guam bombers. On opening night, Guam B–52s hit the priority targets—railyards at Kinh No, Yen Vien, and Gia Lam—while U-Tapao attempted to suppress MiG activity by raiding the airfields at Phuc Yen, Kep, and Hoa Lac (all further from Hanoi than the targeted railyards). While the Guam crews were experiencing especially severe losses on the third night, one U-Tapao crew member even managed some humor by blowing timeout on a whistle; his comrades swore afterward that the North Vietnamese stopped firing missiles for ninety seconds.[64]

The Guam crews were left with far more time than the U-Tapao crews to brood about their losses. During three out of the next four nights, U-Tapao flew all of the Linebacker II B–52 missions and Guam returned to the relatively safe missions over South Vietnam. Even counting the southern runs, Guam crews were expected to fly no more than every other day and most flew less. The long twelve-hour missions that reduced the frequency with which Guam crews could fly also provided many uneventful hours in the air for sharpening grievances.[65]

For the first five nights of Linebacker II, most U-Tapao crews flew every night. While their missions lasted only three hours, night after night of combat was exhausting and Eighth Air Force finally shifted enough crews from Guam to U-Tapao so that crews there would have to fly only every other night. Making maximum use of U-Tapao made sense; a B–52D from there could carry a bomb load to Hanoi (thirty tons) more than three times that of a B–52G flying from Guam (nine tons) and nearly twice that of a B–52D flying from Guam (sixteen tons), four times as fast. The B–52Ds had been modified to carry heavier conventional bombloads in Southeast Asia, while the newer, longer range B–52Gs had continued to prepare for the possibility of nuclear war against the Soviet Union. With a third as many B–52s, U-Tapao crews dropped twice as much tonnage as Guam crews in Linebacker II. When Guam crews were pulled out of Linebacker II following the severe losses of the third night, U-Tapao crews began to bomb easier targets with the improved tactics already being adopted by Strategic Air Command. Since most Guam crews did not participate in this evolution, many got the wrong impression that the Omaha headquarters failed to react until after Christmas.

For U-Tapao, a major upturn in morale came on the fifth night, when new tactics combined happily with an absence of losses. Someone posted a score for the evening; "Christians 30; Gomers 0."[66] The crews called it the Bob Hope Special in honor of the famous comedian who had entertained them before they took off, just as he had entertained so many other servicemen over the years. "The best damn thing that happened during the whole nonstop operation to take a lot of the pressure off was the Bob Hope Show," one captain recalled. "It saved a lot of guys."[67] After the show, Hope met all the crews in their premission briefings. "He was very sober about it," another captain remembered. "He said he didn't know anything funny to tell about the situation," but he did tell a World War II North African story that "calmed the atmosphere."[68]

Another encouraging aspect of Linebacker II was the lackluster performance of the MiGs. A few came up every night, probably to determine the altitude of the B–52s for the missile sites. When the MiGs did threaten the B–52s directly, B–52 gunners proved more than equal to the occasion. The gunners' response to success was less ebullient, however, than the way fighter pilots celebrated victories. Airman First Class Albert E. Moore, who shot down one of the two MiGs for which B–52 gunners received credit, felt some ambivalence. "On the way home," he said afterward, "I wasn't sure whether I should be happy or sad. You know, there was a guy in that MiG. I'm sure he would have wanted to fly home, too. But it was a case of him or my crew."[69]

Meanwhile, Seventh Air Force's newest air-to-air capability had little opportunity to prove itself. Just as Linebacker II was getting underway, a half dozen upgraded "Rivet Haste" F–4Es joined a like number that had arrived at Udorn in November. The December contingent boasted the capability to identify MiGs beyond visual range by interrogating their transponders, a capability heretofore absent in Southeast Asia F–4Es but already possessed for several months by some F–4Ds. All twelve of the new F–4Es, however, had an electronic telescope that would permit daylight identification of enemy aircraft beyond visual range even if their transponders were turned off. All twelve had the leading edge of their wings modified with slats that could be extended to improve dogfighting maneuverability. These new capabilities did not result in any MiG kills during Linebacker II, but the electronic telescope did stop one F–4E from shooting down another F–4E on December 29. The Air Force's three fighter air-to-air victories in December went to aircrews in older F–4s and not to the newcomers, who had ruffled some feathers by replacing seasoned veterans of the famous 555th "Triple Nickel" squadron (which had racked up far more air-to-air victories than any other Air Force squadron in the war).[70]

While very satisfied with the way MiGs were handled from the beginning, B–52 crews complained about their vulnerability to surface-to-air missiles, especially during the first three nights of the campaign. Although many of their complaints were met by improvements in the orders issuing from Strategic Air Command headquarters, other complaints encountered resistance all the way up the chain of command. The big B–52s were far less agile than the fighter air-craft that had proved themselves capable of out-maneuvering missiles, and after the early missions, wing commanders at both U-Tapao and Andersen scolded some of their pilots for making evasive maneuvers during the bomb runs. Not only was this insistence on steady bomb runs an old tradition associated with General LeMay in World War II, but there were new technical reasons to uphold it. A steady run improved accuracy as always, but now in the same way, B–52s could maintain the three-ship cells that best employed electronic jam-ming to fend off surface-to-air missiles.[71]

The temptation to maneuver during the bomb run was hard to resist. The B–52 pilots had not experienced this kind of stress before, and it took them a few days to get used to a more threatening environment. One navigator noted the confusion caused by a particularly bright planet low in the sky on the first night: "The pilots kept seeing the damn thing and thinking it was a SAM and it was just some planet floating out there in space."[72] Although they were above thirty thousand feet and beyond the range of accurate antiaircraft artillery fire, the guns below, nevertheless, put on an unnerving show. As a crew member put it, "it's like watching the Fourth of July from the top looking down."[73]

The problem with Strategic Air Command doing most of the planning for Linebacker II in Nebraska was not distance from Hanoi, but distance from the aircrews. The staff at Offutt was bigger and better equipped, but the men flying combat missions naturally took a dim view of a remote headquarters telling them how to risk their lives. It would have been better to have staff work from Omaha support the Eighth Air Force commander in the theater—rather than tell him exactly what to do. This procedure would not necessarily have produced better orders, but crew members might have been better disposed to receive them from a commander in their midst.

General Meyer's emphasis on bombing railyards and supply depots made sense. They were good area targets, and they had been very little damaged by the summer's laser-guided bombing. Most important, several of them lay on the outskirts of Hanoi and Haiphong where few civilians would be killed, but many in the adjacent cities might be frightened by the unprecedented torrent of bombs exploding so near.

A defect of the railyards as a target system was the location of the largest and most important yard in the heart of Hanoi. While the city train station was hit by laser-guided bombs during Linebacker II, the yard as a whole could only be seriously damaged by B–52 area bombing and that was forbidden to protect civilians downtown. Just across the Red River from downtown Hanoi lay the Gia Lam railyard, which was bombed by B–52s and suffered severe damage not only to locomotives, rolling stock, and track, but also to its important repair facility. This was one of nine yards that Air Force intelligence judged more than 50-percent destroyed by Linebacker II. The nearby storage area at Gia Thuong also suffered heavy damage, and the adjacent Thanh Am oil tank farm was hit again after losing two-thirds of its capacity earlier in the year.[74]

Another badly damaged railyard and storage area was at Yen Vien, across the Canal des Rapides a couple of miles further up the northeast railroad where it intersected with the northwest railroad. Although a longer and less important route to China, the northwest railroad included a railyard of great importance at Kinh No (where the northwest line intersected with a short line running to the ironworks at Thai Nguyen and joining the northeast line at Kep). Around the rail spurs at Kinh No lay the largest storage complex in North Vietnam. For months this had been Meyer's top priority, and here Strategic Air Command had its greatest bomb damage to a railyard in Linebacker II, achieving 75-percent destruction. Although a nearby yard at Duc Noi was judged to be only 50 percent destroyed, its adjacent storage facility was almost entirely gone.[75]

The weight of bombs on Kinh No was exceeded only by the bombing of Lang Dang railyard (sixty miles from Hanoi on the northeast line near the Chinese border), but American intelligence judged that less than a third of this busy facility was destroyed. When Washington demanded that it be hit repeatedly late in the campaign, the thousands of bombs that cratered the yard managed to miss most of the hardware. Better luck rewarded strikes on railyards at Thai Nguyen and Kep, as well as on a rail siding near Haiphong. The railyard in downtown Haiphong, like the one in Hanoi, remained off limits to B–52s, but the oil tank farm on the edge of Haiphong went up in smoke.[76]

As an interdiction campaign, the strikes on railyards and supply areas had limited potential. The summer assault on bridges had caused the North Vietnamese to shift most of their imports to trucks. That shift was even easier during Linebacker II, when pervasive bad weather permitted only one laser-guided bomb attack on a bridge; a flight of F–4s took down the main bridge over the Canal des Rapides. F–111 low-level attacks with unguided bombs failed to bring down two other bridges. The only other bombed targets at all related to truck traffic were the oil tank farms and the vehicle repair shops. The principal truck repair shop was at Van Dien on the southern edge of Hanoi; twenty-one B–52 sorties damaged about a fourth of this facility. Even total destruction could have had only a modest impact, since neighboring China was not only the source of truck cargoes, but also of the trucks themselves.[77]

Fear, not interdiction, was the most promising product of B–52 assaults on Van Dien, Gia Lam, Yen Vien, Kinh No, and other targets ringing Hanoi. The B–52s attacked at night to gain the protection of darkness from MiGs, but night was also the most fearsome time to attack. Hanoi had been accustomed to daylight attacks by a few fighters. Now hundreds of big B–52s dropped thousands of bombs on the edge of the city. An occasional error brought B–52 bombs into the city's heart and underscored the implied threat that more might follow. If the Americans were willing to send fighters against the downtown rail station (albeit with guided bombs), might they ultimately use the B–52s there just as they had against all the railyards in the outskirts? Indeed, the string of B–52 bombs which hit Kham Thien Street on the south side of the Hanoi railyard gave the false impression that the Americans had already done so.

The shock value of Linebacker II was enhanced by an initial element of surprise. The scale of this campaign was probably far beyond anything expected by the North Vietnamese. Nevertheless, there had been warning signs that helped them prepare. The breakdown in the talks on December 13 was followed by a renewal of tactical reconnaissance sorties over the Red River Delta on December 15, together with an increase in SR–71 and drone reconnaissance sorties. Thirty tankers from the United States reached Okinawa on December 17 and 18 to support the compressed B–52 waves from Guam; another twenty-five for refueling fighters would go to the Philippines after the start of the campaign, bringing the total number of tankers working in the theater to nearly two hundred.[78]

On December 16, the North Vietnamese cancelled orders deploying a surface-to-air missile regiment from Hanoi to South Vietnam. That would have reduced the number of Hanoi's active missile sites from twelve to eight. Whatever concern existed at the top of the Hanoi regime failed to stir Hanoi's air defense troops. The commander of the regiment whose move south had been cancelled decided to go on leave, as did his two battalion commanders and many of their men. Even when the General Staff called for the highest state of readiness on December 17, that regimental commander stayed on leave.[79]

Meanwhile, signs of impending attack mounted. Early on the morning of the eighteenth, the North Vietnamese intercepted a Navy carrier message about rescue helicopters and at noon intercepted an RF–4 message reporting weather in the Hanoi area. When more than forty B–52s took off from Guam in the afternoon, there was no way to hide the fact from a Soviet trawler sitting off shore. Always before, Guam had launched three-ship cells more than half an hour apart—except on the seventeenth, when there had been no B–52 launches at all. The North Vietnamese General Staff told the air defense forces to expect a B–52 attack that night. A car was sent to fetch the missing regimental commander. He arrived in time for the first wave, but one of his battalion commanders did not. Nevertheless, another of his battalions shot down the first B–52 lost in Linebacker II.[80]

"The enemy could not achieve the element of surprise," Lt. Gen. Hoang Phuong would brag years later, "because they could not maintain the secrecy of their strategic intentions, the targets they intended to attack, the forces they were going to use, the direction of attacks, the flight paths to attacks, the opportunities for attacks etc. Although this is something that should never be done in military operations, it was a mistake that the enemy made."[81] This postwar bravado at least indicated the importance of shooting down B–52s for North Vietnamese morale. It may well be true that if no B–52s had launched from Guam before U-Tapao B–52s had launched, Strategic Air Command might have achieved greater surprise for the first wave. Thereafter, the element of surprise was bound to shrivel. Greater variation in tactics during the first three nights might have helped in the duel with the missile sites. Although shock effect could be achieved at first despite some warning, Hanoi's citizens were bound to become somewhat inured to the B–52s as night after night most of the bombing remained outside the city. They might begin to feel helpless, however, if bombing were to continue without any opposition from missiles.

Fighter aircraft may also have made a direct contribution to the psychological impact of Linebacker II. Most of the electric lights went out in Hanoi. The city's powerplant, which had been off limits during Linebacker, ceased to operate after a flight of four F–4s dropped laser-guided bombs on its boiler house, generator hall, control building, and machine shop. Linebacker had already done severe damage to the national power grid, and several electrical targets were hit again in Linebacker II. On four occasions, a total of six F–111s made low-level strikes with unguided bombs on the heart of the grid, the transformer station at Dong Anh just north of Hanoi. Once again Dong Anh was put out of operation, as it had been in Rolling Thunder and Linebacker.[82]

Perhaps the most important bomb dropped by a fighter in Linebacker II was one whose malfunctioning laser guidance system caused it to miss the Hanoi powerplant and hit an office building. This occurred on the afternoon of December 21, when a break in the weather afforded the best opportunity for laser-guided bombing during Linebacker II. General Vogt sent three flights of F–4s against three different targets in Hanoi—it was the most he could send since each flight required one of his precious four laser-guidance pods (leaving only one for backup). Despite the relative clarity of the weather, the flight attacking the powerplant ran into some clouds that forced the F–4 with the laser designator to descend to twenty-five hundred feet. Even such risk-taking did not succeed in getting all eight bombs on the target. Two failed to guide. When the flight returned to Ubon, the crews reported that one of the no-guides had struck a big building well south of the powerplant. Seventh Air Force intelligence concluded that the bomb had hit communist party headquarters, and General Vogt expected dire repercussions. But since North Vietnam said nothing about it, it never got into the press. "And you know," Vogt would say after the war, "I think it had a salutary effect on the outcome of the negotiations, because I really think these guys thought we were now going after communist leadership."[83]

Whatever the truth of Vogt's deduction, the decision of the United States at the beginning of the war not to threaten the existence of the North Vietnamese regime had limited the impact of American air operations there. In Linebacker II, the only authorized target linked directly with the leadership was Radio Hanoi. This propaganda tool and symbol of the regime was bombed several times, but not even a laser-guided attack succeeded in putting it off the air. So eager had Washington been to hit this target, that on the first two nights, General Meyer had sent B–52s against it. Area bombing was ill-suited to so small a target. Yet several communications targets and missile sites were bombed by B–52s that had slight chance of doing any effective damage. These awkward missions were born of frustration over the lack of precision bombing capability in bad weather.

Bad weather also kept Strategic Air Command and Seventh Air Force from seeing what, if anything, they had hit. Bomb damage assessment was difficult in the absence of photography that had to wait on better weather. Even reconnaissance drones, which could fly through any weather at low altitude, could still be foiled by the misty conditions of the northeast monsoon. In any case, the Strategic Air Command was launching only four drones a day at the beginning of Linebacker II; after Christmas the launch rate increased to six a day when a third C–130 launch aircraft was deployed. Traveling at a few hundred feet over the Red River Delta, the drones were limited in the number of targets they could photograph. Often, imperfect navigation caused a drone to miss a planned target entirely. Fewer than half the drones followed their planned route. Sometimes route planning was the problem. Two drones missed photographing the Bac Mai hospital because the Defense Intelligence Agency had provided the wrong street address.[84]

Emphasis on photographing the bombing error at the Bac Mai hospital indicated the extent to which drones had to answer to Washington's political requirements rather than to the theater's tactical requirements. Had the destruction of particular targets been truly critical to Linebacker II, the reconnaissance problem would have been more than frustrating. But the critical requirement of Linebacker II was dropping a lot of bombs near Hanoi; so long as they did not kill too many civilians, it did not much matter to the Nixon administration what they hit.

It did matter how many planes were lost, not least because those losses presented the Nixon administration's enemies in Hanoi and Washington with political ammunition. B–52 losses were the most costly, because of the aircraft's fame as a nuclear bomber as well as its size and the size of its crew. The B–52's normal crew of six (pilot, copilot, navigator, radar navigator, electronic warfare officer, and gunner) meant that Hanoi could quickly increase its collection of American prisoners. While five of the fifteen B–52s lost to surface-to-air missiles in Linebacker II managed to limp out of North Vietnam, a radar navigator disappeared after bailing out over Laos and the crash landing at U-Tapao took four more lives. Of the thirty-four B–52 crew members known to have been captured by the North Vietnamese, one died in captivity: Lt. Col. Keith R. Heggen, the deputy airborne commander of the Andersen strike force in the third wave on the third night. Twenty-seven others were missing in North Vietnam and later presumed dead. For many surviving B–52 crew members, Linebacker II had been a close call. In addition to the fifteen B–52s lost, three were severely damaged and six more suffered minor damage.[85]

B–52 losses overshadowed, but did not diminish, the loss of eleven fighter, attack, and reconnaissance aircraft, not to mention an Air Force rescue helicopter and an Air Force EB–66 jammer—the latter brought down by engine failure. The Air Force lost two F–111s (at least one to small arms fire) and two F–4s on air-to-air missions in daylight (both to MiGs). The Navy's six losses included two A–6s, two A–7s, an F–4 and an RA–5; antiaircraft artillery accounted for three, surface-to-air missiles for one, MiGs for one, and for one the cause was unknown. The cause of the loss of a Marine A–6 was also unknown. Although the number of B–52 losses was not much greater than that of these smaller aircraft, three times as many aircrew were involved in the B–52 incidents.[86]

Since fighter aircraft suffered less expensive losses than B–52s while flying more than three times as many Linebacker II sorties, the Pacific Air Forces commander, General Clay, could argue that the entire job of bombing the Red River Delta should be returned to the fighters. On December 28, he declared that there remained "few if any targets" worth losing more B–52s.[87] Given Clay's displeasure over Strategic Air Command's dominance of the campaign and his own limited role, this suggestion did not carry much weight in Washington. In any case, Hanoi's indication that it was eager to complete a cease-fire agreement was all that President Nixon required to call off all bombing north of the twentieth parallel on December 29.[88]

By that time General Haig had already visited President Thieu in Saigon with President Nixon's ultimatum: go along with a cease-fire now or go on alone. By underlining Nixon's promise to react against another North Vietnamese offensive, Linebacker II may have helped this medicine go down a little easier—as did a surge of imported American military equipment (including planes and tanks). Haig tried to get General Vogt to add his assurances that the United States would come to the aid of South Vietnam if North Vietnam attacked, but Vogt refused. "I could see the resolutions that were being introduced in Congress against any resumption of bombing," he recalled years later after the North Vietnamese conquest of South Vietnam. "And I didn't feel I could, in good conscience, offer reassurances to these people under those circumstances. I can sleep nights as a result. I wonder if other people do."[89]

Chapter Eleven

Reverberations

In 1975, two years after signing a cease-fire agreement in Paris, the North Vietnamese completed their conquest of South Vietnam. North Vietnamese forces moved almost unimpeded through Laos or across the Demilitarized Zone to join those already in South Vietnam. This time the United States refused to intervene. Charged with covering up his administration's responsibility for breaking into Democratic party headquarters at Washington's Watergate building, Richard Nixon had resigned the presidency to avoid impeachment. Although Nixon's successor, Gerald Ford, had been House minority leader, he could not muster enough support in Congress for renewed involvement in South Vietnam. Without American air power, the South Vietnamese army disintegrated in two months.

America's sour aftertaste of the Vietnam War was sweetened for the Air Force by the obvious success of American air power in 1972, a success only underlined in 1975 by the disastrous consequences of American air power's absence. While the bitterness of many who had served in a frustrating war was exacerbated by declining Air Force manpower and budgets, the service pursued new technologies stimulated by the Southeast Asian experience—new fighter aircraft, new radar aircraft, new means of countering enemy radar, new means of operating in darkness, and new guided weapons.[1]

The doctrinal legacy of the war was more muddled than the technical legacy. The war's emotional impact sometimes added to the difficulty of determining how best to use the new technologies. In public discussion, the Air Force tended to emphasize the dramatic contribution of the B–52s in Linebacker II rather than the pathbreaking use of laser-guided bombs against bridges in North Vietnam and tanks in South Vietnam. In contrast to laser-guided bombing, B–52 area bombing was an older technology available at the beginning of the war and useable in any weather. B–52s could have attacked North Vietnam in early 1965 without being inhibited by clouds or surface-to-air missiles; B–52 radar could find targets in any weather and North Vietnam had yet to deploy SAMs. By withholding America's all-weather heavy bombers and doling out targets gradually, President Johnson helped the northeast monsoon to shield the Red River Delta of North Vietnam from the much lighter bomb loads of Rolling

Thunder's fair-weather fighter aircraft. Slow gains brought by restricted bombing dribbled away during the annual respite from November to April. Linebacker II bolstered the Air Force's argument that had B–52s been used in the Red River Delta at the outset, the war would have come to a much quicker and more satisfactory conclusion.

The situation in 1972 differed in important respects from 1965. An open invasion exposed communist forces to air power in ways that North Vietnam's earlier support for insurgency had not. Having built relationships with the Soviet Union and China that reduced their support for North Vietnam, President Nixon sought only a cease-fire that left North Vietnamese forces in South Vietnam and brought home the prisoners of war. These differences in the contexts of Rolling Thunder and Linebacker caused doubts about claims that the war might have been won by launching a Linebacker II early in Rolling Thunder. Skepticism inside the Air Force eventually found public expression, most prominently in Maj. Mark Clodfelter's *The Limits of Air Power* (New York, 1989). Too young to have served during the Vietnam War, this Air Force Academy professor found it "difficult to fathom" the "lingering conviction" of Air Force generals that their way of using air power could be decisive in a limited war.[2] Clodfelter was most concerned about guerrilla war, but he also worried about the utility of air power in more conventional forms of limited war under the threat of nuclear retaliation.

Soon after the publication of Clodfelter's book came a radical transformation of world politics. In the waning days of the Soviet Union, American air power proved very effective against an Iraq waging conventional war without any major allies. For those persuaded by the Vietnam War that American air power was ineffective, the Gulf War came as a great surprise—not least for the Iraqi dictator, Saddam Hussein, who had bragged about his ability to emulate Hanoi's victory. In August 1990, Saddam told Dan Rather of CBS Television that "the United States depends on the Air Force. The Air Force has never decided a war in the history of wars."[3]

Since Iraq did not resort to nuclear, biological, or chemical weapons, the Gulf War remained limited not only to conventional weapons, but also to targets that could be hit without endangering civilian residences. The Johnson administration's avoidance of enemy civilian casualties had been so thoroughly inculcated that it was an integral part of the air campaign plan the Air Force produced for President George Bush. But this self-imposed restraint did not cripple air power, because Desert Storm exploited the precision of laser-guided bombing in dramatic new ways.

The laser-guided bombs that "plinked" tanks in Kuwait had their predecessors in the laser-guided bombs that destroyed tanks in South Vietnam. The laser-guided bombing of Iraq, however, was quite different than the laser-guided bombing of North Vietnam. Linebacker's laser-guided bombs had hit mostly bridges. Desert Storm's laser-guided bombs first struck Iraq's command centers and communications nodes. Unlike North Vietnam's rulers, the Iraqi regime and its ability to lead were threatened from the outset. U.S. Air Force surveillance planes had a much better picture of Iraqi air defenses than did Iraqi air leaders. Crippled early, Iraqi air defenses were never able to offer much resistance. Improved air-to-air missiles (especially Sparrows) downed the few Iraqi aircraft that flew within range. Although much larger than North Vietnam's, most of Iraq's air force was destroyed on the ground or fled to Iran. In contrast to the sanctuary enjoyed by North Vietnamese airfields for much of Rolling Thunder, Iraqi airfields were methodically attacked—each hardened aircraft shelter penetrated by a laser-guided bomb.

The improved accuracy of laser-guided bombs meant that their targets in Iraq could be more precisely defined—not just a particular office building, but a particular office. Indeed, the precision of bombs often exceeded the precision of intelligence about enemy activity. The bomb itself could give the first close look at a target, as a camera electronically transmitted imagery showing the target growing larger and larger in the center of the bomb's field of view until detonation. When some of this video tape appeared on commercial television, the American public got a new image of air power. During the Vietnam War, the care of aircrews to avoid civilian casualties had never overcome the image of leveled cities that the public had derived from the Second World War. In Desert Storm, the public saw a precision so amazing that some came to expect air warfare without any civilian casualties at all.

The major incident involving civilian casualties in Iraq occurred when two laser-guided bombs hit a targeted bunker. A great improvement in the newer laser-guided bombs used in Desert Storm was their ability to penetrate bunkers, but intelligence about what was in the bunkers was not equally penetrating. Target planners did not know that the Iraqi leadership was using the bunker as an air raid shelter as well as a command center. Publicity about these casualties caused Washington to restrain bombing in the capital city of Baghdad for the remainder of the Gulf War.[4] Those who fought the air war over North Vietnam were very familiar with enemy willingness to put its military assets amid its civilian population or anywhere else American bombs were apt to yield useful propaganda. In such matters, the Iraqi regime was, in fact, far less skillful than the Vietnamese communists.

Better led than the Iraqis, the North Vietnamese also enjoyed the great advantage of worse weather for bombing. Although American air power made great strides during the 1980s in its ability to operate at night, laser-guided bombing continued to depend on clear weather. Even in the relatively poor Iraqi weather of Desert Storm, the skies were clear enough that, over the course of six weeks, laser-guided bombs fell in Iraq every day but one. The contrast with North Vietnam is evident when it is recalled that in the two weeks of Linebacker II, laser-guided bombing was possible on only two days.

When the weather did break in Linebacker II, General Vogt had only four laser designation pods that could be used in the high-threat area around Hanoi and Haiphong. Two decades later, Gen. Charles A. Horner, the Desert Storm air commander (who had flown in Rolling Thunder and was determined not to repeat its errors), could call upon more than a hundred aircraft with laser designation capability. Horner did not have to build big formations to protect his precision bombers, not only because they were more plentiful, but also because his forces attacked enemy defenses at once. Some of his aircraft used new "stealth" technologies to hide themselves from enemy radar while they were bombing Iraq's air defense control centers; stealth was the product of research animated by North Vietnam's air defenses. In Rolling Thunder, the Air Force had been forbidden to attack enemy airfields for two years. In Desert Storm, enemy airfields were attacked on the first night.

The intensity of laser-guided bombing in Desert Storm was a function of American leadership and planning as well as favorable weather and improved technology. Although some Air Force generals did propose gradual escalation during the early planning for Desert Storm, the old aversion to gradualism reasserted itself in the Air Force and in the White House. There was a realization that, for an air campaign, timing is as important as weight of effort. This fundamental truth had been trampled in the 1960s by the Rolling Thunder campaign. Eventually, almost all the targets in North Vietnam on the original ninety-four target list were bombed, but eventually was not nearly soon enough. Targets that should have been bombed in the first few days were kept off limits for years.

Meanwhile, the bombs kept falling on less important targets, so that in the end, North Vietnam absorbed some eight hundred thousand tons. Yet this was only a tenth of the eight million tons dropped on Southeast Asia as a whole, with South Vietnam bearing the brunt of this onslaught and nearly all the additional eight million tons of artillery shells. No other part of the world had ever been bombed so heavily. In Germany during World War II, the rate of bomb tonnage reached the same level by 1945, but the Vietnam War lasted twice as long; Japan suffered a half million tons in less than a year. Of course, the bombing of Germany and Japan was far more devastating, because their major cities were demolished. A high proportion of the bombing in Southeast Asia did nothing more than tear up the jungle.

American air power dropped about a hundred thousand tons of bombs on Iraq and Kuwait in six weeks—close to the rate bombs had fallen in Southeast Asia, Germany, or Japan. But the Gulf War was over in only six weeks, thanks in part to an acceleration in target destruction permitted by greater precision. Once again, B–52s were largely confined to bombing troop positions in the south rather than urban targets in the north. This time, however, fighter aircraft were better equipped to attack urban targets than they had been in Rolling Thunder or even Linebacker. This time the President authorized urban targets from the beginning.

Laser-guided bombs made urban targeting acceptable to American political leaders early in Desert Storm, but this precision was used with far greater caution four years later when Bosnian Serb military depredations provoked the North Atlantic Treaty Organization (NATO) to launch an air campaign for the first time. Operation Deliberate Force lived up to its name. Avoidance of casualties, even Bosnian Serb military casualties, governed the careful selection of aiming points made personally by NATO's American theater air commander, Lt. Gen. Michael E. Ryan (future Air Force Chief of Staff, veteran of Rolling Thunder, and son of Gen. John D. Ryan, Sr., Pacific Air Forces commander and Air Force Chief of Staff during the Vietnam War). For the first time in so large an operation, most of the bombs dropped were guided; American planes dropped almost nothing else. Despite constraints reminiscent of Vietnam, guided bombing, together with a more favorable situation on the ground, produced an effective air campaign using little more than a thousand bombs and lasting only two weeks.

Three and a half years after Deliberate Force in the spring of 1999, a much bigger NATO air campaign ended a Serbian reign of terror in Kosovo. In deference to the sensibilities of NATO member countries, Operation Allied Force began nearly as cautiously as Deliberate Force. Gradually additional targets were approved. Although, in the end, twice as many unguided bombs would be used, more than seven thousand guided bombs and missiles attacked targets with an accuracy that usually fulfilled NATO's wish to minimize civilian casualties and collateral damage. Faulty intelligence did lead to a deadly attack on the Chinese embassy in the Serbian capital, Belgrade. Nevertheless, this version of gradualism progressed much more rapidly and successfully than Rolling Thunder. Only two NATO planes (both U.S. Air Force) were lost, and both pilots were rescued. There were no bombing pauses. Targets like airfields and powerplants (that were only permitted by the Johnson administration after two years of Rolling Thunder) were hit during the eleven weeks of Allied Force. Allied Force attacks on leadership facilities in Belgrade contrasted with avoidance of targets in downtown Hanoi during Rolling Thunder and Linebacker. Even during Linebacker II, most of the bombs that struck downtown Hanoi were intended for targets on the outskirts.

Once again in Allied Force, the old B–52s played important roles—but nothing like Linebacker II's area bombing near cities. Early in Allied Force, B–52s launched cruise missiles against targets throughout Serbia and later dropped unguided bombs on Serb troop concentrations in Kosovo. Newer B–1s also used unguided bombs, but the Air Force's newest bombers, stealthy B–2s, flew all the way from Missouri to deliver only new all-weather guided bombs. The Air Force employed fighter aircraft (F–117s, F–15s, F–16s, A–10s) that had emerged after the Vietnam War. Except for B–52s and some types of bombs, little of the Air Force hardware used in Vietnam remained in active service. That was true of people as well. One major exception was the air commander for Allied Force, Lt. Gen. Michael C. Short, who had flown F–4s in South Vietnam. This time General Short was serving under President Bill Clinton, who had protested the Vietnam War in his college years and learned to rely on air power in his White House years.

The leading role that the Air Force played in Allied Force, Deliberate Force, and Desert Storm grew out of the post-Vietnam years when the service was widely seen to be filling mostly a supporting role for potential ground operations. While focusing on the defense of Europe in the 1970s and 1980s, many in the Air Force came to see the ground-attack mission of fighter aircraft as restricted to bombing enemy troops and supply lines. The bombardment of Soviet cities would be the job of nuclear missiles and bombers; it was to be avoided if at all possible, because it would mean a nuclear war devastating to friend and foe alike. Strategic bombardment was synonymous with nuclear bombardment. When the Air Force had to think about waging war against Iraq, many Air Force officers had difficulty coming to grips with a "strategic air campaign" that would be waged with conventional bombs dropped by fighter aircraft.

To some degree, this conceptual problem was already present during the Vietnam War. Partly because Rolling Thunder and Linebacker were waged mostly with fighter aircraft dropping conventional bombs, commanders tended to define those campaigns as tactical interdiction rather than strategic campaigns. Since the North Vietnamese had to import nearly all their military supplies, an air campaign confined to bombing North Vietnam could not hit the industries on which the enemy war machine depended. On the other hand, the Air Force did want to threaten enemy leadership—an objective that was traditionally "strategic" and during Rolling Thunder politically unacceptable. The Johnson administration confined Rolling Thunder largely to interdiction, but President Nixon's Linebacker II campaign moved beyond interdiction to intimidation.

Even Rolling Thunder interdiction had a strategic component, for the objective was not merely to limit the flow of supplies to South Vietnam but to hurt the North Vietnamese economy. Indeed, the latter objective may well have been the one toward which the most progress was made. Soviet and Chinese military supplies could more than keep up with American interdiction, but North Vietnam lost the few industries that carried its hopes for modernization. Although the United States refrained from bombing dikes, a considerable portion of the agricultural labor force was diverted to the war effort; North Vietnam had to import rice. Years of bombing had taken a heavy toll on the country's transportation system, especially railroads. Many of the small cities and villages on the principal transportation routes had suffered extensive destruction in contrast to relatively limited bomb damage in the major cities of Hanoi and Haiphong. In 1973, President Nixon offered $3.25 billion for reconstruction, but North Vietnam forfeited the money by persisting with its conquest of South Vietnam.[5]

The North Vietnamese leaders became so accustomed to concentrating on war, that even after the collapse of South Vietnam, they had trouble thinking about anything else. They had to fend off a Chinese invasion while bogged down fighting an insurgency in Cambodia. Together with the severe handicap imposed by their Marxist ideology and by an American trade embargo, the old men of the communist regime in Hanoi permitted their country to fall father and farther behind Thailand and the other booming economies of Southeast Asia. Even gigantic China was quicker to encourage capitalist practices. Not until the late 1980s and a new generation of Vietnamese leaders, did the Vietnamese economy begin to improve.

The war that left Vietnam saddled with an aging leadership actually facilitated an important transition in the leadership of the U.S. Air Force. The dominance of the Strategic Air Command began to unravel in Southeast Asia. Fighter pilots played a more central role than did B–52 pilots, who spent most of the war bombing the jungle of South Vietnam. The very fact that an aircraft designed to drop nuclear bombs on the Soviet Union was used instead to provide close air support signalled the need to reconsider the mission of the Strategic Air Command. Eventually, fighter pilot veterans of Vietnam took charge of the Air Force, eliminated the Strategic Air Command, and put long-range bombers together with fighters in a new Air Combat Command.[6]

Long before those developments, General McConnell began to prepare the way for them as Air Force Chief of Staff. He sent an especially able fighter commander, General Momyer, to take charge of Seventh Air Force and helped Momyer get a fourth star. At the same time, McConnell sent General Ryan from Strategic Air Command to get some fighter experience as commander of Pacific Air Forces before becoming Chief of Staff of the Air Force. McConnell then replaced Momyer at Seventh Air Force with General Brown, who had begun his career as a bomber pilot in the Second World War, but had been a fighter operations deputy in the Korean War. Although Brown had never served in the Strategic Air Command, he became Air Force Chief of Staff in 1973 and Chairman of the Joint Chiefs of Staff a year later. When Brown went to Seventh Air Force, McConnell sent General Holloway, a World War II fighter ace, to take over the Strategic Air Command; this shock led to others for SAC, and their next commander was an even more famous World War II fighter ace, General Meyer.

In 1982 General Gabriel became Air Force Chief of Staff, the first of a succession of Vietnam War fighter pilots in that job. The fact that he had risen to the top even after his involvement in the Lavelle affair demonstrated the degree to which the Air Force had been able to deflect the political currents swirling around the Vietnam War. The Lavelle affair had divided the Air Force for a time, but only Lavelle himself was sacrificed.

The Air Force's essential response to the Vietnam puzzle was to work toward coming out of the war in the best shape possible. Since there seemed to be no permissible way to win the war, the Air Force looked for ways to fight that would build its technology and preserve the precious lives of its aircrews. The other services sought similar ends, and while the Air Force did more to develop new technology, the Navy was quicker to exploit the value of realistic air combat training. Because common sense (supported by the Air Force's own studies) had long indicated that a pilot was most vulnerable and least effective in his first few combat sorties, Seventh Air Force followed the practice throughout the war of keeping aircrews away from Route Package Six until they had flown several sorties in Laos or the panhandle of North Vietnam. But the Navy's Top Gun training program went further and clearly helped the air-to-air performance of their pilots in Linebacker.

After the war, the Air Force began its Red Flag exercises at Nellis Air Force Base, Nevada, where units could attack ground targets in the face of extraordinarily realistic air defenses—not just fighters, but antiaircraft artillery and surface-to-air missiles as well. Here allied air forces learned to work with Americans very much the way they would in the Gulf War. This training would permit remarkably smooth operations with remarkably low losses from the opening night of Desert Storm.

Those who compare the Air Force's concern for aircrew survival in Iraq and North Vietnam unfavorably with the bold expenditure of aircrew lives during World War II miss the fundamental differences in the character of those wars. Whether the U.S. should fight smaller wars with less at stake than World War II is another question—one about which the Air Force has not been given and will not be given much to say. But the Air Force can have considerable impact on the degree of sacrifice that a war exacts.

The Vietnam War cost the lives of more than a million Vietnamese, and more than a million Cambodians died at the hands of Pol Pot's communist regime in the aftermath of the war. While the American sacrifice exceeding fifty thousand lives was painful, it is well to remember that four times as many South Vietnamese government troops died in combat. During the war, most of the killing occurred in South Vietnam. The bombing of North Vietnam probably killed fewer than a hundred thousand North Vietnamese.[7]

Combat over North Vietnam accounted for more than a quarter of the almost two thousand Air Force people killed or missing in Southeast Asia. Of about twenty-two hundred Air Force planes lost in the war, more than six hundred were shot down over North Vietnam.[8] Nearly three hundred of the Air Force men shot down there were captured and came home at the end of the war. Unlike most of the Vietnam veterans who had returned individually to cool or even rude receptions, the groups of released prisoners were welcomed warmly by crowds of Americans. The disturbing fact that the prisoner exchange included only thirteen Americans captured in Laos (where the Air Force alone had lost more than four hundred planes) fed fears that communists might still be holding American prisoners.* The families of the missing were sufficiently well organized to keep the Defense Intelligence Agency at work for decades after the war in an unprecedented effort to determine the fate of every American lost in Southeast Asia.[9]

Except for one Marine who decided to come home after collaborating with the communists, the families of the missing got back only remains.[10] Even the remains came out slowly enough to bolster allegations that the Vietnamese government had a warehouse of them to release little by little, at least until the U.S. government ceased to embargo trade with Vietnam. The end of the embargo in 1994 angered families who believed that the American government had thereby reduced pressure for determining the fate of their relatives. Three years later, a former Air Force prisoner of war and Florida congressman, Douglas "Pete" Peterson, returned to Hanoi as America's first ambassador to the Socialist Republic of Vietnam.

The Vietnam War veterans who commanded air power in the Gulf War sought to ensure that the coalition sacrifice in Southwest Asia would be far less than the allied sacrifice in Southeast Asia, let alone World War II. General Horner told his aircrews that no target was worth their lives unless they were operating in close support of troops. With their new technology and greater freedom to use it to its best advantage, his crews proved able to take out their

---

* Since a much higher percentage of downed aircrew was rescued in Laos than in North Vietnam and the percentage of aircrew who survived a shoot-down was probably no higher in Laos, the percentage captured was probably much lower in Laos. Nevertheless, the number of missing in both regions left room for suspicion that the communists had kept prisoners after the exchange in 1973. In 1993, Stephen J. Morris, an Australian researcher associated with Harvard University and Washington's Woodrow Wilson Center, found a startling document at the communist party central committee archives in Moscow. The document appeared to be a Russian translation of a September 1972 report to the North Vietnamese politburo by Lt. Gen. Tran Van Quang; the document stated that the North Vietnamese then held 1,205 U.S. prisoners of war, not merely the fewer than 600 released about six months later. After Vietnamese and U.S. officials challenged the authenticity and accuracy of the document, relations between the two countries continued to improve. But the document deepened doubts, all the more so because it surfaced in the wake of Russian president Boris Yeltsin's assertion that American prisoners were held in his country during the Vietnam War and that some might still be alive there. For an argument that long after the war American prisoners remained alive in Southeast Asia and the Soviet Union, see John M.G. Brown, *Moscow Bound: Policy, Politics and the POW/MIA Dilemma* (Eureka, Calif., 1993). In the fall of 1996, the U.S. released a national intelligence estimate of 1987, "Hanoi and the POW/MIA Issue" (SNIE 14.3–87), which supported the view that the Vietnamese government had the remains of more than 400 Americans in storage; this estimate also took note of the fact that France had yet to receive the remains of thousands of its soldiers killed in Vietnam during the 1940s and 1950s. But together with release of the 1987 estimate, the national intelligence community also issued an assessment which cast doubt upon that estimate. As to China, in 1973 that country released two CIA officials held since 1952 and two pilots captured during the Vietnam War—one Air Force and one Navy. Air Force Capt. Philip E. Smith's F–104 was shot down by a Chinese MiG–19 on September 20, 1965, when a navigational equipment failure caused him to wander off course near China's Hainan Island; see Smith's *Journey Into Darkness* (New York, 1992).

targets quickly, while sparing almost all their own lives and making possible the survival of almost all coalition troops. The U.S. sent more than half a million men and women to the Gulf, and fewer than two hundred were killed in action.

For General Horner, the Gulf War's extraordinarily low cost in lives was a great relief and a great satisfaction. He knew all too well from his own experience as an F–105 strike and Wild Weasel pilot over North Vietnam during Rolling Thunder that war could be far more lethal. Only a year before the Gulf War, he had occasion to recall a Vietnam dilemma publicly and help change the Air Force's official view of it.[11]

On June 30, 1989, General Horner pinned the Silver Star on Lt. Col. John R. "Bob" Pardo (USAF, retired) and Col. Stephen A. Wayne for an act of life-saving courage over North Vietnam on March 10, 1967. Captain Pardo and Lieutenant Wayne were pilot and backseater of an F–4 bombing the Thai Nguyen iron works. They were hit by antiaircraft fire while pulling off the target. Normally, getting themselves out of North Vietnam would have been enough of a challenge, but another F–4 was in even worse shape and running short of fuel. In a similar situation during the Korean War, Maj. Robbie Risner had pushed his wingman out of North Korea and survived to be shot down more than a decade later over North Vietnam (where he was imprisoned). There "Risner's Push" was joined by "Pardo's Push." Pardo wedged the other F–4's lowered tail hook (a vestige of the F–4's naval origin) against the edge of his windshield; the lowered hook permitted him to stay below the tail wash. Both aircraft made it to Laos before the crews had to bail out, and all four men were rescued.[12]

"Pardo's Push" became famous at air bases throughout Southeast Asia—so much so that a briefing team made the circuit to discourage any more pushing. Logic seemed to dictate that this technique could cost more aircraft than it would save, and that therefore Pardo and Wayne had set a bad example which should not be honored. But a warrior's calculus of risk is as much a matter of emotion as of logic. In the end Pardo and Wayne got their reward, and it was not merely a medal, for on the same day they received the medals the pilot of the other F–4 (Earl D. Aman) retired from the Air Force with twenty-two more years of service than on that much more difficult day over North Vietnam; Aman's backseater (Robert W. Houghton) also completed a full career in the Air Force. In finally honoring Pardo and Wayne, the Air Force was saluting all the men who had taken great risks to bring their comrades home.[13]

When General Horner subsequently told his aircrews in Saudi Arabia that targets were not worth their lives, he echoed senior officers in Thailand. Such admonitions were not always phrased with sufficient care to have the intended effect. On the very morning of Pardo and Wayne's celebrated sortie over North Vietnam, F–4 aircrews were advised that "our little brown brothers aren't worth any one of you getting killed."[14] Pardo was disturbed by the remark, which undervalued the unavoidable risks aircrews were taking. Senior officers walk a fine line between getting crews to avoid unnecessary risks and honoring their courage.

As for most of us looking back upon the men who risked their lives in the deadly skies over North Vietnam, we can honor their courage only with our attention. We may never be able to agree about the political significance of their war, but even across the years we can sense their worth.

Maps

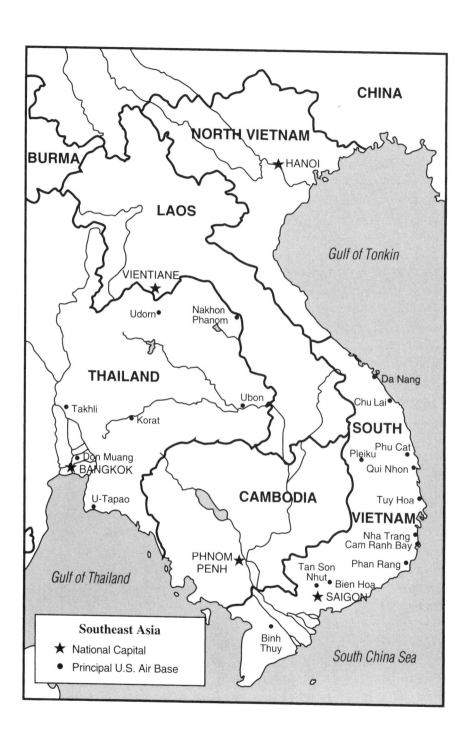

CHINA

NORTH VIETNAM

BURMA

★ HANOI

LAOS

Gulf of Tonkin

VIENTIANE
★

Udorn •

Nakhon
Phanom •

THAILAND

Ubon •

Da Nang •

Chu Lai •

• Takhli

• Korat

SOUTH

Phu Cat •
Pleiku •

Qui Nhon •

• Don Muang
★ BANGKOK

CAMBODIA

Tuy Hoa •

VIETNAM

• U-Tapao

Nha Trang •
Cam Ranh Bay •

PHNOM
PENH ★

Phan Rang •

Gulf of Thailand

Tan Son
Nhut • Bien Hoa •
★ SAIGON

Southeast Asia

★ National Capital

• Principal U.S. Air Base

Binh
Thuy •

South China Sea

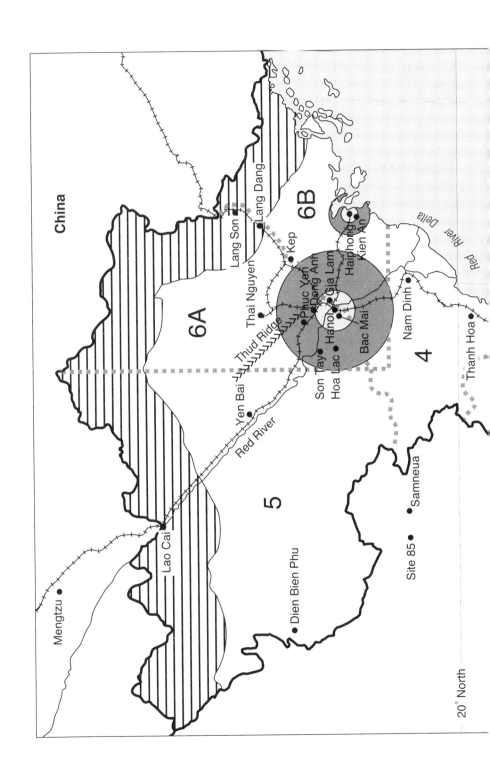

China

Mengtzu

Lao Cai

Red River

Yen Bai

Thud Ridge

Thai Nguyen

Lang Son

Lang Dang

Kep

Phuc Yen

Dong Anh

Gia Lam

Hanoi

Haiphong

Kien An

Bac Mai

Hoa Lac

Son Tay

6A

6B

5

4

Dien Bien Phu

Site 85

Samneua

Nam Dinh

Thanh Hoa

Red River Delta

20° North

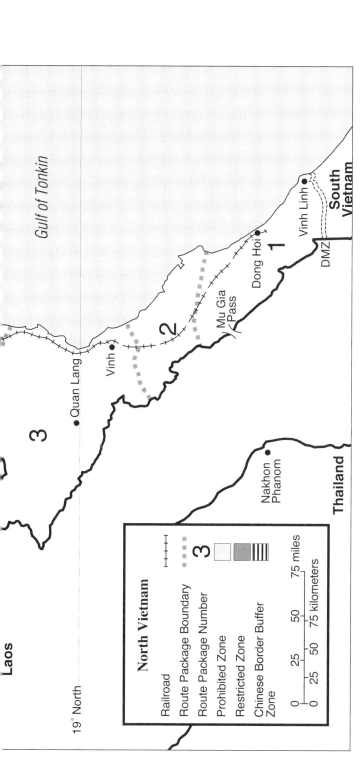

Prior to 1967, the boundary between Route Packages 4 and 5 was a straight-line extension of the southern boundary of Route Package 6 west to the Laotian border. Similarly, the boundary between Route Packages 6A and 6B was a straight line from the southwestern corner of Route Package 6 to Hanoi, after which that boundary followed the northeast railroad to China. While pilots could see the northeast railroad, they could not see imaginary straight lines that completed the boundary between Air Force and Navy operating areas. Consequently, the straight-line boundaries from Hanoi to the Laotian border were bent to follow roads. In 1972, the Hanoi and Haiphong prohibited areas were eliminated, and the Hanoi restricted area was reduced from a radius of 30 nautical miles to a radius of 10 nautical miles.

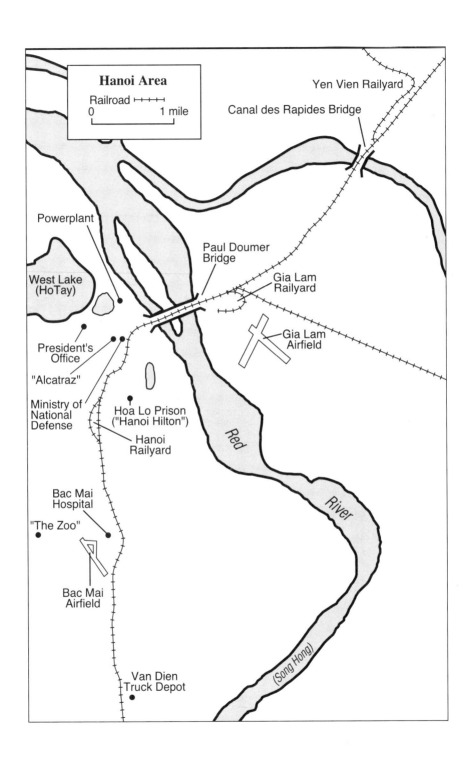

Hanoi Area

Railroad ┠┼┼┼┨
0   1 mile

Yen Vien Railyard

Canal des Rapides Bridge

Powerplant

Paul Doumer
Bridge

Gia Lam
Railyard

West Lake
(HoTay)

Gia Lam
Airfield

President's
Office

"Alcatraz"

Ministry of
National
Defense

Hoa Lo Prison
("Hanoi Hilton")

Hanoi
Railyard

Red

Bac Mai
Hospital

"The Zoo"

River

Bac Mai
Airfield

(Song Hong)

Van Dien
Truck Depot

Statistics

U.S. and South Vietnamese fixed-wing aircraft flew more than 6,000,000 sorties in Southeast Asia from 1962 to 1973. More than 2,000,000 sorties attacked ground targets with about 8,000,000 tons of bombs. Of this total, about 800,000 tons were dropped on North Vietnam by about 350,000 attack sorties. Only about 20 percent of the effort against North Vietnam was directed at Route Package Six, a region that included the country's two largest cities, Hanoi and Haiphong.

In the Southeast Asia of 1967, the Air Force stationed about 1,500 aircraft, of which the 450 in Thailand focused on North Vietnam and Laos; another 150 at Da Nang, South Vietnam, operated both north and south of the demilitarized zone; most other aircraft in South Vietnam expended the bulk of their effort there. The 60 B–52s in Thailand and Guam dropped most of their bombs in South Vietnam, but also hit targets in the North Vietnamese and Laotian panhandles. The Navy normally kept one or two carriers in the Gulf of Tonkin, with about 75 aircraft apiece.

In the Southeast Asia of 1972, there were more than 200 B–52s operating, and the Navy increased its presence to four carriers much of the time. Even after major deployments in response to North Vietnam's invasion of South Vietnam, however, the number of Air Force fighters in the area was fewer than 400, as compared with more than 500 five years earlier. Most Air Force fighters there in 1972 were F–4s operating from Thailand, some of which were replaced by A–7s and F–111s later in the year; by the end of the year, the Air Force had removed all of its aircraft from South Vietnam (except those transferred to the South Vietnamese).

Air Force fighters attacked Route Package Six with about two tons of bombs each, while Navy fighters averaged less than one and a half tons. No B–52 bombed Route Package Six until 1972, when each carried up to thirty tons of bombs. Indeed, the B–52s in 1972 played a much bigger role throughout North Vietnam than they had during Rolling Thunder. In 1972, more than two-thirds of the bomb tonnage used in North Vietnam by the Air Force was delivered by B–52s (compared to less than a quarter during Rolling Thunder).

The tonnage dropped in North Vietnam by Air Force fighters during 1972 was much less than during Rolling Thunder—not only due to the smaller number of fighters available, but also to the emphasis given the new laser-guided bombs. A few guided bombs could do the work of hundreds of "dumb" bombs scattered around a target. Only a half dozen new Pave Knife targeting pods were available for F–4s needing to maneuver in the face of air defenses while keeping a laser guidance beam fixed on a target. Only that small number of new pods could be used in the most heavily defended portion of North Vietnam. To protect those precious pods, the Air Force built large formations in which escort aircraft far outnumbered bombing aircraft.

While the Air Force could supply copious statistics about the weight of its effort in North Vietnam, there was no satisfactory quantitative measurement of results. Estimates of damage to targets (see Table 5 below) were not reliable and, in any case, did not really measure effectiveness. Only by considering the entire situation could any appreciation of possible effectiveness begin to take shape. The Air Force had reason to believe the Linebacker campaigns in 1972 more effective than the Rolling Thunder campaign of 1965–68.

Whatever the effectiveness, the cumulative cost was high. Although aircraft attrition calculated as a percentage of sorties was far lower than for any previous air war, this war's length and scope added up to an unprecedented number of sorties and a large number of losses. The Air Force alone lost 2,257 aircraft, 638 of them over North Vietnam, where Air Force men killed and missing totalled 413 (after 333 Air Force prisoners of war came home, most of them shot down in North Vietnam). This was less than 1 percent of the more than 55,000 American lives lost in Southeast Asia. Vietnamese losses on both sides were much greater. South Vietnamese government forces lost nearly a quarter million killed, and in 1995 the Socialist Republic of Vietnam announced that communist military killed exceeded a million, while civilian deaths approached two million. The new figure for communist military dead was about twice the American estimate and the civilian toll about five times the American estimate. Most of the casualties on both sides were suffered in South Vietnam. American intelligence had estimated civilian deaths from bombing in North Vietnam at about 50,000 for Rolling Thunder alone.

Critics of the air war over North Vietnam often argued that the cost of planes lost (not to mention aircrews killed, wounded and captured) far exceeded the cost of targets destroyed (not to mention people on the ground killed and wounded). But a meaningful comparison was not possible. The real question was how much did the losses of each side mean to their respective war efforts. As usual in war, the answer to that question had at least as much to do with timing and context as with numbers.

Tables:

1. U.S. and South Vietnamese Attack Sorties
2. USAF Combat and Combat Support Sorties in North Vietnam
3. USAF Attack Sorties in Route Package Six
4. USAF Air-to-Ground Munitions Expenditure in North Vietnam
5. USAF Bomb Damage Claims in North Vietnam
6. USAF Aircraft in Thailand and South Vietnam
7. Deployment of USAF Fixed-Wing Aircraft at Selected Bases
8. USAF Aircraft Losses in Southeast Asia by Aircraft Type
9. USAF Aircraft Losses in Southeast Asia by Cause
10. USAF Aircrew Losses in North Vietnam
11. U.S. Military Personnel in Thailand and South Vietnam

Table 1
U.S. and South Vietnamese Attack Sorties

	North Vietnam				
Year	USAF	USN	USMC	VNAF	Total SEA
1965	11,599	*	*	614	133,210
1966	44,762	32,594	3,695	814	291,967
1967	55,680	42,587	8,672	127	359,353
1968	41,743	40,848	10,326	-	416,140
1969	213	72	-	-	352,434
1970	699	404	-	-	245,690
1971	1,195	510	-	-	177,958
1972	21,225	26,754	459	-	244,215
Jan 1973	1,262	787	44	-	21,121

*Total USN and USMC attack sorties in North Vietnam for 1965 were 13,677.

Source: Office of the Secretary of Defense, *Southeast Asia Summary*, Nov 21, 1973, Table 304; the USAF column adds B–52 sorties for North Vietnam from HQ USAF, *Southeast Asia Management Summary*, final semiannual review, 1974, which is also the source of USAF attack sorties for 1965. Total sorties for 1965 are from Table 321 (Apr 19, 1972) of the OSD report.

Table 2
USAF Combat and Combat Support Sorties in North Vietnam

| Year | Attack | | CAP & | | Combat | |
	Fighters	B–52s	Escort	Recce	Support	Total
1965	11,599	-	5,675	3,294	5,554	26,122
1966	44,482	280	9,041	7,910	16,924	78,637
1967	54,312	1,364	5,617	11,714	28,078	101,089
1968	41,057	686	3,015	7,896	24,027	76,681
1969	213	-	939	2,905	3,965	8,022
1970	699	-	2,806	3,320	4,849	11,674
1971	1,195	-	3,419	2,044	2,924	9,582
1972	17,096	4,440	9,658	1,965	4,655	37,815
1973	755	533	526	132	381	2,327
Total	171,408	7,303	40,696	41,180	91,357	351,949

Source: HQ USAF, *Southeast Asia Management Summary*, final semiannual review, 1974.

In addition to the fighter and B–52 attack sorties listed above, there were five gunship sorties—four in 1967 and one in 1972. These have been included in the total column.

Table 3
USAF Attack Sorties in Route Package Six

Month	1967	1972
January	556	-
February	162	-
March	268	-
April	611	63
May	1,040	164
June	1,564	278
July	1,606	256
August	1,478	187
September	878	765
October	1,439	354
November	608	-
December	454	1,521
Total	10,664	3,588

Source: HQ PACAF monthly *Summary Air Operations Southeast Asia.*

This table illustrates seasonal (monsoonal) variation in operations over the Hanoi-Haiphong area for the two years during which it was most heavily bombed. Most Air force sorties in Route Package 6 were in Route Package 6A (Hanoi area), while most Navy sorties were in Route Package 6B (Haiphong area). The decline in sorties for September 1967 was due to unusually bad weather that month. Although the Air Force used fewer attack sorties in 1972, this was more than counterbalanced by the accuracy of F–4 guided bombing and the weight of B–52 bombing; there were 17 B–52 sorties in Route Package 6 for April and 729 in December. In 1967 the Air Force relied upon unguided bombs dropped by fighters. Despite the effectiveness of guided bombing in 1972, there was pressure on Seventh Air Force to increase the number of attack sorties in Route Package 6; some of the increase in September 1972 involved good-weather testing of the Long Range Navigation (loran) system for bombing during the inevitable bad weather later in the year (see Chapter 9).

Table 4
USAF Air-to-Ground Munitions Expenditure in North Vietnam*

Munition Type	March 1965–October 1968	April 1972–January 1973
100/125/250-pound bombs	18,703	202
260-pound fragmentation bombs	3,735	-
500-pound bombs*	227,304	93,292
500-pound laser-guided bombs	-	113
750-pound bombs*	358,941	2,948
1,000-pound bombs	21,058	3,226
1,000-pound TV-guided Walleye bombs	103	-
2,000-pound bombs	5,350	1,918
2,000-pound laser guided bombs	-	3,917
2,000-pound TV-guided bombs	-	299
3,000-pound bombs	10,597	158
3,000-pound laser-guided bombs	-	28
Cluster bombs	43,658	18,959
Rockeye cluster bombs	-	10,552
Mines	3,024	-
Napalm	5,162	36
Bullpup radio-guided missiles	1,944	-
Shrike radar-seeking missiles	2,263	1,032
Standard radar-seeking missiles	8	286
Rockets	868,424	188,513

* The number of munitions is given rather than their cumulative weight. Not included are 750-pound and 500-pound bombs dropped by B–52s (about 150,000 tons, two-thirds of it dropped in 1972). Of the 8,000,000 tons of air munitions expended in Southeast Asia by the U.S., nearly 800,000 tons struck North Vietnam (of which the Air Force share was nearly 500,000 tons).

Source: HQ PACAF monthly *Summary Air Operations Southeast Asia.*

Table 5
USAF Bomb Damage Claims in North Vietnam

Target Type	Mar 1965 – Oct 1968		Apr 1972 – Jan 1973	
	Destroyed	Damaged	Destroyed	Damaged
Vehicles	5,455	3,469	1,635	869
Tanks	-	-	38	20
Locomotives	17	59	1	6
Rail Rolling Stock	1,036	775	56	32
Watercraft	89	128	221	162
Bridges	1,305	1,794	250	55
Railroads	-	1,464 cuts	-	20 cuts
Roads	-	19,324 cuts	-	36 cuts
Ferry Slips	53	166	-	-
Oil Tanks	*	*	2,760	86
Buildings	5,938	4,570	1,207	369
Construction Eqpt.	-	-	35	32
Aircraft	96	25	36	6
Runways	-	19	*	*
AAA Sites	1,682	1,196	217	89
Field Artillery Areas	*	*	9	1
SAM Sites	80	93	40	5
Radar Sites	109	152	55	19

* Bombed but not tallied in this period.

Source: HQ PACAF monthly *Summary Air Operations Southeast Asia.*

While these figures indicate distribution of effort, they should not be taken as an accurate inventory of damage. The difficulty of estimating the degree of damage in the best conditions was compounded by weather, dust, smoke, darkness, deception, repair and repeated strikes in the same area.

Table 6
USAF Aircraft in Thailand and South Vietnam

Year (June 30)	Total	F–105	F–4	B–52*
1965	460	79	18	-
1966	889	126	188	-
1967	1,429	129	182	10
1968	1,768	108	218	28
1969	1,840	70	288	39
1970	1,602	65	212	39
1971	1,132	12 †	216	44
1972	989	30	355	54
1973	675 ‡	24	218	53

* In addition to the B–52s in Thailand, there were B–52s on Guam, where the number varied from about 30 in 1965 to about 150 in 1972.

† After 1970 the remaining F–105s were Wild Weasels carrying radar-seeking missiles to combat surface-to-air missiles.

‡ By this date no USAF aircraft were based in South Vietnam. In addition to F–4s and B–52s, the Thailand-based attack force included 65 A–7s and 45 F–111s which arrived in late 1972.

Source: HQ USAF *Southeast Asia Management Summary*, semiannual review, August 1973.

Table 7
Deployment of USAF Fixed-Wing Aircraft at Selected Air Bases

Base	July 1967 Aircraft Type	July 1967 Number Deployed	July 1972 Aircraft Type	July 1972 Number Deployed
Korat (Thailand)	F–105	76	F–4	39
			F–105	30
			EB–66	19
Takhli (Thailand)	F–105	52	F–4	97
	EB–66	19	KC–135	18
	KC–135	8		
Ubon (Thailand)	F–4	76	F–4	100
	EC–121	6	AC–130	12
	C–130	7	OV–10	9
Udorn (Thailand)	RF–4	25	F–4	105
	RF–101	15	RF–4	20
	F–102	6		
	A–1	14		
	C–130	4		
U-Tapao (Thailand)	B–52	15	B–52	54
	KC–135	28	KC–135	54
			U–2	3
			C–130	10
Andersen (Guam)	B–52	43	B–52	148
			KC–135	6
Kadena (Okinawa)	KC–135	40	KC–135	59
	Other	48	RC–135	5
			SR–71	4
			Other	44
Da Nang (S. Vietnam)	F–4	51	F–4	14
	F–102	6	AC–119	3
	O–1	48	EC–47	12
	O–2	19	A–1	2
			OV–10	32
			O–2	41

Source: HQ USAF monthly *Southeast Asia Management Summary*.

These bases were the ones most heavily involved in air operations over North Vietnam.

Table 8
USAF Aircraft Losses in Southeast Asia by Aircraft Type

Aircraft Type	Combat Losses		Operational Losses*	
	N. Vietnam	Total	N. Vietnam	Total
A–1	18	150	2	41
B–52	18	18	-	12
B–57	5	38	-	18
C–130	2	34	-	21
EB–66/RB–66	3/1	4/2	-	9/-
F–4/RF–4	193/38	382/76	2/1	63/7
F–100	16	198	-	45
F–102	1	7	-	8
F–104	4	8	3	6
F–105	282	334	3	63
F–111	3	8	-	3
HH–3/CH–3	3/1	10/14	1/-	4/3
HH–43	1	10	-	4
HH–53	1	9	-	1
HU–16	1	2	-	2
O–1	2	122	-	50
O–2	3	82	-	22
RC–47	1	2	-	-
RF–101	27	33	1	6
T–28	1	17	-	6
Other	-	177	-	126
Total	625	1,737	13	520

*Operational losses were due to mechanical failure, weather, accident, or pilot error.

Source: HQ USAF *Southeast Asia Management Summary*, final semiannual review, 1974.

Table 9
USAF Aircraft Combat Losses in Southeast Asia by Cause

Year	Ground Fire	Surface to Air Missiles	Aerial Combat	Ground Attack on Air Bases	Unknown/ Other
1962	7	-	-	-	-
1963	12	-	-	-	-
1964	25	-	-	6	-
1965	142	5	3	10	-
1966	267	18	8	6	-
1967	260	28	22	18	6
1968	252	3	9	35	5
1969	206	-	-	12	-
1970	124	-	1	2	-
1971	64	4	1	1	1
1972	78	49	23	6	7
1973	6	3	-	-	2
Total	1,443	110	67 *	96	21

* This figure should probably be somewhat larger (and the unknown/other figure correspondingly smaller). Rob Young, historian of the National Air Intelligence Center, Wright-Patterson Air Force Base, Ohio, credits the MiGs with 74 USAF losses (52 to MiG–21s, 18 to MiG–17s, and 4 to MiG–19s). The USAF claimed to have downed 137 MiGs (68 MiG–21s, 61 MiG–17s, and 8 MiG–19s). For a breakdown of USAF air-to-air victories by weapon employed, see R. Frank Futrell et. al., *Aces and Aerial Victories* (Washington: Office of Air Force History, 1976), p 157.

Source: HQ USAF *Southeast Asia Management Summary*, final semiannual review, 1974.

Michael M. McCrea, *U.S. Navy, Marine Corps, and Air Force Fixed-Wing Aircraft Losses and Damage in Southeast Asia (1962–1973)* (Washington: Center for Naval Analyses, 1976) gives the following causal breakdown for USAF losses in North Vietnam: antiaircraft artillery (253), automatic weapons and small arms (130), surface-to-air missiles (87), MiGs (64), own ordnance (3), unknown/other (80).

Table 10
USAF Aircrew Losses in North Vietnam

Aircraft Type	Rescued	Killed	Missing*	Captured*
A–1	9	2 (2) †	6	2
B–52	44	4	38	24
B–57	4	2	3	-
C–130	-	-	19	-
EB–66/RB–66	7	2	4	12
F–4	130 (4) †	7	128	116
RF–4	22 (2) †	5	30	18
F–100	14	2	5	5
F–102	-	-	1	-
F–104	(3) †	-	3	1
F–105	99 (3) †	18 (1) †	96	99
F–111	-	-	6	-
HH–3/CH–3	10 (4)/1 †	-	3	3
HH–43	-	1	-	3
HH–53	6	-	-	-
HU–16	4	2	-	-
O–1	-	-	2	-
O–2	2	3	-	-
RC–47	-	-	8	-
RF–101	6 (1) †	1	10	10
T–28	-	-	2	-
Total	358 (17) †	49(3) †	364	293

* Of the USAF personnel captured in Southeast Asia, 23 were known to have died in captivity. Subsequent to the prisoner exchange in 1973, none of the USAF's missing men returned home alive.
† Aircrew involved in operational losses are given in parentheses; numbers outside parentheses are for losses to hostile action only.

Source: HQ USAF *Southeast Asia Management Summary*, final semiannual review, 1974.

Table 11
U.S. Military Personnel in Thailand and South Vietnam

Year (Dec 31)	Thailand		South Vietnam	
	USAF	Total	USAF	Total
1960	44	319	68	875
1961	57	542	1,006	3,164
1962	1,212	4,353	2,429	11,326
1963	1,086	4,126	4,630	16,263
1964	2,943	6,505	6,604	23,310
1965	9,117	14,107	20,620	184,314
1966	26,113	34,489	52,913	385,278
1967	33,395	44,517	55,908	485,587
1968	35,791	47,631	58,434	536,134
1969	32,901	44,470	58,422	475,219
1970	27,858	36,110	43,053	334,591
1971	26,851	31,916	28,791	156,776
1972	35,856	43,168	7,608	24,172

Source: Office of the Secretary of Defense, *Southeast Asia Summary*, Sep 26, 1973 (Table 104) and Jul 18, 1973 (Table 103).

Notes

Chapter 1

1. For a more extensive discussion of the early bombing of North Vietnam, see two other volumes in the Air Force's official history of the Vietnam War: Jacob Van Staaveren's forthcoming *Gradual Failure: The Air War Over North Vietnam, 1965–1966* and Robert F. Futrell's *The Advisory Years to 1965*. Futrell deals mostly with South Vietnam, as does another volume in the series, John Schlight's *The War in South Vietnam: The Years of the Offensive, 1965–68*. Jacob Van Staaveren's *Interdiction in Southern Laos, 1960–1968*, a fourth volume in the series, covers Laos. On the development of bombing policy, see especially Mark Clodfelter, *The Limits of Air Power: The American Bombing of North Vietnam* (New York, 1989). See also David M. Barrett, *Uncertain Warriors* (Lawrence, Kan, 1993); Larry Berman, *Planning a Tragedy* (New York, 1982) and *Lyndon Johnson's War* (New York, 1989); Robert Buzzanco, *Masters of War* (Cambridge, England, 1996); Harold P. Ford, *CIA and the Vietnam Policymakers: Three Episodes, 1962–68* (Washington, 1998); Robert L. Gallucci, *Neither Peace Nor Honor* (Baltimore, 1975); Lloyd C. Gardner, *Pay Any Price* (Chicago, 1995); Leslie H. Gelb and Richard K. Betts, *The Irony of Vietnam* (Washington, 1979); William Conrad Gibbons, *The U.S. Government and the Vietnam War*, 4 vols (Washington, 1984–94); David Halberstam, *The Best and the Brightest* (New York, 1972); George Herring, *LBJ and Vietnam* (Austin, Tex, 1994); David Kaiser, *American Tragedy: Kennedy, Johnson, and the Origins of the Vietnam War* (Cambridge, Mass, 2000); Jeffrey Kimball, *Nixon's Vietnam War* (Lawrence, Kan, 1998); Fredrik Logevall, *Choosing War: the Lost Chance for Peace and the Escalation of*

War in Vietnam (Berkeley, Calif, 1999); H.R. McMaster, *Dereliction of Duty* (New York, 1997); Robert A. Pape, Jr., *Bombing to Win* (Ithaca, NY, 1996); Robert D. Schulzinger, *A Time for War* (New York, 1997); R.B. Smith, *An International History of the Vietnam War*, 3 vols (London, 1983–91); Wallace J. Thies, *When Governments Collide* (Berkeley, Calif, 1981); James Clay Thompson, *Rolling Thunder* (Chapel Hill, NC, 1980); Earl H. Tilford, Jr., *Setup* (Maxwell AFB, Ala, 1991); Brian VanDeMark, *Into the Quagmire: Lyndon Johnson and the Escalation of the Vietnam War* (New York, 1991); and Frank E. Vandiver, *Shadows of Vietnam* (College Station, Tex, 1997).

2. Jack S. Ballard, *The United States Air Force in Southeast Asia: Development and Employment of Fixed-Wing Gunships, 1962–1972* (Washington, 1982).

3. For more data on the F–4 and the F–105, see esp Marcelle Size Knaack, *Encyclopedia of US Air Force Aircraft and Missile Systems, Vol I, Post-World War II Fighters, 1945–1973* (Washington, 1978); PACAF, Corona Harvest rpt, "In-Country and Out-Country Strike Operations in Southeast Asia, 1 Jan 65–31 Dec 69," vol II, "Hardware, Strike Aircraft," AFHSO K717.103-13A. See also David Anderton, *Republic F–105 Thunderchief* (London, 1983); Walter J. Boyne, *Phantom in Combat* (Washington, 1985); Glenn E. Bugos, *Engineering the F–4 Phantom II* (Annapolis, 1996); Robert F. Dorr, *McDonnell Douglas F–4 Phantom II* (London, 1984); Jon Lake, ed, *McDonnell F–4 Phantom* (London, 1992); J.C. Scutts, *F–105 Thunderchief* (New York, 1981); and Ron Westrum, *Sidewinder: Creative Missile Development at China Lake* (Annapolis, 1999). For a fighter pilot's analysis of F–4 air-to-air

tactics, see Marshall L. Michel III, *Clashes: Air Combat over North Vietnam, 1965–1972* (Annapolis, 1997). Michel points to the F–4's "adverse yaw" as a problem for pilots, who had to remember to use rudder pedals only (with the aileron stick held in the center) when making hard turns.

4. R. Frank Futrell, et al., *Aces and Aerial Victories* (Washington, 1976).

5. PACAF, Corona Harvest rpt, "In-Country and Out-Country Strike Ops in SEA, 1 Jan 65–31 Dec 69, vol II, Hardware, Strike Aircraft," AFHSO K717.103-13A; Max J. Cleveland, Jim F. Gallagher, and Richard T. Sandborn, "Vulnerabilities of the F–4C and the F–105 Aircraft to Ground Fire in SEA," Aug 1, 1967, doc 18, hist, 7 AF, Jul–Dec 1967. Problems with the survivability of flight control systems in Vietnam led to the introduction of "fly-by-wire" electrical flight controls, first as a backup system in some F–4s and then after the war as a replacement for hydraulic and mechanical controls in the F–16 and subsequent aircraft. See William Elliott's "The Development of Fly-By-Wire Flight Control," Air Force Materiel Command, 1996.

6. Earl H. Tilford, Jr, *Search and Rescue in Southeast Asia, 1961–1975* (Washington, 1980).

7. Charles K. Hopkins, *SAC Tanker Operations in the Southeast Asia War* (HQ SAC, 1979).

8. PACAF, Corona Harvest rpt, "In-Country and Out-Country Strike Ops in SEA, 1965–68," vol III, "People," AFHSO 717.03-14; Capt E. Vallentiny and TSgt D. G. Francis, "Attack on Udorn," CHECO rpt, 1968, AFHSO K717.0413-86; Capt James R. Barrow and Maj Benjamin H. Barnette, Jr, "Base Defense in Thailand," CHECO rpt, 1973, AFHSO K717.0413-200; hist, 8 TFW, Oct–Dec 1972.

9. Trip rpt, Col George G. Loving, Jr, HQ USAF/XOX, 21 Nov 67, WNRC Acc 341-71A-6048, Box 9, RL(67) 38-9, Policy-Asia.

10. Carl O. Clever, "The U.S. Air Force Build-up in Thailand-1966," 13 AF, AFHSO K750.04-9; Warren A. Trest, TSgt Charles E. Garland and SSgt Dale E. Hammons, "USAF Posture in Thailand-1966," CHECO rpt, 1967, AFHSO K717.0413-41; PACAF, Corona Harvest rpt, "In-Country and Out-Country Strike Ops in SEA, 1965–68," vol IV, "Support Facilities," AFHSO K717.03-15J.

11. Barrow and Barnette, "Base Defense in Thailand"; Maj Edward B. Hanrahan, "An Overview of Insurgency and Counterinsurgency in Thailand," CHECO rpt, 1975, AFHSO K717.0413-212.

12. Lt Col Monty D. Coffin and Maj Ronald D. Merrell, "The Royal Thai Air Force," CHECO rpt, 1971, AFHSO K717.0413-173; David K. Wyatt, *Thailand: A Short History*, (New Haven, Conn, 1984); Nigel J. Brailey, *Thailand and the Fall of Singapore: A Frustrated Asian Revolution* (Boulder, Colo, 1986); John L.S. Girling, *Thailand: Society and Politics* (Ithaca, NY, 1981); Robert M. Blackburn, *Mercenaries and Lyndon Johnson's "More Flags": The Hiring of Korean, Filipino and Thai Soldiers in the Vietnam War* (Jefferson, NC, 1994); Robert J. Muscat, *The Fifth Tiger: A Study of Thai Development Policy* (New York, 1994); U. Alexis Johnson with J.O. McAllister, *The Right Hand of Power* (Englewood Cliffs, NJ, 1984).

13. Intrvw, Lt Col Robert G. Zimmerman, Corona Harvest, with Col Roland K. McCoskrie, Washington, Jul 14, 1975; hist, CINCPAC, Annex B, USMACTHAI, 1966.

14. Intrvw, Terry Anderson, Texas A&M University, with Maj Gen Charles R. Bond, Jr., USAF Ret, Jul 21, 1981.

15. Clever, pp 272–75.

16. Richard H. Kohn and Joseph P. Harahan, eds, *Air Superiority in World War II and Korea: An Interview with Gen. James Ferguson, Gen. Robert M. Lee, Gen. William Momyer, and Lt. Gen. Elwood R. Quesada* (Washington, 1983), pp 69–72. On Moore's relationship with Westmoreland, see intrvw, Capt Mark Cleary, Air Force historian, with Lt Gen

Joseph H. Moore, San Antonio, Sep 24–27, 1984. In 1941–42 when he was a P–40 squadron commander in the Philippines, Moore earned a reputation for courage and resourcefulness under fire.

17. Intrvw, Lt Col John Dick, Corona Ace, with Gen William W. Momyer, Pentagon, Jan 31, 1977.

18. Intrvw, Lt Col John N. Dick, Jr, Air Force historian, with Brig Gen Cleo M. Bishop, Ft Walton Beach, Fla, Jul 7–8, 1976; intrvw, Lt Col Arthur W. McCants, Air Force historian, with Gen Louis T. Seith, Oct 27–28, 1980; Bond intrvw; Jack Broughton, *Going Downtown: The War Against Hanoi and Washington* (New York, 1988), pp 105–6; Chuck Yeager, *Yeager: An Autobiography* (New York, 1985), pp 380–91; Schlight, *War in South Vietnam*, pp 139–40, 174.

19. Memo, Momyer, subj: Multi-purpose Fighter, May 7, 1968, CHECO microfilm, CH-23-3-6; memo of conversation with Momyer, Oct 5, 1971, Brig Gen Robert N. Ginsburgh, Chief, Office of Air Force History, Ginsburgh Papers, AFHSO; Momyer, reports on Corona Harvest, 1974–75, AFHSO K239.034-2; William W. Momyer, *Air Power in Three Wars* (Washington, 1978) and *The Vietnamese Air Force, 1951–1975* (Washington, 1977). See also Warren A. Trest, *Air Commando One: Heinie Aderholt and America's Secret Air Wars* (Washington, 2000), pp 157–212.

20. Memo, Momyer, "Command and Control in SEA, 1966–1968," Nov 1970, AFHRA K740.131.

21. See esp Capt Robert M. Snakenberg's intrvw with Lt Col David P. Blackbird, Nov 9, 1969, AFHRA K239.0512-302. Blackbird was an intelligence officer at HQ 7 AF in 1966. See also Capt Russell W. Mank, "TACC Fragging Procedures," CHECO rpt, Aug 15, 1969.

22. PACAF, Corona Harvest rpt, "Intelligence Production, 1962–68, Out-Country Targeting," pp 45–49, 106–12.

23. The most highly placed communist agent in Saigon appears to have been Vu Ngoc Nha, adviser to Presidents Diem and Thieu until 1968; see Bui Tin,

Following Ho Chi Minh: Memoirs of a North Vietnamese Colonel (Honolulu, 1995), pp 58–60. On the difficulty of inserting agents into North Vietnam, see John K. Singlaub, *Hazardous Duty* (New York, 1991), pp 302–6; Sedgwick Tourison, *Secret Army, Secret War* (Annapolis, 1996); John L. Plaster, *SOG: the Secret Wars of America's Commandos in Vietnam* (New York, 1997); Richard H. Schultz, Jr., *The Secret War Against Hanoi: Kennedy's and Johnson's Use of Spies, Saboteurs, and Covert Warriors in North Vietnam* (New York, 1999); Kenneth J. Conboy and Dale Andrade, *Spies and Commandos: How America Lost the Secret War in North Vietnam* (Lawrence, Kansas, 2000); Military Assistance Command Studies and Observations Group (MACSOG) annexes to MACV annual histories; JCS MAC-SOG Documentation Study (1970); Tom G. Abbey, "The Role of the USAF in Support of Special Activities in SEA," CHECO rpt, 1976; Charles F. Reske, "Operation Footboy," *Vietnam*, Oct 1995, pp 30–36. Confronted with the failure of its agent insertions, MACSOG made some attempts to deceive the North Vietnamese into worrying about fictitious agents and resistance movements.

24. Intrvw, Col John E. Van Duyn and Maj Richard B. Clement, Corona Harvest, with Gen Hunter Harris, Apr 21, 1971; Adm U.S. Grant Sharp, *Strategy for Defeat* (San Raphael, Calif, 1978); intrvw, Etta-Belle Kitchen, U.S. Naval Institute, with Adm Sharp, Sep 1969–Jun 1970, San Diego.

25. Ltr, Gen Hunter Harris to Gen John P. McConnell, Mar 12, 1966, Corona Harvest 0222694.

26. A good introduction to the influence of thinking about "limited war" is Stephen Peter Rosen, "Vietnam and the American Theory of Limited War," *International Security*, Fall 1982, pp 83–113. On Johnson and MacArthur, see Robert Dallek, *Lone Star Rising: Lyndon Johnson and His Times, 1908–1960* (New York, 1991), pp 397–401.

27. Gallucci, *Neither Peace Nor*

Honor, argues that Johnson and his advisers did not expect Rolling Thunder to do much more than provide the politically necessary prelude for massive intervention on the ground in South Vietnam. See esp p 53.

28. Thomas M. Coffey, *Iron Eagle: The Turbulent Life of General Curtis LeMay* (New York, 1986).

29. Intrvw, author with Gen LeMay, Pentagon, Sep 14, 1985; Deborah Shapley, *Promise and Power: The Life and Times of Robert McNamara* (Boston, 1993), esp p 620, fn 23; Henry L. Trewhitt, *McNamara: His Ordeal in the Pentagon* (New York, 1971), esp p 37. See also Robert S. McNamara with Brian VanDeMark, *In Retrospect: The Tragedy and Lessons of Vietnam* (New York, 1995), esp pp 114–15 and 121 where McNamara recalls LeMay's "stubbornness."

30. Col Reade F. Tilley, USAF Ret, remarks at dedication of LeMay exhibit, National Air and Space Museum's Silver Hill facility, May 17, 1993.

31. LeMay with MacKinlay Kantor, *Mission with LeMay* (New York, 1965), p 565. See also LeMay with Maj Gen Dale O. Smith, *America Is in Danger* (New York, 1968).

32. LeMay, remarks at Bolling Air Force Base, Apr 13, 1984, transcript in Wayne Thompson, ed, *Air Leadership* (Washington, 1986), p 40.

33. LeMay, quoted in Futrell, *Advisory Years*, p 201.

34. LeMay, Offutt AFB, Neb, Mar 15, 1954, quoted in memo of that date by Capt William B. Moore (USN), *International Security*, Winter 1981/82, p 27.

35. Ibid.

36. Lyndon Baines Johnson, *The Vantage Point* (New York, 1971); VanDeMark, *Into the Quagmire*.

37. Intrvw, Dorothy Pierce McSweeny, Lyndon Baines Johnson Library (LBJ Lib), with Gen John P. McConnell, Pentagon, Aug 28, 1969.

38. Intrvw, Lt Col Bissell and Maj Riddlebarger, Corona Harvest, with Col Henry H. Edelen, Jr, Jan 27, 1970; hist, JCS, Vietnam 1960–68, esp chap 25. Lt.

Gen. Charles G. Cooper, USMC Ret, provides a vivid example of the brutal contempt President Johnson sometimes displayed toward the Joint Chiefs in "The Day It Became the Longest War," *Naval Institute Proceedings*, May 1996, pp 77–80.

39. JCS Bombing Chronology, LBJ Lib, National Security File, Agency Reports, Box 33, # 2. See also David C. Humphrey, "Tuesday Lunch at the Johnson White House," *Diplomatic History*, winter 1984, pp 81–101.

40. The JCS 94 target list was incorporated in CINCPAC Operations Plan 37-64, Dec 17, 1964, as Appendix VII to Annex R. See PACAF, Corona Harvest rpt, "Out-Country Strike Operations, 1965–68," vol V, pt I, "Plans, Concepts and Doctrine," AFHSO K717.03-22, pp A-2-1–6.

41. JCS Bombing Chronology.

42. The growth of the target lists is discussed in PACAF, Corona Harvest rpt, "Targeting Out-Country (NVN), 1962–68," AFHSO K717.03-1, pp 55–62.

43. See 7 AF's Tiger Out-Country Active Target List, Jun 1969, AFHRA K740.323-5.

44. Keith W. Taylor, *The Birth of Vietnam* (Berkeley, Calif, 1983); Alexander Woodside, *Vietnam and the Chinese Model* (Cambridge, Mass, 1971); Joseph Buttinger, *The Smaller Dragon* (New York, 1958) and *Vietnam: The Dragon Embattled* (New York, 1967).

45. Martin J. Murray, *The Development of Capitalism in Colonial Indochina (1870–1940)* (Berkeley, Calif, 1980); Virginia Thompson, *French Indochina* (London, 1937); Charles Robequain, *The Economic Development of French Indo-China* (London, 1944).

46. Cadet Robert L. Cummings, Jr., USAFA, "The Vietnamese Railroad System," 1984, AFHSO; Chen Jian, "China's Involvement in the Vietnam War," *China Quarterly*, Jun 1995, pp 356–87; Xiaoming Zhang, "The Vietnam War, 1964–1969: A Chinese Perspective," *Journal of Military History*, Oct 1996, pp 731–62; John W. Garver, "The Chinese Threat in

the Vietnam War," *Parameters*, spring 1992; Qiang Zhai, "Beijing and the Vietnam Conflict, 1964–1965: New Chinese Evidence," Cold War International History Project (CWIHP) *Bulletin*, winter 1995–96, pp 233–50, "Beijing and the Vietnam Peace Talks, 1965–68: New Evidence from Chinese Sources," CWIHP, Working Paper No. 18, Jun 1997, and *China and the Vietnam Wars, 1950–1975* (Chapel Hill, North Carolina, 2000); Smith, *International History of the Vietnam War*; Allen S. Whiting, *The Chinese Calculus of Deterrence* (Ann Arbor, 1975) and "China's Role in the Vietnam War," in Jayne Werner and David Hunt, eds, *The American War in Vietnam* (Ithaca, NY, 1993), pp 71–76. According to Chen Jian, the number of Chinese troops in North Vietnam peaked at about 170,000 in 1967; Whiting's estimate had been 50,000. In 1998 the Cold War International History Project published the transcript of a 13 Apr 1966 conversation in which both Le Duan of North Vietnam and Deng Xiaoping of China confirmed that at least 100,000 Chinese military personnel were already in North Vietnam. See Odd Arne Westad, et al., eds, "77 Conversations Between Chinese and Foreign Leaders on the Wars in Indochina, 1964–1977," CWIHP, Working Paper No. 22, May 1998.

47. Momyer, *Air Power in Three Wars*, pp 174–88.

48. Col Delbert Corum, et al., *The Tale of Two Bridges* (Washington, 1976).

49. When veterans and other Americans began to visit Vietnam in the 1980s, the Vietnamese made a tourist attraction of the tunnels at Vinh Moc near the coast a few miles north of the former Demilitarized Zone. See Daniel Robinson and Joe Cummings, *Vietnam, Laos and Cambodia: A Travel Survival Kit* (Berkeley, Calif, 1991), pp 309–10; Susan Brownmiller, *Seeing Vietnam* (New York, 1994), pp 173–78; and Janet Gardner's film *A World Beneath the War* (New York, 1997).

50. PACAF, "Summary of Air Operations in SEA," monthly reports, Oct 1966–Oct 1967.

51. Memo, Maj R. N. Smedes, HQ USAF Plans, to CSAF, subj: CINCPAC Meeting with JCS, Sep 15, 1966.

52. Msg, Lt Gen Moore to Lt Gen Compton, HQ USAF DCS/Plans and Ops, 080520Z Nov 1966.

53. Ibid.

54. Ibid.

55. Momyer, *Air Power in Three Wars*, pp 174–75; Sharp intrvw.

56. Van Staaveren, *Interdiction in Southern Laos*, pp 255–83.

57. The gradual evolution of McNamara's thinking on Rolling Thunder can be traced in his *In Retrospect*. See esp pp 207–71.

58. Walt Rostow described his Washington experience in *The Diffusion of Power* (New York, 1972) and London target planning in *Pre-Invasion Bombing Strategy* (Austin, Tex, 1981); see also his *The Stages of Economic Growth: A Non-Communist Manifesto* (Cambridge, England, 1960). For examples of his advocacy of bombing oil and electricity targets in 1965, see the State Department's *Foreign Relations of the United States* (hereafter *FRUS*), *1964–1968*, II, 378–80 and 692–98. On the Bundys, see Kai Bird, *The Color of Truth: McGeorge Bundy and William Bundy* (New York, 1998).

59. Intrvw, Col John E. Van Duyn and Maj Richard B. Clement, Corona Harvest, with Maj Gen Robert N. Ginsburgh, May 26, 1971; Humphrey, "Tuesday Lunch at the Johnson White House," pp 81–101.

60. Intrvw, Maj Samuel E. Riddlebarger and Capt R.G. Swenston, Corona Harvest, with Walt Rostow, Oct 17, 1970.

61. Memo, Ginsburgh for Gen Wheeler, subj: Flooding the Red River, Mar 8, 1968, JCS Chron File, Ginsburgh papers, AFHSO; Ginsburgh intrvw, May 26, 1971; intrvw, Robert Pape with Ginsburgh, Apr 5, 1990; intrvw, James C. Hasdorff, USAF historian, with Brig Gen Noel F. Parrish, Jun 10–14, 1974; McConnell intrvw, Aug 28, 1969; Robert F. Futrell, *The United States Air Force in Korea* (New York, 1961), pp 623–29.

62. On Vietnamese communism and its leaders, see Bui Tin, *Following Ho Chi Minh*; William J. Duiker, *The Communist*

Road to Power in Vietnam (Boulder, Colo, 1981); Bernard B. Fall, *The Two Viet-Nams* (New York, 1963); James Pinckney Harrison, *The Endless War* (New York, 1982); John T. McAlister, Jr., *Viet Nam: The Origins of Revolution* (New York, 1969); Douglas Pike, *History of Vietnam-ese Communism* (Stanford, Calif, 1978); Thai Quang Trung, *Collective Leadership and Factionalism: An Essay on Ho Chi Minh's Legacy* (Singapore, 1985); William S. Turley, "Origins and Development of Communist Military Leadership in Vietnam," *Armed Forces and Society*, Feb 1977, pp 219–47.

63. See esp Bui Tin's memoirs. See also Robert J. O'Neill, *General Giap: Pol-itician and Strategist* (New York, 1969); Peter MacDonald, *Giap: The Victor in Vietnam* (New York, 1993); John Colvin, *Giap: Volcano Under Snow* (New York, 1996); Cecil B. Currey, *Victory At Any Cost: The Genius of Viet Nam's Gen. Vo Nguyen Giap* (Washington, 1997); Douglas Pike, *PAVN: People's Army of Vietnam* (Novato, Calif, 1986); Vo Nguyen Giap, *People's War, People's Army* (New York, 1962) with a foreword by Roger Hilsman and a profile of Giap by Bernard B. Fall; Vo Nguyen Giap, *People's War Against U.S. Aero-Naval War* (Hanoi, 1975).

64. Futrell, *Advisory Years*, pp 230–31; Zoltan Buza and Istvan Toperczer, "MiG–17 over Vietnam," *Wings of Fame*, VIII (1997), pp 100–117.

65. Ilya V. Gaiduk, *The Soviet Union and the Vietnam War* (Chicago, 1996), pp 57–72.

66. On the question of North Viet-nam's fear of excessive Chinese interven-tion, Douglas Pike expresses skepticism in his *Vietnam and the Soviet Union* (Boulder, Colo, 1987) p 86; and Gaiduk, *The Soviet Union and the Vietnam War*, pp 65 and 266, argues the opposite position. See also William J. Duiker, *China and Vietnam: The Roots of Conflict* (Berkeley, Calif, 1986); Eugene K. Lawson, *The Sino-Vietnamese Conflict* (New York, 1984); F. Charles Parker IV, *Vietnam: Strategy for a Stalemate* (New York, 1989); W. R. Smyser, *The Independent Vietnamese:*

Vietnamese Communism between Russia and China, 1956–1969 (Athens, Ohio, 1980); and the works already cited by Allen Whiting, Chen Jian, John Garver, and Qiang Zhai.

67. On the growth of American knowledge about the MiG–17 and the MiG–21, see the USAF Tactical Fighter Weapons Center's Project Red Baron reports on air-to-air encounters in SEA, esp Red Baron II, vol II, pt 1 (Nellis AFB, Nev, 1973), appendices A–C, and Red Baron III, vol III, pt 1 (Nellis AFB, Nev, 1974), pp 5–30. See also Michel, *Clashes*, esp pp 75–81; and Curtis Peebles, *Dark Eagles: A History of Top Secret U.S. Air-craft Programs* (Novato, Calif, 1995), pp 217–43; Robert L. Young, "The Influence of the North Vietnamese MiG–21 Fighter on the U.S. Air Force Air-to-Air Kill Ratio in Southeast Asia," MA thesis, Central Missouri State University, 1995. Early in 1968, HQ PACAF DCS/Intelligence sum-med up the air-to-air combat experience of Rolling Thunder in "North Vietnamese Air Force Fighter Patterns," AFHRA 1000673. Also in 1968, the Air Force tested a MiG–21 (Project Have Doughnut), and the next year two MiGs (Project Have Drill/ Have Ferry); in 1997 the Air Force's National Air Intelligence Center declassi-fied the technical exploitation reports for both projects as well as the Have Drill/ Have Ferry tactical exploitation report.

68. "SA–2" was the North Atlantic Treaty Organization (NATO) designation for the Soviet "V–75 Dvina." See Maj A. Dokuchayev, "'We Too Defended Viet-nam': Participants in Combat Operations Tell Their Story," *Krasnaya Zvezda*, Moscow, Apr 13, 1989, JPRS-UMA-89-015, pp 54–56; Lt Col A. Dokuchayev, article in *Krasnaya Zvezda*, Dec 29, 1990, JPRS-UMA-91-005, pp 133–36; Mark Vorobyov, "Dvina: Guarding Vietnam's Skies," *Military Parade*, Jul–Aug 1998, pp 101–3. See also Steven J. Zaloga, *Soviet Air Defense Missiles* (Coulsdon, England, 1997), pp 36–76. On Dang Tinh, see Turley, "Origins and Development," pp 237–38.

69. Notes of meeting, White House,

May 16, 1965, 6:45 pm, LBJ Lib, Meeting Notes File, published in *FRUS, 1964–1968,* II, 665–68. See also Hist, JCS, Vietnam 1960–68, pp 26–1–5. McNaughton raised an alarm over the danger of Russian SAM sites in North Vietnam as a possible "flash point" even before reconnaissance aircraft provided evidence of their construction. See McNaughton's draft memo of Mar 24, 1965, "Plan of Action for South Vietnam," *The Pentagon Papers: The Senator Gravel Edition* (Boston, 1971), III, 348–51.

70. Notes of meeting in Cabinet Room, Jul 22, 1965, noon, LBJ Lib, Meeting Notes File, published in *FRUS, 1964–1968,* III, 212.

71. Ibid., p 213. Brown did not actually replace Eugene Zuckert as Secretary of the Air Force until Oct 1, 1965.

72. Notes of meetings in Cabinet Room, Jul 26, 1965, 12:30 pm and 6:10 pm, LBJ Lib, Meeting Notes File, published in *FRUS, 1964–1968,* III, 240–57. For Ball's account of his role in the Johnson administration's deliberations on Vietnam, see his *The Past Has Another Pattern* (New York, 1982); see also James A. Bill, *George Ball: Behind the Scenes in U.S. Foreign Policy* (New Haven, Conn, 1997) and David L. DiLeo, *George Ball, Vietnam, and the Rethinking of Containment* (Chapel Hill, NC, 1991).

73. Capt Melvin F. Porter, "Air Tactics Against NVN Air/Ground Defenses," CHECO rpt, Feb 27, 1967. See also John Morrocco, *Thunder from Above* (Boston, 1984), pp 106–10. As a young officer, Gen. Charles A. Horner (who led coalition air forces in the Gulf War) flew on this mission; see his recollections in Al Santoli, *Leading the Way: How Vietnam Veterans Rebuilt the U.S. Military, An Oral History* (New York, 1993), pp 21–22.

74. Bernard C. Nalty, *Tactics and Techniques of Electronic Warfare: Electronic Countermeasures in the Air War Against North Vietnam, 1965–1973* (Washington, 1977), pp 31–52.

75. See Jon M. Van Dyke, *North Vietnam's Strategy for Survival* (Palo Alto, Calif, 1972), a study based on the North Vietnamese press and accounts by foreign visitors.

76. Johnson, *Vantage Point,* p 136.

77. Notes of meeting, President's Office, May 16, 1965, 6:45 pm, LBJ Lib, Meeting Notes File, published in *FRUS, 1964–1968,* II, 665–68.

78. Gravel, *Pentagon Papers,* IV, pp 32–53. McNamara's *In Retrospect* devotes a chap to the "Christmas Bombing Pause." For the North Vietnamese role in these negotiations, see Robert K. Brigham, "Vietnamese-American Peace Negotiations: The Failed 1965 Initiatives," *Journal of American-East Asian Relations,* winter 1995, pp 377–95.

79. See Johnson, *Vantage Point,* pp 578–91 for a list of peace initiatives. The best introduction to the negotiations is Allan E. Goodman, *The Lost Peace: America's Search for a Negotiated Settlement of the Vietnam War* (Stanford, Calif, 1978), supplemented by his later abridged and updated account, *The Search for a Negotiated Settlement of the Vietnam War* (Berkeley, Calif, 1986).

Chapter 2

1. 7 AFP 552, Rolling Thunder Operations, Jul 15, 1968; Hopkins, *Tanker Operations*; Sharp intrvw, Mar 14, 1970.

2. Nalty, *Electronic Warfare,* pp 10–13; DIA/JCS, *Southeast Asia Military Fact Book,* Jan 1967.

3. Msg, JCS to CINCPAC, 110011Z Nov 66.

4. Memo, Maj C. W. Myers, Dir/ Plans, USAF, to CSAF, subj: Rolling Thunder 52, Aug 18, 1966.

5. Gravel, *Pentagon Papers,* IV, 71–74; study, Naval Systems Analysis Group, Effectiveness of Air Strikes Against North Vietnam, Oct 1966.

6. Msg, JCS to CINCPAC, 111708Z Nov 66; Edelen intrvw [Edelen was a USAF liaison on JCS Rolling Thunder tar-

get selection team (65–68)].

7. See note above.

8. David C. Humphrey, ed, *Foreign Relations of the United States, 1964–1968, IV, Vietnam 1966* (Washington, 1998), pp 890–987; Defense Dept, *US-Vietnam Relations 1945–1967* (Washington, 1971), VI, C, 2, published in George C. Herring, ed, *The Secret Diplomacy of the Vietnam War: The Negotiating Volumes of the Pentagon Papers* (Austin, Tex, 1983), pp 209–370; Jerzy Michalowski, "Polish Secret Peace Initiatives in Vietnam," *Cold War International History Project Bulletin*, winter 1995–96, pp 241, 258–59; Wallace J. Thies, *When Governments Collide*; Goodman, *Lost Peace*; David Kraslow and Stuart H. Loory, *The Secret Search for Peace in Vietnam* (New York, 1968).

9. Msg, Wheeler to Sharp, 10 Dec 66, in JCS Official Record, Rolling Thunder 52, sec 13; msgs, US Embassy Poland to State Dept, Dec 7, 1966, and State to embassy, Dec 10, 1966, both in DOD negotiations vols, VI, C, 2, p 44. See also McNamara, *In Retrospect*, pp 249–50.

10. DOD, *US-Vietnam Relations 1945–1967*, VI, C, 2, p 13; msgs, PACAF to 7 AF, 232345Z Dec 66 and 152020Z Dec 66; msg, CINCPAC to CINCPACAF, 151938Z Dec 66. The North Vietnamese may still have been willing to talk after the Dec 2–4 bombing, but not after the Dec 13–14 bombing; see especially James G. Hershberg with L.W. Gluchowski, "Who Murdered 'Marigold'?—New Evidence on the Mysterious Failure of Poland's Secret Peace Initiative to Start U.S.-North Vietnamese Peace Talks, 1966," Cold War International History Project, Working Paper No. 27, Feb 2000.

11. Ibid.

12. William M. Hammond, *The United States Army in Vietnam: The Military and the Media, 1962–1968* (Washington, 1988), pp 272–79; *Baltimore Sun*, Dec 14, 1966; msg, NMCC to JCS, 152025Z Dec 66.

13. *Washington Post*, Dec 30, 1966.

14. Phil G. Goulding, *Confirm or Deny: Informing the People on National Security* (New York, 1970), p 67. See also hearings, Committee on Foreign Relations, Senate, *Trip to North Vietnam*, 90th Cong, 1st sess (Washington, 1967); memo, W.P. Bundy, State Dept, on conversation between British Ambassador Sir Patrick Dean and Secretary of State Dean Rusk, Dec 30, 1966.

15. Tom Wolfe, "The Truest Sport: Jousting with Sam and Charlie," *Esquire*, Oct 1975, p 230.

16. *New York Times*, Dec 25, 1966 Jan 18, 1967; Harrison E. Salisbury, *Behind the Lines-Hanoi* (New York, 1967); intrvw, Paige E. Mulhollan, Univ of Tex oral hist proj, with Harrison E. Salisbury, New York City, Jun 26, 1969. In his *A Time of Change* (New York, 1988), Salisbury revealed his belief that the North Vietnamese sought to send a peace feeler through him to the Johnson administration, but that Johnson would not see him and Rusk would not listen. Rusk did send Johnson a four-page memo describing Salisbury's conversation with Pham Van Dong and suggesting there was probably nothing new in it. See Rusk's memo of Jan 14, 1967, in the LBJ Lib, National Security File, Memos to the President, vol 18, #8a.

17. See note above.

18. *New York Times*, Dec 27, 1966.

19. Ibid.

20. PACAF, "Summary of Air Operations in SEA," Dec 1966; study, Dir/Ops and ACS/Intel, USAF, Analysis of Planned Target Systems in North Vietnam, Mar 10, 1967.

21. *New York Times*, Dec 27, 1966.

22. Intrvw, Tom Belden, Jacob Van Staaveren, and Hugh Ahman, USAF hist prog, with Harold Brown, Pasadena, Calif, Aug 29–30, 1972 AFHRA K239.0512-620 [Brown was Secretary of the Air Force (1965–1969)]; memo, Under Sec State Nicholas Katzenbach to Dep Sec Def Cyrus Vance, subj: Civilian Casualties in North Vietnam, Jan 26, 1967.

23. Rpt, Maj Bernard Appel and Capt Philip R. Meinert, 7 AF, Bombing Accuracy in a Combat Environment, May 10, 1968; rpt, E.H. Sharkey, RAND, Weapon Delivery Accuracy of USAF Strike Fighters, Aug 10, 1966; Bernard Appel,

"Bombing Accuracy in a Combat Environment," *Air University Review*, Jul–Aug 1975, pp 38–52.

24. DIA/JCS, *SEA Military Fact Book*, Jan 1967.

25. PACAF, "Summary of Air Operations in SEA," 1966.

26. *New York Times*, Dec 27, 1966; msg, CINCPAC to JCS, 230440Z Dec 66; msg, 7 AF to PACAF, 181410Z Dec 66.

27. Goulding, *Confirm or Deny*, pp 52–92.

28. *New York Times*, Dec 29, 1966.

29. Salisbury, *Behind*, pp 182–84.

30. *Washington Post*, Feb 12, 1967.

31. PACAF, "Summary of Air Operations in SEA," Jun–Sep 1966; rpt, Col H.W. Hise, J–3, Factors Affecting A/C Losses in SEA, Sep 1966; memos, Dep Sec Def Vance to Sec AF, Sec Nav, and ASD/I&L, Oct 29, 1966; memo, Vance to Sec AF, Sec Nav, CJCS, DDRE, Dir DIA, Jan 10, 1967; CM-2073-67, Study to Reexamine the US Air Campaign Against the North Vietnam Air Defense System, Jan 20, 1967; rpt, JCS Night Song Study Gp, Mar 30, 1967.

32. See note above.

33. See note 31; Nalty, *Electronic Warfare*, p 53.

34. Appel and Meinert rpt; Sharkey rpt. The pattern of increasing dive bomb release altitude and decreasing accuracy repeated the Korean War experience. See 5 AF Operations Analysis Memo No. 69, "History of Bombing Accuracy During the Korean War," Sep 9, 1953.

35. Institute for Defense Analysis, *Analysis of Combat Aircraft Losses in Southeast Asia* (Washington, 1968); Hise rpt.

36. PACAF, "Summary of Air Operations in SEA," Aug 1966, May 1967.

37. PACAF, Corona Harvest rpt, "In-Country and Out-Country Strike Operations, 1 Jan 1965–31 Dec 1969," vol II, "Hardware," sec 2, "Munitions," 1971, pp 29–50; msg, 7 AF to PACAF, 111330Z Feb 67.

38. PACAF, "Summary of Air Operations in SEA," Dec 1966.

39. Ibid.

40. Nalty, *Electronic Warfare*.

41. Institute for Defense Analysis, *Analysis of Combat Aircraft Losses in SEA*; briefing, Brig Gen Robin Olds to Corona Harvest staff, Maxwell AFB, Ala, Sep 29, 1969.

42. Rpt, Robert E. Hiller and Samuel J. Scott, Ops An, 7 AF, Comparison of Dive Bomb Tactics Between 355th TFW and 308th TFW, May 1967.

43. End-of-tour report (EOTR), Brig Gen William S. Chairsell, Cmdr 388th TFW, Jul 8, 1967; Appel and Meinert rpt; 7 AFP 55-2, Rolling Thunder Operations, Jul 15, 1968: Maj John C. Pratt, "Air Tactics Against NVN Air Ground Defenses, December 1966–November 1968," CHECO rpt, 1969.

44. See note above.

45. EOTR, Col Robin Olds, Cmdr 8th TFW, Aug 31, 1967; Olds briefing, Sep 29, 1969; Hopkins, *Tanker Operations*; Col Jack Broughton, *Thud Ridge* (Philadelphia, 1969).

46. DJSM-10-67, atch IIa, Impact of MiG Threat on US Operations Over NVN, Jan 3, 1967; msg, PACAF to AFCP, 142145 Dec 66; msg, CSAF to CINC-PACAF, 151539Z Dec 66.

47. Olds briefing, Sep 29, 1969; intrvw, unidentified Corona Harvest interviewer with Col Olds, Comdr 8th TFW, Jul 12, 1967; Intrvw, Maj Geffen and Maj Folkman, Corona Harvest, with Col Robin Olds, Colo Springs, 1968, AFHRA K239.0512-051.2; Olds EOTR; Ralph Wetterhahn, "Operation Bolo," *Retired Officer Magazine*, Nov 1995, pp 39–43.

48. Rpt, Lt Col C. H. Asay, Maj J.D. Covington, and Capt J.B. Stone, 8th TFW, History of Operation Bolo, no date; Maj Dale F. Tippett, "Operation Bolo," Corona Harvest rpt, 1971; Institute for Defense Analysis, *Air-to-Air Encounters in Southeast Asia*, vol I (Washington, 1967); Lt Charles H. Hefron Jr, "Air-to-Air Encounters in Southeast Asia, 1 Jan–30 Jun 1967," CHECO rpt, 1967.

49. See notes 54 and 55; msg, CSAF to AFLC, 232319Z Dec 66.

50. On Olds' World War II service, see Hub Zemke with Roger A. Freeman,

Zemke's Wolf Pack (New York, 1988), pp 194–201.

51. DIA/JCS, *SEA Military Fact Book*, Jan 1967; rpt, Maj Gordon Y. W. Ow, Ops An, 7 AF, Mission Bolo, Feb 13, 1967.

52. See note above.

53. See note 51; rpt on MiG kill, Olds, Jan 2, 1967.

54. See note above.

55. Msg, 7 AF to PACAF, 240144Z Apr 67; Institute for Defense Analysis, *Air-to-Air Encounters in SEA*, vol III (Washington, 1969).

56. Msgs, Wheeler to Sharp and Westmoreland, 170001Z Feb 67, 181602Z Feb 67, and 222246Z Feb 67.

57. Msg, Wheeler to Sharp and Westmoreland, 181602Z Feb 67.

58. Msg, 7 AF to PACAF, 110905Z Feb 67; msg, CINCPAC to JCS, 242256Z Feb 67; Gravel, *Pentagon Papers*, vol IV, p 144.

59. DOD, *US-Vietnam Relations 1945–1967*, VI, C, 3; Thies, *When Governments Collide*; Goodman, *Lost Peace*; Kraslow and Loory, *Secret Search*; Johnson, *Vantage Point*; Harold Wilson, *A Personal Record: The Labor Government, 1964–1970* (Boston, 1971); Chester Cooper, *The Lost Crusade: America in Vietnam* (New York, 1970); intrvw, Paige E. Mulhollan, Univ of Tex oral hist proj, with Chester Cooper, Arlington, Va, Jul 9–Aug 7, 1969.

60. DOD, *US-Vietnam Relations 1945–1967*, VI, C, 3, p 62.

61. Ibid.

62. Rpt, Dir/Ops and ACS/Intel, USAF, Analysis of Planned Target Systems in North Vietnam, Mar 10, 1967; *Defense Intelligence Digest*, DIA, Jun 1967, p 49; Van Dyke, *North Vietnam's Strategy for Survival*; Fall, *The Two Viet-Nams*.

63. PACAF, "Summary of Air Operations in SEA," Jan 1967 and Feb 1967.

64. Recommendation for decoration, 354th TFS for Capt Merlyn H. Dethlefsen, Jun 12, 1967; intrvw, Hugh N. Ahmann, USAF oral hist prog, with Dethlefsen, Maxwell AFB, Ala, Dec 20, 1971; recommendation for decoration, 357th TFS for

Maj Leo K. Thorsness, Jul 19, 1967; PACAF, "Summary of Air Operations in SEA," Mar 1967.

65. Maj Robert S. Deas, Air Command and Staff College, "Thai Nguyen Iron and Steel Complex," draft Corona Harvest rpt, Jan 1970; Lt Col Deas, Air War College, "Two Days at Thai Nguyen," draft AU SEA mono, Jul 1976; Maj Jack A. Phillips, Air Command and Staff College, "Thai Nguyen Steel Mill," draft Corona Harvest rpt, Feb 1970.

66. See note above; "Weekly Intelligence Summary," 7 AF, Mar 19 and Apr 9, 1967.

67. Msg, 380th TFW to 7 AF, 161225Z Mar 67; "Weekly Intelligence Summary," 7 AF, Apr 2, 1967; PACAF, "Summary of Air Operations in SEA," Mar–Apr 1967; DCS Intel, HQ PACAF, and ACS Intel, HQ HQ USAF, *The Effects of United States Air Operations in Southeast Asia*, 2 vols, (Hickam AFB, Hawaii, 1969).

68. Intrvw, Col John E. Van Duyn and Maj Richard B. Clement, Corona Harvest, with Gen John D. Ryan, CSAF, May 20, 1971.

69. Msg, CINCPACAF to 7 AF, 200310 Feb 67; intrvw, James C. Hasdorff, USAF oral hist prog, with Gen Ryan, San Antonio, Tex, May 15–17, 1979.

70. Rpt, DCS/Plans and Ops, USAF, Combat Target Task Force, Oct 1967.

71. Msg, 388th TFW to 7 AF, 260645Z Jan 67; Chairsell EOTR.

72. Ryan intrvw, May 20, 1971.

73. Msg, CINCPAC to CINCPAC-FLT, 030516Z Apr 67; msg, CINCPAC to CINCPACFLT, 182238Z Mar 67; msg, CINCPAC to COMUSMACV, 240315Z Mar 67.

74. Maj Albert L. Michael, "Ryan's Raiders," Corona Harvest rpt, 1970.

75. Lt Col John A. Ryan, Jr, "LABS," *Air University Review*, spring 1957, pp 92–99.

76. Intrvw, Dr. James C. Hasdorff, USAF Academy, with Col Ben M. Pollard, USAF Ret, May 12, 1992. A radar operator, Maj Pollard was the Raiders' highest-ranking officer.

77. PACAF, "Summary of Air Operations in SEA," May 1967; Pollard intrvw. Maj Pollard was operating the radar when his F–105F was hit by flak just before bomb release on the Kep rail yard strike.

78. Ryan intrvw, May 20, 1971; rpt, Dir/Ops, USAF, Commando Nail, May 9, 1968; msg, 7 AF to CSAF, 201200Z Dec 1967.

79. PACAF, "Summary of Air Operations in SEA," Apr–May 1967.

80. *Baltimore Sun*, Apr 21, 1967.

81. Ibid.

82. Ibid.

83. Msg, CJCS to CINCPAC, 222239Z Apr 67; memo, Maj R. A. Eubank, Dir/Plans, USAF, to CSAF, subj: Operations Against North Vietnam, Apr 22, 1967.

84. Rpt, Dir/Ops and ACS/Intel, USAF, Analysis of Planned Target Systems in North Vietnam, Mar 10, 1967.

85. PACAF, "Summary of Air Operations in SEA," Nov 1967; *Defense Intelligence Digest*, DIA, Aug 1965, Sep 1966, Aug 1967.

86. PACAF, "Summary of Air Operations in SEA," Apr 1967; HQ PACAF and HQ USAF, *Effects of United States Air Operations in SEA*.

87. Msgs, CINCPAC to JCS, 230037Z Mar 67 and 182222Z Mar 67; msgs, CINCPAC to CINCPACFLT and CINCPACAF, 232100Z Apr 67 and 271920Z Apr 67; msg, CJCS to CINCPAC, 222239Z Apr 67; DIA/JCS, *SEA Military Fact Book*, Jan, 1967.

88. Msg, CINCPAC to CINCPACAF and CINCPACFLT, 100539Z May 67; msg, CINCPAC to JCS, 062317Z May 67; Nalty, *Electronic Warfare*, pp 116–46.

89. Hist, 8th TFW, Jan–Jun 1967; msg, 7 AF to CINCPACAF, 150825Z May 67; PACAF, "Summary of Air Operations in SEA," May 1967; Institute for Defense Analysis, *Air-to-Air Encounters in SEA*, vol III.

90. Hist, 366 TFW, Apr–Sep 1967; Maj Gen Frederick C. Blesse, *Check Six: A Fighter Pilot Looks Back* (Mesa, Ariz, 1987) pp 112–52; Blesse, "No Guts-No Glory," reprinted in *USAF Fighter Weapons Review*, spring 1973, pp 1–28. On Gen Momyer's opposition to putting a gun on the F–4, see the interview with Gen Wilbur L. Creech conducted by Hugh Ahmann of the Air Force history program in Jun 1992.

91. *New York Times*, Apr 25, 1967.

92. Ibid.

93. *Washington Post*, Apr 26, 1967.

94. Ibid.

95. Ibid.

96. Msg, JCS to CINCPAC, 022248Z May 67; Sharp intrvw, Apr 4, 1970.

97. Ginsburgh intrvw, May 26, 1971 [Ginsburgh was JCS liaison on NSC staff (1966–1969)]; hist, JCS, SEA 1960–68, pt III, pp 41-9 and 41-10.

98. PACAF, Corona Harvest rpt, "In-Country and Out-Country Strike Operations, 1 Jan 1965–31 Dec 1969," vol II, "Hardware," sec 2, "Munitions," 1971; Melvin F. Porter, "Second Generation Weapons in SEA," CHECO rpt, 1970; Corum, *The Tale of Two Bridges*; draft mono, Off of AF Hist, The Development of Non-Nuclear Air Munitions for Use in Southeast Asia 1961–1973, no date.

99. Msg, CJCS to CINCPAC, 162100Z May 67; msg, CINCPAC to CINCPACFLT, 200250Z May 67; Ginsburgh intrvw, May 26, 1971; PACAF, "Summary of Air Operations in SEA," May 1967; John Colvin, "Hanoi in My Time," *Washington Quarterly*, spring 1981, pp 143–46.

100. *New York Times*, May 20, 1967; Johnson, *Vantage Point*, p 368; memo, Sec Def to CJCS, subj: Hanoi Prohibited Zone, May 22, 1967; msg, CJCS to CINCPAC, 230144Z May 67.

Chapter 3

1. Gen Westmoreland's troop request of Mar 18, 1967 is quoted extensively in Gravel, *Pentagon Papers*, IV, 427–31.

2. JCSM-218-67 to Sec Def, Apr 20,

1967, quoted in hist, JCS, Vietnam 1960–68, III, chap 43, pp 3–7. See also CSAFM-M-57-67 to JCS, Apr 14, 1967, quoted in hist, JCS, Vietnam 1960–68, III, chap 43, p 3.

3. Notes, meeting of President and advisers, Apr 27, 1967, in *New York Times*, ed, *Pentagon Papers*, pp 567–69. See also memo, W. Rostow to President, Apr 27, 1967, LBJ Lib, National Security File, Memos to the President, vol 26, #35; William C. Westmoreland, *A Soldier Reports* (New York, 1976), pp 227–28.

4. DPM, May 19, 1967, in Gravel, *Pentagon Papers*, IV, 170.

5. Draft memo, McNamara to President, subj: Actions Recommended for Vietnam, Oct 14, 1966, in NYT *Pentagon Papers*, pp 542–51.

6. Memo, W. Rostow to President, Jan 19, 1967, LBJ Lib, NSF, Memos to Pres, vol 19, #119. See also Gibbons, *The U.S. Government and the Vietnam War*, pt IV, pp 479–82.

7. Ginsburgh intrvw, May 26, 1971, AFHRA K239.0512-477; intrvw, LBJ Lib with Nicholas Katzenbach, Nov 23, 1968.

8. Memo, W. Rostow to President, May 9, 1967, LBJ Lib, NSF, Memos to Pres, vol 27, #79; W. Rostow memo to President, May 6, 1967, circulated to No Committee members and quoted in Gravel, *Pentagon Papers*, IV, 162–65.

9. Memo, W. Rostow to President, May 19, 1967, LBJ Lib, NSF, Memos to Pres, vol 28, #63.

10. Johnson, *Vantage Point*, pp 256–57.

11. Memo, Harold Brown to McNamara, Jun 3, 1967, LBJ Lib, NSF, Country File, Vietnam, box 83, 3G, #13; Richard Helms to President, 22 May 67, LBJ Lib, NSF, CF, Vietnam, box 83, 3F, #54.

12. Intrvw, Dorothy Pierce, LBJ Lib, with Harold Brown, Pentagon, Jan 17, 1969; Brown intrvw, Aug 29–30, 1972; draft study, Jacob Van Staaveren, "United States Air Force Operations Against Infiltration in Southern Laos, 1960–1968," Office of Air Force History, 1978, pp 587–624.

13. Hist, JCS, Vietnam 1960–68, III, chap 35, pp 21–30.

14. Intrvws with Harold Brown cited in note 12.

15. PACAF, "Summary of Air Operations in SEA," Jun 1967.

16. The scope of North Vietnam's 1967–68 northeast monsoon transportation effort is given in the *History of the People's Army of Vietnam*, vol II, chap 11, sec 3 (Hanoi, 1994); Merle Pribbenow's translation says that on the "strategic transportation route" Group 559 had 5372 trucks to move 61,000 tons of supplies. See also briefing, Capt R. E. Adamson, Jr, USN, to Sec Def, 19 May 1967, Corona Harvest 0216806; JCS 2472/50, Operations Against North Vietnam, Apr 22, 1967; McNamara testimony, Hearings before the Preparedness Investigation Subcommittee of the Committee on Armed Services, Senate, *Air War Against North Vietnam*, 90th Cong, 1st sess (Washington, 1967), hereafter cited as Stennis hearings, p 277.

17. Memo, W. Rostow to President, Jun 28, 1967, LBJ Lib, NSF, Memos to Pres, vol 32, #44; Jul 6, 1967, vol 33, #35J.

18. Defense Intelligence Digest, Sep 1967, pp 32–33; HQ PACAF and HQ USAF, *Effects of United States Air Operations in SEA*, I, chap 4, pp 10–18; Cummings, "Vietnamese Railroad System".

19. See chap 2.

20. See chap 2.

21. See note 18.

22. Momyer, Presentations to Sec Def, Jul 8, 1967, AFHRA 1002619; CIA/DIA, *An Appraisal of Bombing of North Vietnam*, Sep 1967.

23. Ltr, Gen B.K. Holloway, Vice CSAF, to Gen John D. Ryan, CINCPACAF, Jun 30, 1967, AFHRA 165.06-189.

24. PACAF, "Summary of Air Operations in SEA," May 1967; see also chap 2 above.

25. Intrvw, Wayne Thompson with Col Richard D. Vogel, USAF Ret. Melbourne, Fla, Jun 13, 1986; HQ PACAF DCS/Intel, Index of USAF Personnel MIA/POW in Southeast Asia, 1974.

26. JCS Bombing Chronology, Sep 1967, LBJ Lib, NSF, Agency Reports, box 33; hist, JCS, Vietnam 1960–68, III, chap 44, pp 1–2.

27. Ibid.; Momyer briefing cited in note 22.

28. PACAF, "Summary of Air Operations in SEA," Jun 1967.

29. Msg, Sharp to Wheeler, subj: Turkestan Incident, 190245Z Jun 67; msg, Ryan to McConnell, subj: Soviet Ship Incident, 172140Z Jun 67; msg, Ryan to McConnell, 18142026Z Jun 67; msg, Maj Gen William G. Lindley, Jr., Deputy Cmdr 7/13 AF, to Sharp, subj: Turkestan Incident, 181450Z Jun 67; all in PACAF msg file, "Alleged Bombing of Soviet Ship 'Turkestan'," AFHRA K717.052-4.

30. Msg, CINCPAC to NMCC, Jun 2, 1967, LBJ Lib, NSF, Memos to Pres, vol 30, 3108a; memo, W. Rostow to Pres, LBJ Lib, NSF, Memos to Pres, Jun 3, 1967, vol 30, #108; State Dept Bulletin, Jun 26, 1967, p 953, quotes U.S. note delivered to Soviet charge d'affaires, Washington, Jun 3, 1967; Goulding, *Confirm or Deny*, pp 139–52.

31. U.S. notes delivered to Soviet Embassy, Washington, Jun 20, 1967, quoted in State Dept Bulletin, Jul 10, 1967, p 44; memo of conversation, Rusk with Dobrynin, Jun 16, 1967, LBJ Lib, NSF, Memos to Pres, vol 31, #38c; Broughton, *Thud Ridge* and *Going Downtown*; McNamara, *In Retrospect*, p 245.

32. U.S. note delivered to Soviet Ministry of Foreign Affairs, Jul 13, 1967, quoted in State Dept Bulletin, Aug 7, 1967, pp 170–71; msg, CINCPAC to CINCPACFLT, CINCPACAF, and COMUSMACV, 010430Z Jul 1967.

33. Gravel, *Pentagon Papers*, IV, 198.

34. Sharp intrvw, Apr 4, 1970; Sharp, *Strategy for Defeat*, pp 177–85; msgs, Sharp to Westmoreland, 192000Z Jun 1967 and 2703282 Z Jun 67, Westmoreland's Back Channel File, Army Center of Military History; McNamara, *In Retrospect*, p 283.

35. Momyer's second briefing, Jul 8, 1967, AFHRA 1002619.

36. Meeting, White House, Jul 12, 1967, LBJ Lib, Tom Johnson's Notes, box 1, #38a; hist, JCS, Vietnam 1960–68, III, chap 43, p 29; memo, W. Rostow to President, Jul 17, 1967, LBJ Lib, NSF, Memos to Pres, vol 35, #106, and Jul 18, 1967, #88; Evans and Novak column, *Washington Post*, Aug 4, 1967, p 19; Stennis hearings, p 65.

37. Cabinet meeting, White House, Jul 19, 1967, LBJ Lib, Tom Johnson's Notes, box 1, #38a.

38. Memo, W. Rostow to President, Aug 9, 1967, LBJ Lib, NSF, Memos to Pres, vol 37, #17.

39. JCS Bombing Chronology, Sep 1967, LBJ Lib, NSF, Agency Reports, box 33; hist, JCS, Vietnam 1960–68, III, chap 44, pp 1–2.

40. See note above.

41. "CSAF Concept for Isolation of the Port of Haiphong," Jul 19, 1967; hist, JCS, Vietnam 1960–68, III, chap 44, pp 6–7; msg, CINCPACFLT to CINCPAC, 312154Z Jul 1967, PACAF DO Read File, AFHRA K717.312.

42. Hist, JCS, Vietnam, 1960–68, III, chap 44, p 7; see chap 2 above, pp 4–7. Although Gen McConnell argued to increase the Navy's armed reconnaissance authority in the Haiphong donut rather than send Air Force planes there, some of his subordinates continued to call for an end to route packages. See the Jul 1967 study prepared for Secretary Brown by McConnell's targeting staff under Col Edward Ratkovich, "Targeting Concept for NVN," AFHRA 1000574, which lists 22 highway bridges, causeways and ferries around Haiphong together with nearly 300 other recommended targets in North Vietnam: "Route packages and assignment of areas of responsibility to the different air forces must be eliminated." When briefed by Ratkovich on Jul 29, Secretary Brown remarked dryly that "the only targets you have not recommended are fire-bomb raids against the cities, towns, and villages" (quoted by Maj Gen Simler in cover letter). By then McConnell had already skimmed the cream of this study for his Haiphong donut proposal, and

Brown could only ask Ratkovich to develop recommendations for "incremental changes in policy" (i.e., nothing so dramatic as an end to route packages).

43. Memo, W. Rostow to President, Jul 31, 1967, LBJ Lib, NSF, Memos to Pres, vol 36, #12.

44. Memo, W. Rostow to President, Jul 27, 1967, LBJ Lib, NSF, Memos to Pres, vol 36, #50.

45. Intrvw, Joe B. Frantz, LBJ Lib, with Senator John Stennis, Washington, Jun 17, 1972.

46. Memo, W. Rostow to President, Aug 1, 1967, LBJ Lib, NSF, Memos to Pres, vol 37, #121.

47. Intrvw, Michael L. Gillette, LBJ Lib, with Symington, Washington, Nov 28, 1977.

48. "Airpower Probe," *Aviation Week*, Jul 3, 1967, p 7; Stennis hearings, pp 10–11, 406.

49. Summary Report by Preparedness Investigation Subcommittee of the Committee on Armed Services, Senate, *Air War Against North Vietnam*, 90th Cong, 1st sess (Washington, 1967), hereafter cited as Stennis report.

50. Stennis hearings, p 8.

51. Ibid., p 14.

52. Ibid., p 10–11.

53. Ibid., p 13.

54. Memo, W. Rostow to Pres, Aug 9, 1967, LBJ Lib, NSF, Memos to Pres, vol 37, #32.

55. Ibid.

56. Stennis hearings, p 140.

57. Ibid., pp 136–38.

58. Ibid., p 168.

59. Notes by Jim Jones of meeting of President and advisers, Aug 18, 1967, LBJ Lib, Meeting Notes File, #118.

60. Ibid.

61. Stennis hearings, p 209.

62. Ibid., p 335.

63. Ibid., p 281.

64. Ibid., p 307.

65. Stennis report, p 9.

66. Stennis hearings, p 70.

67. Ibid., p 228.

68. Ibid., p 142.

69. Ibid., p 277.

70. Press conf, Sep 1, 1967, *Public Papers of the President*, 1967, II, p 816.

71. Ibid., p 818.

72. CIA intel info cable, Oct 4, 1967, LBJ Lib, NSF, Memos to Pres, vol 44, #59a.

73. NSC meeting, Nov 29, 1967, noon, LBJ Lib, Tom Johnson's Notes, box 1, #136a.

74. Ltr, Moorer to author, Mar 24, 1989; telcon, author with Greene, Mar 20, 1989. The Aug resignation allegation was made public by Mark Perry in his *Four Stars* (Boston, 1989), pp 163–66. The May resignation allegation appeared in Phillip B. Davidson, *Vietnam at War* (Novato, Calif, 1988), p 463. Perry's account has received support from Lewis Sorley, *Honorable Warrior: General Harold K. Johnson and the Ethics of Command* (Lawrence, Kan, 1998), pp 268–70, 285–87 and 303–4.

75. Intrvw, Dorothy P. McSweeny, LBJ Lib, with Gen Wheeler, Pentagon, May 7, 1970. Col Ginsburgh had long sought Wheeler's greater involvement; see chap 1 above.

76. Buttinger, *Vietnam: A Dragon Embattled*, I, 3–43; Cummings, "Vietnamese Railroad System."

77. Corum, *The Tale of Two Bridges*.

78. JCS Bombing Chronology, Sep 67, LBJ Lib, NSF, Agency Reports, box 33.

79. Memo, W. Rostow to President, Aug 11, 1967, LBJ Lib, NSF, Memos to Pres, vol 38, #70. See AFHRA 2K740.3421 for after action msgs from 355 TFW, 1112392 Aug 67; 8 TFW, 111300z Aug 67; 432 TRW, 111100Z Aug 67. See also John Piowaty, "Dropping Doumer Bridge," *Vietnam*, Oct 1993, pp 35–40.

80. Stennis hearings, p 365.

81. CIA/DIA, *Appraisal of Bombing*, Sep 1967.

82. PACAF, "Summary of Air Operations in SEA," Aug 1967.

83. Tactical Fighter Weapons Center, Red Baron II, vol IV, pt 1, pp 97–117.

84. Olds intrvw, 1968.

85. Ibid. See also Col Robin Olds,

"Special Report, 1 Oct 66–31 Aug 67."

86. Intrvws, Wayne Thompson, Office of Air Force History, with Col Robert R. Sawhill, USAF Ret, Bolling AFB, Mar 3, 1982, and Col Kenneth W. Cordier, USAF Ret, Arlington, Va., Mar 25, 1986.

87. Memos, Arthur McCafferty to President, Aug 21, 1967, Bromley Smith to President, Aug 21, 1967, and Arthur McCafferty to Smith, Aug 26, 1967, LBJ Lib, NSF, Memos to Pres, vol 39, #5a, 5, and 71a; Tactical Fighter Weapons Center, Red Baron II, vol IV, pt 1, pp 92–96; Peter J. Kumpa, "Peking Calls U.S. Bombing Near Line Grave Escalation," *Baltimore Sun*, Aug 23, 1967, p 1.

88. Herring, *Pentagon Papers*, pp 717–71; McNamara, *In Retrospect*, pp 295–302; Cooper, *Lost Crusade*, pp 377–81; Johnson, *Vantage Point*, pp 266–67; Kraslow and Loory, *Secret Search*, pp 218–28; Marvin and Bernard Kalb, *Kissinger* (Boston, 1974), pp 70–77; Thies, *When Governments Collide*, pp 180–94; Goodman, *Lost Peace*, pp 59–60.

89. Memo, unsigned, Aug 18, 1967, LBJ Lib, NSF, Memos to Pres, vol 39, #136; notes by Jim Jones, meeting of President with his advisers, Aug 18, 1967, LBJ Lib, Meeting Notes File, #118.

90. Quoted in Herring, *Pentagon Papers*, p 770. See also U.S. Embassy Paris to State, 5545, Oct 20, 1967, in Herring, pp 768–69. For recent Vietnamese views on the relationship between the Kissinger initiative and their planning for the Tet Offensive, see Robert S. McNamara, James Blight, Robert K. Brigham, Thomas Biersteker and Col. Herbert Y. Schandler, *Argument Without End: In Search of Answers to the Vietnam Tragedy* (New York, 1999), pp 292–301.

91. Notes by Jim Jones, meeting of President with his advisers, Sep 5, 1967, LBJ Lib, Meeting Notes File, #2.

92. Notes by Jim Jones, meeting of President with his advisers, Sep 12, 1967, LBJ Lib, Meeting Notes File, #7. See also memo, W. Rostow to President, Oct 6, 1967, LBJ Lib, NSF, Memos to Pres, vol 44, #44.

93. Msg, CINCPAC to JCS, subj: Rolling Thunder, 080726Z Oct 1967, LBJ Lib, NSF, Country File, Vietnam, box 84, 3I, #56a.

94. Memo, W. Rostow to President, Sep 14, 1967, LBJ Lib, NSF, Memos to Pres, vol 41, #5.

95. Memo, Katzenbach to President, Oct 19, 1967, LBJ Lib, NSF, Memos to Pres, vol 46, #16a.

96. Memo, Wheeler to President, CM-2697-67, Implications of Proposal for Cessation of Hostilities, Oct 19, 1967, LBJ Lib, NSF, Memos to Pres, vol 46, #37a.

97. Memo, W. Rostow to President, Sep 27, 1967, LBJ Lib, NSF, Memos to Pres, vol 43, #27; memo, Bromley Smith to W. Rostow, Sep 27, 1967, NSF, Country File, Vietnam, box 219, Reprisal Program, vol VII, #29; Cooper, *Lost Crusade*, pp 381–83.

98. Meeting, White House, Oct 2, 1967, 2:50 pm, LBJ Lib, Tom Johnson Notes, box 1, #103.

99. Notes by George Christian, meeting of President with advisers, Oct 11, 1967, LBJ Lib, Meeting Notes File, #19.

100. Hist, 433 TFSq, Oct–Dec 1967, attached to hist, 8 TFWg, Oct–Dec 1967; PACAF, "Summary of Air Operations in SEA," Oct 1967.

101. Tactical Fighter Weapons Center, Red Baron II, vol IV, pt 1, pp 328–35.

102. PACAF, Corona Harvest rpt, "In-Country and Out-Country Strike Operations in SEA, 1965–69," vol II, "Hardware," sec 2, "Munitions."

103. Olds intrvw, Jul 12, 1967; Olds intrvw, 1968; Olds EOTR; Sawhill intrvw.

104. Tactical Fighter Weapons Center, Red Baron II, vol IV, pt i, pp 366–74.

105. Meeting, President with his advisers, White House, Oct 23, 1967, LBJ Lib, Tom Johnson's Notes, box 1, #119a.

106. PACAF, "Summary of Air Operations in SEA," Oct–Nov, 1967; hist, 388 TFWg, Apr–Dec 1967; HQ PACAF and HQ USAF, *Effects of United States Air Operations in SEA*, vol I, chap 4, p 23.

107. Gene I. Basel, *Pak Six* (La

Mesa, Calif, 1982), p 120.

108. *New York Times*, Nov 19, 1967, p 3; *Washington Post*. Nov 19, 1967, p 17.

109. Colvin, "Hanoi in My Time," p 153. Another sign of disarray in Hanoi was the imprisonment of more than forty "revisionists" apparently for their pro-Russian views, views more likely to lead to a negotiated settlement with the United States than the harder line promoted by the Chinese. See Judy Stowe, "'Revisionism' in Vietnam," a paper for the annual meeting of the Association for Asian Studies, Washington, Mar 1998.

110. CIA/DIA, *Appraisal of Bombing*, Sep 1967, AFHRA K193.56-1.

Chapter 4

1. Momyer, *Airpower in Three Wars*, pp 177–81; msg, PACAF to Dep Cmdr 7/13 AF, 230232Z Sep 67, PACAF DO Read File, AFHRA 717.312. For Ryan's Raiders, see chap 2 above.

2. Intrvw, Lt Col John N. Dick, Jr., USAF historical program, with Gen Gabriel P. Disosway, Dallas, Tex., Oct 4–6, 1977.

3. Momyer, *Airpower in Three Wars*, pp 177–78.

4. Rpt, AF Systems Command, Have Dart Task Force, Mar 1968; HQ PACAF DCS/Intelligence, "North Vietnamese Air Force Fighter Patterns," Mar 1968.

5. Tactical Fighter Weapons Center, Red Baron II, vol IV, pt 2, Event 87, pp 381–92.

6. Msg, Ryan to Momyer, 062202Z Jan 68, AFHRA CHECO microfilm roll TS31.

7. Msg, Momyer to Ryan, 080730Z Jan 68, PACAF DO Read File, AFHRA K717.312.

8. Ibid.

9. Ibid.

10. Maj William E. Reder, "EB–66 Operations in SEA, 1967," draft CHECO rpt, Nov 26, 1968, AFHRA K717.0413-63.

11. Ibid.

12. Tactical Fighter Weapons Center, Red Baron II, vol IV, pt 2, pp 81–89; "Out Country Operations, 1965–68," Corona Harvest final rpt, p 63.

13. Tactical Fighter Weapons Center, Red Baron II, vol IV, pt 3, pp 14–24; PACAF, "Summary of Air Operations in SEA," Jan 1968; computer printout, "SEA Casualties by Date of Incident," USAF Military Personnel Center, Oct 22, 1982.

14. Nalty, *Electronic Warfare*, pp 116–46; Capt Carl W. Reddel, "College Eye," CHECO rpt, 1968; Capt Richard M. Williams, *A History of Big Eye/College Eye* (552d AEW&C Wg, 1969); Grover C. Jarrett, *History of College Eye, Apr 1965–Jun 1969* (ADC, 1969).

15. Olds briefing, Sep 29, 1969.

16. Ibid.

17. OT&E Final Rpt, TAC Test 66-183, USAF Tactical Warfare Center, Eglin AFB, Rivet Top Evaluation Team, Mar 1968, AFHRA CHECO microfilm roll S192; 7 AF OpOrd 510-68, Aug 67, AFHRA CHECO microfilm roll TS16; Pratt, *Air Tactics Against NVN Air Ground Defenses.*

18. Rpt, 7 AF Dir of Tactical Analysis, "Relative Effectiveness of College Eye, Rivet Top, Big Look," Jan 10, 1968, supporting document 14 for Reddel, College Eye.

19. See notes 16 and 17.

20. See note above.

21. Wheeler to McNamara, JCS CM-1798-66, subj: Review of Operating Procedures in Order to Avoid Violating Red Chinese Airspace, Sep 29, 1966; Ryan intrvw, May 20, 1971.

22. Msg, Momyer to Ryan, 080730Z Jan 68, PACAF DO Read File, AFHRA K717.312.

23. Msg, 7 AF to CSAF, subj: A–6A Operations, 201200Z Dec 67, PACAF DO Read File, AFHRA K717.312; Vice Adm Malcom W. Cagle, USN, "Task Force 77 in Action off Vietnam," U.S. Naval Institute Proceedings, Naval Review Issue, 1972, pp 100–101.

24. See above chap X2 hist, Det 1,

428 Tac Fighter Sq, Mar 15–May 31, 1968; Michael H. Gorn, *The TFX: Conceptual Phase to F–111B Termination (1958–1968)* (Air Force Systems Command, 1985); Herman S. Wolk, *Research and Development for Southeast Asia, 1968* (Washington, 1970), pp 27–29; Bill Gunston, *F–111* (New York, 1978); Robert F. Coulam, *Illusions of Choice: The F–111 and the Problem of Weapons Acquisition Reform* (Princeton, 1977).

25. 7 AF OpOrd 523-68, Jan 1968, AFHRA CHECO microfilm roll TS66; Maj Victor B. Anthony, *Tactics and Techniques of Night Operations, 1961–1970* (Washington, 1973), pp 206–7.

26. Intrvw, Maj Richard Clement and Charles Hildreth, AF hist program, with Gen John P. McConnell, Washington, Nov 4, 1970.

27. Brown intrvw, Aug 29–30, 1972.

28. Ryan intrvw, May 15–17, 1979.

29. See chap 2 above.

30. Maj Richard A. Durkee, "Combat Skyspot," CHECO rpt, 1967.

31. The most recent and extensive study of Site 85 at Phou Pha Thi is Timothy N. Castle, *One Day Too Long: Top Secret Site 85 and the Bombing of North Vietnam* (New York, 1999). See also Msg, Col Pettigrew (US Air Attaché Laos) to Gen Momyer, subj: MSQ-77 at Lima Site 85 Laos, 070445Z Jul 67, AFHRA CHECO microfilm roll TS15; msg, Ambassador Sullivan to Secretary of State Rusk, 130930Z Mar 67.

32. For an account (based on American intelligence and a Hanoi exhibit) indicating two AN–2s attacked Phou Pha Thi and were lost while another pair orbited several miles away, see Castle, *One Day Too Long*, pp 76–78. For another account based on Vietnamese sources indicating three AN–2s were lost, see Istvan Toperczer, *Air War Over North Vietnam: The Vietnamese People's Air Force* (Carrollton, Tex, 1998), pp 30–31. See also Victor B. Anthony and Richard R. Sexton, "The War in Northern Laos, 1954–1973," Center for Air Force History, 1993, pp 251–58; Capt Edward Vallentiny, "The Fall of Site 85," CHECO rpt, Aug 1968

with supporting documents on CHECO microfilm TS-70; draft CHECO rpt, "Commando Club Project (OL-26)," CHECO microfilm TS-70; Tactical Fighter Weapons Center, Red Baron II, vol IV, pt 2, pp 398–99; Kenneth Conboy with James Morrison, *Shadow War: The CIA's Secret War in Laos* (Boulder, Colo, 1995), pp 188–96; Timothy N. Castle, *At War in the Shadow of Vietnam: U.S. Military Aid to the Royal Lao Government 1955–1975* (New York, 1993), pp 94–97; Richard Secord with Jay Wurts, *Honored and Betrayed* (New York, 1992), pp 74–92; Roger Warner, *Back Fire* (New York, 1995), pp 200–234; Christopher Robbins, *The Ravens* (New York, 1987), pp 41–85.

33. Msg, Ambassador Sullivan to Gen Momyer, 141248Z Mar 68; intrvw, author with Col Gerald H. Clayton, USAF Ret, Pentagon, Mar 31, 1988; "Chamlong Looks Back at Past," excerpts from the autobiography of Maj Gen Chamlong Simuang, JPRS-SEA-015, 18 May 1990. See also David Corn, *Blond Ghost: Ted Shackley and the CIA Crusades* (New York, 1994) and Jane Hamilton-Merritt, *Tragic Mountains: The Hmong, the Americans, and the Secret Wars for Laos, 1942–1992* (Bloomington, Ind, 1993).

34. Lt Col James Gormley, "Commando Club," Corona Harvest spec rpt, 1970, AFHRA K239.032-31; hist, 388 TFW, Apr–Dec 1967; PACAF, Corona Harvest rpt, "Targeting, Out-Country, 1962–68," pp 333–44; PACAF, "Summary of Air Operations in SEA," Nov 1967–Mar 1968; intrvw, Lt Col Charles M. Heltslcy, Air War College, with Maj Gen John C. Giraudo, Treasure Island, Fla, 8–12 Jan 1985, AFHRA 1105191. As commander of the 355 TFW, Col Giraudo had opposed attempting to use ground radar controlled bombing in the Red River delta.

35. PACAF, Corona Harvest rpt, "Out-Country Strike Operations, 1965–68," vol I, Subtask Id, pp 122–31.

36. Tactical Fighter Weapons Center, Red Baron II, vol IV, pt 2, pp 67–72.

37. See note 33.

38. C.V. Sturdevant, "Effect of Strike Force Formation Size and Spacing on Vul-

nerability to SAMs and Suggested Delivery Tactics for Commando Club Missions," PACAF Operations Analysis Note 68-1, Feb 15, 1968, AFHRA K717.310468-1.

39. PACAF, Corona Harvest rpt, "In-Country and Out-Country Strike Operations, Jan 1965–Mar 1968," vol IV, "Support: Tactical Electronic Warfare," esp pp 78–82, 101–2; PACAF, "Summary of Air Operations in SEA," Nov 1967.

40. See note above.

41. See note 37; Nalty, *Electronic Warfare*, pp 116–46; James E. Pierson, *A Special Historical Study of Electronic Warfare in SEA, 1964–68* (Kelly AFB, Tex, 1973), pp 120–21.

42. See note above.

43. DIA/JCS, *SEA Military Fact Book*, Jan 1968, pp 13–19; Col Gordon E. Danforth, "Iron Hand/Wild Weasel," Corona Harvest spec rpt, 1970; Maj Richard B. Clement, "The SAM Story," Corona Harvest spec rpt, 1970.

44. Msg, 355th TFWg to 7 AF, 190835Z Dec 67, PACAF DO Read File, AFHRA 717.312; Nalty, *Electronic Warfare*, pp 41–49; PACAF, Corona Harvest rpt, "In-Country and Out-Country Strike Operations, Jan 1965–Dec 1969," vol II, "Hardware," sec 2, "Munitions," pp 72–80.

45. Msg, CINCPAC to CINCPACAF, subj: Rolling Thunder, 270447Z Jun 67, AFHRA CHECO microfilm roll TS16.

46. CIA/NPIC, Photographic Interpretation Report, "KH–4 Mission 1042-1, 17–22 Jun 1967, South China and North Vietnam Edition," Jun 1967, in Kevin Ruffner, ed, *CORONA: America's First Satellite Program* (Washington, 1995), pp 307–14. See also Robert A. McDonald, "Corona's Success for Space Reconnaissance, A Look into the Cold War, and a Revolution for Intelligence," *Photogrammetric Engineering and Remote Sensing*, Jun 1995, pp 689–720.

47. William H. Greenhalgh, Jr., "U.S. Air Force Reconnaissance in Southeast Asia, 1960–1975," draft, AFHRA, 1976.

48. Hist, 67th RTSq, Jul–Sep 1967.

49. Msg, 7 AF to CINCPAC, 060700Z Nov 67, PACAF DO Read File, AFHRA K717.312.

50. Msg, CINCPACAF to CINCPAC, 210351Z Nov 67, PACAF DO Read File, AFHRA K717.312.

51. Msg, CINCPACFLT to CINCPACAF, 020354Z Dec 67, PACAF DO Read File, AFHRA K717.312.

52. Msg, CINCPACAF to CINCPAC, subj: NVN Air Defense, 262032Z Dec 67, MACV Records, Federal Records Center, Suitland Md.

53. N. Charzenko and Lt J. D. Reeves, "Analysis of Tactical Employment of the MK–36 Destructors and Other Mines," Innovations Gp, Plans Dir, HQ USAF, Nov 1967; hist, 8th TFWg, Oct–Dec 1967; CIA/DIA, *Appraisal of Bombing* (through Dec 1967).

54. AF Special Communications Center, Comfy Coat Rpt WC3-73, "Evolution of Countermeasures to MK–36 Magnetic Mines," Mar 1973, AFHRA K370.491-1 (1001281).

55. Memo, Rear Adm W. R. McClendon, Deputy Dir for Ops, NMCC, to Sec of Defense, subj: Allied Bombing of Soviet Merchant Ship, 8 Jan 1968, LBJ Lib, National Security File, Vietnam Country File, Box 85, 3J, #32a; msg, Walt Rostow to President, 100714Z Jan 68, CAP80237, LBJ Lib, National Security File, Vietnam Country File, Box 85, 3J, #22; memo for record, Brig Gen James A. Shannon, USAF, Dep Dir for Ops, NMCC, subj: Inadvertent Release of Mark 36 Weapons in International Waters, Dec 31, 1967, LBJ Lib, National Security File, Vietnam Country File, Box 85, 3J, #39a.

56. Hist, JCS, Vietnam, 1960–68, pt III, pp 44–14 and 44–15.

57. Harriman to Rusk, Nov 29, 1967, Bucharest 803, in Herring, *Pentagon Papers*, pp 794–800.

58. Ibid., p 795.

59. Ibid., p 523.

60. Ibid., p 805.

61. Ibid.

62. Msg, Wheeler to Sharp and Westmoreland, 051946Z Jan 68, Westmoreland's Backchannel File, Army Center of Military History.

63. Msg, Bunker, Westmoreland,

Komer, And Locke to Rusk, 050528Z Jan 68, POL 27, Vietnam, 1/1/68, State Dept.

64. Msg, Sharp to Wheeler, 062331Z Jan 68, Westmoreland's Backchannel File, Army Center of Military History.

65. Msg, 355th TFWg to NMCC, 140920Z Dec 67; msg, 388th TFW to NMCC, 141115Z Dec 76; msg, 460th RTSq to PACAF, 182035Z Dec 67; msg, 388th TFWg to NMCC, 180925Z Dec 67; all in PACAF DO Read File, AFHRA 717.312. See also CIA/DIA, *Appraisal of Bombing* (through Dec 1967); HQ PACAF and HQ USAF, *Effects of United States Air Operations in SEA*, vol I, chap 4, 15, and vol II, pp 122–25; Corum, *The Tale of Two Bridges*, pp 75–77.

66. The six Americans shot down near Hanoi 14–17 Dec 1967 and returned in 1973 were Capt James E. Sehorn, Maj James F. Low, 1Lt Howard J. Hill, Maj Kenneth R. Fleenor, 1Lt Terry L. Boyer, Capt Jeffrey T. Ellis.

67. Tactical Fighter Weapons Center, Red Baron II, vol IV, pt 2, events 70–79; Futrell, *Aces and Aerial Victories*, pp 72–74.

68. Tactical Fighter Weapons Center, Red Baron II, vol IV, pt 2, event 75D.

69. Futrell, *Aces and Aerial Victories*, pp vi and 44–64.

70. Hist, 8th TFWg, Oct–Dec 1967, pp 10–12.

71. Tactical Fighter Weapons Center, Red Baron II, vol IV, pt 2, event 54c.

72. Tactical Fighter Weapons Center, Red Baron II, vol IV, pt 2, event 79.

73. Ibid.

74. For the summer 1967 railroad campaign, see chap 3 above.

75. Msg, 7 AF to CINCPACAF, 190355Z Dec 67, PACAF DO Read File, AFHRA 717.312; msg, CINCPAC to 7 AF, 192300Z Dec 67, CH 0243009.

76. Hist, 388 TFWg, Apr–Dec 1967.

77. Hist, 388th TFWg, Apr–Dec 1967; Johnson, *Vantage Point*, pp 378–79.

78. PACAF, "Summary of Air Operations in SEA," Sep 1967, 5-A-8.

79. *Public Papers of the Presidents, Johnson, 1967*, Book II, pp 1182–83.

80. Memo, Col Robert N. Ginsburgh to Gen McConnell, Dec 27, 1967, McConnell's Personal Notebook, vol II, item 507, Office of Air Force History.

81. Ibid.

82. McConnell intrvw, Aug 28, 1969.

83. *Public Papers of the Presidents, Johnson, 1967*, Book II, pp 1077–78. Years later McNamara was asked when he decided to resign, and he replied: "I'm not sure I decided. It would have been the President who decided." See McNamara's deposition in Westmoreland vs CBS, Mar 26, 1984, p 2. See also McNamara, *In Retrospect*, pp 311–14.

84. Goulding, *Confirm or Deny*, pp ix–x; McNamara, *In Retrospect*, pp 303–5.

85. Gallup Poll, Nov 5, 1967.

86. For Johnson versus R. Kennedy, see Gallup Poll of Oct 1, 1967; for Johnson versus Republicans, see Gallup Poll of Oct 22, 1967.

87. Terry Dietz, *Republicans and Vietnam, 1961–1968* (New York, 1986), pp 113–28.

88. Ibid.

89. Gallup Poll, Oct 29, 1967.

90. *Public Papers of the Presidents, Johnson, 1967*, Book II, pp 733–46; Johnson, *Vantage Point*, pp 445–49; Gallup Polls, Aug 13 and Sep 6, 1967. On the Stennis Hearings, see chap 3 above.

91. Notes on meeting of Aug 18, 1967, LBJ Lib, Meeting Notes File, #118.

92. Memo, W. Rostow for President, Oct 20, 1967, LBJ Lib, National Security File, Vietnam Country File, Box 83, 3F, #45 and 45a.

93. For LeMay's departure, see above chap 1.

94. Minutes of Cabinet Meeting, Oct 4, 1967, LBJ Lib, National Security File, Vietnam Country File, Cabinet Papers.

Chapter 5

1. On intelligence reporting before the Tet Offensive, see James J. Wirtz, *The et Offensive: Intelligence Failure in War* (Ithaca, NY, 1991), Ronnie E. Ford, *Tet*

1968: Understanding the Surprise (London, 1995), and John Prados, "The Warning that Left Something to Chance: Intelligence at Tet," *Journal of American-East Asian Relations*, summer 1993, pp 161–84. A revised version of the Prados article appears together with Mark Jacobsen's "President Johnson and the Decision to Curtail Rolling Thunder" and several other informative essays in Marc Jason Gilbert and William Head, editors, *The Tet Offensive* (Westport, Conn, 1996). For the most widely read description of the offensive, see Don Oberdorfer, *Tet!* (Garden City, NY, 1971). For the views of the communist general in charge of the Tet offensive in Saigon, see Tran Van Tra, "Tet-the 1968 General Offensive and General Uprising," in Jayne Werner and Luu Doan Huynh, *The Vietnam War: Vietnamese and American Perspectives* (Armonk, NY, 1993).

2. Westmoreland, *A Soldier Reports*, pp 407–39.

3. Peter Braestrup, *Big Story: How the American Press and Television Reported and Interpreted the Crisis of Tet 1968 in Vietnam and Washington*, 2 vols (Boulder, Colo, 1977).

4. Ibid., I, p 253–60.

5. Ibid., I, p 653–54.

6. Gallup poll, Mar 31, 1968, based on interviews 15–20 Mar 68.

7. On the May 1967 debate, see above chap 3.

8. On the Stennis Hearings, see above chap 3.

9. *Congressional Record*, Jan 30, 1968, p 1398.

10. *New York Times*, Feb 4, 1968, IV, 12.

11. Hearings before the Committee on Armed Services, Senate, *Authorization for Military Procurement, Research and Development, Fiscal Year 1969, and Reserve Strength*, 90th Cong, 2d Sess (Washington, 1968), p. 3.

12. Ibid., pp 12, 26.

13. Ibid., p 754.

14. Ibid., pp 758–62.

15. Ibid., p 765.

16. Ibid., p 770.

17. James Reston, "The Big Peace Battle," *New York Times*, Mar 12, 1968, p 17.

18. Hearings before the Committee on Foreign Relations, Senate, *Foreign Relations Assistance Act of 1968, Part 1-Vietnam*, 90th Cong, 2d Sess (Washington, 1968), p 101.

19. Ibid., p 184.

20. See above chap 3.

21. Memo, W. Rostow to President, May 14, 1968, LBJ Lib, National Security File, Memos to Pres, vol 67, #42.

22. Memo, R. Ginsburgh to W. Rostow, Feb 28, 1968, LBJ Lib, National Security File, National Security Council Hist, Mar 31 Speech, vol 3, #37.

23. Memo, W. Rostow to President, Feb 3, 1968, LBJ Lib, National Security File, Memos to Pres, vol 59, #75; Feb 10, 1968, vol 61, #98; Feb 19, 1968, with att memo from McNamara, vol 63, #35 and 35a. See also msg, Sharp to Wheeler, 020208Z Feb 67, Westmoreland's Back Channel Msg File, US Army Center of Military Hist; press conf, Feb 16, 1968, *Public Papers of the Presidents*, Johnson, 1968–69, I, 234; Herbert Y. Schandler, *The Unmaking of a President: Lyndon Johnson and Vietnam* (Princeton, 1977), pp 89–90.

24. Hist, JCS, Vietnam, 1960–68, pt III, chap 44, p 16.

25. Gravel, *Pentagon Papers*, IV, 234–36.

26. Notes of President's Tuesday lunch meeting, Feb 6, 1968, LBJ Lib, President's Appointment File, box 89.

27. Notes of National Security Council meeting, Feb 7, 1968, LBJ Lib, Tom Johnson's Notes of Meetings and NSF, NSC Meetings File. David C. Humphrey ("Searching for LBJ at the Johnson Library," *Society for Historians of American Foreign Relations Newsletter*, Jun 1989, pp 3–4) has pointed out discrepancies in the two sets of notes. For one thing, Tom Johnson (and no doubt others at the meeting) did not know enough about aircraft to distinguish between an IL–28 and a MiG–21; in his notes, the IL–28s are called "MiGs."

28. Hist, 8th TFW, Jan–Mar 68, pp 27–28; PACAF, "Summary of Air Operations in SEA," Feb 1968, sec 1, p 8 and sec 5, p A-4.

29. Hist, 555 TFS, Jan–Mar 1968.

30. PACAF, "Summary of Air Operations in SEA," Feb 1968, sec 1, p 8 and sec 5, p D-1. Buza and Toperczer, "MiG–17 Over Vietnam," pp 100–117, indicate that the North Vietnamese practice of hiding aircraft off the airfields began as early as 1966.

31. Tactical Fighter Weapons Center, Red Baron II, vol IV, pt 3, pp 159–79; Futrell, *Aces and Aerial Victories*, pp 78–79. Lt Col Wesley D. Kimball and 1st Lt John Daday of the 555 TFS probably shot down a MiG–21 on Mar 29, 1968.

32. CIA/DIA, *Appraisal of Bombing*, Jan–Mar 1968, pp 3–4; hist, 388 TFW, Jan–Mar 1968; hist, 355 TFW, Jan–Mar 1968.

33. PACAF, "Summary of Air Operations in SEA," Feb 1968, chap 1, p 8.

34. See Bernard C. Nalty, *Air Power and the Fight for Khe Sanh* (Washington, 1973).

35. Memo, Art McCafferty (NSC staff) to W. Rostow, Feb 21, 1968, 3:25 pm, LBJ Lib, National Security File Country File-Vietnam, Box 84, 3I, #21. On bombing controlled by Phou Pha Thi's radar (from Nov 1967 until it fell into enemy hands in Mar 1968), see the preceding chap. President Johnson and his advisers discussed radar-controlled "systems" bombing with particular reference to Radio Hanoi and the Hanoi port facilities at Feb 20's Tuesday Lunch meeting. See Tom Johnson's Notes of Meetings, LBJ Lib.

36. Ambassador Taylor had "grave reservations" about the introduction of American ground forces at Da Nnang because he suspected they would be used for more than protecting the air base and that it would be "very difficult to hold the line against an increasing ground involvement." *Foreign Relations of the United States, 1964–1968*, II, 347–49.

37. Gen Bruce Palmer, Jr., *US Intelligence in Vietnam*, a special issue of the CIA's *Studies in Intelligence*, vol 28, no 5, 1984; memo, John A. McCone, Apr 2, 1965, quoted in Gravel, *Pentagon Papers*, III, 352–53.

38. Joint Staff, SEA CABIN Study Group, "Study of the Political-Military Implications in Southeast Asia of the Cessation of Aerial Bombardment and the Initiation of Negotiations," Nov 22, 1967, LBJ Lib, National Security File, Country File, Vietnam, Box 95, 6G(1)b, #26e.

39. Memo, Ginsburgh to Wheeler, Nov 29, 1967, LBJ Lib, National Security File, Country File, Vietnam, Box 95, 6G(1)b, #26b; hist., JCS, Vietnam, 1960–68, pt III, chap 47, p 10.

40. Schandler, *Unmaking of a President*, pp 92–120; Westmoreland, pp 460–77.

41. Hist, JCS, Vietnam, 1960–68, pt III, chap 49, pp 1–8.

42. Westmoreland, pp 465–69.

43. Gravel, *Pentagon Papers*, IV, 575; hist, JCS, Vietnam, 1960–68, pt III, chap 49, pp 10–11.

44. Gravel, *Pentagon Papers*, IV, 547.

45. McPherson's notes of meeting, Feb 27, 1968, LBJ Lib, Meeting Notes File, Box 2, #47.

46. Meeting, Dec 5, 1967, 6 pm, in LBJ Lib, Tom Johnson's Notes, box 1, #146a. On Clifford's opposition to 1965 troop deployment, see Clark Clifford with Richard Holbrooke, *Counsel to the President: A Memoir* (New York, 1991) and George W. Ball, *The Past has Another Pattern: Memoirs* (New York, 1982).

47. McConnell intrvw, Aug 28, 1969. McConnell draft msg to Gen Nazzaro, CINCSAC, Mar 4, 1968, AFHRA 1028520; ltr, McConnell to LBJ, Mar 27, 1968, AFHRA 1028520.

48. A condensed version of the *Pentagon Papers* was published by the *New York Times* in its newspaper and in one volume (New York, 1971). Senator Mike Gravel (Democrat, Alaska) entered more of this classified history into the *Congressional Record* and subsequently sponsored publication in five volumes by

Beacon Press (Boston, 1971). For an account of the "A to Z" reassessment, see the Gravel edition, IV, 238–59, 549–84. See also Gelb and Betts, *The Irony of Vietnam*, and Schandler, *Unmaking of a President*. Schandler wrote the portion of the *Pentagon Papers* relating to the Tet offensive.

49. Gravel, *Pentagon Papers*, IV, 252.

50. Memo with attachments, Secretary of the Air Force Brown to Deputy Secretary of Defense Warnke, subj: SEA Alternative Strategies, Mar 4, 1968, LBJ Lib, Clifford Papers, box 1, Memos to Read (2), #1a; Brown intrvw, Aug 29–30, 1972.

51. Townsend Hoopes, *The Limits of Intervention* (New York, 1969), pp 176–77; Hoopes to Clifford, Feb 13, 1968, LBJ Lib, National Security File, Country File, Vietnam, Box 83, 3G, #5b. On the second JASON report, see also Gravel, *Pentagon Papers*, IV, 222–25. On McNamara's Wall see chap 3 above.

52. Gravel, *Pentagon Papers*, IV, 252.

53. Johnson, *Vantage Point*, p 399. See also memo, W. Rostow to Pres, Mar 4, 1968, 1:45 pm, LBJ Lib, National Security File, NSC Hist, Mar 31 Speech, vol 7, #3.

54. Schandler, *Unmaking of a President*, p 203; Johnson, *Vantage Point*, pp 402–03.

55. Philip E. Converse, Warren E. Miller, Jerod G. Rusk, and Arthur C. Wolfe, "Continuity and Change in American Politics: Parties and Issues in the 1968 Election," *American Political Science Review*, Dec 1969, pp 1083–1105.

56. Intrvw, LBJ Lib with Clark Clifford, Jul 14, 1969.

57. *Public Papers of the Presidents*, Johnson, 1968–69, I, p 404. For Mrs. Johnson's view, see (Claudia T.) Lady Bird Johnson, *A White House Diary* (New York, 1970), esp pp 633–47.

58. *Public Papers of the Presidents*, Johnson, 1968–69, I, p 410.

59. Clifford's handwritten memos of conversations with President and senators, LBJ Lib, Clifford Papers, Notes Taken at Meetings, 2, esp #11, #21, #30, #33; Gravel, *Pentagon Papers*, IV, 589–93; Schandler, *Unmaking of a President*, pp 210–12.

60. Meeting notes, Mar 19 and 22, 1968, LBJ Lib, Meeting Notes File, Box 2, #53 and #54.

61. Ibid. See also memo, Clifford to Wheeler, Mar 5, 1968, attaching Rusk bombing cutback proposal, LBJ Lib, Clifford Papers, Box 2, Memos on Vietnam Feb–Mar 1968, #7a, #7b, #7c; Johnson, *Vantage Point*, pp 397–400.

62. Gravel, *Pentagon Papers*, IV, 233–34.

63. Hoopes, *Limits of Intervention*; Clark M. Clifford, "A Viet Nam Reappraisal: The Personal History of One Man's View and How It Evolved," *Foreign Affairs*, Jul 1969, pp 601–22. Clifford's role in President Johnson's Mar 1968 decisions has been scaled down in succeeding accounts, beginning with Johnson's memoirs, *The Vantage Point*. Schandler, whose account of Tet in the *Pentagon Papers* portrayed Clifford as crucial, retreated considerably from that view in *Unmaking of a President*. Warren I. Cohen followed this line still further in *Dean Rusk* (Totowa, New Jersey, 1980).

64. Walter Isaacson and Evan Thomas, *The Wise Men: Six Friends and the World They Made* (New York, 1986), esp pp 642–741.

65. Memos, W. Rostow to President, Oct 19, 1967 (National Security File, Memos to Pres, vol 46, #30a), Oct 25, 1967 with attachment (vol 48, #80 and 80a), and Nov 3, 1967 (vol 47, #46). The following Wise Men attended the Nov 1967 meeting: Dean Acheson, Clark Clifford, McGeorge Bundy, Supreme Court Justice Abe Fortas, Robert Murphy, Henry Cabot Lodge, Arthur Dean, Douglas Dillon, George Ball, Gen Maxwell Taylor, and Gen Omar Bradley. Two members of the administration with close ties to this group also participated in the meeting: Averell Harriman and William Bundy (brother of McGeorge Bundy and son-in-law of Dean Acheson).

66. Memo, McGeorge Bundy to President, Nov 10, 1967, LBJ Lib, National Security File, Memos to Pres, vol 50, #36b.

67. Ibid. M. Bundy helped Stimson write his memoirs, *On Active Service in Peace and War* (New York, 1947).

68. Clifford intrvw.

69. Johnson, *Vantage Point*, pp 415–17. Attendance at the Mar 1968 meeting of the Wise Men was the same as the Nov 1967 meeting (see note 62 above) with the following additions: Arthur Goldberg, Cyrus Vance, and Gen Matthew Ridgway.

70. Meeting notes, Mar 26, 1968, LBJ Lib, Meeting Notes File, Box 2, #1 and #2.

71. Notes of meeting of President with House and Senate leaders, Apr 3, 1968, LBJ Lib, Tom Johnson's Notes of meetings, Box 2, Apr 1968, #2d; Johnson, *Vantage Point*, esp pp 415–19.

72. "President's Address to the Nation," Mar 31, 1968, *Public Papers of the Presidents*, Johnson, 1968–69, I, pp 469–76; "Statement by the President Following Hanoi's Declaration of Readiness to Begin Discussions," same source, p 492. President Johnson raised the possibility he would not run again on Oct 3, 1967 in a meeting with Rusk, McNamara, Rostow and Helms; see notes of the meeting in LBJ Lib, Tom Johnson's Notes, #105a.

73. Memo, W. Rostow to President, Feb 29, 1968, LBJ Lib, National Security File, NSC Hist, Mar 31 Speech, vol 3, #54; memo, CIA, subj: Question Concerning the Situation in Vietnam, Mar 1, 1968, LBJ Lib, NSC Hist, Mar 31 Speech, vol 4, #2.

74. *Congressional Record*, Apr 2, 1968, p 8569.

75. Ibid., pp 8569–77.

76. Ibid., pp 8572–73.

77. Ibid., p 8574.

78. Meeting notes, Apr 9, 1968, LBJ Lib, Meeting Notes File, Box 2, #61.

79. Draft ltr, Clifford to President, May 4, 1968, LBJ Lib, Clifford Papers, Box 3, Southeast Asia Bombing Pause,

Apr 1968, #2.

80. Meeting note, May 4, 1968, LBJ Lib, Meeting Notes File, Box 2, #3.

81. Memo, Rusk to President, May 18, 1968, with attached Bunker msg, 171048 May 68, LBJ Lib, National Security File, Memos to Pres, vol 77, #7a and #7b.

82. Meeting note, May 25, 1968, LBJ Lib, Meeting Notes File, Box 3, #13.

83. CIA/DIA, *Appraisal of Bombing*, Jul–Oct 1968.

84. PACAF, "Summary of Air Operations in SEA," Apr–Oct 1968.

85. Lt Col John Schlight, "Jet Forward Air Controllers in SE Asia," CHECO rpt, Oct 15, 1969; Ballard, *Gunships*.

86. Hist, 8th TFW, Apr–Jun 1968; HQ PACAF and HQ USAF, *Effects of United States Air Operations in SEA*, esp vol II, chap 7, p 12; memo, George A. Carver, Jr., CIA, to W. Rostow, May 31, 1968, with attached report, "North Vietnamese Truck Losses since 31 Mar 1968," LBJ Lib, National Security File, Country File, Vietnam, Box 83, 3F, #17 and #17a.

87. C. William Thorndale, "Interdiction in Route Package One, 1968," CHECO rpt, Jun 30, 1969.

88. Melvin F. Porter and Maj A. W. Thompson, "Operation Thor," CHECO rpt, Jan 24, 1969.

89. Nalty, *Air Power and the Fight for Khe Sanh*, pp 68–81.

90. See note 83; Col Royal W. Connell, "Operation Thor," Corona Harvest spcc rpt, Feb 1970; C. William Thorndale, "Air War in the DMZ, Sep 1967–Jun 1968," CHECO rpt, Aug 1, 1969; Porter and Thompson, "Operation Thor"; Lt Col Valentino Castellina, "Operation Neutralize: The Pattern is Set," Corona Harvest spec rpt, Jun 1969; Warren A. Trest and Maj Valentino Castellina, "Operation Neutralize," CHECO rpt, Jan 5, 1968. Since the war, the tunnels at Vinh Moc (on the coast east of Vinh Linh) have become a tourist attraction.

91. See note above. Farris R.

Kirkland, "The Attack on Cap Mui Lay, Vietnam, Jul 1968," *Journal of Military History*, Oct 1997, pp 735–60, argues for Operation Thor's success and describes it as the Vietnam War's "only extensive operation involving substantial forces of all four services." The Army used Thor in artillery courses and to justify funding for a new fire control data system.

92. Msg, Abrams to W. Rostow, 231304Z Aug 68. LBJ Lib, Clifford Papers, Box 5, Abroms (1), #1.

93. Thorndale, "Interdiction in Route Package One"; HQ PACAF and HQ USAF, *Effects of United States Air Operations in SEA*, vol I, esp chap 1, pp 9–12, and chap 7, pp 1–13; HQ USAF Operations Analysis and RAND, "Measures of the 1968 Out-Country Bombing Campaign in Southeast Asia," Dec 1968; PACAF, Corona Harvest rpt, "Out-Country Strike Operations, Apr 68–Dec 69," Dec 1, 1970, subtask Ie, North Vietnam, Apr–Nov 68.

94. See note above.

95. See note 93.

96. Brig Gen George J. Keegan, Jr., "7 AF Summer Interdiction Program," appended to Thorndale, "Interdiction in Route Package One."

97. Thorndale, "Interdiction in Route Package One," p 28.

98. Keegan, p 63.

99. The author is indebted to Merle Pribbenow for sharing his translation of the *History of the People's Army of Vietnam*, vol II; the discussion of air interdiction in the North Vietnamese panhandle during 1968 is in chap 11, Sec 3.

100. On McNamara's Wall, see chap 3 above. See also Gary L. Telfer, Lane Rogers, and V. Keith Fleming, *U.S. Marines in Vietnam: Fighting the North Vietnamese, 1967* (Washington, 1984), pp 86–94.

101. Thorndale, "Interdiction in Route Package One," pp 40–42.

102. Keegan, pp 69–70.

103. PACAF, "Summary of Air Operations in SEA," Oct 1968.

104. Msg, Abrams to W. Rostow, 231204Z Aug 68, LBJ Lib, Clifford Papers, Box 5, Abrams (1), #1.

105. Thorndale, "Interdiction in Route Package One," pp 44–52.

106. White House press release, "Summary of General Abrams' View," Aug 23, 1968, LBJ Lib, Clifford Papers, Box 5, Abrams (1), #3; ltr, M. Bundy to President, Aug 15, 1968, with attached memo, LBJ Lib, National Security File, Memos to Pres, vol 91, #2c and #2d; ltr, President to M. Bundy, Aug 25, 1968, LBJ Lib, National Security File, Memos to Pres, vol 91, #2a.

107. *New York Times* editorial, Jul 29, 1968; msg, W. Rostow to President, 191510Z Aug 68, transmitting Adm McCain's msg, LBJ Lib, National Security File, Memos to Pres, vol 91, #35; memo, W. Rostow to President with Brig Gen Ginsburgh's memo attached, Aug 22, 1968, LBJ Lib, National Security File, Memos to Pres, vol 92, #115 and #115a; notes of meeting of President with his advisers, Sep 4, 1968, LBJ Lib, Meeting Notes File, Box 3, #38.

108. Nguyen Tien Hung and Jerrold L. Schecter, *The Palace File* (New York, 1986), pp 21–41.

109. Anna Chennault, *The Education of Anna* (New York, 1980), esp pp 163–214. Clifford's *Counsel to the President* (p 583 in the 1992 edition) confirms that the Johnson administration learned from the FBI, CIA, and NSA about Chennault's efforts to influence the Thieu government and through it the U.S. election. Thieu, of course, probably would have taken the same stand without any prompting from Chennault or Nixon. See also the entries for Jan 9–12, 1973, in H.R. Haldeman, *The Haldeman Diaries: The Complete Multimedia Edition* (Santa Monica, Calif, 1994), and Jules Witcover, *The Year the Dream Died* (New York, 1997), pp 408–52.

110. Bui Diem with David Chanoff, *In the Jaws of History* (Boston, 1987), pp 235–46.

111. Notes, meeting of Oct 14, 1968, 9:40 am, LBJ Lib, Meeting Notes File, Box 3, #68a.

112. Notes, meeting of Oct 14, 1968,

1:50 pm, LBJ Lib, Meeting Notes File, Box 3, #57. These notes were taken by Bromley Smith. See also Tom Johnson's notes of the same meeting in LBJ Lib, Tom Johnson's Notes, #25a.

113. See note above. Despite North Vietnamese eagerness to avoid any public linkage of the "facts of life" with the bombing halt, President Johnson did point to them in his televised address (Oct 31, 1968) announcing the halt: "We cannot have productive talks in an atmosphere where the cities are being shelled and where the demilitarized zone is being abused." See *Public Papers of the Presidents*, Johnson, 1968–69, II, p 1101.

114. Some of Johnson's ambivalence during this period is reflected in Walt Rostow's memos to the President (LBJ Lib, National Security File). See esp Oct 29, 12:40 am, vol 102, #59. See also the chronology of the decision's development in the draft "Briefing Paper" of Oct 30, vol 102, #26a, and the notes for the 6:40 pm NSC meeting on Oct 31 in the Meeting Notes File, Box 3, #69.

115. Memo of Gen Momyer's conversation with the President, Oct 23, 1968, LBJ Lib, National Security File, Memos to Pres, vol 101, #66a. See also notes of meeting, Oct 14, 1968, 9:40 am, LBJ Lib, Meeting Notes File, Box 3, #68a.

Chapter 6

1. *Defense Intelligence Digest*, Sep 1968 (pp 17–18), Nov 1968 (pp 7–9), May 1969 (p1), Nov 1969 (pp 4–9), Sep 1970 (p 13), Oct 1970 (p 13).

2. CIA Intelligence Information Cable, DB-315/03896-68, Oct 25, 1968, LBJ Lib, National Security File, Memos to Pres, W. Rostow, vol 101, #35a; CIA Special Report, "Sino-Vietnamese Relations Over the Last Two Years," SC00791/69A, Dec 19, 1969; *Defense Intelligence Digest*, Oct 1968 (pp 5–7), Apr 1969 (pp 9–11).

3. *Defense Intelligence Digest*, Aug 1968 (pp 15–17), Dec 1970 (pp 26–28).

4. Msg, Maclehose (Hanoi) to Foreign Office (London), Jun 27, 1968, LBJ Lib, National Security File, Memos to Pres, W. Rostow, vol 86, #17a; CIA Intelligence Information Cable, DB-314/10635-68, Jul 2, 1968, LBJ Lib, National Security File, Country File, Vietnam, box 84, 3H(3), #2; CIA/DIA, *Appraisal of Bombing*, Jul–Oct 1968; William S. Turley, "Urbanization in War: Hanoi, 1946–1973," *Pacific Affairs*, Fall 1975, pp 370–97; Nigel Thrift and Dean Forbes, *The Price of War: Urbanization in Vietnam, 1954–1985* (London, 1986).

5. Msg, Stewart (Hanoi) to Foreign Office (London), Sep 12, 1968, LBJ Lib, National Security File, Country File,

Vietnam, Box 85, 3K(2), #5.

6. Msg, W. Rostow to President, CAP82407, 191912Z Sep 68, LBJ Lib, National Security File, Memos to Pres, W. Rostow, vol 95, #83.

7. PACAF, "Summary of Air Operations in SEA," Dec 1969; OASD Comptroller, *Southeast Asia Statistical Summary*, Table 321, Oct 1973.

8. HQ PACAF, *Intelligence Index of USAF Personnel MIA/PW Southeast Asia*, 1974; AFMPC, "Summary of Casualties Due to Hostile Action in Southeast Asia," Nov 1968; PACAF, "Summary of Air Operations in SEA," Nov 1968; Hist, 432 TRW, Oct–Dec 1968; W. Rostow to President, Nov 15, 1968, LBJ Lib, National Security Files, Country File, Vietnam, box 138, Bombing Halt Memos, vol 6, #8.

9. Ibid.; Summary notes, 594th NSC Meeting, Nov 25, 1968, LBJ Lib, National Security File, NSC Meetings, vol 5, tab 76.

10. Memo, W. Rostow to President, Nov 14, 1968, LBJ Lib, National Security File, Memos to Pres, W. Rostow, vol 105, #4; PACAF, "Summary of Air Operations in SEA," Dec 1968.

11. Nixon's version of these events is in his *RN: The Memoirs of Richard Nixon* (New York, 1978) and in his *Six Crises*

(New York, 1962). Recent scholarship has tended to confirm Nixon's view that Hiss was a communist spy. See Allen Weinstein, *Perjury: The Hiss-Chambers Case* (New York, 1978) and Stephen E. Ambrose, *Nixon: The Education of a Politician, 1913–1962* (New York, 1987).

12. Nixon, *RN*, Warner paperback edition, I, 150–53.

13. Ibid., p 187.

14. See above chap XVII. See also Nixon, *RN*, I, 357; Dwight D. Eisenhower, *The White House Years: Mandate for Change, 1953–1956* (Garden City, NY, 1963). Some scholars have been skeptical about the importance of Eisenhower's nuclear threat in ending the Korean War; see Roger Dingman, "Atomic Diplomacy During the Korean War," and Rosemary J. Foot, "Nuclear Coercion and the Ending of the Korean Conflict," both in *International Security*, winter 1988/89.

15. Richard M. Nixon, article, *Foreign Affairs*, Oct 1967.

16. The Soviet proposal to engage in nuclear strikes against China was revealed to the public by H.R. Haldeman, *The Ends of Power* (New York, 1978), Dell paperback edition, p 129.

17. Kraslow and Loory, *Secret Search,* pp 221–24; see above, chap 3.

18. Henry Kissinger, *White House Years* (Boston, 1979), pp 9–10; Nixon, *RN*, I, pp 421–22.

19. Henry A. Kissinger, *Nuclear Weapons and Foreign Policy* (New York, 1957).

20. Ibid., p 418.

21. Ibid.

22. Kissinger, *White House Years*, pp 230–35.

23. Nixon, *RN*, I, pp 399–401; Kissinger, *White House Years*, p 10.

24. Henry A. Kissinger, "The Viet Nam Negotiations," *Foreign Affairs*, Jan 1969, p 224.

25. Ibid., p 233.

26. Kissinger, *White House Years*, pp 24–38.

27. Ibid.

28. Intrvw, Lt Col Lyn R. Officer and Hugh N. Ahman, AFHRA, with Dr.

Robert C. Seamans, Jr., Sep 1973–Mar 1974, AFHRA 1005183. For Ryan's problems with Congress, see intrvw, Lt Col Arthur M. McCants, Jr., and James C. Hasdorff, AFHRA, with Gen John W. Vogt, Annapolis, Aug 8–9, 1978. Seamans' Undersecretary and successor as Secretary of the Air Force, Dr. John L. McLucas, noted years later that Ryan was "quite nervous when we talked at lunch (we had lunch together frequently for business purposes). I would often notice that the whole table was shaking from his legs doing a fast motion beneath." See intrvw, Dr. George Watson, AFHSO, with McLucas, Apr–May 1996, AFHSO K239.0512-2157.

29. Edgar F. Puryear, Jr., *George S. Brown, General, U.S. Air Force: Destined for Stars* (Novato, Calif, 1983), pp 186–87.

30. Ibid., p 173. See also Bishop intrvw.

31. Puryear, *Brown*, p 176.

32. Intrvw, Maj Richard B. Clement and Capt Ralph G. Swenston, AFHRA, with Gen George S. Brown, Oct 19–20, 1970, AFHRA 904349.

33. Ibid.

34. OASD Comptroller, *Southeast Asia Statistical Summary*, Table 351, Apr 18, 1973.

35. Ltr, Gen George S. Brown to Lt Gen Glen W. Martin, DCS/Plans and Operations, HQ USAF, Feb 15, 1969.

36. Memo, Col D.P. McAuliffe, Executive to Chairman JCS, subj: Debrief by Gen George S. Brown on his Meeting with the President, Feb 7, 1969.

37. Kissinger, *White House Years*, pp 235–41; Seymour M. Hersh, *The Price of Power: Kissinger in the Nixon White House* (New York, 1983), pp 48–50.

38. NSSM-1 and responses, *Congressional Record*, CXVIII, pt 13, May 10, 1972; see also *Washington Post*, Apr 25, 1972.

39. Ibid.

40. Transcript, President's news conf, Mar 4, 1969, *Public Papers of the Presidents*, Richard Nixon, 1969 (Washington, 1971), p 183.

41. Ibid., pp 185–86. See also JCS Hist, Vietnam, 1969–70, pp 47–48.

42. Hist, JCS, *Vietnam*, 1969–70, pp 42–47.

43. Memo, Brown to Abrams, subj: Hanoi's Shift in Strategy, Mar 17, 1969.

44. Hist, JCS, *Vietnam*, 1969–70, pp 218–22; Kissinger, *White House Years*, pp 239–54; Nixon, *RN*, I, pp 471–72.

45. *New York Times*, Mar 26, Apr 27, and May 9, 1969. See also *Washington Post*, Apr 27 and May 18, 1969.

46. Kissinger, *White House Years*, pp 252–53.

47. Intrvw, James C. Hasdorff, USAF hist prog, with Lt Gen Robert E. Pursley, Stamford, Conn, Sep 16, 1983; Hersh, *Price of Power*, pp 90–91.

48. News conf transcripts, Melvin Laird, Saigon, Mar 10 and Aug 21, 1969, in SAFAA, *Selected Statements on Vietnam*; *New York Times*, Mar 8, 1969.

49. Nixon, *RN*, I, 476. See also Kissinger, *White House Years*, pp 313–21.

50. Samuel Zaffiri, *Hamburger Hill* (Novato, Calif, 1988).

51. Nixon, *RN*, I, 487.

52. Kissinger, *White House Years*, pp 277–78, 304.

53. Nixon, *RN*, I, 532.

54. *Public Papers of the Presidents,* Nixon, 1969, pp 544–56.

55. Kissinger, *White House Years*, p 280; Luu Van Loi and Nguyen Anh Vu, *Le Duc Tho-Kissinger Negotiations in Paris* (Hanoi, 1996), pp 97–104.

56. Kissinger, *White House Years*, p 283.

57. John E. Woodruf, "Thieu Expects Power Fight Among Ho's Successors," *Baltimore Sun*, Sep 4, 1969, p 1.

58. Kissinger, *White House Years*, pp 284–85. See also Tom Wells, *The War Within* (Berkeley, Calif, 1994), pp 355–79.

59. Hersh, *Price of Power*, pp 120–29.

60. Nixon, *RN*, I, 495.

61. Kissinger, *White House Years*, p 304.

62. Nixon, *RN*, I, 494.

63. Hist, SAC, FY 1970, Historical Study 117, I, 151.

64. Ibid., pp 153–56.

65. Kissinger, *White House Years*, pp 304–5.

66. Gallup poll of Oct. 12, 1969, based on data gathered Oct. 2–7, 1969.

67. Quoted by Eric Pace, "Hanoi Calls Moratorium 'Timely Rebuff' to Nixon," *New York Times*, Oct 15, 1969, p 16.

68. Nixon, *RN*, I, 496.

69. Kissinger, *White House Years*, p 285.

70. Nixon, *RN*, I, 500–501.

71. Nixon, *RN*, I, 503.

72. Ibid., pp 503–4. See also Kissinger, *White House Years*, p 305.

73. "Address to the Nation on the War in Vietnam," Nov 3, 1969, *Public Papers of the the Presidents,* Nixon, 1969, p 902. Nixon also said that the communists had executed 50,000 when they took over North Vietnam in the 1950s. This is the figure given by Fall in *The Two Viet-Nams*, p 156, but it has been questioned by Gareth Porter and Edwin E. Moise. In *Land Reform in China and North Vietnam* (Chapel Hill, NC, 1983), p 222, Moise estimates 5000.

74. "Address to the Nation on the War in Vietnam," Nov 3, 1969, *Public Papers of the Presidents*, Nixon, 1969, p 907.

75. "Address to the Nation on the War in Vietnam," Nov 3, 1969, *Public Papers of the Presidents*, Nixon, 1969, p 909.

76. Gallup poll released Nov 4, 1969.

77. Gallup poll, Nov 23, 1969, based on data gathered Nov 12–17, 1969.

78. Quoted by John D. Carroll, "Nixon Thanks Congressmen," *Baltimore Sun*, Nov 14, 1969, p 1.

79. Twenty years later the crowd on Nov 15, 1969, was still considered to be the largest demonstration ever held in Washington. By then the National Park service had revised its estimate of the size of that crowd upward to 600,000. See Karlyn Barker, "Size of Abortion-Rights March Disputed," *Washington Post*, Apr 11, 1989, p B1.

80. Quoted by Stanley Karnow,

"Hanoi Praises Protests Against War in the U.S.," *Washington Post*, Nov 14, 1969, p 16. See also *New York Times*, Nov 13, 1969, and William Meyers, "November in Hanoi," *The Nation*, Dec 8, 1969.

81. Hist, SAC, FY 1970, Hist Study 117, I, pp 192–95.

82. Hist, JCS, Vietnam, 1969–70, p 347; PACAF, "Summary of Air Operations in SEA," Dec 1969, sec 5, p 8.

83. Hist, 355 TFWg, Jan–Mar 1970; PACAF, "Summary of Air Operations in SEA," Jan 1970, sec 5, pt A, p 1.

84. PACAF, "Summary of Air Operations in SEA," Jan 1970, sec 5, pt A, p 6.

85. Maj Jack Cremin, Aug 8, 1979, quoted by Puryear, *Brown*, p 172. See also Capt Paul W. Elder and Capt Peter J. Melly, "Rules of Engagement, Nov 1969–Sep 1972," CHECO rpt, Mar 1973.

86. PACAF, Summary of Air Operations in SEA," Feb 1970, sec 1, pp 1–2; hist, 8th TFWg, Jan–Mar 1970.

87. Hist, JCS, Vietnam, 1969–70, pp 349–51.

88. Hist, JCS, Vietnam, 1969–70, pp 230–57. For a harshly critical view of Nixon administration policies and actions regarding Cambodia, see William Shawcross, *Sideshow: Kissinger, Nixon, and the Destruction of Cambodia* (New York, 1979).

89. Kissinger, *White House Years*, p 498.

90. Hist, JCS, Vietnam, 1969–70, p 354. The loss of the F–4 was reported in PACAF, "Summary of Air Operations in SEA," May 1970, sec 5, pt A, p 1; in all other respects this report was silent about the early May raids into North Vietnam.

91. Hist, JCS, Vietnam, p 1969–70, p 354.

92. PACAF, "Summary of Air Operations in SEA," May 1970, sec 1, pt A, p 1.

93. Kissinger, *White House Years*, pp 499–501.

94. Elizabeth H. Hartsook, "The Air Force in Southeast Asia: The Role of Air Power Grows, 1970," Office of Air Force History, Sep 1972, p 18.

95. Vice President Agnew, intrvw on CBS Face the Nation, May 3, 1970, quoted in Secretary of the Air Force, Public Affairs, "Selected Statements on Vietnam," Jan–Jun 1970.

96. Daniel Z. Henkin, Assistant Secretary of Defense, Public Affairs, May 4, 1970, quoted in Secretary of the Air Force, Public Affairs, "Selected Statements on Vietnam," Jul–Dec 1970.

97. Gallup Poll, Jun 4, 1970, survey 807-K, question 11, index 61, intrvws May 21–26, 1970.

Chapter 7

1. Marie Smith, "Support for the Captives' Families," *Washington Post*, May 2, 1970, p 4.

2. "Summary of Efforts to Date on Behalf of PW/MIA," 1972, AFHRA K143.430-13; "Operation Homecoming from Inception to Implementation, 1964–1973," AFHRA 1015703; staff summary sheet and attachments, Lt Col Kloberdanz, HQ USAF/XPPGS, subj: Correspondence to Mrs. Rita E. Hauser [UN], Mar 11, 1970, John D. Ryan papers, AFHRA 1024030.

3. Jim Stockdale and Sybil Stockdale, *In Love and War: The Story of a Family's Ordeal and Sacrifice During the Vietnam Years* (New York, 1984), pp 372–76.

4. Robert and Elizabeth Dole with Richard Norton Smith, *Doles: Unlimited Partners* (New York, 1988); histories, 23 TFW, Jan 1966–Dec 1970.

5. Minutes, Interagency Prisoner of War Intelligence Ad Hoc Committee, esp 1970 mtgs, AFHRA 1018954-14.

6. "MiG Sweep," newsletter of the Red River Valley Fighter Pilots Association, Jul 1969.

7. Gardner Hatch and Patti Sheridan, eds, *Red River Valley Fighter Pilots* (Paducah, Kentucky, 1989), pp 27–28.

8. Ltr with numerous attachments, Amarjit Singh Vasir, Bangkok, to author,

Dec 18, 1987; intrvw, author with Amarjit Singh Vasir, Pattaya, Thailand, Nov 7, 1987.

9. Some pilots did think that many prisoners were second-rate pilots. See Zalin Grant, *Over the Beach* (New York, 1986), p 288, who quotes a Navy pilot: "But a sizable portion of the POWs were fuckups. They got shot down either because of their fear or out of stupidity." There was a widespread conviction that increased pilot experience would increase effectiveness and reduce losses. The major study of this relationship during the Vietnam War looked only at air-to-air combat, where despite a relatively small number of engagements, a correlation was found. See Tactical Fighter Weapons Center, Red Baron III, vol III, pt 1, pp 127–53.

10. *New York Times*, Jun 5, 1970, p 8.

11. Ibid.; Arthur Scheer, "H. Ross Perot," in Eleanor W. Schoenebaum, ed, *Profiles of an Era: The Nixon/Ford Years* (New York, 1979), pp 493–94.

12. Goodman, *Lost Peace*, pp 78–122; Gareth Porter, *A Peace Denied: The United States, Vietnam, and the Paris Agreement* (Bloomington, Indian, 1975), pp 79–101.

13. John P. Wallach, "Bombing Cutback Offer Linked to POW Release," *Baltimore News American*, Oct 14, 1969, p 1.

14. Richard Nixon, "Statement on Appointing Frank Borman as Special Representative on Prisoners of War," *Public Papers of the Presidents*, 1970 (Washington, 1971), pp 649 50; *RN*, pp 448 and 531. See also Henry Kissinger memo for Secretaries of State and Defense, Jan 22, 1970, AFHRA 1018954-6; minutes, DOD POW Policy Committee, Mar 9, 1970, AFHRA 1018954-6; minutes, Interagency POW Intelligence Ad Hoc Committee, Aug 7, 1970, AFHRA 1018954-14.

15. Guenter Lewy, *America in Vietnam*, pp 297–99.

16. Gloria Emerson, *Winners and Losers* (New York, 1976), pp 342–50; *Life*, Jul 17, 1970, pp 26–29.

17. The complete text of Borman's speech was given wide distribution by the State Department both in the *Department of State Bulletin*, Oct 12, 1970, and as a pamphlet entitled "U.S. Prisoners of War in Southeast Asia." See also State Department messages relating to Borman's trip in AFHRA 1018953–16.

18. Article 85, Geneva Convention Relative to the Treatment of Prisoners of War, 1949.

19. North Vietnam's reservation to Article 85 is quoted in Richard A. Falk, ed, *The Vietnam War and International Law*, III (Princeton, 1972), p 895.

20. *Against the Crime of Silence: Proceedings of the Russell International War Crimes Tribunal* (New York, 1968).

21. Bernard B. Fall, *Street Without Joy*, 4th ed (New York, 1967), pp 295–311.

22. Albert D. Biderman, *March to Calumny* (New York, 1963); William Lindsay White, *The Captives of Korea* (New York, 1957).

23. Ibid. See Stuart I. Rochester and Frederick Kiley, *Honor Bound: The History of American Prisoners of War in Southeast Asia, 1961–1973* (Washington, 1998) and John G. Hubbell, *P.O.W.* (New York, 1976), for surveys of the American prison experience in North Vietnam. More than thirty Air Force officers who had been prisoners surveyed their own experience in reports prepared at the Air War College in 1974. See esp Armand J. Myers, et al., "Vietnam POW Camp Histories and Studies, vol I," Air War College, 1974, AFHRA 1033169, and Hervey S. Stockman, "Authority, Leadership, Organization and Discipline Among US POWs in the Hanoi Prison System," Air War College, 1974, AFHRA 1033170. Prisoner John M. McGrath, a Navy lieutenant commander, taught himself to draw; his drawings of various methods of torture can be seen in his *Prisoner of War: Six Years in Hanoi* (Annapolis, 1975). Many of the prisoners have published memoirs; these have been discussed by Craig Howes, *Voices of the Vietnam POWs* (New York, 1993) and

Elliott Gruner, *Prisoners of Culture: Representing the Vietnam POWs* (New Brunswick, New Jersey, 1993).

24. Intrvw, Capt Mark C. Cleary, AFHRA, with Col Carlyle S. Harris, Tupelo, Miss, Nov 16, 1982, AFHRA K239.0512-1359.

25. Everett Alvarez, Jr., and Anthony S. Pitch, *Chained Eagle* (New York, 1989), p 164. See also Henry James Bedinger, "Prisoner-of-War Organization in Hanoi," MA thesis, San Diego State University, 1976.

26. HQ USAF, SEA PW Analysis Program Report 800-2, "Places and Dates of Confinement of Air Force, Navy, and Marine Corps Prisoners of War Held in North Vietnam, 1964–73," Jun 1975. On the "Alcatraz Gang," see Sam Johnson and Jan Winebrenner, *Captive Warriors* (College Station, Tex, 1992); an Air Force F–4 pilot shot down in North Vietnam, Johnson later became a Republican congressman from Texas.

27. Capt. Gerald Coffee (USN, Ret), *Beyond Survival: Building on Hard Times- A POW's Inspiring Story* (New York, 1990), pp 195–22.

28. Intrvw, Capt Mark C. Cleary, AFHRA, with Brig Gen Robinson Risner, Austin TX, Mar 1–2, 1983, AFHRA K239.0512-1370; Risner, *The Passing of the Night: My Seven Years as a Prisoner of the North Vietnamese* (New York, 1973); Gen T. R. Milton, "Robinson Risner: The Indispensable Ingredient," in John L. Frisbee, ed, *Makers of the United States Air Force* (Washington, 1987), pp 307–27; Col Jon B. Reynolds, "The Eagle in the Hilton," *Air Force Magazine*, Feb 1983, pp 82–85. As the years in captivity lengthened and newer, younger prisoners sometimes outranked older prisoners, the practice of turning to the senior ranking officer in any group for leadership was not always practical; see, for example, Pollard intrvw, May 11, 1992.

29. The four full colonels were John P. Flynn, David W. Winn, Norman C. Gaddis, and James E. Bean. New prisoners informed the old-timers that subsequent to capture, Risner had been promoted to colonel and Stockdale to Navy captain. But since the prisoners' knowledge of promotion after capture was necessarily incomplete, they determined the identity of the senior ranking officer based on rank at the time of capture. See Col Larry Guarino, *A POW's Story: 2801 Days in Hanoi* (New York, 1990); Stockdale and Stockdale, *In Love and War*; Jeremiah A. Denton, Jr., with Ed Brandt, *When Hell Was in Session: a Personal Story of Survival as a P.O.W. in North Vietnam* (New York, 1976); Richard "Pop" Keirn, *Old Glory is the Most Beautiful of All* (Pittsburgh, 1996); intrvw, Capt Mark C. Cleary, AFHRA, with Brig Gen David W. Winn, Colo Springs, Feb 8–9, 1983.

30. Keirn, *Old Glory is the Most Beautiful of All* pp 7, 64.

31. Risner, *Passing of the Night*, p 31.

32. On German imprisonment of American airmen in World War II, see Arthur A. Durand, *Stalag Luft III* (Baton Rouge, 1988). On Japanese prison camps, see E. Bartlett Kerr, *Surrender and Survival: The Experience of American POWs in the Pacific, 1941–1945* (New York, 1985), and Stanley L. Falk, *Bataan: The March of Death* (New York, 1962). For a survey of the prisoner of war experience from the Hundred Years War to the Vietnam War, see Richard Garrett, *P.O.W.* (London, 1981).

33. Executive Order 10631, Aug 17, 1955.

34. *Report of the Air Force Advisory Committee on Prisoners of War*, Nov 1963. After the Vietnam War, the wording of the Code of Conduct's Article V was changed from "I am bound to give only name, rank, service number, and date of birth" to "I am required to give name, rank, service number, and date of birth." The Code's next sentence, "I will evade answering further questions to the best of my ability," remained unchanged.

35. Suggested Training and Education Guide for the Code of Conduct, Aug 1955, sec 2d(3), in ibid., p 53.

36. Ibid., sec 3a, p 54.

37. *Report of the Air force Advisory*

Committee on Prisoners of War, Nov
1963, p 94.

38. Ibid., pp 27–28.

39. Ibid., pp 92–93.

40. Stockdale and Stockdale, *In Love
and War*, pp 332–36; Denton, *When Hell
Was in Session*, pp 89–98; Scott Blakey,
*Prisoner at War: The Survival of
Commander Richard A. Stratton* (New
York, 1978), pp 113–37; Hubbell, *P.O.W.*,
pp 240–43, 265–69.

41. Hubbell, *P.O.W.*, pp 183–99.

42. Daniel De Luce, "Hanoi Displays
Defenses Against U.S. Air Radio [*sic*],"
Philadelphia Bulletin, Mar 2, 1970;
Blesse, *Check Six*, pp 128–30.

43. Guarino, *A POW's Story*, p 43;
Wilfred Burchett, *At the Barricades: Forty
Years on the Cutting Edge of History*
(New York, 1981); Robert Manne, *Agent
of Influence: The Life and Times of
Wilfred Burchett* (Toronto, 1989), esp pp
51–52.

44. Stockdale and Stockdale, *In Love
and War*, pp 253–54.

45. HQ USAF, "The Special
Exploitation Program for Selected United
States Prisoners of War in Southeast Asia,
1967–1968," Jun 1975, AFCHO K142.04-
31; Guarino, *A POW's Story*, pp 426–28;
Alvarez, *Chained Eagle*, pp 186–87;
Hubbell, *P.O.W.*, pp 320–48, 429–49.

46. Tom Hayden, *Reunion: A Memoir*
(New York, 1988), pp 175–241. See also
Staughton Lynd and Thomas Hayden, *The
Other Side* (New York, 1967) and Herbert
Aptheker, *Mission to Hanoi* (New York,
1966).

47. Maj. James B. Overton, "Enemy
Capture/Release of USAF Personnel in
SEA," CHECO rpt, 1969; Daniel
Berrigan, *Night Flight to Hanoi* (New
York, 1968).

48. John McCain with Mark Salter,
Faith of My Fathers (New York, 1999), pp
189–204.

49. Col George E. Day, *Return with
Honor* (Mesa, Ariz., 1989); Maj Donald
K. Schneider, *Air Force Heroes in
Vietnam* (Maxwell AFB, Ala, 1979), pp
54–59.

50. Stockdale and Stockdale, *In Love

and War*, esp pp 207–13 and 456.

51. Overton, "Enemy
Capture/Release," pp 43–79. See also
Corona Harvest intrvws with Maj Joe V.
Carpenter and Maj Fred N. Thompson,
Jun 1970, AFHRA K239.0512-283 and
K239.0512-284; Thompson and Carpenter,
"Facing Interrogation," Corona Harvest
spec rpt #70-17, 1970. For an admiring
portrait of Kasler as a fighter ace in Korea
by a squadron mate and distinguished
novelist, see James Salter, *Burning the
Days* (New York, 1997), pp 146–56; Low
was an ace in the same squadron.

52. Hubbell, *P.O.W.*, pp 252–87,
312–78, 506–8.

53. Memo for service secretaries
from G. Warren Nutter, Assistant Secretary
of Defense for International Security
Affairs, subj: DOD Policy on Early
Release of POWs by the Enemy, Jul 3,
1970, AFHRA 1018954-1. See also Nutter
memo of Nov 22, 1969, and Charles W.
Havens III memo of Dec 1, 1969, AFHRA
1018964-30; minutes of DOD POW
Policy Committee and Subcommittee, esp
Jan 29, 1970, and Mar 9, 1970, AFHRA
1018954-6; minutes of the Air Staff
E&E/POW Committee, esp Mar 2, 1970,
AFHRA 1018954-16.

54. Excerpt from the Code of
Conduct quoted by Lt Gen Maddox, Cmdr
ATC, ltr to HQ USAF, subj: DOD Policy
on Early Release of PW's by the Enemy,
Aug 26, 1970, AFHRA 1018964-30.

55. Harry S. Ashmore and William C.
Baggs, *Mission to Hanoi: A Chronicle of
Double-Dealing in High Places* (New
York, 1968), pp 112–73. Twenty years
after the Vietnam War, former prisoners of
war continued to be vehement in their
opposition to early release; see, for exam-
ple, intrvw, Dr. James C. Hasdorff, USAF
Academy, with Brig Gen Jon A. Reynolds,
USAF Ret, Apr 20, 1992.

56. Mary McCarthy, *Hanoi* (New
York, 1968), p 111.

57. Ibid., p 112.

58. Hist, JCS, *Vietnam*, 1969–70, pp
501–8.

59. Ibid.

60. Hist, JCS, *Vietnam*, 1971–72, pp

587–88. On negotiations to end the Korean War, see U.S. Department of State, *Foreign Relations of the United States*, 1952–54, vol XV.

61. Article III, Code of Conduct for Members of the Armed Forces of the United States, Executive Order 10631, Aug 17, 1955.

62. Lt Col John A. Dramesi, USAF, *Code of Honor* (New York, 1975), pp 105 and 196–97.

63. Schneider, *Heroes*, pp 54–61.

64. HQ USAF, "US Aircrew Members Escape from Permanent Detention Facilities in North Vietnam," Nov 1975, AFCHO K142.04-33, pp 5–12; Hubbell, *P.O.W.*, pp 355–60.

65. See note above; Dramesi, *Code of Honor*, pp 85–119.

66. HQ USAF, "U.S. Aircrew Members Escape from Permanent Detention Facilities in North Vietnam," Nov 1975, AFCHO K142.04-33, pp 46–48; Guarino, *A POW's Story*, pp 195–208, 283–301; Lt Col Jon A. Reynolds, "Question of Honor," *Air University Review*, Mar–Apr 1977, pp 104–10; Dramesi, *Code of Honor*, pp 22–34.

67. The fullest published account of the effort to extract prisoners from Son Tay is Benjamin F. Schemmer, *The Raid* (New York, 1976), which was based on extensive interviews with participants. See also Tilford, *Search and Rescue in Southeast Asia*, pp 103–12.

68. Tran Van Don, *Our Endless War* (San Rafael, Calif, 1978), pp 1, 16–17, 20–21.

69. Intrvw, Charles Hildreth and William McQuillen, Air Force historians, with Brig. Gen. Manor, Eglin AFB, Dec 31, 1970, AFHRA 239.0512-700; intrvw, Hugh Ahmann, et al., Air Force historians, with Manor, Jan–May 1988, AFHRA K239.0512-1799; rpt, Manor, subj: Son Tay prisoner of war rescue operation, Dec 18, 1970, AFHRA; hearing before the Committee on Foreign Relations, senate, *Bombing Operations and the Prisoner-of-War Rescue Mission in North Vietnam, 91st Cong, 2d sess* (Washington, 1970);

William R. Karsteter, "The Son Tay Raid," annex to hist, Aerospace Rescue and Recovery Service, Jul 1970–Jun 1971; Jay M. Strayer, "The Son Tay Raid: A Personal Perspective," *Friends Journal* (Air Force Museum Foundation), fall 1995, pp 2–6 and 34.

70. *Public Papers of the Presidents, Nixon*, 1970, pp 825–31; Manor intrvws; Kissinger, *White House Years*, pp 699–701, 980–82; Hersh, *Price of Power*, p 304; Schermer, pp 114–15; Lucien S. Vandenbroucke, *Perilous Options: Special Operations as an Instrument of U.S. Foreign Policy* (New York, 1993), p 62.

71. Manor rpt; Manor intrvws; intrvw, Col Robert L. Gleason and Maj Richard B. Clement with Lt Col Keith R. Grimes, 1970, AFHRA K239.0512-478; intrvw, John F. Fuller, Air Force historian, with Lt Col Grimes, Apr 19, 1974, AFHRA K239.0512-1565; John F. Fuller, *Thor's Legions: Weather Support to the U.S. Air Force and Army, 1937–1987* (Boston, 1990), pp 310–12.

72. Manor rpt.

73. Ibid.; Schemmer, *The Raid*, pp 168–71; intrvw, Lt Col V.H. Gallagher and Maj Lyn R. Officer, Air Force historians, with Col Royal A. Brown, Feb 9, 1973, AFHRA K239.0512-657.

74. Kissinger, *White House Years*, p 982.

75. Schemmer, *The Raid*, p 148. But Palmer, "U.S. Intelligence and Vietnam," p 84, found no evidence to support Schemmer's contention that Laird told Nixon.

76. Hearing before the Committee on Foreign Relations, Senate, *Bombing Operations and the Prisoner-of-War Rescue Mission in North Vietnam*, 91st Cong, 2d sess (Washington, 1970), pp 7, 9 and 22.

77. William Beecher, "U.S. Rescue Force Landed 23 Miles from Hanoi," *New York Times*, Nov 24, 1970, p 1; George C. Wilson, "Helicopter Force Hits Camp Near Hanoi," *Washington Post*, Nov 24, 1970, p 1; Charles W. Cordry, "Helcopter Force Finds Camp West of Hanoi Vacated," *Baltimore Sun*, Nov 24, 1970, p 1.

78. Michael Getler, "U.S. Admits It

Hit Bases Near Sontay," *Washington Post*, Nov 28, 1970, p 1; William Chapman, "The Sontay Story: Action Heavier, Scope Greater Than At First Indicated," *Washington Post*, Nov 29, 1970.

79. William Beecher, "Laird Says Raids Struck at Missile and Gun Sites," *New York Times*, Nov 22, 1970, p 1; Peter Braestrup, "Air Raids Limited, U.S. Says," *Washington Post*, Nov 23, 1970, p 1.

80. PACAF, "Summary of Air Operations in SEA," Nov 1970.

81. Msg, McCain to Moorer, subj: SAM sites in RP-1 and Freedom Bait, 230320Z Nov 70, AFHRA CHECO microfilm roll T94.

82. Ltr, Col Irby B. Jarvis, Cmdr 388 TFW to 7 AF/DO, with att rpt, undated, AFHRA CHECO microfilm roll T96.

83. Ltr, Col H. E. Hayes, Dep Cmdr for Ops, 432 TRW to 7 AF/DO, undated, AFHRA CHECO microfilm roll T96.

84. Ltr, Col Daniel C. Perry, Cmdr, 366 TFW to 7 AF/DO, Nov 24, 1970; msg, hand carried, 8 TFW to 7 AF, 241130Z Nov 1970; both in AFHRA

CHECO microfilm roll T96.

85. Ltr, Col H. E. Hayes, Dep Cmdr for Ops, 432 TRW to 7 AF/DO, undated, AFHRA CHECO microfilm roll T96.

86. Guarino, *A POW's Story*, pp 270–301; Hubbell, *P.O.W.*, pp 536–53; Johnson and Winebrenner, *Captive Warriors*, pp 230–53.

87. HQ USAF, "Places and Dates of Confinement of Air Force, Navy, and Marine Corps Prisoners of War Held in North Vietnam, 1964–73," Jun 1975, AFCHO K142.04-13.

88. Hearing before the Committee on Foreign Relations, Senate, *Bombing Operations and the Prisoner-of-War Rescue Mission in North Vietnam*, 91st Cong, 2d sess (Washington, 1970), pp 1–2, 25, and 47; Schemmer, *The Raid*, pp 135 and 193.

89. Valerie Kushner quoted by George Lardner, Jr., "POW Families Praise Rescue Attempt," *Washington Post*, Nov 25, 1970.

90. Mrs. Howard J. Hill quoted by Lardner.

Chapter 8

1. Intrvw, Wayne Thompson with Lt Gen John P. Flynn, USAF Ret, on flight from Randolph AFB, TX, to Andrews AFB, MD, Jun 25, 1981.

2. Intrvw, Lt Col John N. Dick, Jr., AFHRA, with Gen Lavelle, McLean VA, 17–24 Apr 78, AFHRA K239.0512-1036. See also intrvw, Maj Scott S. Thompson, AFHRA, with Gen Nazzaro, Tucson AZ, Feb 3–6, 1980, AFHRA K239.0512-1189.

3. Lavelle intrvw.

4. Ibid.

5. See Bernard Nalty's manuscript on the air war in southern Laos at the Air Force History Support Office, Bolling AFB. See also Van Staaveren, *Interdiction in Southern Laos*.

6. Ryan intrvw, May 15–19, 1979; Lavelle intrvw.

7. Lavelle intrvw. In his 1979 intrvw, almost a decade after the fact, Gen Ryan said he did not remember anything about

discussing the C–5 with Lavelle. In 1990 the author corresponded with a number of people who had been involved with C–5 matters in 1970. Former Secretary of the Air Force Seamans recalled that there had been a proposal for the Air Force to take charge of the Lockheed plant and that he had talked to Lavelle about it, but Seamans doubted that Ryan had favored the idea. Former Undersecretary McLucas thought that Lavelle's account rang true but could not remember the details. Lt. Gen. Harry Goldsworthy, USAF Ret, wrote that he had briefed a proposal to Ryan to force Lockheed into bankruptcy (with greater Air Force participation in plant operations) but that Ryan had shown little interest. Lt. Gen. Otto Glasser, USAF Ret, suspected that Lavelle fabricated his recollection out of bitterness toward Ryan. Maj. Gen. Otis Moore, USAF Ret, who was Ryan's executive officer at the time and later Lavelle's chief of staff in Vietnam, recalled that Lavelle was in trouble with Ryan over something in 1970.

8. Lavelle intrvw.

9. Lavelle intrvw.

10. *Defense Intelligence Digest*, Jan 1972, p 38.

11. PACAF, "Summary of Air Operations in SEA," Oct 1971–Mar 1972.

12. The best introductions to the Lavelle affair are: Col Gordon A. Ginsburg, "The Lavelle Case: Crisis in Integrity," Air War College, Apr 1974; Col James R. Olson, "Preplanned Protective Reaction Strikes: A Case Study on Integrity," Air War College, Apr 1974; George C. Wilson, "The Lavelle Case," *The Atlantic*, Dec 1972, pp 6–27.

13. The Feb and Mar 1971 strikes were called Louisville Slugger and Fracture Cross Alpha. See the msg traffic for those operations in CHECO microfilm rolls T114 and T115, AFHRA.

14. Lavelle intrvw, pp 603–12; PACAF, "Summary of Air Operations in SEA," Sep 1971, p 4-A-4 and p 4-1. See also msg traffic on Operation Prize Bull in CHECO microfilm rolls T110 and T125, AFHRA.

15. Kissinger, *White House Years*, pp 1037–38.

16. Kissinger, *White House Years*, pp 1042–43.

17. See msg traffic on Operation Proud Deep Alpha in CHECO microfilm rolls T110, T125 and S589, AFHRA.

18. Melvin F. Porter, "Proud Deep Alpha," CHECO rpt, 1972, p 50.

19. Porter, "Proud Deep Alpha," pp 32–39.

20. Haldeman, *Haldeman Diaries*, Apr 23, 1970; Mar 30, Jun 2, and Jun 23, 1971; Jan 8, Jan 17, and Feb 5, 1972.

21. Hist, Joint Chiefs of Staff, Vietnam, 1971–73, pt I, pp 254–96; Elder and Melly, "Rules of Engagement"; Lt Gen Phillip B. Davidson (USA, Ret), *Vietnam at War* (Novato, Clif, 1988), pp 669–70.

22. Msg, Adm Moorer to CINCPAC, 241609Z Jul 71, quoted in HQ MACV

memo on protective reaction authority, Mar 18, 1972, CHECO microfilm roll T137, AFHRA.

23. Msg, COMUSMACV, 010940Z Aug 71, quoted in HQ MACV memo on protective reaction authorities, Mar 18, 1972, CHECO microfilm roll T137, AFHRA. See also msg, CINCPAC to MACV, 251345Z Jul 71, quoted in same source.

24. Lavelle presented his rationale extensively and repeatedly in hearings before the House and Senate committees on armed services. See Hearing before the Armed Services Investigating Subcommittee of the Committee on Armed Services, House of Representatives, *Unauthorized Bombing of Military Targets in North Vietnam*, 92d Cong, 2d sess (Washington, 1972); Hearings before the Committee on Armed Services, Senate, *Nomination of John D. Lavelle, General Creighton W. Abrams, and Admiral John S. McCain*, 92d Cong, 2d sess (Washington, 1972).

25. Lavelle intrvw; Moorer testimony, Senate Lavelle hearings, pp 442–59. See also HQ MACV memo on protective reaction authority, Mar 18, 1972, CHECO microfilm roll T137, AFHRA.

26. Lavelle intrvw; Moorer testimony, Senate Lavelle hearings, pp 442–46; Ryan testimony, pp 263–64; Gabriel testimony, pp 205–8; PACAF, "Summary of Air Operations in SEA," Nov 1971.

27. President's news conf, Dec 10, 1970, *Public Papers of the Presidents*, Nixon, 1970, p 1101.

28. Msg, JCS to COMUSMACV, 101716Z Apr 71, quoted in HQ MACV memo on protective reaction authorities, Mar 18, 1972, CHECO microfilm roll T137, AFHRA.

29. Lavelle intrvw.

30. Lavelle intrvw; Moorer testimony, Senate Lavelle hearings, pp 446–47. See also msgs, CINCPAC to MACV, 050410Z Dec 71, and JCS to MACV, 222208Z Nov 71, both quoted in HQ MACV memo on protective reaction authorities, Mar 18, 1972, CHECO microfilm roll T137, AFHRA.

31. Lavelle did not introduce this matter in the 1972 hearings but only in his 1978 intrvw (after Meyer's death). See also PACAF, "Summary of Air Operations in SEA," Dec 1971.

32. Lavelle intrvw; Maj Gen Alton D. Slay testimony, Senate Lavelle hearings, pp 292–95. The two versions differ. Slay said that the raid occurred while Lavelle was still in Washington and was approved by Abrams; and that the raid failed to knock out the radar. 7 AF and PACAF records appear to confirm Lavelle's claim that he had returned and that the radar was out of commission for almost three weeks. The after action msg on the raid by the 388 TFW, 051215Z Jan 72, is quoted in HQ MACV memo on protective reaction authorities, Mar 18, 1972, CHECO microfilm roll T137, AFHRA, as is the JCS response: 051658Z Jan 72 and 072347Z Jan 72.

33. Lavelle testimony, Senate Lavelle hearings, p 7; Slay testimony, Senate Lavelle hearings, p 299; Lavelle intrvw.

34. Gabriel testimony, Senate Lavelle hearings, pp 197–225; Capt Douglas J. Murray testimony, pp 225–39; Sgt Lonnie Douglas Franks testimony, pp 156–95.

35. See Lavelle, Gabriel, and Slay testimonies in Senate Lavelle hearings.

36. See note above.

37. The Franks letter to Senator Hughes was passed to the Secretary of the Air Force by Senator Symington in a letter of Mar 6, 1972. See also Lt Gen Louis L. Wilson, Jr, "Report of Investigation Concerning Alleged Falsification of Classified Reports for Missions in North Vietnam," Mar 20, 1972, with supporting intrvw summaries, Lavelle IG collection, Air Force History Support Office; intrvw, Lt Col Arthur W. McCants, Jr, with Gen Louis L. Wilson, Jr, Tucson, Ariz, Nov 7–8, 1979; Franks testimony, Senate Lavelle hearings, pp 156–95; Daniel St. Albin Greene, "The Sergeant Who Shook Up the Brass," *National Observer*, Sep 23, 1972.

38. On Col Broughton and the *Tukestan* incident, see chap 2. In Lavelle's case the possibility of court martial lingered for some time. In June 1972, Lt.

Delbert R. Terrill, Jr., filed charges against Lavelle on behalf of the Concerned Officers Movement, a group opposed to continuing the war in SEA. Terrill, an Air Force Academy graduate working on the *Air Reservist* magazine at Bolling AFB in Washington, was also featured on a television interview program about his charges. In the fall, Sgt Franks, who had raised the original alarm about false reporting, also filed formal charges. The Secretary of the Air Force held to his original decision not to court martial Lavelle. A transcript of the Terrill interview on WTOP's "Newsmakers" program of Jul 2, 1972, is in the Lavelle IG file, Air Force History Support Office.

39. Seamans intrvw; Laird, memo for Chairman JCS, subj: Command of Air Elements in Southeast Asia, Mar 30, 1972; memo, Lavelle to Ryan, subj: Retirement, Mar 31, 1972; Lt Gen Robert J. Dixon (Deputy Chief of Staff, Personnel), memo to Gen Ryan with attached chronology of Lavelle affair, May 26, 1972. All three memos and the chronology are in the Air Force IG Lavelle files, Air Force History Support Office. The Dixon chronology indicates that Ryan briefed Moorer about the IG report on Mar 23, 1972, before recalling Lavelle. After Ryan told Lavelle on Mar 26 that Ryan intended to relieve him of his command, Laird asked Ryan to withhold action for a few days. While Laird did approve Lavelle's relief on Mar 30, Lavelle requested retirement on Mar 31 and was still offficially commander of 7 AF when he retired on Apr 7.

40. On Lavelle's medical problems, see Maj Gen Thomas H. Crouch's "Resume of Events Leading to the Medical Evaluation and Retirement for Physical Disability of Gen J.D. Lavelle," no date (1972), Lavelle IG Files, Air Force History Support Office. Maj Gen John Giraudo, who was director of Air Force legislative liaison in 1972, later recalled being present when Ryan asked for Lavelle's retirement as a two-star at Andrews Air Force Base just after Lavelle got off the plane from SEA; see Giraudo intrvw. Lavelle's own recollection was

that from the outset Ryan said he would support Lavelle's advancement on the retired list to three stars (but not four); see the Lavelle intrvw.

41. On the 1967 hearings, see chap 3.

42. Report of the Armed Services Investigating Subcommittee of the Committee on Armed Services, House of Representatives, *Unauthorized Bombing of Military Targets in North Vietnam*, 92d

Congr, 2d sess (Washington, 1972); Senate Lavelle hearings.

43. Lavelle testimony, Senate Lavelle hearings, pp 16–17, 59–60; Ryan testimony, pp 263–65; Moorer testimony, pp 444–49.

44. Correspondence relating to Senator Hughes' requests for information, in AF/IG files on Lavelle case, Air Force History Support Office.

Chapter 9

1. *USAF Statistical Digest*, FY 1973, p 86; PACAF, "Summary of Air Operations in SEA," Jan 1973, p 4-A-7; Maj Donald L. Ockerman, "An Analysis of Laser Guided Bombs in SEA," Air Operations Report 73/4, HQ 7 AF, Thailand, Jun 28, 1973, AFHRA K740.041-4, pp ii, 9, 36–46.

2. Hist, USMACV, Jan 1972–Mar 1973, annexes J, K, and L.

3. Msg, Moorer to McCain and Abrams, 040006Z Apr 72, PACAF Source Documents for Corona Harvest V, vol I, Tab 14, AFHRA 717.03-221.

4. Kissinger, *White House Years*, p 1098.

5. Hersh, *Price of Power*, p 506, citing a White House tape recording made public during the Nixon impeachment proceedings.

6. Ibid.

7. Vogt intrvw, Aug 8–9, 1978; Seamans intrvw. Secretary of the Air Force Seamans discussed the Nixon meeting with Vogt shortly after it occurred.

8. *Haldeman Diaries*, Apr 6, 1972.

9. *Haldeman Diaries*, Apr 6, 1972; Kissinger, *White House Years*, p 1111; Lewis Sorley, *Thunderbolt: General Creighton Abrams and the Army of His Times* (New York, 1992), pp 312–16.

10. Kissinger, *White House Years*, p 1112.

11. Intrvw, John T. Mason Jr., U.S. Naval Institute, with Adm Thomas Moorer, Washington DC, 1975–81; memo, Secretary Seamans to Secretary Laird, subj: Southeast Asia Air Operations, Apr

24, 1972, Seamans papers, Air Force History Support Office. See also Seamans' autobiography, *Aiming at Targets* (Washington, 1996), esp pp 194–96. For an example of a backchannel message from Kissinger to Bunker, see Kissinger, *White House Years*, p 1181. The author is indebted to Graham Cosmas of the Army Center of Military History for insight into Bunker's role.

12. Moorer intrvw; Hersh, *Price of Power*, pp 465–79; Gen Alexander M. Haig, Jr., with Charles McCarry, *Inner Circles*, p 245; Walter Isaacson, *Kissinger* (New York, 1992), pp 380–85.

13. Pursley intrvw; Haig, *Inner Circles*.

14. Haig, *Inner Circles*, p 206.

15. Pursley intrvw. See also Hersh, *Price of Power*, pp 576–77.

16. PACAF, "Summary of Air Operations in SEA," esp Mar 1968, Jan 1972 and Jul 1972.

17. Histories of 8 TFW, 49 TFW, 366 TFW, 388 TFW and 432 TRW.

18. A detailed summary of carrier deployments is in Rene J. Francillon, *Tonkin Gulf Yacht Club* (Annapolis, 1988), esp pp 83–86. On the "Rose Garden," see Maj Charles Melson and Lt Col Curtis Arnold, *U.S. Marines in Vietnam: The War that Would Not End, 1971–1973* (Washington, 1991), pp 153–73.

19. Charles K. Hopkins, "SAC Bomber Operations in the Southeast Asia War," HQ SAC, 1983, pp 657–755.

20. Gen Louis T. Seith, USAF Ret, worked for Adm Moorer as Vice Director

of Joint Operations (J-3) in 1972. He recounted Moorer's turkey story in Seith intrvw. See also Secretary of the Air Force Seamans' recollections of Moorer's attempt to persuade Nixon not to deploy more B–52s in Seamans.

21. Quoted in Hopkins, "SAC Bomber Operations," p 690.

22. EOTR, Lt Gen Gerald W. Johnson, Sep 1971–Sep 1973.

23. JCS Hist, Vietnam 1971–73, p 356.

24. PACAF, Corona Harvest rpt, "USAF Air Operations Against North Vietnam, 1 Jul 1971–30 Jun 1972," AFHRA 1007439, pp 68–70.

25. Hist, 307 Strategic Wing, Apr–Jun 1992; Hopkins, "SAC Bomber Operations," pp 733–34.

26. Hist, 307 Strategic Wing, Apr–Jun 1972; Hopkins, "SAC Bomber Operations," pp 734–35.

27. Moorer intrvw; JCS hist, p 367.

28. PACAF, "Summary of Air Operations in SEA," Apr 1972; Bernard C. Nalty, *Electronic Warfare*, p 89.

29. Msg, Vogt to Ryan and Clay, subj: Daily Wrap-up, 161115Z Apr 72, AFHRA 717.03-221.

30. Minutes, 7 AF Commanders Conf, Jul 18–19, 1972, AFHRA 1009446. See also SAC ops input to Corona Harvest, 1 Jul 1971–30 Jun 1972, pp 27–33, AFHRA DABIN 579870.

31. Nixon, II, 65; *Haldeman Diaries*, Apr 16, 1972.

32. SAC intel input to Corona Harvest, 1 Jul 1971–30 Jun 1972, AFHRA DABIN 579869, pp 155–58.

33. Kissinger, *White House Years*, pp 1154–64; Gaiduk, *The Soviet Union and the Vietnam War*, pp 234–37; Anatoly Dobrynin, *In Confidence* (New York, 1995), pp 243–48.

34. Kissinger, *White House Years*, pp 1180–81; Loi and Vu, *Le Duc Tho-Kissinger Negotiations.*

35. JCS Hist, p 378; Nixon, *RN*, II, 78–86; *Haldeman Diaries*, Apr 26, 1972.

36. Nixon, *RN*, II, 79; *Haldeman Diaries*, May 4, 1972. Alexander Haig carried the message from Johnson to Nixon. See Haig, *Inner Circles*, pp 285–86.

37. Kissinger, *White House Years*, p 1180. See also pp 1181–86.

38. Moorer intrvw, Aug 24, 1976.

39. Sorley, *Thunderbolt*, pp 323–25.

40. Moorer intrvw, Sep 10, 1976; MACV hist, Jan 1972–Mar 1973, B–63.

41. PACAF, "Summary of Air Operations in SEA," Apr–Oct 1972.

42. See, for example, Ambrose, *Nixon*, I, 543. Adm Moorer (see intrvw cited above) thought that "Linebacker" was a chance selection from an approved list. But his staff officers might well have selected a name they deemed appropriate.

43. Peter DeLeon, "The Laser-Guided Bomb: Case History of a Development," RAND R-1312-1-PR, Jun 1974; Joan Lisa Bromberg, *The Laser in America, 1950–1970* (Cambridge, Mass, 1991).

44. DeLeon, pp 6–26.

45. Porter, "Second Generation Weaponry in SEA."

46. Ockerman, "Analysis of Laser Guided Bombs"; intrvw, Lt Col Robert G. Zimmerman, USAF hist prog, with Maj Richard M. Atchison, Maxwell AFB, Ala, Jul 16, 1975.

47. HQ 7 AF, Dir of Ops, "History of Linebacker I Operations," AFHRA 1006559.

48. Hist, 8 TFW, Jul 1–Sep 30, 1972.

49. See PACAF, "Summary of Air Operations in SEA," May–Sep 1972.

50. Nixon, *RN*, II, 85–86.

51. Ibid.

52. PACAF, "USAF Air Operations Against North Vietnam," pp 95–96; PACAF, "Summary of Air Operations in SEA," May–Oct 1972.

53. PACAF, "Summary of Air Operations in SEA"; Ockerman, "Analysis of Laser Guided Bombs"; R. L. Blachly, P. A. Conine, and E. H. Sharkey, "Laser and Electro-Optical Guided Bomb Performance in Southeast Asia (Linebacker I)," RAND R-1326-PR, Oct 1973; Capt Edward J. Dunne, Jr., 7 AF Ops Anal Br, "US Air Forces Vs the 130 MM Gun, Apr–Nov 1972," Jan 20, 1973, AFHRA

K740.041-1; Maj Edward J. Dunne, Jr., 7
AF Ops Anal Br, "The US Air War
Against Tanks," May 20, 1973, AFHRA
K740.041-2; David R. Mets, "The Quest
for a Surgical Strike: The United States
Air Force and Laser-Guided Bombs," Air
Force Systems Command, Armament Div,
1987, AFHRA 1003440.

54. RAND R-1326-PR; Maj Calvin
R. Johnson, "Linebacker Operations,
Sep–December 1972," CHECO rpt, Dec
31, 1978, p 39.

55. Hist, 8 TFW, Apr–Jun 1972.

56. David R. Mets, "Background
Notes on Bridge Attack and Defense," HQ
Armament Div, Air Force Systems
Command, Eglin AFB, Fla, 1987.

57. Futrell, *The United States Air
Force in Korea,* pp 291–95.

58. PACAF, Corona Harvest, "In-
Country and Out-Country Strike Ops in
SEA, 1 Jan 65–31 Dec 69," vol II,
"Hardware," sec 2, "Munitions."

59. Corum, *The Tale of Two Bridges.*
For the recent recollections of a North
Vietnamese female soldier, Ngo Thi
Tuyen, who helped to defend the Thanh
Hoa bridge, see Karen Gottschang Turner
with Phan Thanh Hoa, *Even the Women
Must Fight: Memories of War from North
Vietnam* (New York, 1998), pp 51–69.

60. Ibid. pp 84–85.

61. Ibid. pp 85–86.

62. Ibid. pp 88–92; msg, 8 TFW to
HQ 7 AF, Oprep-4 122, 111300Z Aug 67,
AFHRA 2K740.3421; msg, 355 TFW to
HQ 7 AF, Oprep-4 103, 111239Z Aug 67,
AFHRA 2K740.3421.

63. Msg, Cmdr 7 AF to CINCPACAF
and CSAF, subj: Daily Wrap-up, 101130Z
May 72; Jeffrey Ethell and Alfred Price,
*One Day in a Long War: May 10, 1972,
Air War, North Vietnam* (New York, 1989).

64. The author is indebted to Robert
L. Young, historian of the National Air
Intelligence Center at Wright-Patterson Air
Force Base, Ohio, for data on Air Force
and Navy aircraft losses to Chinese
MiG–19s (J-6s). On one occasion a
MiG–21 did bring down an Air Force
F–105 with a gun and on another occasion
a MiG–17 used a missile successfully

against a Navy F–4.

65. Tactical Fighter Weapons Center,
Red Baron III, vol II, pt 1, pp 98–105;
Ethell and Price, *One Day in a Long War,*
pp 151–64.

66. Tactical Fighter Weapons Center,
Red Baron III, vol II, pt 1, pp 136–43;
Randy Cunningham with Jeff Ethell, *Fox
Two* (Mesa, Arizona, 1984); Daniel L.
Haulman and Col William C. Stancik, *Air
Force Aerial Victory Credits: World War I,
World War II, Korea, and Vietnam*
(Maxwell AFB, Al: USAF Historical
Research Center, 1988), pp 63–64.

67. Haulman and Stancik, eds, *Air
Force Victory Credits.*

68. Tactical Fighter Weapons Center,
Red Baron III, Vols I and III; Richard J.
Harris, Doreen K. Wolownik, and Nancy
K. Harris, "Air-to-Air Conflict over North
Vietnam, 1 Apr–30 Nov 1972," Center for
Naval Analyses, Jul 1974.

69. Intrvw, Hugh N. Ahmann, USAF
hist prog, with Lt Gen Carlos M. Talbott,
Alexandria, Va., Jun 10–11, 1985.

70. See preceding chap for Lavelle
affair.

71. Talbott intrvw; EOTR, Maj Gen
Alton D. Slay, Aug 1971–Aug 1972,
AFHSO K740.131 SLAY; minutes, 7 AF
commanders' conf, Jul 18–19, 1972,
AFHRA 1009446.

72. Summaries of the daily
Linebacker confs are in Appendix B of
Tactical Fighter Weapons Center, Red
Baron III, vol III, pt 1. See also minutes, 7
AF commanders' conf, Jul 18–19, 1972,
AFHRA 1009446. On the Red River
Valley Fighter Pilots Association, see chap
7 above.

73. Maj Gen Doyle Larson, USAF
Ret, "Direct Intelligence Combat Support
in Vietnam: Project Teaball," *American
Intelligence Journal*, spring/summer 1994,
pp 56–58; Vogt intrvw, Aug 8–9, 1978;
PACAF, Corona Harvest rpt, "USAF Air
Operations in Southeast Asia, 1 Jul
1972–15 Aug 1973," vol II, pp IV 146–48,
AFHRA 1051287; EOTR, Col Scott G.
Smith, Cmdr, 432 TRW, Apr 1972–Mar
1973, AFHRA K717.131, p 4.

74. Vogt intrvw, Aug 8–9, 1978;

Tactical Fighter Weapons Center, Red Baron III, vol III, pt 1, pp 86–106.

75. Tactical Fighter Weapons Center, Red Baron III, vol III, pt 1, pp 50–51; hist, 8 TFWg, Jul–Sep 1972; hist, USAF Tactical Fighter Weapons Center, Jul 1972–Jun 1973; PACAF, Corona Harvest rpt, "USAF Air Operations in Southeast Asia, 1 Jul 1972–15 Aug 1973," vol II, IV-156–58, AFHRA 1051287.

76. Tactical Fighter Weapons Center, Red Baron III, vol III, pt 1, pp 86–106.

77. Histories, Tactical Air Command, Jul 1972–Dec 1975.

78. Tactical Fighter Weapons Center, Red Baron III, vol III, pt 2, chaps 4 and 5; Red Baron III, vol II, pt 1, pp 148–55.

79. Karl J. Eschmann, *Linebacker: The Untold Story of the Air Raids over North Vietnam* (New York, 1989), p 128.

80. Maj John W. Siemann, "COM-BAT SNAP: AIM–9J Southeast Asia Introduction," CHECO rpt, Apr 24, 1974; Harris, et al., "Air-to-Air Conflict," pp 30–42; Tactical Fighter Weapons Center, Red Baron, vol III, pt 2; intrvw, author with Col Larry D. Griffin, Arnold AFB, Oct 14, 1993. In 1972, Griffin was assigned to the Naval Air Systems Command as a Sparrow product engineer.

81. Futrell, *Aces and Aerial Victories*, pp 123–25. I am indebted to Rob Young, historian of the National Air Intelligence Center at Wright-Patterson Air Force Base, Ohio, for his painstaking statistical analysis of the Air Force's air-to-air losses over North Vietnam.

82. PACAF, "Summary of Air Operations in SEA," 1967–72; rpt, DIA, "Target Systems in North Vietnam," DI-646-43-72, Jul 3, 1972.

83. Intrvw, M.F. Porter, CHECO historian, with Gen John W. Vogt, Jr., Saigon, Nov 12, 1972; DIA Intelligence Study, DI-646-43-72, Oct 16, 1972, p 67; ltr, Lt Col Donald H. Gregory, Air Force Intel Svc, to AF Armament Lab (Eglin AFB), subj: Air Strikes on North Vietnam Airfields, Mar 26, 1973; Air Force Intelligence Service target folders, box 11, Mational Defense University Library.

84. Tactical Fighter Weapons Center,

Red Baron III, vol III, pt 1.

85. Maj David E. Thomasson, "An Analysis of USAF Combat Damage and Losses in SEA, Apr 72–Mar 73," HQ 7 AF Operations Analysis Branch, Jun 30, 1973.

86. Rpt, DIA, "Target Systems in North Vietnam," DI-646-43-72, Jul 3, 1972; PACAF, "Summary of Air Operations in SEA," 1967–72.

87. Harris, et al., "Air-to-Air Conflict."

88. HQ 7 AF, "History of Linebacker I Operations," pp 38–42.

89. Slay EOTR, p 83.

90. Thomasson, "Analysis of USAF Combat Damage."

91. PACAF, Corona Harvest rpt, "USAF Air Operations in Southeast Asia, 1 Jul 1972–15 Aug 1973," pp IV-195–203, AFHRA 1051287.

92. Ibid, pp IV-171–73.

93. PACAF, "Summary of Air Operations in SEA," May–Oct 1972; Kissinger, *White House Years*, p 1098.

94. The North Vietnamese and their Russian advisers claimed to have shot down an F–111 near Hanoi with a SAM on Mar 30, 1968. This claim does not square with USAF records, which show that the F–111 lost on that date never got out of Thailand and crashed there after its crew ejected safely; the loss was attributed to a tube of sealant material carelessly left where it could jam the pitch-roll control mechanism. Like all other F–111 missions in 1968, that one had been sent against a target in Route Package One far from Hanoi. On the Vietnamese and Russian claim, see Gaiduk, *The Soviet Union and the Vietnam War*, p 62. On the 1968 F–111 deployment, see "History of Combat Lancer," Det 1, 426 TFS, by Jack R. Hayes, historian of 474 TFW, Nellis AFB, Nev, and Giraudo intrvw. On Ryan's Raiders, see chap 2 above.

95. PACAF, Corona Harvest rpt, "In-Country and Out-Country Strike Ops in SEA, 1 Jan 65–31 Dec 69," vol II: "Strike Aircraft," Nov 2, 1970, pp 210–12.

96. PACAF, Corona Harvest rpt, "USAF Air Operations in Southeast Asia, 1 Jul 1972–15 Aug 1973," vol I, chap II,

pp 51–61. See also JCS hist, Vietnam 1971–73, pp 430–31.

97. PACAF, Corona Harvest rpt, "USAF Air Operations in Southeast Asia, 1 Jul 1972–15 Aug 1973," May 1975, AFHRA 1008184, vol I, chap II, pp 41–51; Hopkins, *Tanker Operations*, pp 90–94.

98. Don Harten, "Godzilla Versus the F–111" in Hatch and Sheridan, eds, *Red River Valley Fighter Pilots*, p 22. See also Col A.A. Picinich, et al., "The F–111 in Southeast Asia, Sep 1972–January 1973," CHECO rpt, Feb 21, 1974.

99. Vogt intrvw, Aug 8–9, 1978; Herman S. Wolk, *Research and Development for Southeast Asia, 1965–67* (Washington 1969), pp 68–70.

100. Smith EOTR; Johnson, "Linebacker Operations"; Msg, 7/13 AF Security Police to 13 AF, subj: Security of LORAN and TACAN Sites, 041449Z Oct 72, AFHRA 1008707.

101. Seamans intrvw; Vogt intrvw, Nov 12, 1972; Palmer, "U.S. Intelligence and Vietnam." Seamans also got in hot water with Nixon for agreeing with a reporter that it was pssible the war might last three more years. Seamans was widely misquoted as having asserted that the war would last three more years; see Seamans, *Aiming at Targets*, pp 195–96.

102. PACAF, "Summary of Air Operations in SEA," May 1972; HQ USAF Targets Working Group, Bulletin 37, Aug 8, 1972.

103. PACAF, "Summary of Air Operations in SEA," 1967 and 1972.

104. DIA Intelligence Studies: DI-646-40-72 (May 18, 1972), DI-646-43-72 (Jul 3), and DI-646-43-72 (Oct 16); William G. Cooper, Jr., "Communist Chinese Increase Truck Production," *Defense Intelligence Digest*, Jan 1971, pp 34–35.

105. DIA Intelligence Study, DI-646-40-72, Jun 16, 1972. Walt Rostow told Mark Clodfelter (*Limits of Air Power*, p 167) that Gen Haig was Rostow's source for the story that the Chinese held back on sending supplies to North Vietnam for three weeks and stopped transshipment of Soviet supplies for three months. Haig did not discuss this matter in his memoirs. In *Aerial Interdiction in Three Wars* (Washington, 1994), p 377, Eduard Mark raises doubts about the Rostow-Haig account. Clodfelter gives a different version in "Nixon and the Air Weapon," an essay in *An American Dilemma: Vietnam, 1968–72*, edited by Dennis E. Showalter and John G. Albert (Chicago, 1993), p 92. Here Clodfelter claims merely that the Chinese prohibited only Soviet shipments for three weeks and no longer.

106. Minutes, 7 AF commanders' conf, Jul 18, 1972, AFHRA 1009446.

107. PACAF, "USAF Air Operations Against North Vietnam," pp 113–18; DIA Intelligence Study, DI-646-43-72, Oct 16, 1972.

108. DIA Intelligence Study, DI-646-35-72, "The Availability of Rice in Indochina during 1971–72," Apr 1972.

109. AFNIEC, "Basic Target Annex for Campaign against NVN Dike System," Mar 21, 1968.

110. McConnell intrvw, Aug 28, 1969; memo, Brig Gen Ginsburgh to Gen Wheeler, subj: Flooding the Red River, Mar 8, 1968, Ginsburgh Papers, AFHSO; Ginsburgh intrvw, Apr 5, 1990; Futrell, *The United States Air Force in Korea*, pp 623–29. At the Stennis hearings in 1967, McConnell had testified that in both World War II and the Korean War bombing agricultural targets had been permitted; see Stennis hearings, pt 3, p 213.

111. *Public Papers of the President*, 1972, pp 744–52; "Behind the Furor over Bombs on Red River Dikes," *U.S. News & World Report*, Aug 14, 1972; W. Hays Parks, "Linebacker and the Law of War," *Air University Review*, Jan–Feb 1983, pp 12–16. Former Attorney General Ramsey Clark took a North Vietnamese tour of bombed dikes and supported North Vietnamese charges that the dikes were targeted when he testified before Senator Edward Kennedy's Judiciary Subcommittee to Investigate Problems Connected with Refugees and Escapees on Aug 16, 1972: *Problems of War Victims in Indochina, Part III: North Vietnam* (Washington, 1972).

112. Elder and Melly, "Rules of Engagement"; HQ USAF DCS Plans and Ops, "Rolling Thunder-Linebacker: A Preliminary Comparative Analysis," Aug 1972, AFHSO K143.507-9.

113. JCS hist, Vietnam 1971–73, pt 1, pp 377–441.

114. Parks, "Air War and the Law of War," p 169. Laird eventually did approve bombing the Hanoi power plant during Linebacker II in Dec 1972.

115. Vogt intrvw, Aug 8–9, 1978.

116. Associated Press, Jun 14, 1972. See also DIA Intelligence Study, DI-646-40-72, Jun 16, 1972, p 26; Melvin F. Porter, "Linebacker: Overview of the First 120 Days," CHECO rpt, 1973, pp 37–40.

117. Memo for record, Col Richard L. Lawson, Asst Dep Dir for Strike Forces, Dir of Ops, HQ USAF, subj: NVN Air Campaign Coordinating Meeting, Jun 8, 1972; PACAF, "Summary of Air Operations in SEA," Jun 1972.

118. Capt Jack L. Tinius, "Psychological Operations Against North Vietnam, Jul 1972–January 1973," CHECO rpt, May 24, 1974; TSgt John Tomassi, "Stray Goose Crew Remembered During Ceremony," Air Force News Service 98106, Jul 1998.

119. Ibid. The North Vietnamese got some propaganda mileage of their own out of the currency leaflets. Articles appeared in the European press about American counterfeiting, and the North Vietnamese even tried to blame their inflation problem on the leaflets. See Robert W. Chandler, *War of Ideas: The U.S. Propaganda Campaign in Vietnam* (Boulder, Colo,

1981), pp 117–23.

120. Memo for record, Col Richard L. Lawson, Asst Dep Dir for Strike Forces, Ops Dir, HQ USAF, subj: NVN Campaign Coordinating Meeting, Jun 8, 1972.

121. DIA Intelligence Study, DI-646-43-72, Oct 16, 1972, pp 49–53.

122. HQ 7 AF Tactical Analysis Div, Air Operations Rpts 73/1 ("US Air Forces Vs the 130MM Field Gun"), 73/2 ("US Air War Against Tanks"), and 73/4 ("An Analysis of Laser Guided Bombs in SEA"), AFHRA K740.041-1, 2, and 4. For a skeptical analysis of Linebacker's effectiveness, see Mark, *Aerial Interdiction in Three Wars*, pp 367–400.

123. Vogt intrvw, Aug 8–9, 1978; Kissinger, *White House Years*, pp 1341–94; Haig, *Inner Circles*, pp 294–303. See also Hung and Schecter, *The Palace File*; Diem and Chanof, *Jaws of History*; Loi and Vu, *Le Duc Tho-Kissinger Negotiations.*

124. Nixon, *RN*, II, 193.

125. Kissinger, *White House Years*, p 1390.

126. Moorer intrvw, Sep 10, 1976.

127. Pacific Air Forces kept a summary of the many JCS and CINCPAC messages defining air operating authorities and limitations for North Vietnam, Apr–Jun 1972. See PACAF Source Documents for Corona Harvest V, "Study on North Vietnam," vol I, Tab 12, AFHRA 717.03-221. See also Kissinger, *White House Years*, pp 1200 and 1303.

128. Nixon, *RN*, II, 201–2; Kissinger, *White House Years*, pp 1308 and 1329–30.

129. Nixon, *RN*, II, 179.

Chapter 10

1. A thorough accounting of B–52 bombs dropped by target and by unit is in HQ SAC's "Chronology of SAC Participation in Linebacker II," Aug 12, 1973. The data there is more complete than HQ PACAF's "Linebacker II USAF Bombing Survey," Apr 1973, AFHRA 1011707, which accounts for only about 35,000 of the more than 48,000 bombs

dropped by the B–52s in Linebacker II. The figures given in Appendix 1 of Eschmann's *Linebacker* are drawn from the PACAF survey. On bombing statistics for fighter aircraft, see also PACAF, "Summary of Air Operations in SEA," Jan 1973.

2. North Vietnam's official statements on casualties for Linebacker II

were published in a single volume by the DRVN Commission for Investigation of the U.S. Imperialists' War Crimes in Viet Nam, *The Late December 1972 U.S. Blitz on North Vietnam* (Hanoi, 1973). These statements give the number killed at Hanoi (1,318) and Haiphong (305). The number killed in other cities and villages is not always rendered so precisely but appears to be about 400. In this volume the only total figure for North Vietnamese killed by Linebacker II is "thousands," which was probably thought to be the most impressive way of rendering "two thousand."

3. Adm Moorer's testimony, hearings, House Appropriations Subcommittee on Dept of Defense, "Briefings on Bombings of North Vietnam," Jan 9, 1973, pp 18–21; SAC Linebacker II Chronology.

4. Hist, 8 TFWg, Oct–Dec 1972. For North Vietnamese claims that MiG–21s shot down two B–52s, see Toperczer, *Air War Over North Vietnam*.

5. SAC Linebacker II Chronology, p 315; PACAF Linebacker II Bombing Survey. Col Herman Gilster, who wrote the PACAF survey, later published an expanded version as part of his *The Air War in Southeast Asia: Case Studies of Selected Campaigns* (Montgomery, Alab, 1993); here Gilster expresses his skepticism that North Vietnam was running out of SAMs, but intelligence data at least indicates a sharp decline in SAM launches on the last two nights.

6. The text of the cease-fire agreement signed in Paris on Jan 27, 1973, cam be found in the appendices to Goodman's *Lost Peace*. Nixon's letters to Thieu are appended to Hung and Schecter, *The Palace File*; see esp Nixon's letter of Nov 14, 1972, pp 385–86.

7. Ryan intrvw, May 20, 1971.

8. Hist, SAC, FY 1973, pp 98–104.

9. Hist, SAC, FY 1973, p 102.

10. Hist, SAC, FY 1973, pp 102–6; hist, JCS, Vietnam 1971–73, p 436.

11. For Kissinger's own regrets about using this phrase, see his *White House Years*, pp 1399–1400.

12. Nixon, *RN*, II, 209; hist, SAC,

FY 1973, pp 102–6.

13. Kissinger's memoirs stress his differences with Nixon on the urgency of settling with North Vietnam before the election. See *White House Years*, p 1308. Nixon on the other hand, recalls that in Oct he was leery of escalating the bombing after the election. See Nixon, *RN*, II, 201.

14. On the administration's view of Congress, see Kissinger, *White House Years*, pp 1306–7 and 1426.

15. Kissinger, *White House Years*, pp 1418–41; Loi and Vu, *Le Duc Tho-Kissinger Negotiations*, pp 387–422. For evidence that Hanoi had disagreements with its South Vietnameseallies about the details of a cease-fire agreement, see Robert K. Brigham, *Guerilla Diplomacy: The NLF's Foreign Relations and the Vietnam War* (Ithaca, New York, 1999).

16. Kissinger later agreed that his advice had been bad in this case. See *White House Years*, p 1426.

17. Adm Elmo R. Zumwalt, *On Watch: A Memoir* (New York, 1976), pp 412–15; Nixon, *RN*, II, 230; Kissinger, *White House Years*, pp 1420–35; Haig, *Inner Circles*, pp 306–9; Moorer intrvw, Mar 18, 1977; Secord, *Honored and Betrayed*, p 106.

18. *Haldeman Diaries,* Dec 15, 1972; hist, JCS, Vietnam 1971–73, pp 663–70. For the Linebacker II execute order, see msg, JCS to CINPAC and CINCSAC, subj: Linebacker II Operations, 170010Z Dec 72.

19. The long sought photographs appeared in *Aviation Week & Space Technology*, Apr 25, 1972, pp 14–23; see also p 9.

20. Haig, *Inner Circles*, p 308.

21. Sixteen years later, a few months before leaving Hayden, Fonda apologized on national television for her infamous antiaircraft photo. She also apologized for calling former POWs liars in 1973 when they said they had been tortured. These apologies came during an interview with Barbara Walters on ABC's "20/20," Jun 17, 1988. On Ramsey Clark's visit, see hearings, Aug 16–17, 1972, Senate

Judiciary Subcommittee to Investigate Problems Connected with Refugees and Escapees, *Problems of War Victims in Indochina, Part III: North Vietnam* (Washington, 1972).

22. In addition to Telford Taylor's newspaper articles cited below, see Joan Baez, *And a Voice to Sing With: A Memoir* (New York, 1987), pp 193–225.

23. Hearings, House Appropriations Comm, Subcomm on Department of Defense, *Briefings on Bombing of North Vietnam*, p 18.

24. Baez, pp 221–22.

25. Baez's Hanoi album, *Where Are You Now My Son?*, was released by A&M in 1973.

26. Telford Taylor, "Hanoi is Reported Scarred But Key Services Continue," *New York Times*, Dec 25, 1972. See also Frank McGee's televised intrvw with Taylor, NBC, The Today Show, Jan 3, 1973. For bomb damage photography of Bac Mai hospital, see Parks, "Linebacker and the Law of War," pp 22–23. On press reaction to Linebacker II, see Martin F. Herz, *The Prestige Press and the Christmas Bombing, 1972* (Washington, 1980). For the North Vietnamese view, see the Democratic Republic of Vietnam, Commission for Investigation of the US Imperialists' War Crimes in Viet Nam, *The Late December 1972 US Blitz on North Viet Nam* (Hanoi, 1973), pp 41–42.

27. See chap 2 above.

28. Baez, p 213.

29. Telford Taylor, "Hanoi Exhibits Downed Yanks to Boost Morale," *Chicago Tribune*, Jan 10, 1973.

30. Lt Col Jon A. Reynolds, "Linebacker II: The POW Perspective," *Air Force Magazine*, Sep 1979, pp 93–94. Other POW memoirs are cited in chap 7 above. See, for example, Guarino, *A POW's Story*, pp 328–33; Stockdale and Stockdale, *In Love and War*, pp 431–32.

31. Telford Taylor, "Hanoi Under the Bombing: Sirens, Shelters, Rubble and Death," *New York Times*, Jan 7, 1973; SAC Linebacker II Chronology, pp 221–52.

32. For Capt Diefenbach's account, see Col Billy F. Shackelford, Lt Col Charles G. Luse, and Lt Col Neil C. Ray, "Eleven Days in December," Air War College, 1977, AFHRA 1028277, pp 86–88. See also Hist, 307 Strat Wg, Oct–Dec 1972.

33. Nixon, *RN*, p 246. See also *Haldeman Diaries*, Dec 20, 1972.

34. For insight into thinking at SAC HQ, see the long letter from Brig Gen Harry Cordes, USAF Ret, to Brig Gen James McCarthy, undated (1977), AFHRA 1028673.

35. Capt Burke, quoted in hist, 307 SW, Oct–Dec 1972.

36. SAC Linebacker II Chronology, esp pp 221–52.

37. Secord, *Honored and Betrayed*, pp 105–8.

38. See Gerald W. Johnson with John and Charlotte McClure, *Called to Command: A World War II Fighter Ace's Adventurous Journey* (Paducah, Kentucky, 1996).

39. Msg, Meyer to Vogt, subj: Linebacker II, 210220Z Dec 1972, Vogt read file.

40. Msg, Vogt to Meyer, 210540Z Dec 1972, Vogt read file. The fourth night's missions went off as planned against widely separated targets. 7 AF continued the practice begun in Aug of bringing together representatives from each unit involved for after-action discussions. For example, the fourth night's mission was discussed at Udorn on Dec 24. See msg, Col Olsrefski, 7/13 AF, to Gen Vogt, subj: Linebacker Conference, 241715Z Dec 72, AFHRA 1009448.

41. PACAF, Corona Harvest rpt, "USAF Air Operations in Southeast Asia, 1 Jul 1972 15 Aug 1973," vol II, sec IV, pp 195–203, 276–82.

42; PACAF, Corona Harvest rpt, "USAF Air Operations in Southeast Asia, 1 Jul 1972–15 Aug 1973," AFHRA 1008185, pp IV-273–82. In Dec 1982 the official Vietnamese newspaper *Nhan Dan* published an account of SAM operations by Gen Hoang Van Khanh. He attributed SAM success in Linebacker II partly to track-on-jam techniques. A translation appeared in the Apr 1996 issue of *Vietnam* magazine, pp 26–33.

43. Msg, Clay to Meyer and Vogt, subj: B–52 Operation, 221935Z Dec 1972, Vogt read file.

44. Msg, Meyer to Clay and Vogt, subj: B–52 Operation, 232020Z Dec 1972, Vogt read file.

45. PACAF, Corona Harvest rpt, "USAF Air Operations in Southeast Asia, 1 Jul 1972–15 Aug 1973," vol II, sec IV, pp 276–86.

46. PACAF Linebacker II Bombing Survey, pp 16–18. Navy A–6s appear to have had about the same level of success against the Haiphong missile sites that B–52s and F–111s achieved in the Hanoi area. Adm Moorer told a House appropriations subcommittee that in both areas a total of five occupied sites were known to have been damaged. Hearings, House Appropriations Subcommittee on Dept of Defense, "Briefings on Bombings of North Vietnam," Jan 9, 1973, pp 20–21.

47. Hist, 307 Strat Wing, Oct–Dec 1972; SAC Linebacker II Chronology, p 263.

48. PACAF Linebacker II Bombing Survey, pp 14–16.

49. Picinich, "The F–111 in Southeast Asia".

50. PACAF, Corona Harvest rpt, "USAF Air Operations in Southeast Asia, Jul 1972–Aug 1973," vol II, sec IV, p 269; Vogt intrvw, Aug 8–9, 1978; hist, 8 TFWg, Oct–Dec 1972.

51. SAC Linebacker II Chronology, pp 273–309; PACAF Linebacker II Bombing Survey, pp 41–42; HQ USAF Intel photo rpt, "Linebacker II," undated (1973).

52. Vogt intrvw, Aug 8–9, 1978.

53. Moorer intrvw, Sep 10, 1976.

54. SAC Linebacker II Chronology, esp pp 182–99.

55. Ltr, Brig Gen Harry Cordes, USAF Ret, to Brig Gen James McCarthy, undated (1977), AFHRA 1028673.

56. Ibid.

57. Johnson, *Called to Command*, p 206; Brig Gen James R. McCarthy and Lt Col George B. Allison, *Linebacker II: A View from the Rock* (Maxwell AFB, Ala, 1979), pp 85–86; SAC Linebacker II Chronology, p 131. For an account by a crew member on one of the B–52Gs shot down on the third night, see Maj Robert A. Clement, "A Fourth of July in December: A B–52 Navigator's Perspective of Linebacker II," Student Report 84-0540, Air Command and Staff College, Mar 1984.

58. SAC Linebacker II Chronology, pp 184–85.

59. For the perspective of HQ 8 AF on its enlarged planning responsibilities, see McCarthy and Allison, *Linebacker II: A View from the Rock*, pp 121–23.

60. Hist, JCS, Vietnam 1971–73, pp 666–78.

61. Hist, SAC, FY 1973, pp 112 and 120; SAC Linebacker II Chronology, p 303.

62. A former B–52 pilot, Dana Drenkowski, brought crew grievances to public attention with articles in *Soldier of Fortune* and *Armed Forces Journal* (Jul 1977, pp 24–27). The Air Force took these allegations seriously enough to publish an official response in the latter journal (Aug 1977, pp 24–25).

63. For a different interpretation, see Jeff Ethell and Joe Christy, *B–52 Stratofortress* (New York, 1981). They conclude that morale at U-Tapao was worse than on Guam; in gauging morale, much depends on whom you interview. In addition to the B–52 crew member who refused to fly, an F–4 crew member also refused.

64. Hist, 307 Strat Wg, Oct–Dec 1972, pp 70–71.

65. For another account of Guam operations in addition to McCarthy and Allison, *Linebacker II: A View from the Rock*, see "Supplemental History on Linebacker II," 43 Strat Wg and 72 Strat Wg (Prov).

66. Hist, 307 Strat Wg, Oct–Dec 1972.

67. Ibid.

68. Ibid.

69. Ibid.

70. Col Lawrence E. McKenny, "Rivet Haste SEA Introduction Final Report," Apr 1973, hist, Tactical Fighter Weapons Center, FY 1973, vol V, doc 129; Tactical Fighter Weapons Center, Red Baron III, vol II, pt 2, pp 305–8; hist, 432 TFW, Oct–Dec 1972; Smith EOTR.

71. "Supplemental History on Linebacker II," 43 and 72 Strat Wgs (Prov); hist, 307 Strat Wg, Oct–Dec 1972; Col Billy F. Shackelford, Lt Col Charles G. Luse and Lt Col Neil C. Ray, "Eleven Days in December," Air War College, 1977, AFHRA 1028277, pp 63–74. The unpublished study by Shakelford, et al., gives a view from U-Tapao that can be compared with the Guam perspective in McCarthy and Allison, *Linebacker II: A View from the Rock.* See also Brig Gen James R. McCarthy and Col Robert E. Rayfield, *B–52s Over Hanoi: A Linebacker II Story* (Fullerton, Calif, 1996).

72. Hist, 307 Strat Wg, Oct–Dec 1972.

73. Ibid.

74. HQ USAF Intel photo rpt, "Linebacker II," undated (1973), p E–1.

75. PACAF Linebacker II Bombing Survey, pp 40 and 52. The Secretary of Defense's Scientific Advisory Group also examined Linebacker II and came to similar conclusions. See memo, R.F. Linsenmeyer, J35, to J3, subj: Linebacker II Operational Report, Jul 2, 1973, AFHRA 1009451.

76. Hist, SAC, FY 1973, pp 112–20.

77. PACAF, "Summary of Air Operations in SEA," Jan 1973. This issue (which appeared in Mar 1973) covers Linebacker II. See esp pp 4-B-35–38.

78. SAC Linebacker II Chronology, pp 84–86.

79. Maj Gen Tran Nhan, "The Aerial Dien Bien Phu," *Nhan Dan*, Dec 1987, FBIS-EAS-88-006 and 008. Tran Nhan was deputy commander of the Hanoi air defense sector in Dec 1972.

80. Ibid.

81. Lt Gen Hoang Phuong, "The 12-Day Air Defense Campaign in December 1972," *Tap Chi Quan Doi Nhan Dan*, Oct 1987, JPRS-SEA-88-009.

82. Adm Moorer's testimony, hearings, House Appropriations Subcommittee on Dept of Defense, Jan 9, 1973, "Briefings on Bombings of North Vietnam," p 19.

83. Vogt intrvw, Aug 8–9, 1978; see also msg, Vogt to Ryan, Meyer, and Clay, subj: Daily Wrap Up, 211045Z Dec 1972.

84. Maj Paul W. Elder, "Buffalo Hunter," CHECO rpt, Jul 24, 1973, p 35.

85. SAC Linebacker II Chronology, pp 313–15. During the Vietnam War, the Air Force lost a total of 25 B–52s, including 17 in combat and 8 by accident (for example, air refueling collisions); the first combat loss occurred in Nov 1972 and the 17th in Jan 1973 (both over North Vietnam).

86. Michael M. McCrea, "U.S. Navy, Marine Corps, and Air Force Fixed Wing Aircraft Losses and Damage in Southeast Asia (1962–1973)," Center for Naval Analyses, Aug 1976. This report includes microfiche with details on each loss.

87. Msg, Clay to Meyer and Vogt, subj: B–52 Operations in NVN, 281913Z Dec 1972, Vogt read file.

88. Kissinger, *White House Years*, pp 1457–59; msg, JCS to CINCPAC and CINCSAC, 291407Z Dec 72.

89. Vogt intrvw, Aug 8–9, 1978. See also Haig, *Inner Circles*, pp 309–11.

Chapter 11

1. For insight into the attitudes and experience of Air Force leaders in the years immediately following the Vietnam War, see esp two interviews conducted by the Air Force history program: Lt Col Maurice Maryanow and Dr. Richard H.

Kohn interviewed former Chief of Staff Gen David C. Jones in 1985–1986; Dr. George M. Watson Jr., interviewed former Secretary of the Air Force Dr. John L. McLucas in 1996. See also Richard P. Hallion, *Storm over Iraq: Air Power and* the *Gulf War* (Washington, 1992); Santoli, *Leading the Way*; and James Kitfield, *Prodigal Soldiers* (New York, 1995).

2. Clodfelter, *Limits of Air Power*, p 209. See also Raymond W. Leonard, "Learning from History: Linebacker II and U.S. Air Force Doctrine," *Journal of Military History*, Apr 1994, pp 267–303.

3. Transcript of Rather's intrvw with Saddam Hussein, Aug 29, 1990, FBIS-NES-90-170.

4. Wayne Thompson, "After Al Firdos: The Last Two Weeks of Strategic Bombing in Desert Storm," *Air Power History*, Summer 1996, pp 48–65.

5. Henry Kissinger, *Years of Upheaval* (Boston, 1982), pp 37–43; Senator George McGovern, "Vietnam: 1976," Washington: Senate Foreign Relations Committee, 1976.

6. On the role of the Vietnam War in this transition, see Col Mike Worden, *Rise of the Fighter Generals: The Problem of Air Force Leadership, 1945–1982* (Maxwell AFB, Ala, 1998).

7. Estimates of Vietnamese casualties are provided by Lewy, *America in Vietnam*, pp 442–54; Thomas C. Thayer, *War Without Fronts: The American Experience in Vietnam* (Boulder, Colo, 1985), pp 101–8 and 125–34.

8. John M. Granville, "Summary of USAF Aircraft Losses in SEA," TAC, Jun 1974; McCrea, "U.S. Navy, Marine Corps, and Air Force Fixed-Wing Aircraft Losses and Damage."

9. See Paul D. Mather, *M.I.A.: Accounting for the Missing in Southeast Asia* (Washington, 1994); Lewis M. Stern, *Policies of the Vietnamese Government Concerning Captured and Unaccounted For United States Soldiers, 1969–1994* (Jefferson, NC, 1995); Edward P. Brynn and Arthur P. Geesey, "Joint Personnel Recovery in Southeast Asia," CHECO rpt, 1976; Malcom McConnell with Theodore G. Schweitzer III, *Inside Hanoi's Secret Archive* (New York, 1995).

10. For Robert Garwood's version of his collaboration, see Winston Groom and Duncan Spencer, *Conversations with the Enemy: The Story of PFC Robert Garwood* (New York, 1983).

11. Gen Horner has recorded some of his experiences during the Vietnam War in Santoli, *Leading the Way*, pp 19–22, 47–50 and 99–100. See also Kitfield, *Prodigal Soldiers*.

12. On Risner's Push, see John Darrell Sherwood, *Officers in Flight Suits: The Story of American Air Force Fighter Pilots in the Korean War* (New York, 1996), pp 4–5.

13. Hatch and Sheridan, eds, *Red River Valley Fighter Pilots*, pp 55–57; Steve Smith, "Pardo's Push," *Airman*, Dec 1996, pp 38–41. When Col Aman came down with Lou Gehrig's disease, Col Pardo helped to persuade General Motors to donate a van which the Earl Aman Courage Foundation fitted with a lift; see the Red River Valley Fighter Pilots Association newsletter, *Mig Sweep*, fall 1996, p 16.

14. Ibid., p 55.

Glossary

AAA	Antiaircraft Artillery
AF	Air Force
AFB	Air Force Base
AFHSO	Air Force History Support Office (Washington, DC)
AFHRA	Air Force Historical Research Agency (Maxwell AFB, Alabama)
ARVN	Army of the Republic of Vietnam (South Vietnam)
CAP	Combat Air Patrol
CHECO	Contemporary Historical Evaluation of Combat Operations (an Air Force project with offices in South Vietnam and Hawaii)
CIA	Central Intelligence Agency
CINCPAC	Commander in Chief Pacific
CWIHP	Cold War International History Project
DCS	Deputy Chief of Staff
DIA	Defense Intelligence Agency
DMZ	Demilitarized Zone (between North and South Vietnam)
DO	Director of Operations
FBIS	Foreign Broadcast Information Service
FRUS	*Foreign Relations of the United States* (documentary volumes published by the State Department)
FY	Fiscal Year (during the Vietnam War, the U.S. government's fiscal year ran from 1 July to 30 June)
Hist	History
HQ	Headquarters
IG	Inspector General
Intvw	Interview
JCS	Joint Chiefs of Staff
JPRS	Joint Publications Research Service
LBJ	President Lyndon Baines Johnson

Glossary

LORAN	Long-Range Navigation System
Ltr	Letter
MACSOG	MACV Studies and Observations Group
MACV	U.S. Military Assistance Command, Vietnam
MIA	Missing in Action
MiG	Mikoyan-Gurevich (Russian aircraft design bureau or an aircraft designed by it)
Msg	Message
Mtg	Meeting
NSSM	National Security Study Memorandum
NVN	North Vietnam
OASD	Office of the Assistant Secretary of Defense
OSD	Office of the Secretary of Defense
PACAF	Pacific Air Forces
POW	Prisoner of War
PW	See POW
RP	Route Package
Rpt	Report
SAC	Strategic Air Command
SAM	Surface-to-Air Missile
SEA	Southeast Asia
TAC	Tactical Air Command
TFW	Tactical Fighter Wing
TRW	Tactical Reconnaissance Wing
USAF	U.S. Air Force
USA	U.S. Army
USMC	U.S. Marine Corps
USN	U.S. Navy
USSAG	U.S. Support Activities Group (Thailand)
WNRC	Washington National Records Center

Bibliography

This book relies primarily on the records of the United States Air Force and especially the large collection of records maintained by the Air Force Historical Research Agency (AFHRA) at Maxwell Air Force Base, Alabama. Copies of some of those documents are also held by the Air Force History Support Office (AFHSO) at Bolling Air Force Base in Washington, D.C. Not far away in Suitland, Maryland, is the Washington National Records Center (WNRC) that still holds the records of Headquarters U.S. Air Force for the 1960s and 1970s; ultimately many of these headquarters records will be transferred to the National Archives. Target folders prepared by Air Force intelligence personnel in Washington during the war are maintained by the National Defense University library.

The richest repository of documents on Washington decision-making during Rolling Thunder is the Lyndon Baines Johnson (LBJ) Library at Austin, Texas. Access to the papers of Richard Nixon's administration has been more restricted, and the author had not yet begun work in those papers when this book was written.

Most of the Army, Navy, and Marine records cited in this book are copies in Air Force holdings. Parallel historical efforts are underway in the other services to exploit their records on the war. Navy volumes will offer a much fuller picture of the role of the Commander in Chief, Pacific (CINCPAC), and the Army is preparing a volume on the Army generals who led Military Assistance Command, Vietnam (MACV); the MACV records have been transferred from Army custody to the National Archives, but the Army Center of Military History maintains extensive files on Generals Westmoreland and Abrams. The Defense Department has provided casualty files and other records on the missing in action to the Library of Congress.

While the collapse of the Soviet Union opened Moscow's archives to fruitful research and some useful Chinese material has come to light, there remains a dearth of reliable information about Vietnamese communist decision-making. Foreign researchers are only beginning to gain access to Vietnam's less sensitive records. During the war, American intelligence agencies did process a tremendous quantity of data, and some of this raw material survives (e.g., captured documents and prisoner interrogation reports), as do thousands of reports written by intelligence analysts. The U.S. Foreign Broadcast Information Service (FBIS) and the Joint Publications Research Service (JPRS) provided translations of North Vietnamese broadcasts and publications throughout the war. Many of these translations are filed by subject with Vietnamese items in Douglas Pike's collection, which was housed at the University of California, Berkeley, before it was transferred to Texas Tech University at Lubbock. Part of the Pike collection is available on microfilm—as is Cornell University's John M. Echols collection of Vietnamese and other writings on the war. The Cold War International History Project of the Woodrow Wilson International Center for Scholars in Washington has tracked early results of research in Russian, Chinese, and Vietnamese records through its bulletin and published working papers.

Air Force Historical Research Agency

During the Vietnam War, this agency at Maxwell Air Force Base, Alabama, was called the Albert F. Simpson Historical Research Center. While unit histories with supporting documents continued to make up the bulk of the agency's holdings, the Vietnam War caused the establishment of two new document collection programs—CHECO and Corona Harvest. Project CHECO (the changing words behind this acronym eventually became "Contemporary Historical Evaluation of Current Operations") microfilmed about a thousand reels of documents at Seventh Air Force headquarters and at wings in South Vietnam and Thailand. Although much of this microfilm is of poor quality, it is valuable because most of the paper documents never reached the United States. CHECO historians also wrote more than two hundred reports, some of which are listed below in the section on official histories.

Corona Harvest was an elaborate effort to derive lessons from the war. Each Air Force major command submitted assessments of its wartime problems; Pacific Air Forces alone required more than thirty thick volumes for its input. Committees of officers at the Air University (Maxwell Air Force Base, Alabama) integrated and softened input findings; after retirement, General Momyer was asked by the Chief of Staff to read the Corona Harvest reports and recommend improvements in the Air Force. Meanwhile the Corona Harvest team at Maxwell had also produced brief special reports on Air Force functions and problems in Southeast Asia. Throughout the Corona Harvest process, thousands of documents were collected and numbered.

In the wake of CHECO and Corona Harvest, the agency began to microfilm histories and other documents. After documents already in the holdings had been microfilmed, each new item began to receive a computer index ("IRIS") number as well as the old catalog subject number and in many cases a Corona Harvest number. Agency catalog numbers all begin with the letter "K" and include a decimal point in the middle. IRIS numbers are normally seven digits beginning with "1" and not interrupted by a decimal point; some IRIS numbers begin with "8" or "9" and have only six digits. Corona Harvest numbers begin with "CH." CHECO microfilm is cited by giving the reel number.

Agency holdings include teletype messages, correspondence, intelligence reports, plans, orders, after-action reports, trip reports, end-of-tour reports, unit histories, interview tapes, interview transcripts and personal papers (e.g., papers of Generals McConnell and Ryan). A few personal papers are held in the Air Force History Support Office at Bolling Air Force Base in Washington, D.C. (e.g., papers of Generals Ginsburg, LeMay, McConnell, Vogt, and Secretary of the Air Force Seamans); that office also has papers relating to the Lavelle affair. While some Air Force records on the Vietnam War remain classified, the service's declassification program has opened many.

Lyndon Baines Johnson Library

This presidential library on the University of Texas campus at Austin has also made progress in declassifying its important holdings. The Meeting Notes File and Tom Johnson's Notes of Meetings are invaluable; the President's tape-recorded conversations were not yet open when the author was conducting research for this book. Within the voluminous National Security File are the national security adviser's memos to the President (several per day), the files of various aides, a name file (which includes memos by Colonel Ginsburgh), a Vietnam country file, agency files (including, for example, a JCS bombing chronology and reports on JCS war games), minutes of NSC meetings, National Security Action Memoranda, and NSC histories (with supporting documents). The Clark Clifford Papers and the Warnke/McNaughton Papers are also of great value. The Westmoreland Papers came to the library from the Army Center of Military History, which has copies. David C. Humphrey, formerly national security archivist at the library, has published two very helpful articles on its holdings: "Searching for LBJ at the Johnson Library" (*SHAFR Newsletter*, June 1989, pp 1–17) and "Tuesday Lunch at the Johnson White House" (*Diplomatic History*, Winter 1984, pp 81–101.)

Interviews

The author has had the privilege of talking to hundreds of the Air Force's Vietnam veterans, ranging from Generals Momyer and Vogt to the pilots who flew the missions and the airmen who maintained the planes. Over the years, Air Force historians have recorded and transcribed more than two thousand interviews, most of them dealing in some way with the Vietnam War. While the Air Force Historical Research Agency's 1989 catalog of the Air Force Oral History Collection does not have a subject index, the older 1982 catalog does. The Air Force Academy has its own collection of interviews with former prisoners of war.

Bibliography

The Johnson Library has built an excellent collection of interviews with Washington decision makers. The U.S. Naval Institute has conducted extensive interviews with Admirals Moorer and Sharp, among others. Texas A & M University has a useful interview with Maj. Gen. Charles R. Bond, Jr. See also Robert McNamara's deposition in the case of Westmoreland vs. CBS, March 26, 1984, filed in the U.S. District Court for the Southern District of New York.

Published Collections of Documents

After the "Pentagon Papers" were leaked to the press in 1971, they were published in several incomplete editions. The most complete edition was the official one: *United States-Vietnam Relations, 1945–1967*, 12 volumes (Washington: GPO, 1971). It does not, however, have all the documents made available by Senator Mike Gravel (Democrat, Alaska) in his well-indexed version: *The Pentagon Papers: The Senator Gravel Edition*, 5 volumes (Boston: Beacon, 1971–72). The *New York Times* hit the street first with its one-volume paperback edition: *The Pentagon Papers* (New York: Bantam, 1971). More than a decade later, documents on negotiations finally became available in George C. Herring, ed., *The Secret Diplomacy of the Vietnam War: The Negotiating Volumes of the Pentagon Papers* (Austin: University of Texas, 1983). For useful background, see Sanford J. Ungar, *The Papers and The Papers: An Account of the Legal and Political Battle Over the Pentagon Papers* (New York: Columbia, 1989).

The State Department's *Foreign Relations of the United States* series published its Vietnam volumes for 1965–66 (David C. Humphrey, ed.) in 1996–98 with the rest of the war to follow in due course. For the Nixon years, *The Haldeman Diaries: Inside the Nixon White House: the Multimedia Edition*, CD ROM (Santa Monica, California: Sony, 1994) are revealing. The transcripts of Nixon's tape-recorded conversations in Stanley I. Kutler, ed., *Abuse of Power: The New Nixon Tapes* (New York: Free Press, 1997) discuss the Pentagon Papers but contain little else about the Vietnam War. The first published installment of Johnson's tape-recorded conversations covers only 1963–64; see Michael R. Beschloss, ed., *Taking Charge: The Johnson White House Tapes* (New York: Simon & Schuster, 1997). The many volumes of the *Public Papers of the Presidents of the United States* give the text of press conferences and speeches. Beginning in 1965 the Senate Foreign Relations Committee published an annually updated edition of its one-volume document collection: *Background Information Relating to Southeast Asia*. The *Congressional Record* has often published important documents; for example, on May 10–11, 1972, the *Record* included National Security Study Memorandum No. 1, January 1969, and A Summary of Agency Responses. University Publications of America has published microfilm editions of MACV records (Graham Cosmas, ed.) and the National Security Files at the Johnson Library (George C. Herring, ed.).

Congressional Hearings and Reports

This selection is in chronological order:

Air War Against North Vietnam. Hearings, Preparedness Investigating Subcommittee, Senate Armed Services Committee, August 9–23, 1967 ("Stennis Hearings"). Summary Report, 1967.

Bombing Operations and the Prisoner-of-War Rescue Mission in North Vietnam. Hearing, Senate Foreign Relations Committee with Secretary of Defense Laird, November 24, 1970.

Thailand, Laos, and Cambodia: January 1972. Staff report by James Lowenstein and Richard Moose for the Senate Foreign Relations Committee, 1972.

Bombing As A Policy Tool in Vietnam: Effectiveness. Staff study on the Pentagon Papers by Robert Biles for the Senate Foreign Relations Committee, 1972.

Unauthorized Bombing of Military Targets in North Vietnam. Hearing, House Armed Services Committee, June 12, 1972.

Problems of War Victims in Indochina, Part III: North Vietnam. Hearings, Senate Judiciary Committee, August 16–17, 1972.

Nomination of John D. Lavelle, General Creighton W. Abrams, and Admiral John S. McCain. Hearings, Senate Armed Services Committee, September 11–22, 1972.

Bombing of North Vietnam. Hearings, House Appropriations Committee, January 9, 1973.

Thailand, Laos, Cambodia, and Vietnam: April 1973. Staff report by James Lowenstein and Richard Moose for the Senate Foreign Relations Committee, 1973.

Relief and Rehabilitation of War Victims in Indochina: One Year After the Ceasefire. Study mission report for the Senate Judiciary Committee, January 27, 1974.

Vietnam: May 1974. Staff report by Richard Moose and Charles Meissner for the Senate Foreign Relations Committee, 1974.

Weather Modification as a Weapon of War. Hearings, Subcommittee on International Organization and Movements, House Foreign Affairs Committee, September 24, 1974, with appended declassified hearings, *Weather Modification*, Subcommittee on Oceans and International Environment, Senate Foreign Relations Committee, March 20, 1974.

Vietnam: 1976. Senator George McGovern's report to the Senate Foreign Relations Committee, 1976.

Aftermath of War: Humanitarian Problems of Southeast Asia. Staff report for the Senate Judiciary Committee, 1976.

The War Powers Resolution. A special study by John H. Sullivan. House Foreign Affairs Committee, 1982.

Bibliography

U.S. Air Force Histories

This book, like those below, rests in part upon a foundation provided by hundreds of unit histories, as well as by the CHECO and other Air Force historical reports listed after the books.

The United States Air Force in Southeast Asia

Ballard, Jack S. *Development and Employment of Fixed-Wing Gunships, 1962–1972*. Washington, 1982.

Berger, Carl, ed. *An Illustrated Account*. Revised ed. Washington, 1984.

Bowers, Ray. *Tactical Airlift*. Washington, 1983.

Futrell, Robert F. *The Advisory Years to 1965*. Washington, 1981.

Schlight, John. *The War in South Vietnam: The Years of the Offensive, 1965–1968*. Washington, 1988.

Van Staaveren, Jacob. *Interdiction in Southern Laos, 1960–1968*. Washington, 1993.

Other Books

Buckingham, William A., Jr. *The Air Force and Herbicides in Southeast Asia, 1961–1971*. Washington, 1982.

Cooling, Benjamin Franklin, ed. *Case Studies in the Achievement of Air Superiority*. Washington, 1994.

———. *Case Studies in the Development of Close Air Support*, Washington, 1990.

Fox, Roger P. *Air Base Defense in the Republic of Vietnam, 1961–1973*. Washington, 1979.

Futrell, R. Frank, et al. *Aces and Aerial Victories: The United States Air Force in Southeast Asia, 1965–1975*. Washington, 1976.

———. *Ideas, Concepts, Doctrine: Basic Thinking in the United States Air Force, 1907–1984*. Maxwell AFB, 1989.

Gilster, Herman L. *The Air War in Southeast Asia: Case Studies of Selected Campaigns*. Maxwell AFB, 1993.

Lane, John J. *Command and Control and Communications Structures in Southeast Asia*. Maxwell AFB, 1981.

Mark, Eduard. *Aerial Interdiction in Three Wars*. Washington, 1994.

Meilinger, Phillip S., ed. *The Paths of Heaven: The Evolution of Airpower Theory*. Maxwell AFB, 1997.

Mrozek, Donald J. *Air Power and the Ground War in Vietnam*. Maxwell AFB, 1988.

———. *The U.S. Air Force After Vietnam*. Maxwell AFB, 1988.

Nalty, Bernard C. *Air Power and the Fight for Khe Sanh*. Washington, 1973.

Tilford, Earl H., Jr. *Search and Rescue in Southeast Asia, 1961–1975.* Washington, 1980.

———. *Setup: What the Air Force Did in Vietnam and Why.* Maxwell AFB, 1991.

Trest, Warren A. *Air Force Roles and Missions: A History.* Washington, 1998.

Watts, Barry D. *The Foundations of U.S. Air Doctrine.* Maxwell AFB, 1984.

Werrell, Kenneth P. *Archie, Flak, AAA, and SAM.* Maxwell AFB, 1988.

Worden, Mike. *Rise of the Fighter Generals: The Problem of Air Force Leadership, 1945–1982.* Maxwell AFB, 1998.

USAF Southeast Asia Monograph Series

These monographs were written at the Air University Airpower Research Institute, Maxwell Air Force Base, Alabama, by veterans of the war in Southeast Asia. The series includes nine monographs printed in seven volume, with Major, later Lieutenant Colonel, A.J.C. Lavalle the general editor for volumes I through IV, and Colonel Robert E. Rayfield the general editor for volume VI.

Burbage, Paul, et al. *The Battle for the Skies Over North Vietnam.* Volume I, 1976.

Corum, Delbert, et al., *The Tale of Two Bridges.* Volume I, 1976.

Doglione, John A., et al. *Airpower and the 1972 Spring Invasion.* Volume II, 1976.

McCarthy, James R., and George B. Allison. *Linebacker II: A View from the Rock.* Volume VI, 1979.

Momyer, William W. *The Vietnamese Air Force, 1951–1975, an Anaylysis of its Role in Combat.* Volume III, 1977.

Project CHECO Reports

(Written in Southeast Asia or Hawaii and printed in Hawaii.)

Abbey, Tom G. "The Role of USAF in Support of Special Activities in Southeast Asia." 1976.

Barnette, Benjamin H., Jr., and James R. Barrow. "Base Defense in Thailand." 1973.

Bonetti, Lee. "The War in Vietnam, January–June 1967." 1968.

Bonetti, Lee, et al. "The War in Vietnam, July–December 1967." 1968.

Breitling, Patrick J. "Guided Bomb Operations in Southeast Asia: The Weather Dimension, 1 February–31 December 1972." 1973.

Brynn, Edward P. "Reconnaissance in Southeast Asia, July 1966–June 1968." 1969.

Bibliography

Brynn, Edward P., and Arthur P. Geesey. "Joint Personnel Recovery in Southeast Asia." 1976.

Burch, Robert M. "The ABCCC in Southeast Asia." 1969.

―――. "Command and Control, 1966–1968." 1969.

―――. "Tactical Electronic Warfare Operations in Southeast Asia, 1962–1968." 1969.

Burditt, William R. "Rules of Engagement, October 1972–August 1973." 1977.

Colwell, Robert F. "USAF Tactical Reconnaissance in Southeast Asia, July 1969–June 1971." 1971.

Durkee, Richard A. "Combat Skyspot." 1967.

Elder, Paul W. "Buffalo Hunter, 1970–1972." 1973.

Elder, Paul W., and Peter M. Melly. "Rules of Engagement, November 1969–September 1972." 1973.

Fessler, George R., Jr. "Air Refueling in Southeast Asia, 1964–1970." 1971.

Francis, David G., and David R. Nelson. "Search and Rescue Operations in Southeast Asia, 1 April 1972–30 June 1973." 1974.

Garver, Richard B. "Drug Abuse in Southeast Asia." 1975.

Hanrahan, Edward B. "An Overview of Insurgency and Counterinsurgency in Thailand Through 1973." 1975.

Harrison, Philip R. "Impact of Darkness and Weather on Air Operations in Southeast Asia." 1969.

Heffron, Charles H., Jr. "Air-to-Air Encounters Over North Vietnam, 1 January–30 June 1967." 1967.

Helmka, Robert T., and Beverly Hale. "USAF Operations from Thailand, 1964–65." 1966.

Hurley, Alfred F. "The EC–47 in Southeast Asia." 1968.

Johnson, Calvin R. "Linebacker Operations, September–December 1972." 1978.

Lowe, LeRoy W. "Search and Rescue Operations in Southeast Asia, 1 June 1971–31 March 1972." 1972.

Lynch, Walter F. "USAF Search and Rescue Operations in Southeast Asia, 1 July 1969–31 December 1970." 1971.

Machovec, Frank M. "Southeast Asia Tactical Data Systems Interface." 1975.

Melyan, Wesley R.C. "Arc Light, 1965–1966." 1967.

―――. "Arc Light, January–June 1967." 1968.

Melyan, Wesley R.C., and Lee Bonetti. "Rolling Thunder, July 1965–December 1966." 1967.

Montagliani, Ernie S. "Airmunitions in Southeast Asia." 1969.

Morita, Claude G. "USSAG/7AF in Thailand (1973–1975)." 1979.

Nicholson, Charles A. "The USAF Response to the Spring 1972 North Vietnamese Offensive." 1972.

Overton, James B. "Enemy Capture/Release of USAF Personnel in Southeast Asia." 1969.

———. "Rolling Thunder: January 1967–November 1968." 1969.

———. "USAF Search and Rescue, November 1967–June 1969." 1969.

Paterson, L.E. "Air War in the DMZ, January–August 1967." 1968.

———. "Evolution of the Rules of Engagement for Southeast Asia, 1960–1965." 1966.

Penix, Guyman, and Paul T. Ringenbach. "Air Defense in Southeast Asia, 1945–1971." 1973.

Picinich, A.A., et al. "The F–111 in Southeast Asia: September 1972–January 1973." 1974.

Porter, Melvin F. "Air Tactics Against North Vietnam Air/Ground Defenses." 1967.

———. "Control of Airstrikes, January 1967–December 1968." 1969.

———. "The EC–47 in Southeast Asia, April 1968–July 1970." 1970.

———. "Evasion and Escape, Southeast Asia, 1964–1971." 1972.

———. "Interdiction in Southeast Asia, 1965–1966." 1967.

———. "Interdiction of Waterways and POL Pipelines." 1970.

———. "Linebacker: Overview of the First 120 Days." 1973.

———. "Operation Thor." 1969.

———. "Proud Deep Alpha." 1972.

———. "Second Generation Weaponry in Southeast Asia." 1970.

———. "Tactical Control System Operations in Southeast Asia." 1969.

Pralle, James B. "Arc Light, June 1967–December 1968." 1969.

Pratt, John C. "Air Tactics Against North Vietnam Air Ground Defenses, December 1966–November 1968." 1969.

Project CHECO Team. "Possible Communist Counter to Punitive Air Strikes." 1965.

———. "Punitive Air Strikes." 1965.

———. "Rolling Thunder, March–June 1965." 1966.

Reddel, Carl W. "College Eye." 1968.

Render, William E. "EB–66 Operations in Southeast Asia, 1967." 1968.

Sams, Kenneth. "Command and Control, 1965." 1966.

Sams, Kenneth, et al. "The Air War in Vietnam, 1968–1969." 1970.

Schlight, John. "Jet Forward Air Controllers in Southeast Asia." 1969.

———. "Rules of Engagement, 1 January 1966–1 November 1969." 1969.

Seig, Louis. "Impact of Geography on Air Operations in Southeast Asia." 1970.

Sheets, Gary D. "Air Operations in the DMZ Area, 1966." 1967.

Siemann, John W. "Combat Snap: AIM–9J Southeast Asia Introduction." 1974.

Smith, Mark E. "USAF Reconnaissance in Southeast Asia, 1961–66." 1966.

Stevens, Eldon L. "Psychological Operations: Air Support in Southeast Asia, June 1968–May 1971." 1971.

Thompson, A.W. "Strike Control and Reconnaissance (SCAR) in Southeast Asia." 1969.

Thorndale, C. William. "Air War in the DMZ, September 1967–June 1968." 1969.

Bibliography

————. "Interdiction in Route Package One, 1968." 1969.

————. "Interdiction in Southeast Asia, November 1966–October 1968." 1969.

————. "Tactical Recon Photography Request/Distribution." 1969.

Tinius, Jack L. "Psychological Operations Against North Vietnam, July 1972–January 1973." 1974.

Trest, Warren A. "Control of Air Strikes in Southeast Asia, 1961–1966." 1967.

————. "Lucky Tiger Special Air Warfare Operations." 1967.

————. "Operation Tally Ho." 1966.

————. "USAF SAC Operations in Support of Southeast Asia." 1969.

Trest, Warren A., and Valentino Castellina. "Operation Neutralize." 1968.

Trest, Warren A., and Charles E. Gorland. "Counterinsurgency in Thailand, 1966." 1967.

Trest, Warren A., and Dale E. Hammons. "USAF Operations from Thailand, 1966." 1967.

Trest, Warren A., et al. "USAF Posture in Thailand, 1966." 1967.

Vallentiny, Edward. "The Fall of Site 85." 1968.

————. "USAF Posture in Thailand, 1967." 1969.

Vallentiny, Edward, and D.G. Francis. "Attack on Udorn, 26 July 1968." 1968.

Wade, Thomas D. "Seventh Air Force Tactical Air Control Center Operations." 1968.

Weaver, Robert B. "Air-to-Air Encounters Over North Vietnam, 1 July 1967–31 December 1968." 1969.

Wright, Monte D. "USAF Tactics Against Air and Ground Defenses in Southeast Asia, November 1968–May 1970." 1970.

Other Air Force Printed Studies

Anthony, Victor B. *Tactics and Techniques of Night Operations, 1960–1970.* Washington, 1973.

Anthony, Victor B., and Richard N. Sexton. *The War in Northern Laos, 1954–1973.* Washington, 1993.

Drew, Dennis M. *Rolling Thunder 1965: Anatomy of A Failure.* Maxwell AFB, 1986.

Greenwood, John T. *Chronology of SAC Participation in Linebacker II.* Offutt AFB, 1973.

Hartsook, Elizabeth H. *The Administration Emphasizes Air Power, 1969.* Washington, 1971.

————. *Air Power Helps Stop the Invasion and End the War, 1972.* Washington, 1978.

————. *The End of U.S. Involvement, 1973–1975.* Washington, 1980.

————. *Role of Air Power Grows, 1970.* Washington, 1972.

————. *Shield for Vietnamization and Withdrawal, 1971.* Washington, 1976.

Hopkins, Charles K. *SAC Bomber Operations in the Southeast Asia War*. 5 volumes. Offutt AFB, 1983.

———. *SAC Tanker Operations in the Southeast Asia War*. Offutt AFB, 1979.

Nalty, Bernard. *Tactics and Techniques of Electronic Warfare: Electronic Countermeasures in the Air War Against North Vietnam, 1965–1973*. Washington, 1977.

Pierson, James E. *A Special Study of Electronic Warfare in Southeast Asia, 1964–1968*. Kelly AFB, 1973.

Van Staaveren, Jacob. *The Air Campaign Against North Vietnam, 1966*. Washington, 1968.

———. *The Search for Military Alternatives, 1967*. Washington, 1969.

———. *Toward A Bombing Halt, 1968*. Washington, 1970.

———. *USAF Deployment Planning for Southeast Asia, 1966*. Washington, 1967.

———. *USAF Plans and Operations in Southeast Asia, 1965*. Washington, 1966.

Wolk, Herman S. *Logistics and Base Construction in Southeast Asia, 1967*. Washington, 1968.

———. *Research and Development for Southeast Asia, 1965–67*. Washington, 1969.

———. *Research and Development for Southeast Asia, 1968*. Washington, 1970.

———. *USAF Logistic Plans and Policies in Southeast Asia, 1965*. Washington, 1967.

———. *USAF Logistic Plans and Policies in Southeast Asia, 1966*. Washington, 1967.

Air Force Drafts

Cummings, Robert L., Jr. "The Vietnamese Railroad System." Washington, 1984.

Deas, Robert. "Two Days at Thai Nguyen." Maxwell AFB, 1976.

Greenhalgh, William H., Jr. "The U.S. Air Force in Southeast Asia, February 1965–November 1968." Maxwell AFB, 1973.

———. "U.S. Air Force Reconnaissance in Southeast Asia, 1960–1975." Maxwell AFB, 1976.

Nalty, Bernard C. "Interdiction in Southern Laos, 1968–1972." Washington, 1993.

Sunderland, Riley, and Jacob Van Staaveren. "Constraints on the Use of Air Power in Three Wars." Washington, 1971.

Van Staaveren, Jacob. "Gradual Failure: The Air War Over North Vietnam, 1965–66." Washington, 1997.

Bibliography

Other U.S. Government Histories

The classified histories and studies of the Joint Chiefs of Staff, the Pacific Command, the Military Assistance Command Vietnam, the National Security Agency, and the Central Intelligence Agency are invaluable. Several government agencies have published relevant volumes:

Army

Bergen, John D. *Military Communications: A Test for Technology*. Washington, 1986.

Clarke, Jeffrey J. *Advice and Support: The Final Years, 1965–1973*. Washington, 1988.

Hammond, William M. *Public Affairs: The Military and the Media, 1962–1968*. Washington, 1988.

———. *Public Affairs: The Military and the Media, 1968–1973*. Washington, 1996.

Meyerson, Joel D. *Images of a Lengthy War*. Washington, 1986.

Spector, Ronald H. *Advice and Support: The Early Years, 1941–1960*. Washington, 1983.

Navy

Hooper, Edwin Bickford, Dean C. Allard, and Oscar P. Fitzgerald. *The Setting of the Stage to 1959*. Washington, 1976.

Marolda, Edward J. *By Sea, Air, and Land: An Illustrated History of the U.S. Navy and the War in Southeast Asia*. Washington, 1994.

———. *Operation End Sweep*. Washington, 1993.

Marolda, Edward J., and Oscar P. Fitzgerald. *From Military Assistance to Combat, 1959–1965*. Washington, 1986.

Muir, Malcom Jr. *Black Shoes and Blue Water: Surface Warfare in the United States Navy, 1945–1975*. Washington, 1996.

Marine Corps

Cosmas, Graham A., and Terrence P. Murray. *Vietnamization and Redeployment, 1970–1971*. Washington, 1986.

Dunham, George R., and David A. Quinlan. *The Bitter End, 1973–1975*. Washington, 1990.

Melson, Charles D., and Curtis G. Arnold. *The War that Would Not End, 1971–1973*. Washington, 1991.

Shulimson, Jack. *An Expanding War, 1966*. Washington, 1982.

Shulimson, Jack, et al. *The Defining Year, 1968*. Washington, 1997.

Shulimson, Jack, and Charles M. Johnson. *The Landing and the Buildup, 1965*. Washington, 1978.

Smith, Charles P. *High Mobility and Standdown, 1969*. Washington, 1988.

Telfer, Gary L., Lane Rogers, and V. Keith Fleming, Jr. *Fighting the North Vietnamese, 1967*. Washington, 1984.

Whitlow, Robert H. *The Advisory and Combat Assistance Era, 1954–1964*. Washington, 1977.

Office of the Secretary of Defense

Rochester, Stuart I., and Frederick Kiley. *Honor Bound: The History of American Prisoners of War in Southeast Asia, 1961–1973*. Washington, 1998.

National Defense University

Dillard, Walter Scott. *Sixty Days to Peace: Implementing the Paris Peace Accords, Vietnam 1973*. Washington, 1982.

Keaney, Thomas A. *Strategic Bombers and Conventional Weapons: Airpower Options*. Washington, 1984.

Mather, Paul D. *M.I.A.: Accounting for the Missing in Southeast Asia*. Washington, 1994.

Warden, John A., III. *The Air Campaign*. Washington, 1988.

Watts, Barry D. *Clausewitzian Friction and Future War*. Washington, 1996.

Central Intelligence Agency

Ford, Harold P. *CIA and the Vietnam Policymakers: Three Episodes, 1962–1968*. Washington, 1998.

Congressional Research Service

Gibbons, William Conrad. *The U.S. Government and the Vietnam War: Executive and Legislative Roles and Relationships. Parts I (1945–1961), II (1961–1964), III (January–July 1965), and IV (July 1965–January 1968)*. Washington, 1984–94.

U.S. Government Evaluations and Statistical Reports

This list is very selective.

Seventh Air Force

Project CHECO Reports. See list above. Most of these were written at Seventh

Bibliography

Air Force and printed at Pacific Air Forces.
Weekly Air Intelligence Summary.

Pacific Air Forces

Gilster, Col. Herman L., and Capt. Robert E.M. Frady. *Linebacker II USAF Bombing Survey*. Hickam AFB, 1973.
North Vietnamese Air Force Fighter Patterns. Compiled by DCS/Intelligence, March 1968.
Project Corona Harvest Inputs. See discussion of Air Force Historical Research Agency above.
Summary of Air Operations in Southeast Asia. Monthly.

Pacific Command

Rolling Thunder Digest. Quarterly.
Sharp, Adm. U.S. Grant, and Gen. William C. Westmoreland. *Report on the War in Vietnam*. Washington, 1968.

Joint Chiefs of Staff

McPherson, Maj. Gen. John B. *Night Song Study Group Report: An Examination of U.S. Air Operations Against North Vietnam Air Defense System*. 3 volumes. Washington, 1967.

Defense Intelligence Agency

Southeast Asia Military Fact Book. Semiannual. Prepared with JCS.

Office of the Secretary of Defense

Southeast Asia Statistical Summary. Tables frequently updated through 1973.

Headquarters USAF

Trends, Indicators, and Analyses. Monthly.
USAF Management Summary: Southeast Asia. Monthly until final issue in November 1973.
USAF Management Summary: Southeast Asia Review. Semi-annual until final issue in February 1974.
USAF Statistical Digest. Annual.

Tactical Air Command

Granville, John M. *Summary of USAF Aircraft Losses in Southeast Asia.* Langley AFB, 1974.
USAF Tactical Fighter Weapons Center. *Project Red Baron II: Air-to-Air Encounters in Southeast Asia.* 5 volumes. Nellis AFB, 1972–73. *Project Red Baron III.* 4 volumes. Nellis AFB, 1974. For predecessor study, see Institute for Defense Analyses section below.

Air University

Project Corona Harvest Reports. See discussion of Air Force Historical Research Agency above.

Central Intelligence Agency

An Appraisal of Bombing of North Vietnam. At least quarterly. Prepared with Defense Intelligence Agency.
Palmer, Gen. Bruce, Jr. *U.S. Intelligence and Vietnam.* Washington, 1984.

U.S. Government Contract Studies

BDM Corporation

A Study of Strategic Lessons Learned in Vietnam. 9 volumes. Washington, 1979.

Center for Naval Analyses

McCrea, Michael M. *U.S. Navy, Marine Corps, and Air Force Fixed-Wing Aircraft Losses and Damage in Southeast Asia (1962–1973).* Arlington, Va, 1976.
Summary of Air Operations in Southeast Asia. Arlington, Va, monthly.

Institute for Defense Analyses

Air-to-Air Encounter in Southeast Asia. 4 volumes. Arlington, Va, 1974. This is the initial installment of what became Project Red Baron at the USAF Tactical Fighter Weapons Center, Nellis AFB, Nev.
Analysis of Combat Aircraft Losses in Southeast Asia. 5 volumes. Arlington, Va, 1968.
The Effects of U.S. Bombing on North Vietnam's Ability to Support Military Operations in South Vietnam and Laos: Retrospect and Prospect. Arlington, 1966. Better known as the Jason Study.

Bibliography

RAND

Blachly, R.L., P.A. CoNine, and E.H. Sharkey. *Laser and Electro-Optical Guided Bomb Performance in Southeast Asia*. Santa Monica, 1973.

Davison, W. Phillips, and Stephen J. Hosmer. *Some Vietnamese Communist and Anti-Communist Views on Bombing Restrictions and Negotiations*. Santa Monica, 1969.

DeLeon, Peter. *The Laser-Guided Bomb: Case History of a Development*. Santa Monica, 1974.

Dews, Edmund, and Felix Kozaczka. *Air Interdiction: Lessons from Past Campaigns*. Santa Monica, 1981.

Fisk, D.M., P.R. McClenon, and J.J. Surmeier. *Some Methodological Problems of Wartime Costing—A Case Study Using the Southeast Asia Outcountry Air War*. Santa Monica, 1970.

Heymann, Hans, Jr., et al. *Security and Assistance in Thailand*. Santa Monica, 1965.

Hoeffding, Oleg. *Bombing North Vietnam: An Appraisal of Economic and Political Effects*. Santa Monica, 1966.

Hosmer, Stephen T. *The Fall of South Vietnam*. Santa Monica, 1975.

———. *Viet Cong Repression and Its Implications for the Future*. Santa Monica, 1970.

Jenkins, Brian M. *Giap and the Seventh Son*. Santa Monica, 1972.

———. *Why the North Vietnamese Keep Fighting*. Santa Monica, 1972.

Johnson, Dana J. *Roles and Missions for Conventionally Armed Heavy Bombers—An Historical Perspective*. Santa Monica, 1994.

Joint Studies with Headquarters USAF Operations Analysis. Santa Monica, Calif, 1968.

Kellen, Konrad. *Conversations with Enemy Soldiers in Late 1968/Early 1969*. Santa Monica, 1970.

———. *A Profile of the PAVN Soldier in South Vietnam*. Santa Monica, 1966.

Nutt, Anita Lauve. *Prisoners of War in Indochina*. Santa Monica, 1969.

Reinhardt, G.C., and E.H. Sharkey. *Air Interdiction in Southeast Asia*. Santa Monica, 1967.

Simons, William E. *Coercion in Vietnam?* Santa Monica, 1969.

Solomon, Robert L. *Boundary Concepts and Practices in Southeast Asia*. Santa Monica, 1969.

Sweetland, Anders. *Rallying Potential Among the North Vietnamese Armed Forces*. Santa Monica, 1970.

Vick, Alan. *Snakes in the Eagles Nest: A History of Ground Attacks on Air Bases*. Santa Monica, 1995.

Weiner, M.G., J.R. Brown, and R.E. Koon. *Infiltration of Personnel from North Vietnam, 1959–1967*. Santa Monica, 1968.

Winnefeld, James A., and Dana J. Johnson. *Joint Air Operations: Pursuit of*

Unity in Command and Control, 1942–1991. Annapolis: Naval Institute Press, 1993.

Zasloff, Joseph J. *Origins of the Insurgency in South Vietnam, 1954–1960*. Santa Monica, 1967.

———. *Political Motivation of the Viet Cong*. Santa Monica, 1968.

———. *The Role of North Vietnam in the Southern Insurgency*, Santa Monica, 1964.

Vietnamese Perspectives

The Pike and Cornell microfilm collections (described in the introductory section of this bibliography) include Vietnamese publications in English as well as translations by the U.S. government and others. For example, Hanoi published in English a 1973 report of the Commission for Investigation of the U.S. Imperialists' War Crimes in Viet Nam entitled *The Late December 1972 U.S. Blitz on North Vietnam*. A more recent and extensive Vietnamese publication in English is Luu Van Loi and Nguyen Anh Vu, *Le Duc Tho-Kissinger Negotiations* (Hanoi, 1996). Although U.S. government translations of Vietnamese works have become infrequent since the end of the Cold War, in 1996 the U.S. Defense Language Institute translated a 1987 report by the Military History Institute of Vietnam to Gen. Vo Nguyen Giap, entitled *A Consolidated Report on the Fight Against the United States for the Salvation of Vietnam by Our People*. After retiring from the U.S. government, Merle Pribbenow translated the Military History Institute's *History of the People's Army of Vietnam, Volume II: The Coming of Age of the People's Army of Vietnam During the Resistance War Against the Americans to Save the Nation, 1954–1975* (Hanoi, 1994).

Seeking dialogue with Hanoi's historians and other officials, a group of American scholars went there for a conference in 1988; the Americans published their papers together with a summary of views expressed by the Vietnamese in Jayne Werner and David Hunt, eds., *The American War in Vietnam* (Ithaca, New York: Cornell, 1993). In 1995–98, former Secretary of Defense Robert McNamara and colleagues from the Johnson administration together with some American scholars traveled to Hanoi for a series of meetings with Nguyen Co Thach, Vo Nguyen Giap and other Vietnamese experts on the war. A retired U.S. Air Force general, William Y. Smith, participated in those discussions. See Robert S. McNamara, James G. Blight, and Robert K. Brigham, with Thomas J. Biersteker and Col. Herbert Y. Schandler, *Argument Without End: In Search of Answers to the Vietnam Tragedy* (New York: Public Affairs, 1999).

The names of Vietnam's leading figures have been credited as authors of several volumes published in Hanoi. See the entries for Ho Chi Minh, Hoang Van Kanh, Le Duan, Truong Chinh, Van Tien Dung, and Vo Nguyen Giap in the next section of this bibliography, which also lists publications of leaders of South Vietnam (Nguyen Cao Ky, Tran Van Don, Bui Diem, Nguyen Tien Hung, Nguyen

Bibliography

Anh Tuan, Cao Van Vien, and Lam Quang Thi) as well as Vietnamese communists who broke with Hanoi's official view (Bui Tin, Tran Van Tra, and Truong Nhu Tang). For an oral history of female soldiers, see the entry for Karen Gottschang Turner. See also the entries for Don North's interview of Trinh Thi Ngo ("Hanoi Hannah") in *Vietnam* magazine, as well as that magazine's translation of General Hoang Van Khanh's 1982 account (in the Hanoi press) of efforts to shoot down B–52s. Included below are several examples of recent Vietnamese fiction, among them celebrated novels by two authors from the north, Bao Ninh (*The Sorrow of War*) and Duong Thu Huong (*Novel Without a Name*).

Memoirs and Participant Publications

Allison, George B. "The Bombers Go to Bullseye." *Aerospace Historian*, December 1982, pp 227–38.

Alvarez, Everett, Jr., and Anthony S. Pitch. *Chained Eagle*. New York: Donald I. Fine, 1989.

Anthis, Rollen H. "Airpower: The Paradox in Vietnam." *Air Force Magazine*, April 1967, pp 34–38.

Ariel (pseudonym of Morris J. Blachman). "The Stupidity of Intelligence." *Washington Monthly*, September 1969, pp 23–28.

Ashmore, Harry S., and William C. Baggs. *Mission to Hanoi*. New York: Putnam's, 1968.

Baez, Joan. *And a Voice to Sing With*. New York: Summit, 1987.

Ball, George. "A Light that Failed." *Atlantic Monthly*, July 1972, p 39.

———. *The Past Has Another Pattern*. New York: Norton, 1982.

Bao Ninh. *The Sorrow of War: A Novel of North Vietnam*. New York: Pantheon, 1993.

Basel, G.I. *Pak Six*. La Mesa, California: Associated Creative Writers, 1982.

Bedinger, Henry James. "Prisoner of War Organization in Hanoi." MS thesis, San Diego State University, 1976.

Bell, Brig. Gen. Ken. *100 Missions North*. Washington: Brassey's, 1993.

Berent, Mark. *Storm Flight*. New York: Putnam's, 1993. This is the last of five Berent novels giving a veteran's fictional history of the air war over Southeast Asia.

Bingamon, H.W. *Reckonings: Stories of the Air War over North Vietnam*. New York: Vantage, 1988.

Blesse, Frederick C. *Check Six*. Mesa, Arizona: Champlin Museum, 1987.

Bohlen, Charles E. *Witness to History*. New York: Norton, 1973.

Brace, Ernest C. *A Code to Keep*. New York: St. Martin's, 1988.

Broughton, Jack. *Going Downtown*. New York: Orion, 1988.

———. *Thud Ridge*. Philadelphia: Lippincott, 1969.

Bui Diem with David Chanoff. *In the Jaws of History*. Boston: Houghton Mifflin, 1987.

Bui Tin. *Following Ho Chi Minh: Memoirs of a North Vietnamese Colonel.* Honolulu: University of Hawaii, 1995.

Bundy, McGeorge. *Danger and Survival.* New York: Random House, 1988.

————. *The Strength of Government.* Cambridge: Harvard, 1968.

Burchett, Wilfred. *At the Barricades.* New York: Times Books, 1981.

————. *Vietnam North.* New York: International, 1966.

Butler, Jimmie H. *A Certain Brotherhood.* Colorado Springs: Cricket Press, 1996. A novel.

Cao Van Vien. *The Final Collapse.* Washington: Army Center of Military History, 1983.

Carroll, James. *An American Requiem.* Boston: Houghton Mifflin, 1996.

Carson, Don. "Flying the Thud." *Air Force Magazine*, April 1974, pp 18–23.

Clement, Robert A. "A Fourth of July in December: A B–52 Navigator's Perspective of Linebacker II." Air Command and Staff College, 1984.

Clifford, Clark. "A Viet Nam Reappraisal." *Foreign Affairs*, July 1969, pp 601–22.

Clifford, Clark, with Richard Holbrooke. *Counsel to the President.* New York: Random House, 1991.

Colby, William, and Peter Forbath. *Honorable Men: My Life in the CIA.* New York: Simon and Schuster, 1978.

Colby, William, with James McCargar. *Lost Victory.* Chicago: Contemporary Books, 1989.

Colvin, John. "Hanoi in My Time." *Washington Quarterly*, spring 1981, pp 138–54.

————. *Twice Around the World.* London: Leo Cooper, 1991.

Coonts, Stephen. *Flight of the Intruder.* Annapolis: Naval Institute Press, 1986. A novel.

Cooper, Charles G. "The Day It Became the Longest War." *Naval Institute Proceedings*, May 1996, pp 77–80.

Cooper, Chester L. *The Lost Crusade.* New York: Dodd, Mead, 1970.

Cunningham, Randy, with Jeff Ethell. *Fox Two.* Mesa, Arizona: Champlin Museum, 1984.

Davidson, Phillip B. *Vietnam at War.* Novato, California: Presidio, 1988.

Day, George E. *Return with Honor.* Mesa, Arizona: Champlin Museum, 1989.

DeBellvue, Charles. "Navigator Ace—An Interview with Lt. Col. Chuck DeBellvue." *Navigator*, Winter 1983, pp 5–11.

Dobrynin, Anatoly. *In Confidence.* New York: Times Books, 1995.

Dramesi, John A. *Code of Honor.* New York: Norton, 1975.

Duffy, Dan, ed. *North Viet Nam Now: Fiction and Essays from Hanoi (Viet Nam Forum 15).* New Haven: Yale University Council on Southeast Asia Studies, 1996.

Duong Thu Huong. *Novel Without A Name.* New York: Morrow, 1994.

Ellsberg, Daniel. *Papers on the War.* New York: Simon & Schuster, 1972.

Bibliography

Enthoven, Alain C., and K. Wayne Smith. *How Much is Enough?* New York: Harper & Row, 1971.

Fulbright, J.W. *The Pentagon Propaganda Machine.* New York: Liveright, 1970.

Fulbright, J.W., with Seth P. Tillman. *The Price of Empire.* New York: Pantheon, 1989.

Gates, Robert M. *From the Shadows.* New York: Simon & Schuster, 1996.

Gillcrist, Paul T. *Feet Wet: Reflections of a Carrier Pilot.* Novato, California: Presidio, 1990.

Ginsburgh, Robert N. "Strategy and Air Power: The Lessons of Southeast Asia." *Strategic Review*, summer 1973, pp 18–24.

Goldwater, Barry M., with Jack Casserly. *Goldwater.* New York: Doubleday, 1988.

Goulding, Phil G. *Confirm or Deny.* New York: Harper & Row, 1970.

Guarino, Larry. *A POW's Story.* New York: Ivy, 1990.

Gulley, Bill, with Mary Ellen Reese. *Breaking Cover.* New York: Simon& Schuster, 1980.

Haig, Alexander M., Jr., with Charles McCarry. *Inner Circles.* New York: Warner, 1992.

Haldeman, H.R. *The Haldeman Diaries.* New York: Putnam's, 1994. See the section of this note on "Published Collections of Documents" for the complete edition on CD-ROM.

Haldeman, H.R., with Joseph DiMona. *The Ends of Power.* New York: Times Books, 1978.

Hayden, Tom. *Reunion.* New York: Collier, 1988.

Hayslip, Le Ly, with Jay Works. *When Heaven and Earth Changed Places.* New York: Doubleday, 1989.

Hess, Martha. *Then the Americans Came: Voices from Vietnam.* New Brunswick, N.J: Rutgers University Press, 1994.

Ho Chi Minh. *Selected Writings.* Hanoi: Foreign Languages Publishing House, 1977.

Hoang Van Chi. *From Colonialism to Communism: A Case History of North Vietnam.* New York: Praegar, 1964.

Hoang Van Kanh. "Taking Aim at the B–52s." *Vietnam*, April 1996, pp 26–33. Originally published in *Nhan Dan* (Hanoi) December 6–10, 1982.

Hoopes, Townsend. *The Limits of Intervention.* New York: David McKay, 1969.

———. "The Nuremberg Suggestion." *Washington Monthly*, January 1970, pp 18–21.

Humphrey, Hubert. *The Education of a Public Man: My Life and Politics.* Garden City, New York: Doubleday, 1976.

Jensen, Jay R. *Six Years in Hell.* Orcott, California: P.O.W., 1989.

Johnson, Gerald W., with John McClure and Charlotte McClure. *Called to*

Command. Paducah, Kentucky: Turner, 1996.

Johnson, Lady Bird (Claudia T.) *A White House Diary*. New York: Holt, Rinehart & Winston. 1970.

Johnson, Lyndon Baines. *The Vantage Point*. New York: Holt, Rinehart & Winston, 1971.

Johnson, Sam R., and Jan Winebrenner. *Captive Warriors*. College Station: Texas A & M, 1992.

Johnson, U. Alexis, with Jef Olivarius McAllister. *The Right Hand of Power*. Englewood Cliffs, New Jersey: Prentice-Hall, 1984.

Kasler, James H. "The Hanoi POL Strike." *Air University Review*, November–December 1974, pp 19–28.

Keirn, Richard "Pop." *Old Glory is the Most Beautiful of All*. Pittsburgh: Dorrance Publishing Co., 1996.

Kiley, Fred, and Tony Dater. *Listen. The War*. Colorado Springs: USAF Academy, 1973. Poetry.

Kissinger, Henry. "The Viet Nam Negotiations." *Foreign Affairs*, January 1969, pp 211–34.

———. *White House Years*. Boston: Little, Brown, 1979.

———. *Years of Renewal*. New York: Simon & Schuster, 1999.

———. *Years of Upheaval*. Boston: Little, Brown, 1982.

Komer, Robert W. *Bureaucracy at War*. Boulder, Colorado: Westview, 1986.

Kross, Walt. *Splash One*. Washington: Brassey's, 1991. A novel.

Krulak, Victor. *First to Fight*. Annapolis: Naval Institute Press, 1984.

Laird, Melvin. "A Strong Start in a Difficult Decade." *International Security*, fall 1985, pp 5–26.

Lam Quang Thi. *Autopsy: The Death of South Viet Nam*. Phoenix: Sphinx, 1986.

Lansdale, Edward Geary. *In the Midst of War*. New York: Harper & Row, 1972.

Larson, Gerald D. "How a Fighter Pilot Sees the Air War in Vietnam." *Air Force Magazine*, July 1967, pp 45–49.

Le Duan. *The Vietnamese Revolution*. Hanoi: Foreign Languages Publishing House, 1970.

Lchman, John F., Jr. *Command of the Seas*. New York: Charles Scribner's Sons, 1988.

LeMay, Curtis E., with MacKinlay Kantor. *Mission With LeMay*. Garden City, New York: Doubleday, 1965.

Marr, David G., ed. *Phan Boi Chau's "Prison Notes" and Ho Chi Minh's "Prison Diary."* Athens: Ohio University, 1978.

Maurer, Harry. *Strange Ground: Americans in Vietnam, 1945–1975, An Oral History*. New York: Henry Holt, 1989.

McCain, John, with Mark Salter. *Faith of My Fathers*. New York: Random House, 1999.

McCain, John S., Jr. "Admiral McCain Assesses the War in Southeast Asia."

Air Force Magazine, September 1972.

McCarthy, James R., and Robert E. Rayfield. *B–52s Over Hanoi*. Fullerton, California: California State Fullerton Press, 1996.

McCarthy, Mary. *Vietnam*. New York: Harcourt, Brace, 1967.

McCutcheon, Keith B. "Marine Aviation in Vietnam, 1962–1970." *US Naval Institute Naval Review*, May 1971.

McDaniel, Norman A. *Yet Another Voice*. New York: Hawthorn Books, 1975.

McNamara, Robert S. *The Essence of Security*. New York: Harper & Row, 1968.

———. *Out of the Cold*. New York: Simon and Schuster, 1989.

McNamara, Robert S., with Brian VanDeMark. *In Retrospect: The Tragedy and Lessons of Vietnam*. New York: Times Books, 1995.

McNamara, Robert S., James G. Blight, and Robert K. Brigham, with Thomas J. Biersteker and Col. Herbert Y. Schandler, *Argument Without End: In Search of Answers to the Vietnam Tragedy*. New York: Public Affairs, 1999.

McPherson, Harry. *A Political Education*. Boston: Little, Brown, 1972.

Michel, Marshall L., III. *Clashes: Air Combat Over North Vietnam, 1965–1972*. Annapolis: Naval Institute Press, 1997.

Mitchell, James R. "Down on the Ninety-Ninth." *Air Force Magazine*, September 1973, pp 112–16.

Momyer, William W. *Air Power in Three Wars*. Washington: GPO, 1978.

———. "The Evolution of Fighter Tactics in SEA." *Air Force Magazine*, July 1973, pp 58–62.

———. "Our Top Airman in Vietnam: An Interview." *Airman*, May 1967, pp 4–7.

———. "TAC Air's Responsiveness." *Air Force Magazine*, December 1972, pp 32–37.

———. "Tactical Lessons of Vietnam." *Aviation Week and Space Technology*, May 21 and June 4, 1973.

Moorer, Thomas H. "What Admiral Moorer Really Thinks About Airpower's Effectiveness in SEA." *Air Force Magazine*, November 1973.

Mulligan, James A. *The Hanoi Commitment*. Virginia Beach: RIF Marketing, 1981.

Nitze, Paul H., with Ann M. Smith and Steven L. Reardon. *From Hiroshima to Glasnost*. New York: Grove Weidenfeld, 1989.

Nixon, Richard. *In the Arena*. New York: Simon & Schuster, 1990.

———. *Leaders*. New York: Warner, 1982.

———. *Real Peace*. Boston: Little Brown, 1984.

———. *The Real War*. New York: Warner, 1980.

———. *RN: The Memors of Richard Nixon*. New York: Grosset & Dunlap, 1978.

Nguyen Anh Tuan. *South Vietnam: Trial and Experience*. Athens: Ohio

University, 1987.

Nguyen Cao Ky. *Twenty Years and Twenty Days*. New York: Stein & Day, 1976.

Nguyen Tien Hung, and Jerrold L. Schecter. *The Palace File*. New York: Harper & Row, 1986.

Nichols, John B., and Barrett Tillman. *On Yankee Station*. Annapolis: Naval Institute Press, 1987.

North, Don. "Hanoi Hannah Speaks Again." *Vietnam*, April 1996, pp 18–24. An interview with Trinh Thi Ngo.

Olds, Robin. "Forty-Six Years a Fighter Pilot." *American Aviation Historical Society Journal*, Winter 1968, pp 235–39.

———. "How I Got My First MiG." *Air Force Magazine*, July 67, pp 38–44.

———. "The Lessons of Clobber College." *Flight International*, June 1969, pp 1053–56.

Oudes, Bruce, ed. *From: The President: Richard Nixon's Secret Files*. New York: Harper & Row, 1989.

Palmer, Bruce, Jr. *The 25-Year War*. Lexington: University Press of Kentucky, 1984.

Parker, James. *Codename Mule: Fighting the Secret War in Laos for the CIA*. Annapolis: Naval Institute Press, 1995.

Patti, Archimedes. *Why Viet Nam?* Berkeley: University of California Press, 1980.

Piowaty, John F. "Reflections of a Thud Driver." *Air University Review*, January–February 1983, pp 52–53.

Polgar, Thomas. "Managing the Company Store." *Vietnam*, August 1989, pp 42–48.

Pratt, John Clark. *The Laotian Fragments*. New York: Avon, 1985. A novel.

Pratt, John Clark, ed. *Vietnam Voices*. New York: Viking Penguin, 1984.

Price, Raymond. *With Nixon*. New York: Viking, 1977.

Radvanyi, Janos. *Delusions and Reality*. South Bend, Indiana: Gateway, 1978.

Red River Valley Fighter Pilots. 2 vols. Paducah, Kentucky: Turner, 1989–93. Includes aircrew biographical sketches and recollections.

Reynolds, John A. "Linebacker II: The POW Perspective." *Air Force Magazine*, September 1979, pp 93–94.

Risner, Robinson. *The Passing of the Night*. New York: Random House, 1973.

Rollins, Kelly (pseudonym). *Fighter Pilots*. Boston: Little Brown, 1981. A novel.

Ronning, Chester. *A Memoir of China in Revolution*. New York: Pantheon, 1974.

Rostow, W.W. "The Case for the Vietnam War." *Times Literary Supplement*, June 9, 1995, reprinted in *Parameters*, winter 1996–97, pp 39–50.

———. *The Diffusion of Power*. New York: Macmillan, 1972.

———. *The Stages of Economic Growth: A Non-Communist Manifesto*. Cambridge, England: Cambridge University Press, 1960.

Bibliography

Rusk, Dean, as told to Richard Rusk. *As I Saw It*. New York: Norton, 1990.

Safire, William. *Before the Fall*. New York: Doubleday, 1975.

Salisbury, Harrison E. *A Time of Change*. New York: Harper & Row, 1988.

———. *Beyond the Lines—Hanoi*. New York: Harper & Row, 1967.

Santoli, Al. *Leading the Way: How Vietnam Veterans Rebuilt the U.S. Military; An Oral History*. New York: Ballantine, 1993.

Schuyler, Keith C. *Elusive Horizons*. South Brunswick, New Jersey: A.S. Barnes, 1969.

Seamans, Robert C., Jr. *Aiming At Targets*. Washington: NASA, 1996.

Secord, Richard, with Jay Wurts. *Honored and Betrayed*. New York: Wiley, 1992.

Sharp, U.S. Grant. "Airpower Could Have Won in Vietnam." *Air Force Magazine*, September 1971.

———. *Strategy for Defeat*. San Rafael, California: Presidio, 1978.

Singlaub, John K, with Malcolm McConnell. *Hazardous Duty*. New York: Summit Books, 1991.

Smith, Philip E., and Peggy Herz. *Journey into Darkness*. New York: Pocket Books, 1992.

Snepp, Frank. *Decent Interval*. New York: Vintage, 1978.

Sontag, Susan. *Trip to Hanoi*. New York: Farrar, Straus and Giroux, 1968.

Stirling, John Bull. "Voodoo Reconnaissance in the Vietnam War, 1966–1967." *Air Power History*, winter 1996, pp 14–27.

Stockdale, Jim, and Sybil Stockdale. *In Love and War*. New York: Harper & Row, 1984.

Strayer, Jay M. "The Son Tay Prison Raid: A Personal Perspective." *Friends Journal* (Air Force Museum Foundation), fall 1995, pp 2–6.

Strober, Gerald, and Deborah Strober. *Nixon: An Oral History of His Presidency*. New York: Harper Collins, 1994.

Sullivan, William H. *Obligato*. New York: Norton, 1984.

Taylor, Maxwell D. *Swords and Plowshares*. New York: Norton, 1972.

Thompson, Sir Robert. *Make for the Hills*. London: Lee Cooper, 1989.

Tran Van Don. *Our Endless War*. San Rafael, California: Presidio, 1978.

Tran Van Tra. *Concluding the 30-Year War. Vol 5 of History of the Bulwark B–2 Theater*. Arlington, Virginia: FBIS, 1983.

———. "Tet—the 1968 General Offensive and General Uprising" and "The War That Should Not Have Been." Jayne Werner and Luu Doan Huynh, eds., *The Vietnam War: Vietnamese and American Perspectives*. Armonk, New York: Sharpe, 1993.

Trotti, John. *Phantom Over Vietnam: Fighter Pilot, USMC*. Novato, California: Presidio, 1984.

Truong Chinh. *The August Revolution*. 2d ed. Hanoi: Foreign Languages Publishing House, 1962.

———. *The Resistance Will Win*. Hanoi: Foreign Languages Publishing House,

1960.

Truong Nhu Tang with David Chanoff and Doan Van Toai. *A Vietcong Memoir*. New York: Harcourt Brace, 1985.

Turley, G.H. *The Easter Offensive*. Novato, California: Presidio, 1985.

Turner, Karen Gottschang, with Phan Thanh Hoa. *Even the Women Must Fight: Memories of War from North Vietnam*. New York: John Wiley & Sons, 1998.

Tuso, Joseph F. *Singing the Vietnam Blues: Songs of the Air Force in Southeast Asia*. College Station: Texas A&M, 1990.

Van Tien Dung. *Our Great Spring Victory*. New York: Monthly Review Press, 1977.

Vo Nguyen Giap. *Banner of People's War*. New York: Praegar, 1970.

———. *Big Victory, Great Task*. New York: Praegar, 1968.

———. *People's War Against U.S. Aero-Naval War*. Hanoi: Foreign Languages Publishing House, 1975.

———. *People's War, People's Army*. New York: Praegar, 1962.

Vo Nguyen Giap and Van Tien Dung. *How We Won the War*. Philadelphia: RECON, 1976.

Vogt, John W., Jr. "A Commander's View of the Vietnam War." In John Norton Moore, ed., *The Vietnam Debate*. Lanham, Maryland: University Press of America, 1990.

Walt, Lewis W. *America Faces Defeat*. Boston: Houghton Mifflin, 1972.

———. *Strange War, Strange Society*. New York: Funk & Wagnalls, 1970.

Weber, Joe. *Rules of Engagement*. Novato, California: Presidio, 1991. A novel.

Weber, Ralph E. *Spymasters: Ten CIA Officers in Their Own Words*. Wilmington, Delaware: Scholarly Resources, 1999.

Westmoreland, William C. *A Soldier Reports*. New York: Doubleday, 1976.

Wetterhahn, Ralph. "Change of Command." *Air and Space*, August/September 1997, pp 62–69.

———. "Operation Bolo." *Retired Officer Magazine*, November 1995, pp 39–43.

Whitcomb, Darrel D. "Tonnage and Technology: Air Power on the Ho Chi Minh Trail." *Air Power History*, spring 1997, pp 4–17.

Wolff, Robert E. "Linebacker II: A Pilot's Perspective." *Air Force Magazine*, September 1979, pp 86–91.

Zumwalt, Elmo R., Jr. *On Watch*. New York: Quadrangle, 1976.

Biography

Ambrose, Stephen. *Nixon*. 3 vols. New York: Simon & Schuster, 1987–92.

Barrett, David M. *Uncertain Warriors: Lyndon Johnson and His Vietnam Advisors*. Lawrence: University Press of Kansas, 1993.

Berman, William C. *William Fulbright and the Vietnam War*. Kent, Ohio: Kent

State University Press, 1988.

Bill, James A. *George Ball: Behind the Scenes in U.S. Foreign Policy*. New Haven: Yale, 1997.

Bird, Kai. *The Color of Truth: McGeorge Bundy and William Bundy*. New York: Simon & Schuster, 1998.

Bornet, Vaughan Davis. *The Presidency of Lyndon B. Johnson*. Lawrence: University Press of Kansas, 1983.

Brands, H.W. *The Wages of Globalism: Lyndon Johnson and the Limits of American Power*. New York: Oxford, 1995.

Brodie, Fawn M. *Richard Nixon*. New York: Norton, 1981.

Caro, Robert A. *The Years of Lyndon Johnson: Means of Ascent*. New York: Knopf, 1990.

———. *The Years of Lyndon Johnson: The Path to Power*. New York: Knopf, 1982.

Coffey, Thomas M. *Iron Eagle: The Turbulent Life of General Curtis LeMay*. New York: Crown, 1986.

Cohen, Warren I. *Dean Rusk*. Towtowa, New Jersey: Cooper Square, 1980.

Colvin, John. *Giap: Volcano Under Snow*. New York: Soho, 1996.

Corn, David. *Blond Ghost: Ted Shackley and the CIA's Crusades*. New York: Simon & Schuster, 1994.

Currey, Cecil B. *Edward Lansdale: The Unquiet American*. Boston: Houghton Mifflin, 1988.

———. *Victory At Any Cost: The Genius of Vietnam's Gen. Vo Nguyen Giap*. Washington: Brassey's, 1997.

Dallek, Robert. *Lone Star Rising: Lyndon Johnson and His Times, 1908–1960*. New York: Oxford, 1991.

———. *Flawed Giant: Lyndon Johnson and His Times, 1961–1973*. New York: Oxford, 1998.

DiLeo, David L. *George Ball, Vietnam, and the Rethinking of Containment*. Chapel Hill: University of North Carolina, 1991.

Dugger, Ronnie. *The Politician: The Life and Times of Lyndon Johnson*. New York: Norton, 1982.

Edwards, Lee. *Goldwater*. Washington: Regnery, 1995.

Gardner, Lloyd C. *Pay Any Price: Lyndon Johnson and the Wars for Vietnam*. Chicago: Ivan R. Dee, 1995.

Goldberg, Robert Alan. *Barry Goldwater*. New Haven: Yale, 1995.

Hanson, Victor Davis. "The Right Man." *MHQ*, spring 1996, pp 56–65. On Curtis LeMay.

Hendrickson, Paul. *The Living and the Dead: Robert McNamara and Five Lives of a Lost War*. New York: Knopf, 1996.

Herring, George C. *LBJ and Vietnam*. Austin: University of Texas, 1994.

Hersh, Seymour M. *The Price of Power: Kissinger in the Nixon White House*. New York: Summit, 1983.

Hoff, Joan. *Nixon Reconsidered.* New York: Basic Books, 1994.

Humphrey, David C. "Searching for LBJ at the Johnson Library." *Society for Historians of American Foreign Relations Newsletter*, June 1989, pp 1–17.

———. "Tuesday Lunch at the Johnson White House." *Diplomatic History*, winter 1984, pp 81–101.

Isaacson, Walter. *Kissinger.* New York: Simon & Schuster, 1992.

Isaacson, Walter, and Evan Thomas. *The Wise Men.* New York: Simon and Schuster, 1986.

Kalb, Marvin, and Bernard Kalb. *Kissinger.* Boston: Little Brown, 1974.

Kearns, Doris. *Lyndon Johnson and the American Dream.* New York: Harper & Row, 1976.

Macdonald, Peter. *Giap.* New York: Norton, 1993.

Manne, Robert. *Agent of Influence: The Life and Times of Wilfred Burchett.* Toronto: Mackenzie Institute, 1989.

Matthews, Christopher. *Kennedy and Nixon.* New York: Simon & Schuster, 1996.

McConnell, Malcom. *Into the Mouth of the Cat: The Story of Lance Sijan.* New York: Norton, 1985.

McGovern, James R. *Black Eagle: General Daniel "Chappie" James, Jr.* University, Alabama: University of Alabama Press, 1985.

Miller, Merle. *Lyndon: An Oral Biography.* New York: Putnam's, 1980.

Milton, T.R. "Robinson Risner." In John L. Frisbee, ed., *Makers of the United States Air Force.* Washington: Air Force History, 1987.

Morris, Roger. *Richard Milhous Nixon: The Rise of An American Politician.* New York: Henry Holt, 1987.

———. *Uncertain Greatness: Henry Kissinger and American Foreign Policy.* New York: Harper & Row, 1977.

O'Neill, Robert J. *General Giap.* New York: Praegar, 1969.

Powers, Thomas. *The Man Who Kept the Secrets: Richard Helms and the CIA.* New York: Knopf, 1979.

Puryear, Edgar F., Jr. *George S. Brown.* Novato, California: Presidio, 1983.

Quill, J. Michael. *Lyndon Johnson and the Southern Military Tradition.* Washington: University Press of America, 1977.

Schandler, Herbert Y. *The Unmaking of a President: Lyndon Johnson and Vietnam.* Princeton: Princeton University, 1977.

Schlesinger, Arthur M., Jr. *Robert Kennedy and His Times.* Boston: Houghton Mifflin, 1978.

Schoenbaum, Thomas J. *Waging Peace: Dean Rusk in the Truman, Kennedy, and Johnson Years.* New York: Simon & Schuster, 1988.

Schulzinger, Robert D. *Henry Kissinger.* New York: Columbia, 1989.

Shapley, Deborah. *Promise and Power: The Life and Times of Robert McNamara.* Boston: Little Brown, 1993.

Sheehan, Neil. *A Bright Shining Lie: John Paul Vann and America in Vietnam.*

Bibliography

New York: Random House, 1988.

Solberg, Carl. *Hubert Humphrey*. New York: Norton, 1980.

Sorley, Lewis. *Honorable Warrior: General Harold K. Johnson and the Ethics of Command*. Lawrence: University Press of Kansas, 1998.

———. *Thunderbolt: General Creighton Abrams and the Army of His Times*. New York: Simon & Schuster, 1992.

Terrill, Ross. *Mao*. New York: Harper & Row, 1980.

Trewhitt, Henry L. *McNamara*. New York: Harper & Row, 1971.

Valenti, Jack. *A Very Human President*. New York: Norton, 1975.

Vandiver, Frank E. *Shadows of Vietnam: Lyndon Johnson's Wars*. College Station: Texas A&M, 1997.

Woods, Randall Bennett. *Fulbright*. New York: Cambridge, 1995.

Zaffiri, Samuel. *Westmoreland*. New York: William Morrow, 1994.

Ziemke, Caroline F. "Senator Richard B. Russell and the 'Lost Cause' in Vietnam, 1954–1968." *Georgia Historical Quarterly*, spring 1988, pp 36–71.

The Vietnam War and Air Power

Other sections of this bibliography give a more comprehensive indication of official and biographical sources consulted. The concluding section, however, merely offers students of air power some routes into the war's wider literature.

Addington, Larry H. "Antiaircraft Artillery Versus the Fighter Bomber: The Duel Over Vietnam." *Army*, December 1973, pp 18–20.

Ambrose, Stephen E. "The Christmas Bombing." *MHQ*, spring 1996, pp 86–95.

Anderson, William C. *Bat-21*. New York: Prentice-Hall, 1980.

Andrade, Dale. *Trial By Fire: The 1972 Easter Offensive*. New York: Hippocrene, 1995.

Appel, Bernard. "Bombing Accuracy in a Combat Environment." *Air University Review*, July–August 1975.

Bates, Charles C., and John F. Fuller. *America's Weather Warriors, 1814–1985*. College Station: Texas A&M, 1986.

Berman, Larry. *Lyndon Johnson's War*. New York: Norton, 1989.

———. *Planning A Tragedy*. New York: Norton, 1982.

Brigham, Robert K. *Guerrilla Diplomacy: the NLF's Foreign Relations and the Vietnam War*. Ithaca, New York: Cornell University Press, 1999.

Brower, Charles F., IV. "Strategic Reassessment in Vietnam: The Westmoreland 'Alternate Strategy' of 1967–1968." *Naval War College Review*, spring 1991, pp 20–51.

Brown, John M.G. *Moscow Bound: Policy, Politics and the POW/MIA Dilemma*. Eureka, California: Veteran Press, 1993.

Bugos, Glenn E. *Engineering the F–4 Phantom II*. Annapolis: Naval Institute

Press, 1996.

Bundy, William. *A Tangled Web: The Making of Foreign Policy in the Nixon Presidency*. New York: Hill and Wang, 1998.

Buza, Zoltan, and Istvan Toperczer. "MiG–17 over Vietnam." *Wings of Fame*, vol 8 (1997), pp 100–117.

Buzzanco, Robert. *Masters of War: Military Dissent and Politics in the Vietnam Era*. New York: Cambridge, 1996.

Cable, Larry. *Unholy Grail: The US and the Wars in Vietnam, 1965–68*. London: Routledge, 1991.

Cagle, Malcom W. "Task Force 77 in Action off Vietnam." *U.S. Naval Institute Review*, May 1972, pp 68–109.

Castle, Timothy J. *At War in the Shadow of Vietnam: U.S. Military Aid to the Royal Lao Government, 1955–1975*. New York: Columbia University Press, 1993.

———. *One Day Too Long: Top Secret Site 85 and the Bombing of North Vietnam*. New York: Columbia University Press, 1999.

Chaliand, Gerard. *The Peasants of North Vietnam*. Baltimore: Penguin, 1969.

———. *Revolution in the Third World*. New York: Viking, 1977.

Chandler, Robert W. *War of Ideas: The U.S. Propaganda Campaign in Vietnam*. Boulder, Colorado: Westview, 1981.

Chanoff, David, and Doan Van Toai. *Portrait of the Enemy*. New York: Random House, 1986.

Chen Jian. "China's Involvement in the Vietnam War, 1964–69." *China Quarterly*, June 1995, PP 357–87.

Chinnery, Philip D. *Any Time, Any Place: Fifty Years of the USAF Air Commando and Special Operations Forces, 1944–1994*. Annapolis: Naval Institute Press, 1994.

———. *Life On the Line*. New York: St. Martins, 1988.

Clarke, Douglas L. *The Missing Man: Politics and the MIA*. Washington: National Defense University, 1979.

Clodfelter, Mark. *The Limits of Air Power: The American Bombing of North Vietnam*. New York: Free Press, 1989.

Conboy, Kenneth, and Dale Andrade. *Spies and Commandos: How America Lost the Secret War in North Vietnam*. Lawrence: University Press of Kansas, 2000.

Conboy, Kenneth, with James Morrison. *Shadow War: The CIA's Secret War in Laos*. Boulder, Colorado: Paladin Press, 1995.

Coulam, Robert F. *Illusion of Choice: The F–111 and the Problem of Weapons Acquisition*. Princeton: Princeton University Press, 1977.

DeBenedetti, Charles, with Charles Chatfield. *An American Ordeal: The Antiwar Movement of the Vietnam Era*. Syracuse, New York: Syracuse University, 1990.

Deeley, Walter G. "A Fresh Look at Purple Dragon." *Signal*, April 1984, pp

Bibliography

17–21.

DeForest, Orin, and David Chanoff. *Slow Burn: The Rise and Bitter Fall of American Intelligence in Vietnam*. New York: Simon and Schuster, 1990.

Dorr, Robert F. *Air War Hanoi*. London: Blandford, 1988.

Doyle, Edward, Samuel Lipsman, and Terrence Maitland. *The Vietnam Experience: The North*. Boston: Boston Publishing, 1986.

Doyle, Robert C. *Voices from Captivity*. Lawrence: University Press of Kansas, 1994.

Duiker, William J. *China and Vietnam: The Roots of Conflict*. Berkeley: University of California, 1986.

———. *The Communist Road to Power in Vietnam*. 2d ed. Boulder, Colorado: Westview, 1996.

———. *U.S. Containment Policy and the Conflict in Indochina*. Stanford, California: Stanford University, 1994.

Emerson, J. Terry. "Making War Without Will: Vietnam Rules of Engagement." In John Norton Moore, ed., *The Vietnam Debate*. Lanham, Maryland: University Press of America, 1990.

Eschmann, Karl J. *Linebacker*. New York: Ivy, 1989.

Ethell, Jeffrey, and Alfred Price. *One Day in a Long War: May 10, 1972, Air War, North Vietnam*. New York: Random House, 1989.

Fall, Bernard B. *Street Without Joy*. 3d ed. Harrisburg, Pennsylvania: Stackpole, 1963.

Fitts, Richard E., ed. *The Strategy of Electromagnetic Conflict*. Los Altos, California: Peninsula, 1980.

Ford, Ronnie E. *Tet 1968: Understanding the Surprise*. London: Frank Cass, 1995.

Francillon, Rene J. *Tonkin Gulf Yacht Club: U.S. Carrier Operations off Vietnam*. London: Conway Maritime Press, 1988.

———. *Vietnam Air Wars*. London: Temple, 1987.

Franklin, H. Bruce. *M.I.A., or, Mythmaking in America*. Expanded and updated edition. New Brunswick, New Jersey: Rutgers University Press, 1993.

Fuller, John F. *Thor's Legions: Weather Support to the U.S. Air Force and Army, 1937–1987*. Boston: American Meteorological Society, 1990.

Gaddy, David W., ed. *Essential Matters: A History of the Cryptographic Branch of the People's Army of Viet-Nam, 1945–1975*. Ft. Meade, Maryland: National Security Agency, 1994. A translation of a Vietnamese work published in 1990 by the People's Army Publishing House, Hanoi.

Gaiduk, Ilya V. *The Soviet Union and the Vietnam War*. Chicago: Ivan R. Dee, 1996.

Gallucci, Robert L. *Neither Peace Nor Honor*. Baltimore: Johns Hopkins, 1975.

Garthoff, Raymond L. *Detente and Confrontation: American-Soviet Relations from Nixon to Reagan*. Washington: Brookings, 1985.

Garver, John W. "The Chinese Threat in the Vietnam War." *Parameters*, spring 1992, pp 73–85.

Gelb, Leslie H., with Richard Betts. *The Irony of Vietnam: The System Worked*. Washington: Brookings, 1979.

Gibson, James William. *The Perfect War: Technowar in Vietnam*. Boston: Atlantic Monthly Press, 1986.

Gilbert, Marc Jason, and William Head, eds. *The Tet Offensive*. Westport, Connecticut: Praegar, 1996.

Glasser, Jeffrey D. *The Secret Vietnam War: The United States Air Force in Thailand, 1961–1975*. Jefferson, North Carolina: McFarland, 1995.

Goodman, Allan E. *The Lost Peace*. Stanford: Hoover Institution, 1978.

Graff, Henry F. *The Tuesday Cabinet: Deliberation and Decision on Peace and War under Lyndon B. Johnson*. Englewood Cliffs, New Jersey: Prentice-Hall, 1970.

Grant, Zalin. *Over the Beach*. New York: Norton, 1986.

Gropman, Alan L. "The Air War in Vietnam, 1961–73." In R. A. Mason, ed., *War in the Third Dimension*. London: Brassey's, 1986.

———. "Lost Opportunities: The Air War in Vietnam, 1961–1973." In Lawrence E. Grinter and Peter M. Dunn, eds., *The American War in Vietnam*. New York: Greenwood, 1987.

Gruner, Elliott. *Prisoners of Culture*. New Brunswick, New Jersey: Rutgers University Press, 1993.

Guilmartin, John F., Jr. "Bombing the Ho Chi Minh Trail: A Preliminary Analysis of the Effects of Air Interdiction." *Air Power History*, winter 1991, pp 3–17.

———. *A Very Short War: The Mayaguez and the Battle of Koh Tang*. College Station: Texas A&M, 1995.

Halberstam, David. *The Best and the Brightest*. New York: Random House, 1972.

Hannah, Craig C. "Counterflow: The Demise and Rebirth of the USAF Tactical Air Command in the Vietnam Era." MA Thesis, Texas Tech University, 1995.

Harrison, James P. *The Endless War*. New York: Free Press, 1982.

———. "History's Heaviest Bombing." In Jayne S. Werner and Lou Doan Huynh, eds., *The Vietnam War*. Armonk, New York: M.E. Sharpe, 1993.

Harvey, Frank. *Air War: Vietnam*. New York: Bantam, 1967.

Hatcher, Patrick Lloyd. *The Suicide of an Elite: American Internationalists and Vietnam*. Stanford: Stanford University, 1990.

Head, William, and Lawrence E. Grinter, eds. *Looking Back on the Vietnam War*. Westport, Connecticut: Greenwood, 1993.

Herring, George C. *America's Longest War*. 3d ed. New York: McGraw-Hill, 1996.

Herz, Martin F., with Leslie Rider. *The Prestige Press and the Christmas*

Bibliography

Bombing, 1972. Washington: Ethics and Public Policy Center, 1980.

Howes, Craig. *Voices of the Vietnam POWs.* New York: Oxford, 1993.

Hubbell, John G., with Andrew Jones and Kenneth Y. Tomlinson. *P.O.W.* New York: Reader's Digest, 1976.

Jamieson, Neil L. *Understanding Vietnam.* Berkeley: University of California, 1993.

Kaiser, David. *American Tragedy: Kennedy, Johnson, and the Origins of the Vietnam War.* Cambridge, Mass.: Harvard, 2000.

Kattenburg, Paul M. *The Vietnam Trauma in American Foreign Policy, 1945–75.* New Brunswick, New Jersey: Transaction, 1980.

Karnow, Stanley. *Vietnam: A History.* New York: Viking, 1983.

Kimball, Jeffrey. *Nixon's Vietnam War.* Lawrence: University Press of Kansas, 1998.

Kipp, Robert M. "Counterinsurgency from 30,000 Feet." *Air University Review*, January–February 1968, pp 10–18.

Kirkland, Farris R. "The Attack on Cap Mui Lay, Vietnam, July 1968." *Journal of Military History*, October 1967, pp 735–60.

Kolko, Gabriel. *Anatomy of a War.* New York: Pantheon, 1985.

Krepinevich, Andrew F. *The Army and Vietnam.* Baltimore: Johns Hopkins, 1986.

Lanning, Michael Lee, and Dan Cragg. *Inside the VC and the NVA.* New York: Fawcett Columbine, 1992.

Larson, Doyle. "Direct Intelligence Combat Support in Vietnam: Project Teaball." *American Intelligence Journal*, spring/summer 1994, pp 56–58.

Leary, William M. "The CIA and the 'Secret War' in Laos: The Battle for Skyline Ridge, 1971–1972." *Journal of Military History*, July 1995, 505–17.

Leonard, Raymond W. "Learning from History: Linebacker II and U.S. Air Force Doctrine." *Journal of Military History*, April 1994, pp 267–303.

Levinson, Jeffrey L. *Alpha Strike Vietnam: The Navy's Air War 1964 to 1973.* Novato, California: Presidio, 1989.

Lewy, Guenter. *America in Vietnam.* New York: Oxford, 1978.

Lind, Michael. *Vietnam: The Necessary War.* New York: Free Press, 1999.

Littauer, Raphael, and Norman Uphoff, eds. *The Air War in Indochina.* Rev. ed. Boston: Beacon, 1972. Often called the Cornell University study.

Logevall, Frederik. *Choosing War: The Lost Chance for Peace and the Escalation of War in Vietnam.* Berkeley: University of California Press, 1999.

Lomperis, Timothy J. *The War Everyone Lost—And Won: American Intervention in Viet Nam's Twin Struggles.* Baton Rouge: Louisiana State University Press, 1984.

McAlister, John T. Jr. *Viet Nam: The Origins of Revolution.* New York: Knopf, 1969.

McConnell, Malcom, with Theodore G. Schweitzer III. *Inside Hanoi's Secret*

Archives: Solving the MIA Mystery. New York: Simon & Schuster, 1995.

McMaster, H.R. *Dereliction of Duty: Lyndon Johnson, Robert McNamara, the Joint Chiefs of Staff, and the Lies that Led to Vietnam*. New York: HarperCollins, 1997.

Mersky, Peter B., and Norman Polmar. *The Naval Air War in Vietnam*. Second ed. Baltimore: Nautical & Aviation, 1986.

Moise, Edwin E. *Land Reform in China and North Vietnam*. Chapel Hill: University of North Carolina, 1983.

———. *Tonkin Gulf and the Escalation of the Vietnam War*. Chapel Hill: University of North Carolina, 1996.

Morrocco, John. *The Vietnam Experience: Rain of Fire, 1967–1973*. Boston: Boston Publishing, 1985.

———. *The Vietnam Experience: Thunder from Above, 1941–1968*. Boston: Boston Publishing, 1984.

Nalty, Bernard C. "An Uncommon War: The U.S. Air Force in Southeast Asia." *Air Power History*, fall 1994, pp 27–37.

Nordeen, Lon O., Jr. *Air Warfare in the Missile Age*. Washington: Smithsonian, 1985.

Nufer, Harold F. "The Evolution of Frag Orders." *Aerospace Historian*, June 1986, pp 104–13.

O'Connor, Michael. "Aces of the Yellow Star." *Air Combat*, VI (1978), no. 5, pp 77–82.

———. "Duel Over the Dragon Jaw." *American Aviation Historical Society Journal*, winter 1980, pp 273–76.

Pape, Robert A., Jr. *Bombing to Win: Air Power and Coercion in War*. Ithaca, New York: Cornell, 1996.

———. "Coercive Air Power in the Vietnam War." *International Security*, Fall 1990, pp 103–46.

Parker, F. Charles IV. *Vietnam: Strategy for a Stalemate*. New York: Paragon House, 1989.

Parks, W. Hays. "Air War and the Law of War." *Air Force Law Review*, XXXII (1990), no. 1, pp 1–225.

———. "Linebacker and the Law of War." *Air University Review*, January–February 1983, pp 2–30.

———. "Rolling Thunder and the Law of War." *Air University Review*, January–February 1982, pp 2–23.

Peebles, Curtis. *Dark Eagles: A History of Top Secret U.S. Aircraft Programs*. Novato, California: Presidio, 1995.

Pike, Douglas. *PAVN: People's Army of Vietnam*. Novato, California: Presidio, 1986.

Plaster. John L. *SOG: The Secret Wars of America's Commandos in Vietnam*. New York: Simon & Schuster, 1997.

———. *Viet Cong*. Cambridge, Mass.: M.I.T. Press, 1966.

Bibliography

Prados, John. *The Blood Road: The Ho Chi Minh Trail and the Vietnam War.* New York: John Wiley & Sons, 1999.

———. *Keepers of the Keys: A History of the National Security Council.* New York: Morrow, 1991.

———. *The Sky Would Fall: Operation Vulture.* New York: Dial, 1983.

———. "The Warning that Left Something to Chance: Intelligence at Tet." *Journal of American East Asian Relations,* summer 1993, pp 161–84.

Pribbenow, Merle L. "North Vietnam's Final Offensive: Strategic Endgame Nonpareil." *Parameters,* winter 1999–2000, pp 58–71.

———. "North Vietnam's Master Plan." *Vietnam,* August 1999, pp 30–36.

Quester, George H. "The Impact of Strategic Air Warfare." *Armed Forces and Society,* February 1978, pp 179–206.

Qiang Zhai. "Beijing and the Vietnam Conflict, 1964–1965: New Chinese Evidence." *Cold War International History Project Bulletin,* Woodrow Wilson International Center for Scholars, winter 1995–96, pp 233–50.

———. "Beijing and the Vietnam Peace Talks, 1965–68: New Evidence from Chinese Sources." Woodrow Wilson International Center for Scholars, Cold War International History Project, Working Paper No. 18, June 1997.

———. *China and the Vietnam Wars, 1950–1975.* Chapel Hill: University of North Carolina Press, 2000.

Race, Jeffrey. *War Comes to Long An.* Berkeley: University of California, 1972.

Record, Jeffrey. *The Wrong War: Why We Lost in Vietnam.* Annapolis: Naval Institute Press, 1998.

Rendall, Ivan. *Rolling Thunder: Jet Combat from World War II to the Gulf War.* New York: Free Press, 1999.

Reske, Charles F. "Operation Footboy." *Vietnam,* October 1995, pp 30–36.

Robbins, Christopher. *The Ravens.* New York: Crown, 1987.

Schemmer, Benjamin F. *The Raid.* New York: Harper & Row, 1976.

Schlight, John. "Civilian Control of the Military in Southeast Asia." *Air University Review,* November–December 1980, pp 56–69.

Schulzinger, Robert D. *A Time for War: The United States and Vietnam, 1941–1975.* New York: Oxford, 1997.

Scutts, Jerry. *Wolfpack: Hunting MiGs Over Vietnam.* Shrewsbury, England: Airlife Publishing, 1988.

———. *Wrecking Crew: The 388th Tactical Fighter Wing.* New York: Warner, 1990.

Sherwood, John Darrell. Fast Movers: Jet Pilots and the Vietnam Experience. New York: Free Press, 1999.

Showalter, Dennis E., and John G. Albert, eds. *An American Dilemma.* Chicago: Imprint, 1993.

Shultz, Jr., Richard H. *The Secret War against Hanoi: Kennedy's and Johnson's use of Spies, Saboteurs, and Covert Warriors in North Vietnam.* New York: HarperCollins, 1999.

Smith, John T. *The Linebacker Raids*. London: Arms & Armour Press, 1998.

————. *Rolling Thunder*. Walton on Thames, England: Air Research Publications, 1994.

Smith, Melden E. Jr. "The Strategic Bombing Debate: The Second World War and Vietnam." *Journal of Contemporary History*, January 1977, pp 175–92.

Smith, R.B. *An International History of the Vietnam War*. 3 vols. London: Macmillan, 1983–91.

Sorley, Lewis. *A Better War: The Unexamined Victories and Final Tragedy of America's Last Years in Vietnam*. New York: Harcourt Brace, 1999.

Steinberg, David Joel, ed. *In Search of Southeast Asia*. Rev. ed. Honolulu: University of Hawaii, 1987.

Stern, Lewis M. *Imprisoned or Missing in Vietnam: Policies of the Vietnamese Government Concerning Captured and Unaccounted For Unites States Soldiers, 1969–1994*. Jefferson, North Carolina: McFarland, 1995.

Summers, Harry G. *On Strategy: The Vietnam War in Context*. Carlisle, Pennsylvania: Army War College, 1981.

Thayer, Thomas C. *War Without Fronts*. Boulder, Colorado: Westview, 1985.

Thai Quang Trung. *Collective Leadership and Factionalism: An Essay on Ho Chi Minh's Legacy*. Singapore: Institute of Southeast Asian Studies, 1985.

Thies, Wallace J. *When Governments Collide: Coercion and Diplomacy in the Vietnam Conflict, 1964–1968*. Berkeley: University of California, 1980.

Thompson, James Clay. *Rolling Thunder*. Chapel Hill: University of North Carolina, 1980.

Thompson, W. Scott, and Donald D. Frizzell. *The Lessons of Vietnam*. New York: Crane, Russak, 1977.

Tilford, Earl H., Jr. *Crosswinds: The Air Force's Setup in Vietnam*. College Station: Texas A&M, 1993.

Toperczer, Istvan. *Air War Over North Vietnam: The Vietnamese People's Air Force*. Carrollton, Texas: Squadron/Signal Publications, 1998.

Tourison, Sedgwick. *Secret Army, Secret War: Washington's Tragic Spy Operation in North Vietnam*. Annapolis: Naval Institute Press, 1996.

Trooboff, Peter D., ed. *Law and Responsibility in Warfare: The Vietnam Experience*. Chapel Hill: University of North Carolina, 1975.

Turley, William S. "Origins and Development of Communist Military Leadership in Vietnam," *Armed Forces and Society*, February 1977, pp 219–47.

————. "Urbanization in War: Hanoi, 1946–1973." *Pacific Affairs*, Fall 1975, pp 370–97.

Vandenbrouke, Lucien S. *Perilous Options: Special Operations as an Instrument of U.S. Foreign Policy*. New York: Oxford, 1993.

VanDeMark, Brian. *Into the Quagmire*. New York: Oxford, 1991.

Van Dyke, Jon M. *North Vietnam's Strategy for Survival*. Palo Alto, California:

Pacific Books, 1972.

Veith, George J. *Code-Name Bright Light: The Untold Story of POW Rescue Efforts during the Vietnam War*. New York: Free Press, 1998.

Warner, Roger. *Back Fire: The CIA's Secret War in Laos and Its Link to the War in Vietnam*. New York: Simon & Schuster, 1995.

Werrell, Kenneth P. "Did USAF Technology Fail in Vietnam?: Three Case Studies." *Airpower Journal*, spring 1998, pp 87–99.

———. "Linebacker II." *Air University Review*, January–March 1987, pp 48–61.

Westad, Odd Arne, et al., ed. "77 Conversations Between Chinese and Foreign Leaders on the Wars in Indochina, 1964–1977." Woodrow Wilson International Center for Scholars, Cold War International History Project, Working Paper No. 22, May 1998.

Westrum, Ron. *Sidewinder: Creative Missile Development at China Lake*. Annapolis: Naval Institute Press, 1999.

Whitcomb, Darrel D. *The Rescue of Bat 21*. Annapolis: Naval Institute Press, 1998.

Whiting, Allen. "China's Role in the Vietnam War." Jayne Werner and David Hunt, eds, *The American War in Vietnam* (Ithaca, New York: Cornell, 1993), pp 71–76.

———. *The Chinese Calculus of Deterrence*. Ann Arbor: University of Michigan, 1975.

Wilcox, Robert K. *Scream of Eagles: The Creation of Top Gun and the US Air Victory in Vietnam*. New York: Wiley, 1990.

Wirtz, James J. *The Tet Offensive: Intelligence Failure in War*. Ithaca, New York: Cornell, 1991.

Wolfe, Thomas K. "Truest Sport: Jousting With Sam and Charlie." *Esquire*, October 1975, pp 156–59, 229–37.

Xiaoming Zhang. "The Vietnam War, 1964–1969: A Chinese Perspective." *Journal of Military History*, October 1996, pp 731–62.

Young, Robert L. "Fishbed Hit and Run: North Vietnamese MiG–21s versus the USAF, August 1967–February 1968." *Air Power History*, winter 1995, pp 56–69.

Zaloga, Steven J. *Soviet Air Defence Missiles*. Coulsdon, England: Jane's, 1989.

Index

(Numerals in **bold** indicate illustrations.)

Abbott, Joseph S.: **218**
Abrams, Creighton W., Jr.: 135, 138, 146,
        149, 152, 221, 222
    aircraft protection: 207
    B–52 employment: 226, 256
    bombing policy: 163–64, 204–5, 223
    Cambodia: 173
    Lavelle affair: 200–201, 208, 209
Aces, North Vietnam: 186
Aces, U.S.
    Korean War: 64, 183, 189
    Vietnam War: 8, 55, 236–37, 241
    World War II: 52, 86, 221, 266, 287
Acheson, Dean: 137, 138
Agan, Arthur C., Jr.: 99
Agnew, Spiro T.: 174, 176
Aiken, George: 115
Airborne Battlefield Command and
        Control Center: 17
Aircraft, North Vietnam
    An–2: 102
    Il–14: 96
    Il–28: 34, 126–27, 142
    J–6: 236
    MiG–15: 33, 54
    MiG–17: 33, 241
        attacks on U.S. aircraft: 54, 110–11,
            127–28
        capabilities: 34, 92, 237
    MiG–19: 87, 214, 236–37, 242, 289n
    MiG–21: **120**, 240
        attacks on U.S. aircraft: 52–55, 86, 90,
            96, 98, 103, 110, 127, 171,
            201, 242
        capabilities: 34, 127, 237, 241
        losses: 54–55, 90, 203, 226, 236–37,
            241, 242
Aircraft, U.S.: 308–9
    A–1: 9
    A–6: 59, 60, 100–101, 280
        China border violation incident: 87,
            236
        strikes: 87, 90, 108, 128, 203, 223,
            225, 229, 267, 268
    A–7: 203, 225, 226, 246, 267, 269, 280

A–12: 106
AC–130: 231, 233
B–1: 285
B–2: 285
B–24: 234
B–29: 234
B–52: **214**, **216**
    employment
        Abrams position: 223, 224, 226
        airfield attacks: 226, 257, 261, 266,
            268, 273
        arguments against use: 132, 227
        attrition models: 271, 272
        Cambodia raids secrecy: 173–74
        Christmas bombing: 255
        Guam based: 9, 23, 223–24, 255,
            264, 271–74, 275, 277–78,
            280
        Hanoi-Haiphong area: 255–58,
            260–66, 267–68, 270–77,
            279–80
        JCS position: 269
        Johnson position: 3, 20, 26, 35, 39,
            67, 124, 128, 145, 225, 256,
            281
        Laird position: 223, 224
        LeMay position: 21–22, 82, 93
        missile suppression: 266–68
        missiles, vulnerability to: 107, 201,
            275
        mission abort issue: 263, 265–66
        morale: 273–74
        Nixon position: 220, 221, 223–25,
            226–28, 253, 257–58, 259,
            260
        personnel housing: 223, 224
        petroleum facility attacks: 225, 226,
            262, 276
        psychological effect: 277–78
        rail facilities, attacks on: 225, 255,
            257, 261, 263, 270, 272–73,
            275–76
        Rolling Thunder: 3, 20, 27
        Stennis subcommittee position:
            82–83

Index

Thailand based: 5, 10, 128, 223–25,
    255, 263, 264, 268, 273–74
warehouses, attacks on: 227, 262
losses: 240, 255–56, 263, 264, 265,
    268, 271, 272, 279–80
strikes: 39, 82–83, 124–25, 130, 132,
    167–68, 170–71, 220, 223–24,
    228, 251, 256–57, 284
B–52G: 265
B–57: 20
C–130: 201, 231, 234, 251
C–130E: 194
DC–130: **213**
E–3: 17
EB–66: 50, 53, 97, 98, 103, 231, 280
EC–121: 17, 53, 63, 92, 97, 98–99, 103,
    105, 165, **213**, 222, 239
EC–130: 17
F–4: 9, 71, 144, 202, 205, 207, **212**, **214**,
    224, 226, 251, 269
  aircraft downed: 54–55, 90, 92
  capabilities: 7, 10, 34, 59, 225, 226,
    243
  escort mission: 39–40, 50, 97–98,
    103, 205, 227, 243, 246
  employment: 143–44, 245–46, 247,
    265
  pods: 7, 53, 54, 112, 231, 243
  strikes: 9, 58, 63–64, 71, 90, 127, 128,
    172, 175, 202, 203, 205, 207,
    223, 224, 226, 234, 235, 251,
    255, 269, 276, 278
F–4C: 61, 73, 92, 266, 267
F–4D: 61, 74, 91, 102, 108, 223, 239,
    241
F–4E: 223, 241, 243, 266, 267, 274–75
F–5: 240
F–8: 40n
F–100: 233
F–100F: 36, 143–44
F–104: 236
F–105: 64, 111, **118**, 205, **214**, 227, 266,
    267
  capabilities: 6, 60, 245
  employment: 39–40, 266
  jamming pods: 50, 51, 52, 53, 54, 243
  losses: 6, 49, 53, 61, 86, 90, 103, 104
  strikes: 57, 58, 59, 63, 86, 96, 103,
    110, 112, 128, 206–7, 225,
    231, 233, 235, 267
  Wild Weasels: *See* Wild Weasels.
F–105D: 103

F–105F: 36–37, 52, 57, 59–60, 112
  all-weather and night bombers:
    60–61, 73, 95, 101, 245
  employment: 53, 61, 73, 105
  losses: 61, 95, 103
  strikes: 57, 95, 101–2
F–105G: 171
F–111: 59, 61, 101, 245–46, 255, 267,
    268–69, 276, 280
KA–3: 40n
KC–135: 9–10, 40n, 53, **214**, 231
OV–10: 231
RA–3B: 155
RA–5: 256, 280
RF–4: 155, 156, 171, 172, 194n, 196,
    205, **213**, 247, 277
SR–71: 106, 277
T–38: 240
T–39: 194
U–2: 106
WC–130: 194n
Aircraft losses, North Vietnam: 63–64,
    239–40, 256, 274
MiG–17: 92, 111, 112, 128, 226, 236–37
MiG–19: 214
MiG–21: 54–55, 90, 203, 226, 236–37,
    241, 242
Aircraft losses, U.S.: 57–59, 66, 73–74, 89,
    176, 243, 302, 310–11. *See also* Air
    defenses, North Vietnam.
1972: 242
A–1: 195
A–6: 280
A–6, over China: 87
A–7: 226, 268
Air Force vs. Navy: 48
attrition models: 271, 272
B–52: 255–56, 263–64, 265, 268, 271,
    272, 279–80
B–52D: 272
B–52G: 272
Black Friday: 86, 104
Black Wednesday: 86
C–130: 251
EB–66: 50, 98
EC–121: 165
F–4: 6, 8, 35, 50, 54, 61, 86, 90, 92–93,
    103, 104, 110, 113, 127, 187,
    203, 226, 236, 237, 239, 240,
    245, 256, 268, 280
F–4D: 173, 241
F–4E: 241

F–104: 236, 289
F–105: 6, 49, 50, 53, 61, 86, 90, 92–93,
    103, 104, 110, 226, 237
F–105F: 61, 95, 103, 195
F–105G: 171
F–111: 245, 246, 269
helicopters: 171
Laos: 288
Laos vs. Thailand risks: 161
post-target turn: 265
RA–5: 237
rates: 48–49
reconnaissance aircraft: 155–56, 280
Route Package Six: 48–49
Aircraft sorties: 301–5
Aircraft technology. *See also* Electronic
    technology; Bombing accuracy and
    effectiveness.
fuel tanks, self-sealing: 8–9
gun pods: 64, 90, 112, 241
hydraulic control systems: 8–9
survivability: 9
Air defenses, North Vietnam
antiaircraft artillery: 33, 35, 37, 40, 46,
    49, 57, 143, 196, **212**, 269, 275
    downs U.S. aircraft: 57–58, 73, 86,
        93, 143, 156, 242, 280, 290
    estimates of: 40, 242–43
    on irrigation dikes: 46, 250
Atoll air-to-air missiles: 86, 98, 103, **120**
B–52 downing conference: 271n
Christmas bombing: 255
Fan Song radar: 267
flak: 40, 57–58
Hanoi-Haiphong area: 25, 40–41,
    110–11, 143, 277
interlocking radar system: 205
Kep: 74
Lang Dang railyard: **217**, 270
MiGs: 52–55, 74, 86, 89, 92–93, 96, 97,
    98, 110–11, 127–28, 201,
    236–37, 255–56, 268, 270, 274
missile launch rates: 269–70
Moc Chau radar: 206
Nam Dinh: 46, 47
optical controllers, surface-to-air
    missiles: 105
panhandle: 143, 196, 197, 201
Phuc Yen airfield: 54–55, 90, 103–4,
    127–28
radar: 5, 40–41, 105
reconnaissance flights, resistance to:

155–56
Soviet trawlers' role: 277
surface-to-air missiles: 35–37, 40, 50,
    103, 104, 105, 107, **120**, 143,
    171, 225
Team Work radar: 267
Thai Nguyen iron works: 57–59
weather influences: 244
Yen Vien railyard: 86
Air operation coordination and integration.
    See Command and control issues.
Alcatraz prison: 182
Allen, Michael: 261
Aman, Earl D.: 290
Andersen Air Force Base, Guam: 23, **216**,
    223–24, 273–74, 275, 277–78, 280
Anderson, Gregory L.: 171
Anderson, Jack: 222
Anderson, William R.: 179
Antiwar movement: 114, 168–69, 170,
    174, 204, 260–62
Antiwar protest demonstrations: 114, 149,
    168, 170
Aptheker, Herbert: 187
Armstrong, Larry D.: 127
Arnett, Peter: 122
Arnold, Henry H. "Hap": 137
Ashmore, Harry S.: 190
"A to Z" assessment: 132–33
Atterberry, Edwin L.: 192
Aubrac, Raymond: 87

Baez, Joan: 261, 262
Baggs, William C.: 190
Baker, Doyle D.: 111
Baldwin, David L.: 74
Ball, George: 36, 44, 132, 137–38
Barnet, Richard J.: 170
Basel, Gene I.: 93
Bean, James E.: 113
Bell, Holly G.: 171
Berg, Kyle D.: 182
Berrigan, Daniel: 188
Berrigan, Philip: 188
Bien Hoa Air Base: 20, 106
Black, Jon D.: 188
Black Friday aircraft losses: 86, 104. *See
    also* Aircraft losses, U.S.
Black Wednesday aircraft losses: 86. *See
    also* Aircraft losses, U.S.
Blesse, Frederick C.: 64
Blue Chip command center: 16

Index

Bob Hope Show: 113–14, 274
Bolo, Operation: 53–55, 96–97
Bombing accuracy and effectiveness:
17–18, 45–46, 58, 101–2, 154. *See
also* Laser-guided bombs; Walleye
television-guided bombs; Weather.
artillery interdiction: 146
Bac Mai hospital error: **217**, 263, 279
bomb damage claims: 307
Bosnia: 285
bridge interdiction: 247–48
Bullpup missiles: 234
cluster bombs: 244
Combat Skyspot: 102, 225, 260. *See also*
Radar bombing, ground.
Commando Club: 103–4. *See also* Radar
bombing, ground.
Desert Storm: 283, 284
exaggerations: 247–48
F–111: 245, 246
Hanoi-Haiphong area: 226
jungle: 15
Kham Thien street error: **217**, 263
loran sorties: 247
missile suppression: 267–70
night missions: 73–74
oil storage facilities: 203–4
radar. *See* Aircraft, U.S., A–6, B–52,
F–105F, F–111; Radar bombing;
Ryan's Raiders.
railroad interdiction: 248, 276
SA–2: 244
Serbia: 285
Tactical Fighter Weapons Center: 239
Taylor assessment: 262–63
telecommunication links: 252
Vinh raid: 225
World War II: 283, 284
Bombing policy: 82, 83, 124–25, 128, 130,
132, 170–71, 223–24. *See also*
Aircraft, U.S., B–52; Lavelle affair;
Targets.
aircrew survival: 288–89
airfields prohibition: 284
all-weather bombing: 95–96
antiwar movement influence: 204
armed reconnaissance: 232
B–52 cutback in exchange for prisoners:
178–79
barrier concept: *See* McNamara Line.
bombing halts: 37–38, 56, 87–88,
134–36, 138–40, 142, 149,
151–53
bombing resumption: 163, 167–68,
172–73, 196–97, 203
British position: 44
Brown, Harold: 70, 133
Brown, George S.:162, 164
Cambodia: 164–65
China border buffer zone: 63, 87, 248,
250
CIA position: 42, 89, 129, 162, 164
civilians: 82, 279, 282, 285
Clifford position: 133–34, 136–37,
141–42
communist leadership targeting
prohibition: 252, 278–79
congressional position: 44, 62, 64–65,
76, 78–83, 88–89, 115, 122–24,
209, 258
elections, influence: 20, 115–16, 122,
134–35, 138, 149, 254, 258
Ellsberg questionnaire: 162–63
escalation issue: 63
Freedom Train campaign: 229
Ginsburgh influence: 30–31
gradualism: 29, 67, 93–94
ground forces influence: 129
Hanoi-Haiphong area: 24, 42, 62–63,
65–66, 69, 74–78, 87–88, 92,
108–9, 133, 137, 138–39, 203,
225, 226–28, 250–51, 254, 255,
256, 259
illegitimate raids: 202
Institute for Defense Analyses study: 133
irrigation dams and dikes: 46, 249–50
JCS resignation issue: 83–84
Johnson position: 19, 23–24, 30, 41, 42,
43, 62, 65, 67–69, 76–81, 83, 85,
87, 89, 149, 281
Kissinger position: 159, 253–54, 259
Laird position: 162, 221–22, 225,
250–51, 252, 259, 272
land route interdiction: 229
Laos: 4–5
McConnell position: 123–24
McNamara position: 23, 36, 61, 67, 70,
71, 76, 79, 81–83, 85, 115, 126,
131, 133
MiG bases: 55, 77, 126–27, 142
mining: 227–29
Momyer position: 25, 76, 81, 88–89,
95–97, 152
multiweek bombing programs: 24

Nineteenth parallel: 140–41, 142, 143
Nixon position: 150, 162, 228, 259
No Committee position: 68–69
nuclear weapons: 23, 167
political influences: 31, 42, 168–69, 170
protective reaction strikes: 171–72, 206, 207
Rostow, Walt, position: 30–31, 78, 125
route packages system: 18–19, 221
rules interpretation issue: 204–5
Soviet advisors casualty issue: 36
Soviet ship incidents: 75, 108
Salisbury journalism influence: 44–47
Senate Armed Services Committee: 76, 78–83, 88–89, 123–24
Senate Foreign Relations Committee: 124
Sharp position: 79–80, 82
smart bombs: 219. *See also* Laser-guided bombs; Walleye television-guided bombs.
sortie rates: 70–71, 91–92, 92n, 155
Stennis hearings: 82–84, 115
target restrictions: 41–43, 55–56
Tet offensive influence: 122–23, 126
Tet bombing pause: 56
Thailand: 5–6, 107–8
trolling: 205
truck interdiction: 148–49
twentieth parallel: 70, 122, 139, 140, 141, 143, 203, 253, 258
urban targets: 19, 284–85
Wheeler committee: 23
Wheeler position: 80–81, 82, 89, 90, 126, 133–34, 141, 142, 162, 164
Wheeler Study Group report: 129–30
"Wise Men" meetings: 137–39
A to Z assessment: 132–33
Bombing procedures and techniques: 67, 68, 69, 108, 228–29, 260, 270–71. *See also* Bombing accuracy and effectiveness; Command and Control issues; Electronic technology; Tactics.
A–6 employment: 59
anti-MiG sweeps: 96–97, 100
area bombing: 281
chaff: 243, 265
compression issue: 264–65
EC–121 employment: 98–99
escort and support: 231, 255, 266
evasive maneuvers during bomb runs: 275
forward air controllers: 143–44
ground-controlled bombing formations: 102–5
ground forces support: 145
hunter-killer teams: 36, 231, 243, 266–268
Iron Hand hunter-killer flights: 36, 37
jamming, electronic: 97–98
laser designation pods: 284
loran use: 202–3, 246–47, 269
low altitude: 60n
mining: 67, 68, 69, 108, 228–29, 260
night missions: 7, 59, 61, 144
nuclear weapons: 60, 167
photography, area surveillance: 106–7
radar bombing. *See* Radar bombing.
river mining: 108
roads closing: 147–49
Route packages concept: 28–29
sortie rates: 70–71, 91–92, 155, 231–32
surprise element: 278
toss bombing: 60
Bomb tonnage dropped: 284, 301, 306
Bond, Charles R.: 13
Boothby, Harold W.: 113
Border sanctuaries: 164
Borman, Frank: 179–80
Bosnia: 285
Boyd, Charles G.: **218**
Bradley, Omar: 137, 138
Brestel, Max C.: 111
Brezhnev, Leonid: 33
Bridge Busters: 233
Bridge destruction. *See* Bombing accuracy and effectiveness, bridge interdiction; Targets, bridges.
Brinks Hotel car bombing: 20
Broughton, Jacksel M.: 75, 208
Brown, Frederick I.: 147
Brown, George: 42, 65
Brown, George S.: 116, 160–62, 164, 171–72, 201, **211**, 287
Brown, Harold: 35, 70, 91n, 101, 123, 133
Bui Diem: 150
Bundy, McGeorge: 30, 137, 138, 149
Bundy, William: 30, 68
Bunker, Ellsworth: 89, 110, 116, 142, 163, **211**, 222
Burchett, Wilfred: 57n, 88, 187
Burdett, Edward B.: 103
Bush, George: 282

Index

Byrd, Robert C.: 79

Cambodia: 3, 132, 172–74, 227, 287, 288
Campbell, Nathan C.: 40n
Canal des Rapides bridge: 26, 46, 63, 72,
　　85–86, 88, 92, 112, **119**, 276
Cannon, Howard W.: 79, 82
Cappelli, Charles E.: 93
Carver, George: 138
Casteel, John: 40n
Casualties: 20, 44, 45–46, 288, 289, 302,
　　312
Chairsell, William S.: 52n, 176
Chennault, Anna: 150–51
Chennault, Claire L.: 13, 22, 150
China, Peoples Republic of: 26, 33, 141,
　　154, 236, 248, 277
Chinese border
　　airspace violations: 63, 87
　　buffer zone: 24, 44, 71, 72, 77, 250, 254
　　targets hit inside buffer zone: 78, 84, 85,
　　　　217, 270, 272, 273, 276
Choke points: 28, 147–48
Christian, George: 113, 254
CIA, position on bombing policy: 42, 89,
　　129, 162, 164
Civilian casualties: 279
Clark Air Base: 138
Clark, Ramsey: 261
Clay, Lucius D., Jr.: 200, 257, 267, 280
Clifford, Clark: 68, 122, 126, 131, 135,
　　136, 141–42, 143, 156
Clifton, Charles C.: 55
Clinton, Bill: 286
Clodfelter, Mark: 282
Cloud seeding: 194–95
Club bars: 11
Cobeil, Earl G.: 187
Code of Conduct for Prisoners of War:
　　184–85, 190, 191
Collingwood, Charles: 190
Colvin, John: 94
Combat Skyspot radar: 102, 225, 260
Combat Tree equipment: 239
Command and control issues: 15, 16, 22,
　　23. *See also* Lavelle Affair.
　　Abrams-McCain relations: 228
　　Airborne Battlefield Command and
　　　　Control Center: 17
　　air operations coordination and
　　　　integration: 18–19
　　approval procedure: 13

B–52. *See* Aircraft, U.S., B–52.
Bond commission position: 13
Brown, George S., leadership style:
　　160–62
control centers: 16–17
fragmentary orders: 16
Guam discontent: 273–74
interdiction belts authority: 77–78
JCS appointments: 160–61
Kissinger influence: 222
LeMay, as Chief of Staff: 21–22
loran: 246–47, 264–70
McConnell, as Chief of Staff: 22–23
McConnell legacy: 287
McNamara-LeMay conflict: 21
Momyer command: 13–15, 16–18
Momyer leadership style: 160–62
Monkey Mountain control center: 17
Nixon-Laird conflict: 221–22
Nixon-Vogt communication: 221
presidential control: 19–20
Pursley-Haig conflict: 222
Rolling Thunder: v–vii, 3, 18
Rolling Thunder bombing programs: 24
route packages system: 18–19, 28
Ryan appointment as PACAF
　　commander: 59
Sharp-Westmoreland cooperation: 161
Site 85 (Phou Pha Thi): 102–3
Slay appointment: 238
Strategic Air Command
　　declining influence: 287
　　role: 271–72, 275
　　Seventh Air Force conflict: 266
target identification number: 25
target lists confusion: 25
Task Force 77 role: 19
Teaball fusion center: 239–40
theater conflicts: 15, 16
Vogt appointment: 221
Commando Club: 103–4
Congress, U.S.
　　Tonkin Gulf Resolution: 20
　　Vietnam War, position on: 44, 62,
　　　　64–65, 76, 78–83, 88–89, 115,
　　　　122–24, 135, 170, 209, 258
Con Son Island prison: 179–80
Constellation (Connie). *See* Aircraft, U.S.,
　　EC–121.
Cooper, Damon W.: 257
Corder, John A.: 127
Credit, aircraft downing: 111–12, 128, 237

B–52 gunners: 274
　equal for backseater: 8, 111
　rules revision: 111
Cronkite, Walter: 122
Cunningham, Randy: 237
Cuthbert, Bradley G.: 155

Da Nang Air Base: 5, 10, 17, 20, 53, 54, 63, 64, 127, 129, 142, 187, 193, 196, 223
Dang Ngoc Ngu: 186n
Dang Trinh: 35
Davis, Joseph: 230
Davis, Rennard C.: 188
Day, George E.: 188, 189, 191
DeBellevue, Charles B.: **212**, 237, 241
Defense Advisory Committee on Prisoners of War: 184
Defense Intelligence Agency target identification numbers: 25
Dellinger, Dave: 45
Denton, Jeremiah J., Jr.: 183, 185
DePuy, William E.: 138
Desert Storm: 282–83, 288
Dethlefsen, Merlyn H.: 57–58
Diefenbach, Brent O.: 263
Dirksen, Everett: 115, 150
Dirty Bird Prison: 192
Disosway, Gabriel P.: 95–96, 99
Dixon, Robert J.: 172
Dobrynin, Anatoly: 75, 108, 167, 169
Dole, Robert: 175, 176
Don Muang Air Base: 6
Dorsett, Tracy: 127
Douglas, Helen Gahagan: 156
Doumer Bridge: 46, 47, 112, 128, 153
　bombing prohibited: 63, 77, 93, 109
　dropped by bombing: 85, 110, 235
　target for bombing: 84-85, 110–11, 113, 122, 126, 235–36, 251
Doumer, Paul: 84
Draft lottery: 168
Dragon's Jaw. See Thanh Hoa bridge.
Dramesi, John A.: 192–93
Driscoll, William: 237
Drones, reconnaissance: 107, **213**, 279

Easter offensive: 219–20
Edelen, Henry: 23
Eisenhower, Dwight D.: 76, 125, 156, 157
Elections influence on war: 20, 115–16, 122, 134–35, 138, 149, 254, 258

Electronic technology. *See also* Loran; Radar bombing.
　Bolo Operation: 53, 54, 96, 97
　Combat Skyspot radar: 102, 225, 260
　Combat Tree: 239
　electronic countermeasures pods: 39, 40, 49, 50–52, 70, 148–49
　electronic telescope: 274–75
　identification transponders: 98–99
　Pave Knife pods: 231
　radar warning gear: 17, 48, 51, 87, 97, 100, 103, 205
　sensors: 70, 148, 200, 246
　Teaball fusion center: 239–40
　terrain avoidance radar: 59–60, 245
Elliot, Robert M.: 128
Ellsberg, Daniel: 132, 162
Ellsberg questionnaire: 162–63
Emerson, Gloria: 179

Fall, Bernard: 181
Feighny, James P.: 128
Feinstein, Jeffrey S.: 237
Findley, Paul: 115
Flight formations: 40, 51–52, 103–5, 240
Flynn, John P.: 103, 197, 199
Fonda, Jane: **212**, 261
Ford, Gerald: 281
Foreign-object-damage bumps: 241
Fortas, Abe: 135
Forward air controllers: 143–44
Frags, fragmentary orders: 16
Francisco, San D.: 156
Franks, Lonnie D.: 208
Freedom Bait Protective Strikes: 196
Freedom Train campaign: 229
Fuel tanks, self-sealing: 8–9
Fulbright, J. William: 44, 115, 124, 140, 170, 195

Gabriel, Charles A.: 207, 208, 210, 287
Gaddis, Norman C.: 186–87
Gadoury, William: 103n
Galbraith, John K.: 44
Gate Guard interdiction belts: 28–29
Gates, Thomas: 160
Gayler, Noel: 257
Gelb, Leslie: 132
Geneva Accords (1954): 31, 92
Geneva Agreement (1962): 4
Geneva Conventions: 180–81, 184
Ginsburgh, Robert N.: 30–31, 125, 130,

Index

249
Giraudo, John C.: 52n
Goldberg, Arthur: 138
Goldwater, Barry: 20
Goulding, Phil: 61–62
Gradualism: 29, 67, 93–94, 285
Graham, Neil J.: 112–13
Greene, Wallace M., Jr.: 84
Grubb, Wilmer N.: 197–98
Guarino, Lawrence N.: 183, 187
Gulf War: 282–84, 290

Habib, Philip C.: 138, 175
Hague Convention of 1899: 184
Haig, Alexander M., Jr.: 222–23, 259, 260, 280
Hall, James H.: 127
Hamburger Hill, battle of: 165–66
Ham Rong Bridge: See Thanh Hoa bridge.
Hanoi-Haiphong area: 25–27, 33, 41–42, 51, 61, 82, 226
    air defenses: 25, 110–11, 143, 277
    B–52 employment: 261–63, 267, 272
    bombing policy: 24, 42, 62–63, 65–66, 69, 77–78, 87–88, 92, 108–9, 133, 137, 138–39, 203, 225, 226–28, 250–51, 254, 255, 256, 259
    Linebacker II campaign: 267, 272
    mining: 67, 68, 69, 93–94, 125–26, 227–29
    Nixon position: 225, 226, 259–60
    restricted and prohibited zones: 24, 43–44, 62, 71, 72, 75–78, 87, 88, 89, 107–9, 126, 133, 250–51, 254
    targets: 26, 62–63, 261–63, 277
Hanoi Hilton: See Hoa Lo prison.
Harriman, W. Averell: 109, 151
Harris, Carlyle S.: 182
Harris, Hunter: 15, 18, 19
Harris, Jeffrey L.: 236
Hartke, Vance: 44
Hatfield, Mark: 115
Hawkins, Augustus F.: 179
Hayden, Thomas E.: 187–88, 261
Hegdahl, Douglas B.: 189–90
Heggen, Keith R.: 280
Helms, Richard: 69–70, 89, 159
Heltsley, Charles M.: 52n
Hershey, Lewis B.: 168
Hill, Howard J.: 198

Hirsch, Thomas M.: 64
Hiss, Alger: 156
Hoa Lo prison: 182, 197, 262–63
Hoang Phuong,: 278
Hoar, Dean L.: 40n
Ho Chi Minh: 4, 31–32, 87, 167, 193
Ho Chi Minh Trail: 4–5, 9, 28, 56, 59, 70–71, 171, 196–97, 200, 246
Hollings, Ernest F.: 79
Holloway, Bruce K.: 73, 133, 167, 206, 287
Holt, Harold: 113
Hoopes, Townshend: 133, 134, 136
Horner, Charles A.: 284, 289–90
Houghton, Robert W.: 290
House Armed Services Committee: 44, 209
Howerton, Rex D.: 128
Hughes, Harold E.: 208, 209, 210
Humphrey, Hubert: 116, 149
Hussein, Sadam: 282
Hydraulic control systems: 8–9
Hyland, John D.: 76

Ickes, Harold: 116
Income tax exemption issue: 11, 50–52, 161–62
Ingress procedures: 50–52
Institute for Defense Analyses, JASON division: 133
Interdiction belts concept: 28–29
Iraq: 282–84
Iron Hand hunter-killer flights: 36, 37
Iron Triangle: 72
Irrigation dams and dikes: 31, 46, 249–50, 251

Jackson, Henry M.: 79, 159
James, Daniel, Jr.: 54
Johnson, Gerald W.: **211**, 266, 272
Johnson, Harold E.: 58n
Johnson, Lyndon B.
    A–12 employment: 106
    advisors: 23
    airfields targeting: 34
    Armed Services Committee relations: 78–89
    B–52 employment: 3
    bombing halts: 37–38, 134–36, 138–40, 149, 152
    bombing policy: 19, 23–24, 62, 63, 85, 129
    bridges interdiction: 88
    cabinet: 21

Clifford conversion myth: 136–37
escalation: 33–34
Gallup poll ratings: 115, 122
Haiphong area prohibition: 126
Hanoi-Haiphong area: 92, 108–9
McNamara Line: 29
McNamara resignation: 83–84
MiG bases: 89
missiles suppression: 35–36
North Vietnam invasion policy: 4
nuclear weapons: 125
peace negotiations: 56, 69, 109
political influences: 114–16
railroads interdiction: 4, 41, 42
reconnaissance program: 156
reelection refusal: 139
reinforcements: 134, 136
Soviet ship incidents: 75, 108
San Antonio formula: 88
taxes, raising: 115–16
twentieth parallel: 139, 140, 141, 143
visit to Vietnam and Thailand: 113–14
Johnson, Roy L.: 29, 79, 107
Joint Chiefs of Staff: 24–26, 42, 44, 65,
    67–68, 70, 81, 83–84, 125–26, 151,
    162, 164, 269

Kadena Air Base: 106, 224
Kasler, James H.: 183, 187, 189
Katzenbach, Nicholas: 68, 89, 140
Keegan, George J., Jr.: 147, 148, 161
Keirn, Richard P.: 183
Kennedy, John F.: 21, 30, 37
Kennedy, Robert F.: 37, 57n, 135
Khe Sanh siege: 134
Khrushchev, Nikita: 33
Kissinger, Henry: 87, 232
    B–52 employment: 220, 226, 256
    bombing resumption: 169
    Cambodia: 173
    Haiphong mining: 228
    income tax exemption issue: 161–62
    Laird workaround: 222
    Nixon selection: 157–58
    North Korea EC–121 shoot down
        incident: 165
    nuclear strategy: 158
    peace negotiations: 166–67, 227,
        258–59
    peace negotiations, secret: 202–3
    prisoners of war: 195
    "The Viet Nam Negotiations": 9

Korat Air Base: 6, 51, 52, 54, 57, 58, 59,
    73, 85, 90, 103, 112, 114, **118**, 128,
    148, 176, 196, 223, 233, 243, 245
Korat conference: 176–77
Korat plateau: 6, 12
Korea, EC–121 plane incident: 165, 222,
    228
Korean War: 19, 234
Kosovo: 285
Kosygin, Aleksei: 33, 42, 56, 69
Kraslow, David: 157
Ky, Nguyen Cao. *See* Nguyen Cao Ky.

Laird, Melvin R.: **211**, 221–22, 257, 259
    bombing policy: 162, 204, 225, 250–51,
        252, 253–54, 272
    Cambodia: 174
    Haiphong mining: 228
    Nixon–Laird conflict: 221–22
    prisoners of war: 175, 176, 191, 195
    protective reaction strikes: 173–74, 206
    Secretary of Defense appointment:
        159–60
    Vietnamization: 165
Laos
    aircrew losses: 289n
    bombing policy: 4–5
    interdiction bombing: 143, 148
    invasion policy: 4–5
    McNamara Line: 29
    Meo forces: 102
    panhandle: 4, 6, 202
    Site 85 (Phou Pha Thi): 102–3
    truck interdiction: 143
Laser-guided bombs: **215**, 219, 230–31,
    232–33, 243, 247–48, 252, 263
    against Canal des Rapides Bridge: 276
    communist party headquarters hit by
        errant bomb: 278–79
    in Deliberate Force: 285
    during Desert Storm: 282–85
    against Doumer Bridge: 235–36
    against Hanoi powerplant: 251
    against Hanoi radio: 279
    against Lang Chi hydroelectric plant:
        251
Lavelle, John D.: 199–200, 204–7, 208,
    209, 210, **211**, 238
Lavelle affair: 202–3, 287
    after action messages: 207
    bombing authority: 204
    disciplinary response: 208–9

Index

exposed: 208
  false reporting: 201–2, 238
Leaflet and radio drops: 251–52
Le Duan: 32, 167
Le Duc Tho: 227, 253, 258–59
Leeser, Leonard C.: 171
LeMay, Curtis: 21, 82, 116, 150n
Linebacker: 229–30
  after action meetings: 238–39
  air defenses, North Vietnam: 242
  bad weather: 244–45
  bridge busting campaign: 233, 247–48
  deployable strength: 223
  effectiveness: 247
  escorts: 247
  F–111 employment: 245–46
  laser-guided bombs: 219, 230–31, 232–
      33, 243, 247–48, 252
    against Doumer Bridge: 235–36
    against Hanoi powerplant: 251
    against Lang Chi hydroelectric plant:
      251
  leadership targeting prohibition: 252
  leaflet and radio drops: 251–52
  loran: 246–47
  MiG capability degradation: 241–42
  Nixon position: 232
  redeployment: 246
  sortie rates: 231–32
  supplies interdiction: 252–53
  Talbot appointment: 238
  Teaball fusion center: 239–40
Linebacker II. See also Aircraft, U.S.,
      B–52, employment.
  airfield suppression: 273
  civilian casualties: 279
  F–111 employment: 268–69
  Hanoi-Haiphong area: 267, 272
  MiGs performance: 274
  missile suppression: 266–68
  morale: 273–74
  psychological effect: 277–78
  railroads: 272–73, 275–76
Locher, Roger C.: 236
Lodge, Henry Cabot: 42–43, 158, 175
Lodge, Robert A.: 236
Lon Nol,: 172, 173
Loory, Stuart H.: 157
Loose deuce formation: 240
Loran (Long Range Navigation): 200,
      202–3, 246–47, 253, 255, 269,
Lovett, Robert A.: 137

Low, James S.: 189
Luce, Don: 179–80
Lynd, Staughton: 187

MacArthur, Douglas: 19
Macovescu, Gheorghe: 109
Madden, John A., Jr.: 241
Maddux, Sam, Jr.: 190
Maharajah Clothiers party suits: 177
Mai Van Bo: 88, 166
Mai Van Cuong: 186n
Mallon, Richard J.: 171
Manor, Leroy J.: 193–94, 195
Mansfield, Mike: 140
Mao Tse-Tung: 26
March Against Death: 170
Marcovich, Herbert: 87
Marigold peace initiative: 42–43
Marine Corps, U.S.: 5, 15, 20, 59, 84, 90,
      100–101, 111, 121, 128–34,
      145–48, 165, 177, 200, 223, 231,
      280, 289
Marshall, Winton W.: 206
Martin, Graham A.: 13, 15
Matheny, David P.: 188
Maurer, Ion Gheorghe: 89, 109
McCain, John S., Jr.: 149, 161, 196, 199,
      204, 232, 256
McCain, John S., III: 188–89
McCarthy, Eugene: 134–35
McCarthy, Mary: 190
McCone, John: 129
McConnell, John P.: 13, 19, 22–23, 35, 70,
      117, 132
  agricultural targets: 31, 249–50
  air defenses: 82
  B–52 bombing mission: 124–25, 256
  bombing resumption: 151
  command and control issues: 18
  F–111 employment: 101
  Hanoi-Haiphong area: 77
  irrigation dams and dikes: 31, 249–50
  leadership legacy: 287
  troop escalation: 67
McCoskrie, Roland K.: 13
McGovern, George: 254, 258
McKinney, George H., Jr.: 111, 113
McKnight, George G.: 192
McNamara Line: 29, 70, 80, 81, 133, 148,
      200, 202
McNamara, Robert: 20, 21, 75, 123, 131,
      164, 222

barrier concept. *See* McNamara Line.
bombing halts: 37–38, 68, 70, 71, 74, 76, 79, 88, 93, 122, 129, 133, 136
bombing policy: 31, 36, 68–69, 82, 114, 115, **132**, 133, 209
casualties: 45, 126
departure: 83–84, 114, 131
F–111 development: 101, 245
missiles suppression: 35
nuclear weapons: 125
target selection: 81, 82, 85, 90, 221, 250
Tonkin Gulf incident: 20n
McNamara Wall. *See* McNamara Line.
McNaughton, John T.: 23, 35, 68
McPherson, Harry C.: 139
Mengtzu airbase, China: 63
Meo forces: 102
Messett, Thomas: 235
Meyer, John C.: 201, 206, **211**, 256, 265–66, 269, 271, 275, 279
Meyers, William: 170
Mikhail Frunze incident: 75
Military personnel, U.S.: 313
Miller, Carl: 233, 235, 251
Miller, Jack: 79
Mining: 67, 68, 69, 108, 228–29, 260
Missiles, North Vietnam
  Atoll: 86, 98, 103, **120**
  SA–2: 35, **120**, 244
  SA–3: 244
  SA–4: 244
  SA–7: 244
Missiles, U.S.: 7
  AGM–78: 105
  Bullpup: 234
  Cruise: 285
  Falcon: 91–92, 111
  Shrike: 36, 105, 195, 243, 267
  Sidewinder: 7, 55, 90–91, **118**, 236, 241
  Sparrow: 7, 55, 91, **118**, 239, 240–41
  Standard antiradar: 243, 270
Mize, John D.: 268
Momyer, William W.: 13–15, 47, 53, 81, 99, 113, **117**, 160–62, 287
  A–12 employment: 107
  bad weather bombing: 95–97, 100
  bombing policy: 25, 28, 29, 42, 76, 152
  gun pods: 64
  Marine air operations: 145
  MiG bases: 127
  MiGs effectiveness: 88–89
  Site 85 (Phou Pha Thi) evacuation: 102–3
Monkey Mountain control center: 17, 100
Monsoons. *See* Weather.
Moore, Albert E.: 274
Moore, Joseph H.: 13, 14, 28–29, 112
Moorer, Thomas H.: 84, 195, 196, 221
  bombing policy: 160, 220, 222
  Hanoi-Haiphong area strikes: 226, 228, 251, 254, 259, 269, 272
  Lavelle affair: 204, 205, 207, 209
Moratorium, nationwide: 168–69
Morgenthau, Henry, Jr.: 116
Morris, Stephen J.: 289n
Morrison, Anne: 44
Morrison, Joseph C.: 156
Morse, F. Bradford: 115
Morton, Thruston: 115
Munitions: 306. *See also* Bombing accuracy and effectiveness; Laser-guided bombs; Missiles, U.S., Ordnance; Walleye television-guided bombs.
Murphy, Robert: 138

Nakhon Phanom Air Base: 9, 102, 148, 200, 239
National League of Families of American Prisoners and Missing in Southeast Asia: 175–76
Navy, U.S.: 7–8, 11, 18–20, 26–29, 36, 40, 48–53, 59–66, 71, 77–78, 91, 140–41, 185–86, 205, 229, 232, 234, 236–43, 267, 288. *See also* Command and control issues; Denton, Jeremiah J., Jr.; Gayler, Noel; McCain, John S., Jr.; Moorer, Thomas H.; Route packages; Sharp, Ulysses S. Grant; Stockdale, James B.
Nazzaro, Joseph J.: 161, 199, 200
Ngo Dinh Diem: 4
Nguyen Cao Ky: 4, **117**, 193
Nguyen Dinh Uoc: 20n
Nguyen Duy Trinh: 57n
Nguyen Hong Nhi: 186
Nguyen Ngoc Loan,: 122
Nguyen Van Bai,: 186
Nguyen Van Coc,: 186
Nguyen Van Thieu: 4, 150, 167, 191, 253, 256, 280
Nixon, Richard M.
  aircraft losses: 264

Index

air power use: 219–21
anticommunism: 156
antiwar movement: 168–69, 170
B–52 employment: 220, 221, 223–25, 226–28, 253, 257–58, 259, 260
B–52 cutback for prisoner exchange offer: 178–79
bombing policy: 114–15, 228, 253–54
bombing resumption: 163, 167, 172–73
bombing ultimatum: 166–69
cabinet appointments: 159–60
Cambodia: 162, 164–65, 172–73
cease fire: 256, 282
China: 64–65, 157, 203
detente: 227
force withdrawals: 165, 168, 169, 170
Haiphong mining: 228, 229
Hanoi-Haiphong area: 225, 226, 259–60
income tax exemption issue: 161–62
irrigation dams and dikes: 250
Kissinger selection: 157–58
Linebacker: 227–32
Linebacker II: 255–60
military, views on: 204, 240
Nixon Doctrine: 166
North Korea EC–121 shoot down incident: 165
Okinawa: 224
prisoners of war: 175, 179
protective reaction strikes: 171–72, 206, 207
resignation: 281
rocket attacks response: 163
SALT negotiations: 169, 227
secret plan to end war: 150, 157–59, 204
secrecy and suspicion: 164–65
Soviet Union's proposal for nuclear attack on China: 157
summit meeting, Moscow: 227, 254
twentieth parallel, bombing line: 253, 256, 257–58, 280
"No Committee": 68–69
North Vietnam
  agriculture: 249
  air force: 33, 34–35, 241–42
  American antiwar movement: 168–69, 170, 260–62
  Ashmore-Baggs visit: 190
  Berrigan-Zinn visitor group: 188
  Cambodia insurgency: 287
  China assistance: 26–27, 33, 236, 248, 277
  China rail link: 26
  China relations: 154
  economy: 286–87
  electric power: 154, 155
  French influence: 25–26
  Hanoi population growth: 154–55
  Hayden visitor group: 187–88
  invasion threat: 4
  leadership: 31–32, 287
  oil pipelines: 153–54
  pig iron production: 57, 154
  population dispersion: 154
  prisons. See Prisons, North Vietnam.
  railroads: 71–74, 84–86
  SAM inventories: 244
  Sino-Soviet rivalry: 33
  South Vietnam intervention: 20
  Soviet hydroelectric project: 154
  Soviet military assistance: 33, 62, 71, 99
  Soviet ship incidents: 75, 108
  supplies: 56, 82, 141–42, 144, 146–47, 248–49, 276
  transportation infrastructure: 153–54
  truck losses: 248
  typhoon damage: 155
  U.S. reconstruction offer: 286–87
Nuclear weapons: 23, 125
Nuclear Weapons and Foreign Policy: 158
Nugent, Patrick J.: 132

Oil products facilities, U.S. attacks on: 29–30, 41, 43, 47, 50, 68, 82, 202, 203, 225, 226, 262, 276
Okinawa: 9–10, 224
Olds, Robin: 53, 54, 64, 86, 91, 99, 111, **117**
Operation Allied Force: 285
Operation Bolo: 53, 96, 97
Operation Deliberate Force: 285
Ordnance. See also Laser-guided bombs; Missiles, U.S.; Munitions; Walleye television-guided bombs.
  bridge busting: 233–34
  cluster bombs: 49–50
    CBU–24: 231
    CBU–52: 231, 243–44
  F–4 guns: 241
  gun pods: 64, 112
  mines: 234
  Mk–36 Destructor mines: 108
Overly, Norris M.: 188, 189

Pacific Air Forces. *See* Clay, Lucius D., Jr.; Harris, Hunter; Nazzaro, Joseph J.; Ryan, John D.; Vogt, John W.
Pacific Command. *See* Navy, U.S.
Panek, Robert J.: 171
Pardo, John R. "Bob": 290
Paul Doumer Bridge. *See* Doumer Bridge.
Pave Knife pods: 231
Peace negotiations
    Aubrac initiative: 87–88
    bombing ultimatum: 166–69
    cease-fire: 166, 194, 203, 253–54, 256, 257–59, 280
    China position: 141n, 154
    congressional position: 258–60
    informal talks: 139
    international inspection proposal: 258
    Kissinger initiative: 87–88, 90
    Kissinger position: 158–59
    Marigold peace initiative: 42–43
    Nixon position: 150–51
    North Vietnam position: 109, 151, 152, 166, 167, 258–59, 280
    Paris: 142, 150–52, 166–67, 227, 253, 258–60, 277
    Polish initiative: 42–43
    Pope Paul letter: 56
    Rumanian initiative: 109–10
    Salisbury role: 44–47
    San Antonio formula: 88
    Soviet position: 56, 150–51, 253, 280
    talk-fight strategy: 139
    Tet pause: 56–57
    "The Vietnam Negotiations": 159
    Wilson-Kosygin talks: 56–57
Pell, Claiborne: 194n
Percy, Charles: 115
Pereslavl-Zalesskiy ship incident: 108
Perot, H. Ross: 178
Peterson, Douglas: 289
Pham Hung: 141, 141n
Pham Van Dong: 32, 109
Pham Van Ngan: 186n
Phantom backseaters: 8, 10, 55, 58, 74, 111–12, 113, 128, 235, 236, 290
Phantom. *See* Aircraft, U.S., F–4.
Photography, area surveillance: 106–7
Phou Pha Thi (Site 85): 102–3
Phu Cat Air Base: 193, 196
Phuc Yen airfield: 33, 34, 54, 63, 77, 80, 81, 88, 89, 90, 103, 114, **119**, 127–28

Podgorny, Nikola: 254
Preparedness Investigating Subcommittee of the Senate Armed Services Committee: 76, 78
Prisoners, U.S.: 175–76, 191, **218**, 260–61, 288–89
    4th Allied Prisoner of War Wing: 197
    antileadership actions: 183
    B–52 cutback exchange offer: 178
    Borman mission: 179–80
    Camp Unity: 197
    capitol exhibit: 178
    Code of Conduct: 184–85, 191
    collaborators: 289
    conditions: 175, 178
    confession extortion: 181, 185–86
    Defense Advisory Committee on Prisoners of War: 184
    early release: 188, 189, 190
    escape attempts: 191–93
    exchange: 9
    "fink release" program: 187
    Geneva Conventions: 180–81, 184
    Hayden, Thomas E.: 187–88
    Korean War experience: 184–85
    leadership: 183
    National League of Families of American Prisoners and Missing in Southeast Asia: 175–76
    Nixon position: 175, 179
    North Vietnamese in South Vietnam: 178
    North Vietnam position: 180–81, 186
    Perot advocacy: 178
    physical remains: 289
    practice reunion: 176
    prisoner dispersion: 182–83
    propaganda tools: 186, 187
    Red River Valley Fighter Pilots Association: *See* River Rats.
    rescue attempt: 193–97
    River Rats: 176–77
    secret communications: 181–82
    Son Tay prison rescue attempt: 193–97
    Soviet imprisonment: 288–89
    tap code: 182
    Telford Taylor perspective: 261–62
    torture: 181, 183, 187, 188
    Weiss list: 197
Prisons, North Vietnam: 92, 175, 180, 183–84, 188–89, 192, **218**
    "Alcatraz": 182, 183

Index

"Big House": 182
"Country Club": 182
"Dirty Bird": 192
"French House": 182
Hoa Lo ("Hanoi Hilton"): 182, 183, 197, 198, 262–63
"Plantation": 182, 188
Son Tay: 193–97
"Zoo": 182, 183, 187, 192, 197, 262
Prisons, South Vietnam: 179–80
Protective reaction strikes: 173–74, 202, 206
Protests, antiwar, U.S.: 114, 149, 168, 170
Pruett, William D.: 171
Pueblo incident: 123, 130, 175
Pursley, Robert E.: 164–65, 222

Quang Tri: 227
Quesada, Elwood R.: 13–14

Radar bombing
   airborne radar: 59–61, 225
   ground radar: 102–4
Radford, Charles: 222
Radio Hanoi: 129, 279
Railroad car repair shops
   Gia Lam: 72, 112, 272, 276
   Thai Nguyen: 251
Railyards, North Vietnam
   attacks on, U.S.: 39, 72, 87, 112, 245, 255, 261, 263, 275–76
   in Chinese buffer zone: 84, 85, **217**, 270, 273, 276
   Gia Lam: 46, 63, 72, **217**, 263, 272, 273, 276
   Hanoi: 62, 263
   Kep: 61, 73, 272
   Kinh No: 257, 263, 272, 273, 276
   Lang Dang: **217**, 270, 273, 276
   Nam Dinh: 46
   Thai Nguyen: 272, 276
   Vinh: 225
   Yen Bai: 61
   Yen Vien: 41, 43, 45, 46, 65, 72, 77, 85, 86, 112, 272, 273, 276
Rainmaking operations: 194–95
Rather, Dan: 282
Read, Benjamin: 109
Reconnaissance: 17, 106–7, 155, 156, 161, 165, 171, 195, 206, **213**, 273, 277
   armed: 16, 24, 35, 43, 92, 126, 172, 206, 232, 248

attacks upon and losses: 156, 172, 197, 205, 222, 237, 280
drone: 107, **213**, 279
Red Cross: 180
Red Flag exercises: 240
Red River Valley Pilots Association: 176–77
Refueling, aerial: 9–10, 40, **214**, 246
Restricted bombing areas. *See* Chinese border, buffer zone; Hanoi-Haiphong area, restricted and prohibited zones.
Risner, Robinson: 183, 189, 190, 191, 193, 290, 555
River Rats: 176–77
Ritchie, Steve: **212**, 237
River mining: 108
Rivers, L. Mendel: 44, 64
Rivet Top: 99–100
Robb, Charles S.: 132
Robinson, Rembrandt C.: 222
Rockefeller, Nelson: 114, 158
Rogers, William P.: 159, 174
Romney, George: 114
Romo, Barry: 261
Roosevelt, Franklin D.: 116
Rostow, Walt Whitman: 30, 31, 68–69, 71, 75, 78, 79, 80, 85, 88, 89, 114, 125, 129, 132, 149, 151, 155
Route packages
   One: 18, 27, 28, 33, 48, 74, 86, 143, 144, 145, 146, 148, 155, 161, 193, 197, 232, 252, 257
   Two: 18, 141, 143, 161
   Three: 18, 141, 143, 155, 161
   Four: 18
   Five: 18, 61, 233, 248, 251, 254
   Six: 18, 24, 48, 49, 74, 86, 96, 107, 143, 197, 207, 232, 233, 248, 254, 260, 288
Ruhling, Mark J.: 155
Rusk, Dean: 23, 36, 38, 62, 69, 75, 88, 90, 109, 110, 122, 124, 126, 131, 135–36, 139, 143, 151
Russell, Bertrand: 45, 180
Russell, Richard: 62, 79, 123, 135, 140, 151
Ryan, John A., Jr.: 60n
Ryan, John D.: 58, 73, 107, **117**, 160, 199, 287
   B–52 bombing mission: 257
   bad weather bombing: 59–61, 95–97,

100–101, 245
barrier project: 200
bombing accuracy: 206
bombing policy: 246
command changes: 237–38
fighter sweeps: 111
Lavelle affair: 199–201, 208–10
Ryan, John D., Jr.: 111
Ryan, Michael E.: 285
Ryan's Raiders: 59–61

Saigon area offensive: 142, 163
Sainteny, Jean: 166
Salisbury, Harrison: 44, 46, 262
SALT negotiations: 169, 227
Sarit Thanarat: 12
Schemmer, Benjamin F.: 194n
Seamans, Robert C., Jr.: 160, 208, 222, 247
Secord, Richard: 266
Senate Armed Services Committee: 79–83,
        88–89, 123–24
Senate Foreign Relations Committee: 124
Sensors: 70, 148, 200, 246
Seventh Air Force. *See* Brown, George S.;
        Clay, Lucius D., Jr.; Lavelle, John
        D.; Momyer, William W.; Moore,
        Joseph H.; Vogt, John W.
Seventh-Thirteenth Air Force: 13
Sharp, Ulysses S. Grant: 15, 56, 82, 110
    air defense system attack: 63, 65, 106
    nuclear weapons use: 125
    panhandle strikes: 59, 77–78, 161
    targets: 15, 18–19, 41, 47, 56, 79–80, 82,
        161
Shinn, William C.: 171
Short, Michael C.: 286
Shriver, Sargent: 254
Sijan, Lance P.: 191–92
Silent majority: 170
Simmonds, Darrell D.: 112
Simons, Arthur D.: 193, 194, 195
Singkapo Sikhotchounamaly,: 103
Site 85 (Phou Pha Thi): 102–3
Slay, Alton D.: 207, 210, 238
Smith, Margaret Chase: 79, 80, 81
Smith, Philip E.: 289n
Smith, Scott G.: **212**
Son Tay prison rescue attempt: 193–97
Souvanna Phouma: 102
Soviet Union
    advisors: 85, 105
    aircraft furnished: 33

attacks on ships, U.S.: 75, 78, 108
Mikhail Frunze incident: 75
military assistance: 62, 71, 99
North Vietnam hydroelectric project:
        154
peace negotiations: 167, 169
Pereslavl-Zalesskiy incident: 108
Prisoners of War imprisonment: 289
SALT negotiations: 169, 227
Turkestan incident: 75
U.S.-China relations concern: 169
Squadrons, U.S. Air Force
    67th Reconnaissance Technical: 106
    67th Tactical Fighter: 5
    497th Tactical Fighter: 5, 73, 144
    555th "Triple Nickel": 233, 275
Stanfield, Donald N.: 172
Starbird, Alfred D.: 70
Stennis, John: 78, 79, 123, 135, 140, 209
Stilwell, Richard G.: 12–13
Stimson, Henry L.: 137
Stockdale, James B.: 183, 185, 187
Stone, John B.: **117**
Strategic Air Command: 6, 10, 15, 266, 287
Stratton, Richard A.: 185–86
Sullivan, William H.: 102–3, 188
Survival training: 182, 185
Sutton, William C.: 171
Swimming pool construction, Thailand: 11
Sylvester, Arthur: 44
Symington, Stuart: 14, 21, 79, 80–81, 82,
        83, 88, 89, 113, 122, 124, 135, 209

Tactical Fighter Weapons Center: 239
Tactics. *See also* Bombing procedures and
        techniques; Electronic technology.
    388th vs. 355th Tactical Fighter Wing
        procedures: 51–52
    air control development: 98–100, 102
    bombing altitudes: 49, 61, 243
    Combat Tree equipment: 239
    electronic countermeasures: 51–52,
        103–5, 243
    evasive maneuvers: 275
    F–111 employment: 101
    fighter role: 14, 286, 287
    fighter sweeps: 111
    flak suppression: 39, 49
    formations: 40, 51–52, 103–5, 240
    identification, friend or foe: *See* Combat
        Tree equipment, above; radio
        identification transponders,

Index

below.
ingress altitudes: 51–52
jamming pods: *See* electronic
    countermeasures, above.
jettisoning: 47, 53, 96, 103
loran missions: 246–47
MiG defense: 53–55
Navy vs. Air Force bomb release
    altitudes: 49
night missions: 73–74, 248
Pardo's Push: 290
pilot and aircrew training: 240, 288
post-target turn: 265
radio identification transponders: 98–99
Red Flag exercises: 240, 288
Rivet Top mission: 99–100
sortie rates: 70–71, 91–92n, 155, 231–32
surface-to-air missiles: 50–52, 105–7
terrain avoidance radar: 59–60, 245
three-ship cells, B–52: 263–65
Top Gun training program: 288
Taft, Robert A.: 156
Takhli Air Base: 6, 9, 10, 51, 54, 57, 75, 85,
    90, 98, 101, 107, 128, 176, 194,
    208, 223, 233, 245, 269
Talbot, Carlos M.: 238
Tanner, Charles N.: 186
Tan Son Nhut Air Base: 14, 16, 99, 100,
    106, 238
Tap code: 182
Targets. *See also* Route packages;
    Weather.
  agricultural: *See* irrigation dikes, below.
  airfields: 34, 242, 257
  Bac Mai air defense control bunker: 252
  Bac Mai airfield: 92, 93
  Bai Thuong airfield. *See* Thanh Hoa
      airfield, below.
  Ban Karai pass: 172
  bridges: 26, 63, 65, 72–73, 84–85, 88,
      112, **119**, 128, 233–35
  Canal des Rapides Bridge: 26, 46, 63,
      72, 85–86, 88, 92, 112, 276
  Cap Mui Lay sector: 145–46
  China border buffer zone: 44
  choke points: 147–48
  dikes. *See* irrigation dikes, below.
  Dong Anh powerplant: 62
  Dong Hoi airfield: 207
  Doumer Bridge: 47, 63, 77, 84–85, 110,
      112, 113, 235–36
  Duc Noi railyard: 276

  electrical power infrastructure: 251
  Gia Lam airport: 92, 251, 261
  Gia Lam railyard: 62–63, 72, 112, **217**,
      263, 272, 276
  government and leadership immunity:
      31, 35
  Ha Gia tank farm: 50
  Hai Duong bridge: 71
  Haiphong area: 26, 43–44, 71
  Haiphong cement plant: 41–42, 62, 251
  Haiphong powerplants: 61, **215**
  Ham Rong Bridge: *See* Thanh Hoa
      bridge, below.
  Hanoi-Haiphong area: 26, 62–63,
      261–63, 277
  Hanoi oil storage facilities: 276
  Hanoi powerplant: 47, 65–66, **215**, 251,
      272
  Hanoi tank farm: 43, 226
  Hoa Lac airfield: 34, 63–64, 263
  Hon Gai port: 26–27
  Iron Triangle: 72
  irrigation dikes: 25, 31, 37, 46, 130, 133,
      249–50, 286
  Kep airfield: 63, 64
  Kep railyard: 61, 73–74, 272, 276
  Kien An airfield: 65
  Kinh No railyard: 257, 272, 276
  Lang Chi hydroelectric plant: 251
  Lang Dang railyard: **217**, 270, 273, 276
  Longbien Bridge. *See* Doumer Bridge,
      below.
  MiG bases: 39, 41, 63–65, 77
  Mu Gia pass: 60, 172, 173
  Nam Dinh: 46
  oil storage facilities: 29–30, 41, 47
  panhandle: 28, 229
  Phuc Yen airfield: 33, 34, 54, 63, 77, 80,
      81, 88, 89, 90, 103, 114, **119**,
      127–28
  powerplants: 41, 47, 61, 65–66, 251, 272
  Quang Te airfield: 266
  Quan Lang airfield: 203, 205–6, 209
  Quinh Loi: 269, 270
  Radio Hanoi: 279
  railroads: 26–27, 41, 71–74, 84–85,
      272–73, 275–76
  Red River port facilities: 128–29
  Ron ferry: 60–61
  Song Duong bridge: 72
  surface-to-air missiles: 243–44, 256,
      266–68

telecommunication links: 252
Thai Nguyen ironworks: 26–27, 41, 55, 59, **119**, 128, 251
Thai Nguyen railyard: 272, 276
Thanh Am oil tank farm: 276
Thanh Hoa airfield: 34, 142, 226
Thanh Hoa barracks: 203
Thanh Hoa bridge: 24, 27, 65, 85, **215**, 227, 234–35
Thanh Hoa warehouses: 227
transportation infrastructure: 77, 257, 276–77. *See also* railroads, above; trucks, below.
trucks: 144, 146–47, 148–49, 248–49
tunnels: 27
urban targets: 19, 284–85
Van Dien truck depot: 41, 43, 50, 65, 77
Vinh: 225
Vinh Linh: 27, 145–46
warehouses: 45, 226, 227, 256, 262, 264
Yen Bai airfield: 268
Yen Vien railyard: 41, 43, 65, 72, 77, 85–86, 112, 272, 276
Taylor, Maxwell: 137, 138
Taylor, Telford: 261, 262
Teaball fusion center: 239–40
Terrain avoidance radar: 59–60, 245
Terry, Ross R.: 186
Tet offensive of 1968: 121, 122–23, 126, 139, 169
    reaction to: 38, 116, 122, 123, 124, 134
    U.S. military response to: 125–26, 128, 130–31
Thailand: 3
    Air Bases. *See* Don Muang; Korat; Nakhon Phanom; Takhli; Ubon; Udorn; U-Tapao.
    Air Force facilities: 6, 8–9
    income tax breaks for U.S. personnel: 11
    Korat plateau: 6, 12
    prostitutes: 11–12
    U.S. air operations policy: 5–6
    U.S. military assistance: 12
    U.S. relations: 12
Thanh Hoa airfield: 34, 142, 226
Thanh Hoa bridge: 24, 27, 65, 85, 182, **215**, 234–35
Thanom Kittikachorn: 12
Thieu, Nguyen Van. *See* Nguyen Van Thieu.
Thirteenth Air Force: 13
Thompson, Richard: 169

Thorsness, Leo K.: 58n
Thud. *See* Aircraft, U.S., F–105.
Thud Ridge: 51
Thurmond, Strom: 79, 80, 122, 140
Titus, Robert F.: 111
Tonkin Gulf incident: 19–20
Tonkin Gulf Resolution: 20
Toperczer, Istvan: 54n
Top Gun training program: 288
Tour of duty policy: 10–11
Trail, Richard L.: 40n
Transponders, radio identification: 98–99
Tran Van Quang,: 289n
Trautman, Conrad: 192
Trinh: 109
Truck repair shops
    Thanh Hoa: 203
    Van Dien: 276
Truman, Harry S.: 19
Truong Chinh: 32
Turkestan incident: 75

Ubon Air Base: 6, 10, 52, 53, 58, 64, 73, 85, 89, 91, 92n, 97, 98, 99, 108, 127, 128, 144, 172, 176, 198, 223, 224, 233, 241, 251, 278
Udorn Air Base: 8, 10, 13, 17, 100, 147, 176, 177, 194, 196, 207, 223, 236, 238, 241, 246, 274
United Kingdom, bombing position: 42, 44, 56–57
U.S. forces withdrawal: 165, 169, 170, 178–79
U-Tapao Air Base: **216**, 223, 263, 273–74, 278, 280

Vance, Cyrus: 68, 138, 151, 222
Vang Pao: 102
Vasir, Amarjit Singh: 177
Venereal disease: 12
Victory credits: 8, 111–12, 128, 237, 274
Vietnamization: 165, 169–70, 179, 221, 223
Vogel, Richard D.: 74
Vogt, John W.: 200, **211**, 220–22, 226, 243, 253, 266, 267, 269, 280
    all-weather bombing: 270
    armed reconnaissance: 232
    B–52 employment: 220–21
    bombing accuracy: 235
    bombing policy: 246
    F–111 employment: 245

Index

Hanoi-Haiphong area: 278–79
  Long Chi Dam: 251
  Linebacker II: 257
  MiG fighters: 239
  Nixon, meeting with: 220–21
Voight, Ted L., II: 128
Vo Nguyen Giap: 20n, 32–34
Vorybyov, Mark: 244n

Wallace, George: 150n
Walleye television-guided bombs: 65–66,
    85, 91, 97, 128, 232–33, 234,
    235–36
  against Doumer Bridge: 234
  against Hanoi powerplant: 251
  against Phuc Yen airfield: 90
  against Thanh Hoa Bridge: 234
Warehouses, attacks on: 45, 226, 227, 256,
    262, 269
Warnke, Paul: 132
Watergate: 281
Wayne, Stephen A.: 290
Weapon system officers: 7–8, 101, 237
Weather: 28, 39, 41, 43, 61–62, 66, 93,
    95–97, 144, 148, 155, 220, 244,
    279, 283
Weiss, Cora: 197
Welander, Robert O.: 222
Westmoreland, William C.: 14, 15, 59, 67,
    68, 70, 76, 110, 116, 121, 125, 129,
    130, 131, 161
Weyand, Fred C.: 238
Weyland, Otto P.: 95–96
Wheeler, Earle G.: 23, 30, 35, 42, 68, 69,
    75, 89, 123, 138, 160, 163
  air defenses: 82
  bombing halts: 110
  bombing policy: 43, 55–56, 80–81, 82,
      90, 126, 133–34, 141, 142
  bombing resumption: 163, 164, 167
  Haiphong harbor: 78
  MiG bases: 127
  reconnaissance: 156
  resignation threats: 83–84

troop call-up: 130–31
  Wheeler Study Group report: 129–30
White, Theodore H.: 150n
White, Thomas H.: 160
Wild Weasel: 36–37, 195, 205, 227, 231,
    243, 267, 290
  F–4C: 266–67
  F–100F: 36
  F–105F: 36, 52, 57, 95, 105, 112, 197,
      206–7, 225, 226
  F–105F as all-weather and night
      bomber: 59–61, 95, 101, 245
  F–105G: 171
Williams, David O., Jr.: 128
Wilson, Harold: 56
Wilson, Louis L.: 208
Wings
  4th Allied Prisoner of War: 197
  8th Tactical Fighter: 10, 52, 54n, 64,
      108, 233, 235, 243, 247
  49th Tactical Fighter: 223
  336th Tactical Fighter: 5
  355th Tactical Fighter: 10, 51, 128, 223
  366th Tactical Fighter: 10, 64, 223, 233
  388th Tactical Fighter: 10, 51, 59, 103,
      112, 128, 223, 233
  432d Tactical Reconnaissance: 10, 207,
      212, 233, 247
  474th Tactical Fighter: 246
"Wise Men" meetings: 137–39
Wolfe, Tom: 44
Wright, James: 170

Xuan Thuy: 166

Yeltsin, Boris: 289n
Yokota Air Base: 60, 106

Zemke, Hubert: 54n
Zhou Enlai: 141n
Zimer, Milan: 111
Zinn, Howard: 188
Zuckerman, Solly: 30